JOGISHWAR SINGH

BANKS, GODS AND GOVERNMENT

BEITRÄGE ZUR SÜDASIENFORSCHUNG
SÜDASIEN-INSTITUT
UNIVERSITÄT HEIDELBERG

BAND 129

STEINER VERLAG WIESBADEN GMBH
STUTTGART
1989

BANKS, GODS AND GOVERNMENT

INSTITUTIONAL AND INFORMAL CREDIT STRUCTURE IN A REMOTE AND TRIBAL INDIAN DISTRICT (KINNAUR, HIMACHAL PRADESH) 1960-1985

by

JOGISHWAR SINGH

STEINER VERLAG WIESBADEN GMBH
STUTTGART
1989

CIP-Titelaufnahme der Deutschen Bibliothek

Singh, Jogishwar:
Banks, gods and government : institutional and informal credit structure in a remote and tribal Indian district (Kinnaur, Himāchal Pradesh) 1960 - 1985 / by Jogishwar Singh. –
Stuttgart: Steiner-Verl. Wiesbaden, 1989
(Beiträge zur Südasienforschung; 129)
Zugl.: Heidelberg, Univ., Diss., 1987
ISBN 3-515-05396-4
NE: GT

D 16

Dedicated to my children,
Pritam Florian Singh
and
Amrit Hadrien Singh,
who represent the future.

TABLE OF CONTENTS

LIST OF PLATES

LIST OF TABLES

LIST OF GRAPHS

LIST OF GRAPHS

LIST OF MAPS

LIST OF MAPS

FOREWORD

The present work is based on my stay of nearly three years as Deputy Commissioner of Kinnaur District at Kālpa from 1980 to 1983. During this tenure I had ample occasion to come into close interaction with Kinnauras, both rich and poor; to observe the geographic and climatic conditions which govern life in Kinnaur; to visit almost all the 77 villages constituting the district and to have a first-hand experience of being close to nature. When I was posted to Kinnaur in 1980, all that I knew about the area was that it was a "punishment posting", that it snowed there most of the time and that it remained cut off from the rest of "civilization" for months on end. When I left Kālpa in 1983 to proceed to a training course in Paris, it was with a heart full of sadness and the certainty that my time in Kinnaur had been the most interesting and stimulating period of my life. The present work is a small attempt to make known this remarkable area and its people who I remember with fondness and gratitude.

It has been possible to present this work on Kinnaur only because Prof. Dr Dietmar Rothermund, Head of the Department of History, South Asia Institute, Heidelberg University, agreed to act as my guide. He enabled me to come to Heidelberg where I have worked under his supervision. His role is mentioned in the succeeding section on acknowledgements. It has been a challenging task working on Kinnaur, an area about which almost all accounts available are general travelogues or works full of sweeping generalizations unsupported by source material. There was absolutely nothing published available about the rural credit infrastructure in Kinnaur. It is hoped that the present work will prove to be of at least some interest to persons interested in this important aspect of life in Kinnaur. Not having any published material to go by, I have been obliged to rely a lot on original documents in private hands in Kinnaur, on archival material from Herrnhut and Chandigarh, on personal experiences/observations gained during my stay in the district and on personal interviews with Kinnauras.

Kinnaur is not open to free entry by foreigners or non-Kinnaura Indians. An inner line permit is needed to get into most of the area. It has not been opened to mass tourism like Ladakh and Lahaul which have consequently attracted much more media attention and publications. Shielded from the impact of tourist groups, Kinnaur has a traditional, polyandrous society now in the throes of socio-economic change due to development of better means of communication, its upgradation as a district and to increased contact with non-Kinnauras. It is a tribal society trying to adjust to new influences like increasing monetization, stronger government presence and contact with different sets of mores.

Located strategically on the frontier with Tibet, Kinnaur has had centuries of undisturbed evolution in the political, social, economic and religious spheres. It constituted initially the kernel of and later on the most important part of Bushahr State, the largest of the erstwhile Simla Hill States. It has a society in which one can see a slow transition from Hinduism of the hill variety to Buddhism of the Tibetan school as one moves from Nichār Sub-Division to Pooh Sub-Division. The two religions have coexisted harmoniously for centuries and given rise to an intermediate hybrid in which divinities of both sides are venerated. At a time when religious intolerance is becoming the rule rather than the exception in parts of Northern India, Kinnaur offers a welcome contrast where Hindu and Buddhist shrines sometimes share the same courtyard.

Kinnaur has a remarkably developed informal credit sector with the ubiquitous village deity or devta as its pivot. It was observation of the smooth functioning of the devtas' loaning operations vis-a-vis the red-tape ridden functioning of the institutional credit system which first gave me the idea of working on credit networks in the area. The village deity used to be, and continues to be, a central figure of social life in Kinnaur. Giving loans to villagers is one of its important activities. Studying the credit infrastructure necessarily involved me in a study of the social, religious and political aspects of life in Kinnaur, in addition to the economic aspect. The present work has tried in a modest way to touch upon many of these aspects as and when felt necessary.

The approach adopted has been that of a practical administrator and not that of a theoretical specialist. Having had Nuclear Physics and Electronics as special papers for my M.Sc. degree, followed by a M.A. in History, followed by one year as a member of the Indian Police Service, I have since 1976 been an officer of the Indian Administrative Service. Consequently, it has not been easy to readapt to a research environment requiring in many ways the exact opposite of what I have been doing in the preceding ten years. If the reader gets a feeling that the emphasis of the present work is a bit diffuse, that it does not appear to have been done by a trained economist, it would be quite understandable in view of my diverse academic background and administrative training.

Having learnt German, French and Italian in addition to English, Hindi, Punjabi and Urdu, I have used source material in all these languages in an attempt to offer as broad a spectrum of information as I could. It is hoped that this work shall prove of some interest to persons interested in doing research on life in Kinnaur. Any deficiencies found in the work are entirely mine and not my guide's at all. Considering the fact that I remained away from the academic world for more than ten years after finishing my university education at Chandigarh in 1975, I hope that readers will be generous enough not to judge me too harshly.

JOGISHWAR SINGH

Heidelberg

July 1987

ACKNOWLEDGEMENTS

A separate section is needed to thank the persons without whom this work could never have been completed. Their contribution is too important to be dismissed in a general line of acknowledgement. Prof. Dr Dietmar Rothermund has been more than just my guide (Doktorvater). Without his help in securing the necessary financial assistance, his constant availability in spite of his very busy schedule, suggestions for improvement of the text, and generous help in overcoming various bureaucratic hurdles connected with my stay in Heidelberg, I would never have been in a position to begin, let alone finish, this work. I most gratefully put on record my sincere thanks to my guide who has really gone out of his way to be helpful.

The Friedrich-Naumann-Stiftung provided financial assistance in the form of a fellowship to support my work and my family's stay in Heidelberg. Without its help there would have been no question of undertaking this work. I hereby thank the Friedrich-Naumann-Stiftung most cordially for its support.

Prof. Dr Hermann Kulke of the Department of History, South Asia Institute, Heidelberg University, helped a lot in formulating and clarifying my ideas about state formation in Kinnaur and Bushahr. His invaluable help is gratefully acknowledged here.

During my field visit to Kinnaur in November/December 1985 my successor as D.C., Kinnaur, Mr Vivek Srivastava, I.A.S., and his wife, Radhika, offered me personal hospitality, logistical support and full cooperation. Special thanks are due to both of them. The D.C.'s staff, in particular Sarvshri Bhim Sain Negi, Jitendra Singh Negi, Lal Singh Verma, M.S. Chauhan, Keshav Ram, J.P. Kaushik, Kāmi Sherpa and Tegta, compiled information for my work from innumerable files in a short time. I thank all the employees of the D.C.'s Establishment in Kālpa. Thanks are also due to district-level heads of other departments who furnished information promptly to me. Sarvshri B.C. Kāndpāl (D.S.O.), P.N. Negi (D.W.O.), J.S. Chaudhary (D.A.O.), S.G. Negi (D.F.S.C.) and Er R.K. Singha (A.S.C.O.), need special mention in this respect.

Mr Satish Girotra, A.G.M., UCO Bank, Bombay replied promptly to lists of questions sent to him by me. His successor at Simla, Mr Kapoor, provided me with whatever information that I sought from his office. They in particular and bank officers and staff in general have my cordial thanks for their help and cooperation.

Mr Thākur Sain Negi, former Speaker, H.P. Vidhān Sabha, gave me a lot of information about the social and economic fabric of life in Kinnaur in my years of close contact with him from 1980 to 1983. I am grateful to this remarkable Kinnaura personality. I also thank Sarvshri Balwant Singh Negi, Chhering Bhāg Sānā, Dandub Rām, Daulat Rām Negi, Dharam Singh Negi, Ganga Lāl Negi, Goverdhan Singh Negi, Khem Singh Negi, Lama Shimed Chhéwang, Lambardār Keshwa Singh, Medub Dandub and Uday Singh Negi, who gave me long interviews, patiently answered a lot of my questions, provided me with Bahi Khātās and other valuable documents used in this research and translated documents in the Tānkri and Tibetan scripts into Hindi and Urdu for me. That my research could be completed without too much delay is largely due to their generous help.

Frau Pastorin Ingeborg Baldauf, Director of the Archives of the Moravian Mission at Herrnhut, not only provided me with all the archival material that I needed but spent three days reading out texts in the old, gothic German script to me since I knew only the present German script. I thank her for this help.

Dr Friedrich W. Fuhs of the Department of International Agrarian Development, South Asia Institute, Heidelberg University, and I had numerous detailed discussions about rural development and agrarian relations which gave me better insight into different aspects of my work. This has helped me a lot. He and his wife, Frau Antje Fuhs, have provided me generous hospitality at their homes in New Delhi and Heidelberg. I most gratefully acknowledge their help.

Herr E. Dietrich and Herr D. Berger of the Universitäts-Rechenzentrum helped a lot with processing this work on the computer, as did Herr Klaus Müller of the Department of Indology, South Asia Institute, Heidelberg University. All of them gave me a lot of their time and patience for which I formally put my gratitude on record.

Last, but by far not the least, I most heartily thank my wife, Dr Lia Jacqueline née Eberhard, who freed me completely from my household duties so that I could single-mindedly concentrate on my work. Cheering me up in several moments of self-doubt, she has been the pilot keeping me on course. Her family members - father Max Nicolas, mother Agnese Bernardetta, sister Giselle Maxine - supported us liberally, both financially and otherwise. They did much more than can reasonably be expected of even family members. I thank them all most sincerely. My elder brother, Chiranjiv Singh, provided useful ideas for this research and indispensable moral support. All the persons mentioned till now made it possible to complete this work.

ABBREVIATIONS USED FREQUENTLY IN THE TEXT

@ = at the rate of;
A.A.P. = Annual Action Plan;
A.C.R. = Annual Confidential Report;
A.L.R. = Arrear of Land Revenue;
A.S.C.O. = Assistant Soil Conservation Officer;
B.D.O. = Block Development Officer;
C.S. = Chief Secretary;
D.A.O. = District Agriculture Officer;
D.A.H.O. = District Animal Husbandry Officer;
D.C. = Deputy Commissioner;
D.C.C.C. = District Consultative and Coordination Committee;
D.C.P. = District Credit Plan;
D.C.S.O. = District Cooperative and Supplies Officer;
D.D.A. = Desert Development Agency;
D.D.P. = Desert Development Project;
D.F.O. = Divisional Forest Officer;
D.F.S.C. = District Food and Supplies Controller;
D.H.O. = District Horticulture Officer;
D.I.C. = District Industries Centre;
D.M. = District Magistrate, Divisional Manager;
D.R.D.A. = District Rural Development Agency;
D.R.I. = Differential Rate of Interest;
D.W.O. = District Welfare Officer;
E.S.M.A. = Essential Services Maintenance Act;
F.C. = Financial Commissioner;
F.C.(R) = Financial Commissioner (Revenue);
G.M. = General Manager;
G.P. = Grām Panchāyat;
H.D.O. = Horticultural Development Officer;
H.Y.Vs = High Yielding Varieties;
I.R.D.P. = Integrated Rural Development Programme;
I.T.D.P. = Integrated Tribal Development Project;
LDB = Land Development Bank;
M.I.S.A. = Maintenance of Internal Security Act;
N.D.C. = No Dues Certificate;
N.O.C. = No Objection Certificate;
N.R.C. = Non-Recovery Certificate;
P.A.C. = Project Advisory Committee;
PNB = Punjab National Bank;
P.D.S. = Public Distribution System;
P.O. = Project Officer;
RFMs = Rural Financial Markets;
SBI = State Bank of India;
SCB = State Cooperative Bank;
UBI = Union Bank of India;
UCO = United Commercial Bank.

NOTE EXPLAINING ARRANGEMENT OF TEXT

Five levels have been programmed for headings in the text. For example, 'III. INSTITUTIONAL CREDIT NETWORK: COOPERATIVES' is a level-0 heading. Level-0 headings have been used to mark the beginning of each chapter. They have not been indented at all in the table of contents. They appear in capital letters in the text. '3.5 SAMPLE SURVEY IN POOH SUB-DIVISION' is a level-1 heading. Appearing in bold capitals in the text, level-1 headings have been indented 1 column to the right in the table of contents to distinguish them from level-0 headings. '3.5.1 Sample Survey Field Work' is a level-2 heading. Such headings appear in bold italics in the text. They have been indented 5 columns to the right in the table of contents to show that they caption sub-topics of the topic under the preceding level-1 heading which, in turn, does the same for the chapter listed by the concerned level-0 heading. '3.5.1.1 Sample Villages: Fairly Representative' is a level-3 heading. Level-3 headings give the sub-topics of subjects listed under preceding level-2 headings. They (level-3) appear in the text as bold italics. They have been indented 11 columns to the right in the table of contents. '3.5.1.1.1 Household Selection' is a level-4 heading. Level-4 headings appear in bold in the text. They have been indented 19 columns to the right in the table of contents. They indicate sub-divisions of subject matter in the preceding level-3 heading. Level-2, level-3 and level-4 headings do not have every word in capital letters.

The first reference to any book, article, document, interview or other source has been mentioned in full in the footnotes. Subsequent references to the same source have been given in a summarized form. For example, the first reference to Alexander Gerard's book about Kinnaur published in 1841 reads: 'Gerard, Captain (or Capt.) Alexander: Account of Koonawur in the Himalaya Etc. Etc. Etc., edited by George Lloyd, London: James Madden & Co., MDCCCXLI, p. (or Pp)--'. Subsequent references to this work read: 'Gerard, A., 1841, p. (or Pp)--'.

Words have been put in bold, italic or bold italic, particularly in quotations, to only draw attention of the reader. There is no hierarchical order in their choice that words in bold italic are more important than those in bold which, in turn, are more important than those in italic. All these types of print have been used only as devices for pointing out interesting aspects. Changes of font to put a few lines in another type of print have been used in the text to serve exactly the same purpose. Page numbers for graphs attached in the main text have been given in parentheses. The number in parentheses refers to the page number to which the graph pertains. Maps and plates do not carry page numbers. They have been attached immediately after the page number to which they pertain. Much as it was desired to provide maps showing more information about trade routes, mountain passes and similar information, it has not been done because the author, being a government officer, is not free to show these frontier areas in view of security reasons. The lapse is regretted but there was no other choice.

Reference has been made in the text to block diagrams, graphs, histograms and mathematical calculations which were actually carried out but could not be printed in order to keep publishing costs and size within reasonable limits. Actual diagrams and calculations are available at the South Asia Institute of Heidelberg University or with the author for consultation.

CHAPTER I

REMOTE AND AWE INSPIRING: A PROFILE OF THE DISTRICT

This chapter is an introduction to Kinnaur District but not a presentation of general information in the style of a Gazetteer. Only such aspects as have some bearing on the prevailing credit structure of this area have, therefore, briefly been outlined - geographical coordinates and conditions; some facets of its social structure; the administrative structure within which the institutional and informal credit structures operate; the political scenario and economic patterns of certain major surplus generating activities. Major areas of interest like fairs/festivals, ethnicity, folk songs and music, legends and folk tales as well as marriage rites and customs have largely been ignored, being referred to in various chapters as and when necessary.[1]

The official name of the area is now Kinnaur. In the Kinnauri language it is called Kanauring[2] or Kañoriṅ.[3] The name in use in common parlance is **Kanaur.**[4] Different authors have spelt the name in different ways.[5] European travellers began visiting Kinnaur after the proclamation of British paramountcy over Bushahr State in 1816. J.B. Fraser was the first to give information about this area,[6] without actually visiting it. Accounts of Kinnaur contain descriptions like "inhospitable and bleak in climate, barren and unproductive in soil...it is a mass of rocks and wild chasms",[7] "a secluded region, rugged and mountainous in an

[1] Persons interested in more information about Kinnaur please see the following works:

(a) Gerard, Captain Alexander: Account of Koonawur in the Himalaya Etc. Etc. Etc., edited by George Lloyd, London: James Madden & Co., 1841;

(b) Cunningham, J.D.: Notes on Moorcroft's Travels in Ladākh, and on Gerard's Account of Koonawur, including a general description of the latter district, in: Journal of the Asiatic Society of Bengal (J.A.S.B.), Calcutta, Vol.13, No. 147, 1844, Part I: Pp 172-222, and No. 148 (No. 64 New Series), 1844, Part II: Pp 223-253;

(c) Punjab States Gazetteer, Vol. VIII: Simla Hill States, Part 2 A: Bashahr State, Lahore, 1911;

(d) Deuster, R.H.: KANAWAR, Grundriß einer Volks- und Kulturkunde, Studien zur Völkerkunde, Band 14, Leipzig: Jordan & Graimberg, 1939;

(e) Mamgain, M.D.: H.P. District Gazetteers - KINNAUR, Ambala Cantt., 1971, 407 Pages + Appendices.

[2] Negi, T.S.: Scheduled Tribes of Himāchal Pradesh - A Profile, Simla, 1976, p. 11.

[3] Bailey, Rev. T. Grahame: A Brief Grammar of the Kinnauri Language, in: Zeitschrift der Deutschen Morgenländischen Gesellschaft (Z.D.M.G.), Dreiundsechzigster Band, Leipzig, 1909, Pp 661-687.

[4] Negi, T.S., 1976, p. 11.

[5] For example, A. Gerard: **KOORPA, KOONAWUR**; Dr C.H. Gutzlaff, R. Maclagan-Gorrie, W.E. Buchanan, H.M. Glover, A.P.F. Hamilton, Dr Sten Konow, Marco Pallis, R.H. Deuster, Sir G.A. Grierson: **KANAWAR**; James Baillie Fraser, Captain C. Johnson, Captain Thomas Hutton, Captain Madden: **KUNAWUR**; A.H. Francke, Adolf Schulze, Captain H. Strachey, J.D. Cunningham: **KUNAWAR**; Captain H. Strachey: **KUNU, KANOR, KNOR, KANORING**; D. Ibbetson, H.A. Rose, Rev. T. Grahame Bailey: **KANAUR**; Giuseppe Tucci: **KUNAVAR**; Mme. Isabelle Massieu: **KUNOWAR**; Victor Jacquemont: **KANAWER** and Rāhul Sānkrityāyan: **KINNERDESH.** The list is by no means complete. In this dissertation the name Kinnaur will be used.

[6] Fraser, James Baillie: Journal of a Tour through parts of the Snowy Range of the Himālā Mountains and to the Sources of the Rivers Jumna and Ganges, London: Rodwell and Martin, 1820.

[7] Fraser, J.B., 1820, p. 263.

extraordinary degree",[8] "the scenery is indeed grand, but its vastness and barrenness in Upper Kunawar are fatiguing",[9] "the whole scene greatly resembles the Mer de Glace and other glaciers of Savoy and Switzerland",[10] "Sangla may one day be the Zermatt of the Himalaya...it is numbered among the most beautiful valleys in the Himalaya",[11] "the valley of the Baspa is one of the most exquisite alpine valleys, full of the richest changes and natural beauties".[12]

No account can ignore the changing landscape of the area from the picturesque and green valleys in the south to the arid, almost lunar scape-like overpowering barrenness of the north. It is not only the landscape that changes as one moves from Nichār Sub-Division to Kālpa Sub-Division to Pooh Sub-Division. This progression from greenery to barrenness is parallelled by a progression from the monsoon fed zone to the arid zone; from Hinduism of the hill variety to Buddhism resembling that practised in Tibet; from settlements with angular roofs to settlements with the Tibetan-like flat roofs; from a dialect of Kinnauri with few Tibetan words to a dialect resembling pure Tibetan and, most important of all for the purposes of this study, from a zone where the surplus channelled into moneylending was generated mainly through animal husbandry, artisanat or service to one where this surplus was generated largely from cross-frontier trade with Tibet, with Gartok in Western Tibet as its nodal point. Geography and climatic conditions have played a determinant role in the evolution of Kinnauri social relations, economic activities or even creation of a State in this area. Each of these aspects will be examined in this study. We begin by considering what impact geographical location has had on Kinnaur.

1.1 GEOGRAPHICAL COORDINATES

Kinnaur District is situated between 31°-05′-55″ to 32°-05′-20″ N latitude and 77°-45′-00″ to 79°-00′-50″ E longitude.[13] Official publications give differing figures for the surface area of the

[8] Gerard, A., 1841, p. 1.

[9] Cunningham, J.D., 1844, p. 172.

[10] Madden, Captain: Diary of an Excursion to the Shatool and Boorun Passes over the Himalaya, in September 1845, p. 100, in: J.A.S.B., Vol. 15, No. 170, Pp 79-135.

[11] Shewen, Major D.G.P.M.: The Way to the Baspa, Pp 67-68, in: The Himalayan Journal (H.J.), Vol. I, No. 1, April 1929, Pp 67-74.

[12] Kutzner, J.G.: Die Reise seiner königlichen Hoheit des Prinzen Waldemar von Preußen nach Indien in den Jahren 1844 bis 1846, Aus dem darüber erschienen Prachtwerke im Auszüge mitgetheilt, Berlin: Verlag der königlichen Geheimen Ober-Hofbuchdruckerei, 1857, p. 257. The original text reads: *"Das Thal des Baspa ist eins der herrlichsten Alpenthäler, voll der reichsten Abwechselungen und Naturschönheiten"*. Translation mine.

[13] Basic Statistics of Kinnaur District, in: Kinnaur District: Existing Basic Facilites, Directorate of Economics and Statistics, H.P., Simla. The figures mentioned above are given on page 9. The figure 30°-05′-55″ N for the latitude mentioned on page 1 is a printing error. Also please see District Census Handbook: Kinnaur District, 1981, p. 9. Alexander Gerard gives latitude 31°-15′ to 32°-04′ N as the latitude and 77°-50′ to 78°-50′ E as longitude for "Koonawur, called likewise Koorpa" on page 1. (Gerard, A., London, 1841). R.H. Deuster gives 31°-06′ to 32°-04′ N latitude and 77°-50′ to 79°-02′ E longitude as the geographical coordinates of Kinnaur (Deuster, R.H., 1939, p. 1). Geographical coordinates of the erstwhile Bushahr State of which Kinnaur formed part were 31°-06′ to 32°-04′ N latitude and 77°-33′ to 79°-02′ E longitude (Gazetteer, 1911, p. 1). These figures show how Kinnaur was by far the largest territorial constituent of Bushahr State.

district. Some publications give the total surface area of Kinnaur as 6,553 sq. kms.[14] Others have now scaled it down to 6,401 sq. kms.[15] R.H. Deuster gives 5,440 sq. kms. as the area of Kinnaur[16] while A. Gerard pegs it at 2,100 sq. miles.[17] Deuster and Gerard, without specifying it explicitly, seem to be giving the area of Kinnaur beyond Wāngtu which constituted the erstwhile Chini Tahsil. Gerard sums up the difficulty of measuring areas in Kinnaur by observing that the "area of Koonawur...appears to be about 2100 square miles, but this point will probably never be very accurately ascertained from the unsurmountable obstacles that occur at every step".[18] Like much else about Kinnaur, precise information is hard to come by. This is as true today as it was in earlier times.

1.1.1 Boundaries: Cradled Between Snowy Peaks

The eastern boundary of Kinnaur adjoins Western Tibet, roughly along the watershed of the Zaskar mountain chain.[19] The highest mountain of Kinnaur, called the Leo Pargial or the Riwo Phargyul,[20] towers above the area where the Satluj river[21] cuts through the Zaskar mountains below Shipki La pass into Kinnaur.[22] The northern and north-western boundary of

[14] Basic Facilities, Kinnaur District, p. 2;
I.T.D.P. Project Report, Kinnaur, 1981, p. 1;
Statistical Abstract, Kinnaur District, 1974-75, p. 1;
This very value is reiterated in Ibid: 1975-76, 1976-77, 1978, 1979.

[15] Statistical Outline of Himāchal Pradesh, 1983, p. 16;
District Census Handbook, Kinnaur District, 1981, p. ix;
Statistical Abstract of Kinnaur District, 1981, p. vii.

[16] Deuster, R.H., 1939, p. 1.

[17] Gerard, A., 1841, p. 2. This figure of 2,100 sq. miles corresponds to 5,439 sq. kms taking one square mile = 2.5899 square kilometres.

[18] Gerard, A., 1841, p. 2.

[19] Deuster, R.H., 1939, p. 8. The original reads "Die Zaskar-Kette bildet, grob gesprochen, die Grenz-scheide gegen Tibet". Also see: Gazetteer, 1971, p. 1.

[20] Deuster, R.H., 1939, p. 8. A. Gerard calls it the Purgeool. (Gerard, A., 1841, p. 8). Alexander Cunningham calls it Porgyal (Cunningham, Sir Alexander: Ladāk - Physical, Statistical and Historical, Reprint/New Delhi: Sagar Publications, 1970, p. 58) while Thomas Hutton calls it "Purgule" (Hutton, Th., 1839, p. 512). For further information about this mountain which is very important in the legend and mythology of the Pooh area, please see: Pallis, Marco: Gangotri and Leo Pargial, in: H.J., Vol. VI, 1934, Pp 106-126. The part of Tibet bordering Kinnaur is called Nari-Khorsum by Captain H. Strachey. [Strachey, H.: Physical Geography of Western Tibet, p. 15, in: Journal of the Royal Geographical Society (J.R.G.S.), Vol. XXIII, 1853, Pp 1-69]. For different forms of this name, please see:
(a) Körös, A. Csoma de: Geographical Notice of Tibet, in: J.A.S.B., Vol. I, No. 4, April 1832, Pp 121-127;
(b) Gutzlaff, Dr C.H.: Tibet and Sofan, in: J.R.G.S., Vol. XX, London, 1850, Pp 191-227.
These articles give a description of the geographical regions of Tibet.

[21] Written also as the Sutlej or the Satlej. There was for long a controversy regarding its source. For information about this river, see: Cunningham, Alexander, 1970, Pp 127-130; Gerard, A., 1841, Pp 22-28; and Strachey, H., 1853, Pp 34-45. The Tibetan names for this river are Langchen Khabap (Strachey, H., 1853, p. 34), Langzhing Khampa (Gerard, A., 1841, p. 28), Langchin Kabab or Kampa (Cunningham, J.D., 1844, p. 233).

[22] For information about the different passes through the Zaskar mountain chain into Tibet, please see Gerard,

Geographical location of Kinnaur District with respect to surrounding areas like Ladakh, Lahaul & Spiti, Garhwal and Western Tibet

Kinnaur touches the Spiti Sub-Division of Lahaul and Spiti District of Himāchal Pradesh.[23] Running along the Sri Khand range, the boundary touches Kulu District for a while before touching Rāmpur Tahsil of present-day Simla District in the west. The southern boundary of Kinnaur joins Rohru Tahsil of Simla District in the west and Uttarkashi District of Uttar Pradesh in the east. This boundary runs along the crest of the Dhaula Dhār range, dividing the Satluj river basin from the Ganga and the Yamuna river basins.[24]

1.1.2 Topography: Steep Valleys and Hard Lives

Kinnaur lies along both banks of the Satluj river flowing roughly from N.E. to S.W., cutting through three more or less parallel mountain ranges - the Zaskar, the Great Himalaya and the Dhaula Dhār chains.[25] The Satluj valley is the largest valley in the district but is steep and does not lend itself to much settlement or cultivation along its banks. Hence the villages are mostly situated at heights above the river.[26] Next to this valley in order of extent are the Hangrang or Spití valley and the Baspa or Sangla valley respectively.[27] The Sangla valley has the widest and most fertile stretches of cultivable land in Kinnaur. It was in this very valley that the Thākur of Kāmru had his seat. This Thākur was able to establish his sway over other chieftains and evolve into the Rājā of Bushahr, as shall be seen in Chapter II. The other valleys are extremely rugged and steep. Crossing one valley into another meant going over high intervening mountain ridges. If one sought to avoid these forbiddingly high ridges, it meant making long detours over circuitous routes through the Satluj valley over bad tracks and bridges.[28] The rivers are not navigable so there exists no possibility of income generation through river borne commerce. **"The hydrographical basin of the Sutlej nowhere opens into a broad plain, and Kunawar consists of a series of rocky and precipitous ravines descending rapidly to the bed of the principal river".**[29] The steep inclines make it difficult to envisage lift irrigation schemes for lifting water to irrigate large open spaces available at Kā Doghri or near Chāngo village which could generate income through agricultural production if water were available

A., 1841, Pp 48-52.

[23] This district used to form a part of Punjab till 1966. It was transferred on November 1, 1966 to Himāchal Pradesh following the trifurcation of Punjab on linguistic lines.

[24] Gazetteer, 1971, Pp 1-2; and Deuster, R.H., 1939, Pp 4-8.
For information about the passes across the Dhaula Dhār range from Kinnaur to Rohru and Uttarkashi, please see: (i) Gerard, A., 1841, Pp 41-47; (ii) Deuster, R.H., 1939, p. 7.

[25] For more information please see: Gerard, A., 1841, Pp 5-22; Gazetteer, 1971, Pp 4-11; Deuster, R.H., 1939, Pp 4-14.

[26] Alexander Gerard writes that the villages are situated at heights of between 7,000 to 9,000 feet, arable land extends up to 11,000 feet while the elevation of the river bed runs from 4,400 to 8,600 feet. (Gerard, A., 1841, p. 11). He seems to have ignored villages like Hāngo, Nāko, Malling, Chuling, Kuno and Chārang which are all above 9,000 feet.

[27] For information about valleys in Kinnaur, please see:
(i) Gerard, A., 1822, Pp 10-22; (ii) Gazetteer, 1971, Pp 8-11; and Deuster, R.H., 1939, Pp 8-11.

[28] For a description of the different kinds of bridges used in Kinnaur, please see: Gerard, A., 1841, Pp 33-38.
Sven Hedin narrates his experience of a dangerous crossing over the Satluj river using a 'jhoola' or rope bridge at Dubling gorge near Pooh. (Hedin, Sven: Trans-Himalaya, Discoveries and Adventures in Tibet, Vol. III, London: Macmillan and Co., 1913, Pp 369-374). Hedin devotes six pages of graphic description for something which is an everyday routine experience for Kinnauras even today.

[29] Cunningham, J.D., 1844, p. 172.

there.

1.1.3 Climate and Rainfall

"The climate of Kinnaur is as varied as the face of the country...from the heat of the torrid zone almost to the frozen temperatures of a Lapland winter".[30] Alexander Gerard mentions a change from 33°F to 109°F over a distance of 13 or 14 miles.[31] Absolute altitude does not govern the growth of plants as much as the situation and summer temperature.[32] Accounts mention long and hard winters.[33] "By virtue of its elevation, the district may be said to have a temperate zone climate with a long winter from October to May, during which period snowfalls occur, and a short summer from June to September. The transition periods from April to May and from September to October correspond to the spring and autumn seasons of the temperate zone".[34] Practical experience of living three years in Kinnaur showed that autumn extended till the middle or even the end of November before winter set in.[35] Any potential invader of the area could ignore these conditions only at his own peril.[36] R.H. Deuster divides Kinnaur into two climatic zones:

(a) Zone affected by the Monsoons;
(b) Transition zone to Tibetan-type climate.[37]

"Generally, Wāngtu is accepted as the place where the monsoon reaches its end".[38] This is rather inexact as some monsoon currents do reach the Great Himalaya chain around Karchham beyond Wāngtu.[39] Kālpa, however, is spared heavy monsoon rains.[40] Rainfall data measurements are available from the Forest Department at Chini, Kilba and Nichār. It is not known how scientifically such measurements had been carried on earlier. Personal inspection showed that the person actually making the measurements was many times a not very qualified peon who did not have much idea of what he was doing. Artificial means of

[30] Gerard, A., 1841, p. 60.

[31] Ibid.

[32] Ibid.

[33] Cunningham, J.D., 1844, Pp 173-174; Gerard, A., 1841, p. 62.

[34] Gazetteer, 1971, p. 42.

[35] Personal observation from 1980 to 1983.

[36] For more information about the climate in Kinnaur please see: Gazetteer, 1971, Pp 42-43; Gerard, A., 1841, Pp 60-63; Deuster, R.H., 1939, Pp 14-24.

[37] Deuster R.H., 1939, Pp 14-15.

[38] Ibid, p. 19. The original reads: "Allgemein setzt man Wāngtu als den Platz an, wo der Monsoon sein Ende erreicht".
Translation mine.

[39] Personal observation.

[40] (i) Buchanan, W.E.: In the Footsteps of the Gerards, in: H.J., Vol. II, April 1930, p. 78;
(ii) Gorrie, R. Maclagan: Two Easy Passes in Kanawar, in: H.J., Vol. I, No. 1, April 1929, p. 75.
Both acconts state that Chini, as Kālpa was formerly called, was a beloved resort of the Governor-General, Lord Dalhousie, as he could escape here from the damp and humid monsoon of Simla.

irrigation are necessary in Kinnaur for agricultural production. The rainfall is just not enough to carry on purely rainfed agriculture in most areas of the district. With this brief outline of climate and rainfall coming after the geographical coordinates, we can now pass on to consider what impact geographical location, topography and climate have had on various aspects of life in Kinnaur District.[41]

1.2 EXTENDED CREDIT CIRCLES AND UNDISTURBED EVOLUTION

Before considering the impact of geography on state formation in Kinnaur it is relevant to consider its impact on the evolution of the informal credit sector circles because this study primarily deals with the credit infrastructure of Kinnaur.

1.2.1 Skewed Credit Circles: Geography at Work

A study of moneylending operations in the Dhanbad area of Bihar by a German researcher found that moneylenders tended to operate there in well-defined circles as follows:[42]

(a) An "Inner Circle" comprising parties located within the villages under study; and
(b) An "Outer Circle" involving parties in the immediate neighbourhood of the villages under study.

The radius of this **"Outer Circle"** was estimated by the researcher at five kilometres from the place of residence of the moneylender.[43] Even though Dhanbad and Kinnaur are geographically and topographically quite different, some findings of Dr Roth's research in Dhanbad are similar to the situation in Kinnaur as we see.

The traditional credit market in Kinnaur villages consisted of very fragmented, smaller, territorially limited markets. This existence of a multitude of small, limited credit markets suited the needs of both the creditor and the borrower.[44] Physical proximity of the creditor

[41] Those interested in more general information about Kinnaur please see:
(a) Herbert, J.D.: An account of a tour made to lay down the course and levels of the River Setlej or Satudra, as far as traceable within the limits of the British authority, performed in 1819, in: Asiatick Researches, Vol. XV, 1825, Pp 339-428;
(b) Lloyd, W. and Gerard, A.: Narrative of a Journey from Cawnpoor to the Boorendo Pass in the Himalaya..., Vol. I and II, London: James Madden & Co., 1840;
(c) Hutton, Capt. Thomas: Journal of a Tour through Kunawur, Hungrung and Spiti undertaken in the year 1838, in: J.A.S.B., Vol. VIII, No. 7, New Series, No. 95, November 1839, Part I: Pp 901-950; Vol. VIII, Part II, 1839, Part 2: Pp 489-513; Vol. I, Part I - New Series, No. 102, 1840, Part 3: Pp 555-581;
(d) Reeves, H.C.: Notes on the Mountains of Bussahir and Spiti, in: Alpine Journal, Vol. 27, 1913, Pp 332-334;
(e) Stoliczka, F.: Geological Sections across the Himalaya Mountains, from Wāngtu bridge on the River Sutlej to Sungdo on the Indus, in: Memoirs of the Geological Survey of India, Vol. 5, 1866, Pp 1-154;
(f) Stoliczka, F.: Das Setletsch Thal im Himalaya, in: Mitteilungen aus Justus Perthes' geographischer Anstalt über wichtige neue Erforschungen auf dem Gesammtgebiete der Geographie von Dr A. Peterman, Band 16, Gotha: Justus Perthes, 1870, Pp 8-12.

[42] Roth, Hans-Dieter: Indian Moneylenders At Work, New Delhi: Manohar Publications, I edn., 1983, p. 25.

[43] Roth, H.D.: Moneylenders' Management of Loan Agreements, Report on a Case Study in Dhanbad, p. 1167, in: Economic and Political Weekly, Vol. XIV, No. 27, 7 July 1979, Pp 1166-1170.

[44] Ibid.

was a check against delinquency in repayment by the borrower. The creditors belonged to socially and economically dominant groups who could enforce this dominance in, or in close proximity to, their base of operations and not at extended distances. Hence they concentrated moneylending operations in their own villages or their immediate vicinity and did not seek to operate in distant areas where returns on loans might theoretically have been higher.[45]

It is relevant, however, to introduce here a factor important for the informal credit structure in Kinnaur District, viz the role of the village deity or devi/devta as moneylender.[46] Since this phenomenon is dealt with separately later, suffice it to say that the devta remained over centuries as the fulcrum of the credit markets in Kinnaur. There was no wilful default on loans taken from the deities, not just because the borrowers were afraid of divine wrath that would be implacable in case of default. Geography had a role to play in this as well. All devis/devtas were respected but the fear inspired by them seemed to be inversely proportional to the distance from their seats of authority. The local devta was feared the maximum. Even divine power had to manifest itself through human agency for loan disbursement and recovery! Influential villagers dominating the temple committees[47] could make their coercive influence felt best within their own villages because geography had isolated the villages in Kinnaur from each other. The role of the deity has been well summed up by a Kinnaura himself. "The principal village deity is a divinity, a doctor, a magistrate, a judge, the Chief Executive, an astrologer, the village hero, the cynosure of all eyes etc. rolled into one".[48] The "etc. etc.", though the author does not say so, should evidently include "moneylender/credit giver" as a major function. This credit system based on the devtas was Kinnaur's response to the geographical conditions which isolated the area from development of an official credit infrastructure. The deity's capacity of ensuring recovery was most efficient in its own village where it was the presiding divinity. It could not exercise the same coercive power outside its own village as each village had its own deity/deities. Geographical isolation no doubt contributed to this proliferation of deities for each village. The local predominance of most such deities was coterminous with their lending range, thus ensuring the existence of numerous limited credit markets because the deity was generating surplus by virtue of its ritual status and landed property. This coterminous nature of the deity's ritual sway and lending operations was manifested in a pyramidal credit pattern. A geographically spread out and isolated mass of numerous village credit markets functioned as a kind of base plane. Over these existed a middle plane of credit markets based on deities with ritual sway over a 'ghodi' or group of villages rather than over a single village which was covered by a still narrower plane of lending operations by some 'pargana'-level deities having influence over more than one ghodi. This led to an extremely narrow apex formed by deities with ritual sway extending over more than one pargana. This apex had only the Sungra Mahéshras, the Shuwang Chandika of Kothi and the Devta Badrināth of Kāmru as constituents. And even their lending circles showed an overwhelming local market confined to their immediate vicinity with few credit transactions in a regional context.

[45] Ibid.

[46] Please see Chapter VII for more elaboration of this aspect.

[47] Please see Chapter VII for information about temple committees.

[48] Negi, T.S., 1976, p. 39.
For a list of of the village deities in Kinnaur please see:
(i) Negi, T.S., 1976, Appendix IV, Pp 182-184;
(ii) Deuster, R.H., 1939, Pp 82-84;
(iii) Gazetteer, 1971, Pp 369-370.

The credit market pyramid thus had a very wide base and a sharply angled shape leading to an extremely narrow apex plane. Above this pyramid stood the divinity of Bushahr State, Bhimā Kāli of Sarāhan outside Kinnaur. In villages having more than one local deity (Chini, Chagāoṅ, Kāmru - to name a few) each deity functioned as a separate moneylender with its own little credit market. The volume of transactions depended on the surplus available in the deity's 'bhandara' or store. Such deities complemented rather than competed with each other in their credit giving operations. Existence of more than one credit giving source did not lead to variations in the interest rates charged. Interest rates not being different, adherents of one deity would get no advantage even if they took the theoretically possible step of switching their allegiance to another village deity. In any case the deities were generally related to each other and coexisted harmoniously.

Where even the devtas feared to tread commercial banks rushed in! They were quickly taught a harsh lesson by geographical realities. For example, the Punjab National Bank branch at Rekong Peo made extensive loans in the Bhāba valley in Nichār Tahsil, not very far as the crow flies but with two intervening mountain ridges. The bank found out early enough that it was difficult to follow up these loans and ensure their recoveries in view of the terrain involved. Staff members found it hard to trudge from one remotely located hamlet to another. Even though now a motorable road has been constructed up to Katgāoṅ village in the Bhāba valley, people live there in scattered hamlets on the hillsides. In summer many of them leave their homes and migrate with their flocks of sheep and goats into alpine pastures or move up to the 'kandas' for cultivation[49] It is not possible to return home everyday from the kanda. Temporary shelters called doghris are erected by villagers for living there during the summer season.[50] In winter heavy snowfall may either cut off access totally for some time or involve long stretches on foot which not every bank employee, specially one from the plains, may fancy. Again, many shepherds leave Kinnaur before winter with their flocks of sheep and goats and move down to traditional pastures at lower altitudes in Sirmaur, Mandi, Kulu, Kangra, Solan or Simla Districts in Himāchal Pradesh or Dehra Doon, Kumaon and Garhwāl Districts of Uttar Pradesh respectively. These prolonged seasonal absences make the creditor's task hard, unless he/she resides very close in the vicinity, knows the debtor's family well and can bring all his/her social coercive prowess to bear when he/she knows the moment is ripe, for example after the sale of the harvest or some animal or land holding by the debtor. The creditor at long distance can not keep such close track and without close supervision loses out in the form of a high rate of defaults on loans.

Slowly the banks learnt the lesson of Kinnaur's geography and began restricting their loaning operations to the vicinity of their branches. To meet the complaints of villages situated at a distance more and more bank branches have had to be opened regardless of the fact that such branches, at Yangthang for example, cannot be justified by any criterion of viable bankability.[51] Some banks would gladly wind up many of their branches in Kinnaur because these have no chances of showing profits. A bank manager even expressly gave the information that no bank branch in Kinnaur was showing a profit.[52] Political compulsions

[49] A kanda means single cropped land at high altitudes. Each village in in Kinnaur has its kanda. In villages Nāko and Hāngo these kandas extend up to altitudes going till nearly 14,000 feet.

[50] For further information about doghris, please see:
(a) Kleinert, Christian: Siedlung und Umwelt im Zentralen Himalaya, Wiesbaden: Franz Steiner Verlag, 1983, p. 22;
(b) Deuster, R.H., 1939, p. 40;
(c) Smith, C.M.: A Walking Tour through the Himalayas from Hindoostan to Tibet, in: The Alpine Journal, Vol. III, 1867, Pp 52-68.

[51] Please see Chapter IV for information about bank branches in Kinnaur.

and administrative exigencies of financing the integrated rural development programme and other government programmes[53] rule out this easy option dictated by sound banking practice based only on economic considerations. Bankable criteria bow before the new politico-administrative environment and eternal geographical reality in Kinnaur.

Situation rather than radial distance plays an important role in determining loaning patterns. It is easier to follow up loans disbursed in villages up and down the same valley in which the moneylender lives than in adjacent valleys even if villages in the latter may be nearer as the crow flies or at a shorter radial distance. A village situated 10 or 12 kilometres away may mean crossing one or more intervening mountain ridges ranging from 12,000 feet to 18,000 feet or more, while another village in the same valley, even if 20 kms distant or more, may prove far easier of access.[54]

The loaning patterns tend to thus be more elliptical and less circular because of this reality of geography having made access easier up-and-down the valleys rather than across them. Even within the same valley access can be difficult in winter.[55] This makes it unlikely that a moneylender would extend his loaning operations beyond his own village or its immediate accessible vicinity to distant villages even within the same valley. Interestingly enough, the same geographical reality that drastically limited the Inner Circle and the Outer Circle of moneylending activities led to a third circle pitched hundreds of kms away from the moneylenders' villages.

Kinnaur's topography rendered it difficult for a household to flourish economically based solely on one basic occupation like agriculture. This fact drove most households to adopt a mix of occupations like cultivation, trade, animal husbandry, horticulture and moneylending rather than reliance on any one economic activity. The existence of the system of fraternal polyandry and of a joint family system meant that several brothers could devote themselves to different economic activities while one brother always stayed with the common wife at home to look after household affairs.[56]

[52] Personal communication dated December 10, 1985 from the Manager, Punjab National Bank at Rekong Peo.

[53] Henceforth referred to as the I.R.D.P.

[54] For some examples of cases where the radial distance between two villages was short but involved considerable difficulties in crossing, please see:
- (a) Lloyd, W. & Gerard, A., Vol. II, 1840, Pp 65-87;
- (b) Glover, H.M.: Round the Kanawar Kailas, in: H.J., Vol. II, April 1930, Pp 81-86;
- (c) Smith, C.M., 1867, Pp 61-62;
- (d) Theobald, W.: Notes of a Trip from Simla to the Spiti valley and Chomoriri (Tshomoriri) lake during the months of July, August and September 1861, in: J.A.S.B., Vol. 31, No. V, 1862, Pp 480-527.

[55] It took the author nearly eight hours to cover roughly 14 kms distance from village Rakchham to village Chhitkul in the Baspa valley on an easy track of summer which becomes very difficult in winter. The journey was undertaken on December 31, 1980 through heavy snow. The same distance had earlier been covered in summer and autumn by the author many times in between three to four hours.

[56] For information about polyandry in Kinnaur please see:
- (a) Wilson, Andrew: The Abode of Snow, II edn., Edinburgh and London: William Blackwood and Sons, MDCCCLXXVI, Pp 206-217;
- (b) Negi, T.S., 1976, p. 20, Pp 29-30;
- (c) Gazetteer, 1911, Pp 15-17;
- (d) Cunningham, J.D., 1844, Pp 205-206;
- (e) Deuster, R.H., 1939, Pp 36-37;
- (f) Reichelt, G.: Die Himalaya-Mission der Brüdergemeine, Gütersloh: G. Bertelsmann, 1896, Pp 46-47;

As we move from south west to north east in Kinnaur, we pass from the rainfed Nichār Sub-Division in which agriculture was a more important economic activity than trade to Kālpa Sub-Division where the importance of trade as an economic activity, though not as important as agriculture, was higher than in Nichār Sub-Division, to the Pooh Sub-Division where trade overshadowed agriculture as an economic activity. Geographical proximity to Tibet meant that traders from the Pooh area became intermediaries in the trade from Western Tibet to the plains and lower hills through the entrepôt of Rāmpur. Residents of the Baspa valley carried on trade with neighbouring areas of Rohru and Chooara in erstwhile Bushahr State, as well as with areas in Uttarkashi, Garhwāl and Dehra Doon districts of Uttar Pradesh across the Dhaula Dhār range. Residents of Bhāba valley carried on trade with areas in Spiti Sub-Division across the Sri Khand range. In terms of importance, the trade carried on with Western Tibet was far more substantial than that carried on with areas in U.P. or in Spiti.[57] Over time trade patterns stabilized in such a way that traders from particular villages in Kinnaur would trade only with particular correspondents in Western Tibet or other areas year after year. This leads us directly to our third credit circle.

The third circle was one in which Kinnaura traders gave credit at long distance to their borrowers who in return sold their produce only to their creditors. This long-distance trade was financed by giving money in advance to persons in Western Tibet or U.P. In return, the borrowers would furnish the article demanded; mostly shawl wool, borax, salt, butter, sheep and goats from Tibet; rice, wheat, other grains or metal wares from U.P. areas to the lenders only at previously mutually agreed upon rates regardless of the prevailing market prices for these commodities.[58]

Loaning in the third circle was a mechanism for ensuring stability of prices for the coming year by advance payment of loans. The arrangements were a system of specific performance on an annual basis. It assured the supply of commodities at stable prices as an important element of cross border trade. No interest was charged on these loans by Kinnaura moneylenders overtly. They, however, got more than good value for their money by paying lower than the prevailing market rates. The exact terms were a matter of annual negotiations between the moneylender-trader and the borrower-supplier. The absence of overt interest rates should come as no surprise. "Theoretically, a monopolist will lend up to that volume at which his marginal lending costs equal the value of the borrower's marginal product on the loan and he will levy a rate of interest equal to this value of the marginal product where produce markets are competitive".[59] Monopoly profit has been considered as a cause of high interest rates in underdeveloped rural areas like Kinnaur.[60] If interest rates in the third circle did not equal the value of the marginal products, it was because their true values were often subsumed

(g) Schneider, H.: Ein Missionsbild aus dem westlichen Himalaya, Gnadau: Verlag der Unitäts-Buchhandlung, 1880, p. 17;
(h) Jacquemont, Victor: État social et politique de l'Inde du Nord, Paris: Ernest Leroux, 1933, p. 263;
(i) Fraser, J.B., 1820, p. 336;
(j) Gazetteer, 1971, Pp 94-95.

[57] This was shown in everyday life in some cases. Negi Khem Singh told the author in a personal interview in Sangla in December, 1985 that in his school days at Rāmpur children of traders of the Pooh area were better dressed and had more pocket-money than students from other areas of Kinnaur.

[58] Information given in personal interviews by the late Negi Dharam Bhag, then Chairman, Panchāyat Samiti, Pooh, and other former traders like Negi Amar Singh, Medub Dandub and Sanam Narboo.

[59] Bottomley, Anthony: Interest Rate Determination in Underdeveloped Rural Areas, p. 287, in: American Journal of Agricultural Economics, Vol. 57, No. 3, August 1975, Pp 279-291.

[60] Ibid.

under the prices at which Kinnaura trader-creditors bought the Tibetans' produce where such transactions formed an integral part of their loans. Loans were used primarily to facilitate trade as a surplus generating activity.

Creditor-borrower relations in the third circle formed a system in which borrower-producers in Tibet welcomed credit from lender-traders in Kinnaur who were happy to give such credit in order to ensure that the former would sell their produce only through the latter. Kinnauras did not wish to engage in competitive bidding for the output of the Tibetans and claimed their usury in the form of stable lower-than-auction prices at which they bought from their borrowers. Their system of giving credit ostensibly free of interest charges was a device for damping free market fluctuations in prices. Stable prices meant good profits for Kinnauras who repeated this cycle year-after-year. The third credit circle worked well over 150 years till the Sino-Indian conflict of 1962 put a stop to it. A credit system which had well stood the test of time and geographical environment was thus brought to an end. Moneylending operations of the informal sector in Kinnaur have since been confined only to the first two credit circles. That the third circle could flourish for so long without disturbance was partly also due to the fact that geography made Kinnaur difficult for military operations, preventing wars and military depredations from seriously upsetting these long-established long-distance credit patterns.

1.2.2 Quartermasters Not Napoléons: Geography and Military Operations in Kinnaur

Credit operations were not the only aspect relatively unaffected by military operations. Kinnaur was not a terrain where Blitzkriegs could be launched. There is no reliable evidence of major military operations ever having been mounted there. Plundering expeditions rather than sustained military operations seemed the general rule.[61] Even the ordinary traveller had such problems organizing adequate supplies for his party that one can only imagine what a difficult job the quartermaster of an invading army would have had.[62]

Bushahr State never had a standing army. It had only a militia of about 3,000 men.[63] "The military force of Bischur is not great, nor does it appear that any considerable standing army was ever kept up...When a military force was required, the people were summoned by their chiefs to follow them to the field; and they brought with them the means of subsistence for a certain time".[64] A British officer's evaluation was that there was "no standing army or any regular soldiery since the British Government extended its protection to Bussaher, and even before that time it resembled an half-armed mob rather than a military force, having no uniform, and each man being armed according to circumstances, some with matchlocks, some with swords, and others who possessed neither, arming themselves with sticks and branches of trees".[65] Living off the land[66] was ruled out in Kinnaur as a military option by geographical

[61] Legend speaks of plundering expeditions by the Tibetans into the Baspa valley till Kāmru and by the Spitians into Lippa valley through Asrang till Lippa. Please see:
(i) Lloyd, W. and Gerard, A., 1840, Pp 266-267;
(ii) Gerard, A., 1841, p. 52.

[62] For an idea of the problems of organizing supplies for a trek through Kinnaur, please see:
(i) Madden, Captain, 1845, Pp 79-81;
(ii) Theobald, W., 1862, Pp 481-487.

[63] Fraser, J.B., 1820, p. 272.

[64] Ibid, p. 271.

[65] Hutton, Capt. Thomas, 1839, p. 907.

conditions which dictated that the hero of any campaign there would have been the quartermaster, in charge of supply arrangements, rather than a Napoléon-like figure advancing far ahead with mobile units. The absence of a standing army and the existence of a rag-tag militia obliged to feed itself shows that this lesson of geography was not lost on the Bushahr rulers. They were not alone in this perception. Their rivals for influence in the region - Tibet, Ladākh, Garhwāl, Kulu and Sirmaur had similar militias only. This changed only in the early 19th century when the Sikhs and the Gorkhas came on the scene in the Western Himalayas with better organized armies. Unable to cope with this new development, Bushahr had to accept British paramountcy in 1816. Ladākh failed to preserve its independence and had to acknowledge the supremacy of the Sikh Durbār, later becoming a part of Gulab Singh's Kashmir.[67] This military system under discussion is quite similar to the military system used in Switzerland where there was and is a citizens' army with each household required to furnish at least one adult male for military duties in times of war. Geography determined the evolution of such similar structures so far apart and under such different conditions. However, unlike the Swiss, the Kinnauras were not engaged by their neighbours as mercenaries. The Kinnauras as well as the Swiss relied on favourable terrain, in addition to their military prowess, for success on the battlefield.

Attempts made in the Western Himalayas to conduct grandiose military campaigns in defiance of geographical constraints ended in failure. Mirza Haidar Dughlat, the intrepid Central Asian general invaded Western Tibet from Ladākh but had to abandon his plans of marching to Lhāsa and return to his base of operations in Ladākh in 1534 A.D. He was defeated not by any Tibetan force but by inhospitable terrain which made it almost impossible to organize a proper supply line.[68] Zorāwar Singh, the brave Dogra general of the Sikh Durbār, invaded Western Tibet from Ladākh in April 1841.[69] He succeeded in occupying Western Tibet till the Mayum La pass but was annihilated by a Tibetan force near Taklakot in December 1841 in severe winter conditions.[70] Reading about the travails of Zorāwar Singh's troops caught in freezing cold with frost-bitten limbs against enemies better accustomed to the severe climatic conditions one can be struck by a similarity to the sufferings of the invading French and German armies in Russian winter conditions in pursuance of the

[66] A classic example of this concept of living off the land in a military campaign without having a long baggage train is that of General William Tecumseh Sherman's march from Atlanta to Savannah on the coast of Georgia in 1864 during the American Civil War 1861-65.

[67] For information about the military organization of the Ladākhi Kingdom please see:

(a) Datta, C.L.: Ladākh and Western Himalayan Politics 1819-1848, The Dogra conquest of Ladākh, Baltistan and West Tibet and reactions by other powers, New Delhi: Munshiram Manoharlal, 1973, Pp 37-38;

(b) Cunningham, Sir Alexander, 1970, Pp 275-283.

Alexander Cunningham's observations about Ladākh's military system are equally valid for Bushahr/Kinnaur: *"In Ladak there was no regular army; but every family or house...was obliged to furnish one ready-armed soldier at the call of the government" (p. 275). "The soldiers were obliged to find their own food...these bodies of undisciplined militia were not deserving of the name of an army, yet they were generally strong enough to repel all attacks of their immediate neighbours...who were as poor and unsoldierly as themselves" (p. 278). "The best 'means of defence' possessed by Ladak consisted in the general inaccessibilty of the country" (p. 280).*

[68] Datta, C.L., 1973, Pp 52-54.

[69] Datta, C.L.: Zorāwar Singh, Political Mission of J.D. Cunningham, 1841-42, p. 82, in: Bengal: Past and Present, Vol. LXXXIX, Part I, Jan.-June 1970, Pp 82-90.

[70] Datta, C.L., 1973, Pp 159-165; Singh, Khushwant: A History of the Sikhs, Vol. II: 1839 - 1974, New Delhi: Oxford University Press, 1978, Pp 22-23.

grand designs of Napoléon and Hitler respectively. In each of these cases well-drilled military machines ignored the realities of geography and weather and paid the price. The Gorkhas brought Bushahr under their sway but found after a vain attempt that they could not overcome Kinnaur. "The Ghoorkhas attempted to attack Kinnaur, and penetrated three days journey within the valley, but were driven back in consequence of falling short of provisions".[71] This seems an accurate assessment though the Kinnaura legends would have us believe that there was a major battle at Chholtu opposite Tāpri where the Gorkhas were vanquished in a night attack.[72] Even though the Kinnauras were good soldiers, given the state of their weaponry and training they could not have held off the battle-hardened Gorkha veterans without favourable terrain. Personal observation of the supposed battlefield at Chholtu makes it obvious that no major action could have taken place in such a confined space. Victor Jacquemont summed it up well that the destruction "of the Wangtoo sango having blocked the area situated on the right bank of the Satluj river to the Gorkhas, they penetrated on the left bank crossing unheard of obstacles. After marching a few miles in the mountains, they found this torrent before them, and at the end of its course, at its point of flowing into the Satluj, a few hundred Kinnauras waiting for them to dispute them the passage. Inferior in numbers, the Gorkhas were worsted and obliged to retreat but not without having concluded a treaty by which the Kinnauras undertook to pay them an annual tribute".[73]

The only major military campaign in which Bushahr troops, mainly Kinnauras, participated towards the north was the Tibetan-Ladākhi-Mughal War of 1681-83 A.D.[74] Even in this war we find references to the small size of the forces involved. "In return, the Rājā of Bashahr promised to join his small army with dGa-ldan's forces".[75] "The Tibetan army...was quite small".[76] The scale of operations became bigger once Tibetan reinforcements came from Lhāsa and a Mughal expeditionary force entered Ladākh from Kashmir but the numbers of men involved were much smaller than in major battles in the plains. Given such geographical conditions, Kinnaur escaped invasions in recorded history and state formation there could proceed on undisturbed. The moneylenders were thus not the only ones in Kinnaur left to weave the webs of their loans secure in the knowledge of relative safety from the military

[71] Fraser, J.B., 1820, p. 265.

[72] This defeat of the Gorkhas has many colourful accounts in Kinnaur. One legend ascribes the Kinnauras' victory to the supernatural intervention of the Mahéshras Devta of Chagāon who turned stones into soldiers (District Census Handbook, 1981, p. 3). Another legend ascribes the Kinnaura success to the guile of the Poāri Wazir, Fateh Rām, who is supposed to have fobbed off the Gorkhas by giving them stones sealed in boxes to look like the royal treasure (Gazetteer, 1971, p. 60).

[73] Jacquemont, V., 1933, p. 255. The original reads: *"La destruction du Sanga de Wongton fermant aux Gorkhas le pays situé sur la rive droite du Setludje, ils pénetrèrent sur la rive gauche au travers d'obstacles inouis. Après quelques milles de marche dans les montagnes, ils trouvèrent devant eux ce torrent, et dans le fond de son vallon, à son embouchure dans le Setludje, quelques centaines de Kanaweris qui les attendaient pour leur disputer le passage. Inférieurs en nombre les Gorkhas eurent le dessous et fûrent obligés de se retirer, mais non sans avoir fait un traité par lequel les Kanaweris s'engageaient à leur payer un tribut annuel"* Translation mine.

[74] Petech, L.: The Tibetan-Ladākhi-Moghul War of 1681-1683, in: Indian Historical Quarterly, Vol. XXIII, No. 3, Sept. 1947, Pp 169-199. A.H. Francke dates this war to 1646-1647 A.D. in his History of Western Tibet, subsequently published as A History of Ladākh, New Delhi: Sterling Publishers, 1977. C.L. Datta follows Petech's dates in his book 'Ladākh and Western Himalayan Politics'.

[75] Petech, L., 1947, p. 176.

[76] Ibid, p. 178.

angle.

1.2.3 Geography and State Formation: Unspectacular but Steady

A glance at the map shows that Kinnaur is situated at the periphery of all major empires or kingdoms that existed in the neighbourhood - Mughal, Tibetan, Ladākhi, Sikh or Gorkha. It was an area where the supply line of any invading force from these areas would have been stretched to the limit. Behind its snowy barriers, Kinnaura polity was left to evolve till finally the Kingdom of Bushahr encompassed the whole of this region. As will be shown in Chapter II, the Kingdom of Bushahr with its capital at Rāmpur was the culmination of a process of state formation initiated by the efforts of the Thākur of Kāmru to bring other thākurs under his control. The existence of petty chieftains called thākurs ruling over small territories was not a phenomenon peculiar to Kinnaur. It has been said of the hill states in Himāchal that the oldest traditions in the hills "refer to a time when petty chiefs, bearing the title of Rana or Thākur, exercised authority, either as independent rulers or under the suzerainty of a paramount power...In considering the political organization of the hills, at that early period, we must dismiss from our minds all ideas of fully organized principalities, and think of an order of things that was patriarchal rather than monarchical, and very much akin to the clan system of the Highlands of Scotland, down to the eighteenth century".[77] In Kinnaur the process of forming a larger kingdom by reducing the fiefs of the thākurs suffered no violent interruptions or impositions from outside in the shape of a Mughal conquest. Even adjacent valleys were not easy to reach so the process of state formation through the creation of a larger entity evolved slowly over a long time.

Absence of a standing army and geographical remoteness meant that the Rājā's control over Kinnaur was always loose. His trade routes to Tibet and Ladākh passed through this area. As will be discussed in Chapter II, surplus generated by trade played a role in the formation of Bushahr State. The Rājā always ensured that the Kinnauras remained loyal to him. Rebellions in Kinnaur would have been hard to put down without a strong military force capable of coping with hard geographical and climatic conditions. The rājās were conscious of this. As late as 1875 A.D. an English traveller observed about the Kinnauras that though "they were nominally subject to the Rājā of Bussahir, yet their village is so difficult of access that they pay little regard to his commands"[78] while talking about Pooh village. The rājās retained the loyalty of the Kinnauras by giving them sufficient patronage at court. The first European to report about Kinnaur mentions that the district of Kinnaur "once forming the chief part of the territory of Bischur, it is no wonder that Kunawurees should be so highly trusted, and so much in power. Many of the chief families in the state, and the principal officers of the government, are of Kunawar extraction; and the personal attendants on the Rājāh are of that country, and the soldiery are chiefly raised there",[79] about the Kinnaura influence in Bushahr State. The Rājā knew that discontent in Kinnaur would endanger the trade routes of Bushahr to Tibet and also his last place of refuge in case of invasion. With Kinnaur secure, the process of state consolidation could go on expanding southwards and westwards towards agriculturally richer areas. Because of its geographical conditions, Kinnaur provided the kernel from which Bushahr State developed. It was a secure bastion of last refuge for the fledgling state in its early years. Strategic geographical location on the frontier with Tibet made the Kinnauras well-known traders and trade a useful activity.

[77] Hutchison, J. and Vogel, J. Ph.: History of Punjab Hill States, Vol. I, Lahore: Superintendent, Government Printing, Punjab, 1933, p. 12.

[78] Wilson, A., 1876, p. 140.

[79] Fraser, J.B., 1820, p. 265. Also see: (i) Lloyd, W. and Gerard, A., 1840, Vol. II, p. 303; (ii) Gerard, A., 1841, p. 77.

1.2.4 Trade: Silver, Intrepidity, Sheep and Trust!

While it was not accurate to say that the "Koonawurees are all traders, and their chief riches consist in large flocks of sheep and goats, that furnish them with wool, which, together with raisins they exchange for grain"[80] a more realistic assessment would be that the Kinnauras were "mostly agriculturists, but do not on the whole produce as much as they consume; all have some flocks and herds, and the people of the north have of late become enterprizing traders...The Kunawurees are rather all agriculturists than all traders...The people of Lower Kunawar are not traders in the sense meant by Gerard, even now very few of them go to Garoo and Leh".[81] The almost universal ownership of sheep and goats was a factor aiding trade because these animals were used as beasts of burden as well. They were well suited as pack animals to the narrow and precipitous trails followed by traders where heavier animals may not have succeeded. There is testimony from several travellers about the use of sheep and goats as pack animals being an important factor in trade with Tibet. "The people are largely pastoral and own extensive flocks of sheep and goats, but they are also great traders, going far into Tibet, using these animals to carry grain, this they obtain from the outer hills and barter in exchange for wool and borax in Tibet".[82] Prince Waldemar of Prussia reported that "the man guards the herds, trades and brings shawl wool and salt to the valleys of Bushahr on the backs of his packgoats and sheep; to get from there in exchange cereals, rice, raisins, walnuts etc"[83] about activities of Kinnaura men.

There was also testimony about the amount of weight that these sheep and goats could carry. "Each carries according to its strength from six to twenty seers in weight, and they form the chief beasts of burthen throughout the country, travelling ten and twelve miles daily with ease and safety over rocky parts where mules and horses could not obtain a footing".[84] Even now the Deputy Commissioner (henceforth referred to as the D.C.) of Kinnaur District fixes rates of carriage for pack animals and while doing so every year includes sheep and goats in the list.[85] These rates are notified for one year from March 1 to the end of February of the succeeding year. Vide office order no. KNR-V-82(NB)/80-81 dated March 31, 1981, the maximum load permissible for sheep and goats was fixed at six kilogrammes.[86] Geography obliged the Kinnauras to keep sheep and goats because agriculture alone was not sufficient to generate an adequate surplus and this compulsion helped trade in-as-much-as these animals

[80] Gerard, A., 1841, p. 79.

[81] Cunningham, J.D., 1844, Pages 179 and 209. Also see: Herbert, J.D., 1819, Pages 354 and 394; Gerard, Lieutenant A.: Narrative of a Journey from Soobathoo to Shipke in Chinese Tartary, p. 367, in: Journal of the Asiatic Society (J.A.S.), Vol. 11, Part I - New Series, 1842, Pp 361-391.

[82] Glover, H.M.: Round the Kanawar Kailas, p. 83, in: H.J., Vol. II, April 1930, Pp 73-80. For references to sheep as beasts of burden please also see: Lloyd, W. and Gerard, A., 1840, Pages 79, 94, 109 and 121.

[83] Kutzner, J.G., 1857, p. 309. The original reads: *"der Mann die Heerden hütet, Handel treibt und auf den Rücken seiner Lastziegen und Schafe nach den Thälern Bissahirs Shawlwolle und Salz bringt, um dagegen Getreide, Reis, Rosinen, Wallnüsse und so weiter von fort zu holen".*
Translation mine.

[84] Hutton, Th., 1839, p. 912.

[85] These rates for animals and porters are notified in accordance with letter no. F-7/69-III, dated January 1, 1960 from the Ministry of Home Affairs, Government of India, read with letter no. 7/39/66-Him dated March 22, 1961 circulated vide Government of H.P., Finance Department letter no. Fin-10/64/59 dated April 14, 1961, read with S.R. 47 and 81 of the Fundamental and Supplementary Rules, Vol. II.

[86] The author was D.C., Kinnaur in 1981 and issued this order. This very limit was still in force in 1985.

formed convenient pack animals over hard terrain involved in trading with Tibet and Ladākh.

As traders, the Kinnauras established a reputation for reliability, enterprise and honesty. Their patterns of lending money at long range for specific performance rested on this reputation to a certain extent. They were described as "frank, active, generous, hospitable and highly honourable in their dealings...Thieves and robbers are unknown, and a person's word may be implicitly relied upon, in any thing regarding money matters".[87] John Baillie Fraser found a resemblance between the Scots and the Kinnauras. The latter "appear to bear a great resemblance to the Scots highlanders in disposition, being fond of enterprise and travel, and also great traders. Indeed, they are almost exclusively the commercial carriers between Hindostan and Tartary, as also from Tartary to Cashmere; frequenting the routes from Leo in Ludhak, to Lassa and Degurcha and Nepal on trading speculations...an unbounded confidence is placed in them by the people of Ludhak and Cashmere and Tartary who find them strictly honest".[88] Against these rather rosy assessments we have Cunningham's opinion in which he felt that had Gerard "made more careful enquiries than he seems to have done, he would have found that the Kunawarees can lie, cheat, steal and commit murder".[89] Capt. Hutton felt that the honesty of the Kinnauras appeared to be like "the honour which is said to exist between thieves; they are true and honest among themselves, because they find it mutually their interest to be so in a country where each is necessarily more or less dependent on his neighbour for assistance...but in their their dealings with a stranger, they do not hesitate to lie and cheat as much as any of the people of the plains of India".[90] A much more critical assessment was made by the Rev. J.F. Bruske, the founder of the Moravian Mission station at Chini in 1900 A.D., who had this to report about the Kinnauras - *"We have worked in different parts of India, but nowhere met a people which appears so dirty and ragged; is so dull and so lazy and thereby so untruthful, faithless, intriguing and theft-prone like this people. Even the faces of many among them convey an impression of great depravity"*.[91]

Be that as it may, the Rājās of Bushahr recognized fairly early the importance of trade, as evidenced clearly by the treaty signed with Tibet by Rājā Kehri Singh in 1685 A.D.[92] It came to form the cornerstone of trade relations with Tibet which remained in force

[87] Gerard, A., 1841, p. 76.

[88] Fraser, J.B., 1820, p. 264.

[89] Cunningham, J.D., 1844, p. 207.

[90] Hutton, Capt. Th., 1840, Part III, Pp 556-557.

[91] Jahresbericht der Station Chini - Jahr 1900 in German by J.F. Bruske. Available in the archives of the Brüder-Unität at Herrnhut in the GDR under the rubric S.e.1.a, M.D. (Missionsdirektion), Pert. West Himalaya. The original reads: *"Wir haben in verschiedenen Teilen Indiens gearbeitet, aber nirgends ein Volk getroffen, das so schmutzig und so zerlumpt aussieht, so stumpf und faul und dabei so verlogen, treulos, intrigierend und diebisch ist wie dieses Volk. Schon auf Gesichten von vielen unter ihnen liegt ein Ausdruck größer Verworfenheit"*.
Translation mine.

[92] The text of this treaty is a part of the folklore of Kinnaur. It was said to be valid so long as "the black crow does not turn white, the holy Mount Kailash does not melt and the lake Manasarowar does not dry up". This language is similar to that mentioned in a historical document found by Dr Dieter Schuh in 1978 in Kashmir in the Gergan Collection. This document is an officially certified copy of a group of 'Herrscherurkunden' from the time of the Ladākhi king Ni-ma-rnam-rgyal. An oath is said to have been sworn by King Sen-ge-rnam-rgyal-ba and Chos-rje sMu-rjins-pa. The oath partly reads: "So long as the above situated (snow mountain) gans-dkar Ti-se does not melt and so long as the lake Ma-pham does not dry up...". Ti-se is Mount Kailash in Tibetan and Ma-pham is lake Manasarowar. The original reads: "So lange der oben

down to the 20th century up to 1962. The British Trade Agent at Gartok attests in his periodic confidential reports that Kinnaura traders were allowed to go in Western Tibet wherever they could find wool and pasham. No restrictions of any kind were put in their trade.[93] A confidential report of 1912 refers to a "friendly treaty...signed between Bashahr State and Tibet, by that splendid treaty the Bashahris still have free trade rights in Tibet".[94]

This treaty reveals the sagacity of the Rājā of Bushahr. He recognized the importance of cross-border trade with Tibet over mere territorial gain. Instead of demanding substantial territorial concessions for having aided the Tibetans in their war against Ladākh he demanded and obtained only the Hangrang valley, the so-called Upper Kinnaur area of today[95] which gave Bushahr access to direct trade routes to Tibet. The territory so obtained was useful in establishing intensive trade links with Tibet and these were sought to be protected in the treaty. Rather than acquire more arid areas towards Spiti, the Bushahr Rājā cemented good relations with Tibet, a competitor for political influence in the Western Himalayas. In addition, peace with Tibet enabled the Rājā of Bushahr to extend his sway southwards and westwards over areas in present-day Simla District, without having to bother about maintenance of a sizeable military presence on the Tibetan frontier. Bushahr attained its natural frontiers along the Para and Spiti rivers in the north, the Zaskar range in the east. Human and commercial links with Tibet were strengthened, enabling visits by lāmās from Tibet and training of Kinnaura Buddhist monks there. An informal credit network began flourishing through support of trade with Tibet after the treaty.

The Rājā of Bushahr did not directly tax this trade with Tibet but got increased income indirectly. Direct taxation came only towards the end of the 19th century when under the influence of British-appointed managers trade checkposts were established at Nichār and Chini for assessing the flow of goods to- and from Tibet. A duty was imposed at the rate of 6% of the assessed value of the goods. During this period, loans were begun to be given directly from the State Treasury to richer traders at 25% annual rate of interest for carrying on trade with Tibet. The traders made good profits and did not default on their loans, thereby providing the State with a steady source of income. The British Trade Agent refers many times in his confidential despatches to the credit arrangements made by Bushahr for Kinnaura traders as a sort of model worthy of emulation by the British for their own directly administered Bhotia traders in Almora and other areas of U.P. "The Bashahr State is rightly encouraging their traders in this respect by advancing them money without interest".[96] He

gelegene (Schneeberg) gans-dkar Ti-se nicht schmilzt und so lange der See Ma-pham-pa nicht austrocknet...".

Translation mine.

Schuh, Dieter: Zu den Hintergründen der Parteinahme Ladākh's für Bhutan gegen Lhāsa, p. 49, in: Kantowsky, Detlef, Sander, Reinhard (eds.): Recent Researches on Ladākh, Band 1, Schriftenreihe Internationales Asienforum, München, Köln, London: Weltforum Verlag, Pp 37-50.

93 Confidential letter no. 144, dated 30-11-1912, para 11 from Rai Sahib Devi Dās, British Trade Agent, Gartok to the Superintendent Hill States, Simla. The letter is available in the confidential file of the reports of the British Trade Agent, Gartok in the D.C.'s Office at Kālpa.

94 Letter no. 85 dated 15-09-1913 from the British Trade Agent, Gartok to the Superintendent Hill States, Simla, Paras 3 and 4.

95 (a) Petech, L.: The Kingdom of Ladākh C. 950 - 1842 A.D., Rome: IsMEO, Serie Orientale: LI, 1977, p. 79;
(b) Lloyd, W. and Gerard, A., 1840, Vol. II, p. 164;
(c) Hutton, Th., 1839, Part I, Pp 939-940;
(d) Cunningham, J.D., 1844, p. 231;
(e) Deuster, R.H., 1939, p. 102.

Hangrang valley area ceded to Raja Kehri Singh of Bushahr
by the Tibetans in c. 1685 A.D.
after the Tibetan-Ladakhi-Mughal war of 1681-1683

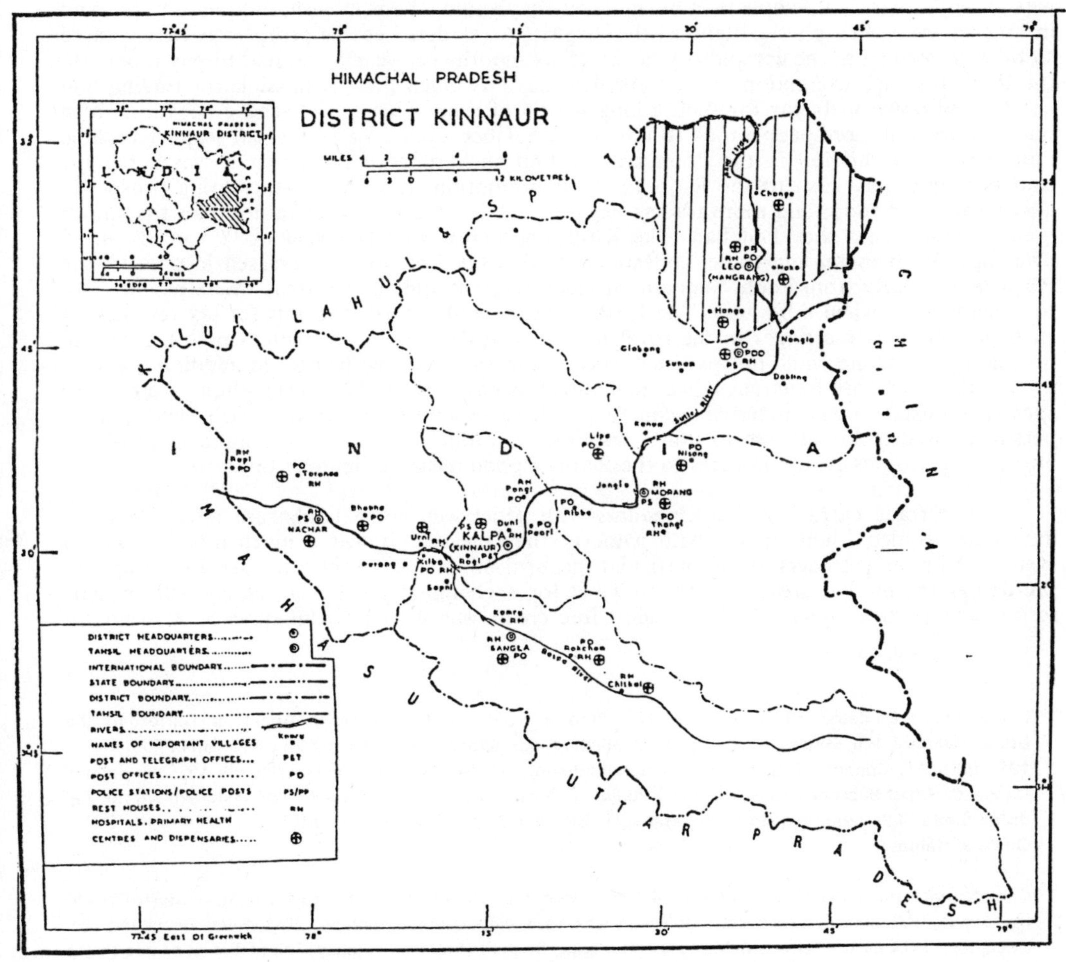

Portion with lines marks the limits of present-day
Hangrang Sub-Tahsil

goes on "...the Garhwālis I think should be afforded facilities of starting cooperative banks as in the case of Bashahris to save them from the clutches of the exacting moneylenders".[97] Obviously, the British Trade Agent had got his facts slightly wrong. Loans were certainly being given by the state to Bushahri traders, mostly Kinnauras, but these were neither interest-free nor was there any cooperative bank which existed from the side of the state to finance such loaning. Lala Devi Dās referred later to the "liberal policy of the Bashahr State by advancing large taccāvi loans" to traders.[98]

Trade brought benefits to the Rājā also indirectly. The taxation system in Bushahr was loosely organized. People paid in whatever they could - be it in cash, in grain, in cash and in kind or even with physical labour, the 'bégār'. As traders became prosperous they wanted to be exempted from the compulsory bégār of six months per year[99] and had to pay money to the Rājā for such exemption. They wanted to have as much time as possible for trading and not be tied down in bégār for such a long period of time. They could send a substitute also but as more and more people took to trading with Tibet, even on a very small scale, it became more and more difficult in the Pooh area to find such substitutes so that it was easier for traders to just pay cash to the Rājā for their exemption from bégār. Increasing prosperity also meant that more and more traders began building 'pucca' houses rather than the earlier mud dwellings that they had had. The Rājā imposed a so-called wall tax[100] on all pucca dwellings. With increasing trade, collections of this tax brought in increased income to the Rājā, particularly from Pooh, Sunnam, Shyāso, Kānam and similar areas where people took to trade with Tibet in a big way. The Rājā used to send special demands for tax revenue on such occasions as marriages in the royal house, special religious ceremonies or other special occasions. If anyone could not pay such special exactions, he/she had to do additional labour in lieu thereof. This functioned like an indirect bégār and to have exemptions from these special imposts traders preferred again to purchase exemption by paying cash. The more a person wanted to be left free to utilize his time in trading with Tibet, the more it translated into paying various exemption fees to the Rājā, a good means of indirect taxation.

The trade carried on by Kinnauras with Tibet was not a haphazard affair in which individuals traded wherever and with whoever they pleased. It was a much more organized system. Kinnaura traders from particular groups of villages went together in groups to pre-designated market areas in Western Tibet for exchanging goods and money with specific respondent parties. Since advance interest-free credit was used by Kinnauras as a means of

[96] Letter no. 119, dated 10 December 1913, Para 8 from the British Trade Agent at Gartok to the Superintendent, Hill States, Simla, a copy of which stands attached to letter no. 22 dated Simla 20 January 1914 from J.F. Connolly Esquire, I.C.S., Superintendent, Hill States, Simla to the Hon'ble Mr C.A. Barron, C.I.E., I.C., Chief Secretary to Government Punjab, Lahore, copy of which was sent vide endorsement no. 254 dated Simla 30th January 1914 to the Manager, Bushahr State, Kotgarh. The last is available in the D.C.'s Office at Kālpa.

[97] Confidential letter dated December 3, 1914, Para 5 from Lala Devi Dās, British Trade Agent, Western Tibet to the Supdt., Hill States, Simla, copy of which was sent vide endorsement no. 2881 dated Simla the 9th. December 1914 by the latter's office to the Manager, Bashahr State at Kotgarh. The last is available in the D.C.'s Office at Kālpa.

[98] Confidential letter no. 23 dated Simla the 13th. December 1915 from Rai Sahib Devi Dās to the Supdt., Hill States, Simla, copy of which was sent vide endorsement no. 3086 by the latter's office to the Manager, Bashahr State at Kotgarh. It is available in the D.C.'s office at Kālpa.

[99] This period of six months per year was reduced to one month after Tikka Raghunāth Singh's Settlement of 1896.

[100] Mauersteuer in German.

obtaining assured supply at stable prices[101] it was in their own interest to carry on trade on strictly organized lines to prevent mutual competition which may have pushed up prices. They sought to ensure this by partitioning out markets in Tibet and evolving strict rules to prevent lone rangers tempted to defy these arrangements from doing so. The Rājā concurred with these rules since organized trade brought him higher income rather than a free-for-all in which some stray Kinnauras may have gained but the majority would have lost profits, thus affecting royal income adversely. Any trader breaking rules evolved by the trading fraternity of Kinnaur risked incurring the Rājā's displeasure. State interest and private interest coincided to keep out adventurers wishing to indulge in free trade anywhere and with anyone. An official estimate of the "number of Kanawari Zamindars genuinely engaged in trade with Tibet"[102] in 1912 was a little under 350, excluding "petty exchanges of salt, grain, cloth etc. which continue in some cases even in winter between Kanawari and Tibetan villages adjacent to the border"[103] showing how much a way of life this trade had become. We can now outline the organization of this trade.

Kinnaura traders constituted themselves mainly into five groups, according to their villages and routes employed by them. These were broadly as follows:

(I) **Hangrang Pargana**: comprising villages in the lower valley of the Spiti river.
Virtually all the villages traded with Tibet. Their route led to Chhumurti area in Tibet, not proceeding to Tashigang. A major number, however, went to Rudok, Langchu and Tso-tso.

(II) **Villages along the line between the termination of the Hindustan - Tibet Road at Namgya and Rārang** i.e. Jāngi, Lippa, Asrang, Kānam, Lābrang, Spillo, Sunnam, Ropa, Gyabong, Rushkalang, Pooh, Dabling, Dubling and Khab.

This group counted about 200 traders, many of them dealing on a large scale. Nearly 75% of them carried on regular trade in wool.[104] Victor Jacquemont talks of a trader of Sunnam village called Patti Rām who had "extended his minor commercial operations" to such an extent that he had "a greater fame in Kinnaur than Mr Laffitte in Paris".[105] Most traders of this group followed the route via Shyalkhar to Chhumurti and beyond, while some went via Shipké. They mainly frequented Rudok, Tok, Rundar, Bongba and Gugé, all far north of Gartok. They brought pasham which went via Suket and Amritsar to Ludhiana, borax, which went via Rāmpur and Simla to Jagadhri. Some of these wealthy entrepreneurs plied their trade as far as Delhi or even Calcutta for china and ironware goods which they exchanged for wool. Payment was mostly effected by them, however, in cash. Cash for trade with Tibet meant silver rupees which were accepted all over Tibet. The Tibetans were keen to receive silver currency which they could use in jewellery as well.

[101] Please see the discussion on the third credit circle in Section 1.2.1.

[102] G. Mackworth Young's Report on Kanawari Traders, Para 3, Section II, sent vide letter no. 2819/S/(Pol.) dated Simla the 25th. Sept. 1912 from C.A. Barron, Chief Secretary to Government Punjab, to the Superintendent Hill States, Simla. This is available in the D.C.'s Office at Kālpa.

[103] Ibid.

[104] Negi Sundar Lal, retired Range Forest Officer, told the author personally that one Opang Negi of Kānam village had unfurled a Lakhpati's flag. His descendents are still a powerful family in Kinnaur. Lakhpati means someone possessing assets worth at least one lakh or 100,000.

[105] The original reads: **"Un des habitants du village a étendu jusqu'à Delhi, Lahor et Cachemir ses petites opérations commerciales; il s'appelle Pattiranme...Il a en Kanawer une plus grande renommée que M. Laffitte à Paris"**. (Jacquemont, V., 1933, p. 277).
Translation mine.

(III) Moorang villagers: Only about ten traders plied their wares from here. They went up the Nésang/Gyamthing valley to Bekhur in Tibet over the Keobrang Pass and further on to Tholing (Totling, Toling or m'Tol-din) and Tsaparang (Chaprang) on the Upper Satluj. One or two went north of Gartok up to Bongba. Nearly all of them dealt in wool and salt. They migrated with their flocks to Garhwāl in winter.
(IV) Ribba, Rispa and Thangi villagers: About 15 traders here went via Thangi to Bekhur and Tsarang, then further on to Tsaparang and Tholing. They also wintered in Garhwāl and hardly any were said to go to Rāmpur.
(V) Villagers of Chhitkul, Rakchham, Kāmru and Sangla: About 35 traders from these areas crossed the Chhitkul Pass towards Chārang (Tsarang) and went on to Tsaparang and Tholing. They brought wool and salt from Tibet which they carried to Garhwāl in winter whence they fetched grain. The Kāmru and Sangla traders were fairly affluent but few of them went to Rāmpur. They did not deal in borax.[106]

The groupings outlined above support Cunningham's contention that not all Kinnauras were traders as mentioned by A. Gerard, J.D. Herbert, J.B. Fraser or Prince Waldemar of Prussia. The Gazetteer of 1911 makes it quite clear. It states that residents of only three (Tukpa, Shua, Shyalkhar) of the five parganas of Kinnaur traded directly with Tibet. The members of each pargana formed a separate group, and no member of one group could join or trade with another group. Business was generally done at Gartok. The traders journeyed thither in large parties, well armed, as the road was infested with robbers. This was a convoy system demanding a high degree of organization. ***"People go for trade in caravans of hundreds of armed men, for the passage is infested with robbers, and for this reason a small number of men cannot safely travel".***[107] It offered its members safety provided they did not flout its rules of sticking only to designated convoys. The State permitted arms to be given for guarding such convoys. Traders from Tukpa and Shyalkhar parganas used the Shipke Pass while the Shua traders used a pass between Shyalkhar and Spiti. At Gartok each group of Bushahr traders had its own group of Tibetan traders as correspondents with whom it traded and with no other group. The Gazetteer shows the list of markets in Tibet allocated as follows:
(A) Tukpa: Gyanam, Kangsang, Gianma, Murbhang, Dubgya and Marbuk;
(B) Shua: Chhang, Rodu, Sangmang, Ladākh, Machang, Gianma and Mongpa;
(C) Shyalkhar: Cho-Chalang and Cho-Gialang.
But the Shyalkhar traders were allowed generally to trade freely with whom they wanted, because, it was said, Gartok had once belonged to Bushahr and Shyalkhar had been a part of Gartok District.[108]

Another account divides the traders into four groups: **Takpais, Gavos, Shawals and Rajgranvis**, named after the names of their parganas. *"If a person belonging to one group joins or trades with another group, then the members of his group punish him as well as the group who admitted him without the consent of his party. The rates of all commodities are fixed by an assembly of all the merchants, and tables of rates are prepared by them. Any one who charges a rate higher or lower than the common rate is considered guilty of disloyalty to the assembly. Commodities cannot be sold before a fixed time. The rate of every article is determined by the merchants and the producers of that article after some days' consideration"*.[109] This, again,

[106] The information till here is all out of G. Mackworth Young's Report on Kinnaura traders.

[107] Singh, Miān Durga: A Report on the Panjab Hill Tribes from the Native Point of View, (communicated by H.A. Rose), p. 274, in: The Indian Antiquary, Vol. XXXVI, September 1907: Pp 264-284, October 1907: Pp 289-315, December 1907: Pp 370-375.

[108] Gazetteer, 1911, p. 62.

[109] Singh, Miān Durga, 1907, p. 274.

Principal routes followed by Kinnaura traders to Western Tibet and other areas

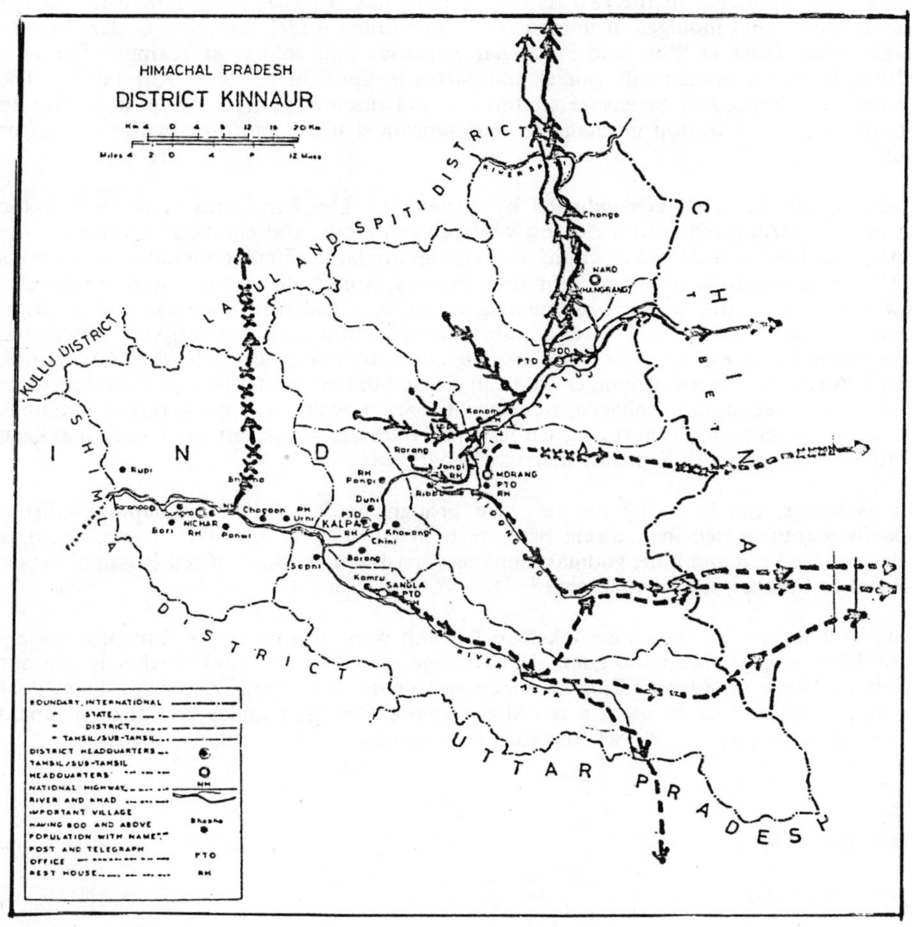

—xxx—xxx→ Route from Pargana Bhaba to Spiti

- - - -→- - -→ Route from the Baspa valley to Tibet and U.P.

— — -→— —→ Route from Ribba, Rispa, Thangi, Kuno, Charang to Tibet

——»——» Route from areas around Moorang and Pooh to Western Tibet

- - -xxx→ - - -xxx→ Route from the Gyamthing valley to Bekhur and Tsaprang

——»»——»» Route from Pargana Hangrang to Rudok, Tso-tso and Langchu

shows a price stabilization mechanism accepted by general consent. Lone rangers out to make a fast buck were not only discouraged but punished as well. The trade was highly organized, with the emphasis being on stability of the market rather than on individual profit. Kinnauras played a leading role in these councils which fixed prices. Behind the guise of fixing fair prices lay disguised usury because the prices were fixed lower than what they might have been in an open market. The residents of the two remaining parganas (Bhāba, Rajgraon) who did not trade directly with Tibet indulged in intermediate short-range trade. Rajgraon traders bought salt brought from Tibet in Shua and Shyalkhar parganas and sold it at Rāmpur fair at a profit. Bhāba residents bought salt, ponies and pattus in Spiti for resale at Rāmpur.[110] The whole system was structured to ensure conformity and discourage freelancing so as not to endanger the price stabilization mechanisms and subsumed usury inherent in the exchanges with Tibet.

"Almost all the trade is conducted by barter".[111] The Kinnauras took to Leh the following articles: strong red cotton clothes; white cotton cloth, and chintzes of various sorts both coarse and fine; a little broad cloth; silks; gongs or large circular metallic instruments struck with a hammer, used by Lāmās for their prayers; iron, both wrought and unwrought, from Newar and Kootlaha of Bushahr; tutenag or spelter; lead from Sirmaur and Jaunsar; copper and brass pots; matchlocks; swords, sabres, shields, bows and arrows, knives, scissors; spectacles; looking glasses; 'shankhs' used in religious ceremonies; crystals; precious stones; sandalwood; porwa or vessels of juniper wood made at Sunnam and Ropa in Kinnaur; otter skins; indigo; oil; ghee, opium, tobacco, rice, wheat, barley, walnuts, apples, raisins, almonds and neozas; cloves, cinnamon, nutmegs, cardamums, mishree, sugar, brown sugar (shakkar), liquor distilled from grapes in Kinnaur, sheep and goats.[112]

In exchange, the following articles were brought back by the Kinnauras: saffron; coarse shawls manufactured in Ladākh; namdās or felts; dochuks or silver ingots; soom, a kind of blanket dyed red and blue; gudmas; punkhees; pashmeena; skins of red Russian leather called bulghal or bulkhal; tiincal and borax.[113]

The very same articles as were taken to Ladākh were also taken by Kinnaura traders to Western Tibet, except sheep and goats. In exchange, they brought back: rock salt dug out of the lakes in Tibet; produce of Tibetan sheep and goats and byangi sheep; pasham; gold dust; tea; borax; nirbissi or zedoary; a few shawl goats; carpets; namdas and charas; rancid butter; sheep dogs for guarding flocks; and yaks in some cases.[114]

[110] Gazetteer, 1911, p. 62.

[111] Gerard, A., 1841, p. 181.

[112] Gerard, A., 1841, Pp 181-182.

[113] Ibid, p. 182.

[114] (a) Gerard, A., 1841, p. 184;
(b) Fraser, J.B., 1820, Pp 273-275;
(c) Gazetteer, 1911, p. 62;
(d) Waldemar, Prinz von Preußen, 1857, Pp 14-16;
(e) Negi, T.S., 1976, Pp 23-24;
(f) Deuster, R.H., 1939, Pp 60-61;
(g) Herbert, J.D., 1819, p. 350;
(h) Lloyd, W. and Gerard, A., 1840, Vol. II, Pages 98, 142, 175, 176 and 231;
(j) Tucci, G. and Ghersi, E.: Secrets of Tibet, London & Glasgow: Blackie & Son, 1935, p. 111.
Also see: Moorcroft, William and Trebeck, George: Travels in the Himalayan Provinces of Hindustan and the Punjab, in Ladākh and Kashmir, in Peshawar, Kabul, Kunduz and Bokhara from 1819 to 1825, Vol. I, Reprint,

The Kinnauras were thus essentially intermediate handlers exchanging the produce of Tibet with that of the lower plains and hills, with a little bit of Kinnauri products thrown in. These exchange relations continued in a series of trade fairs at market places which were essentially 'tent cities' with little fixed population. "There is a series of fairs during the favourable season in these border countries, and at them are carried out even today the principal exchanges with Western Tibet; they begin with those of Kyelang and Patsio in Lahul, then follow those of Dongbara, of Gyanima in Purang and of Gartok, to finish with that of Rāmpur".[115] The Lavi Fair at Rāmpur in November used to be the major culminating exchange market. Also quite important was Gartok. "The true importance of Gartok is not confined to its being the capital, but arises as much from its being the most important emporium in Western Tibet".[116] A great fair used to take place there around September 25 at which merchandize of the most varied kinds: "clothes, which constitute the greater part, things made of tin and aluminium, keys, padlocks, gau of white metal made in Japan, fur caps coming from Shanghai, metal cups, sugar, drugs, paint and varnish"[117] could be found. Descriptions of Gartok talk of the place being a "long, broad plain, absolutely bare, with a dozen wretched hovels in the middle, constitutes at this time of the year what is in summer the chief trading centre of Western Tibet".[118] Another important trade mart was Taklakot in sPurang which "at least equals, if it does not surpass, in importance the summer camp at Gyanema as a trade centre with British India".[119] William Moorcroft pointed out the presence of Russian traders at these fairs. He cited a Tibetan official as asserting that ***"kafilahs (convoys) of 5 or 600 Ooroos (Russians) on horseback had come to the fair at Ghertope.*** Now if the latter intelligence be true the Russians must reach Ghertope by another route than that of Yarkund".[120] All the former traders of Kinnaur interviewed personally during thc course of this research denied ever having seen convoys of Russians at any place in Tibet.

We can now pass on to rough estimate of the volume of Kinnaur's trade with Tibet which meandered from one trade mart to the next. Moorcroft gives no estimate of the trade with Kinnaur, only that of the trade with Kashmir. He estimated that the "amount of wool annually bought by the Rājā was between two and three lakhs".[121] Even the confidential reports of the British Trade Agents make no such estimate. Kinnaura traders when questioned generally mention that the trade was in 'lakhs' without hazarding any specific figure. The only available approximation is that given by J.D. Cunningham during his stay in Kinnaur. He estimated the export trade of Tibet to Rāmpur from 1837 to 1841 A.D., both years inclusive. Graphical representations of these trade estimates follow. The estimations made by him reveal that in the best year, 1840, the estimated value of these exports was just over a lakh of rupees. It fell drastically to around Rs 20,000 the succeeding year but, though Cunningham does not

Delhi: Sagar Publications, 1971, Pages 352 and 358.

115 Tucci, G. and Ghersi, E., 1935, p. 111.

116 Ibid, p. 147.

117 Ibid.

118 Ryder, Major C.H.D.: Exploration and Survey with the Tibet Frontier Commission, and from Gyangtse to Simla via Gartok, p. 389, in: The Geographical Journal (G.J.), Vol. XXVI, No. 4, October 1905, Pp 369-395.

119 Longstaff, T.G.: Notes on a Journey through the Western Himalaya, p. 204, in: G.J., Vol. XXIX, No. 1, January 1907, Pp 201-211.

120 Moorcroft, William: A Journey to Lake Manasarovara in U'n-d'es, a Province of Little Tibet, p. 453, in: Asiatick Researches, Vol. 12, 1818, Pp 380-453.

121 Ibid, p. 452.

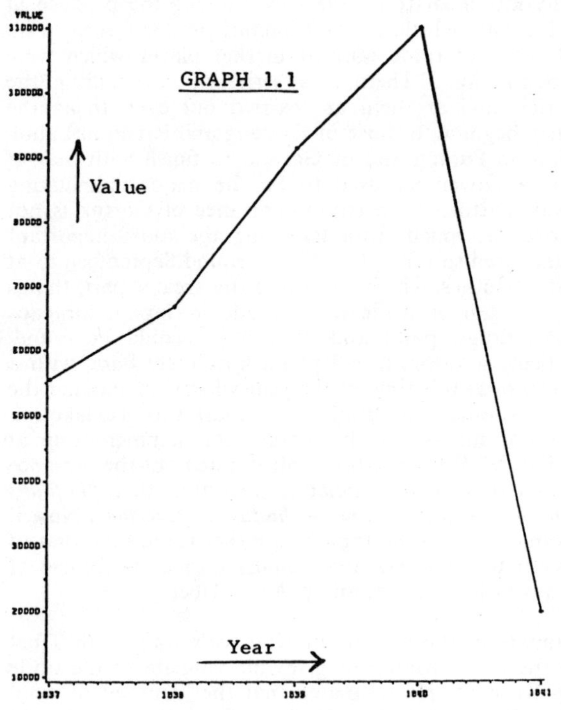

Trade estimates from 1837 to1841 made by Joseph Davey CUNNINGHAM in Upper Kinnaur.

Value = value of trade in Rupees

Year = Year of evaluation

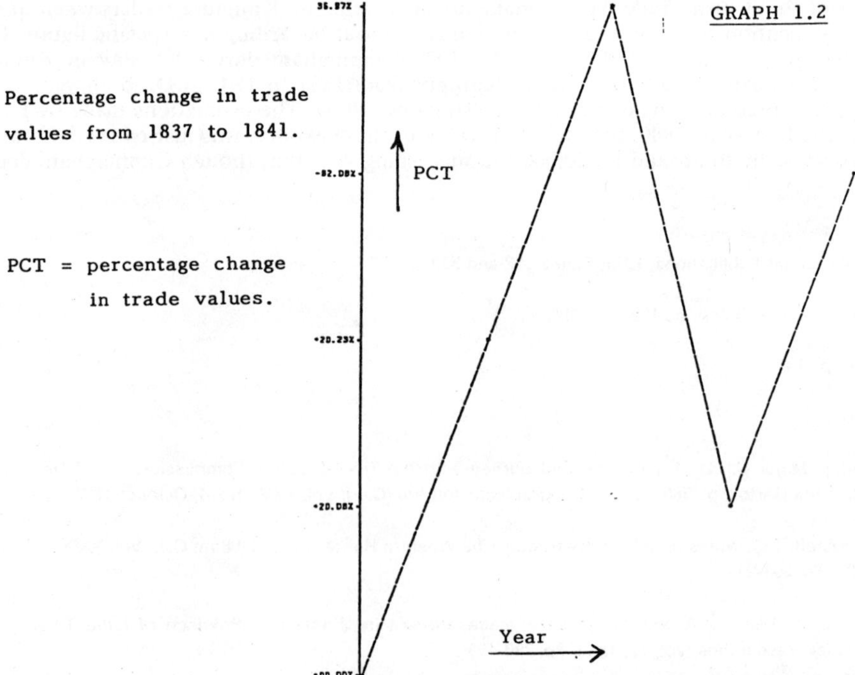

Percentage change in trade values from 1837 to 1841.

PCT = percentage change in trade values.

mention it, this was due to the occupation of Western Tibet by the troops of Zorāwar Singh who had forbidden the Tibetans from trading with anyone other than Kashmiri merchants on pain of severe penalties. Here we can see how important trade was to the politics of the area.[122] Zorāwar Singh was killed in December 1841 and trade picked up again. In the years 1837 to 1840 Cunningham's estimate shows that the volume of the exports from Tibet to Rāmpur rose annually between 20% to 36%.

It should now be considered what were the margins of profit being made on this turnover. According to the Gazetteer of Bushahr State, 20 seers of salt could be obtained for a rupee in Tibet, or in barter two seers of salt for one seer of husked rice. It was then resold in Garhwāl, Rohru or Rāmpur @ 2 or 2.5 seers of husked rice for a seer of salt.[123] Borax was said to be sold at three times its original cost. Other articles, such as wool yielded a profit of about 50%.[124] Butter was "purchased at Rāmpore at about eight seers for the rupee, and sells again in Tartary at four and five seers, so that cent per cent is no uncommon profit on this one article. Tobàcco is also in great demand, and always brings a good profit to the trader".[125] An official despatch, however, differed from this rosy assessment. "Some of the traders bought wool at the rate of Rs 26/- per maund. They would not gain anything if they would get Rs 40/- per maund in India. It costs Rs 12/- per maund for its carriage from Gyanima and Taklakot to Tanakpur. If an interest of -/2/- per rupee is added, the cost price of wool per maund comes to about Rs 42/12/-".[126] If profit margins were high, this was only just. The Kinnauras used to go over hazardous trails over long distances traversing terrain of which a British officer said that "Epithet is heaped on epithet till at length no stores are left to paint the succeeding scene, which rises still higher in the scale of picturesque horror and danger".[127] Geography did not leave the Kinnauras much choice. Population rose slowly but unremittingly, putting ever greater pressure on scarce resources. No single economic activity being adequate, we should now examine some leading economic activities after trade.

1.2.5 Animal Husbandry: Flocks and Transhumance

This is just a short overview of this important occupation of Kinnaur. The number of animals is in excess of the human population by far at any given time. Even a casual visitor to the area cannot fail to be struck by the number of flocks of sheep and goats heading towards the lower hills at the approach of winter and in the reverse direction at the onset of summer. Sheep and goats are no respectors of rank or hierarchy on the road so that even the D.C.'s car flying a flag had to halt before these flocks just like other vehicles! Several factors can explain why animal husbandry is not just another economic activity but a way of life in Kinnaur. The role of sheep and goats as pack animals has already been discussed in the preceding section on trade. Geography rules out spectacular advances through input of modern high yielding technology and mechanization into agriculture in Kinnaur. Tractors cannot run on steep hillsides where even horses and mules have difficulties sometimes and where terracing of even small fields involves hard work! Draught animals are a necessity for cultivation in the area.

[122] Please see, Datta, C.L.: The Importance of the Shawl Wool Trade in West Himalayan Politics, in: Bengal: Past and Present, Vol. LXXXVIII, Part I, January-June 1969, Pp 16-28.

[123] Gazetteer, 1911, p. 63.

[124] Ibid.

[125] Hutton, Th., 1839, p. 905.

[126] Letter no. 11 dated Gyanima Chhakra 30th August 1917, Para Gyanima Chhakra, from Rai Sahib Devi Dās, British Trade Agent, W. Tibet to the Supdt., Hill States, Simla. Available in the D.C.'s Office at Kālpa.

[127] Herbert, J.D., 1819, p. 390.

Apart from yielding wool, manure, goat hair for blankets, milk and meat, the flocks of sheep and goats enabled their owners to generate surpluses through sale of animals, butter, ghee or milk; in addition to trade. This process led to acquisition of some cash or goods by Kinnaura shepherds in Garhwāl, Dehra Doon and Bijnor areas of U.P. and in Mandi, Bilaspur, Sirmaur, Solan and other lower areas of H.P. where they migrated with their flocks in winter. These goods, mostly foodgrains, or money could then be given on credit in Kinnaur which was deficient in both foodgrains and coins. High rates of interest gave good returns on moneylending of this acquired surplus as against its investment in any other occupation. The larger the size of the flocks, the greater the chances for such a cycle of activities. Severe geographical and climatic conditions in Kinnaur put limits on the size of the economic cake there. The areas to which Kinnaura shepherds migrated with their flocks were areas with higher foodgrain production and greater degree of monetization because of easier access and milder climatic conditions. These shepherd-turned-traders began tapping lower lying greater surplus areas and transferring small amounts in money and goods to their own remote valleys for multiplication by lending at high rates of interest there. Those without flocks or very small flocks did not go far in search of pastures in winter and became laggards in this economic transfer of resources through exchanges.

Exchange relations begun at random in lower areas became stabler and more established as the same people came regularly to the same pastures where they slowly acquired grazing rights which were later on recorded even in the revenue record. Thus shepherds from the Baspa valley acquired rights of pasture in Garhwāl, Dehra Doon and Bijnor areas of U.P. across the Dhaula Dhār range. Some of them acquired such rights across the border in Tibet across the Yamrang La pass. Trade and moneylending resulted as a consequence. With the acquisition of rights of pasture and the stabilization of transhumance patterns loans could be followed up at long distances because the shepherd-moneylenders or their family members or servants came for fixed periods to the vicinity of the borrowers and the supervision of loans was consequently easier. Transhumance arising out of animal husbandry enabled two separate spheres of economic surplus generation to be tapped far apart from each other.[128]

No social odium attached to being a shepherd. One member of each household was called upon to shoulder this task. In fact, a Rājā of Rāmpur is said to have been so fond of sheep and goats that he used to himself graze these animals in disguise.[129] The Rājā of Bushahr used to have sizeable flocks which were, however, kept in his wives' names since it

[128] An interesting case study is furnished in this respect by the late Mr Hirpāl of Sangla, father of Negi Goverdhan Singh, retired Tahsildar. Hirpāl began as a shepherd going with flocks of sheep and goats to Dodra Kwār and Garhwāl areas. Slowly as his flocks increased, he commenced petty trade activities and began crossing the Yamrang La pass into Tibet. Ultimately he became a well-known trader. He acquired unbounded influence in the Dodra Kwār area where he had begun his economic march as a shepherd. His influence crossed the frontier into Tibet where he was instrumental in opening the trade mart of Dongbara around the turn of the century. He became a leading 'Seth' or moneylender as well. Such was his influence that when residents of Dodra Kwār were in a state of unrest in the later part of the 19th century, Tikka Raghunāth Singh of Bushahr sent him to pacify the villagers. Today, one of his grandsons, Mr Jawahar Lal Negi, is a Commissioner, Income Tax Department while a second grandson is an officer in the Indian Forest Service. Mr Hirpāl's descendents form a part of a core of the most influential families in Kinnaur. And all this from flocks of sheep and goats a century ago!

[129] According to Negi Goverdhan Singh, this Rājā was Rājā Vijai Singh, son of the famous Rājā Kehri Singh. [Personal interview with Negi Goverdhan Singh, former Pradhān, Gram Panchāyat Sangla on December 6, 1985 in his house at Sangla at 10.00 hours]. Negi Goverdhan Singh is nearly 100 years old and is a treasure house of first-hand information about Bushahr and Kinnaur. He has an invaluable collection of genealogical charts, bahi khātās, official letters and documents. He allowed the author access to his personal collection without reserve. A major debt of gratitude is owed to him and to his son Mr Jawahar Lal Negi, Commissioner, Income Tax.

was considered improper to maintain flocks directly in the Rājā's name. These flocks had to be looked after and their produce sent to the Rājā by designated villagers as a part of long-standing customs and duties. Since the royal flocks were mostly kept in the upper Baspa valley in the names of the queens, a vast pasture in this area came to be called 'Rāni Kanda'. This name dates back to the times when the Rājā of Bushahr was still based at Kāmru. The royal flocks remained in the Ranis' names down to the time of the last Rājā, Padam Singh, in 1947.[130]

This long-established tradition of animal husbandry as a way of life in Kinnaur is now increasingly threatened by a combination of factors. Before the Sino-Indian War of 1962 many Kinnaura traders not only had rights of pasture in Tibet but actually maintained flocks there under care of their local borrower-respondents. Age-old relations had cemented these relationships because Tibet had extensive grazing lands.[131] In Sarchang, a small village 10 miles away from Tashigang, there were on March 29, 1913 "nearly 500 sheep and goats including over 150 of the Bashahri traders who export their wool and pasham to India yearly".[132] In another part of Tibet a first hand official account says that "Chhumurti proper contains some 2000 sheep and goats of Tibetans and some 600 sheep and goats of Bashahris and Piti people".[133] Demchok village, the last on the "northern frontier of Western Tibet has about 400 sheep and goats...including 120 and 50 owned by the Bashahri and Lahauli traders respectively".[134] In Ghiryal village there were "a good number of horses, yaks, and sheep and goats, the wool and pasham of which goes to Bashahr State".[135] In Giyamuk village there were "12 agricultural households which possess about 1200 sheep and goats the wool and pasham of which is sold to Bashahri traders".[136] In Longchoo village there were "over 4000 sheep and goats...They (the inhabitants) sell wool and pasham to the Bashahri and Ladākhi traders from whom they borrow money in advance every year".[137] We can see from these examples from the diaries of the British Trade Agent at Gartok just how widespread was the practice of utilizing Tibetan borrowers to look after the flocks of Kinnaura trader-moneylenders. Trade, animal husbandry and moneylending formed three threads of an integral web. By getting Tibetans to maintain their flocks, Kinnauras subsumed their usurious practices under allegedly interest free loans.

[130] Ibid.

[131] For information about Tibet as a grazing land, please see: Ward, F. Kingdon: Tibet As A Grazing Land, in: G.J., Vol. CX, Nos. 1-3, July-September 1947, Pp 60-75.

[132] Entry for 29th March 1913, Letter no. 26 dated 31st March 1913 from the British Trade Agent, Gartok to the Supdt., Hill States, Simla, copy of which letter is attached to letter no. 1071 dated Simla the 30-05-1913 from J.F. Connolly, I.C.S., Supdt., Hill States, Simla to the Manager, Bashahr State at Kotgarh. Available in the D.C.'s Office at Kālpa.

[133] Letter no. 71 dated 28/29 July 1913 from Idem to Idem, enclosed with letter no. 2132 dated Simla the 5th. September 1913 from Lt. Col. C.P. Egerton, Supdt. Hill States, Simla to the Manager, Bashahr State.

[134] Entry for 27 March 1913 in letter no. 26 from Idem to Idem.

[135] Letter no. 32 dated 8th April 1913, Entry for 2nd April, from the British Trade Agent, Gartok, to the Supdt., Hill States, Simla.

[136] Entry for 20th April 1913, Letter no. 140 dated 23rd April 1913 from the British Trade Agent, Gartok, to Supdt. Hill States, Simla, enclosed with letter no. 1224 dated Simla the 13-06-1913 from Lt. Col. C.P. Egerton, I.A., Superintendent Hill States, Simla to the Manager, Bashahr State at Kotgarh. The last mentioned document is available in the D.C.'s Office at Kālpa.

[137] Entry for 22nd April 1913, Letter no. 41 dated 30th April 1913 from Idem to Idem.

This tradition was rudely shattered by the conflict of 1962. Closure of the Indo-Tibetan border meant not only financial losses in terms of lost credit amounts disbursed by Kinnauras in Tibet but also a sudden stop to availability of extensive pasture lands. New pastures had to be found in India for the flocks that had earlier gone to Tibet over centuries. Coupled with a faster rise in population and subsequent degradation of the environment came other factors impinging upon animal husbandry as a way of life. Government programmes never state it expressly but they are geared towards replacing transhumance with settled animal husbandry. The accent is on quality and stall feeding by distributing improved qualities of animals rather than on quantity. The Forest Department presses for progressively lower ceilings on the numbers of goats to be allowed because the goat is a particularly destructive animal for the environment through its forage. Closure of the frontier with Tibet and the subsequent development of roads in Kinnaur has meant a sizeable reduction in the use of sheep and goats as beasts of burden. Foodgrains and other supplies are now brought in by trucks and then transported from the roadheads on muleback. Distribution of mules as pack animals has shown encouraging results as a part of the I.R.D.P. . Implementation of land reform measures saw some government wastelands allotted to cultivators and a consequent reduction in the pasture land available. Serious disputes have arisen between H.P. and U.P. over grazing rights as greater numbers of animals compete for ever shrinking pasture land. The commencement of fresh Settlement operations in Kinnaur in 1977 caused tensions between neighbouring villages regarding common pastures. The disputes between villages Nichār and Pānwi; Moorang and Nésang and Miru and Yula turned into minor law-and-order problems in 1980 and 1981 as each village sought to have alpine pastures recorded solely for its own use, denying this right to others. This was in marked contrast to the revised Settlement of 1927-28 A.D. when under 'haqooq charai' (pasture rights) villagers freely conceded that if another village had rights of pasture in their pastures such rights should continue without objection.[138] Replacement of polyandrous joint families by monogamous nuclear families makes it difficult to spare an adult male full time to accompany the flocks as a shepherd. The spread of so-called modern education and the subsequent development of a craze for white collar jobs in Kinnaur has meant that a social odium has begun attaching itself to the occupation of a shepherd. A shepherd is considered a good-for-nothing who does not manage to complete his schooling and get a job as a chaprāsi (peon) or as a bābu (clerk). Being a full-time shepherd means giving up full-time education which is increasingly seen as the passport to 'sarkari' jobs. Kinnaura society is in a state of flux. Old socio-economic structures are breaking down ever faster without a matching replacement by newer systems. This is true of animal husbandry as an occupation. Agriculture, the third pillar of the Kinnaura economy alongwith trade and animal husbandry, has changed more slowly perhaps because geographical conditions rule out spectacularly fast change in this remote area. It does remain a way of life but is certainly not what it was in 1817 when Alexander Gerard first came to Kinnaur.

1.2.6. Geography and Agriculture: Toil, Sweat and Tears!

Kinnaur has always been deficit in foodgrains. Local food production has never been enough to feed the populace. "Kunawar has a few villages which produce more grain than their inhabitants require, but considered as a whole, the district imports a portion of its food. The people never willingly part with their grain...and what I required for the few people with me, was sometimes brought from a distance of 60 miles".[139] Lack of adequate quantities of foodgrains was a factor in driving the poorer sections of society into debt of their local deities and trader-turned-moneylenders. We have first-hand reports of this state of affairs from the reports of the Moravian Missionaries in Kinnaur. They had a station in Pooh from 1865 to

[138] Item 4, Wājib-ul-Arz (Village Administration Paper), Ghodi Kāmru, Pargana Tukpa, Tahsil Chini, Riyāsat Rāmpur Bashahr, Zila Shimla, Bābat Tarmim Bandobast Samvat 1984 bikrami, [in Urdu]. Available in the District Record Room at Kālpa.

[139] Cunningham, J.D., 1844, p. 216.

1915 and in Chini from 1900 to 1907.[140] "Since two years the cost-of-living has increased. We have been able to obtain enough cereals to meet just our personal needs only after much effort and with much money".[141] How serious the situation could be can be inferred from this extract of a letter dated 28 June 1906 from J. Bruske in Chini to Bishop La Trobe in Herrnhut. "We have great, lasting drought and also already price rise. Instead of 22 to 24 pounds wheat we are getting only 14 to 17 per rupee and in case it does not rain...we are heading towards famine".[142] The annual report for mission station Pooh for 1887 shows that Pooh with a population of about 600 persons regularly faced a water shortage by May. Agricultural fields could not be watered every 5/6 days as in earlier years but only every 12/14 days, yet there was still not enough water. Potato fields were not getting enough water, leading to violent fights over water.[143] "Our only too overpopulated village cannot feed its 600 inhabitants. There are two crops but even in the best years they fulfil the needs of only one-half of the population. Because of water shortage some fields have even to be left unsown. There can never be any question of cereal export. Cereals are rather an article of all year-round import from the south preferably but also from Spiti and Tibet. Cattle do not have enough nutrition. Besides agriculture and animal husbandry, trade is perceptibly carried on but not with produce and products of the locality in question, the entire trade is much more an intermediate trade in which salt, borax, wool are purchased in Tibet and resold at the Rāmpur mela or fair".[144]

[140] For information about the work of the Moravian missionaries in the West Himalaya, please see:
(a) Reichelt, G. Th.: Die Himalaya Mission der Brüdergemeine, Gütersloh: G. Bertelsman, 1896;
(b) Bechler, Th.: Kulturarbeit der Brüdergemeine im westlichen Himalaya, in: Beiblatt II zur Allgemeine Missionszeitschrift, Band 41, No. 2, März 1914, Pp 18-32;
(c) Beck, Hartmut: Brüder in vielen Völkern, 250 Jahre Mission der Brüdergemeine, Erlangen: Verlag der Ev. Luth. Mission, 1981;
(d) Schneider, H.: Ein Missionsbild aus dem westlichen Himalaya, Gnadau, 1880;
(e) Senft, E.A.: Les Missions Moraves actuellement existantes chez les peuples paiens, Neuchâtel: Delachaux et Niestlé Editeurs, 1890;
(f) Schulze, Adolf: 200 Jahre Brüdermission, Band II, Herrnhut, 1932.

[141] Bruske, J.F.: Jahresbericht der Station Chini - Jahr 1907, [Written in longhand in German], Unpublished. Available in the archives of the Moravian Mission at Herrnhut under the rubric: Alte Sign. S.e.1.a., Prov. Missionsdirektion, Pert. West Himalaya. The original reads: *"Seit zwei Jahren ist hier Teurung. Wir haben nur mit viel Mühe und gegen viel Geld soviel Getreide bekommen, als wir für uns persönlich brauchen"*.
Translation mine.

[142] Handwritten letter in German dated 28 June 1906 from J. Bruske in Chini to Bishop La Trobe in Herrnhut, Unpublished. Available in the archives at Herrnhut under the rubric: J.N. 248, FZ R 66, Sign. R15.U.b.17: Briefwechsel mit Chini 1900-08. The original reads: *"Wir haben große, anhaltende Dürre und bereits auch Teurung. Statt 22 bis 24 Pfund Weizen bekommen wir nur 14 bis 17 pro Rupi, und falls nicht bald reichlich Regen fällt, gehen wir der Hungersnot entgegen"*.
Translation mine.

[143] Weber, J. and L.: Jahresbericht der Station Poo, West Himalaya, [Handwritten report in German], Unpublished.

[144] Ibid. The original reads: *"Unser viel zu sehr übervölkertes Dorf kann seine 600 Einwohner nicht ernähren. Da sind zweimalige Ernten aber selbst in den besten Jahren liefern sie höchstens den Bedarf für die Hälfte der Bewohner. Wegen Waßermangel bleiben sogar manche Felder zur zweiten Ernte brark liegen. Von einer Getreideausführung kann nie die Rede sein. Getreide ist vielmehr ein Artikel, der alljährlich aus dem Süden vornehmlich aber auch aus Spitti und Tibet eingeführt wird. Das Vieh bekommt nicht genug Nahrung...Neben Ackerbau und Viehzucht wird wahrnehmlich Handel getrieben, aber nicht etwa mit Erzeugnissen und Produkten des hiesigen Ortes, der ganze Handel ist vielmehr nur ein Zwischenhandel, in dem in Tibet Salz, Borax, Wolle aufgekauft und auf der Mela oder Messe in Rāmpur wieder verkauft wird"*.
Translation mine.

This observation highlights an interesting aspect that has not been mentioned elsewhere in other accounts of Kinnaur - the fact that grain was imported for Pooh from Spiti and Tibet in times of exceptional need. Julius Weber clearly mentions here that cereal imports were preferably from the South and this is logical because the grain producing areas lay in that direction. Spiti and Tibet were themselves arid, grain deficit areas which imported foodgrains. So when they exported cereals towards Pooh it must have been only at a high price so that the profit motive overcame the normal instinct in these areas of holding on to what foodgrains there were. Since Tibetans were many times under debt to traders from Pooh such exports could have helped to lighten the debt burden. Trader-moneylenders of Pooh could thus obtain repayment in terms of cereals which they could sell in Pooh at higher prices, making good profits. Without debt burdens towards Kinnaura traders of Pooh some Tibetans would not have re-exported their scarce foodgrains. The whole cycle turned to the advantage of the larger trader-moneylenders while the poorer sections of society suffered. Agriculture was certainly a way of life in Kinnaur but never gave the area self-sufficiency in foodgrains.

As so rightly pointed out by Prof. D. Rothermund, the main determinants of peasant agriculture are:

a) Biological;
b) Ecological;
c) Institutional;
d) Economic.

He further points out that the "rich peasant becomes a biological incident",[145] considering the relevance of family labour's availability for agricultural work and patterns of sub-division in generational sequences. Kinnaura agriculture showed some examples of the interplay of these determinants. The evolution of the system of fraternal polyandry in joint family households, such a hallmark of society in Kinnaur over centuries, can be perceived as a response, conscious or otherwise, to the ecological determinant in the shape of a harsh physical environment by trying to influence the biological determinant of generational sequences in-so-far-as it sought to preserve the gains of the "incident" of a rich peasant by replacing the individual peasant's family as the main parameter in generational variations of land holding by the entire polyandrous joint family. Fragmentation of land was thus sought to be reduced as a logical consequence of family multiplication and generational passage. Polyandry as a system was an attempt to limit the vagaries of such biological "incidents". In Kinnaur smaller one-unit families were at a disadvantage because additional avenues of income generation (trade, transhumantic animal husbandry) demanded additional manpower and suffered from the lack of it. The institutional determinant came in because the Rājā's regime encouraged polyandrous joint family units rather than nuclear family units. Taxes were levied on partition of land holdings at a heavy rate (10% of the asset value of the holding sought to be partitioned) and the necessity of furnishing bégār through at least one male adult per household was to the disadvantage of single family households. A Kinnaura thinking of setting up a separate family unit knew that the new unit would have to furnish separate forced labour to the state rather than be treated as a part of the earlier larger unit which had furnished such labour. He also knew that this labour meant prolonged absence for up to six months per year in which help could not be relied upon from the father or brothers who might have resented setting up such a separate unit in the first place. Animal flocks would demand additional absence from the household. This mix of ecological, biological and institutional determinants has now changed under the impact of a new political structure, declining polyandry, closure of trade with Tibet, increasing population pressure, construction of a communications network,

[145] Rothermund, D.: Government, Landlord and Peasant in India, Relations under British Rule 1865-1935, Schriftenreihe des Südasien-Instituts der Universität Heidelberg, Band 25, Wiesbaden: Franz Steiner Verlag, 1978, p. 2. For a general discussion of the four listed determinants of peasant agriculture please see: Ibid, Pp 1-9.

land reform measures and the spread of education. Since biological and ecological determinants cannot by themselves operate in isolation from the institutional determinant, we may perceive the official birth control programme and land consolidation measures as attempts at replacing the old institutional determinant of encouragement of polyandrous joint households by a new system of monogamous households but with controls over the possible deletrious effects of the generational multiplication that would result.

The Rājā of Bushahr had provided another institutional determinant through his free-trade treaty with Tibet which allowed his Kinnaura subjects to exploit the ecological determinant of their strategic location. This determinant no longer operates. It was an incentive to higher foodgrain production in Kinnaur itself. If more foodgrains were produced they could be exported to Tibet and Spiti at good profit. Now most of these foodgrains come in through the public distribution system at subsidized rates so that it is cheaper to buy at government fair price shops rather than produce cereals oneself in some cases. A farmer generating an exportable surplus of cereals cannot sell it in Tibet and has to compete with the subsidized government distribution network. He cannot tap other earlier markets like Spiti or Garhwāl because there also the same subsidized networks are in place. Government have, therefore, sought to modify this institutional determinant to make it conform to prevailing market conditions. Kinnaura agriculturists are being encouraged to raise cash crops like saffron, potatoes and hops, as well as off-season vegetables like peas, tomatoes and onions which fetch good prices in the markets of the North Indian plains. Liberal provision of subsidies, inputs and institutional credit; fixation of procurement prices and organization of cooperative marketing networks are all parts of this new institutional determinant seeking to goad agriculture in Kinnaur from its traditional pre-occupation with production of cereals. Market prices are the economic determinant influencing the choice of the new crops sought to be encouraged in Kinnaur. Ecological conditions make Kinnaur suitable for raising off-season vegetables and seed production, particularly for cauliflower seed and chicory. Seed potato from Kinnaur is also being marketed though it is still far behind Lahaul in volume of export. Good prices for vegetables in the Gulf Countries act as an economic determinant leading the Himāchal authorities to envisage vegetable production programmes in Kinnaur and other areas specifically for this market.

These are all, however, new trends. Many areas in Kinnaur still have the traditional crops of cereals. The kandas are one-crop areas. In areas with two crops the first crop is sown around April (mainly barley) and reaped in July after which the fields are prepared for the staples of ogla (fagopyrum emarginatum) and phaphra (fagopyrum esculentum) which are reaped in October. Where there is only one harvest the crops are ooa (hordeum coeleste), bathoo (amaranthus anardhana), cheena (panicum miliaceum), koda (paspalum scrobiculatum), wheat and barley which are sown around April and reaped in September/October. Potatoes are being produced in the Hangrang valley and the Pooh area. Saffron and cummin seed are being produced on a small scale in the Sangla area. In view of the four determinants outlined by Prof. Rothermund we see that the ecological determinant which restricts agriculture in Kinnaur because of harsh climate and steep slopes favours horticulture as fruit trees are better suited to slopes than cereals. Horticulture has become more and more popular in Kinnaur. Poor means of communication had earlier hindered large scale adoption of horticulture in Kinnaur because of the difficulty in getting horticultural produce to markets in time. Improved roads have gone hand-in-hand with accelerating horticultural production. It is now already a fourth pillar of the Kinnaura economy in addition to the already described traditional three.

1.2.7 Horticulture: Promising but no El Dorado!

Kinnaur was earlier also no stranger to fruit though horticulture was not carried on as systematically as it is being done now. The cold, dry climate of the upper areas of Kinnaur made them suitable for stone fruits, apples and almonds. Almonds of good quality can now be found in Spillo, Kānam and Lābrang and also in the Hangrang valley right up to Shyalkhar and Sumra, the last village. Apples are found all over the district, as are apricots. Grapes flourish in Ribba, Peo and Sunnam. Plums grow in Nichār. Peaches grow in Moorang, Nichār, Gyabong and Sunnam. Kinnaur apples have won renown as disease-free, longer lasting, larger in size and better in taste than other apples. They fetch a premium of Rs 1 to 2 per kilo in the market in cities like Chandigarh.[146] Apples from a small hamlet, Kā, in Hangrang valley have to be tasted to believe just how good an apple can taste! For many years Kinnaur remained free of the dreaded scab disease which ravaged orchards in Kulu District and the Kotgarh area of Simla District, both major apple growing areas. In 1983 scab appeared for the first time in Kinnaur in the orchard of the Devta Mahéshras at Sungra. Since then it has slowly spread northwards and has appeared as far as Kālpa and Pāngi, though not on the scale observed in areas outside the district.

Wild varieties of apricot (called Chuli) and peach (called Baimi) had been standard articles of consumption in Kinnaur since ages. Alcohol was distilled from them. Their oil was used as a medicine, a tonic, as well as a cooking medium. The residues left after pressing their oil were used as cattlefeed. Dried apricots are even today an integral part of the staple diet of Kinnauras in winter. Houses in the Pooh and Kālpa areas have flat roofs so that apricots and other fruit or vegetables can be dried on them under the sun for consumption in winter. Wine and spirits made from grapes form an integral part of the religious rituals and social life in Kinnaur. Alcohol called 'ghanti' is distributed as 'prasad' in the temples of some deities. Travellers mention flourishing fruit trees seen by them. Capt. C. Johnson describes Poāri as "embedded in a growth of apricot, peach, vine and walnut trees".[147] Thomas Hutton found ample apples and apricots at Sunnam. "The finest grapes are produced at the village of Ukpah on the Sutledge. At Soongnum the grapes are neither very abundant nor very good and do not occur across the Hungrung pass at all. Apricots are seen as far as Leeo where they also cease to grow".[148] Capt. Hutton did not either observe too carefully or apricots have since grown in other villages beyond Leo because they can now be found right up to the last village of Kinnaur, Sumra. Alexander Gerard found numerous vineyards in Lippa village where the grapes were "large and of a delicious flavour".[149] Talking of Roghi village he noted that there were "several orchards belonging to Rogee, which contain apples of an excellent kind, nearly as large as those brought from Kabool, which they far excel in flavour".[150] J.D. Cunningham found "an abundance of grapes and apricots, some walnuts, apples and peaches...in Upper and Middle Kunawar...Towards the Tibet frontier the fruits decrease in quantity. The apricot does not produce at a greater elevation than 10,500 feet, and the grapes are inferior at 9,000".[151] Theobald mentions "apricots and walnuts plentiful and thriving around Pāngi, and also excellent blackberries" before talking of "extensive vineyards" in Lippa, thus corroborating what Gerard had found there 40 years earlier.[152]

[146] Personal experience. The author belongs to Chandigarh.

[147] Johnson, Captain C.: Journey through the Himma-leh Mountains to the Sources of the River Jumna, and thence to the confines of Chinese Tartary: performed in April-October 1827, p. 54, in: Journal of the Royal Geographical Society of London (J.R.G.S.), Vol. IV, 1834, Pp 41-71.

[148] Hutton, Th., 1840, Part III, p. 574.

[149] Gerard, A., 1841, p. 383.

[150] Ibid, p. 384.

[151] Cunningham, J.D., 1844, p. 177.

[152] Theobald, W., 1862, Pp 407-408.

All these observations show that the potential for horticulture always existed but the institutional determinant failed to reinforce this ecological determinant towards gainful production. Bushahr State did not provide the necessary infrastructure in terms of roads, credit, marketing facilites, cooperative societies and inputs. This has been done only after 1948 by the Himāchal government. Horticulture requires a long gestation period between the planting of orchards and coming in of the first returns thereof. This period can be anywhere between 7 to 9 years. The horticulturist needs infrastructural support and training because fruit trees need proper maintenance. Their produce cannot be stored by the producer and has to be sold in time or, if the producer is rich enough, be transferred to cold storages which are all located outside Kinnaur. The indigenous wild varieties of fruit had evolved their own balance with nature and did not need such detailed care but their yields were lower and their size smaller than commercially oriented fruit crops.

Horticulture has really caught on in Kinnaur since 1960. Even small landholders have planted orchards in lots of one or two bighās[153] or even in biswās.[154] A ban on the alienation of land to non-tribals has meant that benefits have accrued largely to Kinnauras though some outsiders have profited as well. Laws can always be circumvented to some extent. Outsiders function as commission agents and have an important role in marketing the fruit produce of Kinnaur. Attempts to wean the growers exclusively to the cooperative marketing network do not always succeed because the individual growers want to sell their produce to the highest bidder without being obliged to always sell to the cooperative society. Outsiders functioning as ārhtiyas (intermediaries) have locked the small orchardists in a net of credit advances which cannot be matched by the cooperatives in flexibility of terms and elasticity of supply. In some cases, envoys of commission agents from as far as Delhi come and survey the orchards in Kinnaur, estimate the crop size and buy it up in advance by disbursing credit advances. Nevertheless, a trickle down effect is visible in the horticultural prosperity that has been evidenced in Kinnaur since its creation as a district. Of course, a small core of richer landholders have taken maximum advantage and become prosperous orchard owners. They have also acquired a political role in the Kinnaur polity. This is not something peculiar to Kinnaur. In Himāchal politics in general, the so-called "Apple lobby" consisting of a few rich orchard owners is considered as a political force wielding influence disproportionately large for its size. Its members are represented in the highest echelons of politics and the bureaucracy.

Horticulture has displaced trade as a favoured surplus generating occupation from which returns can be ploughed into moneylending. The devtas have not lagged behind in this respect. The Sungra Mahéshras possesses one of the finest orchards in Kinnaur. Ukha Devi of Nichār also has her own orchard. Larger orchard owners are getting higher returns from, say, 20 bighās of orchard than they would have got by putting the same 20 bighās under agriculture. In addition fruit trees can be planted on sloping hillsides unlike cereals which need terracing. It is horticulture that can be the motor of a counterpart of the so-called "Green Revolution" of the plains for Kinnaur where agriculture can just not be revolutionized to the same extent because of geographical and climatic constraints. It offers better chances than agriculture of generating higher income levels and improving the quality of life because it is better attuned to the physical environment of the area. Higher returns from horticulture have fueled political ambitions. It is now time to switch over to the political scene within which the credit structure must operate.

[153] 1 acre = about 5.333 bighās.

[154] 1 bigha = 20 biswās.

1.3 THE POLITICAL SCENE: INDIVIDUALS RATHER THAN IDEOLOGIES

Kinnaur had no tradition of political activism. Bushahr State left the Kinnauras pretty much to themselves so long as they paid their taxes and performed their customary duties. The customary means of protest was the 'Dhum'. It has been defined as "a kind of satyagraha. Disgruntled people used to leave their houses and fields and collect on mountain sides, refusing to return till their grievances were redressed. Violence was hardly ever used. Abandoning cultivation would lead to reduction in state revenues so that the authorities were obliged to reach a settlement".[155] Dhum has also been defined as "any popular combination raised for the redress of special grievances, or for enforcing claims to certain rights. It was thus a public demonstration of discontent against the ruler".[156] There was a Dhum in 1859 A.D. to protest against the imposition of a new assessment.[157]

A Dhum did not crystallize into any kind of organization. It was a sporadic affair which ended as soon as the specific grievance causing it had been redressed. General political issues did not agitate the people in Kinnaur. What aroused their ire were apprehensions of financial loss. An eyewitness account tells us that the "people of all Bashahr are in a state of unrest. One big assembly after the other is being held sometimes here sometimes there, to which delegates are being sent from every single village. They keep secret the purpose of the gathering. What I have been able to discover till now is that they want to protest against an ordered and already begun new Settlement of fields, because it will lead to increased taxation, and that they want in addition to cause the old Rājā to nominate a successor to the throne. In some villages people are refusing to pay the taxes".[158] Here again we see that the demand was for redressal of specific grievances and not for general changes based on ideology or political conviction. It did not lead to demands for political freedom or for replacement of the Rājā's rule. On the contrary, Kinnauras felt that they had a special relationship with the royal house of Bushahr which had originated in Kāmru and whose loyal defenders they had been over the ages. Right till the merger of Bushahr in Himāchal Pradesh on April 15, 1948 Kinnaur remained free of political unrest. It was not affected by the Praja Mandal Movement organized under the Congress ægis in the 1930s for obtaining greater civil rights for the subjects of princely states. Eyewitness accounts of the events in Rāmpur around April 15, 1948 narrate that there was a lot of unrest in other parts of Bushahr State except Kinnaur.[159] Some prominent leaders of the Praja Mandal Movement (Satya Dev Bashahri, Pandit Padam Dev) belonged to Bushahr State but not to Kinnaur.

[155] Singh, Miāṅ Goverdhan: Bushahr-Kinnaur Rājya, Draft Manuscript in Hindi with corrections in his own handwriting by Mr Thākur Sain Negi, Unpublished, p. 81.

[156] Gazetteer, 1911, p. 10; Gazetteer, 1971, p. 62.

[157] Ibid.

[158] Letter from Bruske to Bishop La Trobe dated 28 June 1906. The original text reads: *"Unter den Leuten von ganz Bashahr herrscht ein Geist der Unruhe. Immer eine große Versammlung nach der anderen wird bald da bald dort gehalten, zu denen von jedem einzelnen Dorf Delegierte geschickt werden. Den Zweck der Versammlung halten sie geheim. Was ich bisher erfahren konnte, ist, daß sie gegen eine angeordnete und bereits begonnene Neuvermessung der Felder Protest einlegen wollen, weil sie Erhöhung der Steuer zur Folge habe, und daß sie ferner den alten Rājā veranlassen wollen, einen Thronfolger zu bestimmen. In einigen Dorfern verweigern die Leute die Steuer".*
Translation mine.

[159] Both Mr T.S. Negi and Negi Goverdhan Singh participated in pacifying this unrest in their capacity as officials of Rāmpur Bushahr State.

Since independence the accent in Kinnaur politics has been more on individuals and much less on parties or ideologies. Elections have been won and lost not on the basis of party programmes but on the personality of the candidate concerned. Mr T.S. Negi was returned four times in succession by the voters of Kinnaur between 1967 and 1985 to the Legislative Assembly as an Independent candidate. Kinnaur had been the very first area in India to go to the polls in the general elections of 1952 because voting was held there on October 25, 1951 in view of the fact that snow would make it impossible for it to go to the polls along with the rest of the country in 1952.[160] The Congress candidate was defeated in this election by an Independent candidate. Elections after 1977 have seen a greater degree of politicisation than before but centred mainly on differences between individuals rather than between ideologies. It does not take long to find out in Kinnaur that prominent politicians who matter are all higher caste Kanaits and not Harijans. They come from affluent clans and families with a long tradition of moneylending and/or trade. Political influence and moneylending operations coexist in many cases. Some Harijan leaders are becoming known but their influence is still very localized. They do not possess the necessary economic resources and social influence to propel themselves onto a wider stage. Remoteness had made the political scene in Kinnaur devoid of passion and dominated by the higher caste groups to the detriment of Scheduled Castes.

No discussion of politics in Kinnaur can ever be complete without a mention of the ubiquitous devis/devtas. No politician can dare to publicly cross swords with a village deity. Candidates for elections begin their campaigns by presenting offerings to the local deity and by seeking its blessings. Should the devta indicate his wrath against a particular candidate, the latter would have an uphill fight on his hands. Campaigners of a candidate in the Assembly election of 1985 were quite flustered when Devta Badrināth of Kāmru hesitated about accepting his offerings.[161] Similarly, Devta Bairing Nāg of Sangla was equivocal in 1985 about the chances of success of another candidate. People watch the devtas' will closely. It will still take some time before politics in Kinnaur can become programme oriented and ideology based rather than being axed mainly on charismatic individuals and the favour of the devtas. This accent on individuals has been marked in administration as well. Bureaucrats are supposed to be faceless but Kinnaur has seen some flamboyant administrators who are still talked about in the area. We can now turn to the administrative set-up of the area.

1.4 ADMINISTRATIVE STRUCTURE: FRIENDS NOT MASTERS?

The traditional administrative structure in Bushahr was a fairly "archaic though inexpensive one".[162] Thomas Hutton gives some idea about it. The Rājā had "three chief vuzeers who manage the affairs of his territories, and who in time of war would take command of his forces, as it is contrary to the custom of the country for the Rājāh to do so in person. These three are equal in rank and their office is hereditary. Below them are several inferior officers also called vuzzeers, whose office is not hereditary but who are elected or rather nominated by the Rājāh annually, and they seem to be thannadars of different pargunnahs...The personal attendants or immediate household of the Rajah conisists of two sets of men called Churriahs and Hazrees. The Churriah derives his name from part of his dury being to carry the Churree or silver stick, on occasions of ceremony before the Rājāh. His duties are chiefly those of a Chupprassee, and he is sent into different pargunnahs to collect the revenue, to report any

[160] Akbar, M. J.: India: The Siege Within, Penguin Books, 1985, p. 71.

[161] Information gathered in public meetings from the villagers of Kāmru and Sangla in Kāmru on December 6, 1985.

[162] Gazetteer, 1971, p. 228.

misconduct, and to see that the people are equitably assessed, that is, to point out who may be taxed more heavily, and who should be excused...and in fact to ferret out and report to the Rājāh the conduct of all his subjects... the Rājāh gives no pay to his servants, their services on the contrary being compulsory. The Churriahs form a body of from sixty to eighty men...they have three officers who are...called 'Pulsur', 'Buttoongee' and 'Naigee', answering to Soobadar, Jemedar and Burkundauze. They are exempt from military service, and remain with the Rājāh. They are drawn from the district of Kunawur, and are compelled to obey summons, unless it graciously please his Highness to excuse them, in which case however he takes good care to exact a fine for their non-attendance...none are taken but men in easy circumstances, who possess either lands or flocks, the Rājāh rightly thinking that those who are well off, will be more likely to keep a sharp eye on the discontented or troublesome characters, than those who have all to gain, and nothing to lose. He has also the satisfaction of reflecting that in case of misconduct they possess the means of paying a heavy fine...The Hazrees are a larger body of men than the Churriahs, and they sometimes perform the same duties...in general they act as Chowkeydars or guards to the Rājāh".[163] The influence of Kinnauras in the administrative set-up of Bushahr is attested to by Gerard as well. "The Rājāh's attendants are all Koonawurees...There are three Wuzeers, or Ministers in Busahir, who have separate control over certain districts. Under them are other officers who have the more immediate management of affairs. The situations of Wuzeer are generally hereditary. These officers acquire their salary by a certain percentage on the collection, a certain percentage of grain; and they have also rent free lands...The Wuzeers have also attendants of two sorts; viz the Mislee and Andree. The former, about 200 in number, wait upon the principal Wuzeer; and the latter, of whom there are seven sets of 100 each, attend on the Wuzeers of their own districts".[164] The Poāri Wazir family has in its possession a 'sanad' (title deed) by which the Rājā had granted all rights of collection, forest produce, forced labour and land in perpetuity to the Poāri Wazir family.[165]

The three hereditary Wazirs were those of Poāri, Shua and Kohāl.[166] They were all Kanaits. "The Poāris are the oldest family".[167] There was also a Sarhaddi Wazir. He was "invested with considerable independent authority, but his post was not hereditary. This was the Sarhaddi Wazir who was in charge of the frontier. The ablest man obtainable in parganas Shua or Tukpa was appointed, and he was practically given a free hand provided that he maintained order. No member of the above mentioned families (Poāri, Shua, Kohal) ever held the frontier district and it was not revived after the expulsion of the Gorkhas".[168] Obviously, the Rājā did not want concentration of too much power in the hands of any of the three hereditary Wazir families by making one of them responsible for the frontier as well.

The Wazirs and their minions were virtually in-charge of affairs. Negi Goverdhan Singh, who has 30 years of experience as an official under the Rājā of Bushahr, said that the Wazirs "had all the rights of income and expenditure. They had only to render annual

[163] Hutton, Th., 1839, Part I, Pp 906-907.

[164] Lloyd, W. and Gerard, A., 1840, Vol. II, Pp 303-304.

[165] This document is in the possession of Wazir Amar Singh Negi of Poāri who is also the Pradhān of the Grām Panchāyat Poāri.

[166] Gazetteer, 1971, p. 228. For more information about these three families, please see: Gazetteer, 1911, Pp 22-25. It gives the genealogical charts for these three families.

[167] Gazetteer, 1911, p. 22.

[168] Ibid.

accounts to the Rājā. After paying the Rājā's due they kept the rest".[169] The traditional administrative structure was thus loose and exploitative but was not perceived by the general public as overly oppressive. British efforts after 1816 to 'modernize' the administration repeatedly met opposition from locals who wanted retention of their former set-up in which they could pay in kind. Payment in kind made the system seem less exploitative than it really was. When cash had to be paid, even at moderate rates, the Kinnauras perceived the new cash system as far more oppressive because of an acute and widespread shortage of coins. Even today the government is a remote concept for many Kinnauras. In the earlier days they hardly ever came into contact with it apart from when they had to pay taxes.

Kinnaur had no tradition of well organized local self government. In case of disputes village elders, mostly upper caste influential persons, would arbitrate and settle the issue. Talking about how disputes were arbitrated in Sangla, Negi Khem Singh, a gazetted officer of the government, explained that "traditionally a few elders decided all disputes. People like Shiv Dhām of Negi Goverdhan Singh's family and two/three other richer people would take all decisions which were accepted by everyone, even in matters pertaining to partition of land. They could levy fines also. Money paid as fine would generally be given to the party in whose favour the decision went. Such Councils allowed marital separations also. Hardly anyone appealed to the revenue authorities".[170] Such councils had no institutional basis or statutory authority, only social sanction. They had no fixed periodicity of meeting and met as and when required. The elders involved were invariably affluent credit givers of the village who could put a squeeze on further credit if a party, generally belonging to the poorer classes, did not accept their decision. They constituted a loose kind of disciplinary mechanism that used control of credit supply as a coercive tool to ensure conformity to its decisions.

There was, of course, always the devta as a sort of final court of appeal but his functionaries through whom he made his will felt were upper caste people related to these affluent elders constituting the decision making councils. There were cases of aggrieved parties going to the devta against the decisions of village councils but such happenings were few and far between.[171] Devtas used to decide cases but the complainants knew that the affluent Kanaits could always choke off their credit in cash and kind if they went too often against the decisions of the latter. If some issue was of importance to more than one village, prominent men of the pargana used to congregate and find a solution. However, there was no institutionalization of this forum.[172] Even now such informal forums exist. Committees exist in Kālpa, Kāmru and other villages to decide matters pertaining to common village welfare like permissions to keep cattle in the village rather than taking them out to the kanda in summer, rates to be charged by weavers, changes in death rites, fees to be imposed on outsiders wishing to graze their cattle in the village pasture and similar matters.[173]

[169] Personal interview in Sangla on December 6, 1985.

[170] Personal interview with Negi Khem Singh, B.D.O., Paunta Block at Sangla on December 6, 1985 in Suite No. 1 of the P.W.D. Rest House from 20.10 till 22.45 hours. Khem Singh used to be B.D.O., Kālpa Block during the author's time as D.C., Kinnaur.

[171] T.S. Negi narrated a case where he had adjudicated the marital dispute of a Harijan couple in his young days because they had come to him for such adjudication. Not satisfied with his decision, the husband presented himself before Devta Janglik of Rohru when the latter came on a visit to the area. The Devta reversed T.S. Negi's decision. [Personal interview with Mr T.S. Negi, retired Chief Secretary, Government of Himāchal Pradesh, former Speaker, H.P. Legislative Assembly, former cabinet minister, on January 9, 1986 from 14.30 hours till 18.30 hours in the Adim Jati Sewak Sangh complex at Salogra near Solan].

[172] Negi, T.S., Personal Interview, January 1986.

[173] Information given by Negi Balwant Singh, then Chairman, Panchāyat Samiti Kālpa in a personal interview in

It merits discussing a case study of such a committee in Kinnaur. We take the village committee of village Chini. The secretary of this committee, a young man aged 28 years named Shamsher Singh, explained that the committee had 15 members, including messengers. He was secretary for the fourth year running in 1985. The 15 members had a term of one year from baisākh (April) to baisākh. Voting was by acclamation and not by balloting, secret or otherwise. The committee was in-charge of the Sering apple farm, a common neoza plantation and minor 'rasam-o-riwāj' (minor customary practices) for the village. It could modify village customs and decide on expenditure on the devta. It had a sub-committee of three members for overseeing the Sering apple farm. It paid the labourers working on that farm. The neoza produce of the community plantation was auctioned off by the committee in an open, public auction. 80% of the proceeds of such auction were distributed equally among the estate right holders while 20% were put into a common village fund meant for financing activities like repair of the devta's temple or for expenditure on common activities. Non right-holders could acquire a share if they paid Rs 150 per annum as fee. Some Tibetans or Nepalese who had married women from Kālpa were also admitted as right holders on payment of this fee. The committee granted no loans. In cases of illness or unforeseen expenditure it gave grants to its members (Kārdārs). It had one Lohār (blacksmith) and two Chāmangs (Harijans) as members out of a total strength of 15, or in other words 20% of the seats consisted of these lower castes. There was no fixed reservation percentage but this number of three had continued since the beginning. The committee had two messengers; one Kanait and one Harijan. General meetings were held twice a year; once in September/October and once in 'Bishu' (April) for the entire village assembly. The smaller committee of 15 met once or twice a month. This committee was a recent phenomenon and was not an ancient institution.[174]

Apart from carrying out Settlement operations, Tikka Raghunāth Singh carried out a reorganization of the administrative structure of Bushahr State in the 1890s. This led to the creation of the Chini Tahsil in 1895 A.D.[175] It consisted of five parganas (Shyalkhar, Tukpa, Shua, Bhāba, Rajgraon) which were further sub-divided into 15 ghodis further divided into 63 revenue estates.[176] Every pargana had a headman called a dashongi who collected 1% of the total revenue collection under his charge as his remuneration. Chini Tahsil was put under the charge of a Naib-Tahsildar with Class III civil and criminal powers. Each ghodi was put under the charge of a Lambardār getting 3% of the total collection under his charge as remuneration. Personal interviews brought out some opinions about this system. "There used to be a Zaildār who used to convey the papers from the Tahsil to the Lambardār and vice versa. One Zaildār based in Poāri looked after all the villages from Chārang to Mebar; another based in Chānsu looked after all the area from Chhitkul to Kilba".[177] A look at the accompanying map would show how the villagers had only loose contact with their remotely located Zaildārs. People hardly saw their field officials more than once or twice a year except in main villages. "The Rājās of Bushahr never came this side, even to Kālpa. They had Kārdārs. The Naib-Tahsildar used to be much greater than the present-day D.C. and used to come regally on tour".[178] Lambardār Keshwa Singh of Sangla, a venerable old man of 85,

the D.C.'s chamber at Kālpa on December, 1985 from 11.00 till 13.30 hours.

[174] Personal interview with Shamsher Singh, Secretary, Village Committee, Chini in the D.C.'s chamber at Kālpa on December 3, 1985.

[175] Gazetteer, 1971, p. 229.

[176] Gazetteer, 1971, Pp 229-230.

[177] Personal interview with Negi Amar Singh Wazir of Poāri on December 9, 1985 in his house in Poāri from 14.30 till 19.15 hours.

[178] Personal interview with Lāmā Shimed Chhéwang on December 10, 1985 in P.W.D. Rest House (Suite No. 2)

Areas marking the jurisdiction of the Zaildars of Poari and Chansu under the administrative system introduced by Tikka Raghunath Singh

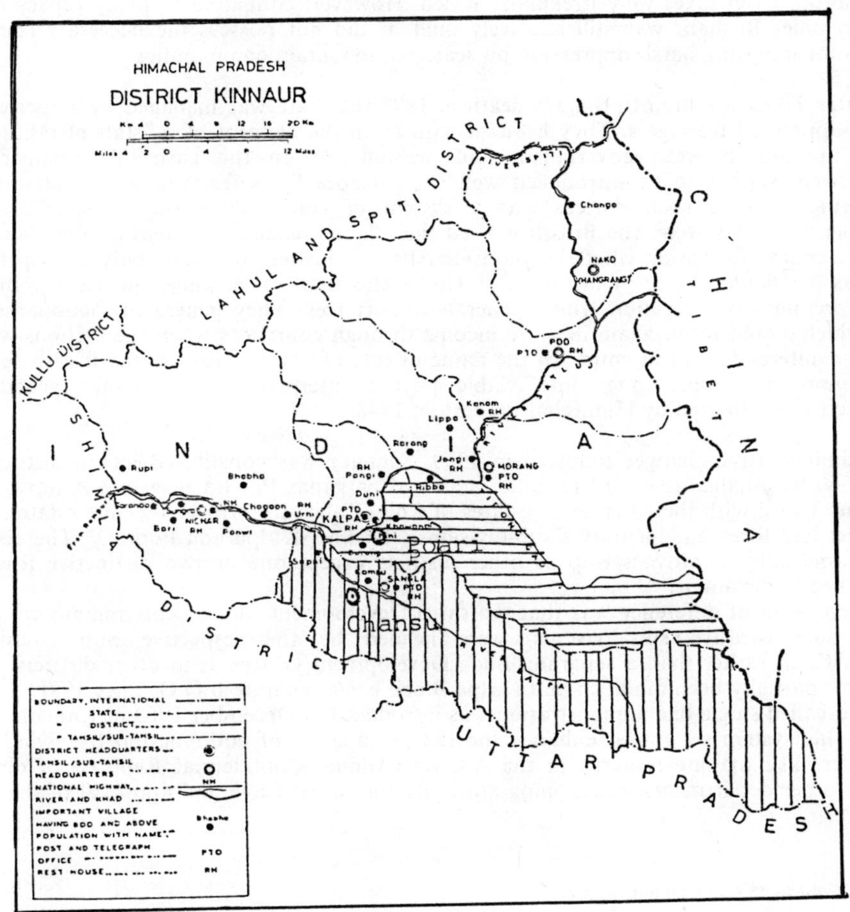

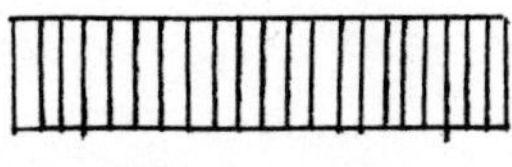

Zail Chansu

Zail Poari

explained that there used to be no "Panchāyats in the Bushahr Rājā's time. Zaildārs and Lambardārs used to take decisions even in criminal matters. All was verbal. They were given respect. My father was the first Lambardār of Sangla. Lambardāri used to be given to only alert persons (hoshiyār ādmi ko lambardāri dī jāti thi). My father used to be the Lambardār from Chhitkul to Shong. Lambardārs had no police powers and used to work under the Zaildār".[179] Chini was still a Tahsil on April 15, 1948 when Bushahr was merged into H.P. Lack of serious crime meant that there were no law and order problems requiring government presence. Development was not considered as one of the essential functions of an administration. Even taxes were irregularly levied. However, compared to really rapacious or despotic regimes Bushahr was still relatively mild. It did not possess the necessary coercive apparatus for imposing harsh oppression on scattered mountain communities.

After Tikka Raghunāth Singh's death in 1898 the State was managed by a succession of British-appointed managers. They brought with them the concept of a "staff of officers to establish the link between government and peasant".[180] In the garb of administrative efficiency were sought to be introduced well tried recipes for safeguarding the interests of colonial rule. Among such devices was a system of courts dispensing "justice". Good businessmen that they were, the British grafted their "comprehensive system of alien law and ubiquitous courts dispensing what they considered to be justice...the monopoly of dispensing justice was a reliable source of income".[181] Under this mask of so-called justice the British placed a premium on litigation which generated court fees. They generated factionalism in villages which would result again in more income through court fees when the factions would battle their differences out in court. In the name of rule of law and justice, the British sought to turn more and more areas into viable paying enterprises. This income generating hotch-potch was inherited by Himāchal Pradesh in 1948.

Administrative changes followed in 1960. Kinnaur was constituted into a district on May 1, 1960 by amalgamating 14 revenue estates of parganas Pandra Bees and Athārā Bees of Rāmpur Tahsil with the 63 revenue estates of Chini Tahsil to form 77 revenue estates. The new district had three administrative sub-divisions - Nichār, Kālpa and Pooh.[182] The district had the same administrative set-up as other districts except one or two distinctive features which we need to examine:[183]

(I) The first point of difference was that the three Development Blocks, coterminous with the three administrative sub-divisions, were headed by the respective Sub Divisional Officer(Civil) rather than a separate Block Development Officer as in other districts. This has now partially been modified and Kālpa Block has a separate B.D.O. since 1981.

(II) The so-called single line administration was introduced in December 1963 in Kinnaur.

Basically, this system sought to enhance the D.C.'s capacity of coordination by giving him extra powers like making remarks in the A.C.Rs (Annual Confidential Reports) of district officers of other departments; sanctioning authority for casual leave and approval of the tour

at Pooh from 19.45 hours till midnight.

[179] Personal interview with Lambardār Keshwa Singh in his house in Sangla on December 7, 1985 at 11.00 hours. He had till then been the Lambardār for 46 years.

[180] Rothermund, D., 1978, p. 11.

[181] Ibid.

[182] Wireless message no. 2-1/60-Border dated 22.04.1960 from the Secretary to the Lieutenant Governor of H.P. addressed to Shri Harish Chandra, Magistrate I Class, Chini.

[183] Order no. 25-35/63-GAD, General Administrative Department, Government of Himāchal Pradesh dated Simla-4 the 24th. Dec.1963.

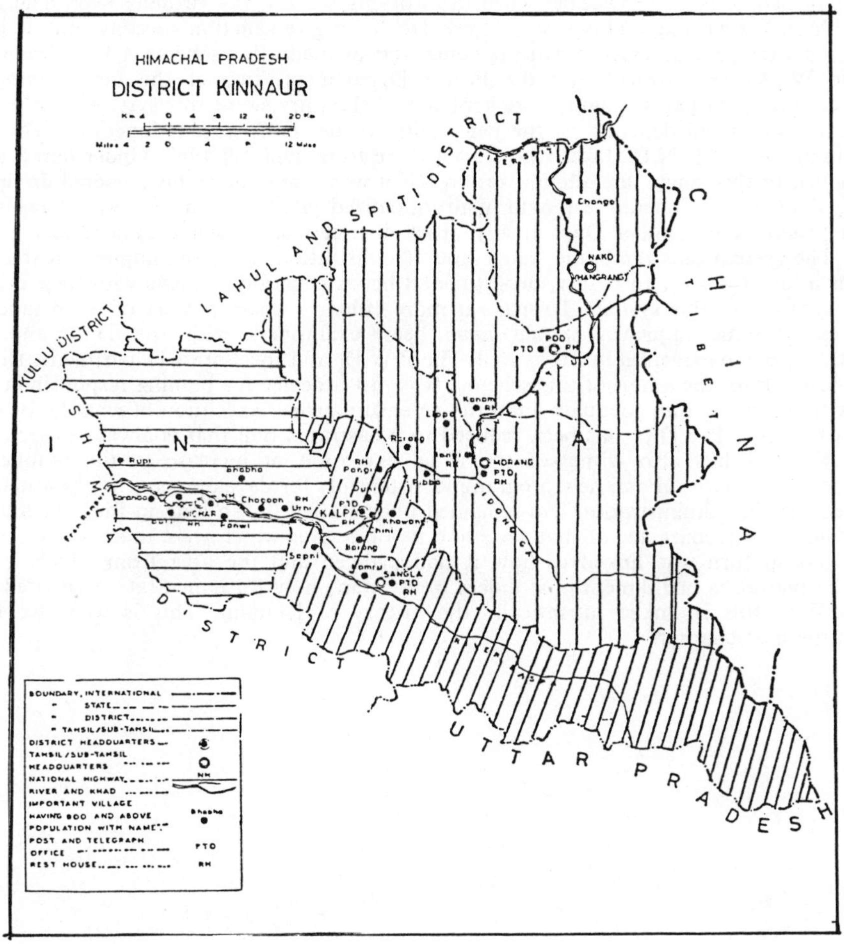

Present-day administrative Sub-Divisions of Kinnaur District

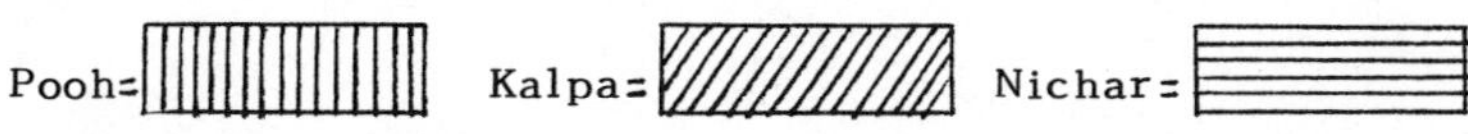

programmes of such officers plus certain powers of financial and administrative sanction. This move was well intentioned because the weather conditions in Kinnaur left time only from May to October, or latest November, for development works. Remote areas and severe winters virtually made work on such projects in winter impossible. If the usual bureaucratic red-tapism of waiting for orders from departmental heads in Simla were to be followed, precious little would get done in the field. Financial and administrative sanctions were sometimes received from Simla in September and October when the working season was virtually over. The D.C. was available in Kālpa, much closer than Simla. He could give sanction speedily. But as in so many other matters, technocrat-bureaucrat controversies made this scheme a toothless tiger. The Public Works Department and the Forest Department, two of the most important departments in an area like Kinnaur, were kept out of the purview of this system. The system is still in force but it all depends on the personality of the D.C. how it functions. The first D.C. of Kinnaur was Mr N.D. Jayal who stayed there from 1960 till 1967. Under him a good start was given to this single line administration but it was more due to his personal drive and personality than to any inherent strength institutionalized in the system. He would probably have been just as successful a D.C. in any other district where such a system was not in operation. The system plus the name 'single line administration' gives the impression that the D.C. wields a lot of power. In reality, departmental heads generally connive with their district officers to circumvent this system. To make it more effective, these powers of leave sanction and tour programme approval should have been exclusively with the D.C. and not concurrently with departmental heads as well. The P.W.D. and the Forest Departments should also have been within the ambit of this scheme. It is just a device for pinning responsibility on the D.C. without giving him adequate authority to ensure proper execution of what he is being held responsible for. The D.C. has been reduced to a castrated bull that is always expected to procreate! Kinnaur has also witnessed the usual explosion of increase in the number of bureaucratic functionaries. Each new programme, ostensibly for development, brings a new set of employees. If the administration had remained understaffed for so long in Bushahr State it was partly due to the character of that state and its objectives which were much more limited in scope. This in turn was linked to how it had evolved and the area from which it had evolved. The picture is one-dimensional unless we examine how Bushahr State originated and developed. With this is linked intrinsically the history of Kinnaur. This is what we shall examine in the next chapter.

Present-day Tahsils and Sub-Tahsils of Kinnaur District

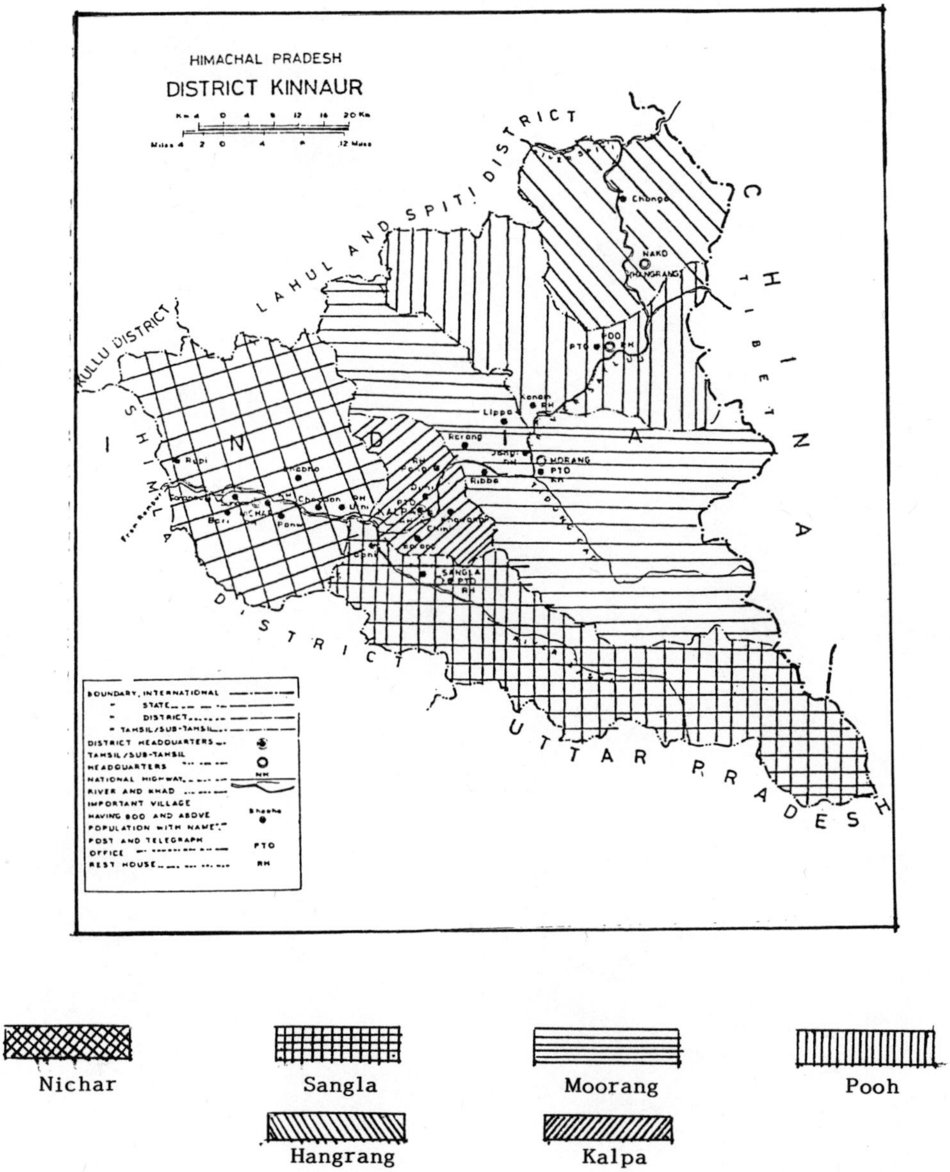

HIMACHAL PRADESH

DISTRICT KINNAUR

Nichar

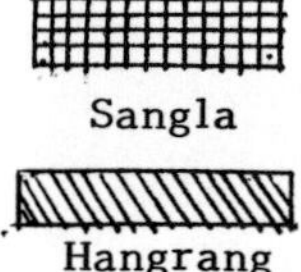
Sangla

Hangrang

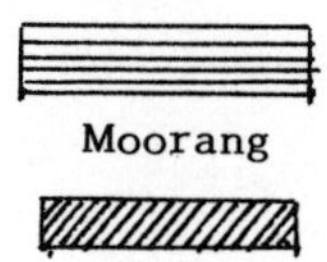
Moorang

Kalpa

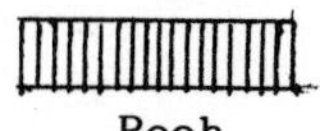
Pooh

CHAPTER II-A

THE HISTORICAL BACKGROUND AND STATE FORMATION

This chapter is not an exposition of the history of Kinnaur. It is an attempt to outline the evolution of Bushahr State within the ambit of which the credit structure in Kinnaur had to operate. No chronological ruler-by-ruler description has been given and only the main factors leading to state formation have been discussed; alongwith the sources available and certain period-divisions of Bushahri/Kinnaura historical evolution in time which throw light on the historical background of the area. Before going on to examine these aspects, we should mention very briefly some features of the already published works on Kinnaur which contain historical accounts of the area.

2.1 EXISTING HISTORY: LONG ON CONJECTURES, SHORT ON FACTS

Accounts about Kinnaur's history build up elaborate chronological sequences without providing enough justification in terms of historical sources for such elaboration. While dividing the history of Kinnaur into what he calls the "following broad periods", T.S. Negi cautions that "what happened, in exact detail, in between, has never yet been studied at length and systematically".[1] He divides the history of Kinnaur as follows:

(A) The original pristine Kinnara Period;
(B) The period when other tribes such as Kiratas and the Khasa arrived on the scene;
(C) The Aryan Period;
(D) The Bhot Period;
(E) The Post-Bhot Period of Thākurs, Village Gods and Rājās;
(F) The British Period;
(G) The Post-Independence Period.

Other accounts reiterate this broad chronological division with minor modifications.[2] None of these accounts attempts to date these sequences even roughly. They do mention the paucity of historical material available but do not try to explore whether this very paucity may itself not be an indicator of something important. Without going into detailed point-by-point refutation of these accounts, certain aspects can be singled out as samples of conjectural prognoses passed off as history.

2.1.1 Gazetteers: Good Information Not Good History

Gazetteers should not be treated as works of history but as compendia giving all sorts of general information about designated areas. However, since they get frequently consulted by researchers interested in the area described, their section giving historical information deserves careful scrutiny. The Gazetteer of 1911 for Bushahr State (referred to as Bashahr) is quite

[1] Negi, T.S., 1976, p. 18.

[2] The periods may not be specifically so entitled but the chronological sequence of other authors comes down essentially to the one outlined by T.S. Negi. For example, see:
(i) Mamgain, M.D.: Himāchal Pradesh District Gazetteers: KINNAUR, Printed at Ambala Cantt., 1971;
(ii) Chib, S.S.: Kanauras of the Trans-Himalaya, New Delhi: Ess Ess Publications, 1984;
(iii) Bajpai, S.C.: Kinnaur in the Himalaya, New Delhi: Concept Publishing House, 1981.
S.C. Bajpai has a similar scheme except that he completely leaves out the Bhot or Tibetan Period. For a discussion of this aspect, please see the Appendix to the present work.

circumspect in this respect and does not attempt to lay out detailed chronological sequences. It mentions legends about the origin of the ruling house of Bushahr but then only mentions some famous rājās before coming to the post-1815 period when information available is more precise.[3] The Gazetteer of Kinnaur District 1971, on the other hand, gives much more detailed information, devoting an entire chapter to the history of the area with chronological divisions.[4] The account is full of phrases like "No written account is available but it can be presumed that...",[5] plus downright absurdities like "The Bhot ruler could not afford to let loose his men to satisfy their lust for women and power and remain a cold and indifferent spectator".[6] There is absolutely no historical evidence to show whether the Bhots lusted after Kinnaura women or whether there were any oppressive manifestations of their rule. It seems to rest on the unsaid assumption that any foreign rulers must necessarily have been rapacious towards the women of the occupied area. These totally unfounded presumptions have found their way into purportedly serious works on Kinnaur. They may be good reading but are not good history. A lengthier discussion of more such unwarranted conclusions is given in the Appendix.

2.2 SOURCES AVAILABLE: REALITY AND INTERPRETATION

It is true that the Gorkhas systematically destroyed archival material during their occupation of Rāmpur.[7] They are said to have destroyed "the archives and the records of the state, leaving behind nothing but rubble. Valuable records which could easily have provided a clue in tracing out the history of the state were also lost".[8] This makes the historian's task harder. But no destruction, howsoever systematic, can completely eliminate all the sources of an area's history. These are not concentrated only at one place. We can broadly categorize the available source material as follows:

2.2.1 Grokch and Chirāning: Gods' Voices, Dances And Trances!

Each village in Kinnaur has at least one deity. Each deity has a human medium through whom it communicates its wishes to the villagers. This mouthpiece of the deity is the person through whom the deity 'speaks'. He is known as the ***'Grokch'***, (also pronounced as the Groks) or the Māli. The grokch has become an institution hereditary in certain families. An overwhelming majority of the grokches belong to the higher caste Kanait group, members of which like to describe themselves as Rājpūts or as Khaushias. When the deity wishes to speak, the grokch becomes possessed, goes into a trance and utters whatever comes to him. Though local people maintain that the grokch's voice is quite different from his normal voice during such possession by the deity, personal observation of four such seances indicated otherwise.[9] While possessed, the grokch talked rather fast and at a higher pitch than his

[3] Punjab States Gazetteer, Volume VIII: Simla Hill States, No. 2, Part A: Bashahr State Gazetteer, Lahore: Government Press, 1911, Section B, Chapter I, Pp 5-11.

[4] Gazetteer, 1971, Chapter II: Pp 48-65.

[5] Gazetteer, 1971, p. 51: Lines no. 26-27 from the top.

[6] Gazetteer, 1971, p. 52: Lines no. 17-18 from the top.

[7] Gazetteer, 1911, p. 7; Gazetteer, 1971, p. 60.

[8] Gazetteer, 1971, p. 60.

[9] Personal attendance at seances in Kāmru, Sangla, Poāri and Nichār from 1980 to 1982 at different periods.

normal voice but the voice did not change unrecognizably. Also, while in personal interviews various grokches maintained that they had absolutely no idea of what they were saying in their trance, in reality some seemed to notice remarkably well whether they had been photographed during the trance or not. When the Grokch of Chini requested a copy of his photograph taken while he was in a trance, he was asked how he knew that such a photograph had been taken at all if he had no idea of what went on around him. This made him feel sheepish but he only smiled and did not say anything.

On festivals or on special occasions the grokch narrates at length the feats performed by the devta or devi. This narration is called the ***'Chirāning'***. It is also sometimes spelt as the ***'Chironing'***. The chirāning of the Devta Badrināth of Kāmru, formerly the Rājā of Bushahr's household devta (kuladevta) narrates the devta's feats and explains how he established the ruling house of Bushahr on the throne. While most of it is a tale of the deity's bravado[10] it does indirectly convey some historical indications. For example, Devta Badrināth mentions that while coming to Kāmru to establish himself there, he crossed the territory of Gugé pargana of Tibet. Then follow references to various thākurs (chieftains) who were purportedly vanquished by him at Sangla, Chini, Tāngling, and Choling. The chirāning further refers to the devta having conferred special rights on the Poāri Wazir family and on certain prominent clans (khāndāns) in different villages - Bauryang of village Shong; Sairyang of Chānsu, Dhansyān (Répalto) of Sangla, Dudhyān of Kāmru, Shañtesto of Batséri, Vilaiñtoo of Rakchham and Baugyato of Chhitkul.[11] All these clans are among the most prosperous and influential families of the Baspa valley even today. The chirāning clearly is an attempt at legitimizing their high standing as some sort of a divine gift. It indicates that these clans could have been possible rivals to the Thākur of Kāmru who later evolved into the Rājā of Bushahr. Since the Rājā sought to legitimize his rule by claiming divine sanction through the medium of the chirānings the leading clans did the same thing on a lesser scale and sought to justify their position through the same medium. The grokch thus served as an important cog in the wheel of legitimizing the status of leading families since he communicated the devta's will. The grokch was not a direct claimant to primacy in village affairs but had to be kept in good humour by the leading families. He was thus an indirect participant in decision making. The hereditary nature of this institution meant that the grokch's family acquired importance as custodians of the devta's expression of will. The greater the importance of the devta, correspondingly greater was the importance of his grokch.

The chirānings of the devta at Poāri which was the seat of the Poāri Wazir family and those of the more important deities of Kinnaur - the Shuwang Chandika of Kothi, the three Devtas Mahéshras of Sungra, Bhāba and Chagāoñ furnish similar historical indices. They narrate how the deities came to the area, what sort of conditions existed at the time of their arrival, which chieftains were defeated by them and how powerful they were. The chains of events narrated in their chirānings must be carefully cross-checked with other sources before their information can be accepted as relevant historical data but they provide at least a starting point. They indirectly convey some historical indices about prevailing political conditions. They mention a plethora of thākurs defeated by deities which hints at a decentralized polity with several petty chieftains having ruled the area before the coming of Bushahr State as the dominating entity of the area.

[10] As T.S. Negi told me in a personal interview on January 6, 1986, "devta apni shaikhi mārta hai" (The devta brags about himself).

[11] Gazetteer, 1971, Appendix III, Pp 362-365; Personal recording of the Chirāning of Devta Badrināth of Kāmru.

2.2.2 Genealogies: Lunar Dynasty and Legitimation

As for other hill states in Himāchal Pradesh, Bushahr State, too, had genealogical charts for its ruling house and for other prominent families for showing their remote and lofty origins. In fact, most genealogies of the Bushahr royal house put Rājā Padam Singh (1914-1948 A.D.) as the 121st in an unbroken line beginning with Parduman Singh, said variously to be the son or

(Specimen of a genealogical chart of the Rajas of Bushahr in Tankri.)

the grandson of Lord Krishna.[12] The royal house of Bushahr claimed a lunar or

[12] Copy of a draft unsigned letter from Rājā Padam Singh of Bushahr to Sir Edward Douglas Maclagan,

Chandravanshi origin. A genealogy found at Kāmru makes Rājā Padam Singh 121st of his line while a genealogy found at Rāmpur makes him the 130th.[13] After giving an explanation of this difference, the Gazetteer points out that except for "the last eleven names the two genealogies...do not fully agree. Much reliance cannot, therefor, be placed on their correctness".[14] The genealogies do, however, clearly hint that a certain reliability can be attached only to the last ten or eleven rulers, indicating a much more recent origin going back only some 250-300 years rather than the 3000 years claimed by legendary accounts. This evidence ties up with other historical material available. During field research a copy of a genealogical chart of the royal house of Bushahr was found at Sangla. It was in the Tānkri script and was said to be a copy of a genealogical table lying in the famous Buddhist monastery at Tholing in Tibet. It has only 96 names and not the usual 121 or more.[15] The last 12 names of this chart match the last 12 names of other tables. Only the last 12 names are considered authentic by H. A. Rose.[16] Giuseppe Tucci also considers only the last 12 names authentic, reconfirming a more recent origin for the royal house.[17]

Of genealogical tables or vanshavalis, it has been said that such documents "are common in the Western Hills, and are preserved with so much care that it is often with the greatest difficulty that a copy can be obtained...Some of them are of doubtful value; while others possess the accuracy of true historical records".[18] For Kāngra State, William Moorcroft observed that he saw a royal vanshavali in which Rājā Sansār Chand of Kāngra "deduces his descent from Mahadeo, and has a pedigree in which his ancestors are traced to their celestial progenitor through many thousand years".[19] Sir Alexander Cunningham attached importance to the Kāngra Vanshavali which he evaluated as having "a much stronger claim to our belief than any of the long string of names shown by the more powerful families of Rājpūtāna".[20]

Bushahr was thus not alone in claiming such ancient lineage. The historical fact is that the hills were not invaded as often as the plains. In consequence, the former suffered less frequent changes of ruling dynasties which could claim undisturbed pedigrees. Their

Governor of the Punjab. The draft letter is in Negi Goverdhan Singh's papers. In para 13(a) of the letter, Rājā Padam Singh writes that the Bushahr chief was a "descendant of Parduman son of Sri Krishan ji of Mahabharata fame. The present Chief is 121st in generation". The Gazetteer of 1911 refers to Parduman as the grandson and not as the son of Sri Krishan (p. 5). Sir Lepel Griffin in his authoritative work on the Chiefs of Punjab refers to Parduman as the grandson of Sri Krishna.
Griffin, Sir Lepel H. and Massy, Col. Charles F.: Chiefs and Families of Note in the Punjab, a revised edition of "The Punjab Chiefs", Vol. II, Lahore: Civil and Military Gazette Press, 1910, p. 439.

[13] Gazetteer, 1971, Pp 366-368.

[14] Gazetteer, 1971, p. 57.

[15] The names were read out to the author by Lambardār Keshwa Singh of Sangla who can read the Tānkri script.

[16] Francke, A.H.: Antiquities of Indian Tibet, Part I: Personal Narrative, A.S.I., New Imperial Series, Vol. XXXVIII, Reprint, New Delhi: S. Chand & Co., 1972 [Calcutta, 1908], Vol. I, Appendix D, p. 124.

[17] Petech, L., 1947, Footnote 8, p. 176.

[18] Hutchison and Vogel, 1933, p. 2.

[19] Moorcroft and Trebeck, 1971, Vol. I, p. 145.

[20] Cunningham, A., 1854, p. 138.

vanshavalis can be cross-checked with those of neighbouring states. For example, for Bushahr we can cross-check with the genealogical charts of Kulu, Garhwāl and Sirmaur States. But in making such comparisons it should always be borne in mind that the vanshavali of the neighbouring state was as liable to fake extension as the document sought to be cross-checked. Hence the necessity of corroboration through epigraphical and numismatic record.

For Bushahr, we can cross-check the information provided by the grokches through their chirānings and that furnished by vanshavalis of the Bushahr dynasty. Unfortunately, while the chirānings provide details about the feats performed by the devtas and also by some rājās like Kehri Singh, the vanshavalis give only a succession of names without any description of what the rājās did or their chronological estimates. Nevertheless, the names given in the vanshavalis tally more or less with the names mentioned in the chirānings, in-so-far-as the latter mention names at all. For example, the chirāning of Devta Badrināth of Kāmru mentions how the devta helped one Deva Purna defeat the demon king Bānāsur and establish Parduman Singh, the grandson of Lord Krishna, on the throne of Bushahr. The genealogical tables all begin with the name Parduman Singh. To this extent the two sets of evidence corroborate each other. But this agreement does not mean that we can accept the 121 generations claimed for the ruling house of Bushahr. It just means that while no sequence of events can be established for the very remote period, such agreement for the period from the 16th century onwards for which we have other supporting evidence puts us on firmer ground. Had the genealogical charts given information about the feats of the various rājās rather than only their names, this process of comparison would have been more meaningful. This process was replicated for leading families as well. During field research, a vanshavali was seen for the Poāri Wazir family. The document showed a chain going back more than 100 generations. It rivalled the vanshavalis of the ruling house of Bushahr in purported longevity. The chirāning of the devta in Poāri village speaks of the Wazir's family's feats and of its having specially been blessed by divinities. Such corroboration needs to be cross-verified with other sources.

2.2.3 Inscriptions: Few and Far Between

The only mention of historically important inscriptions having been found in Kinnaur is by the Rev. A.H. Francke, the famous Tibetologist.[21] He found an inscription in a field in dKor hamlet of Pooh village. The inscription contained the full name of Lha-bla-ma Ye-shes-'od, the "royal priest and early King of Gugé, who had tried in vain to draw the famous Buddhist monk Atisa to his kingdom".[22] Francke describes Ye-shes-'od as "this famous personage of Tibetan history (c. 1025 A.D.)".[23] The king's name was followed by the words "sku-ring-la, meaning in his lifetime...This inscription of King Ye-shes-'od is the first record which can be brought forward to confirm the statements of the Tibetan historians. Fragmentary though it is, it contains some interesting information".[24] This inscription is nowhere to be found now. Even old people in Koro hamlet (the dKor of Francke) remembered nothing at all about such a stone ever having been seen by them. They all felt that in case such a stone had existed, it had long since been uprooted and thrown away.

In addition, Francke noticed votive tablets on several stone walls. None was very ancient. Describing these tablets he said that the "first part may be called devotional, the second part consisted of a eulogy of the country of which the village of Poo (spelt sPu in the inscriptions) was the centre, the third part praised the Rājā of Bashahr who was reigning at

[21] Francke, A.H., 1908, Vol. I, p. 19.

[22] Ibid.

[23] Ibid.

[24] Ibid.

the time, and the fourth part contained the account of the building of the wall, and stated for whose religious benefit it was meant".[25] Rev. Francke and Rev. R. Schnabel, the then resident Moravian missionary at Pooh could decipher the names of only four rājās of Bushahr:

"Rudar (in Tibetan Lurdur) Singh;
Ugar (in Tibetan Urku) Singh;
Mahinder (in Tibetan Metar) Singh;
Shamsher (in Tibetan bSam-gser) Singh".

These names covered the period of the preceding century.[26] Other votive tablets "instead of giving the proper name of the chief simply speak of 'the great king' at Sarāhan (So-ra-rang in Tibetan) This shows that the personal names of the rulers of Bushahr previous to Rudar Singh were not known to the Tibetans".[27] The Rev. Francke says nothing about it but a plausible explanation for the 'great king' could be that it refers to Rājā Kehri Singh, the most famous of the Bushahr rājās and the architect of the trade treaty with Tibet. These votive tablets are also now not to be found in Pooh or its vicinity. Nobody seems to know what happened to them. Prof. Tucci, travelling through the area about 25 years after A.H. Francke, did not find any trace of this inscription. Nor does he mention votive tablets.

2.2.4 Travellers' Accounts: Copious and Important

After Bushahr State came under British paramountcy in 1816 A.D., European travellers were allowed into the area. Their travelogues furnish some information about Kinnaur. They mostly mention then recent historical events and just repeat legends or myths about the past. Since they were just birds of passage, their accounts tend to be superficial at times but nevertheless give help for further research. James Baillie Fraser was the pioneer in this respect. He never visited Kinnaur and came only till Rāmpur and Sarāhan.[28] He was followed by Captain Alexander Gerard who made several journeys into Kinnaur between 1817 and 1821. His books and articles[29] are important for research about Kinnaur. Then followed a whole chain of British visitors - Captain Thomas Hutton, Captain Madden, J.D. Cunningham, who spent a whole winter in the Hangrang valley, C.M. Smith, W. Theobald and Andrew Wilson - to name some. The British were not the only ones who travelled through the area. There were also Victor Jacquemont and Mme Isabelle Massieu from France; Sven Hédin from Sweden and Prince Waldemar of Prussia. It is a pity that the famous Hungarian Tibetologist, Alexander

[25] Ibid, p. 18.

[26] Ibid.

[27] Ibid.

[28] Fraser, J.B., 1820.

[29] Gerard's books are:

(a) Lloyd, Major Sir William and Gerard, Captain Alexander: Narrative of a Journey from Caunpoor to the Boorendo Pass in the Himalaya Mountains via Gwalior, Agra, Delhi and Sirhind, edited by George Lloyd, Vol. II, Book II: Captain Alexander Gerard's Narrative, London: James Madden & Co., 1840;

(b) Account of Koonawur In The Himalaya Etc. Etc. Etc., edited by George Lloyd, London: James Madden & Co., 1841;

His important articles are:

(a) Journal of an Excursion through the Himalayah Mountains, from Shipke to the Frontiers of Chinese Tartary, in: Edinburgh Journal of Science, Vol. I, 1824, Pp 41-51 and 215-224;

(b) A Vocabulary of the Kunawur Language, in: J.A.S., Vol. 11, Part I, New Series, 1842, Pp 478-551;

(c) Narrative of a Journey from Soobathoo to Shipke, in Chinese Tartary, in: J.A.S.B., Vol. 11, Part I, New Series, 1842, Pp 361-391.

Csoma de Körös, who spent nearly three years in Kinnaur at Kānam learning Tibetan from 1827 to 1830 A.D.,[30] has not left any published work about Kinnaur. He could really have produced a work in-depth. Of the Indian travellers who have written about the area more recently, Rāhul Sānkrityāyan and Pran Chopra come readily to mind. None of the accounts published by all these travellers can be regarded as furnishing an authentic history of Kinnaur though. They provide useful information which has to be researched in depth.

2.2.5 Sources in Private Possession: Recent and Few

During field research and an earlier period of service lasting three years in Kinnaur, the present author came across some sources of historical information in private hands. These sources were mainly copies of genealogies; copies of royal seals; documents in the Tānkri script on birch leaves; copies of orders from the Bushahr Durbār; letters from various Rājās of Bushahr and title deeds (sanads) of jāgirs or land grants. None of these was older than 150 years. They furnished good information for the post-1816 period but very little beyond intelligent speculation in what concerned the earlier periods. People are chary about allowing outsiders access to these personal documents. These records pertain mostly to family fortunes and rarely to state formation or political developments. No copies of any treaties were found during field research. Buddhist monasteries at Moorang, Kānam, Rārang, Chāngo, Tashigong and Lippa have only religious works in their libraries according to the lāmās contacted in them. It is possible that historical material is available in some monasteries in Tibet, particularly in those of Tholing and Tsaparang, but these areas are not open to field research. Scholars like Alexander Csoma de Körös and Rāhul Sānkrityāyan, both fluent in Tibetan, do not report any historical material in the monasteries of Kinnaur.

2.2.6 Temples, Gompas and Forts: Scanty Evidence

The remains of old forts, some temples and particularly of Buddhist Gompas offer indirect historical evidence, as do the palaces of the Rājās of Bushahr at Sarāhan and at Rāmpur. Speaking of the Buddhist temple at Chāngo in upper Kinnaur, Prof. Tucci says that its "walls, blackened and smoke laden, bear traces, however, of most remarkable frescoes of great value from the historical, iconographical and religious point of view".[31] There is another such temple at Nāko where there is a rock on which "tradition professes to recognize the imprint of the hand of Padmasambhava".[32] In this very village in another temple "attributed to Rin-chen S'ang-po there is a fine set of stucco images of Vairocana and the other four buddhas".[33] This Rin-c'en-bzaṅ-po was a great missionary and apostle of Buddhism in Western Tibet. He was not only a great translator but a master of spiritual experiences as well. "His name rests indissolubly connected with one of the most important periods of the history of Tibetan art".[34] Temples are said to have been founded by him at Pooh, Chārang, Kānam, and even at Sangla among others. These relics point to a Tibetan connexion in Kinnaura history.

[30] Duka, T.: Life and Works of Alexander Csoma de Körös, London: Trübner& Co., 1885, p. 18.

[31] Tucci & Ghersi, 1935, p. 68.

[32] Ibid, p. 70.

[33] Snellgrove, D.L.: Buddhist Himalaya, Travels and Studies in quest of the Origins and Nature of Tibetan Religion, Oxford: Bruno Cassirer Publishers, p. 185.

[34] Tucci, G.: Indo-Tibetica III, Parte I: Spiti E Kunavar, Roma: Reale Accademia d'Italia, 1935-XIII, p. 5 (Introduction). The original reads: **"Il suo nome resta indissolubilmente connesso con uno dei periodi più importanti della storia dell'arte tibetana".**
Translation mine.

Similarly, Rāhul Sānkrityāyan made a study of the idols in Kothi village.[35] These were Hindu idols and showed a continuous existence of an undercurrent of hinduizing influences at work. The Rev. A.H. Francke mentions a fresco in the palace at Rāmpur as one of the lāmāist frescoes that he had seen. It "evidently represents the treaty between Tibet and Bashahr concluded about 1650 A.D., when Bashahr was supported by the Mughal emperor".[36] This fresco shows no clear detail today and is in a badly damaged condition. In any case, the Bashahris had been allies of the Tibetans whereas the Mughals had come to the rescue of the Ladākhis in the Tibet-Ladākhi-Mughal War so that Francke's conclusion can be challenged. The building style of the palace at Sarāhan shows Tibetan influence in the shape of its roof and design. All this again points to a lasting Tibetan influence exerted through Kinnaur.

2.2.7 Moravian Mission's Archives: Occasional References

The Brüder-Unität at Herrnhut in the GDR, commonly known as the Moravian Mission, had two mission stations in Kinnaur. The first station at Pooh was established by Edouard Pagell in 1865 and lasted till 1915 when the missionaries were interned as undesirable aliens because of World War I. The second station at Chini was established by J. Bruske in 1900 and was wound up in 1907. Copious reports and letters written by the missionaries stationed at these mission stations are available in the archives of the Brüder-Unität at Herrnhut. They yield a wealth of information about the social and economic conditions of Kinnaur in the late 19th century but very little information about the political conditions and history of the area. They do convey an idea of the style of functioning and organization of the admistrative apparatus of Bushahr State. Very little can, however, be gauged from these papers about the early history of Kinnaur and this remains an enigma. We can now evaluate where a discussion of the sources available has led us to.

2.3 PAUCITY OF SOURCES: ALSO AN INDICATOR

Paucity of epigraphical and other source material itself seems to be a source indicating that Bushahr State had not existed since thousands of years as the genealogical charts would have us believe. Otherwise, we would have found more sources; particularly because in some other areas of Himāchal Pradesh where the ruling princes claimed descent from antiquity, epigraphical and numismatic sources have been found for cross-checking such claims. "Richest of all in epigraphical remains is the Hill State of Chamba where we find an almost uninterrupted series from the sixth century A.D. down to the present time".[37] 130 inscriptions had been found in Chamba, excluding those of the last two-and-a-half centuries. The existence of these records is ascribed to the area's having been entirely secluded, with a greater part uninhabited.[38]

Exactly the same conditions were met with in Kinnaur in terms of remoteness and sparse habitation but the latter area has not yielded any similar epigraphical records. We cannot argue that the Gorkha invasion destroyed such artifacts because while this reasoning may have been valid for areas of Bushahr like Rāmpur, Rohru, and Sarāhan which had been occupied by the Gorkhas and plundered, it certainly is not true for Kinnaur which never came

[35] Sānkrityāyan Rāhul: Kinner Desh, Allahabad: Kitāb Mahal, II edn., Pp 302-303.

[36] Francke, A.H., 1908, p. 7.

[37] Hutchison & Vogel, 1933, p. 5.

[38] Ibid.

under Gorkha rule. The Gorkhas could thus not have destroyed any epigraphical evidence in Kinnaur. The only inference seems to be that the process of state formation had not attained the same stage of evolution in Kinnaur as it had in Chamba.

Rock inscriptions were found at Pathyar and Khānyara in Kāngra District. These contain a few characters in brahmi and kharoshthi which "must belong to the centuries anterior to the Christian era".[39] Nothing similar has been found in Kinnaur. Such evidence is an index of an area's having attained a certain level of political development. The absence of any war memorials or edicts commemorating military successes in Kinnaur leads us in the same direction. Wars and invasions reflected to a certain extent the importance of the states attacked. If Ashok had invaded Kalinga it had not been at random. The latter had been important enough politically, economically or otherwise to be perceived as a threat. Hence, it had to be subdued. Closer to Bushahr, Kāngra attracted Muslim invasions because of its fort and its importance as a leading hill state. Its strategically located fort gave whoever commanded it, a certain pre-eminence in the area. No such factor is discernible for Kinnaur. It was never important enough to attract such attention. The so-called forts existing there are puny ramshackle structures compared to a fort like the Kāngra fort.

Had Bushahr really been as important a state as popular accounts say it was, it seems incredible why Muslim chroniclers make no mention of it. We can find numerous and detailed references to some hill states "in the works of the Muhammadan historians, from the time of Mahmud of Ghazni, and more especially during the Mughal period".[40] For example, we can find at least five references to Kāngra in the Ain-i-Akbari of Abu'l Fazl Allami.[41] Muslim chroniclers furnish a major source for the history of hill states. Absence of references to Bushahr in their chronicles is even stranger because Kinnaura/Bushahri tradition maintains that Rājā Kehri Singh of Bushahr had been honoured with the title of Chhatrapati by an unnamed Mughal emperor.[42] Had he really been awarded this title, it is inconceivable that no mention of this event would find place in Mughal chronicles. Reinforcing this tendency is the absence of references to Bushahr in works like Kalhana's Rājātarangini. Of Rājātarangini's importance, it has been estimated that there "is hardly a single principality of any size, then in existence in the hills between the Bias and the Indus, to which reference is not made. In addition to Chamba, the most important of them were Trigarta or Kāngra; Valapura or Balor; Babbapura or Babor...Kashtavata or Kashtwar; Rajapuri or Rajauri, Parnotsa or Poonch...Ursha or Hazara".[43] Bushahr was not important enough to be mentioned in the Rājātarangini. which was a chronicle "replete with information about the eleventh and twelfth centuries".[44] To carry the argument even further back in time, we see that while certain other hill states are mentioned by Hiuen Tsang, Bushahr or Kinnaur finds no such

[39] Ibid.

[40] Ibid, p. 3.

[41] Abu'l-Fazl Allami: Ain-i-Akbari, (Translated into English by H. Blochman), edited by S.L. Goomer, II edn., New Delhi: Aadish Book Depot, 1965, Pp 456-457 and Pages 361, 544, 573.

[42] For information about this title of Chhatrapati having been conferred on Rājā Kehri Singh, please see:
(1) Draft of a personal letter from Rājā Padam Singh of Bushahr to Sir Edward D. Maclagan, Governor of Punjab, Unpublished;
(2) Report on the assessment and revenue rate of Rāmpur Tehsil, Bashahr State, in: Foreign Department, Native States, January 1894, Nos. 18-22, File No. 2, No. 21, Page 17, Para 9;
(3) Gazetteer, 1911, p. 6.

[43] Hutchison & Vogel, 1933, Pp 6-7.

[44] Ibid, p. 6.

mention. "The oldest authentic historical reference to the hill states is to be found in the records of the Chinese pilgrim, Hiuen Tsiang, who visited India in A.D. 629 and remained till 644...The states referred to by him are Urasha or Hazara; Parnotsa or Punch; Rājāpuri or Rājāuri; Trigarta or Jalandhara (Kāngra) and Kuluta or Kulu".[45] The last mentioned is the most important because Kulu had a common border with Bushahr State along the Satluj river and along the Sri Khānd range with Kinnaur respectively. If Hiuen Tsang could mention Kulu he could have also mentioned Bushahr or Kinnaur if these latter areas had been important or significant enough.

Other considerations like the absence of literary or historical works or the absence of a written script for the Kinnauri language also point to the same conclusion. It has been said of state formation that its history is "epitomized in the history of indigenous written records and of script among them. The relation between the formation of the state and the development of script, of writings, is not a chance correlation, but a coordination with interacting consequences in service of the former".[46] Absence of such records or script indicates that state formation had not reached an important enough level. We begin finding such records in the shape of land grants and jāgirs or muāfis for the period after the 17th century in private possession, viz land grants made to the ancestors of the Wazirs of Poāri.

Bushahr seems to have emerged as a leading actor on the regional scene in the Western Hills towards the end of the 17th century. Real historical interest begins in this period towards the end of the Emperor Aurangzeb's rule when he was in the Deccan. Bushahr was not an isolated case. There was a spurt of similar state formation across India. The use of the surname 'Singh' fits in with this analysis as well. As Rev. Francke indicates "All the Rājās are called by the dynastical name Singh...but there is no instance of any ancient Indian family which makes use of that name earlier than the 15th century".[47] H.A. Rose dates it even later, to the 16th century, saying, "the cognomen in question does not seem to have come into use until the 16th century".[48] He also gives a list of 12 rulers of Bushahr, in which Kehri Singh (1639-1696 A.D.)[49] is the fifth after Hari Singh (1464-1512). If the cognomen 'Singh' begins around the time of Hari Singh, it gives about 125 years for state formation to have further developed till the time of Kehri Singh in whose time Bushahr emerged into prominence as a major force.

Events in the neighbourhood of Kinnaur also fit in with this line of reasoning. Around the period of Rājā Kehri Singh, the Ladākhi king Seng-ge-rnam-rgyal had executed some decisions which gave a filip to the importance of Bushahr. After a war in 1639 A.D. with the Balti chief Adam Khān of Skardo, assisted by a Mughal force sent by the Governor of Kashmir, Ali Mardān Khān, the Ladākhi king had prohibited the passage of caravans through Ladākh and even forbidden any person from Kashmir from entering his dominions as an act of economic reprisal against the Mughals who had aided his enemy.[50] These measures of exclusion caused a shifting of trade routes since Ladākh had till then been a major artery for trade between Tibet on one side and Kashmir and the plains of Punjab on the other.

[45] Ibid, p. 3.

[46] Krader, Lawrence: The Origin of the State among the Nomads of Asia, p. 104, in: Claessen, Henri J.M. and Skalnik, Peter (eds.): The Early State, The Hague: Mouton Publishers, 1978, Pp 93-107.

[47] Francke, 1908, p. 8.

[48] Ibid, p. 124.

[49] Ibid. The dates are used as given by H.A. Rose.

[50] Petech, 1977, Pp 50-51.

Francois Bernier, the French traveller, reports that the transit trade through Ladākh was still blocked in 1663, 24 years after the imposition of the ban.[51] "This foolish measure must have proved a real disaster to the economy of Ladākh, which then as always depended above all on transit trade. It is possible that the noticeable weakening of the strength of the kingdom after the death of Sen-ge-rnam-rgyal was due for the greater part to this severe self-inflicted blow to its economy".[52]

One kingdom's self-inflicted wound was the other's healing touch! This sequence of measures by Ladākh between 1640 and 1675 A.D. could not but have diverted some of the trade of the Northern Indian plains, till then passing via Ladākh, towards the Satluj valley route through Kinnaur to Tibet. Confirmation of this fact can be seen in the treaty ensuring free trade between Tibet and Bushahr concluded by Rājā Kehri Singh in 1685 A.D. . There was no need to ensure free trade privileges for Kinnaura traders in Western Tibet in areas like Rudok, Chhumurti and Gartok, which were located eastwards of Ladākh with which they had carried on trade earlier, if trade through Kinnaur were not already increasing or if its importance for the state not already clear enough in Bushahr. Kinnaur, with its geographical location straddling the Satluj valley, provided access to these very areas of so much erstwhile importance for Ladākh. This opportunity given to Bushahr marked the cementing of its trade relations with Tibet towards the end of the 17th century. These relations were later on utilized by the British after 1815. Difficulties in the shawl wool trade "inevitably gave rise to British attempts to open commercial negotiations with the Tibetan and Chinese authorities along their common frontier, either through British officials or through the mediation of native states like Bashahr, which possessed close ties with Tibet".[53] Bushahr was henceforth an actor of note in this region whose politics were significantly influenced by the shawl wool trade with Tibet.[54] Rāmpur with its three annual trade fairs became the major entrepôt for trade with Tibet in this area. Bushahr had already the advantage of a process of state formation going on uninterrupted for the preceding 125-150 years. It was in a position to exploit the opportunity thrown into its lap by the King of Ladākh. Increasing trade furnished an impetus to the next stage of state formation in Bushahr.

The undisturbed evolution of state formation in Bushahr confers authenticity on the legend by which it was considered one of the oldest states in this part of the hills. Since its origins were shrouded in the mystrey of unimportance, its later rulers consolidated their legitimacy by projecting their origins back into unknown antiquity and beyond. How well they succeeded in this task can be seen from the observations made in two well-known works about the hill states of this region. A.H. Francke pointed out that the family of "the Bashahr Rājās...is recognized all over northern India as very ancient and the other rajas are desirous of receiving their caste-mark from the Bashahr Rājā, even if the latter condescends only to put it on their foreheads with his toe".[55] In a similar vein we hear that the "Simla Hill States

[51] Bernier, Francois: Travels in the Mogul Empire, Translated on the basis of Irving Brock's version and annotated by Archibald Constable (1891), II edn., Revised by Vincent A. Smith, London: Humphrey Milford Oxford University Press, 1916, p. 426.

[52] Petech, 1977, p. 51.

[53] Lamb, Alistair: Tibet in Anglo-Chinese Relations 1767-1842, p. 38, in: Journal of the Asiatic Society of Great Britain and Ireland, April 1958, Pp 26-43.

[54] For more information about the shawl wool trade's importance in West Himalayan politica, please see:

(1) Datta, C.L.: Significance of Shawl-wool Trade in Western Himalayan Politics, in: Bengal: Past and Present, Vol. LXXXVII, Part I, January-June 1969, Pp 16-28;

(2) Datta, C.L.: Zorawar Singh: Political Mission of J.D. Cunningham, in: Bengal: Past and Present, Vol. XXXIX, Part I, January-June 1970, Pp 82-90.

are mostly of ancient origin...the oldest of them being probably Bashahr".[56] That Bushahr's claim to such an exalted existence since antiquity was so widely accepted was certainly a remarkable piece of legitimation engineering; available facts point to its having emerged to be taken seriously enough as a state only from the last quarter of the 17th century onwards. To establish this point more clearly, a chronological sequence can now be attempted for Kinnaur.

2.4 CHRONOLOGY FOR KINNAUR: FACTS AND FICTION

Following the trend of reasoning developed till now, the following chronological sequence is proposed for studying the historical background of Kinnaur:-

2.4.1 PRE-BHOT PERIOD (Antiquity-7th Century A.D.)- PROTO HISTORY;
2.4.2 BHOT PERIOD (7th Century A.D.-13th Century A.D.);
2.4.3 PERIOD OF EARLY STATE FORMATION (14 Cen. A.D.-17 Cen. A.D.);
2.4.4 PERIOD OF CONSOLIDATION OF STATE FORMATION (18th Cen.-1815);
2.4.5 PERIOD OF BRITISH PARAMOUNTCY OVER BUSHAHR (1816-1947 A.D.);
2.4.6 POST-INDEPENDENCE PERIOD TILL 1960 (1948-1960 A.D.);
2.4.7 POST-1960 PERIOD (1960-1985 A.D.).

These are not watertight compartments in-as-much-as many of the phenomena listed in one period may have been going on into another. It does not mean, for example, that manifestations of early state formation ceased in the 17th century or that its consolidation began only thereafter. These are just divisions of convenience.

2.4.1 Pre-Bhot Period: Guesswork and Deductions

There is no concrete evidence available for this period. For convenience it shall be discussed under different heads. The first head dealing with ancient Kinnaras means that we are going back in time from the preceding discussion in which we saw how Bushahr State emerged as an important entity in the late 17th century. This liberty has been taken because it was felt that the chronological sequence would be better understood if it were discussed at one place together, rather than from the time of the emergence of Bushahr as an important state. Otherwise, we would have had to begin here from the 17th century onwards and the earliest events of this proposed chronological sequence would have been then scattered between the beginning of the discussion about the sources of history in Kinnaur and the following sequence. To keep a continuous progression in the chronological sequence, it is proposed to now go back in time from the point where the preceding discussion about sources had brought us up to.

2.4.1.1 Ancient Kinners and Kinner Desh: Myth or Reality?

While T.S. Negi maintains that the "Kinnara tribe has a hoary past",[57] the evidence in support of this claim is only tentative, based on legends and mythology. The Kinners are mentioned as a distinct race living in the mountains in various ancient Hindu texts and scriptures, as well as in Jain and Buddhist scriptures and iconography.[58] With a status

[55] Francke, 1908, Vol. I, p. 8.

[56] Hutchison & Vogel, 1933, p. 20.

[57] Negi, T.S., 1976, p. 12.

[58] For information about this aspect, please see:

between humans and gods, various supernatural powers were attributed to these Kinnaras. This is nothing special. Myths and legends about remote regions in most ancient cultures tend to invest their inhabitants with extraordinary attributes. With poor means of communication and little direct knowledge of remote regions beyond majestic snowy mountains, it was almost natural to imagine mysterious beings populating these exotic realms. The Kinners are only one of a series of such beings mentioned in the ancient holy texts.[59] Interestingly enough, there is no mention of the Kinners in the Rig Veda.[60] Kinner could well have been a generic name for the inhabitants of areas in the high mountains, beyond the known centres of population of the-then 'world'. This can well explain assertions that this tribe was spread over a large area from Kashmir to Eastern Nepal covering perhaps the whole West Himalayan region and was "definitely the abode of the Kinnar jāti".[61] Rāhul Sānkrityāyan mentions references to Kinners living on the banks of the Chandrabhāgā river (Upper Chenāb) in an ancient text and as corroboration mentions the fact that even today (sic) Kinnauri language is spoken on the banks of the Chandrabhāgā river. He cites evidence of this language also in village names like Dharāsu in the Uttarkashi area of Tehri Garhwāl.[62]

It is true that certain dialects spoken outside the present-day boundaries of Kinnaur District strongly resemble some Kinnauri dialects. For example, the Kanashi language of Malānā village in Kulu District resembles the Kinnauri language. An area of Kulu District is even today known as Kothi Kanāwar. However, the influence from Kinnaur seems more likely to have come as a result of settlement by itinerant Kinnaura traders in much later times rather than as the remnant of a proto-historical[63] mega-tribe's having stretched from Kashmir to Eastern Nepal. The Kinnauras had ranged widely over these areas because of their trading activities. Since Rāhul Sānkrityāyan laid so much worth on linguistic evidence, we can review some aspects of this field.

2.4.1.2 Philological Evidence: Munda Connexions

The Kinnauri dialect has been classified in the "western group of the 'complex pronominalized' Himalayan languages, and is classified in the tibeto-burman branch of monosyllabic languages".[64] Most tibeto-burman languages spoken in "Western Nepal and still

(a) Negi, T.S., 1976, Pp 13-17;
(b) Gazetteer, 1971, Pp 48-50;
(c) Mishra, D.P.: Studies in the Proto-History of India, I edn., New Delhi: Orient Longmans, 1971, Pp 20-21;
(d) Prakash, Dr Buddha: Studies in Indian History and Civilization, I edn., Agra: Shiv Lal Agarwala & Co., 1962, Pp 32-33 and 354-357;
(e) Mukherjee, Radhakamal: A History of Indian Civilization, Vol. I: Ancient and Classical Traditions, II edn., Bombay: Hind Kitabs Publishers, 1958, p. 69.

[59] Ibid.

[60] (i) Bajpai, S.C., 1981, p. 46; (ii) Chib, S.S., 1984, p. 4.

[61] Sānkrityāyan, 1957, p. 292.

[62] Ibid.

[63] Gratitude is expressed to Prof. Dr Hermann Kulke for having suggested the use of this term 'Proto History' for this very ancient period.

[64] Deuster, 1939, p. 94. The original reads: "Kanawari gehört zur westlichen Gruppe der 'Complex pronominalized' der Himalaya-Sprachen, und wird in den tibeto-birmanischen Zweig der monosyllabischen Sprachen eingruppiert".
Translation mine.

further to the west are dialects of Tibetan. On and about the ethnographic watershed between Tibetan and Aryan there is dotted a series of small dialects which are of a different nature...The most characteristic of this group is the so-called Kanawri, spoken in Kanawar. We there find more traces of the influence of a non-Tibeto-Burman substratum than in any other Himalayan dialect".[65] Based on the studies of the Rev. J. F. Bruske this underlying substratum is ascribed to a language from the Munda family. It is "almost certain that the old language, the influence of which can still be traced in the Kanawri dialect must have belonged to the Munda family...The Munda languages possess a characteristic set of consonants, the so-called semi-consonants...Similar sounds appear to exist in Kanawri...Higher numbers are counted in twenties as in the Munda languages...The personal pronouns have three numbers, and there are double forms of the dual and plural of the first person, just as is the case in Munda".[66] It is also made clear that Kanawri here refers not just to one dialect but to the "dialects spoken in the Sutlej valley from the junction of that river with the Spiti stream".[67] To explain this similarity to Munda languages of Kinnauri dialects, it was explained that it was "due to the influence of an older population which was absorbed by the Bhotias...the old population which has influenced Kanawri grammar belonged to the Munda stock".[68] The Linguistic Survey of India states unambiguously that it is "difficult to help inferring that this state of affairs must be due to the existence of an old heterogenous substratum in the population" which "must then have spoken dialects belonging to a different linguistic family...all those features in which the Himalayan dialects differ from other Tibeto-Burman languages are in thorough agreement with the principles prevailing in the Munda forms of speech. It therefore seems probable that Mundas, or tribes speaking a language connected with those now in use among the Mundas, have once lived in the Himalayas and left their stamp on the dialects spoken at the present-day".[69] These conclusions are based on work done by distinguished philologists.[70] A.H. Francke concludes that "in very early times in these mountain valleys an amalgamation must have taken place between Munda aboriginal tribes and Tibetans".[71]

An interesting skein in the philological picture is provided by the distinct nature of the dialect used by the Kolis or the Harijans of Kinnaur. It can be seen in villages like Sangla, Rakchham, Chhitkul, Nichār and others that the Kolis speak to the higher castes in the prevalent dialect of the area but to each other in their own dialect which is not understood by the higher castes. J.D. Cunningham commented on this as early as 1844 A.D.[72] Alexander

[65] Grierson, Sir G.A., 1909, Vol. III, Part I, p. 427.

[66] Ibid.

[67] Ibid, p. 430.

[68] Ibid, p. 432.

[69] Ibid, p. 179.

[70] For information about the language of Kinnaur, please see:
(a) Konow, Dr Sten: On Some Facts connected with the Tibeto-Burman dialect spoken in Kanawar, in: Zeitschrift der Deutschen Morgenländischen Gesellschaft (Z.D.M.G.), Halle & Leipzig, Neunundfünfzigster Band, 1905, Pp 117-125;
(b) Bailey, Rev. T. Grahame: A Brief Grammar of the Kanauri Language, in: Z.D.M.G., Dreiundsechzigster Band, 1909, Pp 661-687.

[71] Francke, 1908, p. 10; Tucci and Ghersi, 1935, p. 198.

[72] Cunningham, J.D., in: J.A.S.B., 1844.

Gerard had missed out this fact in his classification of the dialects of Kinnaur.[73] "Captain Gerard might have added a sixth language or dialect; viz that of the Kohlis or Chumars differs as much from the Kunawuree, as that does from the Bhotee...the localities of each kind of infinitive may prove that the rest of the tract of the country was occupied by one race in the first instance, and that in the three fertile, but secluded valleys of the N.E., a difference of speech arose. Láppa, Kanám and Sungnam are the principal places in these valleys, and each has its own tongue, the two former differing chiefly in the modifications of the nouns and the verbs, while the dialect of Sungnam owes much to the neighbouring language of Tibet".[74]

Even if we do not agree with this hypothesis about Kinnauri dialects being a result of an admixture of an earlier Munda speaking tribe with Tibetans and believe that such complex pronominalized languages of the Western Himalayan Group have evolved on their own from very ancient, already then-existing pre-tibeto-burman languages, we still do not refute the existence of an earlier tribal group having peopled these valleys. We cannot say whether these were the very people referred to in the numerous ancient texts as the Kinners. But some tribe(s) did exist in this region much before the onset of Tibetan influence. This deduction is corroborated by certain important discoveries made by Rāhul Sānkrityāyan in Kinnaur.

2.4.1.3 Evidence of Graves: Dards or Others?

Rāhul was present in Lippa village in 1948 when old graves were discovered while digging for constructing a house. He examined a skull and bones plus other artifacts found therein. The bone structure hinted at the fact that the dead person had been a man, aged 35-40 years (from his teeth), and had been tall in stature (from bones of limbs). A complete skeleton was not found but it could be deduced that:

(1) The ancient inhabitants of Lippa were not 'gol kapāl' or 'madhya kapāl' like their present-day descendants but 'deergh kapāl', i.e. had a different skull structure;
(2) The dead were buried and not cremated;
(3) The head of the corpse in the grave faced west;
(4) Food and drink were kept in the grave with the corpse;
(5) The corpses were tall statured.

It was reasonable to deduce that the graves dated from a time when the "deergh kapāl" inhabitants of Lippa had not yet established contact with the "gol kapāl" Tibetans; the presence of utensils of food and drink in graves shows that Buddhism had not yet spread to the area i.e. the graves were from such time as when the Tibetan expansion westwards had either not yet taken place or had not had widespread impact.[75] Similar graves with vessels and utensils were found not only downstream from Lippa in Akpa, Rārang, and Jāngi villages but also upstream, in Kānam, Pooh and the last village on the Tibetan frontier, Namgya.[76] During the construction of the Hinduatan-Tibet road (now called the Old H.T. Road) many such graves were found in Kānam. Surprisingly, bones and vessels found therein were thrown away, and this was done not by illiterate people but by the engineers and their staff working on the project.[77]

[73] Gerard, A., 1841, Pp 87-88.

[74] Cunningham, J.D., 1844, p. 224.

[75] Sānkrityāyan, 1957, Pp 297-298.

[76] Ibid, p. 299.

[77] Ibid.

Ancient graves excavated in 1903 near Leh in Ladākh by the Rev. A.H. Francke and Dr Shawe yielded remains of pottery, jars and saucer-like vessels. Most pots were found full of human bones. There were also found some much corroded bronze implements.[78] Prof. Tucci opines that these graves could be attributed to the Dards, a tribe that infiltrated along the course of the Indus river till Leh and may be even further on.[79] Similar artifacts were found near Khalatse and Alchi in Ladākh.[80] While it is not being suggested that the graves found in Kinnaur were also those of the Dards as in Ladākh, their existence does corroborate the philological evidence pointing to the existence of some ancient tribe in Kinnaur pre-dating the onset of Bhot influence. It needs systematic research to establish whether this tribe was an offshoot of the Dards' influx into Ladākh or of some other influx.

2.4.1.4 Folklore: Death Rites and Human Sacrifice

A proverb discovered by the Rev. R. Schnabel in Pooh alludes to the prevalence of the custom of human sacrifice in the area.[81] Songs of the Shar-rgan festival in Pooh also hinted at this fact.[82] Francke discovered a manuscript containing these songs and had it copied. "Although their meaning is not yet intelligible...in every part" they "are of great importance, with regard to the pre-Buddhist religion of Kanāwar as well as of Tibet in general...It is of great importance that the religion they represent is spoken of as Lha-chos and Bon-chos in the Poo songs...And it is very probable that the human sacrifices which used to form part of the Shar-rgan festival belong to the religion of this aboriginal population and not to the Tibetans".[83] It is then explained that the Tibetans had different motives like oaths at important treaties or inauguration of new houses for their practising human sacrifices.[84]

Tucci's study of folk songs in Nāko village reached very similar conclusions about the existence of pre-Buddhist inhabitants. At wedding ceremonies hymns were recited "which originated very long ago, previous, as regards their fundamental nucleus, to the introduction of Buddhism and which have preserved invocations and rites distinctly Bonpo in character. There is no village in which we do not collect some example of them".[85] Further, there "is no doubt that the original races of this country spoke languages different from Tibetan, which, even if they have disappeared from common use or are on their way to disappearing, have left traces in place-names, and sometimes survive side-by-side with the purely Tibetan form".[86] The hymns in Pooh "conclude with a long list of deities who are the protectors or patrons of villages or of simple places, mountains, rivers and bridges - the sole survival of an aboriginal religion now almost completely vanished".[87] To put the point beyond doubt, there existed "a

[78] Vohra, Rohit: Ethno-Historicity of the Dards in Ladākh: Observations and Analysis, Paper delivered at the IV International Seminar on Tibetan Studies, München, July 1985, p. 2.

[79] Tucci, G.: Tibet, Genéve, Paris, Munich, 1973, Pp 51-53.

[80] Vohra, Rohit, 1985, p. 2.

[81] Francke, 1908, p. 21, Footnote 1.

[82] Ibid, Pp 21-22; Also see: Tucci & Ghersi, 1935, Pp 199-200.

[83] Francke, 1908, Pp 21-22.

[84] Ibid, p. 22.

[85] Tucci & Ghersi, 1935, p. 69.

[86] Ibid, p. 70.

Places at which Rahul Sankrityayan found remains of an ancient grave culture in Kinnaur District

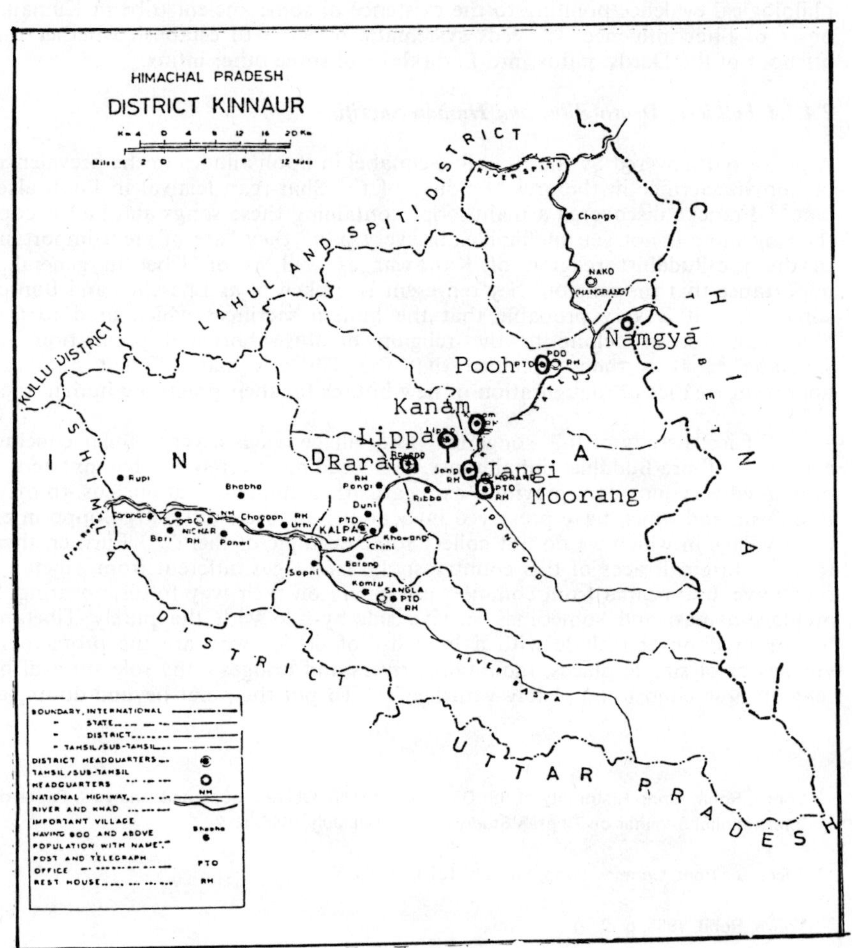

O = site of graves.

mass of beliefs, the origin of which is lost in the night of time, and which Buddhistic missionaries included generically in the term "Bon", the religion which preceded theirs in Tibet"[88] for at least the whole of Northern Kinnaur.[89] Clearly, all this evidence cannot enable us to specify the periods in which the ancient tribe of Kinnaur under discussion flourished or whence it came. To put the fact of its having existed on even firmer footing, we can now discuss a feature discovered during field research in late 1985 in Kinnaur. This feature has existed since centuries for everyone to observe but till now no attention has seemingly been paid to its corroborative value.

2.4.1.5 Two Places of Worship: Ancient and Mysterious

While most village deities in Kinnaur show Hindu or Buddhist influences at work, at least two places of worship indicate that some sort of animistic religion existed there before these influences became important. This hints at the possibility that certain original animist deities were later 'hinduized' or 'buddhized'.

At Astankché, just behind the Tahsil Office at Sangla, there is a site with some stones but no idol. Rājās of Bushahr used to come and offer sacrifices at this spot. Their devta, Badrināth of Kāmru, used to come and pay his respects here. It was considered a great honour to be allowed to offer sacrifice at this place. On special occasions like the 'pranaut' fair, more than 100 sheep and goats used to be sacrificed here.[90]

The fact that even the Rājā and his devta used to come and pay respects at Astankché hints at the existence of some ancient, widespread animist cult which was later on harnessed by the Thākurs of Kāmru to enhance their legitimacy by reserving its use to their devta and to themselves. While tradition narrates tales for the origins of all other devtas/devis, nobody could explain why such sanctity attached to Astankché without there being any idol or image. Clearly, its origins are too buried in antiquity. That it was the seat of some cult can be inferred from legend which says only that it was the seat of some very powerful 'Shakti' or primordial force.

A similar phenomenon exists in village Nésang. Above this village there exists a place with a flat stone without any idol or image. This stone is considered by the people as being imbued with some supernatural force. This belief seems to be the relic of some ancient animist cult practised by the pre-hinduized pre-buddhized inhabitants of Kinnaur.

On the basis of evidence martialled here, we can reasonably state that an ancient tribe did exist in Kinnaur. Where this tribe came from, what ethnic group it belonged to and what its socio-economic structure was are questions which cannot be answered on the basis of the evidence available to us. However, postulating its existence is backed up by reasonable evidence.

[87] Ibid, p. 200.

[88] Ibid, p. 199.

[89] Meaning chiefly the present-day Pooh Sub-Division.

[90] Information given by Sarvshri Gangālal, Goverdhan Singh, Balwant Singh and Khem Singh in personal interviews in Sangla and Kālpa.

2.4.1.6 Khash Influence: Widespread and Lasting

Having reasonably postulated the existence of an ancient tribe in Kinnaur we can now examine whether this tribe was the Khash tribe. The Chairman of the Zila Parishad (District Board) in Kinnaur said in a personal interview, "We may now claim that we are Rājpūt or Kanait. Actually we are Khash". Present-day Kinnaura society is divided into two main groupings -

(A) The higher castes collectively called Khaushiya;
(B) The lower castes collectively called Béru.

Each of these groupings is further sub-divided into other sub-groups which need not detain us for the moment.

The word Khaushiya evidently comes from Khash or Khashia, as the higher caste groups in the Garhwāl hills are called. Khashas, with variants such as Khasa, Khasira are frequently referred to in Sanskrit literature, as also in the Puranas and the Mahābhārata.[91] Sir George Grierson calls them one of the groups of the tribes of the Hindu Kush and the mountainous tracts to the south. The Khasias (or Khashas) were considered as kshatriyas of Aryan origin. They lost their claim to status as Aryans due to non-observance of the dietary rules of the sanskritic people. The Khashas were the earliest immigrants into the hill tracts about whom historical information was available.[92] They were "apparently among those participating in the large movements of Aryan speaking peoples into India. Therefore it is probable that they entered between 1500 and 1000 B.C. from the north-west".[93]

However, another researcher postulates that the Aryans entered India from the mid-Himalayan region. He believes that their entry was from Tibet through Garhwāl into India.[94] If so, then the connexion of Tibet to Kinnaur is even older than commonly believed. The Khash evidently became the pre-eminent group in Central and Southern Kinnaur, as witnessed by the Khaushiya domination of society there even now. It has been said without citing any sources that after "the extinction of the races of the Kinners, Kirāts and Nāgs, the Khash settled themselves to the cultivation of land in addition to their patent occupation of raising and rearing cattle. Khashas were a virile and well-knit race between whom there were no caste distinctions...Among the Khash the affairs of the community were carried out with common consent and the family deities were the guiding hands".[95] What has sometimes been described as the Aryan Period in Kinnaur's history refers presumably to the influx of the Khash into the area. The process may have continued over several centuries. We cannot date it. Khash influence would then have penetrated slowly into Kinnaur. It is not possible to postulate whether they came in one big wave that swamped the original inhabitants of the area or not. Be that as it may, Khash influence became the predominant factor in Kinnaura society. Their sway was partly followed by that of the Bhots, at least in the northern part of Kinnaur.

[91] Berreman, Gerald D.: Hindus of the Himalayas: Ethnography and Change, II edn., University of California Press, 1972, p. 15.

[92] Ibid, Pp 15-16.

[93] Ibid, p. 17.

[94] Ibid. The scholar referred to is F.E. Pargiter.

[95] Gazetteer, 1971, p. 50.

2.4.2 Bhot Period: Lāmās and Buddhism

We cannot pinpoint whether the Bhot Period began in Kinnaur with the expansion of the Tibetan Empire in the 7th century A.D. The available evidence dates from the period of the kingdom of Gugé, 11th to 17th century A.D.[96] It is again a matter of debate how much of present-day Kinnaur was under Bhot or Tibetan influence. A.H. Francke writes that Wāngtu "marks the ancient boundary between Bashahr and Tibet. In fact the West Tibetan Empire reached as far as Wāngtu up to 1650 A.D., when the Satluj valley from Wāngtu to Namgya was made over to Bashahr. Although Tibetan is not yet spoken for several marches up the Satluj, the former Tibetan influence makes itself felt in the frequency of personal Tibetan names".[97] Tucci places the limit of Bhot influence further upstream at Roghi village which he calls the "extreme limit of Buddhist evangelization in the times of the first kings of Gugé".[98] That Kinnaur was never a very important part of the Kingdom of Gugé can be inferred from the fact that the Jesuit missionary Antonio de Andrade (1580-1634 A.D.), who travelled to Tsaparang, the capital of Gugé, in 1624 A.D. and then in 1625-29, where he laid the foundation stone of the first Christian church on April 12, 1626,[99] does not mention Kinnaur at all in his accounts which give detailed information about the Kingdom of Gugé. Nor does Francisco de Azevedo, another Jesuit, the first European to visit Leh in Ladākh on October 25, 1631 A.D.[100] mention anything about Kinnaur. While describing the boundaries of Ladākh he mentions that it "borders in the south on that of Chaparangue or Goge".[101] Spiti was a part of the Kingdom of Ladākh down till the 1840s and so south of Ladākh in Azevedo's time meant south of Spiti as well, meaning Kinnaur. This part is not mentioned as Bushahr but as Gugé. Another Jesuit, Hippolyte Desideri, who was the first European to reach Lhāsā on March 18, 1716,[102] where he stayed till 1721 A.D., mentions Collahor (Kulu), and Sirenagar (Garhwāl) as territories south of Tibet but ignores completely Kinnaur which was obviously not important enough to deserve mention. This also hints at Bhot influence over at least parts of Kinnaur. We can examine further indices of this influence.

[96] For information about the Kingdom of Gugé, please see:
(1) Francke, A.H., 1926, Vol. II, Pp 167-171;
(2) Govinda, Lāmā Anangarika (Anangavajra Khamsum Wangchuk): The Way of the White Clouds, III Printing, Berkeley: Shambhala, 1974, [I Paperback edition, 1970], Appendix 2, Pp 294-297;
(3) Petech, L.: Ya-ts'e, Gu-gé, Pu-rań: A New Study, in: Central Asiatic Journal (C.A.J.), Vol. XXIV, Nos. 1-2, 1980, Pp 85-111.

[97] Francke, 1908, p. 10.

[98] Tucci & Ghersi, 1935, p. 204.

[99] Wessels, C.: Early Jesuit Travellers in Central Asia 1603-1721, The Hague: Martinus Nijhoff, 1924, p. 71.

[100] Ibid, Pp 43-91.

[101] Ibid, p. 108.

[102] Ibid, p. 221.

[103] For some information about this aspect, please see:
(i) Deuster, 1939, p. 94: "Der Wortschatz allerdings weist nach Tibet hin";
(ii) Cunningham, J.D., 1844, p. 224.
Cunningham considers it likely that the Bhots "formerly occupied the Sutlej valley as low down as Cíhní, but

Area under Bhot (Tibetan) influence in Kinnaur District according to the Reverend A.H. Francke

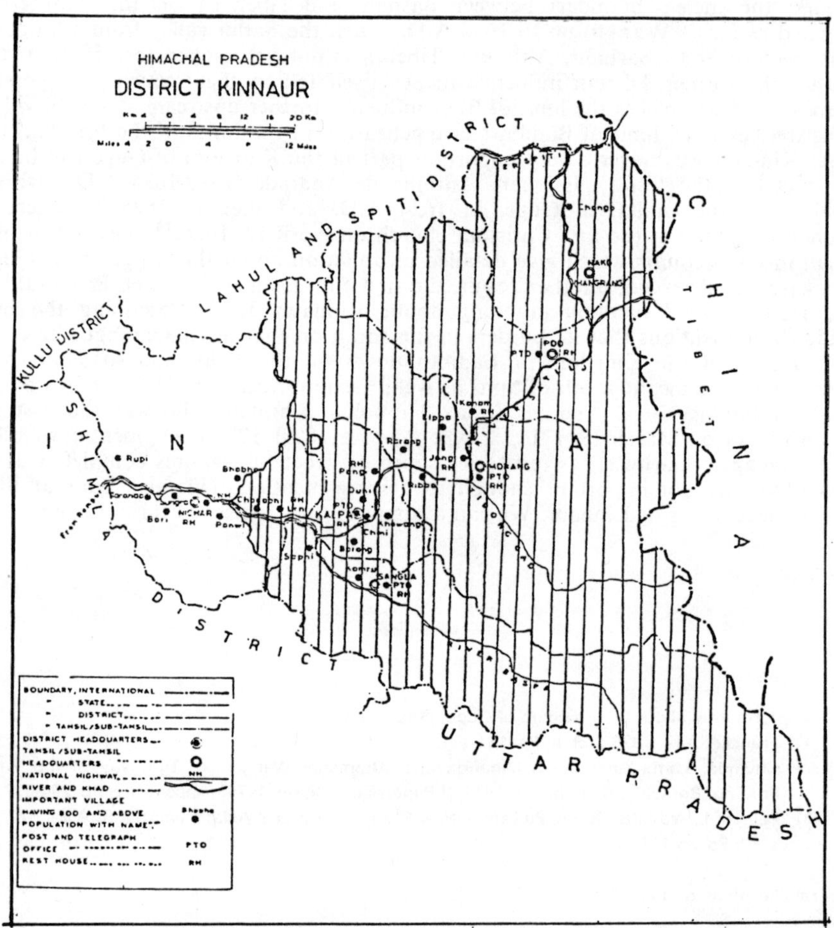

Lined portion marks the limits of Tibetan influence.

2.4.2.1 Philological Evidence: Tibetan über Alles?

The philological evidence[103] clearly points to strong Bhot influence over the area. Present-day Kinnauri is said to be an admixture of between 36% to 60% of original Kirāt language; 25% to 52% Hindi Aryan words and 14% Tibetan words. Among these 14% are most important words like the verb "to be", the negations and the system of numbers.[104] "In most essentials the phonetical system of Kanāwari is apparently the same as that of Western Tibetan".[105] Even lower Kinnauri, which has more Aryan words, "is in its grammar wholly Tibeto-Himalayan".[106] As we move northwards in Kinnaur the spoken dialect shows increasing Tibetan influence till we reach the Nyamskad dialect of Tibetan[107] used in the Hangrang valley. Evidently, so much philological influence could not have arisen without some sort of sustained Bhot presence in Kinnaur.

2.4.2.2 Genetic Evidence: Blood is Thicker than Water!

A few years ago, genetic studies were conducted among Kanait and Koli groups in Kinnaur by researchers from the Department of Human Genetics, University of Newcastle-upon-Tyne in England and the Department of Anthropology, University of Delhi in collaboration.[108] Blood specimens were collected at random from 228 school children from three different schools located at Kālpa, Kothi, and Chini. This sample consisted of children from both the higher caste Kanait group and the lower caste Koli group. The Kanaits under investigation were northern Khashia who "follow the Tibetan form of Buddhism and present more mongoloid facial features, and perhaps are the descendants from the admixture of the local population with immigrant tribes from Tibet during Tibet's expansion towards the south-west during the eighth or ninth century".[109]

Comparison of gene frequency shows conclusive differences between the two groups studied. "The two populations are clearly distinguishable in six systems (ABO, Duffy, Kell, PGM, AK and 6 PGD), and all other systems, especially the combined Rhesus frequencies, P, PGI, and EsD, suggest further divergence between them...The explanation...may be with their possible ethnic associations and the historical settlement of the region. In addition to the more mongoloid features and Buddhist faith of the Kanét, their genetic trait frequencies, with excess of A gene over B, higher Fy^3, low AK^2, and high 6 PGD^C gene frequencies show their positive affinity with the mongoloid populations...Tibetan populations with whom the people of Kinnar (sic) have traded for centuries might be the main source of contributions to the present day gene pool of the Kanét".[110] This gives an interesting indication that higher caste people in the northern part of Kinnaur show greater genetic affinity with the Tibetan population than

gave way before the Kunawurees. This would explain the Bhotee derivatives of the Upper Kunáwar dialects".

104 Sānkrityāyan, Rāhul, 1957, p. 210.

105 Konow, Dr Sten, 1905, p. 118.

106 Bailey, T. Grahame, 1909, p. 661.

107 Ibid, p. 662. For information about Nyamskad, please see: Cunningham, J.D., 1844, Pp 223-228. He calls it Bhoteea or Tartar, as does Alexander Gerard. See: Gerard, A., 1841, p. 88.

108 Papiha, S.S., Chahal, S.M.S., Roberts, D.F., and Singh, I.P.,: Genetic Studies among Kanait and Koli of Kinnar (sic) District in Himāchal Padesh, India, in: American Journal of Physical Anthropology, Vol. 53, August 1980, Pp 275-283.

109 Ibid, p. 275.

110 Ibid, p. 281.

Area under Bhot (Tibetan) influence in Kinnaur District according to Giuseppe Tucci

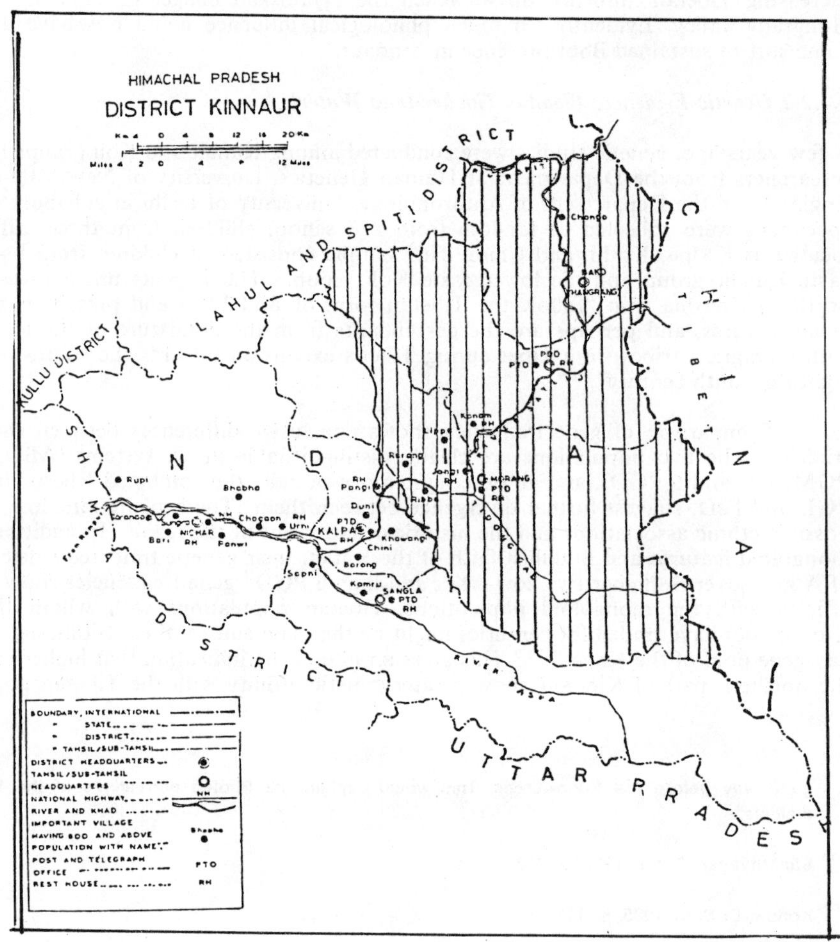

Lined portion marks the limits of Tibetan influence.

the lower castes. To extrapolate this indication to say that the Bhots must have ruled in Kinnaur because their descendants are higher caste predominant people may not be too wide off the mark. Even visually, as we travel into Pooh Sub-Division from lower Kinnaur, the facial features and appearance of the populace become progressively more Tibetan. This genetic affinity could either be the result of a period of Bhot rule over or large scale Bhot immigration into Kinnaur, a phenomenon difficult to envisage without some sort of Bhot pre-eminence having preceded it first in the political sphere. The physical environment is so scarce in resources that unless forced to comply under political domination it is hard to envisage the original inhabitants of the country welcoming or allowing such large scale immigration which would increase competition for already scarce resources to breaking point. In any case, the area was never capable of sustaining a sizeable population, immigrant or otherwise.

2.4.2.3 Historical Evidence: Fragmentary and Disjointed

Having discovered an inscription pointing towards Tibetan rule in Koro village near Pooh the Rev. A.H. Francke explains the existence of ruined castles around Pooh on the ground that this "part of the country was formerly under Gugé and Ladākh, and, as in Ladākh, people were here also compelled to live in fortified places on hilltops round their chief's stronghold".[111] The inscription yielded the information that in the time of King Ye-shes-'od of Gugé, around 1025 A.D., "the villages of sPu and dKor both existed, that Poo even possessed a place (phobrang)...There were ten princes according to the inscription, and all of them were sent to Poo. What was their object in this place, cannot be said with perfect certainty, but from the frequent occurrence of the words lha-chos (religion of the lha) and sngar-chos (former religion) it appears that they were sent here for the propagation of Buddhism. In the end we read that they erected something...probably the first Buddhist temple at Poo of which local tradition asserts that it was erected in the place where now-a-days the inscribed stone is found".[112] This stone was not the only evidence of rule by the Gugé rulers in Kinnaur. Votive tablets were found containing many references to "places beyond the border, thus showing that in the minds of the people, Gugé and Poo were not yet separated".[113] Further southwards from Pooh, a legend about the Thākur of Chini maintains that this ruling chief originally came from 'high land', presumably Tibet.[114] Many European travellers mention that parts of Kinnaur had once been under Tibetan rule.[115]

Whatever be the duration of Bhot rule, it could not have been a very centralized rule. Even as late as the 20th century, official reports from Western Tibet speak of a loose administrative structure prevailing there.[116] Of Gugé it has been said that nothing could be

[111] Francke, 1908, p. 20.

[112] Ibid, p. 19.

[113] Ibid, p. 18.

[114] Please see: (i) Sānkrityāyan, Rāhul, 1957, Pp 213-214; (ii) Deuster, R.H., 1939, p. 102.

[115] For example, J.D. Cunningham, Thomas Hutton, Andrew Wilson, Alexander Gerard and W.G.N. Van der Sleen.

[116] Para 8, Letter No. 4, dated 26th April 1914, from the British Trade Agent, Gartok to the Superintendent, Hill States, Simla, a copy of which was forwarded by the latter's office to the Manager, Bushahr State, Kotgarh vide endorsement No. 1295, dated Simla the 29th May 1914. It reads: "The status of all the Tibetan officials in Western Tibet is very low, they are not paid for the service, they are contractors and traders rather than public servants. There is no check upon them. In reality the Garpons exercise very little power in checking them. The Lāmās are quite independent of the Garpons".

Area under Bhot (Tibetan) influence in Kinnaur District according to Rahul Sankrityayan

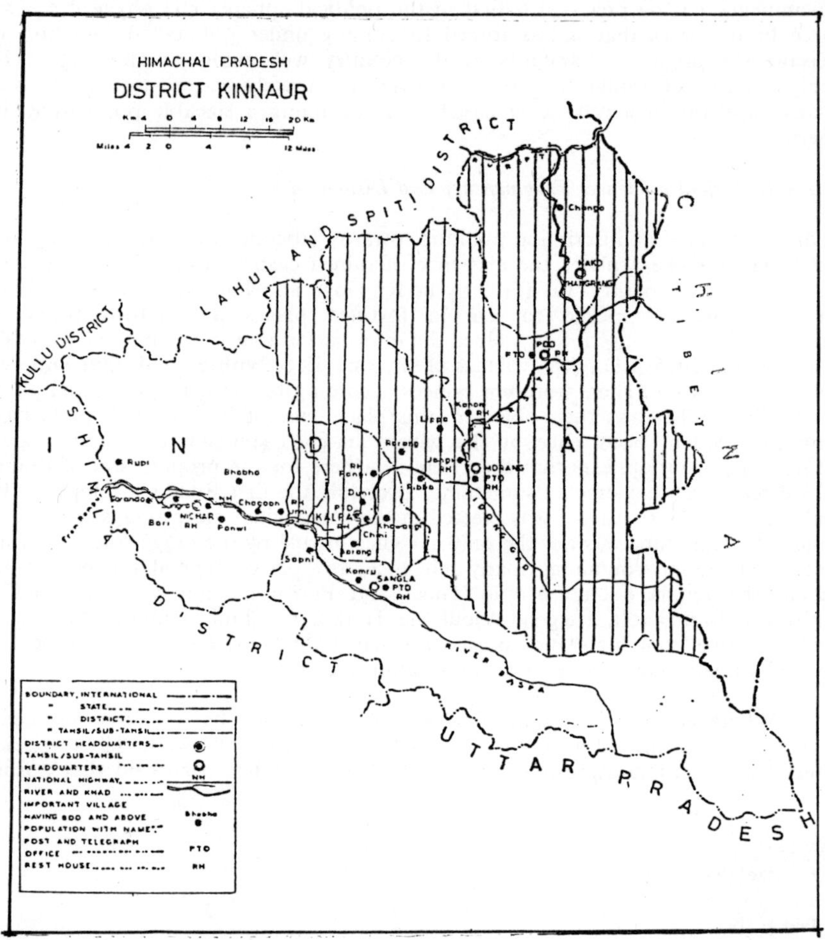

Lined portion marks the limits of Tibetan influence.

said about the "institutions of the kingdom. The one exception is represented by the long-established custom that the brother or uncle of the king became a monk and held the abbotships of the most important monasteries; this secured an efficient control of the king over the dGe-lugs-pa, who were the established church of Gu-gé".[117] A kingdom of Gugé is said to have "continued in existence almost without interruption from the 10th century to 1630".[118]

2.4.2.4 Religious Evidence: Widespread Buddhism and Gompas

Since religion played such an important role in the affairs of Gugé, which had been "greatly flourishing in the 11th century, when it became the starting point for the second introduction (p yi-dar) of Buddhism from India into Tibet, thanks to the patronage extended by the Gu-gé rulers to Lotsawa Rin-c'en-bzaṅ-po (958-1055 A.D.) and to Atisa (983-1054 A.D.). Their work was crowned in 1076 by the so-called council summoned by King rTse-lde-to at Ta-bo in Spiti".[119] Tabo is very close to Kinnaur which also was evidently a fertile field for missionary activity, considering the number of temples scattered all over the district which are ascribed to Lotsawa Rin-c'en-bzaṅ-po.[120] Lāmās are respected a lot in Kinnaur even today. They perform all sorts of religious ceremonies at the time of marriages, births and deaths, that in lower Kinnaur are performed by Hindu priests. Lāmāism did not, however, succeed in completely suppressing local cults and aboriginal deities in Kinnaur. Nevertheless, "Rin-c'en-bzaṅ-po's work of religious propaganda did not lack the king's favour, because it must have accompanied progressive political penetration; conversion of souls that must have prepared and facilitated the submission of heterogeneous tribes that the kings of Gugé, recently come to settle in these western regions, wanted to annex. Not only out of ambition of conquest, but very probably out of vital necessity; Western Tibet, so rocky and sterile, did not have trees and gave no wood, neither for fuel nor for construction; the terrain, even with the greatest labour, was found wanting. The Sutlej valley in Kunu on the other hand had an abundance of forests and more humid climate that rendered the work of the camps easier and more fructuous. It is evident that the new Tibetan conquerors should have focussed their attention towards this green frontier region and sought to utilize religious propaganda for splintering and conquering the resistance of tribes inhabiting the area".[121] How well this effort

Father Hippolyte Desideri also comments on the administrative system of Tibet and says that it was a very loose system of control of the outlying areas. See: Wessels, C., 1924, Pp 256-258.

[117] Petech, L., 1980, Pp 107-108.

[118] Ibid, p. 110.

[119] Ibid, Pp 85-86.

[120] The temples at Pooh, Kānam, Nāko, Sangla, Rārang, Pāngi, Chārang and Lippa, among others, are all said to have been constructed under the supervision of the Lotsawa.

[121] Tucci, G.: Indo-Tibetica III, I Templi Del Tibet Occidentale E Il Loro Simbolismo Artistico, Parte I: Spiti E Kunavar, Rome: Reale Accademia d'Italia, 1935-XIII, Pp 15-16. The original reads: *"Era opera di propaganda religiosa quello di Rin-c'en-bzaṅ-po, cui non mancava il favore di re, perchè ad casa doveva accompagnarsi la progressiva penetrazione politica; conversione degli animi che doveva preparare e facilitare la soggezione di tribù eterogene che i re di Gugé, di recenti venuti a stabilirsi in queste contrade occidentali, volevano annettersi. Non solo per ambizione di conquista, ma molto probabilmente per necessità vitale; il Tibet occidentale cosi roccioso e sterile, non aveva alberi e non dava legna nè per ardere nè per costruire; il terreno, anche con la più grandi fatiche, restio a dare. La valle della Sutlej in quel di Kunu invece abbondava di boschi e il clima più umido rendeva l'opera dei campi più facile e fruttuosa. È evidente che i nuovi conquistatori del Tibet dovessero far convergere le loro mire verso queste verdo paese di confine e cercassero di servirsi della propaganda religiosa per spezzare e vincere la resistenza delle tribù che*

succeeded can be gauged from the fact that even into the 20th century, the entire lāmā hierarchy in Kinnaur considered itself subordinate to Lhāsā, and visiting lāmās from Tibet were treated with great honour and veneration.[122] Kinnaura monks used to go and be trained in Tibet in monasteries. The closure of the border with Tibet in 1962 was thus a big blow in the religious sphere as well.

The influence of Buddhism from Tibet is to be seen in the local deities of the area quite clearly. The central deity of the Pooh Sub-Division is the "Grablà (sgrab Lha or dgrab Lha), the patron of Poo and of Kānam, because everyone of these villages still preserves its tutelary gods. We find - Tañ ta hru at Lippa, Gyan ma gyoṅ at Jāngi (in Tibetan spelling, Gyaṅ riṅ), Man laṅ at Rogi, Pa t'o ro at Rārang, Or mi hru at Morang, K'or mo hru at Rispa, Se śe riṅ at Pāngi (in Tibetan spelling Paṅ riṅ), and Bi śu zu at Chini".[123] This dgrab Lha or Dhabla is the central deity in villages Chāngo, Hāngo, Dabling, Dubling, Namgya, Shyaso, Pooh and Kānam of Pooh Sub-Division. It has been 'buddhized' and has thus stopped accepting animal sacrifice. The eight forms of the Dhabla in the above named villages are said to be brothers and sisters and to have originally come from Tibet, a clear indication of their role as legitimizing agents for acceptance of Bhot rule.

2.4.2.5 Myths and Legends: Frequent References to Tibet

Legends mention frequent raids from Tibet into Pooh Sub-Division and even into the Sangla valley. The famed monastery town of mTol-diṅ (Tholing) in Gugé occurs in the myths about the founding of the ruling dynasty of Bushahr.[124] Legends mention various deities flying into Kinnaur from Tibet. Genealogies are sought to be made more valuable by claiming that they are the copies of originals in Tibet. The main focus of life in Kinnaur was towards Tibet till the 1950s. That this was not a whimsical phenomenon is obvious. Behind this development lay centuries-long interaction of a Bhot Period in the history of Kinnaur. We cannot say whether this period began with Sroṅ-btsan-sgam-po's rise to power in Tibet or not. Such a period did exist and was linked to state formation.

2.4.3 Early State Formation: Thākurs and Castles

The fact that state formation did not become discernible till the 16th or the 17th century in Kinnaur should not be taken to mean that there reigned earlier only chaos and anarchy. The absence of a state did not necessarily equal disorder. People could lead their lives in small settlements in Kinnaur where geographical conditions isolated villages.[125] It is quite likely that villages existed under some sort of system of governance without there having been a state as we understand the term. This did not imply that no culture or religion or political evolution

l'abitavano".
Translation mine.

[122] Information given by Lāmā Shimed Chhéwang of Pooh in a personal interview in Pooh on December 9, 1985. Reports from the Moravian Missionaries in Pooh also give descriptions of such visits by lāmās from Tibet and the veneration with which they were welcomed. Of particular interest from this point of view are the annual reports sent by Edouard Pagell from 1866 till 1882 A.D.

[123] Tucci & Ghersi, 1935, p. 200.

[124] For more information about this aspect, please see:
(A) Singh, Miān Goverdhan: Bushahr-Kinnaur Rājya, Unpublished manuscript in Hindi, [Year not mentioned], p. 5;
(B) Gazetteer, 1971, p. 54.

[125] Please see Section 1.2.3, Chapter I, of this work for the influence of geography on state formation.

took place. State formation did not begin in a total vacuum but on a certain base that had already evolved in Kinnaur. What this pre-state structure was cannot be described on the basis of the evidence available. Beginning from these hazy origins, state formation became discernible towards the latter half of the 17th century, the period of the later years of the Emperor Aurangzeb's rule. This spurt in state formation in the period towards the last years of Aurangzeb's rule was not a phenomenon restricted only to Kinnaur.[126]

It is not possible to state at which point of time this process began. Tradition tells us about Kinnaur's division into seven units called 'Sāt Khund' and the existence of petty chieftains called thākurs.[127] Whether these thākurs originated out of the decline of the Bhot predominance in Kinnaur[128] through the nobles' breaking away and establishing satrapies on their own, or out of 'evolution from below', cannot be separated. We cannot pinpoint a Tibetan descent for the ruling thākur families in Kinnaur, as has been done in neighbouring Lahaul where the "Thākurs are of pure Mongolian origin and spring from the old ruling aristocracy of the country".[129] Of the prominent thākur families of Kolong, Gungrang and Gondla in Lahaul, the Thākurs of Kolong "submitted to the Kulu rajas and espoused their cause so warmly that even the Tibetan names in their genealogy appear to have been altered to show a Rājpūt origin".[130] The difficulty in Kinnaur arises because no such established thākur families exist. The descendants of the legendary ruling thākurs have all died out. Some Thākur families claiming high descent from the erstwhile ruling houses were encountered in village Moorang during field research but their circumstances were not particularly prosperous. They did not enjoy any position of social pre-eminence, unlike the thākur families of Lahaul.[131] The so-called descendants of erstwhile thākur families in Moorang had no idea of their origins and no genealogical charts to back up their claims of illustrious origin. They just said that their ancestors had come centuries ago from the "Rohru side", a clear hint of later hinduizing influence which had preferred origins from Hindu areas rather than from the Buddhist areas of Tibet. They had no idea of what their ancestors had been doing in Rohru before moving to Kinnaur. One sole family in village Spillo also claimed ancient lineage but could offer no specific names or areas of origin. The thākur families encountered during field research had absolutely no points of distinction to show that they were somehow different from the other Kanait families. It is not possible to verify whether they really are the descendants of erstwhile ruling thākurs who did exist as shown by ruins of fortresses in

[126] A similar process of state formation took place in Orissa as well in this very period. For information about this aspect, please see:
(A) Kulke, Hermann: Kshatriyaization and Social Change, A Study in Orissa Setting, in: Pillai, S. Devadas (ed.): Aspects of Changing India, Studies in honour of Professor G.S. Ghurye, Bombay: Popular Prakashan, 1976, Pp 398-409;
(B) Kulke, Hermann: Tribal Deities at Princely Courts: The Feudatory Rājās of Central Orissa and their Tutelary Deities (Istadevatās), in: Mahapatra, Sitakant (ed.): Folk Ways in Religion: Gods, Spirits and Men, Cuttack: Institute of Oriental and Orissan Studies, 1984, Pp 13-24.

[127] (A) Sānkrityāyan, 1957, p. 306;
(B) Singh, Miān Goverdhan: Bushahr-Kinnaur Rājya, Draft manuscript in Hindi, Unpublished, Pages 3 and 7;
(C) Gazetteer, 1971, p. 52;
(D) Manuscript on birch leaf in Tānkri in the possession of Lambardār Keshwā Singh of Sangla.

[128] As maintained in the Gazetteer, 1971, p. 52.

[129] Whistler, Hugh: In the High Himalayas, London: H., F. and G. Witherby, 1924, p. 45.

[130] Ibid.

[131] The meeting with the descendants of a thākur family took place in village Moorang on December 11, 1985 at the time of taking out the procession of Devta Ormik.

Moorang and legends. The "oldest traditions in the hills refer to a time when petty Chiefs, bearing the title of Rana or Thākur, exercised authority, either as independent rulers or under the suzerainty of a paramount power".[132] In case of at least Northern Kinnaur, this paramount power could only have been the Tibetans. These thākurs did not rule over fully organized principalities but an "order of things that was patriarchal rather than monarchical...very much akin to the clan system of the Highlands of Scotland down to the eighteenth century. When this organization came into existence, we cannot say; but its primitive character suggests the possibility of its having been the earliest form of government in force in the hills".[133]

Evolution of the thākurs could also have taken place in another way. As the pastoral Khash settled down in the valleys of Kinnaur to agricultural professions, their egalitarian society slowly yielded place to social stratification due to conquest or a differential availability of limited resources. Some men, maybe owners of better situated land, or those who being bolder went into trade with Tibet, came into prominence, evolving later into chieftains. Such leaders could easily have existed alongside Bhot rule in Kinnaur. Tibetan rule did not extend to the whole of Kinnaur in which areas like the fertile Sangla valley had time to evolve undisturbed, accounting for unbroken long genealogies and claims of descent from antiquity. Bhot rule was loose and did not seek to eliminate the existence of local chieftains. It did not have the military means to do so. In this polity of isolated petty chieftaincies we can now try to discern some factors contributing to early state formation.

2.4.3.1 War or Threat of War: Petty but Significant

Lack of major military campaigns[134] did not mean that the area was all at peace. Tradition speaks of frequent plundering forays from Tibet and Spiti into Kinnaur.[135] Both Gugé and Ladākh were more powerful states than these petty chieftains. For security against such raids, people in Kinnaur would have lined up behind some prominent men and accepted their rule in return for protection of their person and property. Old fortresses in Kāmru, Moorang and Lābrang show that an entire village could come and seek refuge there against marauders.[136] Men who distinguished themselves in such defensive actions would gain prominence. A good defensive position, in conjunction with other favourable factors gave the Thākur of Kāmru a base for a capacity to subdue others. Oppenheimer's theory of conquest[137] cannot be applied to Kinnaur but "the state is also legitimized through repeated actions of a military nature, which serve to show that protection by the state is indispensable".[138] Even the threat of war

[132] Hutchison & Vogel, 1933, p. 12.

[133] Ibid.

[134] Please see Section 1.2.3, Chapter I of this work.

[135] Please see:
(A) Lloyd & Gerard, 1840, Vol. II, Pp 266-267;
(B) Rose, H.A.: A Glossary of the Tribes and Castes of the Punjab and North West Frontier Province, Based on the Census Report for the Punjab, 1883 by the late Sir Denzil Ibbetson and the Census Report for the Punjab, 1892 by the Hon. Mr E.D. Maclagan, Lahore: Aziz Publishers, [First Published, 1911], 1978, p. 483 [I edn. publ. in Pakistan].

[136] Explained by the villagers of these three villages in person on the occasion of visits there during the years from 1980 to 1983.

[137] Oppenheimer, Franz: Der Staat, Frankfurt-am-Main: Mohr Verlag, 1932.

[138] Claessen and Skalník, 1978, p. 615.

Places where ancient fortresses or castles exist, or existed, in Kinnaur according to legends and travel accounts

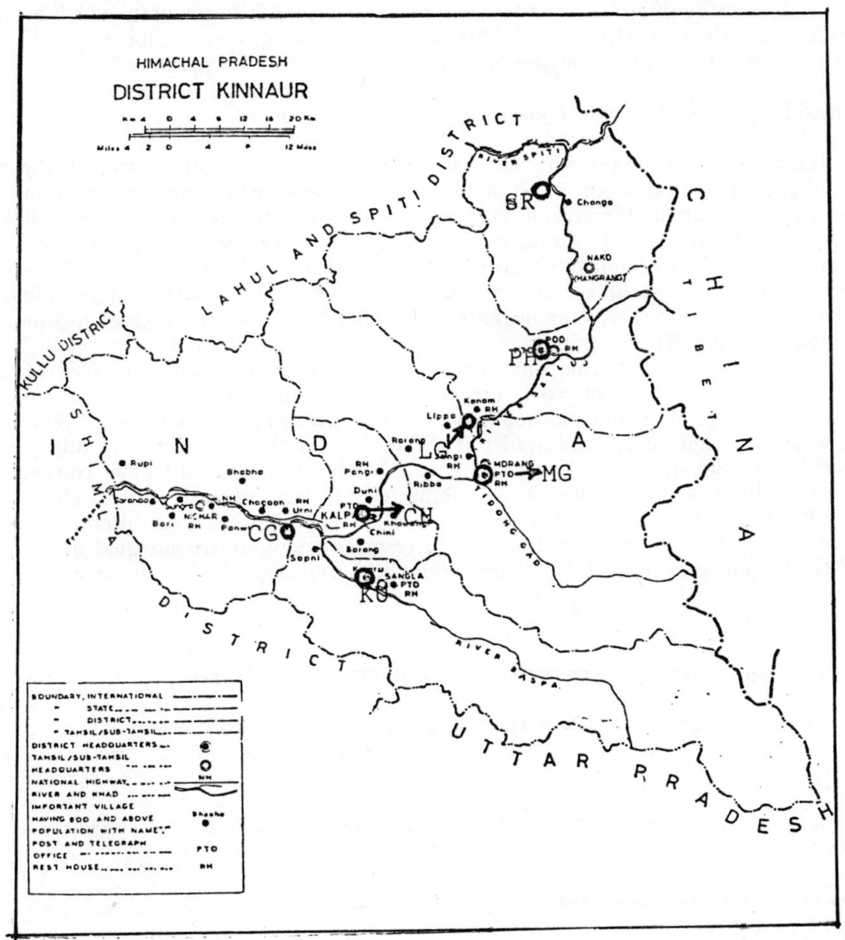

O = site of fortress or castle.

CG = Choling, CH = Chini, KU = Kamru, LG = Labrang, MG = Moorang, PH = Pooh and SR = Shyalkhar

and raids, leave aside actual war or raids, leads to emergence of stronger leaders and a better or stronger organization, be it for the purposes of defence or of attack. Thus state formation was "not caused by war, but is greatly promoted by war, or by the threat of war and by social stress".[139] Service's opinion that the state evolved through voluntary association because the benefits of being a part of it outweighed those of the alternative of remaining outside,[140] reinforces this hypothesis that people needed protection, which could be better assured as a "member of the state than not to be one".[141] Military actions or the threat of such actions generated leadership qualities and the "development of leader-follower units which eventually became rulers and their henchmen".[142] This process generates stratification trends in society and this stratification acts as a contributory factor towards state formation.

2.4.3.2 Stratification: Ancient though more Flexible

Social stratification in Kinnaur was not carried to the extent that it was in the plains. Accounts mention the absence of Brahmins in Kinnaur, with priestly functions being performed by local Kanaits.[143] During field research, some families claiming to be Brahmins were encountered in villages Moorang, Ribba and Kāmru, but they were inter-marrying and inter-dining freely with the Kanaits (Khash) of their respective villages and formed an integral part of the Kanait section of society.[144] The Kanaits have been classified as Shudras by origin.[145] Whether the Kolis were indigenous to the area before being relegated to subordinate status by the invading Khash or not, a two-tier caste-group system has existed in Kinnaur since ancient times. Even Bhot rule was superimposed on this broad division. The ruling Jads of Northern Kinnaur, of Tibetan stock, are now a part of the upper caste Kanait hierarchy. Even though Victor Jacquemont did not find the social distance between classes very great in Kinnaur, it had certainly been exploitative.[146] The Kanaits (Khash) were the rulers and the lower caste Kolis were the ruled. There was no doubt about it. Ronald Cohen considers class structure involving rulers and ruled as an ubiquitous feature of early states. He calls it a "necessary but not sufficient aspect of early states".[147] Though scholars differ regarding the importance of this factor - some defining it in terms of exploitative unequal access to the means of production in a society -[148] there "seems to be no objection to the view that one of

[139] Claessen & Skalník: Limits: Beginning and End of the Early State, p. 626, in: Ibid.

[140] Service, Elman R.: Origins of the State and Civilization, New York: Norton Publishers, 1975.

[141] Ibid, p. 626.

[142] Lewis, Herbert S.: Warfare and the Orgin of the State: Another Formulation, p. 212, in: Claessen & Skalník, 1981, Pp 201-221.

[143] Personal observation. Also, please see:
(1) Lloyd & Gerard, 1840, Vol. I, p. 198;
(2) Lloyd & Gerard, 1840, Vol. II, p. 302;
(3) Deuster, 1939, p. 78;
(4) Bruske, J.: Jahresbericht der Station Chini-Jahr 1900.

[144] Personal observation. Confirmed by T.S. Negi in personal interviews.

[145] (A) Singh, Miān Durga, 1907, Pages 265, 269 and 272; (B) Rose, H.A., 1911, Pp 456-459.

[146] Jacquemont, Victor, 1933, Pp 294-295; Schulze, Adolf, 1932, Band II, p. 532.

[147] Cohen, Ronald: Evolution, Fission, and the Early State, p. 93, in: Claessen & Skalník, 1981, Pp 87-115.

[148] This point of view is supported in:

the characteristics of the state - and perhaps the most important one - is the existence of classes".[149] Classes existed since the Pre-Bhot Period in Kinnaur. Though we cannot establish a complete class-caste nexus in this area, such a nexus does hold good for a large number of villages there. The lower castes are poorer, the upper castes are richer. It was the interest of the ruling upper caste groups to preserve their exploitative advantage. The physical environment itself aided such stratification and exploitation.

2.4.3.3 Environmental Factor: Ubiquitous and Overwhelming

Carneiro considers environmental circumscription as one of two specific conditions leading to formation of a state. This factor was met with where a growing population lived in a confined area, delimited by mountains, jungles, deserts or seas.[150] Carneiro's idea of environmental circumscription has two distinctive and separable aspects. It focusses on the matter of physical control over conquered populations. Where environmental facilities for subsistence are ample, without geographical restraints; a beleaguered populace can just emigrate. However, if "a people is tied to a particular zone, perhaps to the banks of a river, migration would be very costly indeed, perhaps necessitating a total change of subsistence".[151]

Kinnaur is overall remote but some areas like the Baspa valley and Nichār are better endowed in terms of rainfall, availability of irrigation, fertility of soil or presence of forests providing fodder and fuel. This clearly created differences in terms of production of surplus in-as-much-as the areas to the N.E. and to the North were at a disadvantage as far as natural endowments were concerned. People living in Kinnaur were already at the end of their geographical tether and could not migrate. The Sangla valley was an obvious target for plunderers since it was richer in environmental gifts. Its inhabitants faced high passes towards the south, north and east, rendering emigration very tough. Areas that were more fertile, like Rohru to the South over the Dhaula Dhār range, were already more populated, whereas the areas with lesser population, towards Pooh, were arid. The people were obliged to stay on and evolve organizational devices to cope with invasions, or a threat thereof, because of their resources which invited plunder. Nobody would want to go and plunder an arid, desert area with poor people, as in Pooh. The area around Kāmru furnished an optimum combination of environmental factors for state formation - fertile soil; the broadest expanse of any valley in Kinnaur; availability of water; extensive forest cover; trade routes to Tibet, Garhwāl and Rohru; extensive pastures; a sheltered location, which would stretch the supply lines of any invader to the limit and an excess of production over consumption, a most unusual thing in a chronically foodgrain-deficient area like Kinnaur. It is no surprise that Bushahr State originated in Kāmru.

(1) Engels, Friedrich: Der Ursprung der Familie, des Privateigentums und des Staats, Bücherei des Marxismus-Leninismus, Band 11, Berlin: Dietz, 1964;

(2) Engels, Friedrich: The Origin of the Family, Private Property and the State (edited with an introduction by Eleanor Burke Leacock), London: Lawrence and Wishart, 1972;

(3) Wittfogel, Karl A.: Oriental Despotism - A Comparative Study of Total Power, New Haven: Yale University Press, 1957;

(4) Tökei, Ferenc: Zur Frage der asiatischen Produktionsweise, Neuwied und Berlin: Luchterhand, 1969;

(5) Godelier, Maurice: La notion de "mode de production asiatique" et les schémas Marxistes d'évolution des sociétés, in: Sur le 'mode de production asiatique', edited by Roger Garaudy, Paris: Editions Sociales, 1969, Pp 47-100;

(6) Fried, Morton H.: The Evolution of Political Society, New York: Random House Publishers, 1967.

[149] Claessen & Skalník, 1978, p. 20.

[150] Carneiro, Robert L,: A Theory of the Origin of the State, in: Science, Vol. 169, 1970, Pp 733-738.

[151] Lewis, Herbert S., op. cit., p. 211, in: Claessen and Skalník, 1981.

2.4.3.4 Population Pressure: Malthus at Work!

Without getting into a debate whether population pressure is a necessary or a sufficient condition for state formation[152] we can, however, maintain that it has a role to play in the process of state formation. The number of persons per area unit (crude arithmetic density) for Kinnaur worked out to as low as 9 persons/km^2 in 1981. This figure masked the fact that only 2.16% of the total area of Kinnaur was inhabited, leaving 97.84% as uninhabited area. This uninhabited area is also mostly uninhabitable because every inch of land that can be brought under the plough has already been so utilized. To get a better measure of population pressure on land, we consider the number of persons per unit of net cropped area, giving us the average nutritional density. This figure works out to nearly 585 persons/km^2 of cropped land, revealing severe pressure on cultivated land. Population figures from Alexander Gerard's time to 1981 show a continuous (but for one exception) increase, albeit a slow one.[153] There is no reason to presume that this trend was different earlier. The area had not been ravaged by wars, major invasions, diseases or mass migrations. Environmental circumscription favoured settlement, leading to a rise in population. It caused evolution of social institutions and control mechanisms, which later on contributed to the formation of a state in the area. Lack of adequate natural resources converted this growth of population into population pressure on scarce cultivable land. Kāmru was again an obvious place for this phenomenon to manifest itself, for reasons already outlined.

2.4.3.5 Irrigation: Indispensable and Valued

Some scholars consider irrigation works as only a secondary trait of state formation.[154] Others consider these as a major leap forward in the evolutionary process, for "irrigation needed organization, power, and coordination. It opened up the possibility of the large-scale concentration of people and in the end supposedly led to state formation".[155] Claessen considers irrigation as an agent serving to intensify or help in the development of centralization.[156] Scarcity of water, irrigation works, and a conflict-resolving political hierarchy interact to produce further conflict and greater utilization of conflict-resolving institutions.[157]

In Kinnaur, except for some areas in Nichār Sub-Division, where crops can be entirely rainfed, agricultural production occurs only where there are irrigation channels called kuhls. There was a long tradition of constructing and maintaining these kuhls by the villagers themselves. Village councils, formal or informal, decided upon the water quotas, regulation and enforcement thereof. These necessary forums of irrigation management provided occasions for a development of leadership roles. Those who had got more water increased their wealth and importance further. Even nowadays, such village councils serve as training grounds for budding leaders. As settlements became larger, the task of such water management became

[152] Please see Claessen & Skalník, 1978 and 1981, for information about this aspect.

[153] Please see: Gerard, A., 1841, p. 3; District Census Handbook, Kinnaur District, 1981, pp. 23/29.

[154] Claessen & Skalník, 1978, p. 11.

[155] Ibid; also see: Steward, Julian H.: Theory of Culture Change, Urbana: University of Illinois Press, 1955.

[156] Claessen, Henri J.M.: Despotism and Irrigation, p. 56, in: Kloos, Peter & Claessen, Henri J.M. (eds.): Current Anthropology in the Netherlands, Leiden, 1975, Pp 48-62.

[157] Hunt, Eva & Hunt, Robert C.: Irrigation, Conflict and Politics: A Mexican Case, p. 154, in: Downing, T.E., and Gibson, M., (eds.): Irrigation's Impact on Society, Anthropological Papers of the University of Arizona, No. 25, Tucson: University of Arizona Press, 1974, Pp 129-157.

more and more complex, calling for increasing organizational ability and institutions. The Kāmru area was a place where such factors operated at an optimum level. It had many kuhls because of the highest availability of culturable land here in Kinnaur. Managing irrigation systems here provided the embryo of institutional and personal leadership evolution. It begins to look more and more apparent that Kāmru should be the cradle of the development of Bushahr State.

2.4.3.6 Trade: Shifted even the Capital

Having already discussed the role of trade as an economic activity in Chapter I, we consider here its role in the shifting of the capital of Bushahr State from Kāmru to Sarāhan, the first change in a cycle that took the capital finally to Rāmpur via Kalyānpur. This step is important in the process of state formation in Bushahr because it brought the seat of authority closer to the main trade routes and to fertile areas in the south. It cannot be specified when this change took place. It must have taken place at a very early stage of state formation otherwise we would have had some records indicating the circumstances of this shift. Rāhul Sānkrityāyan speculates that this shift from Kāmru to Sarāhan was done by Rājā Chhubal Singh.[158] In the genealogies available, this name is variously at place number 2 or at 3, suggesting that the Rājā in question was one of the earliest rulers who had accomplished the transition from Thākur to Rājā and that the capital was shifted to Sarāhan as an important step in state formation. Whatever be the other reasons for this change, it brought the centre of power closer to a major trade route from the plains to Tibet via the Satluj valley, as opposed to the earlier location at Kāmru which lay on one side, away from this axis. Sarāhan offered a better opportunity for carrying on state formation further. It was the seat of a Kāli cult that later on became the state religious cult of Bushahr State. Sarāhan was closer to more fertile rice growing areas near Nirath or in Rohru; it offered the chance of legitimation of rule by giving land grants to Brahmins who were brought and settled in village Rānwi and gave the Rājā a Rājpūt origin. All this may not consciously have been on the Rājā's mind when he moved the capital but worked out that way in practice. There had been no land available in Kāmru for large scale land grants and Brahmins from outside would not have been very eager to settle down in this geographically remote area. From Sarāhan it was also easier to later on annex richer crop yielding areas. From Kāmru it would have been much more difficult to open up this larger vista of military gain for increasing the surplus generating capacity of the state. It would also have been more difficult to establish Rājpūt credentials with a long noble lineage in Kāmru because other contemporary local families would still have been around to always serve as a reminder of where the true origins lay. In a new place origins could be fudged and shrouded in mystery. These factors emerged later when the dynasty got 'Rājpūtized'. Proximity to major trade routes doubtless aided the change.

Thus, the Thākur of Kāmru was able to exploit all the foregoing factors better than his rivals. There had been other thākurs - in Chini, Lābrang, Moorang, Choling, Sangla and Tāngling, but they were either located in arid areas closer to Tibet where Bhot rule even though not very efficiently organized had narrowed their room for manœuvre with its suzerainty or they did not possess economic resources to match those of the Thākur of Kāmru. Only the Thākur of Sangla had all other factors equal to those of the Thākur of Kāmru since the two villages are in close proximity. In this case, personal capability or some unknown factor seems to have aided Kāmru's victory. According to legend, this factor was treachery and better planning.[159] Legend mentions the victories of the Thākur of Kāmru over the Thākurs of Chini, Sangla, Tāngling and Choling before the founding of the rule of Bushahr at Sarāhan. Clearly, the shift to Sarāhan came first, before the extension of sway over other areas of present-day Kinnaur District. Not burdened by Bhot sovereignty or

[158] Sānkrityāyan, 1957, p. 310.

[159] Sānkrityāyan, 1957, p. 237.

**Locations of Kamru, Kalyanpur, Sarahan and Rampur,
the successive capitals of Bushahr State,
alongwith seats of major deities of the area**

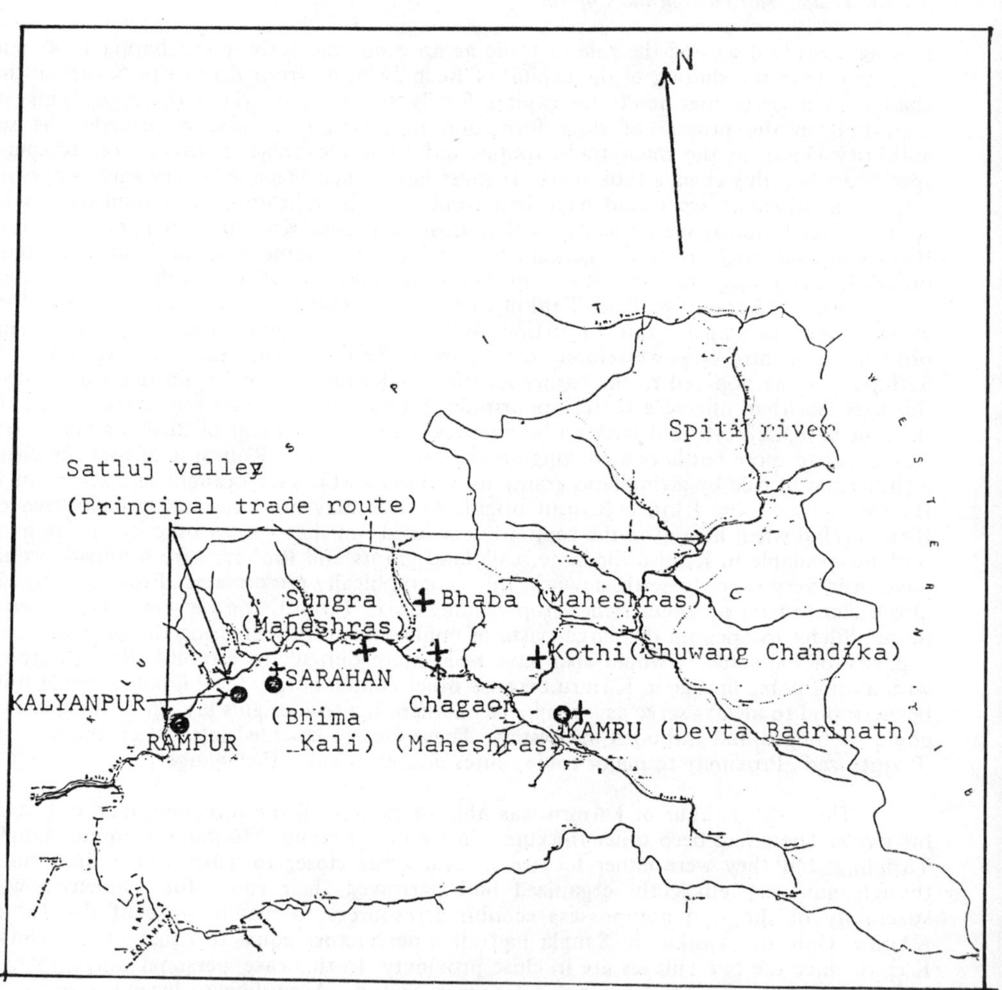

O = site of capital

\+ = seat of deity

suzerainty, as the case might have been, at Sarāhan which was much further away from the border than Kāmru; having access to more productive areas, the incipient Rājā could have enough wherewithal to gain acceptance by winning over the allegiance of his fellow-chieftains in Kinnaur. He had never had a standing army or enough coercive means to control fractious chieftains only by force. Force could only be a part of a package of measures of legitimation. The move to Sarāhan improved the scope of his economic pie, enabling him to better distribute its benefits to consolidate his state.

If early states are classified into three types: ***inchoate, typical and transitional,***[160] the entitiy that we have traced to Sarāhan showed the characteristics allowing it to at least be classified as an ***inchoate early state.*** These features were:[161]

(A) Trade and markets of (as yet) only limited importance;
(B) Succession to high office predominantly hereditary;
(C) Dominance of communal ownership or possession of land;
(D) No codification of laws and punishments and no special formal judges;
(E) Taxes irregular and inaccurately defined, consisting mainly of voluntary tributary gifts and occasional labour for the state.

As the state was consolidated, it began showing more and more features of a typical early state and, in the 20th century, of a transitional early state, as against the features of an inchoate early state at the start. Even at the time of its merger into Himāchal Pradesh in 1948, Bushahr exhibited a mixture of characteristics of typical and transitional early states. It had not evolved into a well-organized state as we understand it in the modern era. The story of this consolidation from the 18th century onwards is a story of Rājpūtization, as shall now be seen.

2.4.4 Consolidation of State Formation: Myths, Rājpūts, even a Chhatrapati

Rājā Chatar Singh (1512-1574 A.D.)[162] is said to have been the first ruler to have consolidated under his sway the whole of the area of the erstwhile Bushahr State, including Kinnaur.[163] This process was carried to its apogee by Rājā Kehri Singh (1639-1696),[164] the hero of legend.[165] However, in spite of some strong personalities we should not imagine Bushahr as a strongly organized state. "In most ways, the power of the King was far less than that of the executive of a twentieth century liberal democracy, despite the institutional and moral constraints on the latter. For one thing, the state apparatus of the twentieth century has a degree of organizational capacity behind it that more than compensates for the increased constraints".[166] The king strengthened his position through "four major mechanisms:

[160] Claessen & Skalník, 1978, p. 22, p. 641.

[161] Claessen, H.J.M. & Skalník, Peter: The Early State: Models and Reality, in: Claessen & Skalník, 1978, Pp 637-650.

[162] Francke, 1908, Appendix D, p. 124.

[163] Gazetteer, 1971, Chapter II, p. 57.

[164] Francke, 1908, Appendix D, p. 124.

[165] Gazetteer, 1971, Chapter II, p. 57. He is said to have been an Ajanuyaku (Ajânu vhay) like Lord Rāma, i.e. he could touch his knees with his hands when standing upright. It is also said that when he was in Delhi to attend a durbār called by the Mughal emperor (conveniently unnamed!), he was protected from the heat of the plains by a small divine cloud covering his head. This cloud went wherever the Rājā went.

[166] Kurtz, Donald V.: The Legitimation of Early Inchoate States, p. 181, in: Claessen & Skalník (eds.), 1981,

bureaucratization, monopolization of force, creation of legitimacy and homogenization of the subject population".[167] In case of Bushahr, bureaucratization, homogenization of subject population and even monopolization of force remained tentative and ill-organized. Creation of legitimacy played the most important role. Legitimacy was not a "once-and-for-all matter. It is a matter of constant compromise".[168]

Legitimation of the authority and of the political structure of early states was essential for their survival. It was the process by which the ruler and his entourage acquired support, either directly or indirectly through acquiescence. "The success of state structures and authority in obtaining the allegiance of the population and reducing antagonisms to them is a gauge of their legitimacy".[169] We can identify five overlapping goals of the state:

(A) Establishment of social distance between the rulers and the ruled;
(B) Validation of the state's authority;
(C) Consolidation of the power of the state;
(D) Socialization of the population regarding the new order that the rulers are creating; and
(E) The restructuring of the economy of the nation.[170]

By increasing the social distance, the ruling strata sought to firm up the class structure existing in society, establish an aura and a mystique for their authority, respect and obedience which state functionaries demand and to symbolize the right of a few to rule over the many. We can now examine how some of these aspects were brought into play in Bushahr.

2.4.4.1 Rājpūtization: A Very Successful Exercise

State formation in Kinnaur/Bushahr reveals some common features with the process pointed out by Surajit Sinha for Central India.[171] Like the existence of chiefs called mānkis in Central India, in Kinnaur there existed the thākurs. Tribal society in Kinnaur showed stratification into "social classes mainly in terms of differential land holding and of the territorial extent of political dominance. This fact of stratification again, has set the various segments of the once relatively egalitarian tribes in a perpetual craze for social upgrading...the peak point of identification of social movements among the tribes is the Rājpūt of north-western India who are regarded as the true representatives of the traditional Kshatriya class...In other words, state-formation in the tribal belt...is very largely a story of Rājpūtization of the tribes".[172] The Brahmins proved invaluable allies for such legitimation through fabrication of spurious genealogies. Rājās of Bushahr gave land grants to Brahmins at Rānwi village. Even though "spurious long genealogies of the aspirant pseudo-Rājpūt tribal chieftains are quite misleading",[173] the Bushahr Rājās succeeded so well in establishing their credentials as

Pp 177-200.

[167] Ibid, p. 182.

[168] Ibid.

[169] Ibid, p. 183.

[170] Ibid, Pp 182-183.

[171] Sinha, Surajit: State Formation and Rājpūt Myth in Central India, in: Man In India, Vol. 42, No. 1, March 1962, Pp 36-80.

[172] Ibid, p. 36.

[173] Ibid, p. 37.

descendants of the lunar dynasty that they were considered of pure Rājpūt stock. As late as 1930 A.D., the Rājā of Bushahr issued a farmān (order) allowing his Kanait subjects to write themselves as Rājpūts.[174] This process of upward social mobility is going on even now. Harijans of Kinnaur have begun writing the title Negi as their surname. This enables them to acquire a certain elevation outside their immediate local environment where their origins are too well known to be masked by such devices. Negi has now become the synonym of a Kinnaura for non-Kinnauras.

The rājputized Rājās of Bushahr became patrons of Brahminism. They inducted ever increasing numbers of higher caste Hindus as secular and ritual officials in order to gain acceptance as Rājpūts by other chiefs. The matrimonial aspect of marrying into high Rājpūt families as a mark of acceptance played its role. It is difficult to pinpoint at which point the ruling house of Bushahr managed to shed its tribal origins and to be accepted as a Rājpūt branch. But the Bushahr Rājās never renounced their connexion with Kinnaur completely. Till the time of the last Rājā, Padam Singh, the ruler underwent a second coronation in Kāmru fort without which he was otherwise not accepted as legitimate.[175] An essential part of the process of Rājpūtization to consolidate legitimacy was the creation of a flattering and miraculous myth of origin.

2.4.4.2 Myths of Origin: Deva Purna, Lord Krishna and the Brahmins

In common with myths of origin of the ruling houses of Central India or Orissa, a pilgrimage to Badrināth and to Tholing monastery in Tibet is mentioned for the ruling house of Bushahr.[176] This effort reveals the necessity of tailoring the needs of legitimacy to the Hindus as well as to the Buddhists in Kinnaur, a remnant of Bhot influence. In fact, the process of mythifying the origins was carried to the extent of claiming a Brahmin lineage for the Rājā.[177] This attempt seems to have been quietly sidelined in favour of a Rājpūt lineage from the son or grandson of Lord Krishna called Parduman Singh.[178] Rāhul was convinced that latter-day Bushahr Rājās were keen on hiding their Kinnaura ancestry in order to avoid being linked to the tribal Kinnauras. Since the expansion of Bushahr State in its latter phases was mainly to the South and West, inhabited by non-tribal non-Kinnaura Hindus more likely to accept a true Kshatriya as ruler, the Rāmpur ruling house "refused to acknowledge Kinnar language and blood".[179]

[174] Information given by T.S. Negi and Negi Goverdhan Singh. The former was then a student in Lahore and the latter a functionary of Bushahr State. This step was taken in the wake of Swami Shraddhanand's assassination when a wave of revivalism swept the area. The Rājpūts felt that their numbers were too small and would render them weak in claiming their rights in society. Therefore, to increase their numbers, Kanaits were allowed to join them as Rājpūts.

[175] Gazetteer, 1971, Ch. II, p. 55. Also, personal enquiries in all the villages of Kinnaur.

[176] Gazetteer, 1971, Ch. II, p. 54.

[177] Gazetteer, 1911, Chapter I.B., p. 5; Gazetteer, 1971, Chapter II, Pp 54-55.

[178] Gazetteer, 1971, Pp 54-55; Draft of a personal letter from Rājā Padam Singh of Bushahr to Sir Edward Douglas Maclagan, Governor of the Punjab, [Unpublished].

[179] Sānkrityāyan, Rāhul, 1957, p. 311. The original line reads: "Rāmpuri Rājvansh nén Kinnauri bhāshā āur raqt sé inkār kar diyā".
Translation mine.

Referring to Orissa, Prof. Hermann Kulke discusses legendary accounts according to which "several founders of the raj families entered their future realms as strangers, many of them on their way back from a pilgrimage to Puri, a story which was certainly introduced as an additional element of legitimacy".[180] What Puri was for legitimation to the Rājās of Orissa; Tholing (in Tibet), Badrināth, Kāshi and Kanchanpuri were to the Rājās of Bushahr. The founder of the Bushahr dynasty, Deva Purna, is said variously to have entered the Baspa valley on his way to Kāmru from these holy places.[181]

Carrying Prof. Kulke's argument a bit further, the first act of the future Rājā used to be the ritual killing of a member of a tribe of that region.[182] Accounts of the origin of the Bushahr dynasty mention that Deva Purna killed or subjugated one Rājā Bānāsur or Bavāsa Deva of Sarāhan before founding the royal house there.[183] This Bānāsur was a tribal chief of renown in the area. His children have subsequently been deified as deities of various parganas in Kinnaur.[184] He appears to have been an important chieftain whose killing set the seal of legitimacy on the transformation of the Thākur of Kāmru into the Rājā of Bushahr. The Rājā was not the only one seeking to glorify his origins. His wazirs did not lag behind though they did not claim pure Rājpūt stock and settled for being kshatriyas instead.

2.4.4.3 Kshatriyaization: Where Rājās Tread, Can Wazirs Be Far Behind?

There were three hereditary wazir families in Bushahr, those of: ***Poāri, Shua and Kohāl.***[185] The Poāri Wazir family in Kinnaur have a genealogical chart rivalling that of the Rājās of Bushahr. Another such chart in the possession of Negi Amar Singh Wazir shows the names of 16 Rājās of Bushahr listed out alongside the names of the corresponding wazirs from the Poāri family, a sequence stretching over 16 generations. Since this number corresponds more or less accurately to the number of rājās to whom some authenticity has been attributed from genealogical charts,[186] it indicates that the heads of the Poāri family were probably rivals for influence of the Thākur of Kāmru who won them over to accept his becoming the Rājā by granting them the status of hereditary wazirs. A similar phenomenon can be attributed to the hereditary status of the Shua Wazir family. The adhesion of these two powerful families to his cause enabled the Rājā to establish his rule on firmer footing. As he turned himself into a pure Rājpūt, his wazirs turned into kshatriyas, thereby putting greater social distance between the rulers and the ruled. This sort of kshatriyaization in Kinnaur was functional rather than ritual and was social change "initiated in tribal areas by the Kshatriyas, i.e. zamindars, chiefs

[180] Kulke, Hermann, 1984, p. 15, in: Mahapatra, Sitakant (ed.), op. cit.

[181] Gazetteer, 1911, Ch. I.B., P. 5; Gazetteer, 1971, Ch. II, p. 53; Foreign Department, Native States, Nos. 18-22, January 1894, No. 21, Chapter I, Para 8, p. 17.

[182] Kulke, Hermann, 1984, p. 17 ff., in: Mahapatra, Sitakant (ed.), op. cit.

[183] Gazetteer, 1911, Ch. I.B., p. 5; Gazetteer, 1971, Ch. II, Pp 54-55.

[184] Bānāsur's three sons are the three devtas Mahéshras of Sungra, Bhāba and Chagāon; patrons of the erstwhile parganas of Athārā Bees, Bhāba and Rājgrāon respectively. His daughters are the Shuwang Chandikā of Kothi, patron of the erstwhile Pargana Shua, and Ukha Devi of Nichār.
Please see: Foreign Department, Native States, Nos. 18-22, January 1894, No.21, Chapter I, Para 9, p. 17.

[185] Gazetteer, 1911, Chapter I. C., Pp 22-24.
(A) Genealogical table of the Poāri family is on p. 23;
(B) Genealogical table of the Shua family is on p. 24;
(C) Genealogical table of the Kohāl family is on p. 24.

[186] Francke, 1908, Appendix D, p. 124.

or rajas to strenghen their claims to legitimacy in the society and to broaden the basis of their economic and political power".[187] It was "initiated mainly by the authorities of the local level of the traditional political system".[188] As in Orissa, so also in Bushahr, divine assistance was martialled for the cause of legitimizing the position of the Rājā.

2.4.4.4 Divine Charter: The Rājā only as a Viceroy

Under the Gangā and the Suryavaṁsa dynasties (ca. 1112-1540/68 A.D.) of Orissa, Lord Jagannāth became the state deity (rāshtradevtā), with the king acting only as his viceroy (rautta).[189] This was a useful device for legitimizing tax collections. Opposition to the king was equated with treacherous attack (droha) on Jagannāth.[190] Something very similar existed in Bushahr. Though there are no inscriptions showing that the Rājā formally handed over his kingdom to a deity, the goddess Bhimā Kāli of Sarāhan was elevated to the state deity (rashtradevtā). Rāhul indicates that the real overlord of Bushahr State was Bhimā Kāli and the Rājā was merely her agent (kāyath).[191] Any resistance to his commands was equated with a crime likely to incur the wrath of the mighty goddess.

Devta Badrināth of Kāmru continued to remain the Rājā of Bushahr's clan god (kuladevta). His chirāning not only seeks to legitimize the Rājā's position by claiming that he himself had put Parduman Singh Chandravanshi on the throne but also serves to achieve the same purpose for certain prominent clans as well, including the clan of the Poāri Wazir.[192]

A letter from Rājā Shamsher Singh of Bushahr in 1875 A.D. calls the Devta Badrināth as 'Krishna rupi' (Krishna incarnate).[193] But in a letter of 1869 A.D., Devta Badrināth's caretaker (Rāwal), Purushottam Sharma, describes the devta as 'Bauddh rupi' (Buddha incarnate).[194] Here again, we discern a clear effort at legitimation vis-à-vis the Buddhists as well as the Hindus. Another letter from Rājā Shamsher Singh, from 1902 A.D., conveys special directions about putting the Devta Badrināth on the throne on his visit to Badrināth.[195] Rāhul feels that the name Badrināth was symbolically given to Kāmru's victor when he became deified.[196] A clear case of such deification is Rājā Kalyān Singh, the predecessor of Rājā Kehri Singh in the genealogical charts, who is now venerated as Devta Kalyān Singh in Kāmru. He is junior to Badrināth as a devta.[197] "As late as the middle of

[187] Kulke, 1976, p. 401.

[188] Kulke, 1976, p. 404.

[189] Kulke, 1976, p. 402.

[190] Ibid.

[191] Sānkrityāyan, 1957, p. 31, Pp 261-262.

[192] Gazetteer, 1971, Appendix III, Pp 362-365.

[193] Letter in the personal papers of Negi Goverdhan Singh in Sangla.

[194] Ibid.

[195] Ibid.

[196] Sānkrityāyan, 1957, p. 237. The original lines read: "devtāoṅ ki kathā badi manorañjak hoti hai lékin itihās méṅ uséy lé baithné par kabhi kabhi gadbadi hoti hai. Ho sakta hai Kāmru ké pratham vijétā ko hi Badrināth kā saṅkétiq nām dé diyā gayā ho".

the last century no act of state was performed without the approval of Bhimā Kāli, who was regarded as the ruler of the land, she having granted the regency to the Rājā's ancestor - just as she had conferred the hereditary priesthood to the senior branch of his dynasty".[198]

On the lines of the droha against Lord Jagannāth in Orissa, we find a custom known as 'Darohi' in Bushahr. This was "a form of oath the Rājā could impose on his subjects, by which he lay a prohibition on any proposed course of action. In its origin it was perhaps a kind of royal taboo, invested with semi-divine attributes of the personage from whom it issued; in its development it proved a source of power in the days when kings were glad to fence themselves around with supernatural safeguards...In its public aspect it is a useful method of ensuring obedience to executive orders with a minimum of friction or delay, and as such is used by certain village officers invested with authority to impose it".[199] We can identify processes of state consolidation that are similar in areas as distant and diverse as Kinnaur and Orissa. Another effort in the same direction was the attempt to imbibe legitimacy from the imperial Mughals.

2.4.4.5 The Mughals and Bushahr: Plenty of Stories, No Proofs

The stories claiming that Rājā Kehri Singh was invested with the title of Chhatrapati by an unnamed Mughal emperor[200] highlight the importance of derived legitimacy emanating from this imperial source, even in areas like Kinnaur where there is no record of the Mughals' ever having brought it under their control. Interestingly, Kehri Singh's reign coincided with the lifetime of Shivāji Mahārāj (1627-1680 A.D.), the famous Maratha ruler. The latter had taken the title Chhatrapati without the sanction of the Mughals. The Rājā of Bushahr thought he could do one better than Shivāji! We see in his case a synthesis between the adoption of a title on the lines of Shivāji and its alleged derivation from the Mughal emperor as a sign of imperial legitimacy. Bushahr had come of age.

The fresco mentioned by A.H. Francke[201] again points towards an attempt to derive legitimacy from Mughal authority representing the imperial ægis emanating from Delhi. This effort was accompanied by a parallel effort at keeping the allegiance of the Buddhists in Kinnaur as well. While the purported stamp of legitimacy from the Mughals was useful in relations with other hill states, many of whom had clearly recognized Mughal suzerainty; the loyalty of Kinnauri Buddhists needed another source of legitimation. The Mughal emperor's role this time was transferred to the Dalai Lāmā in Lhāsā. "The ruling family of Bashahr is...held to be of divine origin, and the Lāmāic theory is that each Rājā of Bashahr is at his death re-incarnated as the Guru Lāmā or Guru of the Lāmās, who is understood to be the Dalai Lāmā of Tibet".[202] The Dalai Lāmā was not only the spiritual but also the de-facto temporal head of Tibet. Situated between two imperial systems - that of Tibet and that of Mughal India - the Rājās of Bushahr thus claimed their legitimacy from both these founts. This was an example of a double-track legitimation calculated to win over and retain the

[197] Devta Kalyān Singh is installed in the temple of Devta Badrināth at Kāmru.

[198] Rose, H.A., 1911, p. 485.

[199] Ibid, Pp 482-483.

[200] Gazetteer, 1911, Ch. I.B., p. 6; Gazetteer, 1971, Ch. II, p. 58; Foreign Department, Native States, January 1894, Nos. 18-22, No. 21, Chapter I, Para 9, p. 17.

[201] Francke, 1908, p. 7.

[202] Rose, H.A., 1911, p. 98;
Gazetteer, 1911, Ch. I.B., p. 5.

loyalties of persons having different religions - Hinduism and Buddhism - and looking towards two different seats of imperial power - Delhi and Lhāsā - as the sources of legitimate political authority. But even vested with such legitimacy, the Rājās of Bushahr did not seek to disturb the animist practices of the devi/devta cults in Kinnaur so as not to unduly upset their subjects.

2.4.4.6 Laissez Faire: Devis and Devtas

As T.S. Negi so rightly points out, the "Rājā of Rāmpur Bushahr seems to have recognized the importance of these village gods and, throughout, an arrangement of mutual respect and 'live and let live' worked satisfactorily to both sides till the last day of the Rājā regime".[203] These deities are still the focus of village life in Kinnaur. Those in areas under Bhot influence adopted Buddhist practices such as giving up human or animal sacrifice.[204] The Rājās of Bushahr always showed respect to the devtas and sent offerings to the more important of these in Kinnaur. In return, the divinities never questioned the legitimacy of the rājās. The management committees of the deities' temples consisted (and consist) of persons called Kārdārs who were (and are) people from the more affluent upper caste families whose interest lay in preserving the position of the Rājā under whom they could continue to hold their social predominance undisturbed. The village deity represented in a way the collective will of the village against unchecked absolutism of the Rājā who moulded the devtas' pre-eminence to his own purposes.

The rājās used the devtas as their representatives for manifesting royal presence in remote areas. For example, Devta Badrināth of Kāmru used to regularly tour areas in Pargana Tukpa on the Rājā's behalf. Divine power was being martialled here in support of temporal power. Since the Rājā did not frequently visit Kinnaur, the devta's frequent tours on his behalf manifested divine sanction for the Rājā's rule. We have an eyewitness account of such a visit to Pooh in October 1866, recorded by the founder of the Moravian Mission station there, Edouard Pagell. He mentions that the Rājā had sent his deities[205] from Middle Kinnaur, with an entourage of 130 persons for residence (Einquartierung). All the costs of this stay were extracted from the locals. The devta was on a chariot (rath). Such persons as could not pay cash, paid in wheat, barley, buckwheat and potatoes.[206] The deity functioned thus as a tax collector as well. With increasing hinduization, these deities, most of whom must earlier have been objects of animist worship, were brought into the Hindu pantheon. They were given appropriate myths of origin showing them to have flown into the area from various centres of Hindu worship. Thus Devta Badrināth is now considered to be equal in status to the deity in Badrināth temple in Uttar Pradesh. His image is put on an equal footing to the right of that of the deity in Badrināth temple whenever he goes visiting there.[207] Devi Shuwang Chandikā of Kothi was turned into a manifestation of Kāli while the Sungra Mahéshras was given the status of being the only devta from Kinnaur who was invited to Sarāhan as the Wazir of Bhimā Kāli for the Udayapan yagya.[208] While the devtas were given full respect within

[203] Negi, T.S., 1976, p. 21.

[204] For indications about a tradition of human sacrifice having existed earlier in Kinnaur, please see: Francke, A.H., 1908, Pp 21-22.

[205] The German word used is "Götzen".

[206] Pagell, Edouard: Jahresbericht der Station Poo, West Himalaya-Jahr 1866.

[207] Information heard in Sangla and Kāmru villages innumerable times in the years from 1980 to 1983. Also given in: Sānkrityāyan, 1957, p. 239.

[208] Gazetteer, 1911, p. 28.

Kinnaur, hinduization was progressively diminishing their role outside this area as agents of legitimation. In the latter areas, rājputization and kshatriyaization were serving this purpose, accompanied by an ever increasing sequence of adoption of Hindu rituals.

The state became in a way the central impulse-giver for the organization of cults around the traditional deities. We can notice here some similarities to the state of affairs found by Dr Günther Unbescheid in the Jumlā area of Nepal. There also, the cult of a goddess had been made into an official cult. "The sudden emergence of a developed temple cult out of a ritual void allows the supposition, that here evidently a finished model was introduced by the ruling house and grafted onto the local holies".[209] Like the deities of Jumlā, who also killed demons, the deities of Kinnaur appear as reclaimers of the country; as oppressors of daityās and rāksasas (demons) and as guardians of the lawful behaviour of kings.[210]

To borrow a phrase from Max Weber, in Kinnaur also we find the "caste system in an irresistible and ever continued expansion".[211] Max Weber's two kinds of hinduization - ***extensive and intensive*** -[212] both had occurred in Bushahr; intensive for areas outside Kinnaur; extensive, followed by intensive, for Kinnaur. The Harijans (Béru) acquired a position of "negative privilege",[213] becoming unclean castes. "This social and economic 'discriminatory integration' was complemented by a rather slow process of Hinduization of tribal customs and beliefs".[214] To again cite Max Weber, this process of hinduization "not only endowed the ruling stratum...with recognized rank in the cultural world of Hinduism, but, through their transformation of castes, secured their superiority over the subject classes with an efficiency unsurpassed by any other religion".[215] All this consolidated state formation which acquired further strength under British paramountcy through improved utilization of its economic means. But before acquiring this umbrella of Pax Britannica, Bushahr State reached its nadir in the period 1803-1815 A.D. during which the Gorkhas occupied the kingdom till Wāngtu.[216] Only Kinnaur remained beyond their grasp. The Rājā of Bushahr remained there in secure refuge, showing that his ancestors' efforts at legitimizing their rule had succeeded well. Kinnaur, the cradle of Bushahr's ruling house, gave Rājā Mahinder Singh a second chance to

[209] Unbescheid, Günther: Göttliche Könige und Königliche Götter, Entwurf zur Organisation von Kulten in Gorkhā und Jumlā, Typewritten Mimeograph, [Year not mentioned], p. 8. The original lines read: *"Das plötzliche Auftauchen eines ausgebauten Tempelkultes aus einem rituellen Nichts läßt vermuten, daß hier offensichtlich ein fertiges Modell durch das Herrscherhaus eingeführt und den lokalen Heiligtümern aufgestülpt wurde"*.
Translation mine.

[210] Ibid, p. 9. The original lines read: *"Die Gottheit tritt darin als Urbarmacher des Landes auf, als Unterdrücker von Daityas und Raksasas und als Wächter über das rechtmäßige Walten der Könige"*.
Translation mine.

[211] Weber, Max: Religion of India: Sociology of Hinduism and Buddhism, Translated by Gerth, H. and Martindale, Don, Glencoe: The Free Press, 1958, p. 130.

[212] Kulke, Hermann: Max Weber's Contribution to the Study of "Hinduization" in India and "Indianization" in Southeast Asia, Pp 100-102, in: Kantowsky, Detlef (ed.): Recent Research on Max Weber's Studies of Hinduism, München & London: Weltforum Verlag, 1986, Pp 97-116.

[213] Ibid, p. 101.

[214] Ibid.

[215] Weber, Max, cited in Ibid, p. 102.

[216] Please see Chapter I, Section 1.2.2 of this work.

take up the work of his ancestors in going on with state formation. As a leading Kinnaura said to the author during field research in 1985, "After all, the Rājā had been one of us. He arose from amongst us and did not fall from the sky".[217]

2.4.5 Period of British Paramountcy: Sāhibs and Natives!

After the expulsion of the Gorkhas from the Western Hills,[218] Rājā Mahinder Singh was confirmed as the ruler of Bushahr by the British Government by virtue of a deed (sanad) dated November 6, 1815 A.D., in possession of all his former territories except Kotgarh and Rāwingarh which were retained as British possessions.[219] Under British paramountcy Bushahr did not suffer any foreign invasions though the Sikhs were perceived as a threat due to their presence across the Satluj river in areas of Kulu and in Spiti both of which they had conquered.[220] The British were chary about an alliance between the Sikhs and the Gorkhas, so they actively followed Zorāwar Singh's military campaign in Western Tibet.[221] But even earlier, the trade with Tibet across Kinnaur had attracted British attention. Under their paramountcy, this trade flourished as an economic activity. The British got constructed the Hindustan-Tibet Road, which ultimately stretched from Nārkanda via Rāmpur and Sarāhan till Shipké village in Tibet. Plans to extend this road till Gartok never materialized.

2.4.5.1 Trade Policy under British Paramountcy: Continuity and Extension

Under the terms of the peace treaty ending the Tibet-Ladākhi-Mughal War (c. 1679-1684 A.D.)[222] the Tibetan authorities agreed to supply the entire quantity of shawl wool from Western Tibet to Ladākh. The East India Company never accepted this monopoly arrangement which later put areas like Almora, Kumaon and Garhwāl, which came under their paramountcy, at a disadvantage regarding trade with Tibet. William Moorcroft managed to purchase a small quantity of shawl wool from Gartok in village Misar. He considered this token purchase in 1812 as the "day of the epoch at which may be fixed the origin of a traffic which is likely to be extremely beneficial to the Honourable Company".[223] It was a direct consequence of this policy to prise open this monopoly granted to Ladākh that when Bushahr came under British paramountcy, the British retained Kotgarh and established a factory there to "try to coax trade in this valuable raw material away from the traditional route to Kashmir through Ladākh, and down on to British territory".[224] Bushahr thus became an important

[217] Personal interview with Negi Goverdhan Singh on December, 1985 at 10.00 hours in his house in Sangla. His original words were: "Rājā bhi to hamāréy beech méṅ sé hi thā. Voh hamāréy beech sé hi chadha thā aur koi āsmān sé thodé hi girā thā".
Translation mine.

[218] For information about the campaign to expel the Gorkhas from Bushahr, please see: Fraser, J.B., 1820, Chapters II to XIV, Pp 13-199.

[219] To see the text of this sanad of November 6, 1815, please see: Gazetteer, 1911, Chapter I.B., p. 9.

[220] Datta, C.L., 1973, Pp 157-158.

[221] Ibid, Pp 158-159. J.D. Cunningham, the future historian of the Sikhs, was sent by the British to upper Kinnaur for the express purpose of monitoring Zorāwar Singh's campaign in Western Tibet. For more information about Cunningham's mission, please see: Datta, C.L., 1970, Pp 82-90.

[222] Ahmad, Zahiruddin,: New Light on the Tibet-Ladākh-Mughal War of 1679-84, in: East and West, New Series, Vol. 18, Nos. 3-4, September-December 1968, Pp 340-361.

[223] Moorcroft, William, 1819, p. 460.

channel of communication in British attempts to open talks with Tibetan officials.[225] "Rāmpur, the capital of Bashahr, also began to develop into a shawl wool trading centre. For the convenient transit of wool, it was thought necessary to have good roads in Kinnaur...Tracks which in 1878 could be used...only with great difficulty were repaired and within two years the Bashahris started bringing sheep laden with wool to Rāmpur".[226] With the encouraging attitude of British officials, Kinnauras began to smuggle shawl wool from Tibet.[227] This was the beginning of the heyday of cross-border trade, with Kinnaur as the entrepôt. An inseparable part of this trade was the complex and intricate relationship of Bushahr and Tibet which the British did not attempt to disrupt.

2.4.5.2 Bushahr and Tibet: Paramountcy, Presents and Confusion

J.D. Cunningham found in 1841 that the Rājā of Bushahr had been receiving a tribute of 30 pieces of woollen cloth from Peri village in Spiti for the preceding 60 years.[228] Thus, a state enjoying British protection (Bushahr) had been collecting tribute, however nominal, from this village in Spiti belonging to Ladākh which was then under the suzerainty of the Sikhs.[229] Similarly, village Giù under Tibetan control used to pay an annual tribute of 7½ Rupees to the Rājā of Bushahr.[230] The Rājā, in return, used to send gifts every three years to the Tibetan Garpon (Governor) of Gartok, because he (the Rājā) was apprehensive that otherwise "his subjects would incur the displeasure of the Tibetans, and consequently their trade would suffer".[231] Conversely, "when a new Rājā of Bashahr took the Gaddi, he received presents from the Governor of Gartok".[232] These practices were continuing as late as 1912 A.D.[233] Trade links between Bushahr and Tibet had fostered this "complex situation where 'multiplicity of relations' and 'divisions of allegiance' existed. In western political parlance it was not clear as to who was the paramount power, who was the sovereign of whom? Cunningham informed his government that the time had come to remodel the relations of the hill states under British protection with the border states under Chinese rule".[234] This remodelling was carried out slowly, without disrupting the traditional skein of trade relations.

[224] Lamb, Alistair, 1958, p. 38.

[225] Ibid, Pp 38-39.

[226] Datta, C.L., 1969, p. 20.

[227] Ibid.

[228] Datta, C.L., 1970, p. 85.

[229] Ibid, p. 86.

[230] Ibid.

[231] Ibid.

[232] Ibid.

[233] Verified from the confidential despatches of the British Trade Agent, Western Tibet, at Gartok to the Superintendent, Hill States, Simla. This correspondence is available in the D.C.'s Office at Kālpa only with the D.C.'s prior permission.

[234] Datta, C.L., 1970, p. 86.

After the Younghusband expedition of 1904, a British Trade Agent was stationed at Gartok. He was to watch over free flow of trade and to ensure that British Indian subjects or Bushahris were not tried under Tibetan law. He was to tour the trade marts continuously to report on the problems, if any, of traders from India. He became an important channel of communication to the Tibetan authorities through his frequent meetings with the Garpons at Gartok and with other Tibetan officials. Finally, the British had succeeded in establishing a direct channel of communication with Tibet.

2.4.5.3 Administrative Reform: Tikka Raghunāth Singh's Legacy

Till the time of Tikka Raghunāth Singh (de facto ruler, 1887-1898 A.D.), Bushahr had had an administrative set-up dominated by the hereditary wazirs. The rājās had been weak, allowing the wazirs to exercise enormous power. The Tikka curbed the power of the wazirs. He was aided in this task by the fact that the umbrella of British paramountcy put his legitimacy beyond doubt. In his struggle against Wazir Ran Bahādur Singh of Poāri the British came down firmly on his side against the Wazir. They did not allow Ran Bahādur Singh to set himself up as a separate ruler of Dodra Kwār and enforced status quo ante.[235] Secure in the knowledge that his hold on the power of the state was beyond challenge, having been totally legitimized through British support, the Tikka (heir presumptive) carried out some administrative reorganization. He laid down the groundwork of a revenue collection system on more scientific lines than hitherto. This system was the setting up of a revenue collection machinery on hierarchical lines and territorial units like ghodis, parganas and tahsils. More reforms were carried out under Rājā Padam Singh (1914-1948 A.D.), but the administrative set-up as late as 1948 was quite ramshackle.

From its earlier characterization as an inchoate early state, Bushahr under Tikka Raghunāth Singh showed some characteristics of a typical early state, viz ***heredity as a principle of succession was balanced by appointment; private ownership of land was still very limited; salaried functionaries were found besides remunerated functionaries, or one and the same functionary was receiving a salary as well as remunerations; a start towards codification of laws and punishments was made; regular tribute, partly in kind and partly in services, was exacted, and major works, organized by government functionaries, were being undertaken with the aid of compulsory labour.***

Trade and markets were of great importance; a characteristic of a transitional early state. Law had not yet become the fulcrum upon which a shift from tradition as the basis of legitimacy to support a regime enforced by prescribed expectations of behaviour could take place. The process of legitimation served covertly and overtly the establishment of an economic foundation upon which the state could build further. The creation of social distance; the validation of state authority; the consolidation of power and the socialization of the population were aimed ultimately at ensuring control of the ruling classes over the economic sphere of the nation. How well this process had succeeded can be gauged from the fact that even though Bushahr State had hardly undertaken any public development works in Kinnaur, the area never showed any signs of revolutionary ferment against the princely order. There was the articulation of minor grievances from time to time but the Kinnauras had looked up to the Rājā for solutions, rather than wanting to replace his regime with another political system. The princely order continued to enjoy the allegiance of most of the Kinnauras right till the end when it was overtaken by events beyond its control - the departure of the British and the creation of independent India.

[235] For information about this struggle, please see: Order dated the 5th December 1898, passed by A. Meredith Esquire, Superintendent Hill States, Simla, on the claim of Ran Bahādur Singh to proprietory and other rights in Dodra Kwār. It is in possession of Negi Goverdhan Singh in Sangla.

2.4.6 Post-Independence Period till 1960: Nothing Spectacular

This period can principally be characterized by two trends:

(A) A slow initiation of public development works;
(B) Introduction of popular participation in political processes.

The political scene came to be dominated by larger landholders[236] and traders-cum-moneylenders, especially in upper Kinnaur. To the poorer peasant it had made little difference that the country had now become free and that the Rājā's regime had been consigned to history. Kinnaur was now a part of Mahāsu District. The district headquarters were located at Kasumpti, nearly 235 kilometres away from Chini. Government still remained a remote concept for the Kinnaura peasant. No banks were present in the area.

The Community Development/National Extension Scheme programme was launched in Kinnaur in October 1956 when a Development Block was established at Chini. But the emphasis of the development programmes was community-oriented rather than individual-oriented. Funds were given for building village roads under the so-called Crash Programme Scheme. Construction of irrigation channels (kuhls) also received priority. The concept of concentrating government development efforts on well-identified target groups through an integrated development programme was missing. Little effort was really made to bring about a change in popular perception about the government being now their own, elected by them, rather than an imposed order, as in earlier days. Kinnauras still saw government functonaries quite seldom. Life went on much as before. Trade went on with Tibet, shepherds migrated with their flocks to their traditional summer pastures, nature was hard and unpredictable. The rhythm of life had not changed.

2.4.7 Post-1960 Period: District, Roads and Bureaucracy

The creation of Kinnaur District on May 1, 1960 brought in its wake some immediate consequences. The Himāchal Pradesh State Cooperative Bank established a branch in Kālpa, as Chini came to be now known. With the establishment of a full-fledged district set-up, the entire range of official agricultural, horticultural, animal husbandry, industries, soil conservation and other development programmes became available to the public at a much closer distance than earlier. Government ceased being a totally remote concept and began to be perceived as a reality closer to home. The Kinnaur District Cooperative Marketing and Supply Federation (KINFED) was created, in place of the hitherto existing Tahsil Cooperative Union functioning from Chini. The KINFED began acting as the apex body of a structure of subsidized inputs which began to be funnelled into Kinnaur, especially after 1962 in the wake of the Sino-Indian conflict.

The Sino-Indian conflict, even without direct fighting in Kinnaur, had two immediate effects. It snapped the ages-old social, cultural, religious, political and economic links of Kinnaur with Tibet. And it forced the Government of India to begin paying much more attention to this hitherto neglected border region. The whole world view (Weltanschauung) of the Kinnauras had to be now turned right around through 180 degrees and focussed totally on India. The black crow had not turned white, the snow on Mount Kailāsh had not melted, the lake Mānasarowar had not dried up,[237] but the entire political situation vis-à-vis Tibet had

[236] It should always be kept in mind that the term 'larger landholders' refers to the context of Kinnaur only. It should not raise visions of landed estates stretching over thousands or even hundreds of acres. In Kinnaur, the terrain being what it is, a landholder owning 15 acres or more of irrigated double-cropped land would qualify for this category.

[237] Please see Section 1.2.4, Chapter I of this work for placing these words in context.

undergone a change. The edifice of good relations and periodic exchanges of presents established by Rājā Kehri Singh and nurtured through more than 250 years by his successors had collapsed; a victim of new power realities and strategic equations in the Himalayan region. Kinnauras were presented with a fait accompli of having to restructure their way of life to cope with these new realities.

The government now went in for accelerated construction of roads. This had become indispensable from the defence point of view. National Highway 22 was laid out from 1968 onwards and opened up the area as never before. Villages could now be reached by bus and by jeep, where over centuries sheep, mules and yaks had held sway. Defence personnel moved into the area in a big way, bringing in their wake problems of adjustment with locals. The establishment of new government offices at the district-level brought in large numbers of non-Kinnaura government employees, generating similar problems of adjustment as in case of soldiers. Government became more visible and sought to intensify development programmes on a much larger scale than before so as not to cause any resentment amongst the tribals of Kinnaur whose unquestioning loyalty to the country was now much more important than ever before, in view of the Chinese troops sitting across the border. Increasing government attention meant the introduction of more and more government programmes. One of the most important of such programmes was the land reforms programme, especially because it is of interest to the main theme of this thesis - the credit structure in Kinnaur. Having examined the historical background of state formation in Kinnaur, we can now turn to the pattern of land reform in the area.

CHAPTER II-B
PATTERN OF LAND REFORM

The pattern of land holding is important for implantation of an institutional credit network in an area.

2.B LAND REFORM: PRE-REQUISITE TO CREDIT-WORTHINESS

Institutional lenders demand security cover for loans. In Kinnaur, with its predominantly agro-pastoral economy, landed property offers acceptable collateral for institutional lenders. To offer land or other immovable property as collateral, the borrower must prove his title to the property in question. If his title itself is doubtful, institutional agencies would not accept him as an eligible borrower. Credit worthiness and private ownership of landed property are indelibly linked together. Absence of an institutional credit system under the Rājās of Bushahr can partly be linked to the traditional land holding pattern prevalent in Kinnaur under which the Rājā held formal title to all the land in his state. Cultivators had no formal title in proprietory terms to the land that they cultivated.

2.B.1 Traditional Land Holding Pattern: Not Credit-worthy

Traditionally, the Rājā was the owner of all land. People of higher caste groups (Brahmins, Rājpūts, Kanaits) were allotted land in order to enable them to discharge a part of their allegiance to their ruler by the transfer of their allotments.[238] The Rājā was the **Ala Mālik** (superior owner) of all lands. Rights of **Adnā Malqiyat** (inferior ownership) were conferred on landholders during the first regular Settlement conducted by Miāṅ Durgā Singh under the supervision of Tikka Raghunāth Singh during the years 1891-92. Prior to conferment of **Adnā Malqiyat** rights, the landholders did not have the rights of transfer of their land by way of sale, gift, mortgage or exchange. The Adnā Māliks could transfer land only among themselves.

It is important to note here that what mattered was actual cultivation on the ground and not formal definition under the law. The fact that the Rājā was the Ala Mālik did not mean that the cultivators in possession were totally defenceless, without any rights whatsoever. Custom and tradition conferred rights in practice on cultivators in possession on the spot. The fact that they lacked formal title to the land that they cultivated could have been a hindrance in transactions where proof of such title was required as a pre-requisite, for example, in case of receipt of institutional credit or for registration of mortgages. No institutional credit agencies existed before the twentieth century so that the first hindrance was purely hypothetical. Credit was obtained from the informal sector which laid worth on cultivating possession of land and not on finer nuances of legal title to such land. As for transactions like mortgages, no Settlement operations had taken place before 1851-52 A.D. so there existed no formal land record as we know it today. This did not mean that no land transfer transactions took place prior to 1854 and began only thereafter. Only, these were not recorded. Actual cultivation on the spot was the determining factor whether a cultivator could informally mortgage a piece of land or not.

Absence of formal title did not override customary rights which relied on actual cultivating possession. The village administration paper (Wājib-ul-Arz) was not recorded in the first legal Settlement (1894 A.D., known as the Qānooni Bandobast) but was prepared for the revision Settlement (Bandobast Tarmim) of 1928 A.D. It lists out the customary rights and practices prevalent in the different ghodis. The Wājib-ul-Arz of Ghodi Kāmru tells us that

[238] Gazetteer, 1971, p. 235.

tenants (cultivators) were of four kinds:-

(a) **Mauroosi (Occupancy);**
(b) **Gair Mauroosi (Non-occupancy);**
(c) **Khidmati (Service);**
(d) **Bilā Sift (Without definition).**

"Bilā Sift tenants (meaning mostly cultivators in actual possession without a formal determination of their titles) were not liable to ejectment, because their rights had not been determined. Accordingly, they could not be ejected through a notice of ejectment. On the issuance of such notice, their rights would be enquired into and the decision of the court of law would specify what category they belonged to. Generally, occupancy tenants are at the service of the Mandir Devta or the Mandir Thākur, at some places also of the zamindārs. Tenants of the Buddhist temple have been in cultivating possession of the temple in question...To the extent that the cultivators are tenants of the temple, they are in possession since long. Without permission of a court, the temple has no right to eject or restore them. If a tenant does not fulfil the conditions of his conduct,...ejectment shall take place through a court order or such order shall be issued as reflects the circumstances revealed during the proceedings".[239] We see that custom gave importance to actual cultivation even while the Rājā remained recorded in papers as the Ala Mālik.

Outsiders could not acquire ownership or mortgage rights to land in Bushahr without the Rājā's prior permission.[240] The ***Adnā Māliks*** were made full owners of their lands only after independence and merger of the erstwhile princely state of Bushahr in the Indian Union.[241] Thus, till 1891 A.D., the landholders had had no formal title at all to their land. They had only the right of inferior or limited ownership. There could be no land offered as collateral or security for obtaining institutional loans in such a system. Clearly, the state did not consider the creation of an institutional credit infrastructure as a necessary adjunct of its functions.

This status of **Adnā Māliks** was not extended to all the cultivators of land but only to larger cultivators from the higher caste groups. When talking about 'larger' cultivators we should not forget the topography of Kinnaur. Landholdings there even today are monitored in bighās rather than acres (roughly 5.333 bighās = 1 acre) or hectares. A cultivator in Kinnaur with more than 75-80 bighās of irrigated double-cropped land would qualify as a large

[239] The original reads: "Jis qadar muzāriyān Tahsil hazā méiṅ haiṅ wéh chār qism ké haiṅ - Mauroosi, Gair Mauroosi, Khidmati, Bilā Sift. Bilā Sift qābil bédakhli nahiṅ haiṅ kyoṅ ké unké haquq ki koi tanqir nahiṅ hui hai. Isliyé yeh notis bédakhli nahiṅ haiṅ. Notis jāri honéy par unké haquq ki tanqih hogi aur faislā adālat ké honéy par qarār diyā jāyégā ki āyā veh kis sift ké haiṅ. Am taur par muzāriyān mauroosi khidmati mandir devta wā mandir thākur ké haiṅ; bāz bāz jagàh zamindārān ké bhi khidmati haiṅ. Muzāriyān mandir bauddh arsā sé zamin hāé ki arāzi ko kāsht kartéy chaléy āyé haiṅ...Jis qadr muzāriyān mandir ké haiṅ, veh log bahut arsā sé qābiz haiṅ. Sivāéy ijāzat adālat ké unké māqāfi wā bahāli kā mandir ko akhtiyār nahiṅ hai. Aur koi muzārā apni shart muqarrar ko poorā nā karéy...to mārfat ad1lat bédakhal kiyā jāyégā yā ki baruéy adālat jaisi soorat muqaddamā zāhir hogi, vaisā huqam munāsib adālat séy miléygā".
Item 12, Ziqr Muazāriyān, Wājib-ul-Arz, Ghodi Kāmru, Pargana Tukpa, Riyāsat Rāmpur Bushahr, Zilā Shimla, Bābat Tarmim Bandobast, Sambat 1985 bikrami [1928 A.D.], Unpublished, [in Urdu].

[240] Lakhanpāl, B.R.,: Assessment Reoprt of the Second Regular Settlement of Nichār Tehsil of Kinnaur District of Himāchal Pradesh (1977-81), Draft Report submitted to the government for approval, Unpublished, 1985, p. 20. The author is extremely grateful to Mr S.S. Negi, I.A.S., Settlement Officer, Simla and Kinnaur Districts, and to Mr I.S. Chandel, H.A.S., A.S.O. Kinnaur, for having allowed him access to this report in their office.

[241] Ibid.

landholder. The predominance of higher caste groups on land holding has not changed even after 1947. This means that the people most in need of institutional credit (poor lower caste groups) had the least to offer in terms of collateral required by institutions. During the latest Settlement operations in Kinnaur, begun in 1977, it was found in case of Nichār Tahsil that the "Rājpūts...hold 70% of total cultivated area. The next come the Kolis who hold 14.4% of the cultivated area".[242] It is not wrong to say that the same phenomenon holds true for the other two Sub-Divisions of Kinnaur (Kālpa and Pooh) where Settlement operations have been carried out but Settlement Reports are still awaited. The percentages will obviously be different but the basic fact of the Kolis' holding much lesser land than the Kanaits will not be different.[243] The traditional pattern of land holding was not favourable to efficient agricultural operation. Without formal title to ownership or tenancy, there was hardly any incentive for investment in land to achieve higher yields. The grip of the Rājā and his minions was not confined only to land but to physical labour and to all spheres of economic activity as well.[244] Where even owners had no formal recorded rights, the plight of the tenants could certainly not be better in this respect.

2.B.2 Tenancy Relations: Karāhads and Bégār

For Rāmpur Tahsil, which included the Athārā Bees Pargana and six revenue estates of the Pandrā Bees Pargana presently in Kinnaur District, there existed various kinds of tenancies as listed below:[245]

(a) Those tenants who like other state subjects had been in occupancy for a long time and had only been paying revenue and fixed habubs (customary payments in kind) to the owners, muāfidārs and jāgirdārs. From such holders the jāgirdārs, etc., had not got rent of any kind, nor any service, only the fixed items;

(b) Those tenants who had been long in occupancy and the muāfidārs and jāgirdārs, besides the fixed cash rent (lagān), could in every way increase the lagān (rate of revenue) and the habubs due from the tenants. They could also get from the latter any kind of service they might choose;

(c) Those tenants who had long been in occupancy and who, in return for the services that they rendered, had been exempted by the jāgirdārs and muāfidārs from the payment of rent. They had, however, to pay from time to time miscellaneous sums imposed on them;

(d) Those tenants who had been exempted by the jāgirdārs and muāfidārs from the payment of their rent;

(e) Those tenants who paid half the produce of their land, and who could be changed and ousted by the muāfidārs and jāgirdārs at their will after two or three years;

(f) Those tenants who had in the Settlement of 1910 samwat (1854 A.D.) been shown as asāmis. Their privileges were the same as of those mentioned in clause (b) of this list;

(g) Those persons who acquired their lands by purchasing these from the holders of jāgirs;

(h) Those persons who had been in possession of land for a short time only, paid cash revenue, as well as a part of the produce of the land (batāi) held by them.

[242] Ibid, Pp 42-43.

[243] Information obtained in person from the Settlement Officer's Office in Sanjāuli, near Simla, on January 6, 1986.

[244] The idea was that everything belonged to the Rājā, including the individual's capacity of physical labour.

[245] Coldstream, W.: Report on the Assessment and Revenue Rate of Rāmpur Tahsil, Bashahr State, No. 21, Chapter III, Para 33, p. 25, in: Foreign Department, Native States, January 1894, Nos. 18-22.

Tenants of clause (a) were shown in Settlement papers in 1894 A.D. as inferior owners; those in clauses (b), (c) and (f) as cultivators without any qualifications (bilā sift). The others remaining were shown as tenants without qualifications whose rights had not been defined (gair mauroosi).[246] Tenants without qualifications (i.e. tenants whose rights had not been defined) could not be ejected from the lands cultivated by them by muāfidārs and jāgirdārs without a court order after the Settlement of 1894 A.D. When, according to rule, an application was made for ejectment of tenants after the kharif crops had been cut, the rights of tenants without qualification were to be fully enquired into. If the tenant was found to have occupancy rights (haquq-i-mustaqil), the landholder's application for ejectment of the tenant would be rejected. Generally, the tenants of the directly controlled royal lands (khālsa lands) had no hereditary rights of occupancy. Khālsa lands belonged directly to the Rājā. Tenants on these lands were shown in the revenue record after Settlement as tenants without occupancy rights.[247]

They had to wait another 60 years to obtain such rights. The concept of occupancy rights was indirectly introduced for the first time after the Settlement of 1894 A.D. through conferment of inferior ownership (Adnā Malqiyat) rights on cultivators belonging to category (a). Tenants of royal lands continued to be recorded as tenants without occupancy rights even after the Revision Settlement of 1928 A.D. It was only after the H.P. Abolition of Big Landed Estates and Land Reforms Act of 1953 that they became entitled to occupancy rights in the lands that they had been cultivating.

Regarding Chini Tahsil, a report of 1897 A.D. clarifies that due to the paucity of cultivated area, very little of it was cultivated by tenants. The greater portion of the land occupied by tenants belonged to jāgirdārs or was held revenue-free by the mahants of temples or the kārdārs of shrines. The tenants on khālsa lands were mostly tenants-at-will. On lands held revenue-free by jāgirdārs and muāfidārs the tenants had often certain rights of occupancy. In addition to whatever rent they paid, bégār (corvée labour) was also due to their landlords.[248] Of the total area cultivated; 47,770 bighās were occupied by proprietors and only 11,083 bighās by tenants. Of the area cultivated by tenants, nearly 50% was rent-free in return for service. Of the area paying rent, 4,210 bighās were held by tenants with occupancy rights and 1,098 bighās by tenants-at-will. On only 616 bighās was half the produce paid as rent. The remaining area (312 bighās) paid cash rents, or (4,886 bighās) combined cash-and-kind rents. The average cash rent on inirrigated land was 4 ānnās 6 pies and on irrigated land 1 rupee 3 ānnās per bighā respectively. Tenants paying rents in kind usually kept all the straw (bhūsa).[249]

Not only were titles to land not legally protected, corvée labour ensured the extraction of services in addition to payment of land revenue. There were broadly three kinds of forced labour:

(A) Bégār;
(B) Athwārā;
(C) Batraul.

[246] Ibid, Para 34, in: Ibid.

[247] Ibid, Para 35, p. 26, in: Ibid.

[248] Steedman, E.B.: Review of the Assessment of Tahsil Chini, No. 6, Para 14, p. 3, in: File No. 9, No. 666 dated 6th April, 1896 from E.B. Steedman, Superintendent Hill States, Simla to the Chief Secretary to Government Punjab in: Foreign Department, Native States, Nos. 5-6, February 1897.

[249] Ibid, Para 15, p. 3, in: Ibid.

Bégār meant carrying of loads; athwārā meant free labour and batraul meant ad hoc labour. The incidence of batraul was less than that of athwārā. The latter had been institutionalized at two months, which term was reduced to 1 ½ months and then to one month.[250] Corvée labour was used for cultivation of royal lands called 'bāsa'. There were not many bāsa lands in Kinnaur, which had hardly any good lands. Bāsa lands were generally the best lands at any location. They did not exceed 25% of the total cultivated area in the village. Labourers working on these lands were called 'béthus'. They belonged generally to the lower castes and got no share in the crop produce; being given only their daily meals as wages. In addition to bāsa lands, the Rājā also got personal income from land holdings called 'halotis', in which the pargana of location also had a share. Villages of the concerned pargana decided who would labour on these lands.[251] There was no distinction between the Rājā's personal income and the income of the state. This distinction began to be made only when the British began sending managers to administer the state after Tikka Raghunāth Singh's death in 1898 A.D. The cultivators had no incentive to make improvements in agriculture, horticulture or other economic activities because the taxation system, being arbitrary, extracted major payments in kind. The more one produced, the more one paid. Taxes fixed in kind were called karāhads.

2.B.3 Traditional Taxation Structure: Little Monetization

In addition to cash revenue, each landholder (asāmi) had to pay according to his means what were called the karāhads or the habubs. Their number was unlimited and large. The major karāhads were as follows:[252]

(A) Khora, apricot oil;
(B) Pinti, ghee;
(C) Batlohi, spirits of grain;
(D) Shiu, spirits of grapes;
(E) Dulgi, spirits of a forest tree called khim;
(F) Hatangnan, elephants' expenses;
(G) Ghortangnan, rent for gharāts or water mills;
(H) Sarkhan, stable expenses;
(I) Manden, Tirni or tax on flocks;
(J) Poksha, Tirni, taken in sheep and goats and not in cash;
(K) Khādu, taken in sheep and goats;
(L) Dhalbaya, 1 ānnā per house taken at the Dhāl fair;
(M) Kothipavali, expenses of Bara or Khud Kāsht (self cultivated land), taken from cultivators, such as devtas, and festival expenses, cash, 2 to 4 ānnās per house;
(N) Mél, share of grain;
(O) Karāhads, cash taken according to status of individual;
(P) Phag, or holi expenses;
(Q) Puthi un, a share of wool taken in Chét and Bhādon, from those who had more than 40 goats or sheep;
(R) Cholumang, assessment to pay for the Rājā's wardrobe;

[250] Information given by Mr T.S. Negi in a personal interview in Salogra on January 10, 1986 in the complex of the Parvatiya Adim Jāti Séwak Sangh from 14.00 hours till 19.00 hours. Also see: Coldstream, W., Foreign Department, Native States, No. 19, 1894, Para 34, p. 14, for Gānwsar Bégār; and Ibid, Paras 35-36, p. 14, for Batrauli Bégār.

[251] Personal interview with Mr T.S. Negi, 1986; corroborated in full by Negi Amar Singh, head of the Poāri Wazir family in a separate personal interview.

[252] Coldstream, W., 1894, Chapter II, Para 19, Pp 19-20; Gazetteer, 1911, Pp 74-75.

(S) Jakat Choudry, payment for servants of Zakat contractors. This pay was recovered by 'Phant' from the cultivators;
(T) Heru, state gamekeeper's pay, recovered from the villagers;
(U) Darai Rāmpur, expenses for the musk men;
(V) Cholti, kārdārs' and wazirs' money levied on cultivators;
(W) Muri, muri grain by the people, in grain;
(X) Indrangnan, cash, Rupees 1 to 4 realized from cultivators;
(Y) Rasaiki, expenses of Sarāhan temples, taken in cash;and
(Z) Chhélu, small goat given for Sarāhan temple.

"The above articles appeared of very little value, but the amount really collected by the officials was practically unlimited. Moreover, there was no proper supervision...for the purpose of checking oppression on the subjects. The value of the articles collected by the officials as their share amounted to twice or thrice as much as that collected for the state as karāhads. When the state officials went to any village for the collection of revenues and the 18 karāhads, each of them was accompanied by about 15 or 20 followers, called piādās (peons) who in their turn collected something from the subjects as their share in addition...They also extracted from each cultivator separately their food expenses etc. The cultivators were consequently obliged to complain against the management of the state to the Deputy Commissioner. With the consent of the subjects an order was accordingly issued in 1851 for the introduction of a new system of management".[253] Thus began the first attempt at land reform, for it was very much that, in-as-much-as it was sought to rationalize revenue collection by recording land holdings, estimating produce and trying to determine titles to land, albeit indirectly. This step began an era in which seven Settlements took place within a period of 74 years.

2.B.4 Era of Settlements: Halting Modernization

Settlement operations were not motivated by philanthrophy or compassion for the oppressed. They were undertaken to modify the revenue collection system so as to render it capable of estimating incomes of tax payers, leading to stable tax revenue proceeds. It was expected that tax revenue would increase as a result. Also, it was used as a political weapon to curb the traditional rights of collection of the wazirs and their positions of power. The fact that Settlements had to be modified so frequently between 1854 A.D. and 1928 A.D. shows that they provoked resistance, fueled by the wazirs who rightly perceived these operations as an attack on their privileges. Table 2.1 gives the fluctuations caused in the assessment of revenue and cesses by these Settlements. The changes wrought by this succession of Settlements are shown graphically. We can now observe the halting trend of reform by briefly examining the main features of each effort, never losing sight of the fact that this process led a century later to a better system of recording of titles to land, thus clearing the way for the introduction of an institutional credit framework.

2.B.4.1 Shām Lāl's Settlement: Quickly Annulled

The first summary settlement of Chini Tahsil was conducted by Munshi Shām Lāl in 1851-52 A.D., with Wazir Mansukh Das of Poāri as co-supervisor. Village to village registers of fields (khasrās) were prepared, with each field being consecutively surveyed and numbered but "surveys made under such an arrangement could not be relied on and considered altogether correct. When khasrā was ready, a khéwat was then prepared in which all the numbers of each owner's fields were shown in the same order as in the khasrā, and thus the total of each person's land was ascertained".[254]

[253] Coldstream, W., 1894, Para 20, p. 20; Ibid, Para 8, Pp 2-3.

[254] Copy of an order (Rubekār), dated 13th. December 1851 issued by Mr Edwards, Para 21, p. 20, in: Foreign Department, Native States, Nos. 18-22, January 1894.

Table 2.1: Settlements in Bushahr State, 1854-1928 A.D.

S	*Year*	*Name Associated*	*Cash*	*Cesses*	*Total*
1	xxxx	Nobody known	7,809	*,***	7,809*
2	1854	Munshi Shām Lāl	16,655	2,664	19,319
3	1856	Lord William Hay	10,797	1,728	12,525
4	1859	Mr G. Barnes	7,809	*,***	7,809*
5	1876	Mr J.W. MacNabb	12,892	1,363	14,225
6	1894	Raghunāth Singh	10,422	2,593	13,015
7	1928	Wazir Chaturbhuj	17,257	4,314	21,571

Legend: Symbol xxxx means the years before 1854 A.D.,

Symbol **** means that the cesses were paid in kind and not in cash. They were paid in the form of 18 karāhads.

Symbol * with the total value means that the cash equivalent of the 18 karāhads has not been added to it since such value had not been calculated.

Code: S = serial number, Year = year of Settlement in A.D., Name Associated = name of person responsible for the Settlement, Cash = cash revenue.

All revenue values are in Rupees.

A statement was prepared showing the produce of each field. The total value of this produce was fixed at Rs 11,854. The 18 karāhads were abolished. The system of bégār was abolished and a new system introduced under which the state had to pay for any service required, @ Rs 2 per month to a peon (chharya); @ Rs 1-12-00 to a messenger (dāgri or piādā) and @ Rs 1-08-00 to a coolie (athwārā). If any one could not pay his revenue in coin, he could give instead grain worth that amount, calculated at the Rāmpur bāzār rate. The revenue was distributed over the owners' holdings according to the means of each asāmi or cultivator. If the revenue was not paid on a fixed day, it was all exacted from the Zaildār (Dashaungi) of the circle, who afterwards realized it from those in arrears by a civil suit if they did not pay up voluntarily. All the agriculturists of a ghodi were made jointly responsible for the payment of revenues of that ghodi. This was one step higher than even the mahālwāri system of dealing with the peasants. In the latter, the state dealt with "estates which could mean villages represented by their headmen or various types of zamindars".[255] In Bushahr, a ghodi consisted of not just one village but of at least 5 to 8 villages which were, however, generally all under one Lambardār. Hence the entire ghodi was taken as the unit of revenue collection because of its being under one and the same Lambardār, rather than each village. In spite of the fact that no attempt was made at giving any sort of protection to tenants-at-will by determining their rights to the land tilled by them, the abolition of the 18 karāhads plus imposition of a cash assessment limited the scope of the wazirs and their minions for exploitation. They did not remain passive spectators in the face of this development but reacted strongly and got this Settlement cancelled within two years.

They had well founded reasons for whipping up opposition to the proposed money Settlement. Even at the time when orders had been issued for a new Settlement (in 1851), it was mentioned that the subjects of Bushahr State had enquired "*as to who was responsible for*

[255] Rothermund, D., 1978, p. 36. For more information about the Mahālwāri System, please see: Baden Powell: Land Systems, Vol. II, p. 531 ff. (As cited in the footnote by Prof. D. Rothermund.)

GRAPH 2.1

CASH REVENUE VARIATION AFTER SETTLEMENTS IN BUSHAHR 1854–1928

1854=SHAM LAL, 1856=LORD HAY, 1859=BARNES, 1876=MACNABB, 1894=TIKKA RAGHUNATH SINGH, 1928=CHATURBHUJ WERE THE PERSONS RESPONSIBLE FOR THESE SETTLEMENT OPERATIONS

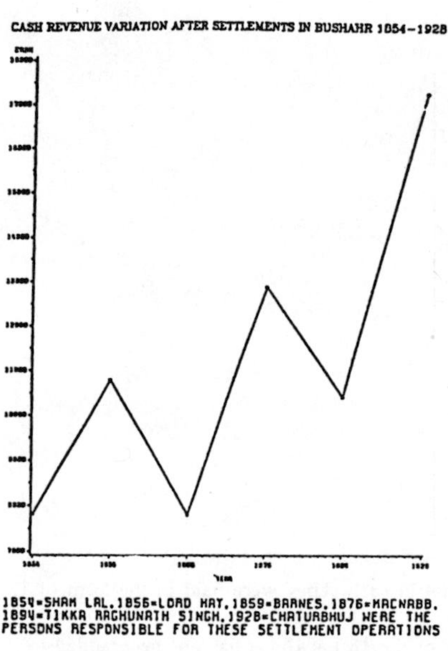

GRAPH 2.3

TOTAL REVENUE VARIATION AFTER SETTLEMENTS IN BUSHAHR 1854–1928

GRAPH 2.2

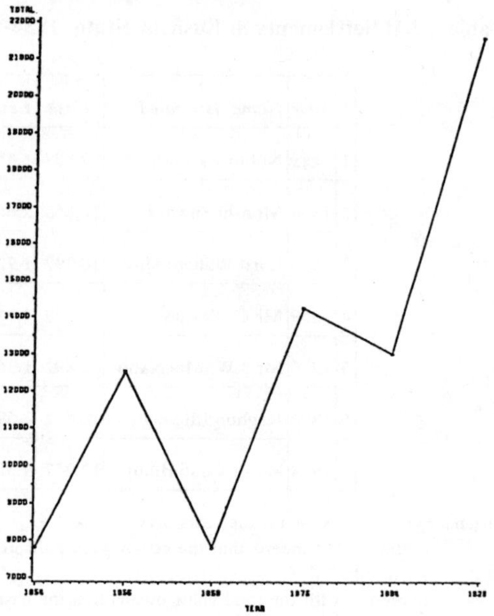

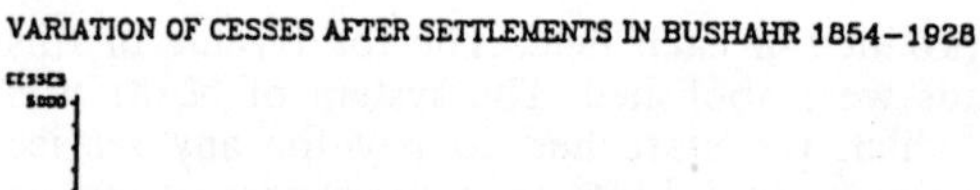

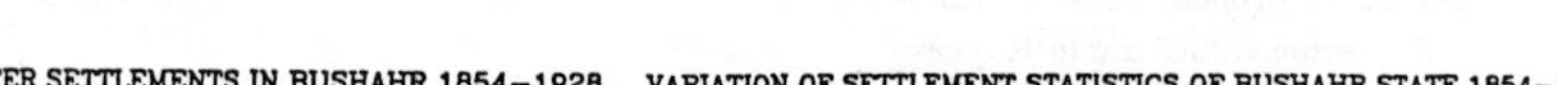

VARIATION OF CESSES AFTER SETTLEMENTS IN BUSHAHR 1854–1928

GRAPH 2.4

VARIATION OF SETTLEMENT STATISTICS OF BUSHAHR STATE, 1854–1928

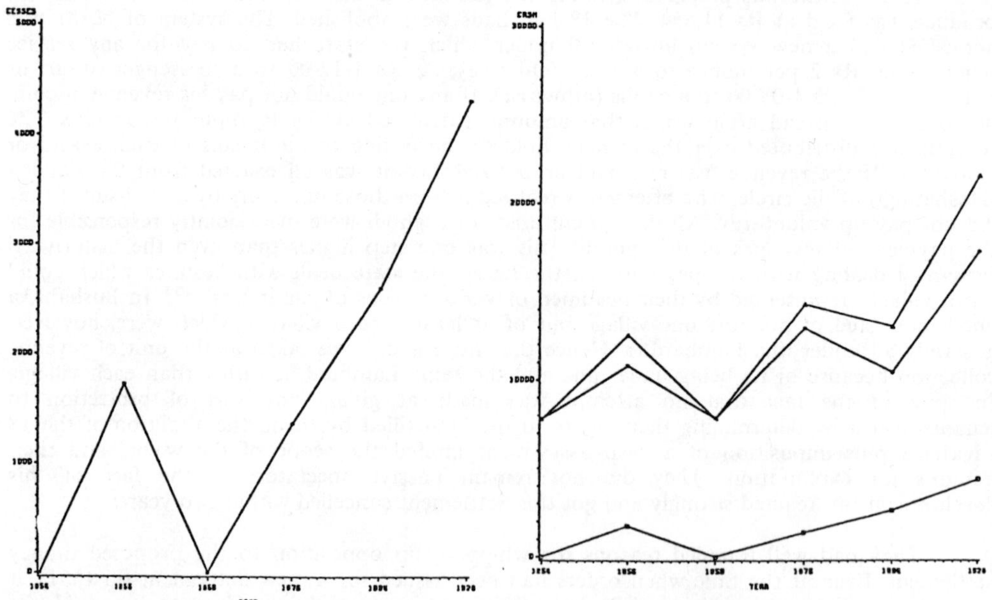

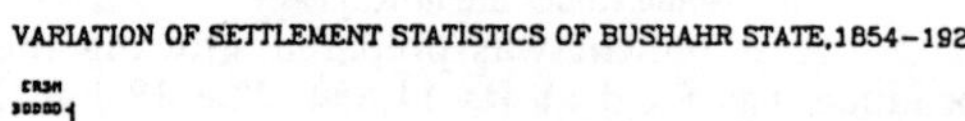

1854 = Munshi Sham Lal's Settlement, 1856 = Lord William Hay's Settlement, 1859 = G. Barnes's Settlement, 1876 = J.W. MacNabb's Settlement, 1894 = Tikka Raghunath Singh's Settlement, 1928 = Wazir Chaturbhuj's Settlement. All years are in A.D.

the loss which might accrue by the new management. After giving this request due consideration, it was ordered that a copy of the order be communicated to the state officials (Motamids) with the object of their explaining it to the agriculturist, that any loss which might result from the new management would be borne by the state, and that the English Government would have nothing to do with it; also that all the revenue of the country under the new management would be paid into the state treasury at the credit of the state".[256]

This shows that people were apprehensive about suffering losses as a consequence of the introduction of a money assessment. They were not used to a money economy but to barter. They were not, as made out by an English administrator,[257] ignorant and barbarous. They had the means to pay in kind but not in cash. It was not that they could not understand the difference between paying less in cash and more in kind. It was a question of availability of the means to pay, which existed in kind but not in cash. They were not defiant subjects who created difficulties about paying their dues. They had been paying their dues to the wazirs who had been collecting more than the specified amounts. The cultivators wanted an end to this extortion, but not a change to a money assessment where they could be even more liable to oppression by the wazirs in case of default in payment of revenue.

The wazirs were able to play on this anxiety and rouse opposition to the assessment, not out of considerations of solidarity with the cultivators but out of a desire to have a greater margin of extortion. They were the ones in active contact with the cultivators. They fanned pubic apprehensions against the money assessment so that petitions were sent to Lord William Hay, Superintendent, Hill States at Simla for a revision of the assessment. This combination of public apprehensions and the wazirs' self-interest proved so potent that Munshi Shām Lāl's Settlement had to be cancelled within two years.

This Settlement had aroused strong public apprehension on another point. "No one was authorized to mortgage or transfer his land to another without sanction of the state. It was therefore ordered that if any land was mortgaged or sold to another without permission the transaction was to be considered illegal, and not to be recognized by the court of law. In case of dispute such a transfer of land was to be considered as null and void. But this rule was never put into force. The people are up to this time mortgaging and selling their landed property to others".[258] Here again, the Settlement had struck at long-established practice by seeking to replace it with legalistic procedures. Cultivators had been mortgaging and selling their land even without formal title. The fact that the ban on such transactions was not actually enforced was no consolation. The wazirs were able to fan public fears by saying that their cherished customary rights of mortgage and sale were under attack. The ban could be enforced unless they pressed for a return to the erstwhile system.

2.B.4.2 Lord Hay's Settlement: Equally Transient

This Settlement was an attempt to respond to the petitions presented by the zamindārs of Kinnaur/Bushahr. New rates were fixed in 1856 A.D. at a conference held in Simla at which the Rājā and representatives of the people were present. The new rate of assessment was reduced by Lord Hay, Superintendent, Hill States, from 25% of the gross produce, as had been fixed by Munshi Shām Lāl, to 15%.[259] The wazirs were required to pay into the state

[256] Foreign Department, Native States, 1894, No. 21, Ch. II, Para 20, p. 20.

[257] No. 19, Chapter II, Para 12, p. 4, in: Ibid.

[258] Chapter II, Para 24, p. 21, in: Ibid.

[259] Brief Abstract of the Order dated 12th October 1856 issued by Lord William Hay, Para 27, p. 21; Fiscal History of Bashahr State, Para 10, p. 3, both in: Foreign Department, Native States, File No. 2, Nos. 18-22,

treasury every month whatever revenue they collected from the agriculturists and were "not to realize a single pie more than the fixed revenue; also they should not allow their servants to oppress the people in order to get money from them".[260]

The usual opposition to money assessment surfaced and the Rājā "professed to approve the money assessment but secretly encouraged the wazirs to oppose it".[261] He used the outbreak of the Mutiny in 1857 to restore the former system of collection of revenue. He justified it by saying that the "principal god of the country had expressed an opinion that the cholera which was then raging was solely attributable to the money assessment".[262]

This Settlement had still tried to stick to the principle of a money assessment and sought to alleviate public apprehensions by reducing the rates of assessment rather than conceding the fact that the idea of a money assessment was convenient from a British point of view but not from a Kinnaura point-of-view. The British were not concerned with the welfare of what they called the 'natives' but with the annual tribute paid to them by Bushahr. A revenue system based on cash payment made it easier for them to extract their pound-of-flesh. What would they have done with grain, apricot oil and sheep? The money assessment was a measure of British self-interest being imposed in the name of administrative efficiency. They sought to convince the cultivators that such a system was in the latter's own interest since it reduced the capacity of the wazirs for exploitation. That the cultivators were not convinced by such reasoning can be seen from the sustained opposition that greeted these money assessments.

The Rājā realized that the British were using money assessment as the thin end of the wedge for installing officials under their own tutelage directly into the administration of Bushahr State. His own powers would correspondingly be under closer scrutiny and interference. It would also be more difficult for him to delay payment of the annual tribute if his revenues were all in cash and could thereby be closely audited. Such an audit ran into difficulties if the revenues were at least partly in kind. The Rājā could not, however, express his resentment overtly. He was afraid that the British could force him to abdicate or even put his state under direct rule from Simla citing his misgovernment. Lord Dalhousie's policy of bringing more and more princely states under direct British rule was too recent to have been forgotten. The Rājā sought to achieve his ends of sidelining the money assessment by covertly encouraging his wazirs to whip up sentiment against it. He knew that they opposed it anyway out of their own self-interest. To avoid having the British holding him directly responsible, he used the ploy of the devta's wrath to escape responsibility. At the same time he played upon his subjects' religious beliefs to make them totally opposed to a money assessment since the devta favoured a return to the old system. Both systems co-existed in confusion for some time. In August 1858 the zamindārs petitioned the Superintendent, Simla Hill States, on 11 points, one of which was that the old Settlement should be reverted to.

2.B.4.3 Barnes's Settlement: Slightly Longer Lasting

This Settlement was done on behalf of the zamindārs who submitted the above-mentioned petition. British official despatches sought, as usual, to describe popular grievances in the following words: "*The arrangements introduced by Lord W. Hay remained in force up to 1858 A.D., when the zamindārs, as usual, raised a cry against it, at the instigation of some of the state*

January 1894.

260 Lord Hay, Ibid, Clause (8), p. 23, in: Ibid.

261 Ibid, Para 10, p. 3; in: Ibid.

262 Ibid.

officials".[263]

Barnes did see the justification in the arguments put forth to him by the cultivators of Bushahr but it was difficult for him to formally concede the fact that the indigenous system was better suited to the needs of the area. To convince his superiors he created a smokescreen of denigration of the indigenous system, behind which he conceded the demand of the zamindārs for a return to the former system of payment of revenue. He knew quite well that after the events of 1857 the British Indian authorities, now under the British Crown, were in no mood to set aside a princely ruler and directly administer Bushahr. Such a step could have caused strong resentment in all the Simla Hill States. The Rājā of Bushahr had a special status, being considered of pure Rājpūt stock and from the oldest ruling house in the area. The British authorities were left with no choice but to approve of Barnes's decisions.

Barnes had got the zamindārs to sign an agreement on October 12, 1858 in writing. He introduced the new management from November 2, 1859 A.D. The zamindārs committed in writing, that as their objections had been accepted, they agreed to *"pay in future the usual revenues and karāhads which were paid hitherto. If they will not be sufficient to cover the expenses of the state, the deficiency will be made up by the zamindārs"* who would have *"no objection to do the bégār service to the state"*.[264] It was also decided that:[265]

"(1) a memo be given to the zamindārs showing the amount of the old revenue, and that the wazirs should enquire where the revenue has been fixed low, and where it is high, and then they should equalize it everywhere;

(2) when any lands are mortgaged or sold (or when there is any unclaimed land) the revenues of those lands are payable by the mortgagor or seller, although the lands have altogether gone out of his possession. He is only caught hold of for the purpose of collecting the revenues, and the person actually in possession of the land and getting the produce therefrom is not made to pay the revenue. In future, all the revenues due on mortgaged or sold lands should be collected from those in possession of the lands. At all times the person holding the lands will be responsible for payment of their revenues. The wazirs will be responsible for seeing that except those jāgirdārs who hold māfi lands, no land escapes from the payment of their fixed revenue (thek bandi); māfidārs are exempt from the payment of karāhads. Although they too, have to pay the usual revenues (thek bandi). The wazirs should in future see that the fixed sum is paid by the māfidārs as shown in the register. They should collect it from their jāgirs also every year and for each crop, without hearing any objections on the part of the subjects. Only those holding sanads (certificates) granted by the previous and present Rājās for their exemption from the payment of fixed revenue will be exempted from their life from such payments. No one else will be exempted".

The principle that exemption from liability to thekbandi was for life only was here introduced.

In April 1859 Mr Barnes, then Superintendent, Simla Hill States, visited Bushahr.[266] People represented to him that their assets consisted of "their crops and their flocks, which owing to the want of markets, they could not readily convert into cash. Money was a scarce commodity except along the line of trade, and their dealings among themselves were almost limited to exchange".[267] They could more easily pay partly in cash, partly in kind rather than

[263] Para 28, Chapter II, p. 23, in: Ibid.

[264] Para 29, Chapter II, No. 21, p. 23, in: Ibid.

[265] Para 29, Ibid, p. 24, in: Ibid.

[266] G. Barnes is a very famous name in the Simla Hills as a revenue officer.

a smaller sum in money. Conceding their demand, Barnes observed self-righteously that the system was "avowedly rude and cumbrous...But...a barbarous race of mountaineers in a remote and secluded part of the Himalaya is not able to discriminate correctly between conflicting systems of revenue...Add to this...the imperfect circulation of coin, the strong attachment of the people to the old system, the opposition of all classes, and it will be seen that Bashahr is not ready for a money assessment; or if such a system must be introduced, we must appoint our own officers and entirely sweep away the native agency".[268] Collection in cash and kind was reverted to. Expediency triumphed over pious professions of better organization under the British. No mention was made at all of protection of tenancy rights or the introduction of an institutional credit system. The merry-go-round continued.

2.B.4.4 MacNabb's Settlement: Unsuccessful

Following the orders in 1874 A.D. from J.W. MacNabb, Superintendent Hill States, Simla, for a new Settlement, this operation was carried out under the supervision of the wazirs, assisted by six respectable men from the six khunds or remote parganas of the state. It was also known as the Settlement of "Saṁbat Teṅtis". Cash payment was enhanced 2.5 times, from Rs 5,372 of the earlier Settlement. Only five karāhads were retained. The value of these five payments in kind was in each case calculated and the option given of paying it in kind, or in the fixed cash equivalent. However, the jāgirdārs did not confine themselves to collection of only the permitted five karāhads but gradually reimposed all the other 13 karāhads on their tenants - "a striking instance of the unblushing rapacity of this privileged class".[269] The British bemoaned the action of the jāgirdārs but did not do anything effective to curb it.

2.B.4.5 Tikka Raghunāth Singh's Settlement: First Regular Settlement

Under the supervision of Tikka Raghunāth Singh, the first regular Settlement was carried out in 1890-1891 A.D. in Chini Tahsil by Miāṅ Durgā Singh. The reasons for this Settlement were as much political as economic. "All the Wazirs in Bashahr were, in practice, more or less hereditary. Owing to the intemperate habits and general want of capacity of the Rājā, they gradually usurped great power, and in 1885 they had practically parcelled out the state among themselves. Then a great change took place. The Rājā was set aside, and he may be said to have abdicated. The management of the state was made over to the heir apparent, Tika Raghunath Singh...The power of the Wazirs was greatly reduced, if not entirely abolished, and the power of the central government was restored".[270]

Settlement operations were an instrument in this struggle for supremacy. "Soon after the Tika had taken over the administration of the state he commenced a regular settlement. This settlement, among other purposes, has been used as a means of depressing and controlling the Wazirs. For these Wazirs are the chief jagirdars, and the Tika has kept the enquiry into jāgirs in his own hands. He has not yet decided which are to be maintained and which are to be resumed and he is in no hurry to do so. By keeping the matter in suspense and by dealing with it piecemeal he conceives that he maintains a powerful hold upon the

[267] Extract from Letter No. 122, dated 30th April, 1859 from G. Barnes, No.19, Para 12, p. 3, in: Ibid.

[268] Ibid, No. 19, Para 15, p. 5, in: Ibid.

[269] Draft Settlement Report of Nichār Tahsil, Unpublished, 1985, Pp 30-31.

[270] No. 8, Para 3, p. 3, Memorandum by R.G. Thomson Esquire, Superintendent, Hill States, Simla on the state of affairs in the Dodra Kwār Pargana of the Bashahr State - dated Camp Sangri (Bashahr) 14th November 1897, attached to No. 7, Confidential Letter no. 2290 dated 20th November 1897 from Idem to the Chief Secretary to Government, Punjab, in: Printed K.-Ws, Foreign Department, Native States, Nos. 29-47, File No. 3, June 1898.

jagirdars. In the meanwhile, as far as possible, jagir revenue is collected directly by the state, and payments, on account, are made to the jagirdars out of the state treasury".[271]

The survey was carried out in accordance with the principles then prevalent in Punjab. A field map (Shajrā Kishtwār) and a standing record (Misal Haqiyat) were prepared. However, assigned lands (Muāfis) were not scrutinized and the village administration paper (Wājib-ul-Arz) was not prepared. No copy of this Settlement Report has ever been found. This first regular Settlement had several flaws. The field map and standing record were not duly signed by any officer. Popular sentiment had been incited against measurement (paimāish) to such an extent that the Settlement Superintendent was prevented from inspecting revenue estates to judge assessable capacity. Be that as it may, athwārā was reduced from six months to one month. All the karāhads were abolished and the landowners granted inferior proprietory (Adnā Malqiyat) rights. These gave them leeway in mortgage and transfer of land.[272]

Even after this Settlement, proprietory right "as it is recognized in British territory does not exist in Bashahr, but at the same time so long as a zamindar cultivates his lands and pays his revenue, restrictions on alienation excepted, his status differs but little from that of a proprietor. Possession is the measure of right. Joint rights exist in the village site and the grazing area only. There is no shamilat deh, as the unappropriated waste is the property of the state, subject to the rights of user enjoyed from time immemorial by the zamindars. The hay fields are held in severalty, and are just as valuable as cultivated land. Waste land when broken up belongs to the man who breaks it up".[273] De facto ownership of land was not, however, de jure title to land. Legally, the cultivator could not pledge as security what did not formally belong to him.

2.B.4.6 Chaturbhuj's Settlement: Not Thorough Enough

After years of procrastination,[274] Settlement work was begun in 1926 A.D. under the supervision of Wazir Chaturbhuj, designated as Settlement Officer. The patwaris' copy of the field map (Shajrā Parchā) of the Settlement of 1894 had become so soiled, worn out and spoilt through repeated use as to be largely useless for practical purposes. Fresh copies could not be prepared from original maps (Musāwis) because land grants made subsequently had not at all been incorporated into those maps. Since large areas of state-owned waste lands had been encroached upon, a substantial increase in land revenue was tacitly anticipated even without enhancement of the revenue rate. The emphasis was on increasing land revenue rather than protecting the title of the cultivator to land.

2.B.4.7 Present Settlement Operations: Not Yet Concluded

A general re-assessment of land revenue in Kinnaur was ordered by the Financial Commissioner (Revenue), H.P., on November 23, 1976.[275] Special revision of the existing

[271] Para 4, Ibid, in Ibid.

[272] E.B. Steedman's Report On The Assessment Of Tahsil Chini, 1896, Para 13, p. 3.

[273] Draft Settlement Report, Unpublished, 1985, Pp 30-31.

[274] Ibid.

[275] Please see: Notification No. 17-4/70-Rev. II, dated Simla the 23rd November 1976, of the Revenue Department, Government of Himāchal Pradesh, issued by Mr P.K. Mattoo, I.A.S., Financial Commissioner-cum-Secretary (Revenue).

record of rights and estate formation was also ordered.[276] Preparatory work for survey and settlement was begun in early 1977. Survey work in Nichār Tahsil was almost over by 29-11-1980[277] but preparation of the revenue record had not even begun. Survey operations are now almost over but the Assessment Report in respect of Nichār Tahsil was completed only on September 2, 1985. Till February 1986 assessment reports were not ready in respect of Kālpa and Pooh Tahsils.[278] Even the Report for Nichār Tahsil had not yet been approved by the government.

Frequent Settlement operations between 1851 and 1928 did not lead to the creation of a reliable record of rights, rather they only highlighted the absence of such record. As so rightly pointed out by Prof. D. Rothermund, "in most parts of India a reliable record of rights was conspicuous by its absence".[279] To the extent that rights in land were recorded during revenue settlement this record "was meant only to fix the responsibility for the payment of revenue, if it also provided a certain security of land titles this was purely accidental. The revenue record was a record of land and not of titles. A detailed and up-to-date revenue record was maintained only in those parts of Northern India where proprietory village communities had been assessed jointly".[280] Kinnaur was only slowly brought into this cadre. Revenue records began to reflect the record of rights better after 1953 when the first major land reform legislation was passed in Himāchal Pradesh. Even so, land which had been "transferred to moneylenders would still be registered under the previous owner's name, the moneylender was not keen to have his name in the revenue list and the previous owner often harboured the illusion that as long as his name was still recorded by the government he may hope to recover his land after all which in many cases he continued to cultivate as a tenant of the moneylender".[281] Examples of this phenomenon were found during field research in late 1985 and early 1986. Bābu Narayan Singh and Shyam Saran Negi, both large landholder/moneylenders of village Chini, had obtained cultivating possession of lands from defaulters of loans without getting the entries made formally in their names in the revenue record. Jawāhar Singh of village Rupi had also obtained actual possession of plots of land as compensation for default by his debtors without having the transactions recorded in the revenue record. Formal recording of such land transfers was avoided to pre-empt difficulties with the Ceiling on Land Holdings Act, 1972.[282] Moneylenders in Kinnaur generally belong to large landholding families whose holdings could exceed the limits of 10 acres of double-crop land under assured irrigation, 15 acres of single-crop land under assured irrigation and 70 acres of land of other classes in Kinnaur[283] if they kept on formally having titles of land accruing to them in lieu of repayment of loans recorded in their names in the revenue record. What mattered to them was the right of user on such lands and not the formal title.

[276] Notification Ibid.

[277] Draft Settlement Report of Nichār Tahsil, Unpublished, 1985, p. 72.

[278] Information given in person by Mr I.S. Chandel, Assistant Settlement Officer, Kinnaur in his office in Sañjauli near Simla on January 6, 1986.

[279] Rothermund, D.: The Record of Rights in British India, p. 443, in: The Indian Economic and Social History Review, Vol. VIII, No. 4, 1971, Pp 443-461.

[280] Ibid.

[281] Ibid, p. 444.

[282] Please see Section 2.B.5.5 of this chapter.

[283] Sections 4(1) and 4(2), H.P. Ceiling On Land Holdings Act, 1972.

Rām Singh of village Tāngling pointed out that moneylenders in the area around his village obtained possession of lands in case of default on repayment, but did not bother to get the change recorded in revenue papers.[284] Duni Chand s/o Kālu Rām of Chini explained how his grandfather Jiunar had taken a loan from Negi Bhoop Singh of the same village and had subsequently lost possession of his land to the latter without any record in writing.[285] The prevalence of such transactions was common in the Hangrang valley. The account books (bahi khātās) of Dandub Rām, Sāhukār of Pooh village, showed at least 15 instances where possession of land had been transferred to him without any entry having been made in the record-of-rights. Thus this phenomenon stretched from the Rupi/Chhota Kamba area of lower Kinnaur to Poāri, Chini, Sangla areas of middle Kinnaur to Pooh, Hangrang areas of upper Kinnaur, in short all over the district. Actual inspection of Jamābandis (record-of-rights registers) for the villages named in the preceding lines showed that transfers of possession had not been recorded therein even though it was common knowledge that such transactions had taken place. Because of this inseparable lien between moneylending, title to land and record of rights, it is relevant to very briefly review post-1948 land reforms in Kinnaur.

2.B.5 Land Reform Measures since 1948: Largely Cosmetic

The inadequacy of land records was felt keenly after independence when land reforms were sought to be introduced. It hampered the work of abolition of the zamindāri system in Northern India. This task of abolition necessitated the stepping in of the government as collector of rent and revenue in areas in which this work had formerly been done by the zamindārs.[286] A realistic agrarian policy was "almost impossible in view of this lack of an accurate record of rights, not to speak of a record which would distinguish between ownership and tenure so as to provide information about the actual units of cultivation".[287] Land revenue which had at one time been the mainstay of state finance was now relegated to a secondary role. "The land reform measures of independent India were undertaken without any reference to the land revenue system which was allowed to decay further until some states actually abolished land revenue".[288] Himāchal Pradesh was no exception to this diminution in the role of land revenue as a means of state finance. The latest Settlement operations in Kinnaur are not so much an effort to increase land revenue as to record more accurately the rights of tillers of land. With the introduction of institutional credit on a major scale, such a record of rights was badly needed. The chain of events of land reform begins really in 1953.

2.B.5.1 The H.P. Abolition of Big Landed Estates and Land Reforms Act, 1953

Prior to the passage of the Abolition of Big Landed Estates Act, 1953, certain land reform measures had already prepared the ground for this major piece of legislation. The Punjab Tenants (Security of Tenures) Act, 1950, had been extended to H.P. in 1951. It imposed a ceiling of 250 bighās on a landlord's holding.[289] Tenants, especially other than occupancy tenants or tenants for a fixed term, were given security of tenure for at least four years.

[284] Personal interview in Tāngling, December 9, 1985, 20.15 hours.

[285] Personal interview, Chini village, December 9, 1985, 09.15 hours.

[286] Rothermund, D., 1971, p. 460.

[287] Ibid.

[288] Ibid, p. 461; also Rothermund, D., 1978, Pp 41-45.

[289] Gazetteer, 1971, p. 249; Also, Basu, A.R.: Tribal Development Programmes and Administration in India (With special reference to Himāchal Pradesh), New Delhi: National Book Organization, I edn., 1985, p. 93.

Tenants ejected between May 1-30, 1950 were entitled to restoration of possessions.[290] The Punjab Tenancy (Himāchal Pradesh Amendment) Act, 1952, added Section 25-A which fixed maximum rents chargeable from tenants at 1/4th the produce. Tenants were given the right of pre-emption in respect of their tenancies by the H.P. Tenants (Rights Restoration) Act, 1952.

The H.P. Abolition of Big Landed Estates and Land Reforms Act, 1953 "was the first major land reforms legislation. The Act governed the law relating to tenancies in agricultural lands and also contained provisions of land reforms of a far-reaching importance".[291] Landowners could resume land for personal cultivation up to a maximum of five acres, subject to the proviso that no tenant could be evicted from more than 1/4th of the area held by him. The term for exercise of this right was originally fixed at one year from the date of commencement of the Act, but was later extended to March 1, 1956 and then to September 1, 1956. All rights, titles and interests of landowners holding land in excess of Rs 125 of annual land revenue, and which was with tenants, were vested in the state government which could transfer these in favour of cultivating tenants in lieu of payment of nominal compensation. Tenants with rights of occupancy could not be ejected from their tenancies except if they rendered land in their possession unfit for the purpose for which it was originally held; or for failing to cultivate the land according to local custom; or for sub-letting land without the consent of the landlord. Rights of widows, minors, armed forces personnel, students and prisoners were specially protected.

The operation of this Act in Kinnaur till February 28, 1966 showed the following results:

(1) Total no. of tenants to acquire proprietory rights = 8,302;
(2) Total no. of tenants having acquired proprietory rights = 1,161;
(3) Area involved for granting proprietory rights = 238 acres;
(4) Total no. of landowners affected by Sec. 27(1) = 10;
(5) Total area vested in the state government = 375 acres;
(6) Total no. of tenants = 2,785;
(7) Total no. of tenants involved in proprietory rights = 1,996;
(8) Total no. of tenants awaiting proprietory rights on 30-11-65 = 789;
(9) Amount of compensation realized from the tenants = Rs 18,064;
(10) Amount of compensation to be realized from tenants = Rs 6,333;
(11) Amount of compensation to be paid to the landowners in lieu of their land vested in the state government (paid to five landowners only) = Rs 21,029;
(12) Amount of compensation due to the landowners = Rs 5,476.

(I) Big landowners affected in Kinnaur = (a) Devta Mahéshras, Sungra;
(b) Devta Mahéshras, Chagāoṅ;
(c) Devta Mahéshras, Bhāba;
(d) Devta Badrināth, Kāmru;
(e) Devta Bairiṅg Nāgjee, Sangla;

All the affected landowners were village gods. The Rājā had conferred land holdings upon them so that they would remain his allies and act as agents of legitimation of royal authority. In addition to the lands received from the Rājā, the village gods were also sometimes gifted lands by rich devotees in gratitude for having received some boon. wazirs also gifted them lands in order to ape the behaviour-pattern of the Rājā and to bask in his reflected legitimacy. More information about the role of devtas as landholders is given in Chapter VII where their moneylending operations are also discussed.

[290] Gazetteer, 1971, p. 249.

[291] Basu, A.R., 1985, Pp 93-94.

Table 2.2: Landowners Affected by the Land Reforms Act, 1953

sn	*Landowner*	*Adclsp*	*Alwt*	*Taiot*
1	Devta Maheshwar, Sungra	2745-17	54-17	2800-14
2	Devta Maheshwar,Chgaon	1669-19	36-05	1706-04
3	Devta Maheshwar, Bhāba	1030-08	30-06	1060-14
4	Devta Badrināth, Kāmru	1245-05	741-06	1986-11
5	Devta Nāgjee, Sangla	2421-04	22-03	2443-07
6	Total	9112-13	884-17	9997-10

Legend: sn = Serial Number,
Adclsp = area declared surplus and ownership rights thereof granted to tenants, Alwt = area left with temple, Taiot = total area in ownership of temple.
All areas are in Bighās-Biswās.

(II) Area declared surplus as a result of the Act: This area is shown in Table 2.2 .

(III) Numbers of tenants acquiring rights of ownership from big landowners:
(a) From Devta Mahéshras, Sungra = 1,253;
(b) From Devta Mahéshras, Chagāon = 226;
(c) From Devta Mahéshras, Bhāba = 188;
(d) From Devta Badrināth, Kāmru = 190;
(e) From Devta Bairing Nāgjee, Sangla = 427;
Total = 2,284.

Landowners' could keep the best land under their share of resumption. Measures for the protection of tenancies presumed that such rights were at least recorded in the revenue record. This was not always the case. As aleady seen, Settlement operations in Kinnaur till 1948 had not been thorough affairs and the records of right resulting as a consequence were full of lacunae. This was sought to be remedied by the next major legislation.

2.B.5.2 The H.P. Land Revenue Act, 1954

This Act laid down a comprehensive regulation of the entire land revenue system and revenue collection machinery. Chapter II gives the classes of revenue officers (Section 7) and their powers (Section 11); outlines the administrative control of revenue officers (Sections 12-13); procedure of appeal (Sections 14-15); review (Section 16) and revision (Section 17). Chapter IV deals with the record of rights and annual records. Section 32 is extremely important, stating that there shall be a record-of-rights for each estate [Section 32(1)]. In Section 32(2), the documents constituting such record are defined as:[292]

"*(a) statements showing, so far as may be practicable:-*
(i) the persons who are landowners, tenants or assignees of land revenue receiving any of the rents, profits in the estate, or who are entitled to the produce of the estate or to occupy land therein;

[292] Thākur, Ravinder (Advocate): The Himāchal Pradesh Land Revenue Act, 1954 With Rules, Simla: Saraswati Publishing House, 1982, p. 37.

(ii) the nature and extent of the interests of these persons and the conditions and liabilities attaching thereto;
(iii) the rent, land revenue, rates, cesses or other payments due from and to each of these persons and to the government;
(b) a statement of customs respecting rights and liabilities in the estate;
(c) a map of the estate; and
(d) such other documents as the Financial Commissioner may, with the previous sanction of the state government prescribe".

Section 33 provides for special revision of the record of rights, under which Settlement operations could be ordered. Section 34 specifies the annual record, including a register of mutations [Section 34(3)]. Chapter IV (Sections 68-101) deals with the collection of land revenue, including coercive processes. These processes for the recovery of dues as arrears of land revenue (henceforth always referred to as the A.L.R.) are of extreme importance for institutional credit givers. This Act laid the foundation on which an institutional credit network could be raised later on. It defined titles to land in the revenue record and installed an elaborate revenue hierarchy. To cater to Kinnaur's being a tribal area with special problems, the alienation of land by tribals to non-tribals was restricted in 1968.

2.B.5.3 The H.P. Transfer of Land (Regulation) Act, 1968

Section 3 of this Act bars Scheduled Tribes' members from transferring interest in any land by way of sale, mortgage, lease, gift, or otherwise to non-tribals, except with the previous permission in writing of the District Collector. Section 5 provides for ejectment of non-tribals after due process of law in case they have acquired the interests of a tribal in land in contravention of the provisions of this Act. Section 9 lays down fines for contraventions of Sections 3 and 5. This Act did succeed to a large extent in preventing a wholesale influx of plainsmen into tribal areas where they acquire monopoly control over business activities. This has been the case with the influx of traders and liquor contractors in the tribal areas of Bastar in Madhya Pradesh; Kolhan area in Bihar and the tribal areas of Orissa. But it has not totally plugged the loophole of such transfer. Any statutory provision can only be as successful as its enforcers and framers care to make it. The provision for lease [Section 3(1)(a)] means that many non-tribal shopkeepers have managed to take land on lease from tribals for carrying on business activities. They are in some cases not even recorded in the revenue papers. They give consumption credit to make themselves indispensable. Tribal debtors are loath to complain against them, lest their channel of consumption credit be choked off. This can have grave consequences just before winter when rations have to be stored up for around four months in advance to cope with the problem of the disruption of communication links due to heavy snowfall.

An unsavoury aspect of the Tribal Land Regulation Act was the scope for corruption that it provided to unscrupulous politicians and officials. The politicians could not directly take action against offenders under this Act but could pressurize officials to either proceed against such non-Kinnauras as did not meet their demands or to abstain from such process in case the demands had been met. The officials proceeded speedily if they were not properly "taken care of". Legal proceedings were slowed down in direct proportion to the pecuniary or other gratification provided. Regular bribes in cash or kind sometimes ensured that violation of this law was either not proceeded against at all or that such proceedings were stalled. The revenue staff were remarkably reluctant to proceed under this Act. The offenders were not poor people who could fearlessly be tackled since they had no political influence. They were moneyed shopkeepers, almost always in alliance with at least one local political faction. By proceeding against them too severely officials risked losing a good source of regular gratification. Attempts made by the D.C. between 1980 and 1983 to enforce this Act stringently ran into opposition from local politicians and obstructive delays from within the Revenue Department. The revenue staff did not want to kill the non-tribal goose that laid the golden eggs! Shopkeepers continue to flout the law or have got their land acquisitions regularized under it through misrepresentation of facts to officials well aware of the actual state of affairs but won over by extra-legal considerations.

An analysis of land transfer mortgages in some major villages of Kinnaur reveals that all the recorded land transfers; by sale, gift or mortgage, were from tribal to tribal.[293] An order dated April 4, 1981, passed by the author in his capacity as the District Collector, Kinnaur District,[294] under Section 5 of the Act under discussion reveals how non-tribal shopkeepers found in possession of land took the plea that they had been resident in Kinnaur from before 1968 when the law came into force. Efforts to genuinely enforce the Act incur the risk of the enforcer's being dragged into political controversies. The resident non-tribals are well-off and are aligned politically to local groups by giving the latter monetary contributions and as providers of credit. They have their tribal borrowers who act as their protagonists in this struggle to cow down the officials genuinely wishing to implement this Act. No case of a non-tribal having been actually evicted under this Act came to notice during field research. Even a casual visitor can notice non-tribal shopkeepers in possession of land for shops along major roads, chiefly along the N.H. 22. The Act is nevertheless a handy sword of Damocles to dangle over the heads of these shopkeepers, without using it too effectively to drive them actually out. The locals need them as credit suppliers.

2.B.5.4 The H.P. Nautor Land Rules, 1968

These rules allowed the grant of government wasteland for purposes such as *horticulture; agriculture, including raising of fodder; growing of vegetables; growing of any special grasses, herbs, shrubs and trees for domestic use or for cash income and dairy farming; construction of any building subservient to agriculture, threshing floor, water mill and water channel; construction of a building for residence; consolidation of holdings and for genuine public purposes like construction of a dharamsālā [Rules 5(a), 5(b), 5(c)(i) to (iv), 5(d), 5(e) and 5(f)].* Land up to 20 bighās could be granted for horticultural and agricultural purposes [Rules 6(i), 6(ii)]. Rule 7 laid down the eligibility conditions, giving preference to owners of less than 10 bighās of land; Scheduled Castes and Scheduled Tribes; serving defence personnel and ex-servicemen. Rule 17 barred legal practitioners from appearing in proceedings under these rules. Under Rule 27-A, for applications received up to December 31, 1963, adverse possession was to be regularized for limits of 30 years, between 10 and 30 years; between 5 and 10 years; and less than 5 years, on rising terms of payment in terms of multiples of land revenue assessed.

These rules have widely been misused, not only in Kinnaur but also in other districts. Cases were found in Kinnaur in which land had been acquired from private owners for public purpose on payment of a certain compensation. This very land had then subsequently been regularized as Nautor (newly broken land) in the names of sons of locally influential political figures at much lower rates of payment. It had resulted in transfer of land from poorer owners to richer owners at lower prices, with the government suffering a loss by paying higher sums as compensation than it obtained for regularization. In another case, an influential politician owning much more than 20 bighās of land was allotted choice government wasteland as Nautor on the false manipulation that he had earlier transferred 5 bighās of his land to his son who was then allotted 15 bighās of government land to bring his holding up to 20 bighās. The father also got allotted 5 bighās to bring his own holding up to the same ceiling of 20 bighās as well. This case was not untypical. Influential people thoroughly misused these Rules with the full connivance of officials. However, some poor people did get lands under the scheme as well. The lands allotted to the latter were for the most part unproductive. They

[293] This data has been copied from field reports sent by the Patwāris of Patwār Circles Pooh, Kānam, Akpa, Thangi, Rupi, Paunda and Chholtu. It was compiled in December 1985 for the author by officials of the Sadar Kānungo Branch of the D.C.'s Office at Kālpa.

[294] Case number 3/80, instituted on 26.06.1980, decided on 04.04.1981.

could nevertheless be pledged as security for obtaining institutional credit. Private credit givers were well aware that the lands being offered in collateral were mostly lands in the kanda which were unproductive. They did not give loans against such security of doubtful value. Institutional lenders, however, were generally devoid of adequate local knowledge and could be made to disburse loans against such unproductive security out of ignorance.

2.B.5.5 The H.P. Ceiling on Land Holdings Act, 1972

This Act specified the highest permissible area for a landowner or a tenant or a mortgagee in possession or partly in one capacity and partly in another of a person or a family consisting of husband, wife and up to three minor children as:-

(a) 10 acres for land under assured irrigation, capable of growing two crops a year;
(b) 15 acres of land under assured irrigation, capable of growing one crop in a year; and
(c) 70 acres for Kinnaur District (and six other areas, all listed in the Act) for land of classes other than described in (a) and (b) above, including land under orchards [Sections 4(1), 4(2)].

The maximum limit for cases where additional units were permitted was fixed at two units. The Wazir family of Poāri was affected by this Act. Proceedings in respect of their estate had still not been finally consigned as late as January 1986 because of appeals and revisions ordered in the case. Figures available in the District Office at Kālpa were as follows:-

1. Total area declared surplus = 8,973 acres;
2. Land allotted out of surplus area = 0.70 acres.

A large portion of the area declared surplus[295] was unfit for allotment, being cliffs and slopes. Nevertheless the figure of 0.70 acres shows what a measly progress has been made in distributing surplus land to needy persons. This much trumpeted measure has hardly brought any benefit to the landless and eligible persons in Kinnaur.

2.B.5.6 The H.P. Tenancy and Land Reforms Act, 1972

This Act was a comprehensive legislation for giving protection to tenants. Occupancy tenants (defined in Sections 3-8) were made landowners vide Section 94. Non-occupancy tenants were also conferred proprietory rights in some cases under Section 104. Under 104(i), landowners could resume up to 1.5 acres of irrigated or 3 acres of unirrigated land under tenancy, for personal cultivation. Section 104(v) gave the tenant the first right of selection of land in case of a dispute and not to the landowner. The provisions of the Act of 1953 were thus reversed in this respect. Non-occupancy tenants were made owners with effect from October 3, 1975. The maximum rent payable by a tenant was fixed. Section 20(1) fixed the maximum rent to be paid by a tenant at 1/4th of the crop produce of any land or the value of such produce. Grass and straw (bhūsa) were not to form part of the produce for the purposes of such calculation. Collection of rent in excess of this ceiling would render the landowner liable to imprisonment of up to six months or a fine of up to Rs 1000 or both, according to Section 20(3). The importance of the role of land as security for loans from institutional sources was being realized. Provisions were made in the Act for safeguarding the interest of institutional lenders. Under Section 104(5), if the land in question was subject to a mortgage debt from a bank, the mortgage debt would be first charge on the amount payable for such land.

[295] These figures have been prepared for the author by Shri Bhim Sain Negi, Superintendent Grade IV, D.C.'s Office, Kālpa in December 1985 from the records of the Land Reforms Branch.

2.B.5.7 Land Allotment Programmes after 1975

Crash programmes for allotment of land to landless and eligible persons were launched during the Emergency in 1975 and 1976. Landless persons were to be allotted 5 bighās of land out of government wastelands and surplus lands. Eligible persons were defined as landholders owning less than 5 bighās of land. They were to be allotted such an area of land as would bring their land ownership to 5 bighās.[296] This was subsequently incorporated into the 20 Point Programme and thus enshrined as an article of faith. Even a change of the political regime in 1977 did not result in altering the substance of this programme. Only its name was changed and it was carried on as a part of the Antyodaya Programme instead of the 20 Point Programme which temporarily passed into history! After a second change of regime, in 1980, the 20 Point Programme staged a comeback and the Antyodaya Programme fell by the wayside as a victim of political changes. The 20 Point Program has since then continued as an icon under revised names and points.

Lands were allotted in undue haste. In many cases field officers of the Revenue Department were given only 72 to 96 hours to prepare title deeds (pattās) for the parcels of land to be allotted; alongwith lists of all the landless/eligible persons. No proper survey was done. Revenue officers were bombarded with wireless messages asking them to finish the work on time. Threats of unpleasant consequences were conveyed in such messages. Deadlines were set, that on such and such day a prominent politician would be distributing the pattās to the beneficiaries with a lot of fanfare. Faced with an impossible task, revenue officers summoned Kānuṅgos and Patwāris to tahsil headquarters where plot maps (tatimās) were made from the existing revenue record without physical verification on the spot. After such pattās had been granted and the abolition of landlessness publicly proclaimed at functions, it was found that parcels of uncultivable land had been allotted on cliffs, in stream beds strewn with boulders or on rocks. Resurveys were then ordered to make good the lapses of the earlier haste. Unculturable lands that had been allotted were to be exchanged against culturable lands. But there was just not enough culturable land available to be given. Geography had made Kinnaur unsuitable for propagandist programmes to be given concrete practical shape! Land improvement loans up to Rs 500 were lavishly doled out to the new allottees who promptly used them as consumption loans. The purpose of the programme had been laudable but its execution had left much to be desired. It had been hasty and improper. The figures under this programme for Kinnaur are shown in Table 2.3 . These figures represent the data from 1975 till 1983 which was communicated to the state government vide Letter No. KNR-VIII-1(SK)/80-IX-2050 dated October 19, 1983 from the Deputy Commissioner, Kinnaur. The scheme was reported as having been completed, vide this letter. 14 landless and 146 eligible persons had not been covered because there was just not enough allotable land available. Landlessness had thus not been completely eliminated. But its extent had been reduced. Graphical representations of the data are attached.

The allotments of land did, however, provide a better foundation on which to build an institutional credit network than what had been legated by the earlier centuries-old regime of Bushahr. Many of the allottees given land under this programme were later on identified under the I.R.D.P. and other development programmes as target groups for preferential credit disbursement. Attempts were made by them to exchange their allotted lands for better situated lands by filing exchange applications before the District Collector under Rule 27 of the Nautor

[296] Instructions regarding this land allotment programme were received vide Financial Commissioner, H.P.'s Letter no. 9-14/75-Rev-A, dated Simla the 27th October 1975. Further instructions were received vide the F.C.'s Letter No. Rev-2-5-(7)-12/82 dated July 11, 1983. Earlier instructions for land allotment had been conveyed vide the F.C.'s Letter No. 10-4/73-Rev-A dated February 2, 1973. These letters were sent to all the Deputy Commissioners in Himāchal Pradesh through their respective Divisional Commissioners. In the D.C.'s Office at Kālpa, these instructions are available in File No. KNR-VIII-1(SK)/80-IX of the Sadar Kānuṅgo Branch.

Table 2.3: Land Distribution Statistics for Kinnaur, 1975-1983

S	*Tahsil*	*Lds*	*Elg*	*Land Allotted*			
,,	*...do...*	-"-	-"-	*Lds*	*Area*	*Elg*	*Area*
1	Hangrang	30	79	26	128.75	79	188.40
2	Kālpa	23	143	21	102.70	132	348.65
3	Moorang	48	171	44	200.00	131	358.90
4	Nichār	43	238	39	197.15	214	269.60
5	Pooh	56	192	56	261.35	178	554.20
6	Sangla	13	146	13	69.35	89	218.55
7	Total	213	969	199	939.30	823	1938.30

Legend: Areas are in bighās,
S = serial number,
Lds = number of landless persons identified,
***Elg = number of eligible persons identified,* Hangrang = Sub-Tahsil Hangrang,**
Land Allotted = land allotted to persons of both categories.

Rules, 1968. Between 1980 and 1983, more than 300 such cases had been decided by the author, mostly against the applicants. In four cases of Nésang village, for example, exchange was allowed in 1981 because the lands granted earlier had all been in kandas so high that they remained under snow for up to nine months in a year.

The task of land allotment was brought to a standstill by the Forest Conservation Ordinance of 1980 issued by the Union Government. This Ordinance laid down that land with a slope of more than 15 degrees and having more than two trees per bighā could not be allotted for non-forestry purposes without prior permission from the Prime Minister's Secretariat in New Delhi. The competence of not just the district authorities but the state authorities as well was curtailed drastically by this measure. 64 cases were sent up from Kinnaur for such permission in 1981. Till January 1986 no permission had been conveyed in these cases.

The process begun by Munshi Shām Lāl in 1854 A.D. had thus culminated more than a hundred years later in a chain of reform measures reflecting a changed perception of the role of the state in Kinnaur. Mere collection of taxes had given way to an active role by the state as an agent of socio-economic change, in which institutional credit was to be used as a major instrument for trying to alleviate the lot of the poor. We can now pass on to a review of the institutional credit infrastructure through which this attempt at socio-economic engineering is being carried out. Beginning with cooperative societies, this effort is now spearheaded by commercial banks, with the ubiquitous district administration very much in the foreground. We begin our review in the following chapter by first dealing with cooperative societies and banks.

Dimensions of Kinnaur District within the territory of the erstwhile Bushahr State

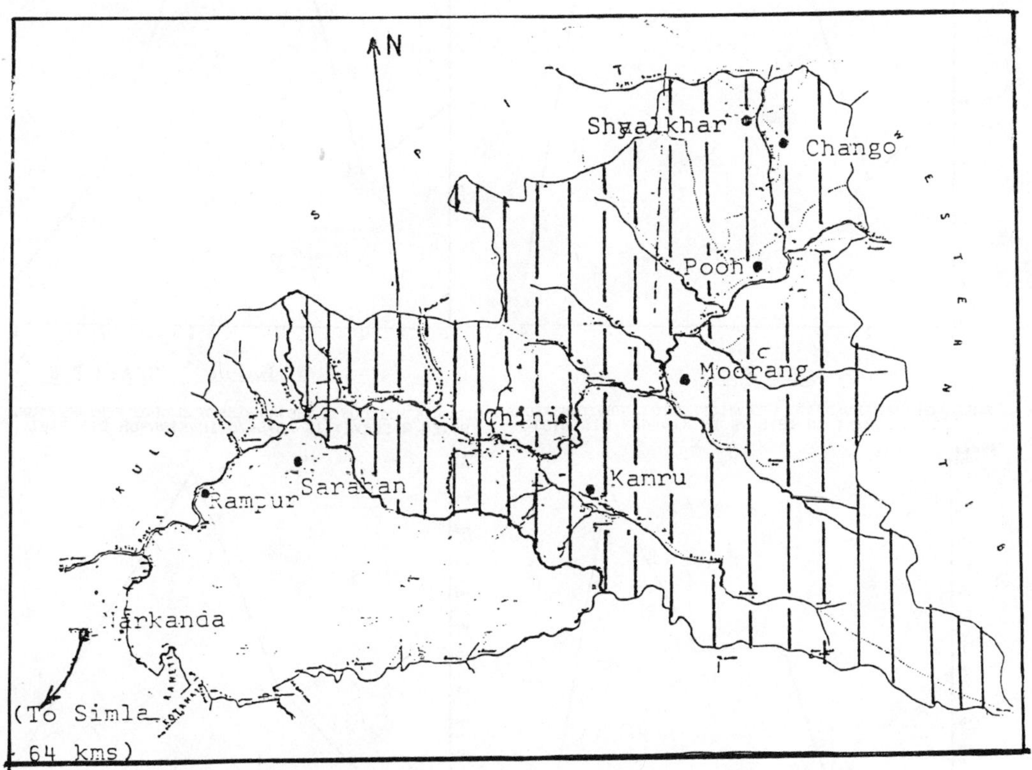

Lined portion marks the boundaries of Kinnaur District.

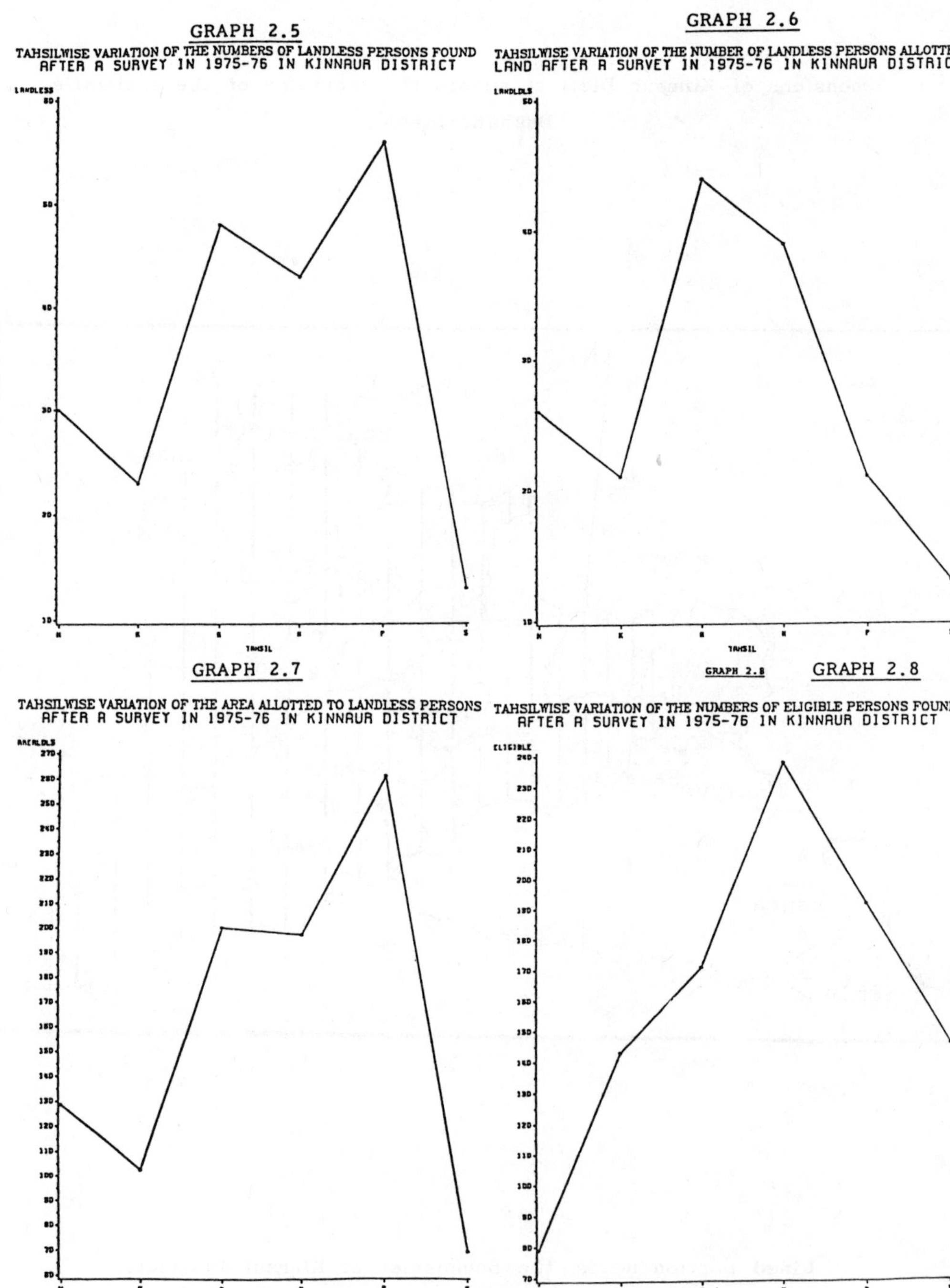

Tahsil H = Hangrang Sub-Tahsil, K = Kalpa, M = Moorang, N = Nichar,
P = Pooh and S = Sangla.

Landless = No. of landless persons, Landldls = No. of landless persons allotted land, Arealdls = Area allotted to landless persons in bighas.

CHAPTER III

INSTITUTIONAL CREDIT NETWORK: COOPERATIVES

Having examined the evolution of Bushahr State, we know now that Kinnaur entered the post-independence era after Bushahr's merger into Himāchal Pradesh on April 15, 1948. There was then a negligible institutional credit network in Kinnaur. The degree of development of such a credit network was an indication of just how well the economic underpinnings of the state had evolved. A sizeable share in the local credit market enables the State to act as a major influence in the economic sphere. The credit markets in Kinnaur were almost totally in the hands of private moneylenders. The state either left them undisturbed, or even came to their succour by establishing tribunals before whom they could enforce their claims against defaulters.[1] In the name of judicial reform, legal coercion was added to the moneylenders' armoury of social coercive measures for enforcing repayment. This stranglehold began to weaken only very slowly in post-British India. The taccāvi loans given by the Revenue Department continued to be the mainstay of the institutional credit system.

3.1 INSTITUTIONAL CREDIT: BETTER LATE THAN NEVER!

The area was completely devoid of banking facilities in 1948. The first post-1948 efforts at building up an institutional credit network came in 1950-51 when cooperative societies were organized in Kinnaur. Cooperatives formed the core of the institutional credit infrastructure till 1960 when Kinnaur's upgradation to a district brought in its wake the opening of a branch of the H.P. State Cooperative Bank (henceforth referred to as the SCB) at Kālpa on November 10, 1960.[2] This was the first bank branch ever in Kinnaur.

With the establishment of a full-fledged district set-up; a number of loans for agricultural, horticultural, industrial, housing and other purposes were made available through institutional channels. A noteworthy step was the upgradation of the hitherto existing Tahsil Cooperative Union at Kālpa to the Kinnaur District Cooperative Marketing and Supply Federation (henceforth referred to as the KINFED).[3] It was constituted as the apex secondary cooperative institution in the district. KINFED began to arrange supplies of consumer articles to member-societies at subsidized rates and to market agricultural produce. Already in 1961-62, it supplied consumer goods worth Rs 351,000 to member-societies and distributed 6,500 maunds of foodgrains as a distributing agency on behalf of the government.[4] In terms of credit needs, these figures were small but they did signal the first time that private moneylenders were going to face even modest competition. How far this process would have gone on had the Sino-Indian conflict of 1962 not taken place remains an interesting conundrum. The socio-political impact of this event on life in Kinnaur has already been

[1] Information given by Mr T.S. Negi and Mr Goverdhan Singh Negi in personal interviews. Both of them had been senior officials in Bushahr State.

[2] Gazetteer, 1971, p. 181; also see: Role of the Cooperative Banks in the Development of Agriculture, Note prepared for the author on the orders of Mr B.S. Chauhan, H.A.S, Managing Director, SCB, Simla by his office staff, January 1986, Typewritten Manuscript, Unpublished, p. 5. This document mentions November 11, 1960 as the date of opening of the SCB branch at Kālpa.

[3] Gazetteer, 1971, p. 179.

[4] Ibid; also confirmed in person from the office files of the D.C.S.O., Kinnaur District at Rekong Peo in December 1985.

discussed in Section 2.4.7, Chapter II.

3.1.1 Conflict and Credit: Sino-Indian War of 1962

Kinnauras were faced in 1962 with a fait accompli of having to restructure their economy to compensate for the stoppage of border trade. Diversion of traders into other occupations which became necessary as a consequence required major credit inflows. The larger traders were themselves moneylenders and might not have required institutional credit in a big way but low rates of interest of the institutional loans acted as an incentive for taking such loans for further lending at higher rates of interest.[5] The medium and small traders, in any case, did not have the necessary fiscal liquidity to branch out into other gainful occupations without government help. Absence of institutional credit would have driven them further into bondage of the moneylenders. To keep the allegiance of these sections of society in the newly-important geo-strategic region of Kinnaur institutional credit was to serve as an effective instrument. Traders were to be helped in re-establishing themselves as shopkeepers, transporters or in other activities so as to dispel the notion that trade with Tibet was indispensable.

The conflict of 1962 abruptly lopped off the extended third circle of moneylending in Kinnaur.[6] Moneylending by Kinnaura traders across the border was no longer feasible. This cessation removed a price stabilization mechanism practised for surplus generation by trader-moneylenders.[7] They suffered major losses. Source capital was blocked in Tibet instead of being available for profit generation through trade and partial ploughing back into moneylending in Kinnaur. Moneylenders became wary. A major prop of the informal credit sector was knocked away. It offered a window of opportunity to cooperative institutions to take up the slack and gain the allegiance of the borrowers. Cooperatives were in the vanguard of the fledgling institutional credit infrastructure that had to cope with this development. The newly established SCB branch at Kālpa took over a motor role in building up an adequate institutional credit network because cooperative credit societies by themselves were found wanting. They had to be reinforced with a cooperative banking framework. Commercial banks were still mostly in private hands and not interested at all in moving into remote areas like Kinnaur, notwithstanding its newly-found strategic importance from the military point of view. The banker looked at the profits to be had, and not at the strategic advantages from a military point-of-view! The cooperative network was the only convenient agency available to the government for using institutional credit as a tool for winning the hearts and minds of the Kinnauras.

To study the institutional credit infrastructure in Kinnaur, we must first concentrate on the cooperative credit sector which enjoyed a monopoly of institutional credit till 1974. Commercial banks have since assumed such a predominant role as agents of official credit in recent years that there is a tendency to forget that it was not they but the cooperative credit societies that laid the foundation of any kind of institutional alternative to the informal sector. The cooperative banks, being inseparable components of the cooperative credit package, have to be thus grouped with cooperative societies and not with commercial banks which shall be discussed in Chapter IV.

[5] Please see Section 1.2.1, Chapter I of this work.

[6] Ibid.

[7] Please see Sections 1.2.1 and 1.2.4, Chapter I of this work.

3.1.2 District Creation: Bābus and Soldiers!

The creation of a district in Kinnaur on May 1, 1960 meant the implantation of the usual resident apparatus of district administration. Since the available government housing was totally inadequate to cope with the sudden influx of newly posted government functionaries, large numbers of newly posted staff had to rent private accomodation as best as they could. Rents were paid in cash and local houseowners suddenly found monetary liquidity on their hands. The employees paid cash for their purchases. This impact may not have mattered much in more developed areas but in Kinnaur's primarily barter internal economy its impact was multiplied in importance. Civilian employees were even greater agents of monetization of the economy than their military counterparts. Soldiers could exchange, of course illegally, their quota of duty-free liquor or excise-exempted consumer articles from military canteens against local produce like fruit and neozās. Civilians lacked such canteen facilities and had to pay cash for what they required or bought locally. They received higher allowances for serving in this remote tribal area. The onset of winter in October/November saw large money inflows into the local markets because the civilian employees bought up to four months' rations to stock up for the coming winter months. They received (and still do today) four months' salary in lumpsum in order to enable them to make such purchases.

The establishment of the Deputy Commissioner's Office at Kālpa meant the induction of nearly *"300 persons of various grades, who live in the village of Kālpa, whose own population does not exceed that number and even the population of the Kālpa revenue estate, which includes several surrounding hamlets and settlements, is not more than about four times the number of the district employees of the government living in their midst"*.[8] If this be true of just the D.C.'s Office, the impact was multiplied manifold by the induction of employees of other district offices. These outsiders had not formed part of the traditional local web of credit exchange relations of a predominantly barter economy. They wanted institutional credit rather than credit from the local moneylender. They wanted banks, not just to deposit their money in but also for transferring their money to their families or relatives outside Kinnaur. The presence of this monetized cash revenue acted as an agent of change. It was only a matter of time before a bank opened its doors in Kinnaur. Even if a bank came only to mop up this available monetary reserve, it necessarily brought its entire gamut of loans along. However, banks kept a low profile in institutional credit till they were forced to accelerate in the late 1970s as integral parts of the politically sponsored programmes like the Integrated Rural Development Programme (henceforth referred to only as the I.R.D.P. or the I.R.D. Programme).

For many years before 1974 the institutional credit infrastructure had remained synonymous with cooperatives. Regardless of the fact that the they did not measure up to all the hopes pinned on them as agents of social change, the cooperatives did nevertheless provide the sole alternative to the ubiquitous village moneylenders. They tried to stimulate economic activity by using institutional credit as an input. Nowadays they are so much overshadowed by commercial banks that it is almost forgotten that they were the ones who built up a foundation on which later entrants like the banks could build upon. It is relevant to consider the role of cooperatives in Kinnaur very briefly.

3.2 COOPERATIVES: DECEPTION, CRITICISM AND INDISPENSABILITY

Cooperatives are important in a remote area like Kinnaur where topographical conditions deter expansion by commercial banks. They were needed not only as outlets for funnelling in institutional credit but also for becoming the backbone of the public distribution system for supply of essential commodities, agricultural inputs and consumer goods, as well as for

[8] Chopra, Pran: On An Indian Border, London: Asia Publishing House, 1964, p. 95.

providing marketing channels for agricultural and horticultural produce. Marketing the increasing horticultural production of Kinnaur necessitated the organization of marketing societies on an ever larger scale. In addition, cooperatives were to be the main mechanisms of mobilization for ensuring the participation of targeted socio-economic groups in the development process. Their success in mobilizing village masses' participation would be a reliable indicator of judging whether the development process had become a two-way street with its targets being also actively involved in it or had remained a one-way street with government functionaries dishing out development programmes and foisting these on indifferent villagers as necessary curative medicine prescribed by those who knew best what was good for the villagers! The latter eventuality involved the risk of distorted feedback in which the non-participation of villagers would lead district officials to formulate pre-determined benefit indices. We shall focus here on the primary agricultural credit societies (henceforth referred to as P.A.C.S.) which were in the vanguard of the institutional effort to try and make a dent in the predominance of the moneylenders in the credit markets of Kinnaur. Criticism of their performance and disappointed expectations partly show that too much may have been expected of them in the first place. They were expected to take on centuries-old established systems of credit of proven durability and to vanquish them.

3.2.1 The Beginnings (1951-60): Shaky and Limited

The cooperative movement was organized in Kinnaur District in 1951-52 with the registration of the Chini Cooperative Multipurpose Society. Rather than provision of institutional credit, its main aim was to cater to the needs of the surrounding areas in Chini Tahsil with respect to essential consumer items to be supplied at controlled rates.[9] *"It was subsidized by the government but the people have not shown any enthusiasm to enroll themselves as its members as has happened elsewhere also".*[10] Simultaneously, agricultural multipurpose societies were also organized in 1951-52 for the first time. Six such societies were organized, one for each Patwār Circle.[11] This number rose to 18 by the year 1962. This shows a rate of increase of roughly one society per year. In addition to providing credit to agriculturists, they also supplied implements at controlled prices. In 1961-62 these societies had advanced Rs 10,000 as loan and implements worth Rs 32,000 at subsidized rates.[12] Thus, ten years after their launch, the credit input through this institutional channel remained meagre. Rs 10,000 worked out to roughly Rs 0.244 per capita, or only about 25 paise per head in Kinnaur.[13] Clearly, a decade of operation by cooperatives had made only a superficial impact in the credit markets of Kinnaur, even though income and expenditure levels there were not high.

A detailed socio-economic survey carried out in 1965 revealed expenditure levels from as low as Rs 150 per annum for landless persons in Moorang Tahsil to a high of Rs 7,390 per annum for landowners possessing 10 hectares or above of cultivated land for Pooh Tahsil. Since recorded per annum incomes for these two categories correspond to Rs 1,200 and above to Rs 4,200 respectively, we see a greater credit gap for families with higher incomes than for the poorest families. A family with income just above Rs 4,200 per annum had an average expenditure of Rs 7,400, revealing a deficit of Rs 3,200, almost 76% of the annual income. Even if we consider this family to be consisting of 10 members, in view of the polyandrous family system in Kinnaur, the cooperative credit falling to its share would work out to a

[9] Gazetteer, 1971, p. 179.

[10] Ibid, p. 180.

[11] Ibid, p. 179.

[12] Ibid, p. 180.

[13] Using the figure of 40,980 persons as the total population of Kinnaur, as per the 1961 census.

VARIATION IN THE NUMBER OF COOPERATIVE SOCIETIES IN KINNAUR

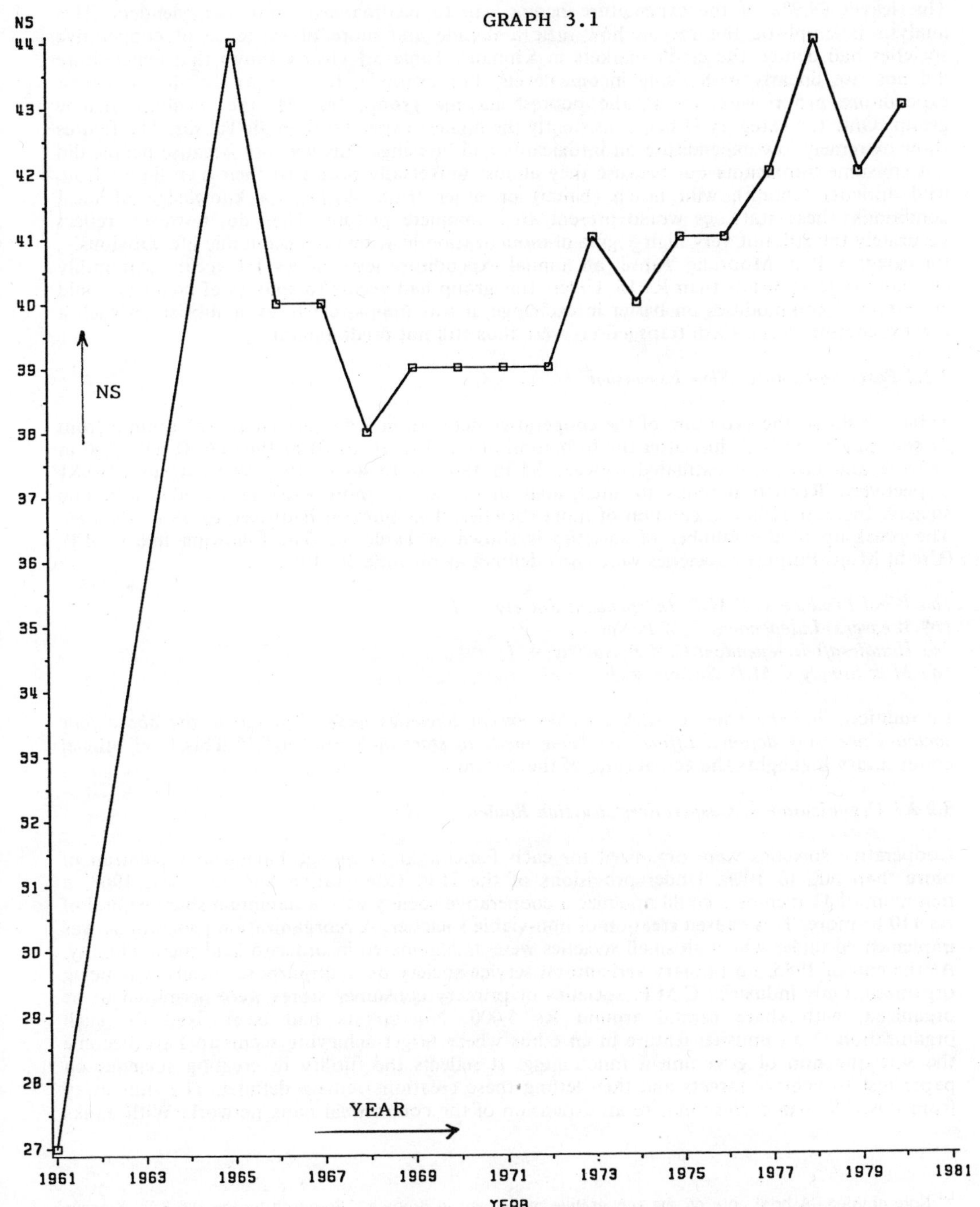

NS = number of cooperative societies in Kinnaur District.

meagre Rs 2.50, on the basis of 25 paise per capita figure worked out in the preceding lines. This leaves 99.9% of the expenditure-income gap to be financed from moneylenders. This analysis is simplistic but reveals how little a decade and more of existence of cooperative societies had dented the credit markets in Kinnaur. Table 3.1 clearly shows that expenditure did not rise linearly with rising income levels. For example, for Nichār Tahsil the lowest expenditure group was not P, the poorest income group, but M, the medium income group. Only the category H had consistently the highest expenditure in all Tahsils. The figures show extremely low expenditure on intoxicants and housing. This was not because people did not consume intoxicants but because they almost universally produced their own liquor from wild apricots (chooli), wild peach (baimi) or other fruit. Without a knowledge of local conditions, these statistics would present an incomplete picture. They do, however, reflect accurately the still not very high degree of monetization in Kinnaur's economic life. Obviously, for category P in Moorang Tahsil, an annual expenditure level of Rs 150 meant a monthly expenditure level of less than Rs 15. Unless this group had access to sources of credit or could get essential commodities on barter in exchange, it was impossible to even subsist on such a low expenditure level. Cash transactions were thus still not predominant.

3.2.2 Post-1960 Phase: Slow Expansion

Table 3.2 shows the evolution of the cooperative network in Kinnaur. There was a jump from 27 societies in 1961-62, just after the formation of the district, to 44 in 1965-66. It fell to 40 in 1967-68 and has since oscillated between 38 in 1968-69 to 44 in 1978-79 to 43 in 1980-81 respectively. Reduction refers to amalgamation of two or more existing societies into one society. Increase refers to creation of more societies. This number had risen to 58 in 1985-86. The break-up of the number of societies is shown in Table 3.3 The following five C.M.P. (Credit Multi-Purpose) Societies were lying defunct as on June 30, 1985:

(a) Wool Producers' C.M.P. Independent Society = 1;
(b) Weavers' Independent C.M.P. Society = 2;
(c) Handicraft Independent C.M.P. Society = 1;
(d) Milk Supply C.M.P. Society = 1.

In addition, *"all the other C.M.P. societies except Societies under liquidation and above four societies are lying defunct. Efforts are being made to start their working"*.[14] This brief official commentary highlights the actual state of the system.

3.2.2.1 Organization of Cooperatives: Russian Roulette!

Cooperative societies were organized for each Panchāyat or village having a population of more than 500 to 1000. Under provisions of the H.P. Cooperative Societies Act, 1968, a minimum of 11 members could organize a cooperative society with a minimum share capital of Rs 110 or more. This caused creation of non-viable societies. A reorganization programme was implemented under which all small societies were amalgamated in order to lend them viability. At the end of 1985, no primary agricultural service society or multipurpose society was being organized. Only industrial C.M.P. societies or primary consumer stores were permitted to be organized, with share capital around Rs 5,000. No targets had been fixed for such organization,[15] an unusual feature in an ethos where target-achieving seems to have become the sine qua non of government functioning. It reflects the futility of creating societies on paper just to achieve targets and then letting these creations remain defunct. The shift away from P.A.C.S. also corresponds to an expansion of the commercial bank network. With banks

[14] Note entitled "A brief note on the cooperative movement in Kinnaur", Prepared by the D.C.S.O., Kinnaur District in December 1985 for the author, Handwritten, [In English], Unpublished, p. 3.

[15] Ibid.

Table 3.1: Annual Average Family Expenditure in Kinnaur.

s	Tahsil	FC	Expenditure Item							Total
,,	**--do--**	**do**	**f+b**	**intx**	**f+l**	**hsg**	**c+s**	**f+u**	**mscl**	**expdr**
a	Nichār	P	1150	000	00	00	150	000	50	1350
b	--do--	L	150	000	10	00	60	00	70	290
c	--do--	M	90	00	30	00	90	00	20	230
d	--do--	H	900	00	25	00	100	00	90	1115
e	Kālpa	P	730	36	00	00	40	00	00	806
f	--do--	L	2400	132	12	00	776	00	170	3490
g	--do--	M	2100	84	00	00	248	00	248	2680
h	--do--	H	3285	510	24	00	526	00	90	4434
i	Sangla	P	460	00	10	00	200	00	20	690
j	--do--	L	300	60	20	00	200	00	00	580
k	--do--	M	560	60	00	00	270	00	20	910
l	--do--	H	1430	30	15	00	700	00	200	2375
m	Moorang	P	120	00	00	00	30	00	00	150
n	--do--	L	750	00	12	00	180	10	50	1002
o	--do--	M	1380	36	00	00	250	00	60	1726
p	--do--	H	1680	90	15	00	380	00	95	2260
q	Pooh	P	700	50	00	00	470	25	100	1345
r	-do-	L	1200	50	00	00	780	25	100	2155
s	-do-	M	800	50	00	00	560	25	100	1535
t	--do--	H	1830	200	00	00	1260	100	4000	7399
u	Hangrang	P	720	00	12	05	200	05	50	992
v	--do---	L	1138	150	24	100	275	20	440	2147
w	---do---	M	2160	90	40	00	450	00	755	3495
x	---do---	H	2640	150	70	00	650	50	1390	4950

Code: **s = serial number, FC = family category, f+b = food + beverages, intx = intoxicants, f+l = fuel + lighting, hsg = housing, f+u = furniture + utensil, mscl = miscellaneous,**

c+s = clothing + shoes, expdr = expenditure. (All amounts are in Rupees).
P = Landless, with no other means of livelihood, income up to Rs 100 per month (P = Poorest); L = Lower = Landowners with up to 4.04 hectares of cultivated land, income from Rs 101 to Rs 200 per month; M = Medium = Landowners having more than 4.04 hectares but less than 10.11 hectares cultivated land, income between Rs 201 and Rs 350 per month; H = High = Landowners holding 10.11 hectares or more of cultivated land, income of Rs 351 per month or above.
(Source: Survey Registers in the D.C.'s Office at Kālpa).

Table 3.2: Evolution of the Cooperative Structure in Kinnaur

s	Period	NS	MSP	WC	SC	LI
1	1961-62	27	2,244	4.89	1.02	11.19
2	1965-66	44	5,441	6.12	1.72	79.49
3	1966-67	40	5,937	7.07	2.30	70.41
4	1967-68	40	6,227	6.38	2.42	56.37
5	1968-69	38	6,165	6.98	2.41	92.85
6	1969-70	34	6,367	7.38	2.60	69.71

Code: NS = no. of societies, MSP = membership of cooperative societies,
WC = working capital, SC = share capital, LI = loans issued.
LI is in thousands of Rupees while WC, SC are in lakhs (1 lakh = 100,000).
(Source: Evaluation Study of Kinnaur District, 1971, p. 35.)

replacing cooperatives as the leading institutional credit givers, the creation of P.A.C.S. has been switched on to the back burner. These structures relied exclusively on government assistance for survival.

3.2.2.2 Assistance to Cooperatives: Life-Support System

All cooperative societies are eligible for the following types of assistance from the government:-

(a) Managerial subsidy;
(b) Subsidy for construction of godowns or sheds;
(c) Subsidy for the purchase of machinery, implements, furniture and fixtures;
(d) Share capital, which is to be refunded to the government after eight years in equal instalments without interest but the Society has to pay dividend @ 10% or less, being the profits earned each year by it.
(e) Loans for purchase of machinery, implements, furniture and fixtures, to be paid annually in equal instalments with interest.
(f) Interest subsidy as working capital.

The assistance distributed in 1984-85 is shown in Table 3.4 .

3.2.2.3 Government Loans: Backbone of the System

Government loans received by cooperatives during the year 1985 amounted to Rs 491,500 in Kinnaur District.[16] For the year 1985-86, proposals for the sanction of managerial subsidy, share capital, interest subsidy, working capital subsidy, loan and subsidy for the construction

[16] Ibid, p. 4.

Table 3A: Evolution of the Cooperative Structure in Kinnaur

sn	Type of Societies	Unit	Year										
1.0	**Number of Societies**	**No.**	**67**	**68**	**69**	**70**	**71**	**72**	**73**	**74**	**75**	**76**	**77**
1.1	central/other secondary	No.	01	01	01	01	01	01	01	01	0	01	01
1.2	agricultural	-,,-	034	033	034	034	034	034	036	036	036	037	037
1.3	non-agricultural	-,,-	005	004	004	004	004	004	004	003	04	04	04
1.4	TOTAL	-,,-	040	038	039	039	039	039	041	040	041	041	042
2.0	**Membership**	-,,-											
2.1	Central	-,,-	016	017	022	022	023	024	025	025	025	026	028
2.2	Agricultural		5701	5665	5832	6000	6084	6307	6713	6782	6974	7300	7843
2.3	Non-Agricultural	-,,-	510	483	513	563	577	614	609	399	423	453	328
2.4	Total		6227	6165	6367	6586	6684	6995	7347	7206	7422	7779	8199
3.0	**Working Capital**	**lakhs**											
3.1	Agricultural		1.35	1.87	1.99	2.64	4.05	4.92	5.15	8.08	6.63	10.59	14.77
3.2	Non-Agricultural		3.18	3.13	3.48	4.09	4.91	5.09	5.22	7.51	10.52	19.35	24.07
3.3	Total		1.85	1.98	1.91	2.13	2.37	2.14	1.47	1.54	2.06	2.18	3.23
4.0	**Share Capital**	**'000**											
4.1	Central	-,,-	7.90	7.90	13.60	18.70							
4.2	Agricultural	-,,-	194.91	193.54	207.22	221.42							
4.3	Non-Agricultural	-,,-	39.30	39.26	39.08	39.42							
4.4	TOTAL	-,,-	242.11	240.70	259.90	279.50							
5.0			56.37	92.82	68.71	71.81	78.60	68.50	77.10	149.40	421	878	1162
6.0	**Loans Outstanding**	-,,-											
6.1	Agrl					124.60	117.2	123.3	130.70	197.60	481	909.1	1292.4
6.2	Non-Agricultural	-,,-											98.70

Code: **Agrl = agricultural cooperative society;**

Year 67 = 1967-68; 68 = 1968-69; and so on till 77 = 1977-77.

(Source: Statistical Abstract of Kinnaur District, 1981, p. 63;

Review of Achievements Kinnaur District, 1970-71, p. 63;

Statistical Abstract of Kinnaur District, 1970-71, p. 43;

Statistical Abstract of Kinnaur District, 1974-75, p. 43;
Statistical Abstract of Kinnaur District; 1975-76, p. 43)
Blank boxes in the Table mean zero value for that year.

of godowns had been sent to the state government. The sanction was awaited around March 31, 1986 after which the amount sanctioned would be accounted for by the SCB in a savings bank account duly pledged in the name of the Assistant Registrar Cooperative Societies, District Kinnaur. The Assistant Registrar would release these amounts as and when demanded by the Societies in question after proper verification of their need. Each case has to be verified meticulously and decided on merit so that funds are not released just as a matter of course. In practice, such verification is seldom thoroughly made. Funds are released as a matter of normal bureaucratic routine.

Dependent heavily on government doles, cooperative societies have evolved into adjuncts of the Cooperative Department rather than into self-help autonomous bodies. They have become just like a government department in the public mind which does not distinguish them from the Cooperative Department. The entire structure has evolved into four layers. There is the base layer of primary societies at the village or the panchāyat level. Then come primary societies at the Tahsil level. Only one Tahsil Union was existing in Kinnaur in the beginning of 1986 (at Pooh).[17] Then came the secondary society at the apex of the district-level in the shape of the KINFED. At the state-level apex came the tertiary society called the Himāchal State Cooperative Marketing and Supply Federation (HIMFED). This whole structure is propped up by the SCB.

3.3 STATE COOPERATIVE BANK: BUREAUCRATIC BUT NECESSARY

From the very beginning of the development process in 1952 when the Community Development Scheme was launched, the provision of an adequate, easy and timely supply of institutional credit has been essential policy of the government. The Managing Director (henceforth referred to as the M.D.) of the SCB went to the extent of believing that *"from Rome to Scotland...an essential of agriculture is credit. Neither the condition of the country nor the nature of the land tenures, nor the position of agriculture affects the one great fact that agriculturists must borrow"*.[18] To cater to this need and at least partly protect the agriculturists from the moneylenders' clutches, a cooperative credit structure based on an interlocking system of cooperative societies and cooperative banks was built up. In those days, commercial banks had still not been nationalized and martialled into acting as the spearheads of the institutional credit effort. The necessary banking support for the soon enough burgeoning cooperative credit network had to be provided by a cooperative bank.

3.3.1 Cooperative Loan Structure: Multi-tiered

The cooperative credit structure in Kinnaur, like in other districts, can very broadly be classified into two categories as follows:-
(a) Short- and Medium-term credit; and
(b) Long-term credit.
Each of these categories has further sub-categories because the short- and medium-term credit requirement is met by the SCB while the agency responsible for meeting long-term credit requirements is the ***State Cooperative Land Development Bank (henceforth, LDB).*** These two apex organizations are responsible for the entire State. They have established their branches in different districts for being present in the field and to not have everything centralized at state

[17] Personal observation during field research.

[18] Note entitled "Role of the Cooperative Banks in the Development of Agriculture", op. cit., January 1986, p. 2.

GRAPH 3.2

VARIATION IN THE LOAN AMOUNTS GIVEN BY COOPERATIVES IN KINNAUR

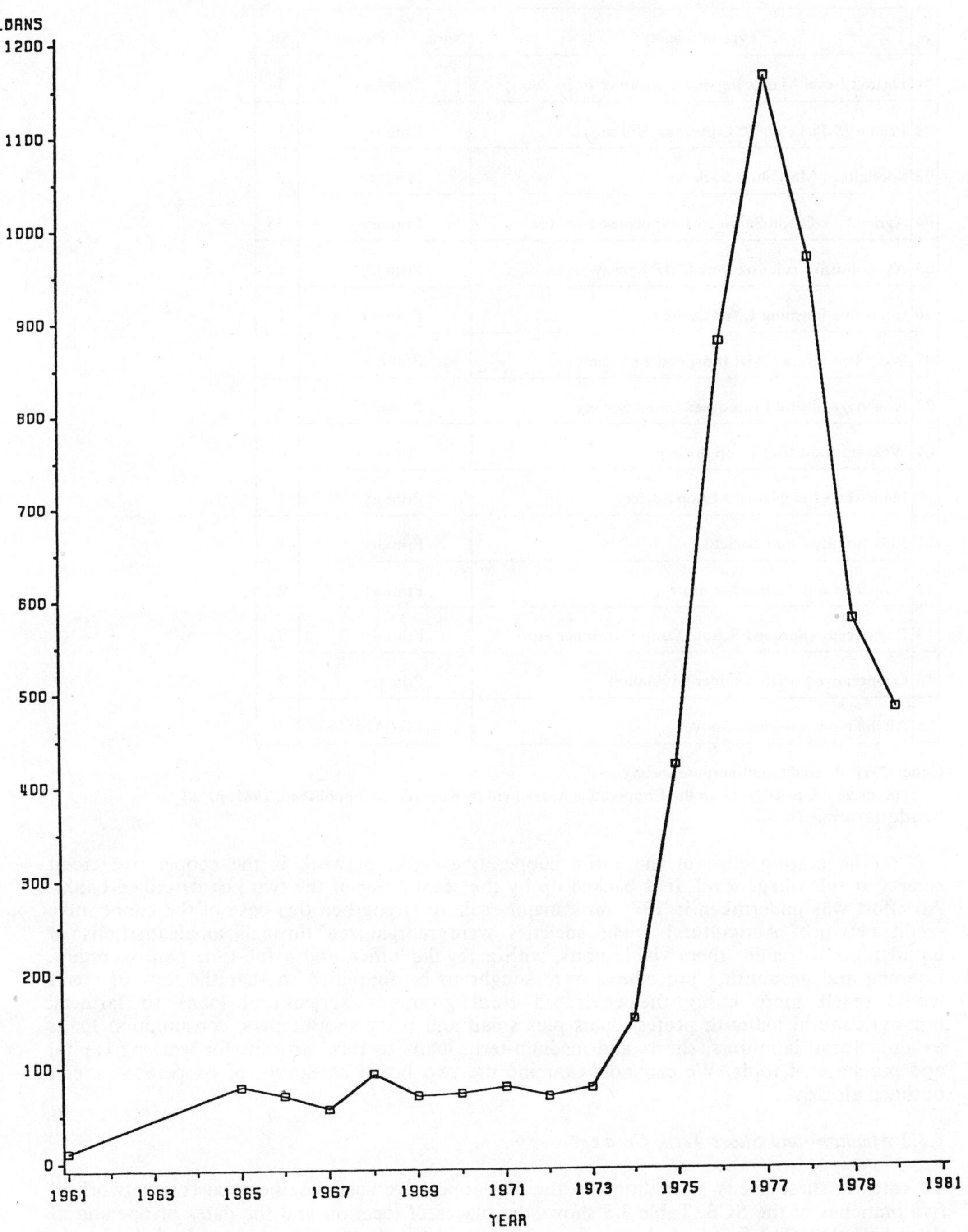

Table 3.3: Total No. of Cooperative Societies in Kinnaur District at the End of 1985

sn	Type of Society	Nature of Society	No.
01	District Level Marketing and Consumer Federation	Secodary	1
02	Primary Marketing & Consumer Union	Primary	1
03	Specialized Marketing Societies	Primary	3
04	Agriculture Credit Service/Multipurpose Societies	Primary	35
05	Agricultural Fruit Growers CMP Society	Primary	1
06	Collective Farming CMP Society	Primary	1
07	Wool Producers CMP Independent Society	Primary	1
08	Non-Agricultural Employees Credit Society	Primary	2
09	Weavers Industrial Coop Society	Primary	4
10	Handicraft Independent Coop Society	Primary	1
11	Milk Supply Coop Society	Primary	1
12	Primary Coop Consumer Store	Primary	2
13	Registered/Approved School Coop Consumer Store	Primary	3
14	Cooperative Societies under liquidation	Primary	2
15	All the types described above	TOTAL	58

Code: **CMP = credit multipurpose society.**

(Source: "A Brief Note on the Cooperative Movement in Kinnaur", Unpublished, 1985, p. 2.)

headquarters.

The cutting edge of the entire cooperative credit network is the cooperative credit society at the village level. It is backed up by the second tier of the two just described banks. An effort was undertaken in 1976 on a major scale to strengthen this base of the cooperative credit network. Agricultural credit societies were reorganized through amalgamations or liquidations to render them viable units, with a regular office and a full-time paid secretary. Loaning and accounting procedures were sought to be simplified so that the flow of credit would reach more easily the envisaged rural groups - agricultural loans to farmers; non-agricultural loans to professionals plus small and petty shopkeepers; consumption loans to agricultural labourers; short- and medium-term loans to rural artisans for working capital and purchase of tools. We can now examine the two broad categories of cooperative credit outlined already.

3.3.2 Medium- and Short-Term Credit

To cater to these needs, in addition to the 58 cooperative societies there exists a network of five branches of the SCB. Table 3.5 shows the places of location and the dates of opening of these branches. The first branch was located at the district headquarters six and a half months

VARIATION IN THE NUMBER OF MEMBERS OF COOPERATIVES IN KINNAUR

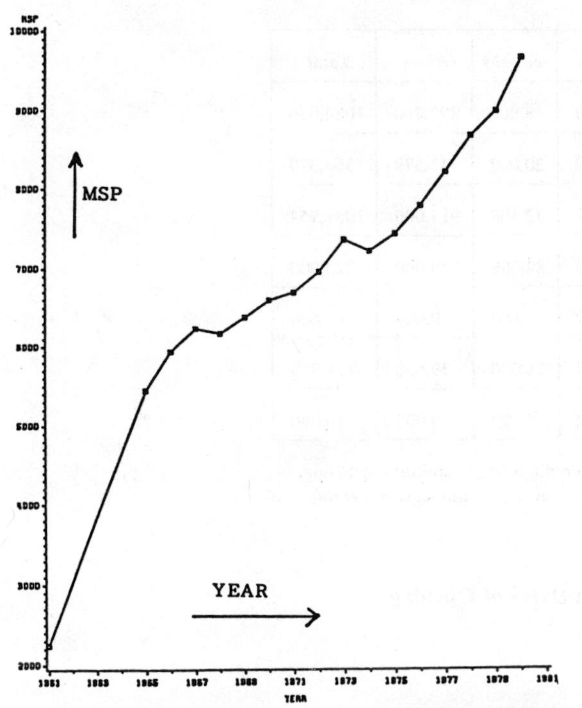

Graph 3.3

MSP = number of members of cooperative societies in Kinnaur.

VARIATION IN THE WORKING CAPITAL OF COOPERATIVES IN KINNAUR

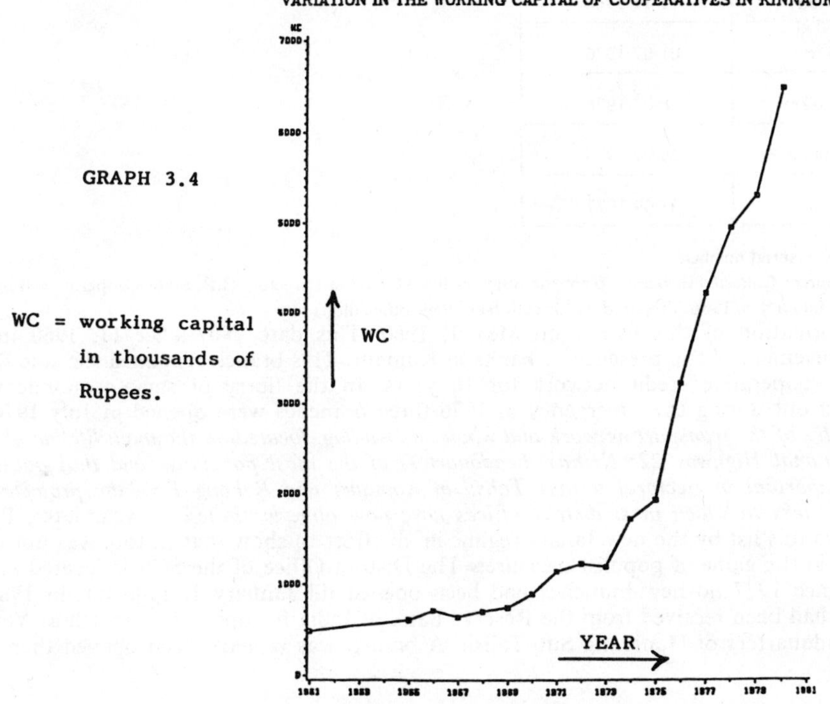

GRAPH 3.4

WC = working capital in thousands of Rupees.

Table 3.4: State/Central Government Assistance to the Cooperatives in Kinnaur, 1984-85

s	*Society*	*shcptl*	*intsby*	*mngsby*	*Others*	*Total*
1	District Federation	165,000	18,280	8,000	892,750	1084,030
2	Tahsil Union	0,000	0,000	20,000	343,579	363,579
3	S.M. Societies	70,000	12,454	32,500	917,000	1031,954
4	Agricultural MPS	0,000	0,000	84,000	239,000	323,000
5	Agricultural NCdt	0,000	0,000	,600	0,000	,600
6	Industrial Societies	87,400	0,000	24,000	39,650	151,050
7	Primary Consumer Stores	10,000	0,000	0,000	0,000	10,000

Code: MPS = multipurpose societies, NCdt = non-credit, S.M. = special marketing, ***shcptl = share capital, intsby = interest subsidy, mngsby = managerial subsidy, All amounts are in Rupees.***
(Source: As for preceding Table, p. 4)

Table 3.5: SCB Branches in Kinnaur, with Dates of Opening

sn	Location	Date of Opening
1	Kālpa	11-11-1960
2	Tāpri	01-07-1976
3	Nichār	28-07-1976
4	Rekong Peo	28-07-1976
5	Pooh	03-09-1977

Code: **sn = serial number.**
(Source: Collected in person from the office of the Managing Director, H.P. State Cooperative Bank at Simla on January 6, 1986. Prepared by his staff from their office files.)

after formation of the district on May 1, 1960. This date, **November 11, 1960** marks the commencement of the presence of banks in Kinnaur. This branch remained the sole flagbearer of the cooperative credit network for 16 years. In the flurry of socio-economic measures churned out during the Emergency in 1976 three branches were opened in July 1976: *Tāpri, the centre of the transport network and wholesale trading, located on the main lifeline of Kinnaur, the National Highway 22; Nichār, headquarters of the most populous (and thus politically the most important in electoral terms) Tahsil of Kinnaur; and Rekong Peo, the projected district headquarters to which most district offices have now already shifted.* A year later, Pooh was added to this list by the new Janata regime in an effort to show that it, too, was not to be left behind in the game of populist measures. The District Office of the SCB is located at Rekong Peo. Since 1977 no new branches had been opened till January 1, 1986 but in 1985 a new licence had been received from the Reserve Bank of India for opening a branch at Yangthang, the headquarters of Hangrang Sub-Tahsil. A branch was to have been opened there without delay.[19]

During field research data was found pertaining only to the Kālpa and Peo branches of the SCB and that also only from 1977 onwards. During the shifting of the District Office of the Cooperative Department from Kālpa to Peo, documents had just been dumped into jute sacks and nobody seemed to know what had been dumped where.[20] The staffing pattern for the SCB branches shows staff strength at a minimum so that establishment costs remain low, particularly because higher allowances have to be paid in Kinnaur, it being a geographically hard area. Branches in Kinnaur were category C branches, except those at the district h.q.

A category C branch was headed not by a full-fledged manager but by a grade III officer (presently the grade of accountants) and should have at least one clerk-cum-cashier. The SCB has assumed (taking into account the norms in the banking sector and the level of efficiency of its own banking staff) that a clerk can easily handle up to 40 vouchers per day. Based on this norm, a category C branch should be provided with a second clerk if the average number of vouchers exceeds 40 per day. Having briefly reviewed the cooperative banking infrastructure available in Kinnaur, we can now examine the scope of the short- and medium-term credit schemes existing for these bank branches.

3.3.2.1 Short-Term Agricultural Loans

These loans are the commonly called crop loans which were launched in 1969 with so much hope. They constitute a production-oriented lending system and can be availed of through the P.A.C.S. Crop loans can be given to agriculturists for growing various cereal crops and vegetables; for seasonal agricultural operations and for seasonal horticultural operations for fruit plants. These loans are provided both in cash and in kind or in a mixture of the two. The scales of finance for different crops are fixed on the basis of recommendations made by district- and state-level technical groups. Their objective is to finance current expenditure and their term is one year. In Kinnaur, such loans are available for the kharif and for the rabi crops and also for apple and potato production.

1% penal rate of interest is charged extra on overdue amounts. The SCB charges primary societies 10% as the annual rate of interest for providing finance under this scheme. These societies further charge 12% as the annual rate of interest from the agriculturist borrowers. The interest so charged is reimbursed by the state government to the tune of 6% under the general scheme of giving 50% subsidy on inputs in tribal areas to low income groups. This reimbursement is not paid directly in cash to the borrowers but is credited to their interest accounts in the books of the bank/loaning primary society.

3.3.2.1.1 Procedure: Fixation of Credit Limits

Two limits, *the maximum credit limit and the normal credit limit,* are prepared at the primary cooperative society-level for each borrower keeping in view his land holding, the trees on it and other assets, as per periodic norms prescribed by the government. As per directions in force at the end of 1985,[21] the total loan amount could not exceed Rs 10,000 upper ceiling limit. The limits so prepared by the society remain valid for three years, after which time they must be refixed taking afresh into account the economic earning capacity of the borrower.

[19] Information given in person by the M.D., SCB and the D.C.S.O., Kinnaur District in January 1986 to the author.

[20] Personal observation on the spot during a field resarch trip in December 1985 and January 1986.

[21] As seen in the D.C.S.O., Kinnaur's Office at Rekong Peo in Dec. 1985.

VARIATION OF CROP LOANS GIVEN BY COOPERATIVES IN KINNAUR

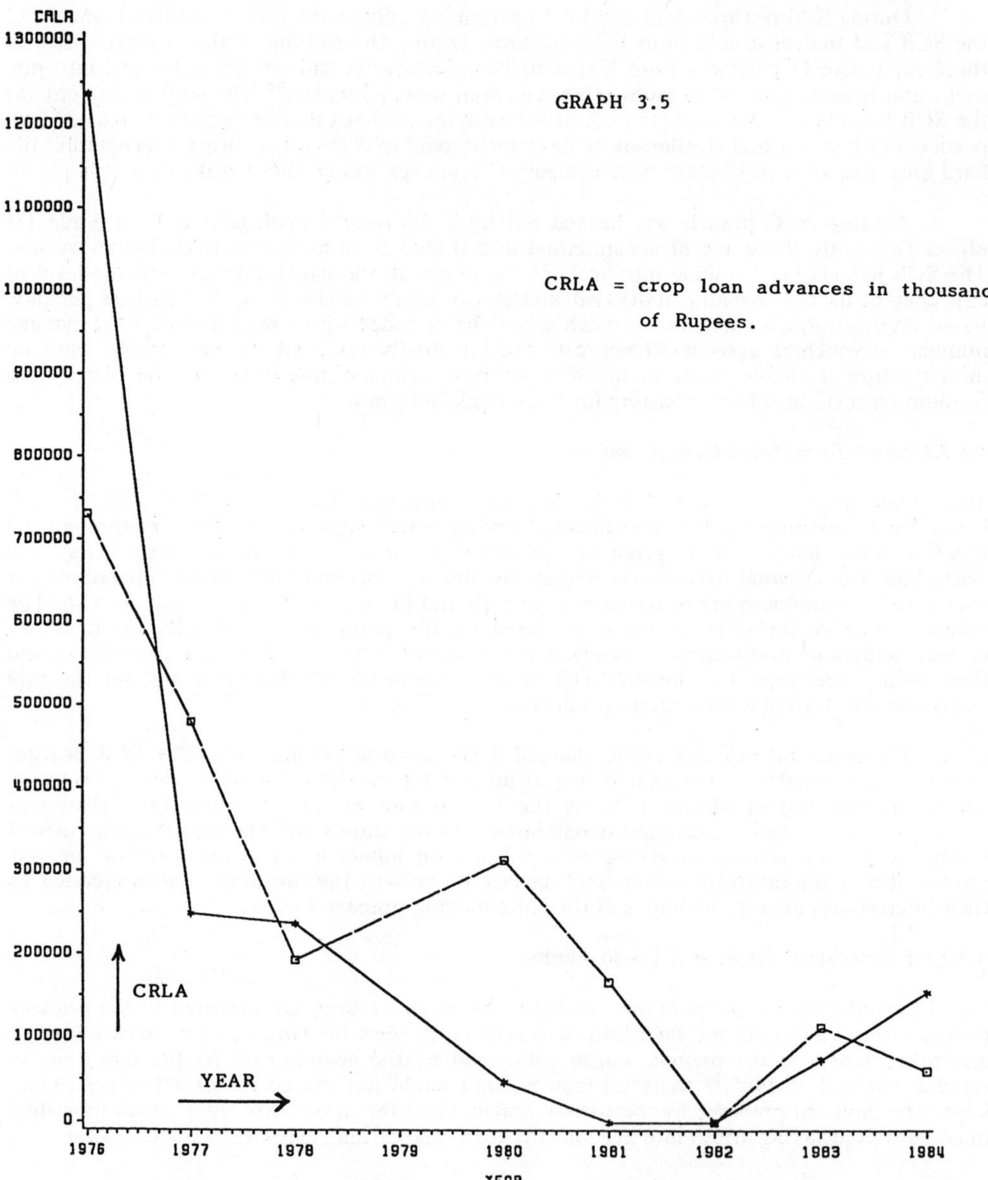

CODE FOR YEARS: 1976=1976-77, 1977=1977-78----1984-85=1984
UNBROKEN LINE JOINING STARS IS FOR LOAN AMOUNTS ADVANCED
BROKEN LINE JOINING SQUARES IS FOR LOANS RECOVERED

Once such limits have been fixed, the borrower approaches the cooperative society of which he is a member as and when he requires a crop loan. The society examines his loan application and files it before the assigned SCB branch from where loans are advanced to individual borrowers. Financing norms envisage a component in cash and a component in kind which are fixed differently for irrigated and unirrigated areas. Components in kind mean the farmer directly gets fertilizers, seeds or modern equipment. Disbursement figures for the

Table 3.6: Crop Loan Advances and Recoveries of the SCB, Kālpa

sn	*Year*	*Crop Loans in Rupees*		*pct*
,,	-do-	advanced	recovered	-do-
1	1976-77	1235,787.07	730,390.63	59.10
2	1977-78	753,418.20	478,790.79	63.55
3	1978-79	510,335.47	192,377.90	37.70
4	1979-80	510,335.47	192,370.90	37.70
5	1980-81	46,994.00	313,331.00	666.75
6	1981-82	0.00	188,285.22	00.00
7	1982-83	45,830.00	29,518.18	64.41
8	1983-84	112,253.96	112,253.96	100.00
9	1984-85	239,154.61	183,902.76	76.90

Code: **Pct = Percentage of recovery to advance, sn = Serial Number,**

(Source: Office Files of the D.C.S.O., Kinnaur District at Rekong Peo. Information collected in person in December 1985.)

Kālpa branch of the SCB are given in Table 3.6 .

3.3.2.2 Medium-Term Agricultural Loans

Medium-term loans are repayable in three to five years depending upon the type of loan raised by the agriculturist. Instalments are repayable on a half-yearly basis. Maximum borrowing has no fixed absolute limits but varies from borrower to borrower on the basis of his/her assessed capacity for income generation and loan repayment. The purposes for which medium-term agricultural loans are available are as follows:-[22]

(A) Purchase of bullocks;
(B) Minor repair works of wells and irrigation channels (kuhls);
(C) Purchase of minor agricultural implements;
(D) Purchase of metal storage bins;
(E) Installation of electric motor/diesel pumpset;
(F) Purchase of mules;
(G) Purchase of indigenous/imported buffaloes;
(H) Purchase of indigenous/imported cows;

[22] Note "Role of Cooperative Banks----", op. cit., p. 3.

Table 3.7: Crop Loan Advances made by the SCB, Rekong Peo Branch

sn	*Year*	*Crop Loans in Rupees*		*pct*
„	-do-	advanced	recovered	-do-
1	1976-77	0.00	0.00	0.00
2	1977-78	0.00	0.00	0.00
3	1978-79	0.00	0.00	0.00
4	1979-80	34,332.45	6,500.00	18.93
5	1980-81	10,435.00	18,385.00	176.19
6	1981-82	138,665.81	20,959.50	15.12
7	1982-83	0.00	24,105.71	0.00
8	1983-84	63,580.64	78,579.88	123.59
9	1984-85	2,385.00	312.00	13.08

Code: **Pct = recovery as a percentage of the advance, sn = serial number,**

(Source: Office files of the D.C.S.O., Kinnaur District at Rekong Peo. Information collected in person in December 1985.)

(I) Purchase of poultry birds;
(J) Purchase of sheep and goats;
(K) Land levelling;
(L) Reclamation of land; and
(M) Improvement of land.

3.3.2.2.1 Procedural Formalities of Cooperative Loans

As for crop loans, the maximum and the normal credit limits of each borrower, who has to be a member of the loaning cooperative society, are prepared at the primary society-level with the help of the Cooperative Department and in line with government instructions in force at the time. Cooperative Department here means the concerned Cooperative Inspector or Sub-Inspector to each of whom panchāyats and villages stand earmarked for intensive touring and supervision purposes. The borrowers' repaying/borrowing capacity is assessed on the basis of his total land holding and the pattern of crops adopted by him. The actual repayment instalment is generally fixed equal to one-third of the total assessed repaying capacity or one-sixth of the total anticipated crop produce so as not to impose too heavy a repayment burden on borrowers.

The primary society sends the loan case file to the assigned cooperative bank branch which releases the loan amount. In cases involving purchase of milch animals, pack animals, sheep, goats or draught animals, the loan amount is paid directly to the seller and not to the buyer. A team consisting of the Block Development Officer (henceforth referred to as the B.D.O.) or his nominee; the District Animal Husbandry Officer (henceforth to be referred to as the D.A.H.O.) or his nominee; the manager of the loaning branch or his nominee, scrutinizes the health and cost of the animal before allowing purchase. Agricultural implements are purchased by the B.D.O. from manufacturers and supplied to borrowers. The loan amounts are passed directly to the equipment supplier and not to the borrower.

The SCB charges 10% as the annual rate of interest for financing P.A.C.S. which in turn charge 12% from the borrowers. The state government subsidizes these loan amounts, as also the interest amounts, to the tune of 50% in Kinnaur District. In practice it means that if a borrower wants to purchase an animal worth Rs 3,000 he need raise only Rs 1,500 as medium-term loan since the government release a matching amount of Rs 1,500 as subsidy, subject to an upper ceiling of Rs 5,000 subsidy. Beyond this limit of Rs 5,000 subsidy amount, the borrower is free to raise further loan amounts which shall, however, remain unmatched by a matching subsidy. Interest repayment amounts subsidized by the government are credited directly into the accounts of the borrowers in the SCB branch which makes the necessary adjustment in its books.

3.3.2.2.2 Conversion of Short-Term Loan into Medium-Term Loan

Loanee members of cooperatives have been provided with a facility of conversion of their short-term agricultural loans into medium-term agricultural loans if drought or other natural calamities affect the area and damage crops to the extent of more than 50%. This is of special importance in Kinnaur which is prone to natural calamities like cloud bursts, landslides and avalanches. Cases for such conversion are considered only if 'ānnéwāri' (crop damage recorded in the Khasra Girdāwari or crop inspection register) is officially declared at 50% or more by the District Collector. It was observed from 1980 to 1982 that borrowers clamoured for such conversion on the plea that their crops had been completely ruined. The revenue authorities, however, had declared ānnéwāri to the tune of 50% or above only in certain villages like Gharsu, Nāthpa, Rokcharang, Kācharang, Rupi, Chhota Kamba and Bada Kamba and not in other places. Only borrowers from these villages were eligible for this facility. It created political pressures on the district administration to declare similar ānnéwāri in other villages also. Annéwāri is the name given to the system of assessment of expected crop produce. It is based on the fact that a rupee had 16 ānnās. If the forecast said that the damage to the standing crop was assessed at 4 ānnās in the rupee, it meant a damage of 25%. Another way of saying the same thing was that the crop was expected at only 12 ānnās to the rupee. Similarly, if the field inspection spoke of damage of 8 ānnās in the rupee (or a crop produce of 8 ānnās in the rupee), it meant that the crop was damaged to the extent of 50%. A damage report of 8 ānnās or more to the rupee made the affected borrowers eligible for conversion of loans.

Where conversion of crop loans into medium-term loans is allowed it is only the instalment next due that is to be recovered over a period of three years. Other already fixed instalments are to be recovered as scheduled. To have an idea of the scale of medium term financing and conversion, we observe the figures of the Kālpa branch of the SCB. This scheme of medium-term loans was introduced only in 1980 and conversion was done for the first time in 1983. Table 3.8 shows that the amounts involved are less than Rs 50,000 and do not even reach the level of Rs 1 per capita in Kinnaur.[23]

3.3.2.3 Short-Term and Medium-Term Non-Agricultural Loans

The short-term non-agricultural loan facility has not so far been utilized at all and remains a hypothetical option on paper. Should loans be advanced under this head, the SCB would charge societies giving such loans an annual interest rate of 11%.[24] Lending societies would charge an interest rate of 13.5% per annum. No eventualities have really been specified for which such loans would be given and how the procedural formalities would operate. This sector has been left exclusively for commercial banks.

[23] Considering the total population figure of the 1981 census (= 59,547 persons) for Kinnaur District.

[24] Note "Role of the Cooperative Banks---", op cit., Annexure A.

Table 3.8: Scale of Cooperative Medium-Term Financing in Kinnaur

sn	Year	M.T. Loans in Rupees		M.T. Conversion Loans	
,,	-do-	advanced	recovered	advanced	recovered
1	1980-81	41,100	0,000	0,000	0,000
2	1981-82	0,000	5,142	0,000	0,000
3	1982-83	0,000	1,512	0,000	0,000
4	1983-84	0,000	0,000	33,790	0,000
5	1984-85	0,000	34,444	0,000	3,631

Code: sn = serial number, M.T. = medium-term.
All loan amounts are in Rupees
(Source: Supplied in person by the Manager, SCB, Kālpa Branch from his office files on December 3, 1985 at Kālpa.)

The medium-term non-agricultural loan facility involves an interest rate of 11.5% per annum for funds loaned by the SCB to societies. It is for government employees who form their own society and have it registered with the Registrar Cooperative Societies (henceforth, R.C.S.) through the Cooperative Department. The SCB then fixes their loan limits in proportion to their share capital. Repayment of such loans is made in monthly instalments. Two such societies were functioning in Kinnaur at the end of 1985. These were providing direct credit to members but were also relevant because by providing essential commodities at controlled rates they were reducing the need to borrow for these items, had the members been obliged to purchase these at open market rates. Amounts loaned out and recovered under this

Table 3.9: Medium-Term Non-Agricultural Loans by the SCB, Kālpa

sn	*Year*	*Loan Amount(Rupees)*		*PCT*
,,	-do-	advanced	recovered	-do-
1	1980-81	27,800	19,400	69.78
2	1981-82	69,100	16,570	23.98
3	1982-83	76,730	28,005	36.50
4	1983-84	106,221	39,609	37.29
5	1984-85	193,351	9,761	05.05

Code: sn = Serial Number, PCT = Recovery as percentage of advance.
(Source: Office Files of the D.C.S.O., Kinnaur District. Handed over in person by the District Cooperative Inspector in Peo on 06-12-85).

scheme are shown in Table 3.9. The rate of interest on such loans is 12.5% per annum.

3.3.2.4 Financing of Marketing and Consumer Activities

The SCB not only provides term loans as discussed till now but also provides the facility of cash credit limits to individuals as well as to P.A.C.S. for carrying on the following activities:[25]

(1) Wholesale procurement of fertilizers, insecticides, pesticides and their distribution through P.A.C.S. or individual depot holders;
(2) Trading in controlled commodities;
(3) Procurement and sale of essential commodities under the public distribution system (P.D.S.);
(4) Marketing of cash crops like potatoes, apples, vegetables and ginger;
(5) Procurement of raw material and marketing of woven fabrics by weavers' cooperatives;
(6) Processing/canning and marketing of agricultural/horticultural produce by processing cooperatives.

3.3.2.4.1 Cash Credit Pledge Limits

The SCB allows cash credit pledge limits to individuals or societies according to the working efficiency of the borrower concerned. These limits can be up to any amount. The borrower and the bank both maintain their own locks on the godown as security. The bank allows delivery of goods from the godown on demand from the borrower. A reserve margin of 25% is usually kept on the sanctioned limit. The interest rate charged is 13.5% per annum, except for fertilizers for which the interest rates are as follows:

(a) 11.5% per annum up to Rs 5,000 loan;
(b) 13.5% per annum above Rs 5,000 and up to Rs 25,000;
(c) 16% per annum above Rs 25,000.[26]

The interest charged by the bank is reimbursed by the state government to the societies. Amounts advanced and recovered under this head for the Kālpa branch of the SCB are shown in Table 3.10 .

3.3.2.4.2 Cash Credit Hypothecation Limits

These limits are sanctioned according to an assessment of the working of the society in question. Interest is charged at the rate of 13.5% per annum on such accounts. The bank keeps a margin of 40% in the limit as a security reserve. The interest charged by the bank is reimbursed to societies by the government. Loans disbursed under these hypothecation limits and the amounts recovered for the years 1976-77 to 1984-85 by the Kālpa branch of the SCB are shown in Table 3.11 .

3.3.2.4.3 Cash Credit Marketing Limits

Special limits to deal with the marketing of potato, cummin seed, neoza, apple and other produce (almonds, apricots etc.) are sanctioned by the head office of the SCB in Simla for operations in Kinnaur by marketing societies. These limits carry an annual rate of interest to the tune of 13.5%. To encourage marketing societies, government usually reimburse this interest charged by the bank. Government also help such societies by giving them share capital. Cash credit marketing limits' statistics are shown in Table 3.12 . Data was available for only these two years.

[25] Ibid, p. 4.

[26] Ibid, Annexure A.

Table 3.10: Pledged Amounts Advanced and Recovered from Cooperatives by the SCB, Kālpa

sn	*Year*	*Pledges to Societies*		*PCT*
,,	-do-	advanced	recovered	-do-
1	1976-77	63,907	61,963	96.96
2	1977-78	1,946	,111	05.70
3	1982-83	1242,541	967,754	77.89
4	1983-84	953,575	814,046	85.37
5	1984-85	370,881	370,491	99.90

Code: **sn = Serial Number; PCT = Recovery as percentage of advance.**
The years from 1978-79 to 1981-82 have been left out as the value for all the variables was zero.
(Source: Given in person by the Manager, SCB, Kālpa Branch from his office files in Kālpa on December 3, 1985.)

3.3.2.4.4 Cash Credit Public Distribution System Limits

At the end of 1985 there were 37 registered cooperative societies and seven individual depot holders (in villages Rakchham, Chhitkul, Choling, Asrang, Leo, Chāngo and Sumra) distributing consumer goods under the P.D.S. . All these dealers had been sanctioned cash credit limits under the P.D.S. subject to an upper ceiling of Rs 30,000. The SCB charged an annual rate of interest of 13.5% which was reimbursed into their account books by the government. Data under this scheme for the Kālpa branch of the SCB is shown in Table 3.13

In addition to this gamut of institutional credit inputs, credit is further available to individuals as members of cooperatives on lines similar to those followed by commercial banks as shall be discussed in the following Chapter.

3.3.3 Loans to Individuals: A Business Necessity

Loaning schemes for individuals were a sign of recognition by cooperative banks that they could not ignore the principle of individual service in banking. After the nationalization of 14 major commercial banks in 1969 and their subsequent branch expansion into Kinnaur the potential borrower had the choice of going either to the cooperative banks or to the commercial banks. Not only was the absolute monopoly of the SCB, lasting from 1960 till 1974, broken but also, the newly arrived parvenus offered a much wider choice of loans for the individual borrower than had the SCB. Initially this did not cause much problem because the commercial banks preferred to focus their lending on economically viable schemes like the purchase of trucks. All this changed once they were railroaded by the government into liberally financing development schemes in rural areas. The SCB had to cope with this new reality that it could not just smugly watch rural people coming to its doors for development loans because no other bank was willing to meet their requests. Monopolizing the cooperative network's credit requirements was no longer enough. The individual, too, had to be catered to. Schemes were devised keeping the individual borrower in view.

3.3.3.1 Loans Against the Bank's Own Deposits

Customers of the SCB were sanctioned loans on the security of their own deposits in the form of fixed deposit receipts (F.D.Rs) or term deposits. The bank was willing to finance such customers to the extent of 85% of their own deposits. Such finance was also made available on the basis of interest accrued on such term deposits. The bank, in return, would charge an

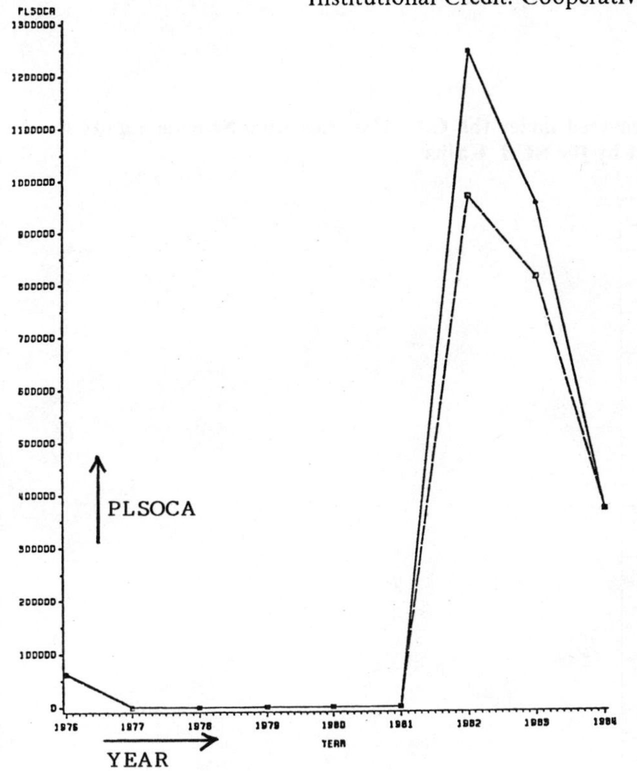

GRAPH 3.6

Variation of amounts pledged to cooperative societies by the Cooperative Bank in Kinnaur District.

PLSOCA = amount pledged in Rupees.

VARIATION OF C.C.HYPOTHECATION AMOUNTS FOR COOPERATIVES

PLSOCA = Amounts loaned out under the pledges to cooperatives in thousands of Rupees.

CCHYPA = Amounts loaned out under the cash-credit hypothecation limits' scheme to cooperatives, in thousands of Rupees.

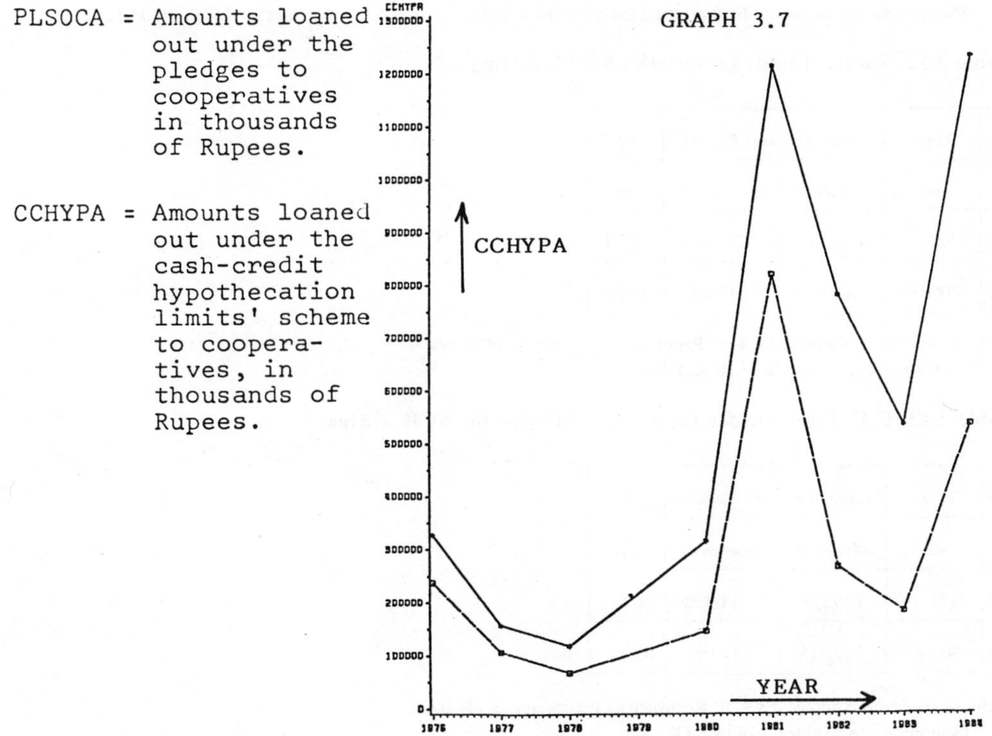

GRAPH 3.7

CODE FOR YEARS: 1976=1976-77, 1977=1977-78----1984-85=1984
UNBROKEN LINE JOINING STARS IS FOR LOAN AMOUNTS ADVANCED
BROKEN LINE JOINING SQUARES IS FOR LOANS RECOVERED

Table 3.11: Amounts Advanced and Recovered under the C.C. Hypothecation Scheme Limits to Cooperative Societies in Kinnaur District by the SCB, Kālpa

sn	*Year*	*C.C. Hypthcn Limits*		*PCT*
,,	-do-	advanced	recovered	-do-
1	1976-77	63,907	61,963	96.96
2	1977-78	1,946	,111	05.70
3	1978-79	117,148	66,900	57.11
4	1979-80	0,000	0,000	00.00
5	1980-81	312,853	144,074	46.05
6	1981-82	1211,230	818,169	67.55
7	1982-83	778,952	264,400	33.94
8	1983-84	533,097	180,045	33.77
9	1984-85	1230,317	534,138	43.41

Code: sn = serial number; PCT = recovery as percentage of advance.
C.C. Hypthcn Limits = Cash Credit Hypothecation Limits.
(Source: Given in person by the Manager, SCB, Kālpa Branch from his office files in Kālpa on 03-12-85.)

Table 3.12: Special Limits to Societies for Marketing

sn	*Year*	*Limit Amount (Rupees)*		*PCT*
,,	-do-	advanced	recovered	-do-
1	1982-83	865,518	726,046	83.39
2	1983-84	814,873	811,531	99.59

Code: sn = Serial Number; PCT = Recovery as percentage of advance.
(Source: As for Tables 3.10 and 3.11)

Table 3.13: C.C. Limits under the P.D.S. Data for the SCB, Kālpa

sn	*Year*	*Loan Amount (Rupees)*		*PCT*
,,	-do-	advanced	recovered	-do-
1	1983-84	176,256	11,562	06.56
2	1984-85	127,815	114,080	89.25

Code: sn = Serial Number; PCT = Recovery as percentage of advance.
(Source: As for Tables 3.10 to 3.12)

annual rate of interest 2% higher than what it was giving to the borrower on his own fixed deposit per annum. This margin rose to 2.5% per annum if loan was granted to a third party on the security of the term deposit of an intermediary account holder. The account holder has, of course, to signify his agreement to such an arrangement on legal paper. These schemes have been in operation in Kinnaur at least since 1976-77. They have shown a steady and perceptible rise in the amounts loaned out, as can be verified from the figures available for the Kālpa branch of the SCB in Table 3.14. Deposit figures are also listed alongside for easy

Table 3.14: Loans against own Term Deposits by the SCB, Kālpa

sn	*Year*	*Loan Amounts (Rupees)*		*Deposits*	*Recovery as %of*	
,,	-do-	advanced	recovered	—do—	advances	deposits
1	1976-77	26,267	19,522	3086,635	74.32	0.06
2	1977-78	51,539	48,217	2374,847	93.55	02.03
3	1978-79	690,527	654,618	2768,322	94.80	23.65
4	1980-81	1784,500	1543,416	4075,433	86.49	37.87
5	1981-82	1843,100	1556,790	4199,252	84.47	37.07
6	1982-83	2321,637	1945,170	4240,684	83.78	45.87
7	1983-84	2826,779	2296,157	5391,707	81.23	42.59
8	1984-85	3400,744	2701,504	6103,140	79.44	44.26

Note: % = percentage, sn = serial number, Deposits = bank deposits.
(Source: As for Tables 3.11 to 3.13).

cross-reference. The Reserve Bank of India has allowed cooperative banks to finance individuals on the lines of cooperative societies. Accordingly, the SCB has introduced the following schemes from the year 1983 onwards.

3.3.3.2 Cash Credit Hypothecation Limits to Individuals

Loan amounts sanctioned depend upon the economic activity being carried on by individual borrowers. Usually these cash credit limits are sanctioned to very reliable clients whose bona fides are not in doubt by the bank. Such limits can be availed of for marketing activities in easily disposable commodities like foodgrains, oil seeds, edible oils, sugar, cloth in mill packed bales, iron and steel and electrical goods - all with margins of security in reserve of not less than 40% of the invoice/market value. Maximum ceilings on such loans have been fixed at Rs 10,000. The annual rate of interest charged is 18%. Amounts loaned under this scheme by the Kālpa branch of the SCB are shown in Table 3.15 .

3.3.3.3 C.C. Limits under Pledge to Individuals

Such cash credit pledge limits are granted to individuals on the security of easily marketable commodities such as foodgrains, oil seeds, edible oil in sealed tins, sugar, cloth in mill packed bales, iron and steel. The bank enforces effective control by having its own lock put on the storage godown and by insisting on a security reserve margin of 25% of the invoice/market value. This advance is subject to an upper ceiling of Rs 25,000 and carries an annual rate of interest to the tune of 17.5%. Data for such transactions is shown in Table 3.15 .

Table 3.15: C.C. Hypothecation Limits to Individuals by the SCB

sn	*Year*	*Loan Type*	*Loan Amount(Rupees)*		*Pct of*
„	-do-	—do—	advanced	recovered	adv/rvy
1.1 -"-	1983-84 ---do--	C.C.Hypothecation to individuals	121,189	112,790	93.07
1.2 -„-	---do--- ---do---	Overdrafts to Individuals	8,044 --,--	5,200 --,--	64.64 --.--
1.3	---do---	Consumer Durables	20,410	2,780	13.62
1.4	---do---	Against Salary	0,000	0,000	00.00
1.5	---do---	Against N.S.C	0,000	0,000	00.00
2.1 -„-	1984-85 ---do---	C.C.Hypothecation to Individuals	234,157 ---,---	198,227 ---,---	84.66 --.--
2.2 -„-	---do--- ---do---	Overdrafts to Individuals	0,000 -,---	2,891 -,---	00.00 --.--
2.3	---do---	Consumer Durables	31,142	16,334	52.45
2.4	---do---	Against Salary	18,902	12,547	66.38
2.5	---do---	Against N.S.C	0,000	0,000	00.00

Code: **C.C. = Cash Credit, N.S.C = National Savings Certificates, adv/rvy = Percentage of Recoveries to Advances.**
(Source: As for Tables 3.11 to 3.14.)

3.3.3.4 Advances Against Salary Bills, Life Insurance Policies, National Savings Certificates and for Purchase of Consumer Durables: Vive La Bourgeoisie!

These loan amounts are sanctioned at the bank's discretion up to 75% of the value of the surrender document in the shape of a L.I.C. policy, a salary bill of a government servant or a national savings certificate. Such loans are also granted for the purchase of consumer durables like refrigerators, scooters, T.V. sets, radio sets etc., subject to an upper ceiling of Rs 7,500. These loans carry an annual rate of interest of 17.5%. Amounts advanced and recovered under this scheme by the Kālpa branch of the SCB are shown in Table 3.15.

In addition to providing such loans, the SCB pays 0.25% higher rate of interest per annum on deposits than those paid by commercial banks. Figures for the total deposits of the Kālpa branch of the SCB have aleady been shown in Table 3.14. The bank issues drafts on banks in important cities in India and transfers money for its customers at par. This is all part of the effort aimed at providing the same services as are being rendered by commercial banks to their customers. Having thus examined the palette of short- and medium-term loan schemes offered by the SCB, we can now pass on to the other string in the bow of cooperative credit banking institutions, namely, long-term credit. This is handled by the H.P. State Cooperative Land Development Bank (henceforth to be referred to as the LDB) with its head office at Simla. It has one branch in Kinnaur District at Kālpa since 1981. The thrust or raison d'être of its lending operations is to enable agriculturists/horticulturists to improve their productive capacities and hence their income earning capacity by giving loans on a long-term basis.

3.4 THE H.P. STATE COOPERATIVE LAND DEVELOPMENT BANK (LDB)

The LDB is not an agency for providing long-term credit for any and every purpose. On the lines of the SCB, specific purposes have been pinpointed by the LDB for such lending. These are as follows:[27]

(1) Provision of irrigation facilities and water taps for land;
(2) For rendering waste land cultivable;
(3) For checking land erosion and levelling land;
(4) For providing fencing all around or in any direction on one's land;
(5) For planting apple, pear, plum, citrus, mango, mandarin or other fruit orchards and for tea plantations;
(6) For purchase of tractors, threshers, electric motors, spraying machines for orchards or for other operations that increase the agriculturists'/horticulturists' land production capacity;
(7) For redeeming mortgaged land; and
(8) For purchase of land, subject to the condition that the land being purchased is surrounded by or adjacent to the buyer's land. Preference is given to purchases helping to consolidate the borrowers' land holdings.

Clearly, none of the purposes listed above, yields quick returns. That is why the LDB's loans cover periods of more than five years. Limits have been placed on these loans since there are just not enough funds available for giving unlimited loan amounts.

3.4.1 Ceilings on Long-Term Loans

These ceilings are as follows:

(1) For purchasing a tractor = Rs 80,000;
(2) For planting a tea estate = Rs 50,000;
(3) For other listed purposes = Rs 30,000.

They are subject to periodic revision.

3.4.2 Rates of Interest Charged

Unlike the multifarious variety of interest rates charged for its schemes by the SCB, the LDB has a dual pattern of interest rates.

(a) For small farmers/horticulturists = 10% per annum;
(b) For other farmers/horticulturists = 12.5% per annum.

These interest rates are periodically fixed by the National Bank of Agriculture and Rural Development (henceforth to be referred to as the NABARD).[28]

3.4.3 Loan Repayment Periods

The repayment period depends on the economic activity for which the loan is taken. Four broad classifications have been made for repayment periods, as follows:[29]

[27] Note entitled "Himāchal Pradesh Bhoomi Vikās Bank logoṅ ki séwā meiṅ", Prepared on the orders of the M.D., LDB, for the author in Simla in January 1986, Typewritten Hindi Document, Unpublished, p. 3.

[28] Ibid, p. 5.

[29] Ibid.

(1) 15 years for repayment of loans taken for planting apple orchards. The first instalment of repayment commences from the eighth year onwards;
(2) 15 years for repayment of loans taken for planting citrus orchards. The first repayment instalment falls due from the sixth year onwards;
(3) 7 years for loans for tractor purchase; and
(4) 10 years for repayment of other loans.

As with all government or semi-government agencies, the procedural aspect should not be ignored. Loans are released only when all procedural formalities have been duly completed. What this involves in a bureaucracy-ridden infrastructure shall be seen later.

3.4.4 Procedural Formalities: Intricate Labyrinth!

A prospective borrower must fill up a proforma or loan application form prescribed by the LDB. This duly filled-in form has to be submitted to the nearest LDB branch alongwith the following land record copies pertaining to the applicant's land holding:

(a) Copy of the latest Jamābandi (Record of Rights Register);
(b) Copy of the latest Khasrā Girdāwari (Crop Inspection Register); and
(c) Assessment chart of the quinquennial average purchase-sale prices of the revenue estate in which the land in question may be.

In addition to filing this loan application form and accompanying documents, the applicant must enrol himself as an 'A' class member of the LDB. For this purpose he/she has to deposit Rs 100 as membership contribution (security) and Rs 5 as membership fee. Once the loan amount has been sanctioned, the borrower-applicant must mortgage the land in question in favour of the bank by signing a mortgage deed in the presence of an authorized employee of the bank. On completion of mortgage formalities, at the time of getting the loan amount released, the borrowers have to purchase necessary/additional shares on the basis of the loan amount and deposit the necessary sum. To calculate this, a share of Rs 100 has to be purchased by depositing this amount for every Rs 2,000 of loan. Hence to obtain Rs 10,000 as loan, the prospective borrower has to purchase five shares of the LDB of value Rs 100 each, totalling Rs 500 in all. The operations of the LDB in Kinnaur have been on a very limited scale, as will be seen in the tables of bank statistics in the next Chapter. We can now turn our attention to the operation of the cooperative credit network in the remotest sub-division of Kinnaur (= Pooh).

3.5 SAMPLE SURVEY IN POOH SUB-DIVISION

Pooh Sub-Division was the hub of the cross-border trade with Tibet before 1962.[30] It suffered the maximum losses when this trade was stopped. It is relevant to examine how far the cooperative credit network has succeeded in meeting the credit demands of the area thus affected. Till the advent of commercial banks, the area was dependent wholly and solely on cooperatives for institutional credit. Credit needs that had been met earlier by the informal sector through surpluses generated by trade were now turned inwards. Poohwas the fittest area was, after 1962, for large-scale introduction of institutional credit. What were the actual results?

[30] Please see Section 1.2.4, Chapter I of this work.

3.5.1 Sample Survey Field Work

Under the ægis of the Desert Development Agency (henceforth referred to as the D.D.A.), the special agency set up to implement the Desert Development Programme (henceforth, the D.D.P.) in Pooh for its accelerated development,[31] a comprehensive Bench Mark Survey was initiated in August 1983 for which the field work was completed during August/September 1983. The survey was carried out under control of the Director of Economics and Statistics, H.P., assisted by his Joint Director, Deputy Director (Planning) and the District Statistical Officer (henceforth referred to as the D.S.O.), Kinnaur, all senior officers. Before seeing how the cooperative credit network actually performed, we must see the sample villages chosen and the income, expenditure and credit need patterns therein.

3.5.1.1 Sample Villages: Fairly Representative

Table 3.16: Sample Villages of Pooh Sub-Division

sn ,,	*Village Name*	*Tahsil/ Sub-Tah*	*Tla hec*	*Tlpn -do-*	*Hds No.*	*Avgpn --do--*
1	Sumra	Hangrang	35	229	47	04.87
2	Leo	Hangrang	76	477	103	04.63
3	Dābling	Pooh	107	284	66	04.30
4	Namgya	Pooh	135	434	97	04.47
5	Kānam	Pooh	601	874	145	06.03
6	Chārang	Moorang	60	213	48	04.44
7	Jāngi	Moorang	169	925	164	05.64
8	Moorang	Moorang	246	1534	317	04.84

Code: **sn = serial number, Tla = total area, Tlpn = total population,**
Hds = number of households,
Avgpn = average population per household,
Sub-Tah = Sub-Tahsil, hec = Hectares.
(Source: District Census Handbook, 1981, p. 46 for villages Sumra and Leo, p. 52 for villages Dābling, Namgya, Kānam and p. 58 for villages Chārang, Jāngi and Moorang.)

Table 3.16 gives some data about the sample villages chosen. Sumra is the last village in Kinnaur towards the North. Chārang is one of the two remotest villages (the other being Kuno), to reach which one has to walk about 45 kms from the roadhead. It is very close to the frontier with Tibet. Namgya is the last village before the Shipki La pass. Moorang and Kānam are two of the largest villages in Kinnaur. They lie close to N.H. 22, as do Dābling and Jāngi. None of the villages lies, however, on N.H. 22. They cover both the Tahsils and

[31] The Agency was established in 1981 with the author as its first Chairman in his capacity as the D.C., Kinnaur District. He personally prepared the Draft Five Year Plan for the D.D.P., on the basis of which funds were released by the Union and State Governments. This task could be completed successfully only because of the total and unreserved support extended to the author by the late Mr C.D. Parsheera, I.A.S., Director, R.I.D. Department, Simla.

Sub-Tahsil Hangrang of Pooh Sub-Division.

3.5.1.1.1 Household Selection

20 households were selected in each sample village on a circular systematic sampling basis, arranged according to means of livelihood classes. The method of hamlet group selection had to be adopted in Moorang on account of its large population. Two hamlet groups were formed here, of which one was selected randomly and the survey work restricted to this hamlet group only. The total population covered in these eight sample villages was 3,791 persons, constituting about 21% of the total population of Pooh Sub-Division. The total number of households was 987, giving an average household size of five persons. The following indicators are of special interest to us:-

(1) Consumption expenditure;
(2) Per household per mensem income and consumption expenditure by income ranges;
(3) Consumer expenditure per household by broad groups of items of consumption;
(4) Distribution of population by monthly per capita consumption expenditure;
(5) Extent of indebtedness and debt liabilities by ranges of values of assets owned; and
(6) Credit requirements by tenurial classification and asset groups.

3.5.1.1.2 Consumption Expenditure Per Household Per Month

Table 3.17 shows the consumption expenditure per household per month by total annual

Table 3.17: Consumption Expenditure per Household per Month

sn ,,	*Receipt Class* (Rupees)	*Shd* No.	*Total c.e.* (Rupees)	*Per HH* C.e.p.m
1	Below-2,000	000	00.00	00.00
2	2,000-3,500	005	944.20	188.84
3	3,500-4,200	003	639.45	213.15
4	4,200-6,000	008	3114.95	389.36
5	6,000-7,200	007	2257.40	322.48
6	7,200-7,500	002	1436.15	728.07
7	7,500-9,000	017	8422.05	495.41
8	9,000-12,000	023	14,638.77	636.46
9	12,000-Above	095	82,863.80	872.25
10	All-Classes	160	114,336.79	714.60

Code: **sn = serial number, Shd = number of sample households, c.e. = consumption expenditure,**
Per HH = per household, C.e.p.m = consumption expenditure per month.
(Source: An Economic Profile of Pooh Cold Desert Area: A Benchmark Survey, A Study carried out for the Desert Development Agency, Pooh, p. 56.)

receipt classes. The table reveals that while the average per household consumption expenditure per month is about Rs 715, nearly 41% of the sample households have consumption expenditure levels below this average. These are just prima facie conclusions as this data does not lend itself to detailed analysis in view of its inappropriate classification form. It is better to study it relative to income ranges.

3.5.1.1.3 Per Household Per Mensem Income and Consumption Expenditure by Income Ranges

Table 3.18: Per Household Income/Expenditure by Income Range

sn ,,	*Receipt Class* (Rupees)	*Shd* No.	*Total c.e.* (Rupees)	*Per HH* C.e.p.m
1	Below-2,000	00	00.00	00.00
2	2,000-3,500	5	243.42	188.84
3	3,500-4,200	3	321.11	213.15
4	4,200-6,000	8	440.31	389.36
5	6,000-7,200	7	553.99	322.48
6	7,200-7,500	2	619.38	728.07
7	7,500-9,000	17	711.57	495.41
8	9,000-12,000	23	862.77	636.46
9	12,000-Above	95	2125.82	872.25
10	All-Classes	160	1,529.46	714.60

Code: **sn = serial number, Shd = number of sample households,**
c.e. = consumption expenditure,
Per HH = per household, C.e.p.m = consumption expenditure per month.
(Source: An Economic Profile of Pooh Cold Desert Area, A Benchmark Survey, A Study carried out for the Desert Development Agency, Pooh, Unpublished, p. 57.)

All household classes show a propensity to save. This is born partly out of the historical style of living in this geographically remote area where lifestyles had to be frugal. The area was not easily open to imports so people tried to make-do with what they had. A positive correlation between the per month per household income and the per month per household consumption expendture is clearly discernible. Higher income groups show a higher propensity to save. This should, however, not be used to infer that credit needs would be determined accordingly, with the poorer income groups borrowing more and the richer income groups borrowing less.

3.5.1.1.4 Per Household Consumption Expenditure in the 30 Days Preceding the Survey Date

To have a better idea of consumption expenditure, it was calculated per household per month on the basis of the actual expenditure incurred during the 30 days preceding the date of survey. This cross-sectional data is shown in Table 3.19. Food items accounted for nearly 66% of the total consumption expenditure. The expenditure percentage for clothing and footwear was also significant, being nearly 16%. There is no perceptible "conspicuous" consumption even in higher per capita income groups above Rs 200. Having examined these consumption patterns, we can now try to form an estimate of the indebtedness and the developmental credit requirements of the sample households.

Table 3.19: Consumption Expenditure during 30 Days before the Survey

sn	*Monthly p.c.*	*Hds*	*Expenditure on(in Rupees)*						
,,	Exp. Class	No.	Cereals	Pulses	o.f. item	f+1	c+f	misc	Total
1	00-60	0	0.00	00.00	000.00	00.00	00.00	00.00	000.00
2	60-76	7	179.57	17.57	173.41	58.57	46.71	08.88	484.71
3	76-100	39	232.15	24.85	181.12	83.08	82.75	29.71	633.66
4	100-110	20	222.58	24.80	229.45	106.70	42.30	22.65	648.43
5	110-150	37	221.55	28.27	216.12	92.54	118.49	26.05	703.03
6	150-200	27	263.65	35.78	330.36	110.42	216.89	48.43	1005.58
7	200-250	11	149.45	27.91	334.63	112.12	154.09	81.55	859.75
8	250-Above	19	95.45	21.36	222.36	63.54	174.55	58.53	635.59
9	All-Classes	160	209.60	26.96	235.55	91.44	113.0	37.21	713.76
% to Total Consumption			29.37	03.78	33.00	12.81	15.83	05.21	100.00

Code: **Monthly p.c. = monthly per capita, o.f. item = other food items,**
f+l = fuel + lighting, c+f = clothing and footwear, misc = miscellaneous, Exp. Class = expenditure class. % = percentage, Hds = number of households.
(Source: As for Table 3.18, p. 58)

3.5.1.2 Indebtedness and Credit Requirements

The area in question revealed a lack of conspicuous consumption, coupled with a propensity to save amongst all income groups. This can not, however, be taken as an index of a lack of demand for development credit available from the institutional infrastructure. In common with other areas, the higher income groups tended to reveal greater readiness towards availing institutional credit facilities than lower income groups. This could have been a priori presumed as a valid axiom but was actually borne out by the survey. Table 3.20 contains the field survey data about indebtedness of households and per household indebtedness by classes of value of assets owned by sample households. 73 out of 160 households (45.625%) in the sample were under debt but their distribution amongst asset value groups was markedly uneven. As many as 55 out of 73 (75.34%) indebted households belonged to the asset value range group of Rs 25,000 and above. The total number of households in this range was 110 (68.75% of the total sample households = 160). 55 (34.38%) of the total sample households belonging to the two highest asset value range groups of Rs 25,000 and above had outstanding debt liabilities amounting to Rs 183,105 on the date of survey. This constituted 90.44% of the total debt liability of Rs 202,455 on this date for all sample households. Per household debt liability for these groups of Rs 25,000 and above came to Rs 3329.18, if we divide Rs 183,105 by the number of households (55) in these groups. Of the 110 households in this group, 55 had outstanding debt liabilities, i.e. 50% of the total number of households in this range were indebted. Even though the average figure of indebtedness for the whole sample was Rs 2,776.36, the per household average indebtedness for households in the asset value range of Rs 30,000 and above was Rs 3,634.80; Rs 861.44 higher than the overall sample average. Rs 861.44 equals 31.06% of Rs 2,773.36 and 23,70% of Rs 3,634.80. Thus the per household indebtedness of the Rs 25,000 and above asset range is 31.06% higher than that of the average

Table 3.20: Indebtedness & Debt Liabilities by Asset Value Ranges

sn	*Asset Value Group*	*No. of Hds*		*O.d.l on*	*Extent of*
"	**(Rupees)**	**Ttl**	**owi**	**d.o.s**	**inds.p.h**
1	Below-5,000	12	00	0,000	00.00
2	5,000-7,500	2	0	0,000	00.00
3	7,500-10,000	3	1	,600	600.00
4	10,000-12,500	3	1	1,000	1000.00
5	12,500-15,000	3	1	,800	800.00
6	15,000-18,000	2	0	0,000	00.00
7	18,000-21,000	9	5	3,750	750.00
8	21,000-25,000	16	10	13,200	1320.00
9	25,000-30,000	9	6	5,000	833.33
10	30,000-Above	101	49	178,105	3634.80
11	Total	160	73	202,455	2773.36

Code: **Hds = households, O.d.l = outstanding debt liabilities, Ttl = total, owi = of which indebted, d.o.s = date of survey, inds.p.h = indebtedness per household.**
(Source: As for Table 3.18, p. 61.)

of the whole sample. We can calculate similar percentages for the entire sample. Their results are shown in Table 3.21. Column 5 of Table 3.21 shows no correlation between the abrupt changes in per household indebtedness of an asset value range over that of the preceding asset value range in terms of percentage. The biggest jump of +336% comes as we pass from the asset value range of 25,000-30,000 to that of Rs 30,000 and above. This value is nearly 1.5 times higher than Rs 2,773.36, the average per household indebtedness figure for the whole sample. The lowest asset value group (0-7,500) which should borrow the maximum in terms of needed improvement in economic standards, did not borrow at all. The debt amount per household does not increase linearly with rising asset value but makes a quantum leap at the highest asset value range. Having made these empirical calculations, we can examine the survey results in terms of term-credit requirements.

3.5.1.2.1 Short-, Medium- and Long-Term Credit Requirements

Having already seen the schemes offered by the cooperative credit network, we can now examine the term-credit requirements of the sample households. Table 3.22 contains the results of this examination. This can be represented in terms of percentages of total credit requirement, for the asset value group and for the grand total. The results are displayed in Table 3.23. These Tables reinforce the conclusions of Tables 3.20 and 3.21 that credit requirements rise in general with asset value range. Except for a drop at 25,000-30,000 from the level of 21,000-25,000, we have a constant rise in the credit requirement. Not that the lowest asset value ranges do not need credit. They lack enough asset value to offer as security and are thus considered as credit risks by official credit agencies. None of the sample

Table 3.21: Indebtedness Statistics for Sample Households

sn	*A.V. Group*	*O.D.L.*	*E.O.I.*	*%Change*	*P.H.I.*
1	0-5000	0,000	0.00	0.00	0.00
2	5,000-7,500	0,000	0.00	0.00	0.00
3	7,500-10,000	,600	600.00	0.00	21.63
4	10,000-12,500	1,000	1000.00	+66.67	36.06
5	12,500-15,000	,800	800.00	-20.00	28.85
6	15,000-18,000	0,000	0.00	0.00	0.00
7	18,000-21,000	3,750	750.00	0.00	27.04
8	21,000-25,000	13,200	1320.00	+76.00	47.60
9	25,000-30,000	5,000	833.33	-36.87	30.05
10	30,000-Above	178,105	3634.80	+336.18	131.06

Code: **A.V. Group = asset value group, sn = serial number,**
O.D.L. = outstanding debt liabilities as on the date of survey,
E.O.I. = extent of indebtedness per household,
%Change = percentage change of per household indebtedness over preceding asset value range,
P.H.I. = per household indebtedness as percentage of total average indebtedness per household.
(Source: As for Table 3.20)

households indicated a need for short-term credit. Only the three top asset value ranges stated a requirement for medium-term credit. Long-term credit requirement was indicated by nearly 90% of the sample households. It formed 90.57% of the total credit requirements. The survey explains the total absence of short-term credit requirement as a matter of satisfaction indicating that the "*short-term credit needs are generally possible to be met by the households themselves. It indicates the resilience of the households to meet their needs for bulk of the farm operations internally. This fact is also borne out by the fact that all households had been assessed to be having propensity to save*".[32]

Of the 144 sample households expressing a need for long-term credit, only 38 had approached some agencies for obtaining credit to meet their needs. The official document smugly concludes that it was "*a matter of great satisfaction that all these households had approached the government agencies for their long-term credit needs. The institution of private moneylenders appears to be almost non-existent in the study area. This may be due to the stringent legislation operating in the area*".[33] These rosy conclusions are not borne out by facts. It is unrealistic to infer a near absence of private moneylenders from the absence of an expressed requirement for short-term credit. As shall be seen in Chapter VII, short-term credit requirements almost everywhere in Kinnaur were mostly being met from private sources, one of the most important of which were (and are) the village deities. Since these sources

[32] Bhatnagar, R.S, Sharma, K.K., Sharma, D.K.,: An Economic Profile of Pooh Cold Desert Area, (A Bench Mark Survey), A study carried out for the Desert Development Agency, Pooh, Cyclostyled Mimeograph, Pp 62-63.

[33] Ibid, p. 63.

Table 3.22: Term-Credit Requirements of Sample Households

sn	*nhd*	*A.V.Group*	*Credit Requirement (Rupees)*					
„	-do-	(Rupees)	L.T. Loan as		M.T. Loan as		S.T.L as	
-"-	-do-	—do—	%G.T	%avtl	%G.T	%avtl	%gt	%avt
1	012	Below-5,000	00.00	00.00	00.00	00.00	nil	nil
2	002	5,000-7,500	00.00	00.00	00.00	00.00	nil	nil
3	003	7,500-10,000	0.02	100.00	00.00	00.00	nil	nil
4	003	10,000-12,500	0.04	100.00	00.00	00.00	nil	nil
5	003	12,500-15,000	0.09	100.00	00.00	00.00	nil	nil
6	002	15,000-18,000	00.00	00.00	00.00	00.00	nil	nil
7	009	18,000-21,000	01.18	100.00	00.00	00.00	nil	nil
8	016	21,000-25,000	08.29	92.35	00.07	07.65	nil	nil
9	009	25,000-30,000	03.58	83.91	00.07	16.09	nil	nil
10	110	30,000-&Above	76.37	90.81	07.72	09.19	nil	nil

Code: **sn = serial number, nhd = number of households, A.V. Group = asset value group,**
L.T. = long-term, M.T. = medium-term, S.T.L = short-term loan,
%G.T = percentage of grand total, %avtl = percentage of asset value group total, %gt and %avt are the same as %G.T and %avtl respectively.
Grand Total for all categories of loan requirements = Rs 1,018,800.

confine their lending mostly to annual terms, the official data reflect only long- and medium-term credit requirements. Legislation pertaining to moneylending activities has had limited impact, as shall be discussed in Chapter VII. The amounts involved in Table 3.22 are small - Rs 926,100 for long-term credit and Rs 78,700 for medium-term credit, giving Rs 1,018,800 in all for 160 households or Rs 6,367.50 per household. Of this amount, Rs 915,800 was for the 126 households in the three highest asset value groups, showing a per household credit requirement of Rs 7,268.25. This is not a high figure. Yet even this figure has not been met by the cooperative credit network, as can be seen from the actual loaning performance in these villages.

3.5.2 Performance of the Cooperative Credit Network

Of the eight sample villages, six had cooperative societies, with a total membership of 110 persons. Their share capital was Rs 117,220. This meant an average share capital per member of Rs 105.70. Table 3.24 gives the village-wise data for our sample villages. It is worth noting from Table 3.24 that out of 1,534 persons in Moorang only 319 (or 20.79%) were members of cooperative societies. Of course, minor children have to be excluded but even so this gives a low membership figure. There were 317 households in Moorang, so roughly only one member per household, presumably the head of the family, was registered as a member. For Kānam there were 145 households but 295 members, roughly 2 members per household. Only two cooperatives were active in advancing loans to members. The average per member loan amounts worked out to Rs 245.22 for village Jāngi and Rs 325.42 for village Kānam which

Table 3.23: Credit Requirements of Sample Households by Terminal Classifications and Asset Groups, Expressed as Percentages

sn	*A.V.Group*	*nhd*	*Credit Requirements (Rupees)*			
„	(in Rupees)	-'-	Long T.	Med.T.	s.t.	Total
1	Below-5,000	012	0,000	0,000	nil	0,000
2	5,000-7,500	002	0,000	0,000	nil	0,000
3	7,500-10,000	003	2,000	0,000	nil	2,000
4	10,000-12,500	003	4,000	0,000	nil	4,000
5	12,500-15,000	003	9,000	0,000	nil	9,000
6	15,000-18,000	002	0,000	0,000	nil	0,000
7	18,000-21,000	009	12,000	0,000	nil	12,000
8	21,000-25,000	016	84,500	7,000	nil	91,500
9	25,000-30,000	009	36,500	7,000	nil	43,500
10	30,000-Above	101	778,100	78,700	nil	856,800
11	All-Classes	160	926,100	92,700	nil	1018,800

Code: **sn = serial number, A.V. Group = Asset Value Group, nhd = no. of households, Long T. = long-term, Med.T. = medium-term, s.t. = short-term.**

Table 3.24: Cooperative Network's Extent In The Sample Villages

SN	*village name*	*smp*	*shcptl*	*loans*	*a.l.p.m*
1	Chārang	106	3,740	0,000	00.00
2	Moorang	319	41,210	0,000	00.00
3	Jāngi	157	20,270	38,500	245.22
4	Namgya	82	5,000	0,000	00.00
5	Leo	150	5,000	0,000	00.00
6	Kānam	295	42,000	96,000	325.42

code: **SN = serial number, smp = society membership, shcptl = share capital, a.l.p.m = average loan amount per member. shcptl and a.l.p.m are both in Rupees.**
(Source: As for Table 3.18, p. 76)

were far less than the average per household credit requirement of Rs 6,367.50 calculated earlier. In fact, the average per member loans amount to 3.85% and 5.11% of this figure for villages Jāngi and Moorang respectively. The official survey document makes no attempt at examining where the rest of the credit requirement was to come from. It is true that the credit requirements stated during the survey may not all be necessarily covered by actual borrowing but it is equally true that at least some of the gap left uncovered by cooperative lending would doubtlessly have to be filled by loans from private moneylenders. Moorang, the largest village in the sample in terms of population, had no cooperative loans at all, as also Chārang and Leo, both remote but important villages. Even according to this official survey, the role of the cooperative credit network in meeting the credit needs of assorted villages has been marginal. Within this overall cadre, we can now analyse the data pertaining to cooperatives in Kinnaur.

3.6 STATISTICAL ANALYSIS: APPROXIMATE CORRELATIONS

This analysis was carried out using the S.A.S. (Statistical Analysis System) programme in the Heidelberg University Rechenzentrum with its HADES facility. This has not been a superfluous exercise, but has furnished convincing corroboration of certain general features discernible in the cooperative credit network from intensive personal experience. Apparent discontinuities arise in the cooperative credit network essentially out of the fact that it is influenced as-much-as, if not more, by political and administrative decisions as by economic factors, being a quasi-government agency. A private agency would function much more autonomously, based on considerations of profit and economic viability. For example, if it is economically not viable to open a retail outlet in remote villages like Chārang, Kuno, Hāngo, Chuling, or Asrang because the costs of transportation are too high, the number of consumers and their purchasing power rather low, the environment remote and hostile to expansion into gainful activities like the cultivation of cash crops, a private party would just not establish such an outlet. Cooperatives, on the other hand, are obliged by government policy to run such an outlet as a public service because a political decision has been taken to establish P.D.S. outlets in all villages. These outlets are a matter of public service rather than profit-making-mechanisms. Not only this, the P.D.S. outlets have to deal in items like exercise books, rapeseed oil etc. which have been specified by the state government rather than themselves deciding which articles to deal in, as any private sector dealer would do.

Changes in the political environment like approaching elections or in the administrative environment like the launching of special drives cause discontinuous changes in the credit framework. As elections are announced, credit begins to be disbursed more liberally while recoveries are slackened. This means that statistical variables like loan amounts disbursed, recoveries, membership of cooperatives and their numbers do not vary consistently. It is then not easy to establish correlation equations between the variables. Rationally, if loan disbursements increase recoveries should also increase proportionately so as to avert choking up of the credit inflows and enable better recycling of limited funds. But near elections the reverse happens. Loans go up sharply, recoveries decline and the mathematical correlations go awry. The Emergency period (1975-76) marks a particularly sharp discontinuity. There was a sudden rise in loans disbursed, lands granted (at least on paper!), the membership of cooperatives and their number. Graphs and histograms should show abnormal variations for this period upsetting smooth correlation curves.

If the state government decided that more cooperative societies should be formed, this was done in Kinnaur regardless of the fact whether the performance of the cooperative structure warranted such an increase or not. These increases were not always linked to increases in the working capital so that their variation became dissimilar in reality and not correlated as it should be on purely economic considerations. The variation of all the variables should be non-symmetrical because of this unpredictability of political and administrative factors. However, the correlation between cooperatives' membership and working captal should be better than that between loan amounts disbursed and working capital. Loan disbursement was more affected by political/administrative changes than membership or working capital. Politicians were more concerned about liberal doling out of loans near elections than about technicalities like working capital and membership. Their pressure, coupled with the readiness of many officials to comply with such wishes, distorted the smooth correlation between loan amounts disbursed and working capital much more than that between membership and working capital.

The attitude of the Cooperative Department depends on the latest set of rules and instructions issued by the government whether loan amounts are to be increased or decreased, regardless of membership or working capital. Loans are advanced liberally under special programmes under which specified targets have to be achieved or at the approach of politically important events like elections or other changes of government; or as inputs of programmes enshrined as holy cows, like the I.R.D. Programme. The entire cooperative credit mechanism has become just another cog in the wheel of government programmes rather than an independent input whose magnitude should be left to the governing bodies of the supposedly autonomous cooperative societies for decision. Our statistical analysis, if accurate, should corroborate these characteristics and show mathematically just how important political and administrative influences are as determinants of the cooperative credit structure. It has just not been possible to run this network purely on economic principles of demand and supply or of profit and loss. It is a hostage to the overall cadre of government programmes.

3.6.1 Graphical Representations: Aesthetic and Illustrative

The data contained in Table 3.2 was processed by defining the following variables:

WC = Working capital;
NS = Number of Cooperative Societies;
LOANS = Loan amounts actually advanced ; and
MSP = Membership of cooperative societies.

In a cooperative credit network responsive to public demand, more loans should be advanced as the working capital rises. Membership should also rise with rising working capital because the latter phenomenon should mean that the societies should meet more and more credit needs, thereby providing practical incentive for more and more villagers to enroll themselves as members, leading to a rise in MSP. Thus WC was kept as the independent variable and Loans as well as MSP were tested as dependent variables. Before doing so, the yearly variations of these variables were plotted graphically. Graphs 3.1 to 3.4 show the resultant variation of WC, NS, MSP and Loans separately.

The variations of NS are sharply compressed and appear as a straight line because the magnitude of this variable was very low as compared to the magnitudes of the other variables. Loan amounts were also similarly compressed. They follow the curve of NS till 1974-75 after which they show a slightly parabolic curve. This means that we should also test for a parabolic relation of the type $y^2 = 4ax$ while examining the correlations between the variables. The WC curve follows a near straight line till 1969-70 after which it rises slowly till 1975-76 after which it shows a sharper rise. This bears out our earlier expectation that in a period of special drives (like the Emergency certainly was) the increases should be sharper. This very phenomenon is observable in the MSP graph as well. Membership rose sharply between 1961-62 to 1966-67, then fluctuated in a slowly rising curve till a sharper rise in 1975-76. Loans also showed a sharp rise in 1975-76, rose further till 1977-78 and then fell sharply till 1980-81.

These changes correspond, as predicted earlier, to major political changes. Cooperative credit disbursements increased sharply during the Emergency which forced the pace in populist measures. Membership and the number of societies continued to rise in the period of the Janata regime but loan amounts disbursed declined sharply. This was a part of returning reality after the euphoria of the Emergency. As predicted, politico-administrative factors were affecting the credit network even more than purely economic considerations. The need for cooperative credit was always there. The supply of such credit varied with changing political climate. Political decisions injected vastly increased loan amounts into Kinnaur in 1975-76. Similarly, political decisions reduced these amounts in 1978. This reduction did not mean that the need for cooperative credit had declined, just as it had not increased all of a sudden in 1975. These extra-economic influences make the credit network's fluctuations not very easy to interpret in purely economic terms.

3.6.2 Vertical Bar Charts: Visually Clear

The overall conclusions shown by the vertical bar charts would necessarily be the same as those deduced from the graphs. However, the vertical bar charts show the variations visually more clearly than graphs. The value 39 had the maximum relative percentage (nearly 24%), followed by 40 and 41 (each 18%). This means that 60% of the time, the number of cooperative societies remained between 39 and 41. Loan amounts are concentrated towards the lower end of the midpoint scale. 64% of the loan amounts are grouped around the lowest midpoint (200). There is a sharp fall to 12% for midpoints 400 and 1000 and to 6% each for midpoints 600 and 800 respectively. Membership values are concentrated around the middle, rather than the lower end as in case of loans amounts disbursed. The value distribution is uneven and not regular but less so than that for loans. We can see that variables like loans, membership and working capital do not vary in a synchronized manner. They vary without a fixed correlation, a clear mathematical manifestation of a cooperative network in which the important variables vary with no definite correlation visible. The loan amounts around midpoint 200,000 are all between 11,190 and 149,400 - far below the figure of 200,000 as indicated in the bar chart. These are obviously amounts insufficient to cover the credit needs of Kinnaur. It is unrealistic to imagine that this level of provision of credit would be enough to replace the centuries old network of village moneylenders. Now we can examine the existence of a correlation or otherwise between WC as the independent variable and MSP, Loans as dependent variables.

3.6.3 Relationships between Cooperative Loan Variables

The existence/absence of such relationships was tested for by using regression analysis and the general linear models procedure. MSP and Loans, being dependent variables, were plotted along the ordinate while WC, being the independent variable, was plotted along the abscissa. The graphs show a curvilinear relation which approximates a straight line before it curves off. Without going into statistical details, we try to deduce some results. The vertical bar charts have already shown that the variation of loans, WC and MSP was not symmetrical. This very result was confirmed by a univariate analysis for these variables. In view of the non-symmetrical variation of the variables under examination, we should use a non-parametric procedure (Spearman or Kendall) rather than a parametric procedure (Pearson) for testing the correlation between them.

3.6.3.1 Spearman's Correlation Test: Interesting Results

The results of the Spearman non-parametric correlation test show a stronger correlation between membership of cooperative bodies and their working capital (Correlation coefficient = 0.98) than that between loan amounts disbursed and working capital (Correlation coefficient = 0.78). We can mathematically see that the increase in membership of societies follows the increase in their working capital more closely than shown by the loan amounts disbursed.

Increasing membership of cooperatives means more share capital for the society. This in turn means a greater matching share in capital grants and working capital sanctions from the state government. More members means greater demand for loans. Increased availability of loans is one of the factors attracting Kinnauras to join cooperative societies. This has not happened to an appreciable extent in practice in Kinnaur as should have been warranted by the increase in membership. The reason is partly that the cooperatives are considered as extended arms of the government rather than autonomous bodies functioning on their own; increasing their lending when their membership and consequently their working capital increased and vice versa. This would have been the modus operandi of a private loan giving agency, for example a Chit Fund Organization.

Chit Fund Organizations are unofficial credit unions constituted by an initial kernel of members (generally 10 or so. They expand later) who specify a fixed amount (Rs 50 to Rs 200, or higher, depending upon their economic capacities) as the per mensem contribution for forming a credit pool. The amount so collected is either directly given as credit to one member per month or in the form of a durable consumer article (refrigerator, T.V. set). The members themselves decide how the sequence should run. Generally, they follow an alphabetical order in deciding how the credit cycle should cover all members. For example, if there are 12 persons who decide to constitute such a union with Rs 200 per month as the fixed contribution, then each of them would receive Rs 2,400 once in a period of 12 months after which the cycle can begin again, either with an increase or a decrease or the same amount as desired by members. Changes can be made only once the credit cycle has run its course over all members and not inbetween because each member has to receive exactly the same amount as every other member.

There are other versions of this arrangement. The 12 members of our example could have been paying Rs 200 per month as fixed contribution but giving out only Rs 1,800 per member as credit, thereby saving Rs 600 (or Rs 50 per member per month) per month in a reserve pool which could then be put in a savings bank account to gain interest. The group decides how this reserve is to be used. There can be many choices. Each member can get an equal share of the saved amount at the end of the year by equal division; or one member at-a-time can get the entire accumulated reserve, with the circle so going on till each member has had his turn; or the pool can be used as an emergency reserve out of which the members can take loans, interest-free or at previously mutually decided upon rates of interest, for any purpose or for previously agreed-upon purposes like a marriage in the family. Everything depends upon how the group has laid down the ground rules. It also decides whether a designated member acts as the coordinator for the distribution of pooled funds or whether this role also rotates from member to member in an alphabetical or otherwise specified order. Whatever the arrangement, Chit Fund Organizations are flexible bureaucracy-free mechanisms for managing pooled amounts. They are autonomous and responsive to the relations between demand and supply because their members decide everything between themselves. The name Chit Fund Organization seems to come from the fact that names were written on slips of paper (called chits) which were all put in a vessel. One chit was pulled out at random, like in a lottery, to decide the name at which the round of credit giving should begin. The cycle could then proceed in an alphabetical order or similarly by draw of chits each time, with of course the names of the persons having already received loans being left out in each succeeding lottery till every member of the group had had his turn and the cycle could begin again. If members of Cooperatives want such flexibility, they have to depend on sanction from the Cooperative Department. They cannot function as free agents operating according to local conditions.

3.6.3.2 Relationship between Loans and Working Capital

The general linear models procedure was utilized to test the interrelation between the working capital and the loan amounts disbursed. Since the graphs between these two variables were curvilinear in part, the G.L.M. procedure was used not just to test a relation between loans and WC but also between higher terms (square, cube) as well. Combinations of these terms were employed as well to find the best fit for the interrelation we are seeking. The R-Square value, an indicator of the degree of justification of our model, fell sharply from 0.61 to 0.44 as we moved from terms in (WC) to terms in $(WC)^2$.

The resultant equations, giving the interrelation of loans to terms of working capital come out as follows:

$$y = 0.15\,x - 6.47;$$

$$y = 0.30\,x^{1/2} - 6.47;$$

$$y = 0.45\,x^{1/3} - 6.47;$$

$$y = 0.60\,x^{1/4} - 6.47;$$

$$y = 0.07\,[x^{1/4} + x^{1/3} + x^{1/2} + x] - 6.47.$$

Here y = loans disbursed and x = working capital.

Since the extent of reliability does not increase beyond 61% whether we retain the simplest term, a linear relation, or retain more complicated terms, we make the former choice without losing out on accuracy. From a purely mathematical point of view, we should look for a relation giving us a reliability quotient of 95% or higher but in the cooperative credit network too many human, political and social factors rule out such high degrees of accuracy. Factors other than economic play such a dominant role that we cannot quantify these in precise measurable units and have to be satisfied with the degree of reliability that we have. The resulting equation set is then:

$$\mathbf{y = 0.15\,x - 6.47}$$

In this equation, x = **abscissa = working capital, y = ordinate = loan amounts advanced, and 6.47 = intercept value on the Y-axis.**

This very equation can be rewritten as:

$$\mathbf{x = 6.67\,y + 43.13}$$

3.6.3.3 Relationship between Membership and Working Capital

Regression Analysis was used to examine the relationship between the membership of cooperatives and different terms of working capital. The graphical representation had already indicated that this interrelation was closer than that between loans and working capital. This observation is now mathematically confirmed. We get the following set of equations:

$$M = 1.36\,(WC)^{1/2} + 5483.67,$$

$$M = 2.04\,(WC)^{(1/3)} + 5483.67,$$

$$M = 2.73\,(WC)^{1/4} + 5483.67,$$

$$M = 0.37[(WC)^{(1/3)} + (WC)^{1/2} + WC] + 5483.67,$$

$$M = 0.68\,WC + 5483.67$$

Leaving aside the equations involving complex higher or lower powers of the variable WC because the R-square value remains the same, we get the following set of equations:

$$\mathbf{a = 0.7\,b + 5484}$$

$$\mathbf{b = 1.4\,a - 7834}$$

In these equations, the variable a = membership of cooperatives in Kinnaur and the variable b = working capital available. This marks the first time that such a calculation has ever been attempted, let alone derived, even if the derived equations have a reliability quotient of only around 62%.

3.7 ANALYSIS OF DATA PERTAINING TO THE SCB, KALPA BRANCH

On lines similar to those used for the analysis of the data for cooperative societies in Kinnaur, we can analyse the data available for the Kālpa branch of the SCB to check whether any correlation equations can be derived or not. If such equations emerge, they would enable us to calculate dependent variables knowing the independent or base variable. The Kālpa branch was chosen for such analysis because it was the longest existing bank branch in Kinnaur.

The choice of the base variable was important. In our case, it should logically be total deposits because the higher such deposits in the bank, the higher should be the amounts loaned out so that the credit-deposit ratio (henceforth referred to as the C.D. Ratio) does not sink too low. The C.D. Ratio is regularly reviewed in district-level meetings and is an important index of banking statistics in Kinnaur. We thus select the variable TD (= Total Deposits) as the base variable. We begin our analysis again with graphs and bar charts.

3.7.1 Vertical Bar Charts: Tools for Analysis

Vertical bar charts help us examine the variation of the variable in question, whether it varies symmetrically or asymmetrically. On such choice will depend whether the succeeding analysis needs to be based on parametric or non-parametric coefficients.

3.7.1.1 Frequency Bar Charts with all Values Displayed

These charts were plotted to study the variation of the amounts advanced under the various schemes being implemented by the SCB. Newer schemes for loans to individuals were not considered because these began only from 1983-84 onwards, thus giving only two values, not sufficient for proper analysis. It would be useless to draw general conclusions from a set of only two values. The distributions were not symmetrical. No variation pattern could be discerned at all. Values for all loan amounts disbursed and recovered varied from as low as zero to high figures like Rs 1,235,787 in the case of crop loans advanced; from zero to Rs 1,242,541 for advances of amounts pledged to cooperative societies. We observe at once that the amounts recovered under all schemes are lower in magnitude than the amounts advanced. This means the first signs of a blockage of institutional credit funds.

3.7.1.2 Vertical Bar Charts Showing Year-wise Values

Bar charts showing year-wise values show that crop loans advanced had the highest value in 1976-77 from where they decreased dramatically in 1977-78, remained constant in 1978-79 and fell again in 1980-81. They became zero for two years, rose slightly in 1983-84, rose further in 1984-85 (remaining nevertheless well below the level of 1976-77). Crop loan recoveries followed a different pattern. Overall, they also declined from their peak value in 1976-77 to a low of Rs 100,000 in 1984-85 but the fall was not so abrupt as that for crop loan advances and there was a perceptible intermediate rise to above Rs 300,000 in 1980-81. This was partly due to the fact that the value of the crop loan advances in 1976-77 (Rs 1,250,000) was much higher than that for the recoveries (Rs 740,000) so that the falls of the former are sharper than those of the latter.

The advances under the scheme of limits pledged to cooperative societies began in earnest only in 1982-83 when more than Rs 1,200,000 were advanced. Since then their values have declined regularly. The recoveries under this scheme show values more comparable to the amounts advanced than was the case for the crop loan scheme. The behaviour here corresponds closely for advances and recoveries. A good correlation exists for the two variables.

Loan amounts advanced under the Cash Credit Hypothecation Limit Scheme (called CCHYPA in the graphs/histograms) and recovered (called CCHYPR) show similar behaviour from 1976-77 to 1984-85 but the increase for both is proportionately much higher for CCHYPA than for CCHYPR. Every graph/bar chart indicates a lagging of recovery behind disbursement. The correlation between advances and recoveries is not so good as that observed for the preceding scheme.

Amounts advanced against the borrowers' own deposits (called OWNDEPA) show an almost regular and continuous rise from 1976-77 till 1984-85. Recoveries of such advances (called OWNDEPR) follow a corresponding pattern of regular rise. The sums involved are comparable to each other and do not show recoveries lagging far behind advances. This means that a good correlation is to be expected between these two variables. Their equation of correlation is linear, of the type $y = mx + c$, as their rise is regular and linear. They exhibit a positive correlation. Graphs showing the yearwise variation of CCHYPA and CCHYPR confirm these presumptions.

3.7.1.2.1 Graphs: Corroboration of Earlier Findings

Graphs for the crop loan amounts advanced (called CRLA) and recovered (called CRLR) show a negative slope i.e. a falling trend. The graphs show a weak correlation between the these two variables (CRLA and CRLR).

The case is reversed for the amounts advanced and recovered under the scheme of pledged limits to cooperative societies (called the variables PLSOCA and PLSOCR respectively). The two curves (one for advances, one for recoveries) are similar in shape, showing a good correlation. This is true to a lesser extent for the graphs for CCHYPA and CCHYPR which do not show a good linear relation, being haphazard in their changes in magnitude.

Loans given against the borrowers own deposits (OWNDEPA, OWNDEPR) show an excellent correlation, a positive slope and an almost perfectly linear rise. The graph of total deposits (variable TD) at the end of each banking year shows a fall from 1976-77 to 1977-78 but then a rise for two years, an almost constant value for a further two years and then a sharp rise in 1982-83 and 1984-85. We shall now try and pinpoint the significance of all these findings. The starting point is a non-parametric correlation test since no symmetrical distribution has been revealed by the graphs or bar charts.

3.7.2 Spearman's Correlation Test: Useful Corroboration

Spearman's correlation test indicates that we have to exclude a correlation except between the following pairs of variables:

(a) CRLR to OWNDEPA and OWNDEPR;
(b) PLSOCA to PLSOCR; and
(c) OWNDEPA to OWNDEPR and CRLR.

We can treat any of these variables as the base variable and the other as the dependent variable. We choose advances (PLSOCA, OWNDEPA) as the base variables and the recoveries (CRLR, OWNDEPR, PLSOCR) as the dependent variables because advances precede recoveries. Had no advances been made to begin with, no recoveries would have been necessary. Once advances had been disbursed, recoveries would have to be effected. If in an extreme case advances were completely stopped after once having been commenced, their recoveries would then be carried on till no principal and interest amounts were left pending. Once this stage was reached, recoveries would then fall to zero, unless in the meanwhile further loans had been advanced. In practice, recoveries tend to follow advances. If increased amounts are disbursed as loan, recoveries should normally be increased so that defaults do not choke off the credit system by blocking limited available liquidity. Political considerations can demand that loaning be increased without increasing (or even accompanied by decreasing) recovery but these exigencies have till now in Kinnaur been transient aberrations that have not endured. There are just not enough funds available to keep doling out loans without matching incrases in recovery. Before establishing equations correlating our selected base variables with the dependent variables, we plot the latter against the former. The graphs then give us visual indications about their correlation.

3.7.2.1 Correlation Graphs: Useful Evidence

Plotting CRLR, PLSOCR and OWNDEPR along the Y-axis as ordinate and OWNDEPA, PLSOCA and OWNDEPA respectively along the X-axis as abscissa, an excellent fit was found for the PLSOCR-PLSOCA and OWNDEPR-OWNDEPA graphs. Both show straight lines with very little deviation for points lying off the line of best-fit. We anticipate a linear equation between these pairs. The CRLR-OWNDEPA plot reveals a worse fit. It is a curvilinear graph with a declining slope. Any equation found to fit this pair will not have the same degree of accuracy as for the other two pairs.

3.7.3 Regression Analysis: Solution of Best-Fit

We try and find a fit that minimizes the sum of the squares formed from the perpendicular distance and horizontal distance of points lying off the line of best-fit on to this line. There is an inverse relationship between the sum of these squares and the degree of validity of the curve of best-fit. The smaller the sum of these squares, the better the accuracy of our model and vice versa.

3.7.3.1 CRLR-OWNDEPA Equation

Taking CRLR as the dependent variable and OWNDEPA as the independent variable, the R-square value is 0.6746. This means that our model has a reliability quotient of nearly 67.5% accuracy. Within this limit of accuracy we get the following equations:

$$\mathbf{y = 514032 - 0.2\ x}$$
$$\mathbf{x = 5y + 2570160}$$

In these equations, x = OWNDEPA, y = CRLR, and the intercept values have been rounded off to the nearest integer values.

3.7.3.2 PLSOCR-PLSOCA Equation

Spearman Correlation Coefficients indicate that we should get a much higher degree of accuracy (R-square value) and a more normal distribution for the present regression analysis than for the preceding case. The R-square value is 0.9937 which means an accuracy of 99.37%. The equation that we get is:

$$\text{PLSOCR} = 0.81\ \text{PLSOCA} + 9990.32$$

If we put PLSOCR = ordinate = y and PLSOCA = abscissa = x, then this equation is rewritten as:

$$y = 0.81\ x + 9990$$
$$x = 1.24\ y - 12334$$

3.7.3.3 OWNDEPR-OWNDEPA Equation

Here again, a high degree of accuracy is expected. The R-square value is 0.9973, even higher than what we had in the preceding Section (3.7.3.2). This indicates an accuracy-level of 99.73% or nearly 100%. The equations are:

$$a = 0.8\,b + 50554$$
$$b = 1.25\,a - 63193$$

where a = OWNDEPR and b = OWNDEPA.

3.7.3.4 Regression Analysis on Total Deposits as the Base

Using total deposits as the base variable for regression analysis we obtain no correlation between TD and CRLA, PLSOCA or OWNDEPA. The R-square value is at an unacceptably low level of 0.2594. Thus, we cannot correlate other variables to TD as the base variable. This means that rising deposits in banks do not correspondingly lead to increased loans for the masses. It certainly means more profits for the banks but these profits can always be ploughed into any investment that the bank considers profitable, for which there exist hardly any opportunities in Kinnaur. Deposits have risen constantly but the crop loans advanced, for example, have been drastically reduced. The equations derived by us are not for mathematical beauty but as concrete manifestations of certain correlations between the amounts disbursed as loans and the amounts recovered. It is no random hazard that only two variable pairs show close correlation, one pair shows a tolerable correlation and all the others show no correlation at all. In any case, these equations are not general relations true for all times to come. They do foretell the probable evolution pattern provided the credit network continues functioning as it has functioned till now. If the political authorities suddenly decide that the parameters of operation of the cooperative credit system should be changed, these equations will obviously not give accurate results.

3.7.3.5 Interpretation of Results: Economics versus Politics

It may appear as a fictional correlation that recovery of crop loans rises linearly with advances against own deposits rather than with crop loan advances. To people familiar with the working of the bureaucracy in Kinnaur in general, and of the Cooperative Department in particular, this is no surprise. The crop loan scheme was a favourite child of politicians and officials who saw in it a way of distributing largesse to fulfil politico-administrative targets. They could then crow about their achievements and reel off speeches and brochures to show how much they had done for the 'janata'. Bankers never liked this scheme.[34] It involved several small loans at rates of interest lower than those possible for more profitable schemes like transport advances.[35] Each case meant paperwork and formalities to be gone through. Loans in larger consolidated blocks meant having to deal with financially sounder parties, involving lesser paperwork. Crop loans had to be distributed under political pressure to small cultivators, a group singularly unloved by the bankers, also cooperative bankers. For crop loan advances, the spadework was all done at primary society-level and the cases were presented to the cooperative bank branches as virtual faits accomplis. The bank staff could theoretically refuse to release such funds but it would subject them to heavy pressure from local politicians anxious to win goodwill by causing distribution of money not their own and by government staff anxious to fulfil targets. The SCB manager was caught in a fix. In Kinnaur, even such people as were not keen to get crop loans were induced to apply by being

[34] Opinion almost universally expressed by bank officers from the rank of Assistant General Manager, Regional Manager to Branch Managers to the author in innumerable private conversations. None of them was willing to be so frank in public.

[35] Note "Role of Cooperative Banks---", op. cit., Annexure A.

misinformed that these were grants or subsidies and not loans.[36] Subsidies or grants did not have to be repaid. It came as a rude shock to borrowers, when they later on got recovery notices after many years, to learn that what they had obtained had not been doles but loans which had to be repaid. Bank staff did not like these loans in which their room for manœuvre was circumscribed by fear of extraneous pressure.

On the other hand, they had their full discretion and freedom of choice when it came to making loan advances to individuals against the latter's own deposits. These loans were not the focus of attention of politicians and government officials. Bank staff could proceed on rational criteria of financial viability of borrowers. These loans could be released in cases where past repayment record or other factors, including personal familiarity, convinced the bankers that the loans would be repaid; an instance not possible in crop loan cases in which the bank just released the funds and did not really process the cases. Since the funds available were not unlimited, greater lending under the scheme of loans against own deposits could be carried on smoothly only if the recoveries were made more conscientiously, in order to recycle limited liquidity more efficiently. An important factor in such recycling was the threat of cutting off further loans to defaulters. This could not work in the case of crop loans where the amounts per individual were much smaller, so that the borrowers could well afford to forego further loans in case of default. We thus clearly discern the excellent correlation between loan amounts advanced and recovered under the scheme of advances agaist own deposits. The borrower here knew that the bank held his term-deposit as security which could be confiscated on non-payment. In crop loans there existed no such built-in coercive incentive to repay. They were released either without security or, even if crop produce or land was pledged as security, it was only through a complicated procedure before the revenue authorities or civil courts that the bank could turn such security into tangible repayment. It was in the borrowers' own interest to repay on time in both categories of loans, but whereas this need was perceived very clearly in the scheme of bank loans against own deposits, it was not the case for the poorer borrowers under the scheme of crop loans since they did not mostly have term-deposit accounts in the SCB, a sine qua non of the former scheme. Crop loans were perceived as merely another government aid programme rather than as a banking scheme. Our regression analysis equations giving excellent correlation between OWNDEPA and OWNDEPR are mathematical confirmation of this fact.

We see that crop loan advances have virtually ceased. Recoveries of crop loans show an approximately linear correlation to OWNDEPA because the SCB prefers to recover pending CRLR amounts. It keeps these as liquidity for advancing against the borrowers' own deposits rather than recycling them into an enlarged crop loan framework. Since crop loans have to be recovered within one year, efforts are focussed on their recovery otherwise these defaults quickly show up in the books of the SCB, causing problems for the manager whose career advancement depends upon his annual confidential report (henceforth referred to as the A.C.R.). One of the leading criteria of assessing a bank officer in his A.C.R. form is recoveries or the extent of default on loans given by him. More crop loans mean more defaults appearing in the succeeding year in the A.C.R. Thus efforts have been concentrated on recovery of crop loans, rather than their disbursement which leads to more problems. So it is CRLR which gives a good correlation with OWNDEPA and not CRLA because the funds recovered as CRLR are presumably diverted into the more profitable lending under OWNDEPA. However, crop loan recoveries are not easy to make and have not linearly followed the rising trend of OWNDEPA so that their mutual correlation is not too close. In cases where a borrower has taken a crop loans and also wants to avail of OWNDEPA, it is obviously in his own interest to repay the crop loan so that he is not deprived of the latter loan as a defaulter. This gives a rising trend in CRLR, matching a rising trend in OWNDEPA. Since the number of such borrowers is not large, the correlation has a low coefficient. Borrowers under OWNDEPA tend to be wealthier persons; those under crop loans include many poor borrowers.

[36] Personal observation during visits to villages in Kinnaur.

The excellent correlations between PLSOCA, PLSOCR and CCHYPA, CCHYPR corroborate the fact that these limits affect more the cooperative societies as a whole than individual borrowers as in crop loans. The rates of interest under both these schemes are higher than those for crop loans so that the SCB makes more efforts to make these schemes a success by recovering and relending money. The societies are also keen to repay and get further loans for lucrative activities like marketing of commodities or purchase of trucks since the benefits accrue mostly to the richer members anyway. These two schemes have not been politicised and distorted in the public mind into schemes for individual doles as were the crop loans. The cooperative department functionaries pay more attention to their smooth operation because otherwise the cooperatives under their care may wither, reducing the number of functioning cooperatives which could mean a black mark in their A.C.Rs. Crop loan defaults are considered in a different light as headaches of the SCB and the individual borrowers. The officials of the Cooperative Department are not motivated in this case to the same extent as when their own A.C.Rs are involved. They adopt a laissez faire attitude. Individuals getting loans under the CCHYPA scheme are traders or horticulturists who need to remain in the good books of the SCB in order to ensure the smooth running of their occupations. So they repay on time so as not to risk losing this facility. Thus while the PLSOCA, PLSOCR and CCHYPA, CCHYPR relations reveal excellent correlations, between each other, the same does not hold true for crop loan schemes. There is no spill over effect. Our mathematical equations are thus formulations revealing the functioning of the cooperative credit network in Kinnaur. We have to now proceed to examine the second prop of the institutional credit infrastructure - commercial banks. We shall see in the coming chapter (IV) whether commercial banks exhibit trends similar or dissimilar to those displayed by the cooperative credit network.

CHAPTER IV

INSTITUTIONAL CREDIT INFRASTRUCTURE: COMMERCIAL BANKS

Till the creation of Kinnaur District in 1960 Rāmpur, the focal point of trade, had also remained the focal point of the credit network of commercial banks. These banks were latecomers in Kinnaur. The first branch of any commercial bank was opened at Rekong Peo on April 25, 1974; 37 years after independence and five years after the nationalization of 14 major banks in 1969. Had it not been for this measure by the Union Government it is doubtful whether the commercial banks would really have moved into this remote area.[1] They were made to move into Kinnaur because of a government policy decision to use institutional credit as an important input in its efforts to promote social engineering by launching socio-economic development programmes in rural areas.

The impetus towards widening the existing cooperative kernel of the incipient institutional credit infrastructure was provided by political and administrative rather than economic reasons. Commercial banks had not decided to expand their network into areas like Kinnaur in order to earn profits but to fulfil new obligations forced on them as a part of a national campaign against poverty. Major credit inflows had been decreed as necessary for ensuring gainful economic activities for the rural poor. These inflows were supposed to generate a viable cycle of income generation and improvement in the quality of life of the rural poor.

Cooperative societies and the Kālpa branch of the SCB had shouldered this burden alone in Kinnaur till 1974. Now they were to be joined, and gradually even sidelined to a certain extent, by commercial banks. The government had decided that commercial banks offered a useful instrument for rural uplift. They had trained and well-paid staff; years of banking experience on a large scale and much larger reserves of funds available than cooperative credit societies and banks. They were not confined for their funds to only Himāchal Pradesh, as were the cooperative banks, but had their branches all over India. For example, a commercial bank was not obliged to loan out only such amounts as it had obtained in the form of deposits in H.P. If it considered enough schemes viable, it could draw upon its deposits from States other than H.P. for loaning out in Kinnaur or other areas of Himāchal. Commercial bank staff were supposedly more capable of deciding the economic viability of loan schemes, unlike cooperatives which had become politicised and dominated by influential, richer classes. Commercial banks were considered more resistant to such domination. They would better withstand pressures to dole out loans liberally to undeserving people. This aspect would become increasingly important as credit inflows were increased manifold. Cooperatives alone could not cope with such sharply rising credit amounts. Particularly in areas like Kinnaur, with traditionally low degrees of monetization where people were not much used to cash transactions, large monetary inflows needed better monitoring. Commercial banks were considered better equipped for this task than cooperatives.

4.1 BRANCH EXPANSION PROGRAMME

Starting from one in 1974 there were 13 commercial bank branches in Kinnaur at the end of 1985, not including five branches of the SCB and one of the LDB. The block-wise distribution of commercial bank branches at the end of 1985 is shown in Table 4.1 . This branch network is shown in the banking map of Kinnaur District attached herewith. All Tahsils and Hangrang

[1] Honest opinion conveyed in private conversations by senior bank officers to the author. This would, however, not be maintained publicly.

Table 4.1: Block-wise Distribution of Commercial Bank Branches

sn	*Block*	*Tahsil*	*Bank*	*nb*	*Places*
1a	Nichār	Nichār	PNB	01	Nugalsari
1b	Nichār	Nichār	UCO	03	Tāpri
do	--do--	---do---	-do-	do	Katgāon
do	--do--	---do---	-do-	do	Nāthpa
1c	---do--	---do--	UBI	01	Nichār
1d	---do--	---do--	SBI	01	Sungra
1e	---do--	---do--	Ttl	06	As Above
2a	Kālpa	Kālpa	PNB	02	R. Peo
do	--do--	---do---	-do-	do	Kālpa
2b	--do--	Sangla	UCO	01	Sangla
2c	---do--	---do--	Ttl	03	As Above
3a	Pooh	Moorang	UCO	02	Spillo
do	--do--	---do---	-do-	do	Akpa
3b	-do-	Pooh	SBI	01	Pooh
3c	-do-	Hangrang	UCO	01	Yangthang
3d	-do-	---do---	Ttl	04	As Above
4a			Gtl	13	As Above

Code: **nb = number of branches, Ttl = total, Gtl = grand total.**

(Source: Personally collected from the Office of the Divisional Manager, UCO Bank, Simla on January 10, 1986.)

Sub-Tahsil are covered by at least one commercial bank branch. More important than their territorial-unit-wise distribution is their valley-wise distribution. It would make little sense if all administrative units were covered but major valleys left without bank branches. Even on this score, Kinnaur is now well covered. The maximum concentration is naturally along the N.H. 22 which runs along the biggest two valleys - Satluj and Spiti. The next two biggest valleys - Baspa and Bhāba - are also covered by UCO Bank branches at Sangla and Katgāoṅ respectively. The concept of 'Talschaft' (rough translation = valley brotherhood) has not been ignored for these four largest valleys.

The smaller valleys like the Nésaṅg, the Tidong, the Yula and the Taiti are without banks. They have no chance of getting bank branches in the foreseeable future because of a complete absence of motorable roads and other infrastructural facilities. Villages situated in these valleys are covered by bank branches situated in the Satluj valley. Villagers of Kuno and Chārang have, for example, to cover nearly 45 kms on foot to reach the nearest commercial bank branches at Aren Jhula and Spillo. This disadvantage causes lots of discomfort to villagers from remote areas during completion of loan formalities but turns full circle and becomes their ally when the bank staff have to pursue them for recoveries of loans. Geographical remoteness with respect to location of bank branches is thus not an unmixed blessing!

Locations of commercial and cooperative bank branches in Kinnaur District

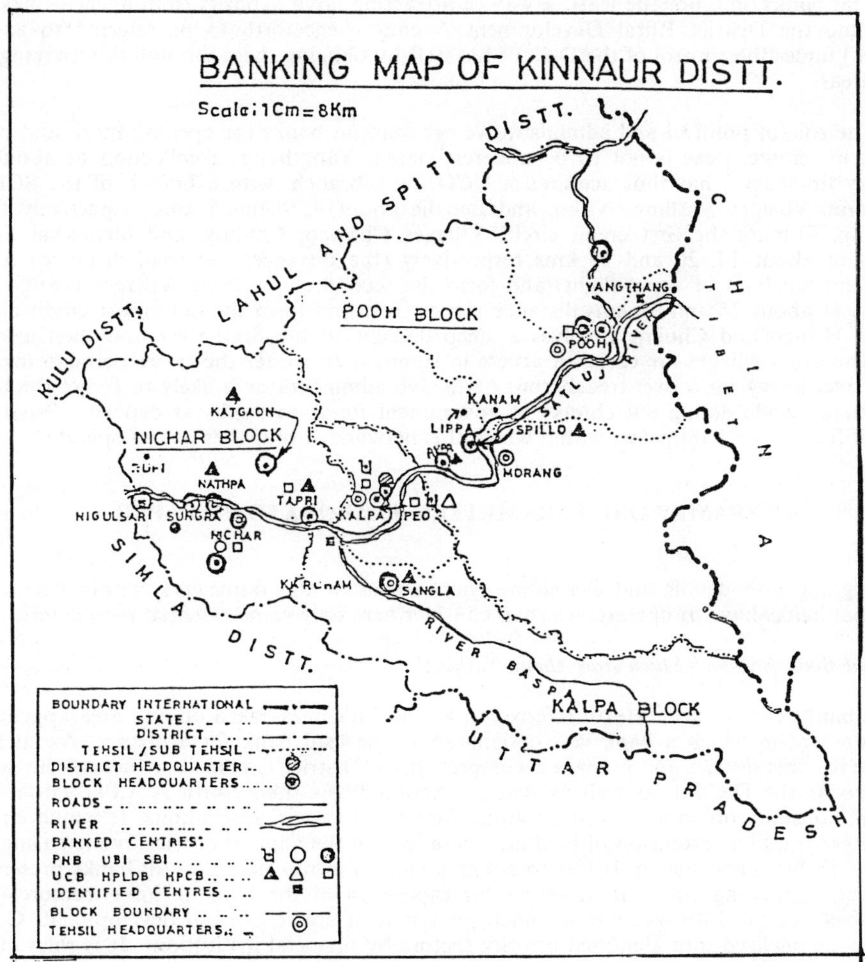

O = site of bank branch.

This was the number of branches on January 1, 1986.

Branch expansion, apart from providing banking services to increasing numbers of Kinnauras, was supposed to provide more focal points of supervising recovery operations by reducing the distance to be covered; mop up savings from hitherto unbanked remote regions; enable bank staff to get better first hand knowledge of the area to be covered for better formulation of loan schemes; shorten the radius of the credit circles being built up by commercial banks and, not the least, a way of attracting large deposits from agencies like the D.D.A. and the District Rural Development Agency (henceforth to be referred to as the D.R.D.A.) under the control of the D.C. or his staff by obliging them through this coverage of remote areas.

The role of political and administrative pressure on banks for opening more and more branches in remote areas is not to be underestimated. Yangthang, a collection of about 25 temporary tin shacks, has thus acquired a UCO Bank branch, with a branch of the SCB to follow soon. Villages Mālling, Nāko, and Leo lie about 9, 9 and 5 kms respectively from Yangthang, forming the first credit circle. Villages Chāngo, Chuling, and Shyalkhar lie at distances of about 14, 20 and 20 kms respectively (the distances are road distances to be covered and not lines of aerial flight) and form the second credit circle. Villages Hāngo and Sumra lie at about 25 and 32 kms distance respectively and form the outermost credit circle. Going to Hāngo and Chuling involves a steep descent to the Spiti river and then a steep ascent. The other villages are easier of access in summer. In winter the entire belt can involve trekking over heavy snow over treacherous paths. No administrator is likely to forget the bank at Yangthang while doling out chunks of government funds to banks as deposits. What are the broad framework parameters within which this network of branches has to operate?

4.2 FRAMEWORK PARAMETERS: ELABORATE ON PAPER

Without going into details and examining each aspect of the framework within which the commercial banks have to operate, we shall consider here only some essential parameters.

4.2.1 Lead Bank Scheme: Much Ado About Nothing!

The lead bank scheme[2] (henceforth referred to as the LBS) was based on an "area approach" to development in which a bank was designated as the lead bank for a district. As such, it would survey this district and prepare a comprehensive District Credit Plan (henceforth to be referred to as the D.C.P.), as well as Annual Action Plans (henceforth A.A.Ps) within this D.C.P., in consultation with the district authorities and financial institutions. It would ensure adequate geographical extension of banking operations in the allotted district by increasing the number of its branches therein. It was to act as a kind of group leader for all banks present in the district, suggesting coherent measures for expansion of the banking infrastructure. The overall object of the LBS was not so much provision of credit as rural development. Credit was to be channelized into identified priority sectors by financial institutions. It is relevant to study the criteria for allocation of districts to lead banks.

[2] The name 'Lead Bank' is quite a misnomer because it suggests some sort of a leading role. In reality, it means only acting as compilor of information and as a sort of post box between the banks and the D.C. The name seems to be a reward for the thankless task of compiling information from all banks! A better name would be 'Compiling Bank .

4.2.1.1 District Allocation Criteria: Paradox for Kinnaur

Certain factors can be identified as constituting the core of the criteria for district allocation to banks. These are:

(a) Bank deposits in the district;
(b) Spatial distribution in the district;
(c) Contiguity of districts;
(d) Availability of necessary staff; and
(e) Political-administrative support.

Normally a lead bank should have more deposits than other banks in its allocated district(s). Its banking operations therein should be spatially well spread-out through an extensive branch network. If it has to be the lead bank for more than one district, such districts should be contiguous as far as possible. It should have adequate technical, extension and field staff. It should have close rapport with the political and administrative authorities.

The PNB, the lead bank for Kinnaur District, failed all these criteria. It seems to have been designated as the lead bank for the historical reason that it had been the first commercial bank to open a branch in Kinnaur. Its deposits have since then fallen behind those of the

Table 4.2: Bank-wise Deposit and Loan Advance Figures for Kinnaur

s	Date	Bank											
,,	-do-	PNB			UCO			SBI			UBI		
,,	-do-	TD	TA	cdr	TD	TA	cdr	TD	TA	cdr	TD	TA	cdr
"	-do-	'000	'000	%	'000	'000	%	'000	'000	%	'000	'000	%
1	31-12-82	7,741	1,577	20	4,002	1,991	41	7,208	3,236	45	1,224	186	15
2	31-12-83	10,136	2,012	20	11,528	3,386	29	7,391	5,791	73	1,526	677	44
3	31-12-84	11,427	2,975	26	17,926	4,400	25	9,209	4,340	47	1,478	929	63
4	31-06-85	12,179	4,496	40	15,274	5,108	33	15,730	5,475	35	1,049	844	78
5	31-09-85	11,799	4,744	40	15,474	5,117	33	x,xxx	x,xxx	xx	1,036	803	77

Note: x,xxx = not available, '000 = in thousands, % = percentage,
TD = total deposits, TA = total advances, cdr = credit-deposit ratio.

UCO Bank, as can be seen from Table 4.2 . Total deposits of the UCO Bank (at Rs 4,002,000 on December 31, 1982) were nearly 48% lower than those of the PNB (at Rs 7,741,000). On September 30, 1985 i.e. in less than three years' time the former had total deposits of Rs 15,474,000 which were 31% higher than those of the latter at Rs 11,799,000. The percentage rise in total deposits had thus been 287% for the UCO Bank and only 52% for the PNB respectively. In fact the maximum total deposit figures on June 30, 1985 were those of the SBI (Rs 15,730,000).

In spatial distribution also, the UCO Bank had left the lead bank (PNB) far behind by establishing seven branches distributed over all the Sub-Divisions while the lead bank had only three branches distributed over only two of the total three Sub-Divisions. Two of these three branches, at Kālpa and Rekong Peo, are within 5 kms of each other as the crow flies while the third, at Nugalsari, is at one corner of the district. The UCO Bank branches are much more evenly spaced out.

Allocation of Kinnaur to the PNB did not conform to the criterion of contiguity of lead districts either. The UCO Bank was the lead bank in the most important adjoining district (Simla). The PNB was not the lead bank in the districts adjoining Kinnaur. It had fewer staff available in Kinnaur than the UCO Bank. For example, the latter had two Field Officers stationed in Kinnaur whereas the former had only one. Going by the criteria listed out earlier, it is the UCO Bank that should be the lead bank in Kinnaur and not the PNB.

This is borne out by another index as well - the level of political and administrative support. The total deposit figures do not distinguish between government and private funds. Major chunks of these deposits are official funds. The fact that the SBI with only two branches in Kinnaur had the maximum deposit figures on June 30, 1985 does not mean that its clients were richer than those of other banks or that its staff had worked harder but that the D.D.A.'s funds had been placed in it because of the location of the D.D.P. at Pooh where no other commercial bank had a branch. Panchāyat pradhāns (presidents) and other political figures used to very often request that the UCO Bank should replace the PNB as the lead bank in Kinnaur.[3]

4.2.1.2 Functions of the Lead Bank: Deceptive Impressions!

The lead bank was supposed to perform the following functions:

- ***(a) Conduct thorough economic surveys of the district for estimating the potential sources of development funds;***
- ***(b) Locate potential growth centres where it was desirable to open bank branches to geographically extend banking facilities;***
- ***(c) Identify areas and sectors with few or no bank dealings that depend on the informal sector to meet credit needs;***
- ***(d) Pinpoint credit gaps;***
- ***(e) Maintain close contacts and liaison with government or semi-government agencies;***
- ***(f) Formulate suitable development oriented schemes after locating potential project areas; and***
- ***(g) Prepare the D.C.P. in collaboration with other financial institutions in the district.***

The scheme assumes that provision of institutional credit is a main pre-requisite for rural development. Such credit is to be channelized within the cadre of the D.C.P. and the A.A.Ps. The lead bank was supposed to play a motor role as an initiator of development and not as a follower of communicated projects or schemes. We can now examine the preparation of the D.C.P. within which bank credit is estimated and provided for.

4.2.2 District Credit Plan: Elaborate Jugglery!

The so-called second round of the D.C.P. (1980-82) was, as the lead bank itself admits, a modest attempt towards adopting a *"coordinated and planned approach for assessing the credit needs of the priority sectors of the district's economy"*.[4] The D.C.Ps are drafted for a term of three years. Their concept was first introduced in 1973 when there was no commercial

[3] An official request to this effect was made by the author as D.C., Kinnaur District in 1982 to the Reserve Bank of India through the Finance Secretary, Government of H.P., Simla. The request was not acceded to but the PNB authorities did become more responsive to the D.C.'s requests after this episode than they had hitherto been.

[4] District Credit Plan (1983-85) Kinnaur (H.P.), Punjab National Bank, Regional Office, Simla, 1983, Cyclostyled Document, Chap. II, p. 14.

bank branch at all in Kinnaur. These plans could not be left to the whims and fancies of the lead bank but had to conform to certain guidelines issued by the Reserve Bank of India (henceforth, only R.B.I.).

4.2.2.1 Guidelines for D.C.Ps: Sweeping and Lofty

According to the guidelines issued by the R.B.I., a D.C.P. should be geared to:[5]

(a) Removal of unemployment and underemployment;
(b) Improving the standard of living of poorer sections of society; and
(c) Provision of basic consumption needs of people belonging to poorer sections of society.

These were overall objectives, within which the lead bank was obliged to frame a D.C.P. emphasizing the following points:

(A) Formulation of bankable loan schemes that were labour intensive in character, generating mass employment;
(B) Disbursement of loans to the agricultural and allied sectors aimed at reducing underemployment and raising incomes; and
(C) Maximum credit to the weaker sections, viz marginal farmers, small farmers, agricultural labourers, artisans, scheduled castes and scheduled tribes.

The lead bank is not alone in preparing the D.C.P. Other banks and official institutions like the Scheduled Caste Welfare Corporation are also involved. The lead bank acts as a leader of the team. As such, for preparing a D.C.P., a task force is constituted. The task force consists of the representatives of all those departments and institutions in the district that are partners in the development of the district. D.C.P. formulation can be classified into three stages:

(1) Identification of economically viable activities deserving financing by institutional credit givers;
(2) Collection of data aiming at formulating bankable schemes; and
(3) Estimation of credit needs foreseen under each bankable scheme for different sectors and different Development Blocks in the district.

These three stages involve consideration of some important factors.

4.2.2.1.1 Determining Factors: Determining Cadre

Formulation of a D.C.P. necessarily involves taking into account the following factors:-

(a) Existing number of banks and distribution of their branches in different Development Blocks of the district;
(b) Deposit mobilization by various banks, their past growth rate and projected future evolution;
(c) Availability of personnel in the banks present in the district, particularly field staff;
(d) Total advances loaned out, credit deposit ratio and amounts recovered by banks present within the district;
(e) Infrastructure of various government departments involved in social and economic development of the district;
(f) Perspective future plans of government departments in the district;

[5] Singh, Ajit: Rural Development and Banking in India, Theory & Practice, New Delhi: Deep and Deep Publishers, 1985, Chapter 6, p. 76.

(g) Existence of development plans drafted by Development Block authorities for all Blocks in the district so that financial requirements can be estimated and capital made available;
(h) Availability of liquidity from different banks, with a view to attaining a C.D. ratio of at least 60% for all banks;
(i) Pinpointing/specification of the responsibilities of government departments on one side and banks on the other side, for implementation of development plans; and
(j) Functioning of forums of coordination at which the problems faced by government agencies and credit giving banks could be sorted out vis-a-vis one another.

In spite of such elaborate consideration and detailed guidelines, practical difficulties still dog the implementation of D.C.Ps. Experience has certainly been gained since 1980 when the first D.C.P. was launched in Kinnaur but the difficulties to be narrated in the following lines are as true today as they were then. Their extent may inbetween have been reduced, the sharp edges rounded off, but their existence can unfortunately not be denied. They stymie the D.C.P., the principal vehicle of institutional credit, and hinder the free flow of credit.

4.2.2.2 Difficulties in Implementing a D.C.P.

These difficulties are not theoretical postulates but practical observations made between 1980-83 in Kinnaur as Chairman of the District Coordination and Consultative Committee (henceforth to be referred to as the D.C.C.C.), the principal forum for resolving problems of liaison between banks and government departments. In addition, these were discerned in innumerable discussions with government officials and bankers, both officially and privately.[6] The list is by no means exhaustive and can differ from district to district. Some principal hindrances observed were:

(A) There was no conscious commitment by bankers and government officials that the D.C.P. had to be made a success to reduce the stranglehold of moneylenders on credit markets in Kinnaur. There was no sense of mission. The motivation, if it existed at all, was career advancement. In this optic, the D.C.P. came to be considered as a necessary evil that had to be gone through. The requisite sense of commitment and zeal, so important to such a sweeping credit input mechanism involving so many departments, institutions and individuals was missing;
(B) The concept of the D.C.P. as the overall cadre within which all ongoing credit injection schemes had to be dovetailed was not clearly understood, either by bankers or by officials. The latter considered it as just another "sarkāri" programme, another prescribed proforma to be filled in. The former considered it more as an exercise in putting some odd schemes in document form to satisfy nosey superiors than as a real effort at bank credit management on scientific lines;
(C) The lead bank did not carry out comprehensive field surveys to determine credit needs. Such surveys, where carried out, were superficial exercises confined to settlements near to roadheads. In some cases data was taken over lock, stock and barrel from surveys made many years earlier by the Development Block staff. The presumption that trained bank staff would be better able to assess credit needs through comprehensive surveys than less trained, lower paid Block staff was not really realized. Such surveys were cosmetic exercises. Geographical remoteness, lack of adequate transport facilities and of field staff and severe climatic conditions were always cited as mitigating excuses when bankers were reminded about the lack of proper credit surveys;
(D) The necessary data was almost never supplied in full and in time by banks as well as by government departments. Several reminders had to be sent as a matter of routine;
(E) Banks were not keen to supply details of their total deposits, fearing revelation of this banking secret. They feared sharper competition from other banks present in Kinnaur if it became known that they had been able to mobilize higher deposits;

[6] Personal experience. The author was D.C., Kinnaur during this period.

(F) Some government departments had no cogent development plans from the perspective of credit management. They had just administrative schemes to spend the annual budgetary allocations;

(G) Disputes between banks over shares of credit allocation and disbursement were frequent and prolonged affairs which took months to settle. These delays could prove fatal in Kinnaur with a working season effectively restricted to the months May-October;

(H) Lack of trained staff in bank branches delayed processing of loan cases;

(I) Bankers did not come well prepared in many D.C.C.C. meetings where the implementation of the D.C.P. was reviewed. They either lacked the necessary statistical data or sent representatives of lower rank who could neither take decisions on their own nor give clear replies to queries concerning their branches. For example, pleading lack of any available substitute capable of taking over his duties for even one day, the manager of the UBI at Nichār or of the SBI at Sungra absented themselves from several meetings;

(J) Government departments and banks tended to go their own ways. There was no sense of spontaneous coordination. Since the D.C. could not always promptly attend to each and every issue requiring liaison, this lack of spontaneous coordination delayed proper implementation of the D.C.P. ;

(K) Banks other than the lead bank considered the D.C.P. as the lead bank's baby and not their joint responsibility. They tended to point accusing fingers at the lead bank for improper implementation;

(L) Since the entire approach was target-oriented, both in terms of numbers of persons to be covered and amounts to be loaned out, it was difficult to be selective and improve the quality of the lending being done under the D.C.P. ;

(M) Proper identification of target beneficiaries was lacking. Bankers complained that land records were not complete and did not provide correct information about borrowers. Bankers had to figure out previous liabilities themselves and cases got delayed; and

(N) Lacking any powers whatsoever of disciplining other banks not sending information on time or not cooperating fully in implementing the D.C.P., the lead bank could only remind, cajole and complain (to the D.C.). It was a typical case of responsibility without authority.

We can now examine D.C.P. statistics for Kinnaur.

4.2.2.3 D.C.P. Statistics for Kinnaur

A credit gap of Rs 6,657,000 was assessed for three years for Kinnaur District in the D.C.P. 1980-82. The sector-wise distribution of this credit gap, its allocation between various banks and their achievements in the period from January 1, 1980 to December 31, 1982 are shown in Table 4.3 . The D.C.P. document crows that the *"overall as well as sectoral gaps envisaged...were not only achieved by participating banks but surpassed by substantial margins"*.[7] It does not mention that all this was true only in relative terms. In absolute terms, Rs 20,878,000 disbursed over three years came roughly to Rs 350 per head, according to the 1981 Census figure of 59,547 persons for the total population of Kinnaur. This meant Rs 117 per head per annum. Also, the biggest excess (420%) was in the services or tertiary sector, meaning loans for purchase of trucks amongst other things. This scheme had obviously benefited rich borrowers. Poor people do not buy trucks! In the small scale industries (henceforth to be referred to as the S.S.I.) sector also, the break-up does not specify how much loan went to needy artisans and how much to rich sawmill owners establishing new units.

Lumping all categories of borrowers together to show an overall overshooting of targets is a typical official statistical manipulation masking whether needy target groups benefited or not. It is clear that the LDB, the long-term loan cooperative outlet, fulfilled only 33% of its target of Rs 1,000,000. No targets had been specified for the UCO Bank which did not have any branches at all in Kinnaur when this D.C.P. was launched in 1980. Starting late

[7] D.C.P. 1983-85, op. cit., Chapter II, p. 14.

Table 4.3: Progress under D.C.P. 1980-82 in Kinnaur District

s	*Bank*	*Agriculture*		*ssi*		*Service*		*Total*	
,,	Name	T	A	T	A	T	A	T	A
1	PNB	290	403	354	320	440	649	1084	1372
2	UCO	000	978	000	219	000	1177	0000	2374
3	UBI	537	163	181	135	270	243	988	541
4	SBI	303	1157	122	554	365	2918	790	4629
5	LDB	1000	330	000	000	000	0000	1000	330
6	SCB	1725	5786	70	000	1000	5786	2795	11572
7	Ttl	3855	8817	727	1228	2075	10773	6657	20818

Code: T = Target, A = Achievement, s = Serial Number,
ssi = Small Scale Industries Sector,
Ttl = Total. All amounts are in thousands of Rupees.
(Source: District Credit Plan 1983-85, Kinnaur District, p. 14)

in 1980, this bank ended up disbursing double the loan amount given out by the lead bank. The UBI fell well short of its targets, in spite of having its branch at a sub-divisional h.q., Nichār. Nevertheless, a beginning had been made. The only way that lay ahead was forwards, as can be seen from the D.C.P. figures for 1983-85.

4.2.2.3.1 D.C.P. Statistics for 1983-85

This plan was more detailed than that of 1980-82. Fresh credit disbursement of Rs 12,084,000 was envisaged, an increase of 81.52% over the figure of the preceding D.C.P. and 58% of the total actual achievement shown in Table 4.3. Evidently, actual achievement was not pegged as the target for the succeeding years, as in the postal small savings programme. The banks were more prudent! They kept the targets reasonably low so that achievement could be trumpeted as quite high in terms of percentages. The target of Rs 12,084,000 was sure to be exceeded by the end of 1985 since it had alrady been even at the end of 1982 when the figure achieved stood at Rs 20,818,000. Table 4.4 shows the progress made till September 30, 1985. With a whole quarter still to go, achievement was already running at 143% of the target. However, none of the banks had achieved their targets in the S.S.I. sector, so important for raising income levels in Kinnaur with its large population of artisans and the necessity of finding occupations away from agriculture which was not remunerative because of climatic conditions. The I.R.D.P. accounted for more than 50% of the total target with an outlay of Rs 6,897,000 but only 23.73% of the total achievement with Rs 4,109,000. The percentage of achievement rose to 60% if only the I.R.D.P. figures were considered, but this was nevertheless 83% lower than the figure for all sectors combined. Clearly, in the I.R.D. sector, catering to the "poorest of the poor",[8] the percentage of achievement lagged behind. The high rates of achievement were in sectors other than this sector - truck purchase loans, retail trade loans, purchase of sawmill equipment - not indicated as such on the achievement chart.

[8] Nomenclature current in official documents. It gained currency during the period of the Antyodaya Programme (1978-80) launched by the Janata regime in Himāchal Pradesh.

Table 4.4: Targets/Achievements D.C.P. 1983-85 (Amounts in '000)

s	*bank*	*agriculture*		*ssi*		*others*		*total*		*of which under IRDP*			*oa%*
,,	name	T	A	T	A	T	A	T	A	T	A	%	-do-
1	PNB	656	1019	476	350	423	535	1555	1904	1036	465	45	122
2	UCO	2298	1981	1860	999	1291	1103	5449	4083	3988	2171	54	75
3	SBI	766	935	759	146	607	1440	2132	2521	1361	821	60	118
4	UBI	247	520	279	080	199	187	725	787	512	652	127	108
5	SCB	1000	1858	000	000	600	5789	1600	7647	000	000	000	477
6	LDB	623	372	000	000	000	000	623	372	000	000	000	60
7	GTL	5590	6685	3374	1575	3120	9054	12084	17314	6897	4109	60	143

Code ; T = **Target, A = Achievement, s = Serial Number,** % = Percentage, GTL = Grand Total,
ssi = Small Scale Industry, oa% = Overall Percentage.
All amounts are in Thousands of Rupees (Rs '000).
(Source: Annexure to personal letter dated July 16, 1986 from Mr S.C. Girotra, Assistant General Manager, UCO Bank, Bombay to the author)

The SCB had a remarkably high figure of 477% achievement of which the major part (237.23%) was in the tertiary sector, meaning the inclusion of loans given for purchase of new trucks for the KINFED. Without the two cooperative banks, the percentage of achievement fell from 143% to 94% because Rs 9,295,000 had been disbursed as loan against a target of Rs 9,861,000. The lead bank lagged behind the UCO Bank in all sectors in terms of achievement in absolute terms, though it had higher relative achievement percentage overall. Long-term credit from the LDB was only 60% of the target. A new round of the D.C.P. was to begin on January 1, 1986, data for which was still not available at the time of field survey for this research in December 1985 and January 1986.

Rather than wait three years before seeing how the D.C.P. was progressing in terms of achievement of targets, overall targets are divided into year-wise targets and annual achievements are reviewed under the so-called A.A.Ps. Achievements under the A.A.Ps should at least together equal the targets set for the D.C.P., if not exceeding them, when added up over three years. Under the D.C.P. lasting three years, three A.A.Ps were prepared. These allowed scope for mid-course corrections in institutional credit inflows, if it was felt that achievements in a certain sector necessitated diversion of credit outlays to other sectors where achievements were below expectation. For example, if it were observed after reviewing the first A.A.P. that achievement in the agriculture sector had far exceeded targets whereas achievement in the S.S.I. sector had lagged far behind; depending on priorities two choices were available. The succeeding A.A.P. could emphasize concentration of efforts on the S.S.I. sector to righten this imbalance or funds could be diverted away from the S.S.I. sector in which demand for credit had not been proved compatible with outlay. Keeping in view the changing needs of the economy, the A.A.Ps are a sort of rolling plan mechanism within the overall fixed plan cadre of the D.C.P. In practice, such concepts hardly mean much as we shall now see. Targets are sub-divided without much overall cohesive design in mind.

4.2.2.4 Annual Action Plans: Impressive Statistics!

To understand the functioning of the A.A.P. concept we can consider the yearwise targets and achievements for the three A.A.Ps of the D.C.P. for 1980-82 given in Table 4.3. Each A.A.P. is

Table 4.5: A.A.P. for Kinnaur District, 1980 (Rupees '000).

s	*bank*	*sectors*								
,,	-do-	agri/alld		ssi		svcs		total		
,,	-do	T	A	T	A	T	A	T	A	%
1	pnb	112	69	108	21	195	30	415	120	29
2	ubi	174	84	42	10	50	27	266	121	46
3	sbi	127	17	61	100	170	86	358	203	57
4	scb	1206	3264	26	000	400	00	1632	3264	200
5	ldb	300	38	00	000	000	00	300	38	13
6	ttl	1919	3472	237	131	815	143	2971	3746	79

Code: **T = Target, A = Achievement, ttl = Total,** s = Serial No., % = Percent,
agri/alld = Agriculture + Allied; ssi = Small Scale Industries; svcs = Services.
All amounts are in thousands of Rupees.
(Source: As for preceding table)

given separately in Tables 4.5 to 4.7 respectively. The lead bank itself labels the A.A.P. 1980 as the ***"year of the Cooperative Bank"***,[9] which disbursed Rs 3,264,000 as loans in the agriculture and allied sector against a target of Rs 1,206,000; a percentage of achievement of 271%. The commercial banks could, however, disburse only Rs 170,000 as loans in this very sector against a target of Rs 1,919,000, giving a percentage of achievement of 8.86% only. ***"The reason for this poor performance of the commercial banks in the agriculture sector was the financial strength and wide coverage of the cooperative bank in the district"***.[10] This explanation is not credible as the commercial banks between themselves had the same number of branches in Kinnaur (five) as the SCB at this time. The latter had proved more amenable than the former to pleas from the district administration to liberalize credit inflows by not being too rigid about procedural formalities.

A new D.C. had taken charge of the district in 1980 and he was keen on increasing credit inflows. Since commercial banks were hesitant, he found better cooperation from the SCB through direct persuasion and the good offices of his D.C.S.O. It was only due to the SCB's sterling performance that overall A.A.P. targets were achieved in 1980 because the commercial banks fell far short of their targets in the S.S.I. and services sector as well. Things changed in 1981 by when the commercial banks had realized that the D.C. would not relent in his pressure for injecting more institutional credit into Kinnaur and that he was willing to be very helpful by distributing government funds as deposits in commercial banks and by accelerating overdue recoveries for agencies cooperating with him. He was equally unhelpful to

[9] D.C.P. 1983-85, op. cit., Chapter II, p. 16.

[10] Ibid.

such banks as acted too finicky on procedural red-tapism or refused to dovetail their loaning to overall district-level targets. He constantly harped on the fact that credit inflows had to be increased to consciously try and begin competing with moneylenders as sources of credit. The institutional credit infrastructure would not be allowed to shirk its responsibility of making a dent, howsoever small, in the near total domination of the regional credit markets by local moneylenders, chiefly village deities. The district set-up was geared up to help institutional credit agencies by strict enforcement of laws curbing the activities of local moneylenders, as shall be discussed later (in Chapter VII). Commercial banks were put under heavy pressure to

Table 4.6: A.A.P., 1981 for Kinnaur District

s	Bank	Sector (Rupees'000)											
,,	name	agri + alld			ssi			tertiary			total		
,,	-do-	T	A	%	T	A	%	T	A	%	T	A	%
1	pnb	140	42	30	90	108	120	245	345	141	475	495	104
2	uco	115	240	209	40	59	148	305	294	96	460	593	129
3	ubi	65	12	19	50	65	130	90	13	14	205	90	44
4	sbi	75	199	265	50	46	92	285	1285	451	410	1530	373
5	ttl	395	493	125	230	278	121	925	1937	209	1550	2708	175
6	scb	1475	400	27	000	000	000	400	1132	283	1875	1532	82
7	ldb	300	111	37	000	000	000	000	000	000	300	111	37
8	gtl	2170	1004	46	230	278	121	1325	3069	232	3725	4351	117

Note: T = Target, A = Achievement, % = Achievement as percentage of target,
agri + alld = Agriculture & Allied Sector, ssi = Small Scale Industries Sector, ttl = Total, gtl = Grand Total.
(Source: D.C.P. 1983-85, p. 15.)

be more liberal. It can at once be noticed that except for the UBI all other commercial banks achieved and exceeded their targets in 1981. The lead bank achieved its targets in the S.S.I. and tertiary sectors but failed to do so in the agriculture sector. The UBI's performance was very poor. It disbursed only Rs 90,000 as loans, less than the lending of a rich moneylender per annum. The UCO Bank and the SBI achieved their targets in all sectors except shortfalls for the SBI in the S.S.I. and for the UCO Bank in the tertiary sector respectively, but the magnitudes of failure were rather small. The new D.C.'s efforts had begun yielding results! The lead bank points out that there was ***"good coordination between the block authorities/district authorities and commercial banks. The development agencies in the district sponsored the loan cases to the banks and the loans were disbursed by the banks in a well planned manner".***[11]

We can notice the rolling plan effect here. Since Rs 3,472,000 had been disbursed against a target of Rs 1,919,000 during the A.A.P. 1980, the district administration focussed more on the S.S.I. sector and did not exert much pressure on the banks to reach the targets in the agriculture and allied sector. As a result, Rs 278,000 were disbursed in the S.S.I. sector against a target of Rs 230,000. In the agriculture sector, only Rs 1,004,000 were advanced

[11] Ibid, p. 17.

against a target of Rs 2,170,000 but if the A.A.Ps 1980 and 1981 were added up, Rs 4,476,000 had been disbursed as loan in this sector against a target of Rs 4,089,000. There was still a shortfall in the S.S.I. sector because only Rs 409,000 had been advanced against a target of Rs 467,000 but in terms of relative achievement percentage even here there had been a rise from 55% in 1980 to 121% in 1981. The mid-course correction was working!

The inauguration of a UCO Bank branch (at Sangla) in November 1980 marked the entry of this bank into Kinnaur. The local legislator and the D.C. had both worked hard to get this bank to Kinnaur. Its Divisional Manager was quite development minded and cooperative. He had instructed his officers to reduce red-tapism, cooperate closely with the district administration and be liberal in advancing loans. Within one year, this bank had already pumped in Rs 593,000 as credit into Kinnaur as against Rs 495,000 loaned out by the lead bank (PNB). Contrary to the guidelines of the LBS, the PNB continues to be the lead

Table 4.7: A.A.P., 1982 for Kinnaur District: Apex of Achievement

s	*Bank*	*Sector (Rupees'000)*											
,,	name	agri + alld			ssi			tertiary			total		
,,	-do-	T	A	%	T	A	%	T	A	%	T	A	%
1	pnb	321	292	91	157	191	122	205	274	134	683	757	111
2	uco	599	738	123	289	160	55	281	883	314	1169	1781	152
3	ubi	192	67	35	57	60	105	182	203	112	431	330	77
4	sbi	323	941	291	91	408	448	206	1547	751	620	2896	467
5	ttl	1435	2038	142	594	819	138	874	2907	333	2903	5764	199
6	scb	963	2122	220	000	000	000	1150	4654	405	2113	6776	321
7	ldb	350	181	52	000	000	000	000	000	000	350	181	52
8	gtl	2748	4341	158	594	819	138	2024	7561	374	5366	12721	237

Note: T = Target, A = Achievement, % = Achievement as percentage of target, agri + alld = Agriculture & Allied Sector, ssi = Small Scale Industries Sector, ttl = Total, gtl = Grand Total. (Source: D.C.P. 1983-85, p. 16.)

bank in Kinnaur.[12] The S.S.I. sector finally showed satisfactory results in 1982 because the functioning of the District Industries Centre at Rekong Peo had been toned up. Against a total target of Rs 5,366,000 for all the sectors, Rs 12,271,000 (more than double the target amount) were disbursed as loan. Even the habitual laggard, the UBI, managed to exceed its targets in the S.S.I. and the tertiary sectors! The LDB also improved its performance, in spite of having only one staff member to perform all functions. The I.R.D. Programme was extended to the remaining two Blocks (Kālpa and Pooh) on October 2, 1982. The lead bank concluded that in spite of the geographical remoteness of Kinnaur District and the lack of civil amenities there, ***"the performance of the financial institutions operating in the district can be rated as good. The trend of achievements during the three years covered by the plan is very***

[12] Please see Section 4.2.1, this Chapter.

encouraging".[13]

This optimistic outlook had been brought about through sustained pressure by the D.C. on bankers to disburse more loans and on Revenue and Cooperative Department officials to be severe in dealing with wilful defaulters of bank loans. Bank officers were allowed ready access to discuss their difficulties. They were provided transportation in government vehicles to make field visits. They were given the feeling that they were in no way considered as **"outsiders"** on whom the incompetence of government departments could be blamed. Close personal rapport between the D.C. on the one hand and the Divisional Manager, UCO Bank and the Regional Manager, PNB on the other, facilitated coordination. Theoretically, individuals should have mattered much less than institutions but in practice it was repeatedly experienced that where individuals were not in good rapport, the institutions also functioned slowly. We can now briefly examine the further evolution of the banks during the third round

Table 4.8: A.A.P. 1983 for Kinnaur District: New D.C.P. Round

sn	*Bank*	*Sector (Rupees ' 000)*														
do	-do-	Agri + Alld			SSI			Tertiary			Total			IRDP		
do	*-do-*	*T*	*A*	*%*	*T*	*A*	*%*	*T*	*A*	*%*	*T*	*A*	*%*	*T*	*A*	*%*
1	pnb	171	674	394	150	137	91	262	236	90	583	1097	188	296	208	70
2	uco	683	1048	153	433	630	146	1210	378	31	2326	2048	88	1103	1207	109
3	sbi	319	467	146	166	61	37	675	885	131	1160	1413	121	473	472	99
4	ubi	180	195	108	100	55	55	200	93	47	480	343	71	245	266	109
5		1353	2376	176	849	933	110	2347	1592	68	4549	4901	108	2117	2153	10
6	scb	510	455	89	000	000	00	900	909	101	1410	1364	97	000	000	000
7	ldb	308	97	32	000	000	00	000	000	000	308	97	31	000	000	000
8		2171	2988	135	849	933	110	3247	2501	77	6267	6362	102	2117	2153	

Code: **T = Target, A = Achievement, % = percentage (A/T), ttl = Total,**
sn = serial number, SSI = Small Scale Industries, gtl = Grand Total.
(Source: Annual Action Plan For District Kinnaur, Cyclostyled PNB Document, Unpublished, Undated, Simla, Chapter II, p. 9)

of the D.C.P. Achievements declined in all the sectors from the levels attained in 1982. The target for all sectors at Rs 5,400,000 was higher than that for A.A.P. 1982 (Rs 5,366,000). The achievement exceeded this target but was Rs 10,952,000 as against Rs 12,721,000 attained in 1982. The most striking feature was in the S.S.I. sector in which the target had been raised to Rs 1,405,000 from Rs 594,000 in 1982 but the achievement was only Rs 642,000, much below the Rs 819,000 attained already in 1982. Also, while overall total target was surpassed, only 66% achievement was done for the I.R.D. cases, the "poorest of the poor". This pattern remained unchanged. 1983 was the first year of a new round of the D.C.P. (1983-85). A new D.C. had taken over at the beginning of 1983 in Kinnaur, just as his predecessor had taken over in early 1980 at the beginning of the preceding D.C.P. The figures up to December 31,

[13] D.C.P. 1983-85 Draft Document, op. cit., 1983, p. 18.

Table 4.9: A.A.P. 1984 till 30.09.1984 for Kinnaur District

sn	*Bank*	***Sector (Rupees ' 000)***														
do	**-do-**	**Agri + Alld**			**SSI**			**Tertiary**			**Total**			**IRDP**		
do	*-do-*	*T*	*A*	*%*	*T*	*A*	*%*	*T*	*A*	*%*	*T*	*A*	*%*	*T*	*A*	*%*
1	pnb	815	900	110	225	348	155	505	369	73	1545	1697	110	535	382	71
2	uco	1140	725	64	650	310	48	1150	179	16	2940	1214	41	1270	813	64
3	sbi	525	122	23	215	81	38	570	1332	234	1340	1535	115	565	95	17
4	ubi	240	145	60	70	26	37	240	40	17	550	219	40	185	54	29
5		2720	1892	70	1160	765	66	2465	1920	78	6375	4665	73	2555	1344	53
6	scb	622	696	112	000	000	00	000	200	000	622	956	154	000	00	000
7	ldb	400	195	49	000	000	00	000	000	000	400	195	49	000	000	000
8	gtl	3742	2863	77	1160	765	66	2465	2120	86	7397	5816	79	2555	1344	53

Code: gtl = **Grand Total, T = Target, A = Achievement, % = Percentage (A/T), ttl = Total,**
sn = Serial Number, SSI = Small Scale Industries.

(Source: Annual Action Plan For District Kinnaur, Cyclostyled PNB Document, Unpublished, Undated, Simla, Chapter II.)

1984 were not available but would be higher. Already targets were higher than those for 1982 but overall achievement lower. Achievement was 48% lower in the agriculture and allied sector, 14% higher for the S.S.I. sector, 202% lower in the tertiary sector and 100% lower overall. Sectoral adjustments can also be discerned. Targets had been lowered for the agriculture and allied sector and raised for the S.S.I. and tertiary sectors. The target had also been lowered for the I.R.D.P. from Rs 2,952,000 in 1983 to Rs 2,117,000 in 1984, a reduction of about 39%. This was hidden by a rise in the percentage of achievement from 66% to 102%, a typical case of official jugglery with statistics to mask decreases in absolute terms.

The final field data available covered the period from January 1, 1985 till June 30, 1985 after which no data was available. There was an 18% increase in the target for bank credit disbursement in 1985 over 1984. We can clearly see how the SCB, which had a target of Rs 1,206,000 in the agriculture and allied sector in 1980 at the beginning of the D.C.P. process in Kinnaur, a figure more than ten times the target for the PNB and nearly eight times that for the UCO Bank, had been now reduced to a target in this sector of Rs 622,000 in 1985 as against a target of Rs 1,140,000 for the UCO Bank, nearly double that of the SCB. Even the lead bank (PNB) had a target in this sector of Rs 815,000 in 1985, 31% higher than that of the SCB. The cooperative banks had yielded the motor role to commercial banks in all sectors, 16 years after the nationalization of 14 major banks and 25 years after the establishment of the first SCB branch at Kālpa. The UCO Bank had become the institutional credit leader. It had established seven branches all over Kinnaur. Having seen the changes in the credit distribution sectoral pattern, we can now examine the schemes for which loans were given. Having observed the credit disbursement sector-wise, we consider now the targets which had been decided upon for 1986. Roughly 11.5 million rupees were to be given as credit in 1986. This yields a per capita figure of about Rs 193 according to the population statistics taken from the 1981 Census.

Table 4.10: A.A.P. 1985 till June 30, 1985, for Kinnaur District

sn	*Bank*	***Sector (Rupees ' 000)***														
do	-do-	Agri + Alld			SSI			Tertiary			Total			IRDP		
do	*-do-*	*T*	*A*	*%*	*T*	*A*	*%*	*T*	*A*	*%*	*T*	*A*	*%*	*T*	*A*	*%*
1	pnb	279	345	124	178	163	92	209	299	143	666	807	121	449	257	57
2	uco	944	941	100	769	369	48	790	725	92	2503	2035	81	1688	964	57
3	sbi	341	468	137	345	85	25	375	555	148	1070	1108	104	594	349	59
4	ubi	108	325	301	113	25	22	18	94	522	239	444	186	221	386	175
5		1672	2079	124	1405	642	46	1392	1673	120	4478	4394	98	2952	1956	66
6	scb	400	1403	351	000	000	00	250	4890	1956	650	6283	967	000	00	000
7	ldb	272	275	101	000	000	00	000	000	000	272	275	101	000	000	000
8		2344	3757	160	1405	642	46	1642	6553	399	5400	10952	203	2952	1956	

Code: gtl = Grand Total, T = Target, A = Achievement, % = Percentage (A/T), ttl = Total,
sn = Serial Number, SSI = Small Scale Industries.
(Source: Annual Action Plan For District Kinnaur, Cyclostyled PNB Document, Unpublished, Undated, Simla, Chapter II, p. 8.)

Table 4.11: Credit Disbursement under A.A.Ps in Kinnaur

sn	*D.C.P.*	*Year*	***A.A.P. Data(Rs'000)***			
„	-do-	--do--	TT	TA	%Change	
„	*-do-*	*--do--*	*do*	*do*	*T*	*A*
1	1980-82	1980	2,971	3,746	0000	0000
2	1980-82	1981	3,725	4,351	+25%	+16%
3	1980-82	1982	5,366	12,701	+44%	+192%
4	1983-85	1983	5,400	10,952	+.6%	-14%
5	1983-85	1984	6,267	6,362	+16%	-42%
6	1983-85	1985	7,367	5,816	+18%	-09%

Code: sn = Serial No.; D.C.P. = District Credit Plan; A.A.P. = Annual Action Plan;
TT = Total Target; TA = Total Achievement; %Change = Percentage Change from preceding year;
Figures for 1984 are till September 30, 1984.
Figures for 1985 are till June 30, 1985.

Table 4.12: Financial Allocations under A.A.P. 1986 for Kinnaur

sn	*Bank*	*Allocation(Rs '000)*		
do	-do-	–do–	%Change from	
do	*-do-*	*-do-*	*1984*	*1985*
01	PNB	2,785	+378%	+80%
02	UCO	4,240	+82%	+44%
03	SBI	1,720	+48%	+28%
04	UBI	,845	+76%	+54%
05	SCB	1,300	-08%	+109%
06	SCB	,590	+92%	+48%
07	TTL	11,510	+84%	+56%

(Source: Information collected in person from the D.C.'s Office at Kālpa and the Regional Office of the Punjab National Bank at Simla in December 1985 and January 1986 respectively.)

4.3 BANKABLE SCHEMES: I.R.D.P. TO THE FORE

Since nearly 33% of the total credit outlays in 1984 and 1985 were earmarked for distribution under the I.R.D.P., we can divide bankable schemes for Kinnaur into two broad categories:
(a) I.R.D.P. Schemes; and
(b) Other Schemes.
The I.R.D.P. relies on an integrated strategy, including institutional credit inputs, for increasing production and productivity. The poorest sections of society were to be given subsidy and credit facilities. Beneficiaries would be financed partly through subsidy and partly through bank loans. The subsidy varies with the income level of the beneficiary from 25% to 50% of the capital cost. All beneficiaries under the I.R.D.P. in Kinnaur, being either Scheduled Castes or Scheduled Tribes, are considered eligible for 50% subsidy. Every year 600 families per Development Block are to be assisted for productive activities with follow-up measures to ensure that they cross the poverty line fixed at Rs 3,500 per family per annum. The programme is focussed on small and marginal farmers, tenants and share croppers, landless labourers and rural artisans, with special emphasis on the S.Cs and the S.Ts which means that virtually everyone in Kinnaur can become eligible. S.C./S.T. beneficiaries are eligible for maximum subsidy up to Rs 5,000. Their bank loan components carry a rate of interest @ 10% per annum.

4.3.1 I.R.D.P. Loan Schemes: Most Important

In the agricultural sector loans could be taken from banks for the following purposes:

(a) Minor irrigation schemes;
(b) Farm implements @ Rs 500 per unit with matching subsidy;
(c) Plough animals meaning bullocks or churus (crosses between a yak and a cow) @ Rs 4,000 per pair;
(d) Land development; and

(e) Horticulture and hop cultivation.

In the allied sector loans were available for the following:

(A) Dairy, @ Rs 3,500 per unit for purchase of jersey cows and improved breeds of milch cattle;
(B) Sheep and goat rearing @ Rs 1,400 per sheep/goat unit;
(C) Pack animals (donkeys, mules etc.) @ Rs 2,000 for a pair of donkeys and Rs 8,000 for a pair of mules.

In the S.S.I. sector, loans were provided for the following schemes:

(a) Handlooms and weaving, @ Rs 8,000 per unit;
(b) Carpentry, @ Rs 2,500 per worker;
(c) Blacksmithy, @ Rs 2,500 per beneficiary;
(d) Tailoring/Sewing Machines, @ Rs 500 per sewing machine and Rs 4,000 per tailoring unit;
(e) Sheet metal units, @ Rs 8,000 per unit;
(f) Auto repairs workshop, @ Rs 10,000 per unit;
(g) Furniture units, @ Rs 14,000 per unit;
(h) Composite units, @ Rs 37,000 per unit;
(i) Dry cleaning units, @ Rs 14,000 per unit;
(j) Washing soap units, @ Rs 14,000 per unit;
(k) Shoemaking, @ Rs 3,000 per unit/worker; and
(l) Sawmills, @ Rs 15,000 per unit.

In the tertiary or services sector, the major activities eligible for bank loans were as follows:

(a) Small retail trade, @ Rs 8,000 per occupational unit; and
(b) Small business, @ Rs 5,000 per unit.

The limits stated are upper limits or ceilings and not obligatory amounts that must invariably be borrowed. If an I.R.D.P. beneficiary wants to purchase a pair of mules, he can avail up to Rs 8,000 financial assistance of which Rs 4,000 would be bank loan and Rs 4,000 subsidy. In case he wants more loan he can take more, only that matching subsidy cannot exceed Rs 5,000 in all. If he wants Rs 15,000 for a saw mill, the subsidy component would be Rs 5,000 and the loan component Rs 10,000 of which Rs 5,000 would carry interest @ 10% per annum and the rest at higher rates of interest. In addition to these schemes, commercial banks had parallel schemes carrying higher rates of interest.

4.3.2 Non-I.R.D.P. Loan Schemes

In the agriculture sector, crop loans were available from commercial banks on exactly the same terms as from cooperative banks.[14] In addition, loans could be obtained as follows:

(a) Short-term loans up to Rs 5,000 carrying 11.5% annual rate of interest;
(b) Short-term loans over Rs 5,000 up to Rs 10,000 carrying 12.5% annual rate of interest;
(c) Short-term loans over Rs 10,000 up to Rs 25,000 with an annual rate of interest not to exceed 14%; and
(d) Short-term loans above Rs 25,000 carrying an annual rate of interest not exceeding 16.5%.

Medium-term loans for not less than three years were:

[14] Please see Section 3.3.2.1, Chapter III of this work.

(a) Minor irrigation and land development loans, with a rate of interest 10% per annum;
(b) Other purposes (agricultural implements, pack animals, sheep, poultry, piggery), with rate of interest = 10% per annum for small farmers and 12.5% for other farmers.

In the S.S.I. sector, loans were available for all types of small scale industries, including village and cottage industries (including all schemes already listed under the I.R.D.P.). The rates of interest on these loans were as follows:

(a) Composite loans up to Rs 25,000, rate of interest = 10% per annum;
(b) Short-term advances up to and inclusive of Rs 200,000, rate of interest = not to exceed 14% per annum;
(c) Short-term advances over Rs 200,000 and up to Rs 2,500,000, rate of interest = not to exceed 16.5%;
(d) Short-term loans above Rs 2,500,000, rate of interest = not to exceed 18%; and
(e) For term loans of not less than three years, rate of interest = 12.5%

In the tertiary sector, commercial banks provided loans for:

(a) Retail Trade
(1) Up to and inclusive of Rs 5,000, rate of interest = 12.5% per annum;
(2) Over Rs 5,000 and up to Rs 25,000 (inclusive), rate of interest = 15% per annum; and
(3) Above Rs 25,000, rate of interest = 17.5% per annum;
(b) Small business, rate of interest = 15% per annum;
(c) Transport
(1) Owner-Driver Scheme, up to two vehicles, rate of interest = 12.5% per annum;
(2) Transport Ownership Scheme, rate of interest = 15% per annum.
(d) Professional and self-employed persons, rate of interest = 12.5% per annum.

The scale of finance was Rs 150,000 per truck in Kinnaur. There were some special schemes introduced by commercial banks in Kinnaur.

4.3.2.1 Special Schemes: Still in a Trial Stage

It was recognized that giving loans for only productive economic activities would leave the borrowers totally dependent on moneylenders for consumption purposes. It had nevertheless long been a rule that banks would not give consumption loans. This principle has now been diluted in recognition of the fact that without making a dent in this monopoly of moneylenders on consumption credit, the risk of diversion of funds borrowed for productive economic purposes towards consumption purposes would remain unacceptably high. Some tentative steps have been taken by banks to redress this imbalance.

4.3.2.1.1 Consumption Loans for Weaker Sections from Banks

Consumption loans could be given for the following purposes:
(a) General consumption, up to maximum Rs 75;
(b) Medical expenses, up to maximum Rs 250;
(c) Educational needs, up to maximum Rs 100;
(d) Marriage ceremonies, up to maximum Rs 250;
(e) Funerals, births etc., up to maximum Rs 75; and
(f) Religious ceremonies, up to maximum Rs 75.
These loans would all carry rates of interest @ 4% per annum for S.Cs and S.Ts. Loans were permissible for more than one of these listed purposes, provided the aggregate finance did not exceed Rs 500 per family. However, the purpose-wise ceilings were not to apply where loans were secured against gold and silver ornaments pledged as security. In such cases, a ceiling of Rs 1,000 was to be stipulated. Anyone familiar with expenditure on marriage ceremonies and religious rites in India knows that these ceilings are laughably low! These petty sums would certainly not challenge the hold of moneylenders on consumption credit.

4.3.2.1.2 Loans for Educational Purposes

This scheme was for graduate and post-graduate courses in India in fields like engineering, commerce and other sciences or arts. Loans could be taken to meet expenses incurred on course fees, hostel fees, cost of books, stationery and equipment required for the course, as well as examination fees. Maximum permissible amounts of such loans were as under:

(a) Graduate studies in engineering, technology and medicine = Rs 15,000;
(b) Post-Graduate studies in engineering, technology, medicine and post-graduate research studies abroad = Rs 25,000; and
(c) For all other purposes eligible under the scheme = Rs 10,000.

Due consideration had to be given to any financial assistance such as stipend or scholarship for which the student might have been eligible. The actual disbursement would be done on a quarterly basis to avoid misuse of the loan amount. Before disbursing the loan amount for the quarter, the manager would examine receipts, fees and room rents paid, cash memos in respect of books or stationery purchased during the preceding quarter.

The rates of interest for S.Cs and S.Ts were as below:

(a) For loan amounts up to Rs 6,500(inclusive) = 4% per annum;
(b) For loan amounts more than Rs 6,500 = 2% over the bank rate with a minimum of 11% per annum; and
(c) For studies abroad = 5% over the bank rate with a minimum of 15% per annum.

The figures under these special schemes were zero in Kinnaur District till the end of 1985. Very few villagers knew of the existence of these schemes, and even they seemed to feel that there were too many procedural constraints. The banks were not making any perceptible effort to publicize these loan schemes. They felt that wide publicity would only increase the number of bad debts. These schemes remained purely options on paper. In any case, they had no appeal to the poorest sections of society. To cater to them, there was the Differential Rate of Interest Scheme (henceforth, D.R.I. scheme) which was tending to become more and more popular, in spite of passive resistance by banks. The rate of interest was 4% per annum under the D.R.I. scheme and this was too low for the bankers' liking. The risk factor was high because persons eligible to get loans under this Scheme were indigent, unable to offer guarantees or securities.

4.3.3 D.R.I. Scheme: People's Darling but Bankers' Nightmare!

This Scheme was announced in the Lok Sabha on March 25, 1972. It aims at fixing very low rates of interest for poor borrowers on a sliding scale on which rate of interest would rise in proportion to rise in income. Hence the name Differential Rate of Interest Scheme. As per R.B.I. directives,[15] every commercial bank with deposits more than Rs 250 million is required to lend at least 1% of its total advances under the D.R.I. scheme. Such loans could be given directly to the beneficiary or be routed through institutions like the Scheduled Caste Welfare Corporation. The R.B.I. guidelines amplify conditions of eligibility for these loans.

4.3.3.1 Eligibility for D.R.I. Loans

These conditions are calculated to ensure that really the "poorest of the poor" become eligible.

(1) The borrower should lack any tangible security of much worth on his/her own;
(2) There should exist the possibility that the borrower can be assisted in bettering his existing economic status through a productive endeavour by the banks. He should have some artisan skill so that the productive endeavour in question can render his situation economically viable in about three years;

[15] Singh, Ajit, 1985, Chapter 21, p. 280.

(3) *The borrower should not incur liability to two sources of institutional finance at the same time, otherwise he would be overburdened with a loan repayment charge beyond his capacity to repay;*
(4) *The annual income of the borrower's family, including husband, wife and dependent children, should not exceed Rs 3,000 per annum in urban/semi-urban areas and Rs 2,000 per annum in rural areas. This family income comprises the income earned by all the members of the family, whether earned or unearned or whether obtained in cash or in kind;*
(5) *The borrower should not own any land. If he does own some land, the size of his holding as per revenue record should not exceed 1 acre of irrigated land or 2.5 acres of unirrigated land. This stipulation can be waived in case of S.C./S.T. borrowers provided income criteria are strictly observed;*
(6) *Preference should be given to S.C./S.T. borrowers and to officially designated backward areas or tribal areas (like Kinnaur); and*
(7) *Beneficiaries recommended by the State S.C. Corporation are also eligible under the Scheme. The income ceiling per annum is fixed at Rs 3,000 by the Corporation itself.*

These conditions of eligibility are complimented by a specification of the activities which can be financed under the D.R.I. scheme.

4.3.3.2 List of Activities to be Financed under D.R.I. Scheme

These activities are supposedly grouped on the basis of the segment of society to which the borrower belongs. This is a recognition of the fact that borrowers eligible under this Scheme are more likely to belong to certain social groups that practise certain occupations. They do not conform to the principle of randomness. Accordingly, some favoured occupations have been selected under the D.R.I. scheme for loans:

(a) *Agriculture on a small scale;*
(b) *Activities allied to agriculture, like dairying, poultry, piggery, sheep rearing on a small scale;*
(c) *Processing of forest produce and collection of fodder;*
(d) *Rural and cottage industries/vocations, like sale of cheap food items, cloth cutting, garment stitching, home delivery service of commodities/articles of everyday use, roadside tea stalls, plying of self-owned cycle rickshaws, fabrication/repair of shoes on modest scale, basket making by hand and bicycle repair sheds;*
(e) *Physically handicapped persons possessing productive skills in which a continuous supply of raw material was required. Institutions employing such persons for these productive occupations were also eligible for bank loans under the D.R.I. scheme; and*
(f) *Indigent students, particularly from backward areas, who have merit and are interested in higher studies but are unable to get scholarships/stipends from the government or educational institutions can be given bank loans under this Scheme.*

The amount of credit to be disbursed per person is not unlimited but is limited by ceiling norms.

4.3.3.3 Credit Ceiling Norms under the D.R.I. Scheme

The amount of credit permissible obviously varies with the purpose and costs of the intended project. However, this amount is not limitless. The maximum amount of loan permissible is Rs 6,500, of which Rs 5,000 maximum can constitute a term loan and Rs 1,500 maximum working capital. R.B.I. directives permit loaning banks to ignore the separation between term loan and working capital in cases from the decentralized sector involving small industries and village artisans. The loan can be given as a composite loan wherever the distinction between term loan and working capital is not easy to make. This limit of Rs 6,500 can be relaxed only in case of institutions and on merits. It cannot be waived in case of individual borrowers. This is an incentive for individual artisans to group themselves together into cooperatives or work for centres run by existing institutions in case they want loans in excess of Rs 6,500. The presumption is that for very poor people, economies of scale could become possible only when they work together in groups and not if they work on an individual basis. Since it was not possible to exclude individual borrowers, a ceiling was imposed on the amount of loan admissible whereas groups or institutions could be exempted from this ceiling.

The rate of interest is a uniform concessional rate of 4% per annum simple interest. Moreover, no penal rate of interest should be imposed on loans under the D.R.I. scheme. This was to remove one of the biggest fears of poor borrowers who felt that in cases of default penal interest imposition would make their repayment burden unacceptably heavy. No margin money was to be demanded, in view of the non-existent savings capacity of borrowers. Demanding margin money was clearly against the norms of the Scheme. The figures for actual advances under the D.R.I. scheme in Kinnaur show that bankers have not done badly at lending at such low rates of interest, but there is no way of knowing whether all the loans went to really needy people.

4.3.3.4 D.R.I. Scheme Statistics for Kinnaur District

Table 4.13: D.R.I. Scheme Disbursement Figures for Kinnaur District

s	*Year*	*BANK*							
"	-do-	**PNB**		**UCO**		**UBI**		**SBI**	
"	*-do-*	*dria*	*pct*	*dria*	*pct*	*dria*	*pct*	*dria*	*pct*
1	1982	334	21	,897	45	102	54	490	15
2	1983	404	20	1,255	37	104	15	781	13
3	1984	505	17	1,684	38	144	16	751	17
4	1985	842	19	1,938	38	162	20	705	13
5	82-85	2085	05	5,774	13	512	11	2727	06

Code: **dria = D.R.I. advances in thousands of Rs, pct = percent of total.**

Table 4.13 shows the advances under the D.R.I. scheme in Kinnaur. The percentage of D.R.I. advances as fraction of total advances varied between 17% and 21% for the PNB; between 37% and 45% for UCO Bank; between 13% and 17% for the SBI and between 15% and 20% for the UBI, with an exception of 54% in 1982. These percentages are much higher than the mandatory 1% of total advances decreed by the R.B.I. Most of these cases were I.R.D. cases sponsored by the Development Block authorities. The number of cases financed directly by the banks under this scheme was low. Bank managers agreed in private conversation that they were not keen to be liberal under this scheme. It involved much paper work for small loan amounts; furnished no security and carried a high risk of default. Cases financed directly by banks under D.R.I. revealed that this was often the result of pressure by local political figures like panchāyat pradhāns, lambardārs etc. In one case a bank had given a D.R.I. loan to the son of a political figure who was one of the richest men of Kinnaur. On paper, the loanee had been separated from his father; had less than 2 acres of unirrigated land in his own name and had obtained an income certificate saying that his annual income was less than Rs 2,000 per annum. However, had the bank manager made even a minor enquiry he would have found out that the borrower was one of the richest persons in Kinnaur. In fact, the manager did know it but had to yield to pressure. Such cases should not detract from the fact that poor borrowers have also been covered, albeit mostly under the I.R.D.P. The D.R.I. scheme has become an integral part of the I.R.D.P. and is hardly perceived as a separate scheme for aiding the poorest sections of society.

4.3.3.5 Banking Statistics for Kinnaur District

Overall banking statistics from 1983 to 1985 for Kinnaur District show that in terms of advances to the priority sector, all commercial banks had reached figures between 85% and 93% for 1985. There had been a rise in total bank deposits from Rs 47,125,000 on December 31, 1983 to Rs 66,913,000 on June 30, 1985. Of course, it was not specified how much of this increase came through government funds and how much genuinely from deposits from private parties. The C.D. ratio, an important indicator to gauge whether a bank was squeezed for credit availability or not, was 40% for the lead bank, 33% for UCO Bank, 35% for the SBI, 33% for the SCB and 78% for the UBI in 1985. The high figure for the UBI is a result of the low deposit mobilization by this bank so that even a figure as low as Rs 814,000 for total advances gave such a high C.D. ratio. Commercial banks have otherwise not been able to bring their C.D. ratios up to the figure of 60% recommended by decisions made many times in the D.C.C.C. Enough funds were thus available for further loaning to try and raise this ratio to 60%. Even the cooperative bank had a ratio as low as 33%. Evidently, there was no problem of refinance or paucity of funds. How the structure functioned can perhaps be better perceived by considering data for the first commercial bank branch established in Kinnaur District at Rekong Peo.

4.4 DATA FOR THE REKONG PEO BRANCH OF THE PNB

This branch was the only one which furnished statistical data from 1976 onwards till 1985. Branches of other banks could furnish data only from 1982 onwards. Table 4.14 shows the data about loans advanced by the Rekong Peo branch of the PNB. Graphical representations of these figures show fluctuating curves but a sharp rise from 1984 to 1985. Loan inputs increased in the D.C.P. 1983-85. The rise in 1985 was partly a response to the fact that the UCO Bank was building up pressure for permission to be allowed to open a branch at Rekong Peo. The PNB, already left behind by the UCO Bank in the number of branches in Kinnaur, resisted this proposal. To show that it was capable of catering to the needs of the Peo area and that it was not unduly bureaucratic in its approach, as alleged, loan amounts disbursed were increased. Competition between these two banks was turning to the advantage of the borrowers in terms of greater readiness to be flexible. Since there was no difference in the interest rates, the PNB feared competition only through credit disbursement without too many formalities if the UCO Bank were to have a branch at Peo. It sought to pre-empt this by adopting the latter bank's lenient approach. Hence the sharp rise for 1985 was a corroboration of the fact that credit availability variations in Kinnaur depended not so much on popular demand as on political and administrative factors.

Employing the Kendall Tau B non-parametric correlation test to determine whether there existed any correlation between the loan amounts disbursed under different heads, it was found that no two loan variables were significantly correlated, positively or negatively. Loans were disbursed in various sectors independently of each other. This results from a low C.D. ratio, leading to adequate liquidity availability for loaning in all sectors. Had this ratio been more than 60%, we may have observed significant correlation between some variables because limited funds would have had to be partitioned between various sectors. This would have meant that a rise in lending in one sector may have led to parallel increases in similar sectors but corresponding decreases in dissimilar sectors. We can now examine the performance of the bank that had pumped in the maximum credit into Kinnaur: the UCO Bank.

Table 4.14: Loans from the Rekong Peo Branch of the PNB

sn	*Year*	*Sector(Rs '000)*							
"	-do-	agri	ssi	trty	labd	tpt	rta	sle	total
01	1976	057	043	13	026	087	000	000	226
02	1977	025	007	13	010	000	000	000	055
03	1978	078	020	00	026	095	000	000	219
04	1979	051	041	24	146	000	021	000	283
05	1980	047	049	30	134	000	060	000	320
06	1981	076	076	26	168	300	040	000	686
07	1982	092	088	20	160	150	043	000	553
08	1983	089	098	24	147	000	045	000	403
09	1984	199	149	42	166	000	075	125	756
10	1985	472	391	58	357	000	569	130	1977

Code: sn = serial no., Rs '000 = Rupees in thousands, agri = agriculture, ssi = small scale industries, trty = tertiary, labd = loan against bank deposit, tpt = loans for transport, rta = retail trade advances, sle = loans to self-employed persons.
(Source: Collected in person from the Office of the Manager, PNB Branch, Rekong Peo on December 14, 1985. Compiled from branch ledgers pertaining to loan categories.)

4.5 DISBURSAL MADE BY THE UCO BANK DURING THE PERIOD 1980-84

The UCO Bank had rapidly increased credit inflows into Kinnaur. The expansion has been matched by an increase in the number of its branches. The first branch opened its doors in Sangla on November 20, 1980 and already by the end of the year had disbursed Rs 18,000 as loan in the priority sector, nearly 56% of it to small business. The disbursement rose to Rs 593,000 in 1981, an increase of 3194% over the figure for 1980. 181 borrowers benefited, giving an average loan per borrower of Rs 3,276. This figure fell to Rs 2,254 for 1982, a decrease of 31%. The corresponding figures were Rs 3,026, +34% for 1983 and Rs 2,587 and -15% for 1984 respectively. These average amounts were significant, showing that a real dent was sought to be made in the credit market in Kinnaur. The average amount of loan per marginal farmer was Rs 5,111 for 1981; Rs 1,511 for 1982; Rs 2,131 for 1983 and Rs 2,070 for 1984 respectively.[16] Parallel figures for small farmers were Rs 2,722 for 1981; Rs 3,625 for 1982; Rs 3,065 for 1983 and Rs 3,028 for 1984 respectively. After the aberration of 1981 when average loan amount per marginal farmer was nearly double that per small farmer, the situation became more 'normal' from 1982 onwards when the amount per small farmer became higher than the amount per marginal farmer. This was conforming to the results found in field surveys[17] in Kinnaur that credit demand rose with rising income and asset ownership range.

[16] All the figures mentioned in this Section are taken from a personal letter dated May 13, 1985, from Mr S.C. Girotra, Assistant General Manager, UCO Bank, Bombay, to the author.

The average of Rs 5,000 plus per marginal farmer in 1981 was abnormally high and could be ascribed to the bank's desire to make an impact in a major fashion by handing out loan amounts even in excess of repaying capacity of the average marginal farmer. Agriculture and allied sectors accounted for 0%, 40%, 39%, 44% and 53% of the loan amounts advanced in 1980, 1981, 1982, 1983 and 1984 respectively. Transport accounted for 0% in 1980, 1981 and 1984; for 11.5% in 1982 and 26.8% in 1983 respectively of the total advances in the priority sector. Consumption loans were nil for all the years. Loans for retail trade, small business and self-employed professionals formed a significant part of total lending. Having seen the loan disbursement pattern for a leading branch and the largest bank in Kinnaur, we can now analyse the bank loan data at our disposal.

4.6 ANALYSIS OF BANK LOAN STATISTICS IN KINNAUR

This analysis consists of bar charts, graphs, correlation tests, pie diagrams, regression analysis and general linear model analysis for some selected variables. We have already seen[18] how political and administrative factors influence the entire framework of the cooperative credit network. The fact that such impact cannot be mathematically quantified leads to weak correlations in general between variables under consideration. Needless to say, similar considerations affect the commercial bank credit network as well. Variables should show abnormal changes in election years (1977, 1982, 1985) or when the political complexion of the regime changed (1977, 1980, 1983). The changes in 1977, when the Janata Party replaced the Congress(I) at the helm, and 1980, when the Congress(I) returned to power (without elections in Himāchal Pradesh. Enough M.L.As crossed the floor!), involved wholesale replacement of programmes and personnel. Our loan variables should reflect these political upheavels through discontinuities.

If the commercial banks have been operating their credit schemes in a coordinated manner according to a comprehensive D.C.P., statistical variables should also vary in a highly correlated fashion. But if this were not so, or that there was only weak coordination, this variation should not be very strongly correlated. Practical experience of working with commercial bank staff leads to the presumption that commercial banks do not operate according to a well-planned cohesive strategy. Statistical analysis should corroborate this presumption by giving weak coefficients of correlation after parametric or non-parametric tests as the case may be. Competition between commercial banks for deposit mobilization means that they are willing within limits to oblige government officials, the source of large sums as deposits, by giving credit as suggested by the latter. Since each department seeks to fulfil its own targets without bothering about other departments, this competition of target-fulfilling should also contribute to uncoordinated movements in the loan variables and weak statistical correlations. The commercial bank network should show less discontinuity caused by political pressure in its variation than in the case of cooperative banks. The former have a professional management which depends much less than cooperative bank staff on politicians for career prospects' advancement. Their recruitment is done centrally. The basic influence of politics is going to be reflected in the statistical analysis of commercial bank data but its amplitude should be less than that observed for cooperative banks in the preceding chapter.

[17] See Section 3.5.1.2, Chapter III of this work.

[18] Sections 3.6-3.7, Chapter III of this work.

4.6.1 Graphs for Different Banks: Dissimilar Patterns

Graphs were plotted for the following variables:

(a) TD = Total Deposits;
(b) TA = Total Advances;
(c) TPPA = Advances under the 20 Point Programme;
(d) DRIA = Advances under the D.R.I. Scheme;
(e) SCSTA = Advances to Scheduled Castes and Scheduled Tribes;
(f) WSA = Advances to Weaker Sections; and
(g) PSA = Advances in the Priority Sector.

There were two points on the graphs for 1985, the lower one for the quarter ending June 30 and the upper one for the quarter ending September 30. All the variables showed a rise for the PNB; the TD value fell for the UCO Bank while TPPA reached a plateau while other variables rose continuously. The SBI's advances behaved differently - TD rose continuously while TA rose, fell and rose again but not to the level attained in 1983. TPPA rose continuously till 1984 and then fell sharply in 1985 while DRIA rose to their highest level in 1983 and then fell two years running. SCSTA rose sharply in 1985. For the UBI; TD fell sharply in 1985, TA rose till 1984 and then fell slowly in 1985, TPPA rose continuously alongwith DRIA while SCSTA rose sharply in 1984 and fell in 1985. There was no consistent pattern for all banks which might have reflected across the board institutional credit coordination in Kinnaur.

4.6.2 Bar Charts: Numerous Possibilities

Vertical bar charts were obtained in different configurations.

4.6.2.1 Bar Charts with the variable Bank as Sub-Group

These charts revealed a non-symmetrical distribution of loan variables, including the C.D. ratio. This indicated a non-parametric test for correlation.

4.6.2.2 Bar Charts Showing Yearwise Variation of Variables

This set of bar charts corroborated exactly the credit variation patterns revealed by separate graphs for each bank. There was no consistent up or down movement in credits given by different banks. No coherent credit market pattern applicable equally to all banks could be found.

4.6.2.3 Bar Charts Showing Bankwise Variation of Sums

The results revealed a non-symmetrical distribution for credits advanced under different heads/sectors. This corroborated the results obtained earlier.

4.6.2.4 Target and Achievement Histograms for Banks in Kinnaur

The targets and achievement figures were summed over different years and displayed bank-wise. The distribution was non-symmetrical. It could be seen straightaway that targets and achievements in the agriculture and the I.R.D.P. sectors were higher for the UCO Bank than for the lead bank (PNB).

4.6.2.5 Block Diagrams with C.D. Ratio as the Block Variable

Banks were grouped here in groups of two. The PNB and UCO Bank were grouped together as the two largest commercial banks present in Kinnaur; the SBI and UBI were grouped as the smaller commercial banks, while the SCB and LDB constituted the cooperative banking sector.

For TPPA, maximum lending took place in the C.D. ratio block 33% to 38% in the cooperative sector. About half of this amount was lent as maximum in the C.D. ratio group of 40% to 47%. Values higher than this C.D. ratio block were found only for the UBI, SBI group. The most prevalent value of this ratio ranged between 33% to 38% and then between 40% to 47% for the three loan categories considered. This was far below the figure of 60% desired by the D.C.C.C. for banks in Kinnaur.

4.6.2.6 Block Diagrams with the Number of Branches as the Block Variable

The classification for group variables was changed to match the different values for the number of branches as the block variable. The LDB, UBI and SBI were grouped together because they all had only one or two branches each in Kinnaur. Similarly, the PNB and SCB were grouped together, having 3 and 5 branches respectively; while the UCO Bank was given a category of its own, with 7 branches. The block diagrams clearly reveal the importance which the UCO Bank had acquired in the institutional credit framework of Kinnaur. It disbursed more credit as TPPA than the UBI, SBI and LDB grouped together; in D.R.I. Scheme loans it exceeded the sum of the credit given by all other banks while in loans to S.Cs and S.Ts, its contribution was nearly 87% of the loans given by all the other banks combined together.

4.7 CORRELATION BETWEEN LOAN VARIABLES FOR BANKS IN KINNAUR

Spearman's non-parametric test was applied to determine the correlation between loans advanced in different sectors. Total deposits show a reasonable correlation with total advances, PSA, WSA and SCSTA. This amounts virtually to a repetition because TA, PSA, WSA and SCSTA are overlapping variables. Borrowers in Kinnaur were to a large extent S.C. or S.T. so that most advances would fall under SCSTA. Since a large percentage of bank loans is tied to official programs like the I.R.D.P. or the D.D.P., advances made would also fall under the heads PSA and WSA since at least the I.R.D.P. is confined only to the weaker sections by definition. Naturally, if TD value rises, advances made under these sectors rise as well. But TA rise was not linked to TD rise 1:1. The coefficient of correlation was only 0.89. The correlation to DRIA was very weak for OTHERA (other advances), showing that DRIA increased more slowly than OTHERA. From this set of variables we choose TD as the independent variable because advances under different heads depend on this base. Amongst the advances, we choose TPPA because the 20 Point Programme has become the most important framework for guiding institutional credit inputs as part of the development process. We now try to establish a relation between TPPA and TD by regression analysis. Our equation giving the highest degree of reliability is the following:

$$\mathbf{y = x^2 + 809}$$

where y = TPPA and x = TD; decimals have been rounded off to the nearest integers in this relation which comes out in the form -

$$TPPA = 0.00000973608\,(TD)^2 + 809.50758$$

The equation means that TD vary in proportion to the square root of TPPA because the above relation can be rewritten as:

$$\mathbf{x = (y - 809)^{1/2}}$$

This is not a linear relation and gives a curvilinear graph. The increase in the advances under the 20 Point Programme is thus faster than the rise in the total deposits of banks in Kinnaur, considered as a proportion. By similar analysis we get the following equations:

where x_1 = **Total Deposits = TD; y_1 = Total Advances = TA;**
y_2 = Priority Sector Advances = PSA; y_3 = Advances To Weaker Sections = WSA;
y_4 = Advances To S.Cs And S.Ts = SCSTA

$$x_1 = (3.23\, y_1 - 1713) = (4.35\, y_2 - 2291) = (5y_3 - 2555) = (5.56\, y_4 - 2428)$$

We thus get the value of x_1 = TD, in terms of different loan advances. Hence we can find the inter-relation of these variables. The equations are:

$$3.23\, y_1 - 1713 = x_1 = 4.35\, y_2 - 2291;$$
$$\text{or } 3.23\, y_1 + 578 = 4.35\, y_2;$$
$$y_1 = 1.35\, y_2 - 578.$$

We must, therefore, calculate better by appoximating the results without these intercept values, otherwise we land up with a patently absurd result as the one above: $y_1 = 1.35\, y_2 - 578$ meaning that PSA have a value higher than TA (in all sectors). This is impossible that a part can be greater than the whole. Therefore, ignoring the segments we get:

$$y_1 = 1.35\, y_2$$
$$\text{or } y_2 = 0.74\, y_1$$

This means that 74% of the total advances by banks were in the priority sector. Similarly,

$$3.23\, y_1 = 5y_3$$
$$y_3 = 0.65\, y_1$$

65% of the total advances given by banks in Kinnaur thus went to the weaker sections.

Lastly, $3.23\, y_1 = 5.56\, y_4$

$$y_4 = 0.58\, y_1$$

We have derived the rather interesting result that only 58% of the total advances were to S.Cs and S.Ts, meaning that as much as 42% of the total advances went to non-S.Cs and non-S.Ts. And this in a district in which, according to the 1981 Census, 74.87% of the population were S.Ts and 10.63% were S.Cs - together constituting 85.50% of the total Kinnaura population. More than 2/5ths of the total loans thus went to the non-tribal, non-harijan population of Kinnaur which constituted only 14.5% of the total population. These were primarily shopkeepers, government servants or military personnel.

Our results give the overall variation of the bank credit inputs. This behavioral pattern can be assumed to hold reasonably for future evolution of the institutional credit network but not completely. Political decisions can always shift this behaviour in a manner not explicable by these equations. For example, a complete credit freeze could be decreed on all credit under the 20 Point Programme, as happened once in the past when this programme was replaced by the Antyodaya Programme in 1977 when the Janata regime came to power in Himāchal Pradesh. The Antyodaya Programme became a kind of flagship of the Janata government and in turn was re-replaced by the 20 Point Programme when the Congress(I) came back to power in 1980. Under such a freeze, changes in the total deposits of banks would not result in an increase in TPPA as predicted by our parabolic equation. No mathematical relation can reflect these political realities. Governments can, and do, write off the loans of poor people, thus distorting recoveries and subsequent changes in the deposit amounts of banks. We can now see how the banking credit network has practically functioned in Kinnaur till now.

4.8 FIELD SURVEY IN CHAURA VILLAGE: INTERESTING RESULTS

This field survey was carried out in village Chaura of Nichār Tahsil with the help of the halqa (area) Patwāri and the Grām Séwak between December 1, 1985 to December 15, 1985 for this research work. Chaura village was selected because it is the first village in Kinnaur as one enters the district from Simla District. The village is almost on National Highway 22; is almost never cut off from communication with the outside world in winter, unlike other villages in the interior areas of Kinnaur; has a lead bank branch at Nugalsari the next village, about 8 km down the N.H. 22; is connected by bus to Simla and is in frequent contact with Jeori, 10 kms away, in Simla District, a focal point for the area with a bank branch, many shops and a sheep-breeding farm.

Chaura thus has a good location where productive economic activity can succeed better than at many other places in Kinnaur. It is optimally situated. If the institutional credit network could succeed somewhere in Kinnaur, Chaura is one of the first places that come to mind. According to the 1981 Census, it had a population of 372 persons, living in 72 households. It had a total cultivated area of 92 hectares, giving an average land holding of 1.28 hectares per household. It forms the point of access for village Rupi in the 15/20 area, and its hamlets like Huruwā. Supplies have to be carried to the 15/20 area's villages from Chaura on pack animals because there is a bridge on the Satluj river, albeit a very rickety one, below it. Other points of crossing till the Wāngtu bridge are only 'jhulās' which can not take loaded pack animals. An economic activity that suggests itself in Chaura is purchase of pack animals for ferrying supplies to- and from the 15/20 area across the Satluj river.

4.8.1 Loan Statistics for Chaura Village

It was found that 29 households (or 40% of the total number of households in the village) had availed of bank loans. All the loans had been taken under the ægis of the I.R.D.P. and there had been no personal initiative for securing a bank loan. The results of the field survey are summarized in Table 4.15 . The mean for average loan amounts was Rs 1,759 for the sample. These amounts should in reality be doubled because a matching subsidy of 50% was released in each case by the government. Loan amounts till Rs 1,000 constituted 17.2% of the total loan amount; between Rs 1,200 and 2,000, made 68.8% and between Rs 3,000 to 5,000 the remaining 14%. It is thus an approximately symmetrical distribution in terms of percentage, with five households in the lower fifth of the borrowed amounts; 20 families in the central three-fifth; and four families in the highest end of the range. All the families claimed that they were repaying their instalments on time and that they had benefited from the loans but this proved difficult to verify on the spot. We can now see the purposes for which these loans had been taken.

4.8.1.1 Loan Pattern with Purpose of Loans

The 29 borrower households had taken loans for eight purposes, all components of the I.R.D.P., viz

AH = animal husbandry, meaning milch animals of improved varieties;
AT = artisanat tools;
LD = land development;
MP = multipurpose loans;
PA = pack animals, meaning mules or donkeys;
SH = sheep units;
SM = sewing machines; and
TN = tarpaulin.

Land development loans accounted for 34.48% of the total number of loans. The amounts varied from Rs 600 in one case; Rs 1000, Rs 1,200, Rs 1,500 each in one case; Rs 1,600 in two cases; Rs 1,700 in three cases to even Rs 3,000 in one case. The beneficiaries had ostensibly constructed soil conservation works and fences around their fields with this money. On the spot inspection revealed no special retaining walls or check dams. Walls were found around fields but it was not possible to know whether they had been built using the loan amounts or not. The chance of diversion of land development loans for consumption purposes is significant. A usual explanation for non-existence of land development works on the spot was that these had been destroyed during the preceding winter by landslides or avalanches. Chaura

Table 4.15: Field Survey Data for Chaura Village

sn	*Loan*	*n*	*PCT*	*cf*	*c%*
1	0165	1	3.4	01	03.4
2	0225	1	3.4	02	06.9
3	0262	1	3.4	03	10.3
4	0600	1	3.4	04	13.8
5	1000	1	3.4	05	17.2
6	1200	1	3.4	06	20.7
7	1250	1	3.4	07	24.1
8	1500	5	17.2	12	41.4
9	1600	2	6.9	14	48.3
10	1700	3	10.3	17	58.6
11	1750	6	20.7	23	79.3
12	2000	2	6.9	25	86.2
13	3000	2	6.9	27	93.1
14	5000	2	6.9	29	100.0

Code: **sn = serial no., n = frequency,**
cf = cumulative frequency, c% = cumulative percentage, PCT = percentage.
All Amounts are in Rupees.
(Source: Own Survey.)

does not suffer many avalanches, one reason for its selection for field survey. It all depends on proper supervision whether land development loans are properly utilized or not. In other purposes, the chance of misuse of loan amounts is reduced because money is paid directly to the seller or supplier. No new crop rotations or new varieties of seeds were found in the fields of the borrowers of land development loans.

The next highest number of loans (six), constituting 20.69% of the total loan number, was for purchasing improved varieties of cows. There was perfect symmetry here because all six had borrowed Rs 1,750 each. The cows had been provided in reality but no perceptible improvement in income or living standards had taken place. The cows were not giving more than 2-3 kgs of milk per day, leaving no surplus for sale. There was no organized milk collection service by a cooperative or a government agency. The beneficiaries hoped that once the Animal Husbandry Department's milk collection centre at Sungra began functioning they could hope for regular sales. The plant was still not in operation at the end of 1985.

13.79% of the total number of loans were for artisans' tools. There was no functioning artisans' cooperative in Chaura. All four loans were for Rs 1,500 each, paid directly to the suppliers, leaving no chance for loan diversion. The borrowers said that their income levels had improved but could not specify by how much. Since there had been no proper calculation of their income levels earlier or later, no comparisons could be made. Survey papers in the Block did mention income levels but nobody knew how exactly these had been calculated. Mostly, the beneficiaries had themselves been asked how much they earned. The respondents were likely to understate their incomes so that they could be covered under the I.R.D.P. or D.R.I. Schemes. There is also a social belief that exact income should not be divulged lest the evil eye be attracted. People generally tended to understate their income and assets.

Three borrowers each for sheep units and pack animals constituted 10.34% of the total number of loans each. For sheep, there were two loans of Rs 2,000 each and one of Rs 1,250. At the time of this survey, the sheep were said to have gone towards the plains for winter so it was not possible to verify whether the sheep were actually alive or had been sold further or sacrificed to the village deity, or eaten up. On the contrary, pack animals, involving two loans of Rs 5,000 each and one of Rs 3,000, had made a perceptible difference in income levels. The borrowers admitted that they were able to make between Rs 12 to Rs 20 per day. Two of them had land holdings of 2 and 5 bighās respectively, so that they derived more income from their pack animals than from their land. The third had 8 bighās 10 biswās of land and was a tribal whereas the earlier two were both Harijans.

There was no clear link between loan amounts and land holding. We observe that amongst the S.C borrowers, three had borrowed the same amount (Rs 1,750) for animal husbandry but had land holdings of 18, 5.6 and 1 bighās respectively. On the contrary, of the two cases of animal husbandry loans for S.Ts, land holding was 12 bighās each for the same loan amount. This was at variance with the finding that loan amounts borrowed rose with rising asset value range.[19] This shows the element of official domination of this loan disbursement and the absence of individual selection of loans according to asset value. This holds true for both groups of borrowers - S.Cs as well as S.Ts.

4.8.1.1.1 Loan Purpose Distribution for Scheduled Tribes

Tribal borrowers constituted 13 cases out of 29 or nearly 45% of the sample. This is much lower than their percentage in the population of Kinnaur (75%)[20] or of Chaura village, constituting 3.5% of Kinnaur's population.[21] This again shows deliberate official priority to S.Cs who are generally poorer, rather than an independent evolution of the regional credit market. There was one loan of Rs 225 to a tribal for a sewing machine which was to form part of the daughter's dowry rather than really adding to the family income. 8 out of 12 cases of land development loans were for S.Ts, showing that comparatively more affluent borrowers (S.Ts) secured 80% of the total number of loans in which misuse was easier to hide than in other loans, while poorer borrowers (S.Cs) managed only 20% of such loans. Tribal borrowers accounted for Rs 22,390 of the total loan amount of Rs 51,002 (or 44%). Evidently, Rs 22,390 was not enough to cover the loan needs of all tribal families in Chaura. The gap could have been filled by moneylenders.

[19] Please see Section 3.5.1.2.1 (Tables 3.23, 3.24), Chapter III.

[20] The exact figure was 74.87%. District Census Handbook, Kinnaur District, 1981, p. (x). The percentage was 68.16% for males and 82.45% for females, showing that many non-tribals (mostly government employees) had come into the district leaving their spouses at home.

[21] Figures according to the 1981 Census. The population of Chaura was 372. (Section 1: Village Directory, p. 72.)

4.8.1.1.2 Loan Purpose Distribution for Scheduled Castes

16 S.C borrowers (constituting nearly 55% of the sample) borrowed a total of Rs 28,612 (56% of the total loan disbursement of Rs 51,002). They constituted 100% of the loan amounts borrowed for artisanat tools, conforming to the social custom of only S.Cs carrying on activities like shoemaking. They had an average land holding of 5.44 bighās per borrowing family, as compared to an average of 12.17 bighās for S.T borrowers. The average land holding per borrowing family was 124% higher for S.T borrowers than for S.C borrowers who, however, had an average per family loan amount of Rs 1,788 or 3.8% higher than the corresponding figure of Rs 1,722 for S.T borrowers.

4.8.1.1.3 Block Diagram Showing Loan Distribution for Chaura

This diagram shows visually how loan amounts varied with the purpose of the loan and with S.C. or S.T. as origin. S.T. borrowers lag behind S.C. borrowers in all purposes except land development principally and for minor amounts in sewing machine and multipurpose loans. This distribution pattern is confirmed by bar charts as well.

4.8.1.1.4 Bar Charts Showing Loan Distribution by Origin

The loan distribution patterns were similar for S.Ts and S.Cs. The pattern of distribution was more symmetrical for S.T. borrowers than for S.C. borrowers. The chart for Scheduled Castes peaked at loan amounts of Rs 1,500 while that for Scheduled Tribes peaked at Rs 1,700. The threshold for S.Ts was lower (at Rs 165) than that for S.Cs (at Rs 262). The credit distribution pattern is dependent on outside (government) manipulation all through. It rests on channelization of institutional credit towards identified target groups regardless of regional credit market tendencies. Neglect of poor borrowers by institutional channels had lasted for centuries during the time of Bushahr State.[22] Now, an effort was being made to compensate for this neglect, but the amounts involved were still small. A major hurdle being encountered in the smooth functioning of the bank credit network, especially by poorer borrowers, was the insistence by bank managers on security or collateral even in schemes where no such security was required.

4.9 SECURITY AND DIFFERENT LOAN SCHEMES: DIFFICULT PROBLEM

One of the factors inhibiting borrowers in Kinnaur from going to banks for meeting their credit needs is the **"wide opinion among the public that commercial banks demand security from the people and that loan proposals are delayed unnecessarily".**[23] Questioned about this, bank managers in Kinnaur stated[24] that even though R.B.I. guidelines exempted certain categories of borrowers from furnishing security, their superiors cautioned them unofficially to demand security where the bona fides of the borrower were suspect. This led to complaints by non-official members in meetings of the D.R.D.A and the D.C.C.C. where the same bank managers coolly denied that that they were insisting upon such security, and then continued it

[22] Please see the introduction immediately after the commencement of Chapter III for more information on this aspect.

[23] Note entitled "Commercial Banks in Kinnaur", prepared on the orders of the Divisional Manager, UCO Bank, Simla by his staff for the author, January 10, 1986, Typewritten, Unpublished, p. 9.

[24] These opinions were always expressed in private. There is a lot of hypocricy involved in what bankers and government officials honestly feel in private and what they are willing to concede in public. Careerism is rampant. If it is felt that an honest conviction publicly expressed could harm one's career, it is kept private.

in practice. The R.B.I. guidelines[25] on security norms are as follows:

Nature Of Loan	Loan Amount	Security Needed
1. Crop Loan	*(a) Till Rs 1000*	*DPn/Loan agreement only;*
	(b) Rs 1,001-5,000	Hypothecation of crops;
	(c) Over Rs 5,000	Hypothecation of crops & Mortgage of lands at the bank's discretion or Third Party guarantee.
2. Investment Loan (i) Where movable assets are created	(a) Up to the cost of economic unit (where applicable) or Rs 5,000, whichever is lower.	Hypothecation of assets.
	(b) Others (i.e. for amounts over those under (a) above.	(a) Hypothecation of assets and (b) Mortgage of land at bank's discretion/ III party guarantee.
(ii) Where movable assets are not created e.g. dugwell, land development etc.	Rs 1,000	Mortgage of land at the bank's discretion.

The guidelines clearly state that in cases "*where mortgage of land or third party guarantee has not been indicated as security, banks **should not** take such security*".[26] In Kinnaur a simple declaration creating a charge on land offered as security would be sufficient so that mortgage of land was not necessary.

In the S.S.I. sector security norms are as follows:

Type of Borrowers	Loan/Credit Limits	Security To Be Furnished
(a) Artisans, village and small.	Composite Loan up to Rs 25,000.	Pledge/Hypothecation/ Mortgage of Assets created out of the loans
(b) Other small industries.	Limits up to and inclusive of Rs 25,000.	Security/III party guarantee should not be taken.
(c) -do-	Limits over Rs 25,000.	As determined by the bank on the merits of each case.

The R.B.I. guidelines clarify that in respect of advances over Rs 25,000 collateral security "*by way of immovable properties or third party guarantees may be asked for only in cases where primary security is inadequate or for other valid reasons and not as a matter of routine. Proposals otherwise viable should also not be turned down merely for want of such collateral security or third party guarantees*".[27] Other borrowers in the priority sector have been defined as:[28]

[25] Guidelines for Advances to Priority Sector, Reserve Bank of India (R.B.I.), Bombay: Rural Planning and Credit Department, First Published, June 1984.

[26] Ibid, Section I: Agriculture, Item 1.11: Security Norms, Note (a), p. 4.

[27] Ibid, Section II: Small Scale Industries, Item 2.7, p. 6.

(a) Small road/water transport operators;
(b) Retail trade;
(c) Small business operators;
(d) Professional and self-employed persons;
(e) Students for education purposes;
(f) Scheduled Castes/Scheduled Tribes/Weaker Sections borrowing loans for housing purposes;
(g) Borrowers belonging to the weaker sections taking pure consumption loans.

For these categories security norms are as follows:

Credit Limit	Security Required
(i) Credit Limit up to and inclusive of Rs 25,000.	Pledge/Hypothecation/Mortgage of assets created out of loan.
(ii) Credit Limit in excess of Rs 25,000.	As determined by the banks on the merits of the case.
(iii) Housing Loan	Mortgage of properties or government guarantee.
(iv) Consumption Loan	Guarantee of one or more individuals or groups of persons.

The citation given below the S.S.I. security norms is equally applicable here as well. Wherever feasible, equitable mortgage instead of registered mortgage ahould be taken to save stamp duty. In respect of advances granted *"on clean basis for edcation, guarantee/collateral security may be taken on merits of each case"*.[29] These guidelines were sent by the Chief Officer of the R.B.I. to the Chairmen/M.Ds of all scheduled commercial banks vide his letter no. RPCD No. BC29/PS2-84 dated March 16, 1984, Rural Planning and Credit Department, Bombay. 40% of the total advances of commercial banks were to go to the priority sector, within which 15% was to be for direct agricultural advances. This target was exceeded for Kinnaur District by 1985.

4.10 PRELIMINARY EVALUATION OF INSTITUTIONAL CREDIT

The prevailing consensus behind the institutional credit infrastructure in Kinnaur involves stock figures like conservative peasants and wicked moneylenders. Individual credit transactions having productive purposes like the *"purchase of fixed capital, working inputs, labour or land"*[30] are sought to be fostered. But in Kinnaur the borrowers live with the lenders in **"multiplex social relationships within a village community, and do so in ways that invalidate neat distinctions between credit for production and for consumption"**.[31] In estimating institutional credit demand, it is sought to value the inputs used currently. Then follows calculation of the fraction purchased, as opposed to availability of family labour, saved seed and plough animals. Finally, the percentage of such purchases financed through the farming family's own savings and earlier profits is assessed. The fraction left uncovered by such savings needs to be covered by borrowing, either from *"relatives and friends, sellers' credit, formal financial institutions, advance buyers of crop, and moneylenders, in (usually) increasing order of*

[28] Ibid, Section III: Other Borrowers in the Priority Sector, 3.1, p. 6.

[29] Ibid, Item 3.9, p. 7.

[30] Lipton, M.: Agricultural Finance and Rural Credit in Poor Countries, 1. Introduction, p. 543, in: World Development, Vol. 4, No. 7, 1976, Pp 543-553.

[31] Ibid.

both interest rate and risk of default".[32] According to Prof. Michael Lipton the requirement for extra agricultural credit comprises:[33]

(a) The part of that residual that is, in some sense unsatisfactory and in need of replacement - in particular, debts at interest rates so high as to remove much of the farmer's investable surplus;
(b) Extra production loans to small/marginal farmers who, even if capable of generating satisfactory income generation effects, are considered too risk prone or poor to be judged credit-worthy by existing lenders; and
(c) The extra credit requirement of new technologies.

The third factor was still not very prominent in Kinnaur where high yielding varieties with intensive input packages are hindered by climatic conditions. Small and marginal farmers are disfavoured by rural credit systems in Kinnaur. Of the total advances to the priority sector by the largest institutional lender (UCO Bank), only 7.8% went to farmers cultivating below or equal to 2 hectares of land in 1981; 10.4% in 1982; 15.5% in 1983 and 25.2% in 1984. The switch from cooperative to commercial bank credit has not helped overmuch because of the ***"borrowers' lack of conventional collateral...even for institutions aimed directly at small farmers"***.[34] This can partly be attributed to the demand side comprising aversion to risk or propensity to keep some reserve credit for consumption emergencies or high administration costs of smaller loans on the supply side or the covariance of risks upon small local loans.

Institutional credit projections ingore the fact that most farms in Kinnaur feed and are worked by chiefly the families that run them. With such farming meeting, say, 50% of their alimentary needs, isolation of their cash-flow position from that of the farm's is unjustified. Failure to realize this has led to endless time-wasting by credit agencies seeking to tie loans to particular productive purposes. The associated formalities can deter small borrowers. More seriously, attempts to solve the small farmer's credit problem by giving him access to loans at competitive rates of interest that he can repay and will want to repay regularly founder because the agencies concerned, often by statute, omit consumer credit from their calculations. Credit is not taken in Kinnaur in isolation for productive purposes, as the official credit institutions ardently desire and base their projections on.

The farming/trading Kinnaura households constitute enterprises which decide in totality how much credit is required as a whole, whether conventionally classified as consumption, education, investment or producer inputs; for fertilizers, agricultural implements, purchase of food items like wheat and rice not grown on their own farms; weddings or religious festivals; and how best to allocate available credit among these possible uses. If purchase of woollen clothing for winter or stockpiling of purchased foodgrains for winter is deemed more necessary in view of the Lāmā's forecast for a severe coming winter, available credit will be diverted for such purchases. If cash in the form of institutional credit is tied to production purposes, it is utilized for only such purposes as would have been pursued, without the loan, using the family's cash which then becomes fungible towards consumption purposes.[35]

[32] Ibid, Part 2, p. 544.

[33] Ibid.

[34] Lipton, Michael, 1976, Part 2., p. 546.

[35] Ibid, Part 3., p. 547.

"Any sensible person, given a loan, first sees that he and his family do not starve; second, uses the residual for high priority outlays, notably the repayment of existing debt...costing 30-50% yearly, as is common with rural moneylending, and only then considers what profitable investments (e.g. on his farm) he can make".[36] The Kinnaura is no exception to this axiom. Institutional credit in Kinnaur ignores consumption credit demand, resulting in overlooking of a major source of potential expansion of production credit; its diversion not from scarce total family savings but from consumption lending, by means of redistribution of incomes and assets, through land reform for instance. Seriously implemented land reform could probably reduce the number of net dissavers in Kinnaur; thereby diminishing demand for and hence the profitability of misusing scarce investible funds to supply consumption loans. What to talk of a chronically foodgrain-deficit area like Kinnaur, even in Illinois State (U.S.A.), small borrowers were wary of taking production loans to avoid running too high a debt burden to maintain credit ratings against a consumption emergency like a bad harvest.[37]

Small institutional credit amounts injected by banks to foster productive purposes in Kinnaur may instead have strengthened the traditional village system of consumer loans. Institutional credit drifted towards the bigger farmer/trader who was often the village moneylender. Field surveys for this research in villages Chaura, Nigāni, Roghi, Yuwaringi, Sangla, Kāmru, and Pooh revealed that loans taken from banks for land development, small business or retail trade did not manifest a perceptible utilization on the ground or any upward change in income levels. Replies as to their actual utilization were hedged. Private enquiries from prominent persons gave the impression that these loans had been utilized, in part if not wholly, for repaying earlier loans from local farmer/trader moneylenders. Institutional credit, at annual rate of interest of 4% (D.R.I. scheme) or 10% (I.R.D.P.), thus gets recycled to the local moneylenders to cover production costs which they would have anyway incurred. This freed their cash for increased lending at higher rates of interest, sometimes touching 30%-40%. However, such rates of interest have been rare in Kinnaur. This is discussed at length in Chapter VII about the informal credit sector.

Even if outside credit does go to the small farmer, it may pay him best to use it to repay the moneylender who then uses it to lend out again to even poorer people who expect to repay interest for ever and capital never. Banks thus unwittingly become **refinancing agents for local farmer moneylenders in Kinnaur.** That this was no peculiarity of this remote region can be seen from the work of Dr Hans-Dieter Roth in Dhanbad District of Bihar where he found banks serving as refinancing agents for moneylenders in a similar fashion.[38] Dr Michael Lipton feels that it is not necessarily bad to so underpin traditional consumer credit. People must eat. Financial institutions like banks are not good at swift consumption loans which demand intricate local knowledge. A higher supply of money-to-lend, desired or otherwise, in a village could even bring down interest rates by competing with moneylenders' interest rates that had traditionally been forced up by local monopoly. ***"It is no good sweeping away traditional credit arrangements before the state, the banks, or the cooperatives can replace them...But the small-scale, outside injection of institutional credit used for unplanned purposes, reinforcing the traditional moneylenders it purports to replace that is likely, even if in theory 'supervised', to be wasteful, frustrating, and randomly unfair. One cannot wag the dog, total community finance, by the tail, individual producer credit".***[39]

[36] Ibid.

[37] Ibid.

[38] Roth, Hans-Dieter: Indian Moneylenders at Work, New Delhi: Manohar Publishers, 1983.

[39] Lipton, 1976, Part 3., p. 547.

The D.C., Kinnaur, made a conscious effort during 1980-82 to check whether liberal bank loans focussed on certain villages could make an impact on the local credit market. He knew well that some of these loans would be used to repay debts of private moneylenders. Nevertheless, he wanted to try whether it was possible to push interest rates downwards or not. In Sungra village, seat of the Sungra Maheshwar, a leading moneylender, loans were liberally sanctioned under the D.R.I. and I.R.D. schemes through the SBI branch at Sungra and the UBI branch at Nichār. An average of between Rs 35,000 and 50,000 were pumped in per year, in addition to additional direct financing by these banks to horticulturists, shopkeepers and sawmill operators. Sungra village had 686 households as per the 1981 Census.[40] Thus, institutional credit amounts in excess of an average of Rs 60 per household per annum were injected to compete with local moneylenders. The results were striking.

According to Negi Daulat Rām, Chairman, Zila Parishad, Kinnaur, a leading Kinnaura of Nichār, and other residents of Sungra, the rate of annual interest charged by Devta Maheshwar was reduced from the earlier 25% to 12.5% and then to 10%.[41] Once the dèvta reduced his interest rate, local farmer-moneylenders followed suit and reduced the rate of interest on their loans to 12.5% per annum. This reduction could be achieved partly because the economy of the area had traditionally had a low degree of monetization where local residents had frugal lifestyles with low credit needs so that even sums around Rs 65,000 per annum offered competition to local moneylenders. It was also due to the fact that horticulture had brought increased income to even marginal landowners whose needs of consumption credit had to that extent been controlled, if not reduced. The Maheshwar Devta, owner of the biggest apple orchard in the area, benefited from this horticultural boomlet and had sizeable cash inflows, over Rs 50,000 in good years,[42] at the same time as others also obtained higher incomes albeit on a much lower scale. In such conditions, a sudden influx of bank credit on low rates of interest succeeded in aiding a downward revision of the moneylenders' interest rates. This could not be repeated on a district-wide level as the banks were reluctant to inject large loan amounts without adequate security. Administratively also, such a conscious policy of competing indirectly with moneylenders became difficult.

A necessary concomitant of liberal lending was stricter recovery and stringent action against defaulters if finances were to be recycled. Strictness in recoveries was begun from the top because richer borrowers were bigger defaulters. They had been securing bank loans more easily because of their ability to offer credible security. They went less to the local moneylenders than poor borrowers but blocked up more bank funds through default on loan repayments. The D.C. decided that they should be squeezed more to repay so that more funds could be diverted to poorer borrowers who were regular clients of village moneylenders. A political storm was raised by rich defaulters. Even some bankers, who were overtly ardent advocates of a better recovery performance, pleaded in private for a go-slow policy. With elections scheduled for 1982, it became difficult to sustain this policy. Sungra was an example of the dictum that isolation of the *static economies of farm finance was unlikely to tackle very effectively problems rooted in the social dynamics of rural credit.*[43]

[40] District Census Handbook, Kinnaur District, 1981, Part A: Village and Town Directory, Section - 1: Village Directory, p. 72.

[41] Personal interview with Negi Daulat Rām, Chairman, Zila Parishad, Kinnaur, on December 12, 1985 at 13.00 hours in the D.C.'s chamber at Kālpa.

[42] Personal assessment on the basis of going rates for orchard auctions in Kinnaur between 1980 and 1983. The figure given by the Devta's Kārdārs is much lower (around Rs 10,000) since they do not want to reveal the Devta's real income.

[43] The author was subjected to heavy pressure to go easy on influential persons in the matter of loan recoveries. Soon enough, he came to know how influential people of differing political allegiance could be

4.10.1 Interest Rates on Bank Loans in Kinnaur

The supply of formal bank credit in Kinnaur has expanded rapidly, with increases of 16% to 44% between 1980 and 1985.[44] Government have attempted to direct a sizeable portion of these funds to the rural poor. An important element in this strategy has been maintenance of interest rates at low levels.[45] In spite of such low rates of interest, relatively little of the additional available funds have gone to the really needy poor. One explanation for this concerns supply allocation problems within financial institutions. Widely used concessional interest rate policies, combined with relatively high lender loan transaction costs for servicing small or new borrowers, discourage financial institutions from lending more to the rural poor.[46] This partly negates the basic intention behind concessional interest rates. To understand the interplay of interest rate, we can discuss differences in borrowing costs among various types of formal borrowers. It has been proposed that differential borrowing costs **"strongly affect the willingness of the rural poor to seek loans from formal lenders".**[47]

4.10.1.1 Borrowing Costs for Institutional Credit

In official credit analyses, the nominal rate of interest charged on a loan is equated to the price of the loan. This price of credit should be widened to include real net costs incurred in the process of obtaining the loan. The borrowing costs (BC) may include three separate elements:[48]

(a) Nominal interest payments made to the lender = **NI**;
(b) Additional loan transaction costs incurred by the borrower = **TC**;
(c) Changes in the purchasing power of money over loan period = ΔP.

The borrowers in Kinnaur can usually estimate the **NI and TC** elements of their total borrowing costs, though some of the poorest borrowers have difficulties comprehending even the NI element. However, since the I.R.D.P. loans carry a flat rate of interest of 10% per annum and the poorest borrowers are supposedly covered under this Scheme, explaining that interest constitutes 1/10th of the principal is not too hard. ΔP has a close correlation with recent changes in purchasing power of money experienced by prospective borrowers. The expected borrowing cost used by the prospective borrower in finalising loan demand decisions would equal:

$$BC = NI + TC - \Delta P$$

played off against each other in the game of trying to enforce recoveries from them. Criminal cases were registered against panchāyat pradhāns for embezzlement of public funds but it was ensured that of the four proceedings started, two were against pradhāns of one political faction and two against those of the opposing faction. This was to ensure a kind of balance of Schadenfreude (negative satisfaction) that the opposing party was in the same soup as well.

[44] Tables 4.5 to 4.10, Section 4.2.2.4, this Chapter.

[45] Sections 4.3.1, 4.3.2, 4.3.3, this Chapter.

[46] Adams, D.W. and Nehman, G.I.: Borrowing Costs and the Demand for Rural Credit, Part I, Introduction, p. 165, in: Journal of Development Studies, Vol. 15, January 1979, Pp 165-176.

[47] Ibid, p. 166.

[48] Ibid, Part II: Borrowing Costs, p. 166.

4.10.1.1.1 Borrower Transaction Costs (TC)

Experience shows that borrowers of small amounts and persons lacking prior borrowing experience are likely to incur relatively high transaction costs to acquire a loan. At least three kinds of borrower transaction costs could be discerned:[49]

(a) Loan charges collected by the lender beyond interest payments, through such things as application fees, forced purchase of other lender services, service fees, bribes, compensatory balances and closing costs. TC may also be raised through deduction of interest charges in advance or collection of interest charges on the entire loan amount though only a part is withdrawn by the borrower;

(b) In some cases, borrowers may have to negotiate with someone outside the institutional lending agency before a loan application is formally reviewed. This intermediary may be a local official or leader or a cosigner as guarantor. In some cases expenses may be unofficially deducted for a visit by an assessor to visit and evaluate the applicant's farm operation. Gifts and/or bribes may be involved in some of these cases;

(c) In many cases, the largest and most important time costs are the borrower's time and travel expenses involved in the loan transaction. A number of visits are necessitated to the Block and bank branch headquarters to negotiate the loan, withdraw portions of the loan, and make repayments. In Kinnaur these visits sometimes mean long waits and travel over long distances. Lost work time may become significant, particularly if loan transactions get concentrated during the planting and harvesting periods when the opportunity costs of the borrowers' time are substantial.

This problem exists often in Kinnaur where means of access to bank branches are easier in summer or autumn than in winter. Summer happens to be the planting time and autumn the harvesting time for the single/double crop seasons in most of the area. A visit to the bank can easily mean a day lost, a day in which the Kinnaura could have worked on a P.W.D. scheme or in his fields.

4.10.1.1.2 Changes in Purchasing Power of Money

Kinnaur has been relatively shielded from fluctuations in the purchasing power of money by an extended network of government subsidies. Wheat flour, rice, cooking oil, and sugar were all subsidized and sold at rates below prevailing market rates in the plains. Potatoes and apples were purchased by the Horticultural Produce and Marketing Corporation (the **H.P.M.C.**) at fixed prices if the open market price fell below pre-specified levels. But complete isolation was not possible. Unlike Brazil, or Argentina, where persistent inflation causes borrowers to include expected price changes in calculations of expected borrowing costs, this factor is limited in Kinnaur. Price fluctuations in the apple and neoza market do influence the calculations of large orchardists but their number is small. The larger mass consists of small borrowers who hardly account for inflationary or deflationary changes in the value of money while determining their loan requirements.

4.10.1.1.3 Farm Household Level Information: Illustrative

There was no research or field data available on Kinnaur to determine the relative importance of TC and Δ P in loan demand decisions. Hence, a field survey was carried out in November-December 1985 with the help of area Patwāris and Field Kānungos in five villages comprising 1,207 households and 8.45% of the total population of Kinnaur according to the 1981 Census: villages **Roghi and Yuwaringi of Kālpa Block, Chaura and Nigāni of Nichār Block and Pooh of Pooh Block.** The sample of households consisted of about 50% small farmers. About 20% of the total households interviewed had formal bank loans. The average nominal

[49] Ibid, (a) Borrower Transaction Costs, Pp 166-167.

rate of interest was 10% (under the I.R.D.P.) because there were only 17 cases under the D.R.I. scheme at 4% rate of interest. To facilitate calculation, the nominal rate of interest was

Table 4.16: Farmers' Costs of Borrowing from Institutional Sources in Five Villages of Kinnaur by Farm-Size Groups.

sn	*FSB*	*AFLS*	*ATCGL*	*NIPLH*		*ICDCB*		*ADCBL*	
0	1	2	3	4	5	6	7	8	9
do	-do-	Rs	Rs	6mnths	12mnths	$6ms^{\alpha}$	$12ms^{\beta}$	$6ms^{\gamma}$	$12ms^{\delta}$
1	00-05	1,935	050	96.75	193.50	66	80	15	13
2	06-10	2,039	100	101.95	203.90	50	67	20	15
3	11-15	1,361	100	68.05	136.10	40	58	25	17
4	16-20	1,375	125	68.75	137.50	35	52	28	19
5	21-25	1,700	150	85.00	170.00	37	53	28	19

Code: sn = **Serial Number, FSB = Farm size in bighās,**
AFLS = Average formal loan size, ATCGL = Average transaction costs of getting loans, NIPLH = Nominal interest payment on loans held for, ICDCB = Interest charges as percentage of direct costs of borrowing, ADCBL = Annualized direct costs of borrowing as percentage of loan amount, Rs = Rupees, mnths = ms = Months.

Note

α = [Col. 4 / (Col. 3 + Col. 4)];

β = [Col. 5 / (Col. 3 + Col. 5)];

γ = [(Col. 3 + Col. 4) / Col. 2] into 2, to convert it to annual rate;

δ = [(Col. 3 + Col. 5) / Col. 2]

These calculations are on the lines done by G.I. Nehman in Sao Paulo State, Brazil (Adams and Nehman, 1979, p. 170).

(Source: Own Survey)

taken as 10% per annum. The field survey data is summarized in Table 4.16 .

Borrowers claimed that they had had to make between four to nine visits to various offices for completion of formalities; each time wasting a day's work on which they could have earned between Rs 6 to Rs 10 per day. They had had to eat outside and pay transportation costs in some cases. TC figures are according to their estimations of what they lost. Institutional loans were for mostly one year periods or more, in some cases for a single crop period of six months. Borrowers in the smallest farm size incurred TCs of Rs 50 on average loan amounts of Rs 1,935 while borrowers in the three highest farm-size groups incurred twice, two-and-a-half times and three times this figure for smaller average loan amounts respectively. These results differ from those obtained by G.I. Nehman in Brazil.[50]

However, annualized direct costs of borrowing as a percentage of loan value varied inversely with loan size, except for farm-size group of 6-10 bighās. Smallest farm-size holders faced rates of 15% on 6-months' loans and 13% on annual loans while the highest farm-size group borrowers faced rates of 28% and 19% respectively. To this extent the institutional credit network had indeed been successful in its objectives but a field study of borrowing costs

[50] Ibid, Part III: Farm-Household Level Information, (b) Brazilian Case, Pp 169-172.

of loans from informal lenders revealed rates of interest between 12.5% to 15% per annum, with rates of around 25% for loans for six month periods. Very few TCs were involved and the number of visits required to be made was far fewer. Small to medium farmers were thus **"often indifferent as to whether to seek a formal or informal loan because they felt that total costs of acquiring a loan from either source were very similar".**[51]

Borrower loan transaction costs above and beyond NI payments appear to be significant in Kinnaur, discouraging smaller and new borrowers from demanding institutional loans in spite of lower nominal rates of interest. Adjustments in nominal interest rates would not affect directly borrowing costs and loan demand of small and new borrowers as much as reduction in borrower transaction costs by reducing the travel expenses and number of visits required, a factor significant in an area like Kinnaur where borrowers from some villages may have to cover 15-20 kms, if not more, on foot to reach the nearest bank branch. Mobile banks and small bank branches located in remote villages have not yet been tried as solutions to this problem in Kinnaur. It cannot be denied[52] that **"formal lenders impose substantial loan transaction costs on small and new borrowers as a way of keeping unprofitable business away from the bank",**[53] though no banker admits it formally. Concessional rates of interest combined with significant lender costs of making small loans push banks to prefer direct loans to richer borrowers. Higher nominal rates of interest could possibly cause these richer borrowers to demand, directly or through poorer proxies, fewer loans; encourage banks to service smaller and new borrowers by raising profit margins on such loans and indirectly motivate them to reduce borrowing costs by simplifying procedural formalities. **"The net result of increasing nominal interest rates on agricultural loans may be to reduce the borrowing costs for the rural poor".**[54]

However, this step needs a tougher political consensus that does not yet exist. Low rates of interest on subsidized loans in Kinnaur are insufficient to generate an increasing fund of revolving credit. **"Low interest rates, combined with inflation and tolerated default, underlie the collapse of credit institutions"**[55] in Kinnaur as a whole. Similar has been the experience not only in other parts of India but in other countries like Sri Lanka, Colombia, Costa Rica, Turkey and Thailand as well.[56] Institutional credit at around 20%-25% annual rate of interest could present a much more serious challenge to traditional moneylenders than a trickle of such credit at 4% or 10% **"in theory steered to the poor but in practice rationed and allocated by the strong, attracted by the low rates. Such low rates mean inadequate capital, little competition with such local monopoly as does prevail, constantly collapsing institutions, and low morale in the lending agencies".**[57] In addition, we can now examine a second sacrosanct aspect of institutional credit programmes - that banks credits should be a part of a package of inputs.

[51] Ibid, p. 171.

[52] As bank managers do all too often in India in public!

[53] Adams & Nehman, 1979, Part VI: Conclusions, p. 174.

[54] Ibid, p. 175.

[55] Lipton, Michael, 1976, Part 4., p. 548.

[56] Ibid.

[57] Ibid, p. 549.

4.10.2 Loans as Package Components

The I.R.D.P. and other government influenced development programmes envisage institutional credit as part of an integral package of inputs. Further, these packages are inextricably linked to major schemes of regional change (like the D.D.P. in the Pooh Sub-Division of Kinnaur). A specified public rural outlay is divided among many components of an integrated programme instead of concentrating it on removing key constraints on individual or group action. In countries like Taiwan and South Korea where rural credit programmes have succeeded admirably, institutional inputs of credit followed *"radical equalization of rights in land through distributive reform. It is this deeper sense of 'production structure' - the scale, type and distribution among individuals of rights to the product of the land they till - which is probably the most crucial to the design, and prospects, of even an appropriate programme of rural credit. Land redistribution will reduce the demand for consumer credit; drastically increase, in the early years, the demand for producer credit; and alter the mix of inputs, outputs and timings for which producer credit is sought"*.[58] To a certain extent these observations apply to Kinnaur where agriculture is still a way of life. Figures for land distribution[59] show that traditional land holding patterns have been disturbed only slightly. With the onset of horticulture on a mass scale, lands too steep to be used for crop production can sometimes be utilized for fruit production. Serious land redistribution measures are needed.

It is true that packaging loans and use of similar non-market rationing devices **"diminishes the most attractive and useful property of finance, fungibility. It is the fungibility of money that allows it to be converted into any good or service available in the market".**[60] Institutionally packaged credit programmes in Kinnaur do not conform to this essential property of finance (**fungibility**) by allocating loans in pre-subscribed quotas, supply of credit direct to suppliers, loans made in kind and trying to specify the ultimate use of loans. It is implicit in this approach that the borrower is ignorant of what is best for him; that loans can be allocated like physical inputs and, most important, that bankers and official planners are competent enough to make efficiency and equity decisions for poor borrowers. In some cases in Kinnaur, to fulfil already-decided-upon I.R.D.P. targets this planning approach was used as a sort of return to a barter economy.

Jersey cows obtained under the I.R.D.P. in at least three cases in village Kangos[61] had been bartered away to bigger farmer-moneylenders in exchange for cash for consumption purposes. The ability of government planners to diminish fungibility of institutional loans is thus limited through such barter transactions which generate secondary markets in which beneficiaries receiving ostensibly-controlled inputs sell these to others. Borrowed liquidity at controlled interest rates was many times substituted for personal liquidity by Kinnaura borrowers when their priorities differed from those of planners/bankers. The impact of non-market rationing devices in Kinnaur for PSA has to a certain extent increased the total costs of financial intermediation for borrowers and undermined the viability of lenders. No attempt has been made to modify the approach of considering institutional credit inputs as just like any other input as seeds, fertilizers, milch cattle or farm labour and instead treat them as claims on financial resources for enabling the borrowers to command additional goods and services that may or may not be used for the objectives stated on loan applications. Proper incentives have not been provided for lenders-mobilizers to perform in socially more desirable

[58] Ibid, p. 550.

[59] Please see Table 2.3, Section 2.B.5.7, Chapter II - B of this work.

[60] Adams, Dale W. and Graham, Douglas H.: A Critique of Traditional Agricultural Credit Projects and Policies, p. 355, in: Journal of Development Economics, Vol. 8, June 1981, Pp 347-366.

[61] Personal inspection in December 1985.

ways. "*The focus should be on inducing rural financial markets as a whole to service better the credit and deposit needs of a much broader clientele in rural areas...RFMs should also be given strong inducements to adopt innovations that reduce the total costs of financial intermediation. RFMs cannot be used to transfer cheap credit to thousands or millions of small, previously unserviced farmers. If governments attempt to push this strategy, the cheap credit will mostly end up in the hands of the wealthy*".[62]

No political or administrative consensus has evolved in Kinnaur about effecting changes in the direction discussed in the preceding lines. An **integrated approach** has been enshrined in the 20 Point Programme and no officer dares to pose fundamental questions about the utility of this approach. More and more targets have to be fulfilled; prescribed proformæ filled in and returns sent on time. There is an assumption that bankers and officials know best what is good for the borrower. More and more supervision seems to be deemed necessary. There are so many returns to be sent that keeping track of them becomes difficult. The routine administrative burden makes it difficult to consider fundamental questions of policy in depth. People concentrate on sending returns on time rather than thinking about how many of the returns are necessary at all.

4.10.3 Supervision of Bank Loans: A Real Achilles' Heel

Fungibility of credit reduces institutional attempts to supervise and survey credit money. Corruption in the system means that many times such attempts harass honest borrowers. It exposes them to blackmail by officials and indirectly works to the advantage of the private moneylenders. Particularly in the co̅operative sector, cooperative societies' secretaries/presidents indulged in embezzlement of funds, as in panchāyats Urni, Bari, Rāmni, Jāni and Chhota Kamba. This aspect will be discussed at length in the following Chapter (V). There were two Field Officers of the UCO Bank and one of the PNB stationed in Kinnaur. For other banks, they came from Simla. Considering the topographical conditions in Kinnaur, this strength of Field Officers was (and is) patently inadequate for proper supervision of commercial bank loans. A fuller discussion of the performance of the institutional credit network is possible only if the very important aspect of recoveries of bank loans is considered first. This is what we are going to do now.

[62] Adams & Graham, 1981, p. 357.

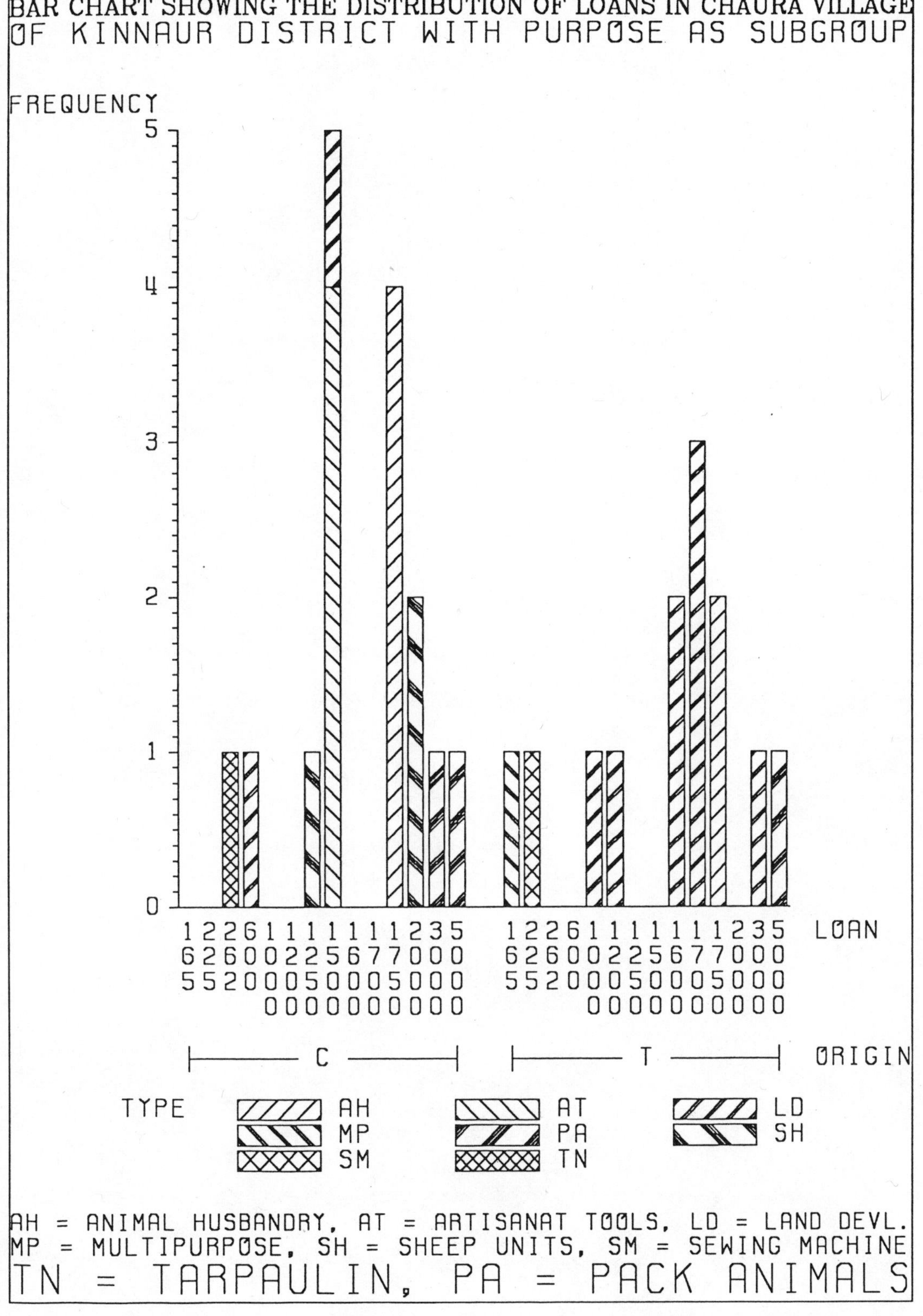
BAR CHART SHOWING THE DISTRIBUTION OF LOANS IN CHAURA VILLAGE
OF KINNAUR DISTRICT WITH PURPOSE AS SUBGROUP
FREQUENCY
5
4
3
2
1
0
LOAN
C
T
ORIGIN
TYPE
AH
AT
LD
MP
PA
SH
SM
TN
AH = ANIMAL HUSBANDRY, AT = ARTISANAT TOOLS, LD = LAND DEVL.
MP = MULTIPURPOSE, SH = SHEEP UNITS, SM = SEWING MACHINE
TN = TARPAULIN, PA = PACK ANIMALS

CHAPTER V

RECOVERY OF INSTITUTIONAL CREDIT

The performance of the institutional credit network depends to such an extent on recovery of funds loaned out that a complete chapter has been devoted to this aspect. It is defaults in repayment which choke up the institutional credit system. It is in recovery procedures that political and social pressures come into full play and stymie the smooth functioning of the credit cycle. Without considering these pressures we cannot form an overall picture of the institutional credit infrastructure. As will be seen in Chapter VII, village moneylenders score over institutions in having a much more efficient recovery system which relies on socio-economic realities and not on administrative and legislative measures like the institutional network. Village devtās and moneylenders prove themselves to be better by far at recovering their dues in Kinnaur than the entire phalanx of government recovery, with its officers, decrees, courts, laws and rules. Recoveries form the theme of innumerable official meetings, campaigns, special drives and harangues because everyone vaguely seems to feel that unless recoveries are stepped up, the institutional system cannot go on. Special Tahsildārs have been appointed for accelerating recoveries. More and more Acts have been passed in the hope of plugging legal loopholes, as if the sheer weight of legislation can somehow overcome socio-political constraints that prevent these laws from showing results in practice.

The system of recovery has become slow and sporadic. There is no regular, consistent level of performance. Each recovery case becomes almost a special drive in which officials have to be repeatedly exhorted to perform their normal recovery work, what they are being paid for. The normal reflex is not to recover but somehow to procrastinate so that some general administrative instruction can be received as the consequence of some natural calamity (drought, avalanche, glacier) or political decision. In some cases, loans of Rs 500 or less had not been recovered during 20 years while their case files became thicker progressively, with each summons, order or postponement. Penal interest payments accumulated in the meanwhile to such an extent as to render interest payments eight or ten or more times the original principal amounts. In some such cases, though rare ones, borrowers had to pawn or sell family jewellery to repay originally petty sums which had grown to much larger amounts in the meanwhile. The system works in fits and starts, as if to prove that it still exists! It seems to be not pure chance that richer and influential defaulters seem to escape without too much difficulty while the poorer ones have to be harshly forced to repay so that official returns can show their quota of recoveries made. An assessment, especially of the cooperative credit network, is not possible without examining how funds are sought to be recycled, meaning how the recovery system was able to fit into the projections made by planners. It is relevant to begin this review by examining the administrative rules and legislative acts forming the cornerstone of the recovery system.

5.1 LEGISLATIVE AND ADMINISTRATIVE BASES: A WHOLE SERIES

Apart from certain legislative measures, administrative instructions have continually been issued by the government regarding recovery procedures. It is obviously not possible to discuss all such measures. Only major laws/instructions need consideration. The basic law for recovery remains the H.P. Land Revenue Act of 1954.

5.1.1 Recovery Provisions in the Land Revenue Act 1954

A whole chapter (Chapter VII, Sections 102-105) of the Land Revenue Act 1954[1] deals with recoveries. In addition, a whole set of measures for recovering land revenue arrears becomes applicable to recoveries of institutional loans under provisions of Section 105 of this Act. Historically, land revenue was a major source of state income. Default in land revenue payment was not tolerated. In British times a whole panoply of coercive measures had been laid out carefully to enforce payments of land revenue. The Act of 1954 has borrowed most of the coercive provisions from the Punjab Land Revenue Act, 1887. Coercive measures are listed out in Chapter VI of the 1954 Act.

5.1.1.1 Arrears of Land Revenue: Debtors' Nightmare!

The revenue staff got involved in recoveries becase the state got involved in private transactions such as credit. "*The manifestations of government particularly if they appear in the form of oppressive subordinate officers may often be regarded as a nuisance but government as such is respected or even thought of in terms of ritual sanctity*" by peasants.[2] The structure of British colonial rule relied on administrators who maintained their alien identity and were "*supported by a comprehensive system of alien law and ubiquitous courts dispensing what they considered to be justice...the monopoly of dispensing justice was a most reliable source of income*".[3] The British were not content to restrict their judicial ambition to the "*sphere of criminal jurisdiction which is a hallmark of sovereignty but involves the state only in unprofitable trouble. The sphere of private law had been left almost exclusively to the arbitration of autonomous bodies. But the British-Indian courts intruded into this sphere and attracted an immense amount of litigation as well as lucrative court fees*".[4] This process of extension of authority into areas left undisturbed by previous régimes was not confined only to courts. The revenue machinery was drawn into it as well.

As Prof. D. Rothermund rightly points out, the landlord as such "*was a creature of the British legal system but lords of the land had existed before*".[5] All such lords of the land, "*whether petty or large were only entitled to a customary share of the agricultural surplus. They did not interfere with peasant agriculture*".[6] With the establishment of British rule, the "*public role of the lord of the land became the private role of the landlord. The area from which he had received the agricultural surplus became his "real estate". His power was reduced but his credit expanded. The peasantry became a tenantry and the share of the produce which they gave to the lord was now called rent, with all the dire consequences which this semantic change implied. Protected by law rather than by their retainers the landlords accepted their new role as rentiers and the wealthy and literate among them left the countryside and became absentee landlords*".[7]

[1] This Act is basically an edited version of the famous Punjab Land Revenue Act of 1887 which forms the basis for most of the land revenue acts of states in the North Western region of India.

[2] Rothermund, D., 1978, Chapter I, 1.2 The Roots of Government, p. 10.

[3] Ibid, p. 11.

[4] Ibid.

[5] Ibid, 1.3: The Role of the Landlord, p. 12.

[6] Ibid, p. 13.

[7] Ibid, p. 13.

Land revenue had been a traditional mainstay of government finance in India. The British made the system of revenue collection quite rigid, not permitting remissions of revenue but at the most suspensions of payment in bad years. *"This rigidity and pseudo-scientific ruthlessness were the major innovations which the British added to the indigenous system which was certainly transformed in this way"*.[8] Innovations by the British were "*mainly in terms of greater rigidity and less tolerance of any deviation between assessment and collection of the revenue*".[9] Even though the British flaunted their revenue system as scientific and fair, "*overassessment and rigorous collection or the merciless sale of land for arrears of revenue were the order of the day...unlike in earlier times arbitrariness was no longer tempered by inefficiency*".[10] Prof. Rothermund points out three major reasons for what he calls a **"fundamental transformation"** of the British Indian revenue administration in the period from 1860s to 1935:[11]

(a) The completion of the era of survey and settlement;
(b) The increase of quasi-judicial work under the various tenancy acts; and
(c) The decline of land revenue itself and the progress of constitutional reforms.

"The incidence of judicial functions of revenue officers varied with the nature of legislation for different provinces...Where the Bengal precedent prevailed much was left to the civil courts, but where statutory tenancy, the record of rights and the fixing of rents by revenue officers was the mainstay of tenancy protection the revenue authorities...had to shoulder an enormous burden. The district collector who was quite accurately called "Collector" in keeping with his main duty in earlier times became more and more a dispenser of justice. In a way this function provided the revenue administration with a new lease of life when its more narrowly conceived duties of settlement, assessment and collection of land revenue were in gradual eclipse".[12]

Faced with unrest amongst the peasantry as a result of changing over to cash assessment and rigidity in collection of land revenue, the British made a transition from rent acts to tenancy acts because the initial problem of rent recovery had been replaced by that of rent enhancement and such enhancement could usually be achieved only through a termination of the tenancy. "*The problem of rent enhancement and its instrument, the dreaded notice of eviction, arose only with the commutation of rents in kind into cash rents...The British rulers who had themselves put this instrument into the hands of the landlord feared its effects just as much as that of the notorious ex parte decrees which they had placed at the disposal of the moneylender. They felt that they had to protect the customary occupancy right of the Indian peasant in order to prevent unrest. Of course, legislative correction of the relation between landlord and tenant meant an interference with the freedom of contract, and the British concern about this freedom was an obstacle to sweeping measures in this respect. Therefore all kinds of measures had to be taken into consideration which would restrict this freedom without abolishing it altogether, and customary occupancy right had to be restored by means of prescription and similar devices of British jurisprudence*".[13] By making the Revenue Department responsible for collection of sums declared as arrears of land revenue, the British sought to quell possible unrest amongst

[8] Ibid, Chapter 3 Revenue and Property, 3.1 Land Revenue Systems, p. 36.

[9] Ibid, p. 37.

[10] Ibid.

[11] Ibid, 3.3: The Transformation of Revenue Administration, p. 45.

[12] Ibid, p. 45.

[13] Ibid, 6.1 The Relation of Landlord and Tenant, p. 89.

landlords and protected tenantry against cash assessments. Playing upon traditional respect for the 'sarkār' (government), the British interposed the Revenue Department as a mediator for allaying popular apprehensions about the harshness of their revenue system of assessment and collection. Rent-paying cultivators were sought to be reassured through this measure that they needed not fear cash assessments since the Revenue Department would enforce collection of rents in a just way, taking cognizance of the state of affairs of each cultivator. If landlords or protected tenants had given land out to tenants-at-will for cultivation and the latter did not regularly pay their share of rent or agricultural produce to the former, the Revenue Department would then step in as the collecting agency to ensure that the former could pay their rent to the government by coercing the latter on behalf of the former. Involvement of the Revenue Department in what were essentially private matters of rent collection and credit was thus a measure to mollify opposition of protected categories of landlords and occupancy tenants by getting them to pay cash rents fixed after assessments by the British. Non-occupancy tenants and sharecroppers were ignored. They were to become the objects of coercion by the Revenue Department to pay arrears of land revenue. They were not considered politically important enough to qualify for protection which was motivated by no humane considerations of social justice but by purely practical considerations of optimising income from land revenue.

In order to qualify for recovery through the Revenue Department, a defaulted sum must be certified by the District Collector as an arrear of land revenue (Called A.L.R. in official parlance) for the purposes of recovery. Declaration of a pending sum as A.L.R. creates a charge in the books of the Revenue Department which then swings into formal action to recover it. The following sums can be recovered as arrears of land revenue:[14]

(a) Fees, fines, costs and other charges, including the village officers' cess;
(b) Revenue due to the government on account of pastures or other natural products of lands, or on account of water, or on account of all mines of metal and coal and all earth, oil and gold washing;
(c) Fees payable to local bodies including the Panchayats formed under the H.P. Panchayati Raj Act for use of or benefits derived from the following works:-
  (α) Constructions and repair of embankments and the supply, storage and control of water for agricultural purposes; and
  (β) Preservation and reclamation of soil, and the drainage and reclamation of swamps.
(d) Sums leviable by or under the authority of the state government as water-rates, or an account of the maintenance or management of embankments and other irrigation works, not being sums recoverable as A.L.R. under any enactment for the time being in force;
(e) Sums payable to the state government on account of rent and other dues in respect of land;
(f) Sums payable to the state government by a person who is surety for the payment of any of the foregoing sums or of any other sum recoverable as A.L.R.

We notice that cooperative or commercial bank loans were not listed under these provisions. An A.L.R. may be recovered by any one or more of the following processes:[15]

[14] The H.P Land Revenue Act 1954 (Act No. 6 of 1954), Chapter VII: Recovery of Other Demands by Revenue Officers, Section 103.

[15] Act Ibid, Chapter VI: Collection of Land Revenue, Section 74.

*(A) By service of a **writ of demand** on the defaulter;*
(B) By distress and sale of his movable property and uncut or ungathered crops;
(C) By transfer of the holding in respect of which the arrear is due;
(D) By attachment of the assessment of that estate or holding;
(E) By annulment of the assessment of that estate or holding;
(F) By sale of that estate or holding; and
(G) By proceedings against other immovable property of the defaulter

This is a formidable array of coercive measures to match those of any village moneylender. It reveals how important a role land revenue had. In fact, collection of land revenue was considered one of the basic raisons d'être of the state, meriting this array of harsh recovery options in case of default. Institutional credit was not treated in the same light. Banks were then mainly in private hands. Social control and nationalization of banks were many years away! It was only slowly that the realization dawned that institutional credit expansion should be complemented by similar draconian provisions for enforcing recovery. This led to the passing of the H.P Agricultural Credit Operations Act of 1972. This Act forms a cornerstone of recovery of bank loan overdues. The bank network was armed with this legal safeguard before the coming of the PNB in 1974 to Kinnaur.

5.1.2 H.P. Agricultural Credit Operations and Miscellaneous Provisions (Banks) Act 1972

This Act was passed to *"facilitate adequate flow of credit for agricultural production and development through banks and other institutional credit agencies"*.[16]

5.1.2.1 Definitions: Oriented towards Agriculture

The title of the Act makes it clear that it caters to agricultural credit chiefly. This is amply corroborated by its definitions. Agriculture was meant to include the following:[17]

(a) Making land fit for cultivation;
(b) Cultivation of land;
(c) Improvement of land, including development of resources of irrigation;
(d) Raising and harvesting of crops;
(e) Horticulture;
(f) Forestry planting and farming;
(g) Seed farming;
(h) Pisciculture;
(i) Apiculture;
(j) Sericulture; and
(k) Piggery, poultry farming and other such activities as are generally carried out by agriculturists, dairy farmers, cattle breeders, poultry farmers and other categories of persons engaged in similar activities including marketing of agricultural produce, its storage and transportation and the acquisition of implements and machinery in connection with such activity.

An agriculturist was defined as **"a person who is engaged in agriculture".**[18] This is important because no reference is made at all to the capacity in which the agriculturist works on land. No distinction was made between proprietors, occupancy tenants, non-occupancy

[16] The H.P. Agricultural Credit Operations and Miscellaneous Provisions (Banks) Act, 1972, (Act No. 7 of 1973), opening lines, p. 1.

[17] Act Ibid, Chapter I: Preliminary, Section 2(a).

[18] Act Ibid, Section 2(b).

tenants, sharecroppers, lessees or tenants-at-will. Institutional credit was sought to be linked to an occupation (agriculture, broadly defined) and not to formal title to the land on which this occupation was carried out. This fact was clearly highlighted in the debate on the bill in the Vidhān Sabha (Legislative Assembly).

5.1.2.2 Legislative Debate on the Bill: Short and Cursory

The then Chief Minister, Dr Y.S. Parmār, while introducing the bill, called it a *"significant step towards socialism"*,[19] and a measure for showing agriculturists that such **"doors of credit as were earlier closed, were now being opened".**[20] It was meant to sizeably increase institutional credit amounts because the money which *"should have gone to the villages had not reached there"*.[21] A major reason for this was analysed as being the difficulties feared by banks in enforcing recovery of their loans. Thus even before the entry of the first commercial bank into Kinnaur, the problem of default on bank loans had already come to the fore. It was conceded that even nationalization of banks had not produced desired results because banks faced problems in recovering their loans. Dr Parmār clarified that the bill was a *"revolutionary step"*[22] because the *"ordinary man even if he be a farmer, even if he not be a proprietor, has no land of his own, can carry on his occupation by taking loans...Non-proprietors of land, who can produce only grain, would be eligible for loan in spite of not being owners"*.[23] Earlier, cultivators not owning land could not mortgage the land they cultivated, could not hypothecate the crops or produce of such land to obtain loans. *"The biggest obstacle why loans could earlier not be obtained...was the absence of a right to recover such loans"*.[24] Such right was created by the Act in question.

Mr J.B.L. Khāchi pointed out that in Mahāsu District *"as much as 87% of the total loans which have been given either as takavi or by the Land Mortgage Bank or by the State Cooperative Bank or by any credit giving agency, **87% of the credits are in arrears.** Money is in arrears. The money is not being paid back...The area, the most affluent area, Kumhārsain today is a defaulter tehsil...if after all the credit giving agencies have to function they must function in an atmosphere where there are no defaulters"*.[25]

The Chief Minister admitted that there were defaulters. Lists of defaulters were progressevely lengthening, *"affecting the entire economy of the Pradesh, cooperative societies get less money...needs of farmers could not be met due to such defaults"*.[26] Each stage of discussion saw this point being discussed repeatedly.

[19] Himāchal Pradesh Vidhān Sabha ki Kāryavāhi (Adhikrat Vivaran), Khand 2, Aṅk 3, 7 June 1972 (Tratiya Vidhān Sabha), The Himāchal Pradesh Agricultural Credit Operations and Miscellaneous Provisions (Banks) Bill 1972 par vichār aivaṃ pāran, Introductory address by the Chief Minister, Dr Y. S. Parmār, [In Hindi], p. 107. These proceedings of the Legislative Assembly are not open to general inspection. Special prior permissio has to be obtained from the Speaker of the House through the Secretary, Vidhān Sabha.

[20] Ibid.

[21] Ibid.

[22] Ibid, p. 108.

[23] Ibid.

[24] Ibid.

[25] Ibid, Speech of J.B.L. Khāchi, [In English], Pp 112-113.

[26] Ibid, Reply of the Chief Minister, [In Hindi], p. 120.

5.1.2.3 Provisions of the Act

Recovery of dues was dealt with in Chapter IV of the Act. Section 12 gave legal sanction to banks to attach and sell, through a civil court, any land or any interest therein charged or mortgaged to them. Proceeds of such sale would be applied towards all money due to the bank, including costs and expenses awarded by the court. Section 13(1) provided for the appointment of a **"prescribed authority".**[27] This authority could, on the application of a bank, order any agriculturist, his legal heir or his legal representative to pay any sum due to the bank on account of financial assistance availed, by sale of any land or any interest therein upon which the payment of such money is charged or mortgaged. However, no such sale was to be effected without first serving a formal notice on the defaulter to repay the amount due. Sub-Divisional Magistrates (henceforth referred to only as S.D.Ms) were notified as the **"prescribed authority"** under this Act. Section 13(2) gave every order passed by the S.D.M. as prescribed authority the status of a civil court decree. Section 13(3) gave banks the unfettered right to enforce their rights in any other manner open to them in any way for the time being in force. Section 14(1) empowered the banks to themselves acquire agricultural land or interest therein or any other immovable property which had been charged or mortgaged to them, provided the said land or interest therein or any other immovable property had been sought to be sold by public auction where no person had offered to purchase it for a price sufficient to pay them the money due. Such acquired land could be leased out by the bank, pending sale, for a period not exceeding one year at a time, according to Section 14(3). The lessee would not acquire any interest in that property not withstanding anything to the contrary contained in any other law for the time being in force. Section 14(4) puts some restrictions on sale by a bank of such land or interest therein. Sales had to conform to any law in force placing restrictions purchase of land by non-agriculturists or by non-tribals. They had also to conform to laws in force about ceilings on land holdings and those against fragmentation of land. Section 15 exempted the banks from restrictions on acquisition of land in excess of the prescribed ceiling.

Chapter V (Sections 16 to 25) provided for financing of cooperative societies by banks. Under Section 24(1), if a cooperative society defaulted on its loan from a bank by reason of its members not repaying, the bank could direct its committee to proceed against defaulting members under the H.P. Cooperative Societies Act, 1968. Under Section 24(2) if the committee fails to act within 90 days on the receipt of such notice, the bank may itself proceed against the defaulting members, in which event the provisions of the H.P. Cooperative Societies Act, 1968 as well as the rules and bye-laws made thereunder shall apply as if all references to the society or its committee were references to the bank. Section 24(3) empowers a bank, which has obtained a decree or award against a cooperative society indebted to it, to proceed to recover such amounts first from the assets of the society and secondly from the members of the society to the extent of their debts due to the society.

Chapter 6 (Sections 26-29) provided additional miscellaneous provisions. Section 26 provided that nothing in any law for the time being in force dealing with money lending or agriculturists' debt relief would apply to financial assistance availed of by an agriculturist from a bank. Under Section 27(1), an agreement of mortgage executed by the manager of a Joint Hindu Family in favour of a bank for securing financial assistance for an agricultural purpose would be binding on its every member.

Subsequently, two new Sections (26-A and 26-B) were inserted into the Act through legislation. Section 26-A dealt with loans given by banks on applications sponsored by a government corporation under tie-up arrangements. In case of default, a certificate sent by a bank or its authorized officer stating the sum due, alongwith interest accrued up to date alongwith the collection charges was to suffice for converting the amount due into an A.L.R.

[27] Act op. cit., 1972, Section 13(1).

Under Section 26-B a bank availing the services of the Collector under 26-A would have to pay collection charges to the government. The Act was supplemented by Rules framed in 1975.

5.1.2.4 H.P. Agricultural Credit Operations and Miscellaneous Provisions (Banks) Rules, 1975

These Rules were to complement provisions of the preceding Act. A gap of three years can be noticed between the passing of the Act and the promulgation of the Rules thereunder. Rule 3(1) authorized the loaning bank to move the Collector for distraint and sale of such crop produce or property as had had a charge created on it in favour of the bank. Such application was to be made in Form A. Under Rule 4, if the bank satisfied the Collector of the genuineness of its efforts, the latter could cause to be served a written notice of demand on the defaulting agriculturist, his heir or legal representative; calling upon the defaulter to repay the amount specified in the notice within 15 days from the date of service thereof, or to show cause why the property charged may not be distrained and sold. Rules 5 to 11 outline the procedure for service of notice; custody of distrained property and procedure for auction/sale of seized property. The Rules are in conformity with the provisions of the Civil Procedure Code (henceforth to be referred to only as the C.P.C.).

5.1.2.5 H.P. Public Moneys (Recovery of Dues) Act, 1973

This Act was meant to provide further safeguard for funds loaned out by the state government. It indicates that it was not just banks which constituted the sole outlet for institutional credit. The government itself also functioned as a giver of credit, as shall be seen in Chapter VI. As in the Banks Act of 1972 and its Rules, defaults of public money are to be converted into A.L.Rs because it is an A.L.R. which affects the Revenue Department's balance sheets and, being a factor in the A.C.Rs of Tahsildārs and Naib-Tahsildārs, makes for quicker action. An important point can be noticed here.

These legislative measures, by relying on conversion into A.L.R. for expeditious recovery, were meant to motivate financial institutions to reach more agriculturist-borrowers who might otherwise go only to village moneylenders. But this very motivation to the institutional lenders frightened the borrowers - not all borrowers but the most needy ones. These were the small/marginal farmers and agricultural labourers who were primarily to be reached out to by the lenders. Borrowers were well-aware of the consequences of any sum declared as A.L.R.. While the relatively well-off borrowers had enough political clout and links with revenue officials to escape draconian measures possible for recovering A.L.Rs, the poorer borrowers had no such buffer of influence. They became the objects of the full force of the coercive authority of the Revenue Department. They could neither pay bribes to officials to stall such coercion, nor get politicians to intercede with government machinery in their favour because they were not important enough in electoral calculations! The coercive pressure sought to be exercised through conversion of bank/other institutional overdues into A.L.Rs caused fear only amongst the poor, politically/economically unimportant classes. Instead of repaying their loans promptly, as was envisaged in the Act, they preferred not to take loans from institutional lenders. They could always negotiate with their traditional moneylenders whereas default in payment of A.L.Rs would lead straight to distraint/sale of their land, depriving them of their primary source of livelihood. They could not avoid such distraint by paying in kind or by doing physical labour for the credit-giver, as they could for the devtas or other village moneylenders. Institutional loans had to be repaid in cash and nothing else. Government were not interested in keeping family jewellery or utensils as collateral in lieu of not enforcing demanded repayment! In an area like Kinnaur with its long tradition of barter and repayments in kind, forced cash repayment drives poorer borrowers towards the informal sector. The richer borrowers utilize institutional funds, obtained either directly or through poorer proxies, since they are influential enough to escape the full force of coercive measures foreseen by conversion to A.L.Rs. Streamlined recovery procedures through such conversion may have reassured institutional lenders that their loans would be recovered by the Revenue

Department. In practice they did not help much since borrowers vulnerable to coercion shied away from institutional loans as a consequence. The borrowers actually taking credit were in a position to deflect the severity of the measures envisaged. As with so many other legislative measures, there was a rather wide slip between the cup and the lip! In addition to legislative provisions there were many administrative instructions.

5.1.3 Administrative Instructions: Frequent and Repetitive

The series of such instructions goes back nearly 80 years in time.

5.1.3.1 Standing Order 29 of the Financial Commissioner, Punjab

The Standing Orders of the Financial Commissioner (henceforth to be referred to only as the F.C.) have quasi-judicial importance for Revenue Officers. Standing Order Number 29 of the F.C., Punjab is applicable even today in Himāchal Pradesh. It was originally issued on July 28, 1909 and outlined coercive processes for effecting recovery of amounts due as A.L.Rs. The following coercive processes[28] were outlined:

(a) Writs of Demand;
(b) Arrest and Detention;
(c) Distress and Sale;
(d) Transfer of Holding;
(e) Attachment of Estate or Holding;
(f) Annulment of Assessment; and
(g) Sales of Land.

The Tahsildār was designated as a key figure in the recovery process. *"It is the duty of tahsildārs to see that all instalments are paid punctually"*.[29] Writs, warrants and other processes for the collection of revenue are ordinarily served through the agency of the Tahsil peons (chaprāsis) and the fees recovered credited to the government. The possibility of corruption was candidly mentioned. *"Arrears of revenue may not be realized from defaulters and brought to the tahsil by talbana or other low-paid peons. Such a practice is liable to lead to abuse. Defaulters and lambardars should be ordered to pay sums due from them into the treasury either in person or through an agent or by postal money order"*.[30]

5.1.3.2 Chief Secretary's Letter Dated June 21, 1975

This communication from the seniormost civil servant in H.P. only stated what had been complained about by almost all Revenue Officers in Kinnaur and elsewhere. Having discovered that getting an overdue amount declared as A.L.R. meant transferring the headache of recovery to the Revenue Department, other government departments and banks began sending cases for recovery en masse to the former without making proper efforts to recover the overdue amounts themselves. Instead of being used as an exceptional means of last resort, A.L.Rs were sought to be used as routine procedures of first instance. Institutional lenders would just send a letter or two to the borrowers asking them to repay. When such routine letter(s) showed no concrete results, the case was dumped onto the Revenue Department for recovery. The Chief Secretary (henceforth referred to as the C.S.) clarified unambiguously that

[28] Standing Order No. 29: Coercive Processes, Orders of the Financial Commissioners Punjab, III Reprint, 18 December 1951, Part A: Sections 3 to 11, Part B: Sections 16 to 18, Part C: Sections 19 to 21, Part D: Sections 22 to 23, Part F: Sections 24 to 30 and Part G: Sections 31 to 33.

[29] Ibid, Part A: Writs of Demand and Execution of Processes, Section 8.

[30] Ibid, Section 10.

it was **"primarily for the loaning departments themselves to make efforts for effecting the recoveries".**[31] Cases were to be sent to the Revenue Department for recovery only if all efforts of the institutional lender failed.

5.1.3.3 Chief Secretary's Letter Dated October 8, 1976

The C.S.'s clarification of June 21, 1975 caused confusion. Revenue authorities happily redumped recovery cases back onto the institutional lenders while the latter did not quite know how to cope with this new situation in which the Revenue Department was not always willing to bail them out. Accordingly, a detailed letter was issued by the C.S. directing the lenders to use recovery of overdues as A.L.R. as a measure of last resort and not as a normal routine. Loaning departments were advised to prescribe a recovery procedure in their rules. Measures like civil litigation or arbitration could be included in bonds of agreement governing such loans. Cases were to be sent to the Collector for recovery as A.L.R. only if no other measures had succeeded in effecting recovery. The C.S. sought to dispel the impression of loaning departments that recovery was the responsibility of only the Revenue Department. Financial irresponsibility by institutional lenders was sought to be curbed. Lenders had liberally distributed money when they felt that recovery was not their responsibility but that of the Revenue Department. They were forced to become more careful once recovery became primarily their baby. They were to themselves ensure that loans were not handed out as largesse but given for viable schemes to carefully vetted borrowers. With this brief background, we can now see how the recovery procedures have actually performed in Kinnaur in terms of recovery of outstanding debts. This is an important indicator of the degree of efficiency with which the institutional credit network was functioning.

5.2 RECOVERY OF BANK LOANS IN KINNAUR

As per information furnished by the manager, PNB at Rekong Peo, banks adopted mainly three procedures for effecting recoveries:[32]
(a) **Personal contacts;**
(b) **Notices of ordinary/registered post; and**
(c) **Civil suits.**
Interestingly enough, proceedings under the Banks Act 1972 were not mentioned at all. The recovery procedures have thus not relied much on this legislation which was supposed to be the major pivot on which the whole bank credit infrastructure was to rest. When asked about how much help bankers received from government agencies in effecting recoveries, the branch manager of the PNB at Peo stated **"generally no help".**[33] On the contrary, the former Divisional Manager of the UCO Bank for H.P. felt that bankers received more than adequate help in this respect.[34] These contradictory views could be due to differing personal experiences and levels of perception because the D.M. was the highest UCO Bank officer in Himāchal

[31] Letter No. 1-13/72-Rev. I(II), dated Simla-171002, the 8th. October, 1976 from Mr U.N. Sharma, Chief Secretary to Himāchal Pradesh Government to 1. All Administrative Secretaries to Himāchal Pradesh Govt., 2. All Heads of Department in Himāchal Pradesh, and 3. All Deputy Commissioners in Himāchal Pradesh, Subject: Recovery of Government Dues - Instructions regarding, Para 2(i).

[32] Personal Communication No. Nil dated Nil from Mr Negi, Manager, PNB Branch, Rekong Peo to the author. Handed over in person in Peo on December 15, 1985.

[33] Ibid.

[34] Personal Communication dated July 13, 1985 from Mr S.C. Girotra, Assistant General Manager, UCO Bank, Bombay to the author, Para 5.

whereas the branch manager was only one of many such officers in the district. Tables 5.1 to

Table 5.1: Bankwise Recovery Position as on 31-12-1983 in Kinnaur

sn	*Bank*	*Demand*	*Amount*	*Odues*	*R%*	*O%*
01	PNB	741	453	288	61	39
02	UCO	1168	695	473	60	40
03	SBI	357	221	136	62	38
04	UBI	099	073	026	74	26

Code: sn = serial no., R% = percentage of recovery, Amount in Rs'000.
O% = percentage of overdues, Odues = overdues,
(Source: Collected in person from the Regional Office of the PNB in Simla on December 27, 1985)

5.3 show recovery from 1983 onwards. The UCO Bank gave figures for 1982 as well. At the end of 1983, nearly one-third of the total amounts due were in default. In terms of absolute amounts, total overdues left unrecovered amounted to Rs 923,000; not a very large figure in itself. But the percentages of overdues pointed towards the fact that even in absolute terms larger sums of money would get blocked with an expansion of institutional credit supply. This

Table 5.2: Bankwise Recovery Position in Kinnaur on 31-12-1984

sn	*Bank*	*demand raised*		*amount recd*		*Overdues*		*R%*
do	-do-	A/Cs	Amnt	A/Cs	Amnt	A/Cs	Amnt	do
01	PNB	433	1,183	338	596	385	587	50
02	UCO	1552	1,742	1054	880	985	862	50
03	SBI	679	1,030	214	380	465	650	37
04	UBI	304	,110	273	081	031	029	74
			Of which under IRDP					
01	PNB	320	,309	238	123	280	186	40
02	UCO	1243	,931	837	530	705	401	57
03	SBI	415	,348	134	135	281	213	39
04	UBI	302	,104	273	081	030	023	78

Code: A/Cs = Accounts, Amnt = Amount, Amount recd = Amount recovered during the half year,
Odues = Overdues at the end of the half year, demand raised = Demand raised during the present half year plus previous overdues (Total Demand).
All amounts are in thousands of Rupees.
(Source: As for preceding Table.)

is corroborated by similar statistics for the years 1984 and 1985 respectively. We notice that the percentage of recovery fell from 61% to 50% for PNB; from 60% to 50% for the UCO

Bank and from 62% to 37% for the SBI from 1983 to 1984. This fall occurred even though the amount recovered in absolute terms rose from Rs 453,000 to Rs 596,000; an increase of about 32% over the figure for 1983 for the PNB; from Rs 695,000 to Rs 880,000 (increase of 27%) for the UCO Bank and from Rs 221,000 to Rs 380,000 (increase of 72%) for the SBI respectively. Only the UBI managed an increase both in its percentage of recovery for the I.R.D.P. and in absolute terms. Recovery stayed at 74% of the amount advanced for the UBI while the amount recovered rose from Rs 73,000 to Rs 81,000; an increase of nearly 10% over the 1983 figure. The percentage of recovery was higher in the I.R.D.P. sector for the UCO Bank, SBI and UBI. It fell only for the lead bank (PNB). The UBI's lending was almost entirely in the I.R.D.P. sector.

Higher percentages of recovery in I.R.D.P. for three out of four banks go contrary to the widespread fear of bankers that recovery necessarily falls if increasing numbers of poorer people are given loans because they lack adequate collateral and are loan security risks. If I.R.D.P. assistance has been obtained through a proxy (a poor borrower), the real beneficiary ensures prompt repayment so that the proxy's credit rating does not suffer through default, undermining eligibility for further I.R.D.P. assistance. Credit at concessional rates of interest can thus continue to flow to relatively affluent farmer-moneylenders for refinancing their loan-giving operations. Banks were sometimes aware of this cycle of the flow of institutional credit but overlooked it so long as their repayment instalments were deposited on time. Everyone was satisfied. The commercial banks were satisfied because it increased their I.R.D.P. loans' quota and improved their recovery performance. Proxy borrowers were satisfied because such loans helped them to repay dearer money overdues with cheaper institutional credit. Real beneficiaries were satisfied because it increased their supply of money

Table 5.3: Statement of Recovery on June 30, 1985, in Kinnaur

sn	*Bank*	*total demand*		*amount recd*		*Overdues*		*R%*	*O%*
do	-do-	A/Cs	Amnt	A/Cs	Amnt	A/Cs	Amnt	do	do
01	PNB	627	1613	431	982	355	631	61	39
02	UCO	1762	2039	1207	818	1181	1221	40	60
03	SBI	688	4980	559	4154	899	826	83	17
04	UBI	370	162	345	130	027	032	80	20
05	SCB	052	2112	055	988	029	1124	47	53
06	LDB	006	014	006	005	003	009	36	64
07	TTL	3505	10920	2603	7077	2494	3843	65	35

Code: R% = percentage of recovery, O% = percentage of overdues,
Odues = total overdues, recd = recovered, Amnt = amount,
All amounts are in thousands of Rupees, TTL = grand total.
(Source: As for preceding Table.)

to be lent out. The percentage of recovery rose for the PNB from 50% to 61%; for the UCO Bank it fell from 50% to 40%; for the SBI it rose from 37% to 83% and for the UBI it rose from 74% to 80%. In comparison, the percentage of recovery for the SCB was only 47%, even though in absolute terms it had recovered Rs 988,000; second only to the SBI's recovery of Rs 4,980,000. The latter's performance was the best and also the highest in absolute terms. The progressive choking up of the cooperative sector is shown by the low percentages of recovery for both long-term credit (LDB) and short-term credit (SCB). The overall recovery percentage of 65 hides substantial bank-wise variations between 36% and 83%. On the whole, however, the percentage of recovery showed no consistence for commercial banks. There was no coordinated evolution. We can now examine whether this pattern was similar or dissimilar if we take only one bank with the maximum credit disbursement in Kinnaur.

5.2.1 Recovery Performance of UCO Bank Branches in Kinnaur

Figures were available for the UCO Bank network's recovery performance from June 1982 till June 1984. June 30th was the date of closing of the banking year, which runs in India from

Table 5.4: Recovery Performance of UCO Bank Branches in Kinnaur

sn	*As On*	*Sector*	*dmnd*	*clcn*	*odues*	*%c/d*
01	June 1982	Agriculture	149	083	066	55.70
02	June 1982	S.S.I.	009	000	009	00.00
03	June 1982	Services	378	355	023	93.71
04	June 1982	Total	536	438	098	81.72
05	June 1983	Agriculture	275	195	080	70.91
06	June 1983	S.S.I.	031	019	012	61.29
07	June 1983	Services	596	419	177	70.30
08	June 1983	Total	902	633	269	70.18
09	June 1984	Agriculture	540	212	328	39.26
10	June 1984	S.S.I.	127	035	092	27.56
11	June 1984	Services	1205	420	785	34.85
12	June 1984	Total	1872	667	1205	35.63

Code: **dmnd** = **Demand, clcn** = **Collection, odues** = **Overdues, %c/d** = Percentage of Collection to Demand.
All amounts are in thousands of Rupees.
(Source: Personal Communication dated May 13, 1985 from Mr S.C. Girotra, then-Divisional Manager, UCO Bank, Simla to the author.)

July 1 to June 30 of the succeeding year. Percentage of recovery in the agriculture sector rose from 55.70 in 1982 to 70.91 in 1983 but then fell to 39.26 in 1984 even though in absolute terms collection rose from Rs 83,000 in 1982 to Rs 195,000 in 1983 to Rs 212,000 in 1984. A similar pattern existed in the S.S.I. sector where recovery rose from 0% in 1982 to 61.29% in 1983 and then fell to 27.56% in 1984 even while collection in absolute terms rose from 0 in 1982 to Rs 19,000 in 1983 to Rs 35,000 in 1984 respectively. In the services sector percentage of recovery fell regularly; from 93.91 in 1982 to 70.30 in 1983 to 34.85 in 1984; even as collection rose from Rs 355,000 in 1982 to Rs 419,000 in 1983 to Rs 420,000 in 1984 respectively. While the total collection rose from Rs 438,000 in 1982 to Rs 633,000 in 1983 to Rs 667,000 in 1984; the percentage of overall recovery fell from 81.72 in 1982 to 70.18 in 1983 to 35.63 in 1984.

We see that the percentage of recovery was falling while demand was rising. As the institutional credit funnelled into Kinnaur rose manifold, the percentage of recovery did not keep pace but lagged behind. Compulsions of lending by specified targets under the I.R.D.P. and other programs meant that this hiatus between increased institutional lending and declining percentages of recovery to demand kept widening. There were no sound principles of bankability in evidence. We can begin by examining the correlations between various variables.

5.2.1.1 Analysis of UCO Bank Recovery Data: Representative

The first step was to see whether the distribution of demand, collection and overdues variables was symmetrical or non-symmetrical. The easiest way of seeing it was optical examination of vertical bar charts.

5.2.1.1.1 Vertical Bar Charts Showing Yearwise Distribution

Since the number of observations for each variable was only three, it was not much use plotting bar charts except to examine year-wise variation. The distribution was non-symmetrical. The rise in total overdues was steeper than the rise of total collection. Overdues in the agriculture sector rose sharply in 1984. Similar rises were observed in overdues for the S.S.I. and services sectors in 1984 as well. Expansion of institutional credit was accompanied by a rise in overdues in all sectors, a fact better brought out by block diagrams.

5.2.1.1.2 Block Diagrams for all the Sectors for UCO Bank

Block diagrams were plotted for recovery demand, collection and overdues for all sectors combined. The year was kept as the block variable and number of bank branches as the group variable. Total recovery demand rose sharply to Rs 1,872,000 in 1984. Overdues were low in 1982 and 1983 but much higher in 1984. As was to be expected, an increase in the number of branches meant corresponding higher overdues because of more channels of bank credit input without matching streamlining of the recovery mechanisms. Since the distribution of variables was non-symmetrical, a non-parametric test was used to examine correlations.

5.2.1.1.3 Spearman's Correlation Test

The results of Spearman's Non-Parametric Correlation Test show that demand for recovery was totally related to demand, collection and overdues for all sectors, combined as well as separately. Same was the case for total amount collected and total overdues; as well as for these variables in individual sectors. Correlation coefficients for all these correlations were 1.00000, the highest possible correlation value. It shows that the entire set of variables moved in a correlated fashion. Such a perfect correlation is not due to any super-coordination of the UCO Bank but only due to the fact that there is a paucity of observations available, only three in each case here. This paucity affects the analysis.

5.2.1.1.4 General Linear Models Procedure for Recovery Variables

Since all the variables in our set are highly correlated, any of them can be pegged as the independent variable and the others derived out of it. Total collection was chosen as this variable because it would determine demand, collection and overdues for the succeeding banking years. No mathematical equation can be written between variables in the set because of paucity of adequate values.

5.2.1.2 Recovery Performance of the PNB Branch at Rekong Peo

Recovery data was made available for this branch, the first in Kinnaur, from 1976 to 1985. Trends could be observed better than for UCO Bank where only three values were available, too few to discern any evolutionary trends. Total advances and recoveries made by the Peo

Table 5.5: Total Advances and Recoveries of the PNB's Peo Branch

sn	*Year*	*advs*	*rcrs*	*%ra*
01	1976	226	070	031
02	1977	055	122	222
03	1978	219	163	074
04	1979	283	204	072
05	1980	320	180	056
06	1981	686	232	034
07	1982	553	246	045
08	1983	403	330	082
09	1984	756	512	068
10	1985	1977	158	008
11	Total	5478	2217	041

Code: advs = **total advances, rcrs = total recoveries, %ra = percentage of recovery to advances,**
All amounts are in thousands of Rupees.
(Source: Personal Communication dated December 12, 1985 from the manager, PNB, Rekong Peo to the author. Information compiled from bank ledgers and registers.)

branch of the PNB are shown in Table 5.5 . There was no consistent rise or fall in the amounts advanced or recovered. To see whether any method can be found in this apparently chaotic evolutionary pattern, we observe how it looks on a graph.

5.2.1.2.1 Graphs Showing Year-wise Variation of Recovery

The graph showing the year-wise variation of recovered amounts shows a continuous rise from 1976 to 1979 and a fall in 1980. It rose again in 1981 till 1984 and fell sharply in 1985. The rise from 1981 to 1982 was slow; being only from Rs 232,000 to Rs 246,000 (only 6%). However, total advances rose from Rs 756,000 in 1984 to Rs 1,977,000 in 1985; a spectacular annual rise of +162%.

From Chapters III and IV we are well aware that both 1982 and 1985 were election years in H.P. In 1980 there had been a change in the ruling party with the Congress(I) replacing the Janata Party. This change is marked by an immediate drop in recoveries by the PNB branch at Rekong Peo. The rate of recoveries slowed down markedly in the election year of 1982. In 1985 the rate of recovery registered the sharpest fall (-69% over the figure for 1984) and total advances showed the sharpest rise (+162%). The figures speak for themselves! Politicians may seek to explain the variations in recovered amounts as sheer coincidence but the facts speak otherwise. Recoveries fell or their rate of rise slowed down perceptibly in the years in which there were elections. The data points to a bank-credit infrastructure in which advances and recoveries worked in dissonance with each other. The process of recycling institutional credit was not functioning efficiently. The overall average percentage of recovery to advances between 1976 and 1985 was only 41%, and this for the leading branch of the lead bank which was expected to set an example in efficiency for other banks. This flagship branch of the lead bank was not worthy of emulation in so far as its recovery performance was considered. This very impression of lax working of the recovery structure was reinforced by the lack of any effective action under the Banks Act of 1972 which had been meant to streamline recoveries in particular and the functioning of banks in general.

5.2.2 Institution and Disposal of Cases under the Banks Act 1972

Cases had been instituted for recovery under the Act of 1972 only in Kālpa Sub-Division before the S.D.M. . There were 7 cases filed in all, pertaining to loans given by banks between 1978 and 1982. Interestingly, six out of these were for land development loans. Only one case related to loan for a jersey cow. Against Bishan Das of Sangla and Inder Singh of Chānsu cases (Nos. 2/84 and 3/84 respectively) were instituted on October 18, 1984. Already on November 6, 1984, less than three weeks later, the full amount had been recovered and paid to the loaning bank. Personal enquiries from the Tahsildār Sangla revealed that the Banks Act had not been used at all. He had used administrative pressure to make the defaulters repay. In the loan case for a jersey cow in village Kālpa no charge had been created on movable or immovable property of the loanees. It shows a lack of adequate procedural preparation before filing these cases. Creation of charge on property should have been a necessary pre-requisite before filing such suits. In the case of Joban Sukh of Sangla, payments had been coming in amounts between Rs 100 and Rs 500 already before October 18, 1984 when the suit was instituted. Eleven instalments totalling Rs 1,900 had already been repaid. This was not a habitual defaulter who needed to be taught a lesson, particularly when habitual defaulters were being allowed to go scot free. The application of the Banks Act seemed to be arbitrary, inadequately prepared and seldom used.

Revenue Officers pointed out that the Act had no provision for mandatory creation of charge on movable or immovable property before banks could give loans. The provisions for creation of charge were optional and were not always applied before loans were released. Banks did not create charge on property but wanted the revenue authorities to seize or auction it to enforce repayment when the loans fell into default. Revenue Officers felt that bankers did not have adequate knowledge of the legal aspects of recovery proceedings. The latter thought that the Tahsildār was some kind of magician who could recover their loans by some means somehow. If the revenue authorities pointed out that procedural formalities had not been fulfilled, bankers thought that the former were only stalling. Of the seven cases under process in Kinnaur, charge on property had been created in only one case. Very clearly, the Act of 1972 has not been utilized as an effective instrument for streamlining institutional credit operations.

The preceding conclusion can also be inferred from the fact that so few cases were filed. This did not mean that there were no defaulters in Kinnaur. To get an idea of chronic defaulters, bank managers of selected bank branches were requested to furnish lists of such persons. The list provided by the manager of the PNB branch at Rekong Peo contained the names of 35 chronic defaulters, further establishing how the seven cases filed under the Banks Act of 1972 covered only a fringe of the problem of default. In case of other bank branch managers also, the number of chronic defaulters was on the average between 40 and 75 per branch.[35] Since there were 13 commercial bank branches and 5 cooperative bank branches in Kinnaur by the end of 1985, taking even the lower end of the preceding average figure we get

[35] Personal consultations with branch managers in Kinnaur.

about 720 chronic defaulters. The 7 cases filed under the Act of 1972 thus constituted only 0.0097% of such defaulters.

Interest payments had accumulated over time and become significant percentages of the principal. In the case of Chhodub of village Brélingi; suspended interest payments were Rs 319.50 and recorded interest payments were Rs 173.94 versus a balance of Rs 278.80. In the case of Amarjeet Singh Bedi, Rs 4,312.27 stood as the recorded interest on Rs 11,739.35 balance amount. A civil suit had been filed by the loaning bank and decreed in its favour by the Senior Sub-Judge at Kālpa. Decrees had been issued in two other cases while civil suits stood filed in two cases; civil courts had thus been moved in five cases out of 35. Non-Kinnauras accounted for six cases but formed an overwhelming majority (67%) of the loans given for small businesses. These six had an outstanding balance of Rs 51,413.82 (or 51% of the total outstanding balance of Rs 101,453.46). Six major defaulters or nearly 17% of the total sample of 35 defaulters accounted thus for 51% of the total debt of the sample. None of them had been proceeded against under the Banks Act 1972 though civil suits had been filed against three of them. Asked as to why the more intricate C.P.C. procedure had been preferred over the simpler procedure under the Banks Act of 1972, the manager of the Peo branch of the PNB felt that to be really sure they used civil suits because political pressure could not be brought to bear in such proceedings and decrees issued therein had to be executed with more despatch.

The loaning pattern was spread geographically wide. Villages Batséri, Rispa, Rārang, Kāfnoo, Yula, Ribba and Katgāoṅ were covered from Peo. In addition, there were defaulters from Rāmpur, Hamirpur, Punjab and even Bārāmula in Kashmir. It should be no surprise that they defaulted. Distance makes execution of even civil court decrees difficult. It would be no easy process to confiscate the property of a defaulter in Kashmir. The revenue authorities in Kinnaur would have to send the decree to their counterparts in the district in which Bārāmula falls. From there, the papers would be sent to the concerned Tahsildār for execution. The money recovered would then be transferred to the Kinnaur revenue authorities and then to the civil court. It would not be too difficult for the defaulter to so manipulate things in collusion with field revenue staff in Bārāmula that recovery would be repeatedly delayed. For example, it could be easily reported (falsely) that the defaulter was not traceable at his home address or that he had no property which could be seized to enforce repayment, or a host of such delaying excuses. Such risks were not carefully weighed by the banks at the time of giving loans to non-Kinnauras in Kinnaur. The bank could not follow up loans in Katgāoṅ, Urni and Batséri from Rekong Peo. They were simply too far in winter and even in summer it required at least some walking to get there. For a single defaulter, each visit to Batséri meant a day spent in travelling for the bank official. We can now examine how the recovery pattern varied for cooperative loans.

5.3 RECOVERY OF COOPERATIVE BANK LOANS IN KINNAUR

Since the SCB was the pioneer in introducing banking operations in Kinnaur, it is revealing to consider its recovery figures for the first decade of its existence.

5.3.1 SCB Statistics for the First Decade in Kinnaur

As can be seen from Table 5.6, recovery followed no regular pattern. There was no consistent rise or fall. However, even at this early stage we can observe that during election years (here 1962 and 1967) recovery tended to fall or to slow down. This phenomenon has become almost an inbuilt part of the system. Even in the absence of the degree of politicization that has affected Kinnaur since 1977 recovery procedures tended to slow down perceptibly just after its creation as a district in 1960. It seems difficult for the supposedly non-political district administration to dip its hands into the pockets of voters in election years when its political masters are going around with outstretched hands for votes. From the very beginning of banking operations in Kinnaur this development distorted popular perception of recovery. Since elections, coming every five years or earlier, showed how recoveries slowed down under political compulsions, people could not see why they should not try and use pressures for delaying recovery at other times as well. Regular repayment, instead of being established as a

Table 5.6: Recovery Statistics for the First Decade of the SCB

sn	*Year*	*advances*	*recoveries*	*%R/A*	*%Change*
01	1960-61	52,401.89	32,430.68	061.89	00.00
02	1961-62	318.22	18,725.37	5884.41	-42.26
03	1962-63	229,953.63	166,801.45	072.54	+790.78
04	1963-64	362,300.35	375,876.14	103.75	+125.34
05	1964-65	302,412.31	340,697.72	112.66	-009.36
06	1965-66	7,143.53	9,876.32	138.26	-097.10
07	1966-67	110,554.68	37,327.15	033.76	+368.06
08	1967-68	95,938.95	84,813.43	088.40	+127.22
09	1968-69	112,939.85	82,230.16	072.81	-003.05
10	1969-70	102,131.69	121,966.34	119.42	+048.32

Code: **%R/A = percentage of recoveries to advances,**
%Change = percentage change from figure of preceding year.
(Source: Gazetteer, 1971, p. 182.)

habit, became an exception. Table 5.6 shows how percentage values fluctuated from year to year. There was no clear correlation between the variables. Percentage of recovery to advance could be artificially pushed up by lowering amounts advanced. This is seen clearly in 1961-62 when this percentage had an exorbitantly high value of 5884% not because recoveries registered a dramatic increase but because loans advanced fell to an extreme low of Rs 318. In fact recovery fell by 42% over the preceding year's collection. Collection was more than 100% higher from 1963-64 to 1965-66 (falling to 34% in 1967, an election year) and 1969-70. This pattern of the first decade was continued in later years in commercial banks' recoveries as well.[36] In all, Rs 1,376,095 were loaned out by the SCB, Kālpa of which Rs 1,270,744.80 stood recovered, giving an average overall recovery percentage of 92%, a good figure. Unfortunately, this performance was not maintained as larger loan amounts were given out in succeeding years. On June 30, 1985 the percentage of recovery to demand stood at 47%[37] for the SCB in Kinnaur. We can now compare the performance of recovery of cooperative loans in different sectors.

[36] Please see Section 5.2.1, Tables 5.1 to 5.5, this Chapter.

[37] Personal Communication dated December 10, 1985 from the manager, SCB, Kālpa branch to the author.

5.3.2 Recovery under Different Heads of Cooperative Loans

Tables 3.1 to 3.16 of Chapter III contain the statistical data for the loans advanced and recovered under different schemes from the Kālpa branch of the SCB.

5.3.2.1 Crop Loans: Desirable But Default Ridden

The percentage of recovery for crop loans was 59% in 1976-77, 193% in 1977-78, 82% in 1978-79, 667% in 1980-81, 152% in 1983-84 and 39% in 1984-85 respectively. In absolute terms, recovery was nil in 1982-83 (while advances were nil in 1981-82), from a high point of Rs 730,390 in 1976-77 during the Emergency. From a recovery of Rs 313,331 in 1980-81, there was a continuous fall to Rs 60,131 in 1984-85 for crop loans. This progression shows the mounting overdues in this key sector of cooperative loaning. Amounts advanced increased from Rs 46,994 to Rs 153,678 while recoveries fell, creating a choking effect on the system.

5.3.2.2 Recoveries of Amounts under Pledge to Societies

Table 5.7 gives the fluctuations in recoveries under the scheme of limits pledged to cooperative

Table 5.7: Recovery Data for Amounts under Pledge to Cooperatives

sn	*Year*	*recovery*	*Pct*	*r %change*
01	1976-77	61,963	097	00.00
02	1977-78	,111	006	-99.80
03	1978-79	0,000	000	-100.0
04	1979-80	0,000	000	-100.0
05	1980-81	0,000	000	-100.0
06	1981-82	0,000	000	-100.0
07	1982-83	967,754	078	-000
08	1983-84	814,046	085	-15.90
09	1984-85	370,491	100	-54.50

Code: **Pct = percentage of recovery to advances,**
r%change = relative percentage change from preceding year.
(Source: Table 3.11; Chapter III of this work.)

societies.[38] Here again, large fluctuations are to be observed. The figures speak for themselves. Recoveries remained zero over four years for which no cogent reasons could be had from the manager of the SCB, Kālpa Branch. There was no government directive to completely stop recoveries. The percentage of recovery rose to nearly 100% in 1984-85 but only because advances were nearly three times lower than those of the preceding year. Once again, lower absolute performance was masked by higher percentage figures. Recoveries fell in absolute terms.

[38] Please see Section 3.3.2.4.1, Chapter III, of this work.

5.3.2.3 Recovery of Amounts under C.C. Hypothecation Limits

Cooperative credit availability under the Cash Credit Hypothecation Limits has already been

Table 5.8: C.C. Hypothecation Limit Recoveries for the SCB, Kālpa

sn	*Year*	*recovery*	*Pct*	*r %change*
01	1976-77	237,971	073	00.00
02	1977-78	106,524	068	-55.00
03	1978-79	66,900	057	-37.00
04	1980-81	144,074	046	+115.0
05	1981-82	818,169	068	+82.00
06	1982-83	264,400	034	-68.00
07	1983-84	180,045	034	-68.00
08	1984-85	534,138	043	+197.0

Code: **Pct = percentage of recovery to advances,**
r%change = relative percentage change from preceding year.
(Source: Table 3.11, Chapter III of this work.)

outlined.[39] Table 5.8 gives the recovery figures under this scheme.
Recovery reached a maximum value in 1981-82 when it was over Rs 800,000. Since then it has remained well under this figure. The percentage of recovery also fell from 68% in 1981-82 to 43% in 1984-85. Table 5.8 shows no consistent trend in recovery. This fact was quite in conformity with recovery under other schemes. Defaults meant interest accumulation on overdue amounts and a worsening of the debt burden. This scheme involved cooperative societies or better-off individuals as borrowers and not poor borrowers. A poor borrower had no chance of obtaining a hypothecation limit, having nothing much to hypothecate in the first place! Cooperative societies were dominated by relatively more affluent persons. Table 5.8 hints at the fact that even in a scheme where conventional credit risks, meaning poor borrowers lacking assets, were a priori sidelined, recovery performance was fairly low on the average. Against total advances of Rs 4,667,589 recoveries stood at Rs 2,352,221 giving a rough percentage of recovery to advances of 50%.

5.3.2.4 Recovery of Loans Against Own Deposits by the SCB, Kalpa

Provisions of this scheme have already been explained in Chapter III.[40] Statistical data for recovery under this scheme is given in Table 5.9 . Here again, poor borrowers would play no role because they would not be having own deposits in the bank to offer as tangible security to cover the bank's risk. The risk factor for the bank was lower as security was available in the form of borrowers' own term-deposits. The borrowers were aware of this fact only too well! They were also aware that recovery process in this case was less likely to be impeded by external pressures than in other schemes lacking such guaranteed collateral. Banks did not

[39] Section 3.3.2.4.2, Ibid.

[40] Section 3.3.3.1, Ibid.

Table 5.9: Recovery Data for Loans Against own Deposits for SCB

sn	*Year*	*recovery*	*Pct*	*r %change*
01	1976-77	19,522	074	00.00
02	1977-78	48,217	094	+147.0
03	1978-79	654,618	095	+1258
04	1979-80	x,xxx	xxx	-xxxx
05	1980-81	1543,416	087	xxxx
06	1981-82	1556,790	084	-00.87
07	1982-83	1945,170	084	+25.00
08	1983-84	2296,157	081	+18.00
09	1984-85	2701,504	079	+18.00

Code: Pct = **percentage of recovery to advances,**
r%change = relative percentage change from preceding year,
x,xxx, xxx, xxxx = not applicable or data not available.
(Source: Table 3.11, Chapter III of this work.)

need to go through complicated procedures through revenue authorities or civil courts to enforce recovery. They could simply waive repayment of the term-deposits and interest accrued thereon on maturity and block the funds as recovery amounts. Logically, shorn of much of their political and social pressure exerting mechanisms, borrowers would have lesser room for recovery-delaying manœuvres here. Hence recoveries should be higher than those for preceding schemes, fact amply corroborated by the actual figures in Table 5.9. It can straightaway be noticed that the percentages of recovery to advances are higher, as expected. Secondly, percentage change from recovery figures of preceding years was always positive and never negative, unlike in Tables 5.5 to 5.7. Total recovery was Rs 10,765,394 against total advances of Rs 12,945,093, yielding an overall recovery percentage of 83%, higher than the average under other schemes.

Obviously, when the scope for usual hindering pressures was reduced, recovery performance improved considerably. The bank was in a position to directly enforce recovery rather than be helplessly dependent on other agencies. But it would not be easy to point to this scheme as a model to be emulated for other schemes because this would mean steering the focus of the entire institutional credit network towards more affluent borrowers who could afford to have own term-deposits to offer as security. Banks would naturally prefer such guarantees but it would negate the entire evolution of the institutional credit philosophy that such credit should be made more and more easily available to poor people and deliberately manipulated as an instrument of socio-economic improvement. This implies discouraging bank schemes emphasizing cast iron guarantees in the form of long-term deposits or land holdings and motivating the banks to prefer schemes calling for waiving insistence on securities. The whole structure was to be pushed towards the poorest borrower and not towards the richest borrower. However, many difficulties stood in the way of such evolution of the institutional credit network, partly through difficulties in recovering outstanding loans.

5.4 DIFFICULTIES FACED IN RECOVERING LOANS

A banker himself concedes that despite the "*good work done by the commercial and cooperative banks in the field of agriculture and rural lending, the aspect of recovery continues to be a major problem. It has, in fact, become a limiting factor for many practical bankers, particularly branch managers, in playing a more ambitious role in rural financing. Recovery of advances is vital for recycling of funds in the development process. During the past decade this problem has generated enough discussions at the academic and administrative levels but they have yet to offer any effective solution*".[41] This statement applies in its totality to Kinnaur. The UCO Bank staff, followed by the SBI, were such practical bankers who felt hindered by the low percentage of recovery. Endless discussions at the district and state levels have taken place about improving recovery figures. However, no practical compromise has been found where exactly should lie the weightage between the need to fulfil targets under various government programmes for poorer socio-economic groups and the need to sharply increase recoveries of bank loans. The impression got from such discussions was one of repeated generalities which were long on what needed to be done and very, very short on how to do what needed to be done!

A persistent feature of such meetings was the division of the participants into more or less three overall blocks - **non-officials, officials and bankers.** The non-officials pressed for easing up of recovery drives and pressure from officials to curb the bankers' penchant for recovery. Officials privately understood the predicament of bankers in being asked to be liberal with loan funds in the face of poor recovery performance but preferred to avoid saying it in meetings so as not to get on the wrong side of non-officials. Also, they felt that if they supported the bankers' pleas for increased recovery as a pre-condition for more loans, their targets under the I.R.D.P. and other development programmes would not be met, which might cause problems for their A.C.Rs. Such careerist motives made them in many cases to join up with non-officials in pressurising bankers for more liberal lending policies without a matching upswing in recoveries. Bankers were then left alone in pleading for improved recovery performance in practice before being urged to distribute more loans. Instead of working as a harmonious whole, bankers and officials were often at cross-purposes. It is not possible to give an exhaustive list of all difficulties met with in recovering bank loans. Only some major difficulties are being outlined here.

5.4.1 Lack of Transport Facilities: Immobile Bankers!

It not being possible to always be in the vicinity of the borrowers in a remote area like Kinnaur with its scattered villages, it is important that bank managers have adequate transport facilities to closely monitor problematic recovery cases. Bus services are not very frequent in Kinnaur. Roads are often blocked by landslides or avalanches. It is necessary for bank staff to be able to cover as large a number of villages as possible as often as possible in as short a time as possible. Bank branches in Kinnaur did not have large staff strengths to spare staff members for extended periods to do this task.

No bank branch had any motorized means of transport. The Divisional Manager of the UCO Bank at Simla opined that the "area is risky and roads are...non-motorable, it is difficult to drive the vehicles. Only one petrol pump is there in the whole district. Availability of transport is very less. No vehicle has been provided to our staff in these branches. Whole job is performed on foot and by public transport. However, motor cycles are sanctioned for Field Officers. Jeep is provided from headquarters on intervals for follow-up and special campaigns".[42] Enquiries from bank staff in Kinnaur showed that motor cycles may have been

[41] Singh, Ajit, 1985, Chapter 29, p. 364.

sanctioned on paper at headquarters but had not been made available to Field Officers. No vehicles had been sent from headquarters at periodic intervals or for special campaigns. The only time they saw bank vehicles was when their seniors came to Kinnaur from Simla to attend meetings or otherwise on tour, which was seldom. All branch managers listed complete lack of motorized transport as a major hindrance in the task of streamlining recovery operations. Lacking such means, they were dependent on government officials with transport to help them to move around on non-busable roads in Kinnaur. As on March 31, 1984; against a length of 200 kms of double-lane motorable roads there were 193 kms of single-lane motorable roads and 110 kms of jeepable roads.[43] A jeep could perceptibly widen the radius of reach, especially to important villages like Nāko, Moorang, Kānam, Purbani, Rārang, Urni, Chagāon, Leo, Namgya, Thangi and Ribba which could be reached only by jeep. Dependence on government jeeps meant that bankers could not afford to come into confrontation with officials over recovery of loans. Only someone who has lived in Kinnaur can fully appreciate what an advantage it is to have motorized transport. It is impractical to talk of streamlining recoveries by bankers so long as they do not have jeeps and motor cycles. Their dependence on government officials for transport merely adds to other problems between them.

5.4.2 Bankers and Officials: Differing Perceptions

With some exceptions government officials feel that bankers do not make enough efforts to recover loan amounts but wait till they can just dump the problem onto the revenue authorities as A.L.Rs. Bankers feel that officials exert a lot of pressure on them to be liberal in giving loans but once the loans have been given out do not consider recovery as an essential part of the bargain. They treat recovery purely as a problem of bankers. Officials feel that bank employees receive much higher salaries than their counterparts in government departments for doing much less work. They feel that such highly paid bankers should exert themselves more to justify their salaries instead of just sitting in their branch offices while low paid revenue officials do the **"dirty"** work of enforcing recoveries of bank loans. At senior levels there was good rapport between the D.C., Kinnaur and the D.Ms/R.Ms of banks at Simla but this rapport did not percolate downwards. Even senior officers like S.D.Ms felt that bank managers were obstructive and retrograde in their approach. Bank managers thought that the S.D.Ms did not pay enough heed to their problems. There were clear **"we"** versus **"they"** feelings. This made for dissonance rather than consonance. Revenue authorities wanted banks to be primarily responsible for recoveries while bankers felt that revenue authorities had a monopoly on coercive processes for enforcing repayment so they should be more helpful. Tahsildārs reacted negatively almost every time bank loan overdues were declared as A.L.Rs and sent to them by the Collector for recovery. In almost every revenue officers' meeting, Tahsildārs felt that such cases should be sent back to the banks for further efforts on their own.[44] Bankers said in every meeting that they lacked the necessary authority to obtain recoveries and that more overdues should be declared as A.L.Rs to be passed on to Tahsildārs.

[42] Personal communication dated May 13, 1985 from Mr S.C. Girotra, erstwhile D.M., UCO Bank, Simla, Page 3, Section (F).

[43] Information obtained from the Office of the Superintending Engineer, II Tribal Circle, Kālpa in December 1985 in person.

[44] Personal experience. Such meetings were regularly held once a quarter during the tenure of the author as D.C., Kinnaur at all Tahsil headquarters by rotation. Mr Devi Chand, Tahsildār Pooh; Mr S. B. Réwāl, Tahsildār Kālpa; Mr Laiq Rām Mohil, Tahsildār Sangla and Mr Pratap Singh Kutlahria, Tahsildār Moorang - all extremely capable Revenue Officers with whom the author had the pleasure of serving - were unanimous on this point. They all felt that the banks were not doing enough to recover loan arrears.

Asked to point out which steps commrcial banks took on their own for recovery before passing the problem onto the Revenue Department, a senior banker listed out the following steps:[45]

(a) Branch Managers/Field Officers of the concerned branches meet the borrowers for recovering loans;
(b) Follow-up through correspondence is done vigorously;
(c) The guarantors are contacted to help in recovering the amount from the borrowers;
(d) Notices are sent to defaulters;
(e) After giving two notices at monthly intervals, if no response is received, the case is referred to the Collector/S.D.M. under the H.P. Agricultural Credit Operations and Miscellaneous Provisions (Banks) Act 1972;
(f) Thereafter, cases are prepared to attach the movable property of defaulters and sent to the Collector/S.D.M.;
(g) If recovery is not effected, then cases are prepared for attaching immovable property. Collection is then made by the S.D.Ms who then remit the amounts to the banks concerned; and
(h) Direct suits are also filed in civil courts in agricultural and non-agricultural accounts.

Detailed interviews with borrowers and extensive touring in villages of Kinnaur, however, revealed that steps (a) to (c) in the preceding list were honoured more in the breach. Notices were sent to defaulters who routinely ignored them. Bankers then moved to step (e). This meant that recovery became the responsibility of revenue authorities. Revenue Officers complained that after two or three routine postal notices the bankers could not be allowed to claim that they had exhausted their channels of recovery. This constant tug-of-war hampered recovery as neither side was fully motivated to perform its task. Bank managers then became cautious with mounting overdues as this affected their A.C.Rs and consequently their career prospects. They were held personally responsible for bad debts accumulated by their branches. Revenue Officers driven by similar careerist considerations sought to prevent bank loan recoveries from being declared as A.L.Rs. Recoveries were stalled, and the whole thrust of more liberal institutional lending to rural poor in Kinnaur impeded. This was further aggravated by a communication gap between bankers and local borrowers.

5.4.3 Banker-Borrower Communication Gap: Outsiders and Insiders

As Kinnaur became a district there was a large number of non-Kinnaura officials who moved in to man various offices. The phenomenon of **"insider"** and **"outsider"**, never really absent,[46] now became sharper. This mistrust of outsiders never took virulent forms as in some parts of India like Assam or in West Germany but has nevertheless grown in intensity. In view of this reciprocal feeling of unease between Kinnauras and Kochās it became important that bank staff consist of ever greater numbers of Kinnauras so that recoveries were not hampered by communication gaps between Kinnaura borrowers and non-Kinnaura bankers. A non-Kinnaura banker could not talk the borrowers' language; did not know their socio-economic obligations and could not liaise properly with them. He could not know who to contact so as to persuade the borrower to repay on time. On the contrary, a Kinnaura banker would know the borrowers personally in some cases; know important villagers to bring pressure for repayment on defaulters and communicate with borrowers in their own language and metaphor. Kinnauras posted in banks would be less likely to regard a posting in Kinnaur

[45] Letter from Mr S.C. Girotra, op. cit., May 13, 1985.

[46] Insider and outsider are only generic terms. The Kinnauras use the word **kochās** for non-Kinnauras. Kochā is an impolite word. Initially it was used during the time of Bushahr State for all persons originating from beyond the Nogli river, 5 kms from Rāmpur towards Simla. It has now been widened by Kinnauras to include any non-Kinnaura, even people from Rāmpur.

as a punishment and to try all means to get a posting outside as quickly as possible.

Banks have recognized the importance of narrowing this communication gap with borrowers. More and more Kinnauras are being sent by them to Kinnaur, both as officers and as lower staff. The staffing pattern for the bank with the largest number of branches in Kinnaur (UCO) showed that five out of seven branch managers were Kinnauras while only one head cashier out of seven was a Kinnaura. This heavy preponderance of Kinnauras as branch managers makes sense because the branch manager comes maximum in contact with government officials and locals. He functions as the lynchpin of the branch's banking operations. But lack of transport[47] curbed the effectiveness of local branch managers by curtailing their supervisory capacity and reducing them from field bankers to cabin bankers in Kinnaur, which geography has rendered essentially a field banking area. Other banks were also beginning to see the advantage of sending more Kinnauras as members of their staff to Kinnaur. However, merely sending locals was of only limited use if proper follow-up was not made on loans.

5.4.4 Lack of Proper Follow-up on Loans: Major Lacuna

Some bankers and government officials believe that since institutional credit is parcelled out in nicely pre-planned driblets into designated ***"productive purposes"***, and borrowers are aware of the coercive capability of the Revenue Department to recover loans, repayments should follow as a matter of course. Unfortunately, matters do not work out so neatly in Kinnaur, a completely rural area. The village moneylenders there constantly follow up their loans; being around on occasions of joy and of sorrow. They can choose an opportune moment for enforcing repayment. Bankers, on the contrary, remain alien figures ensconced in their managerial cabins. Their follow-up is cursory and incomplete. Loans are disbursed extensively under the I.R.D.P. so that the Grām Séwak (Village Level Worker, now called Village Development Officer or V.D.O.) or Block staff are thought by the bank to have primary responsibility for such follow-up. These officials say that they regularly visit I.R.D.P. beneficiaries but in practice few of them do regular follow-up. It is pointless giving an improved variety milch animal to a borrower without regularly following up whether there is a regular supply of fodder for the animal; whether the animal is being medically looked after; whether additional income is accruing to the borrower and if so to what end is it being utilized. Only with such follow-up can an opportune moment be chosen for demanding repayment. Bank staff keep mechanically sending demand notices without first ascertaining whether the borrowers are really in a position to repay or not. They do not pay enough attention to crop and weather conditions, both of which affect repaying capacity of Kinnaura borrowers to a significant extent. Proper follow-up would let bankers know which area was in a position to repay and which was not. By insisting routinely on repayment without proper follow-up, bankers arouse defaults from sullen borrowers. This problem is compounded by popular perceptions of institutional credit inputs as a veiled sort of subsidy, largesse being distributed by the **'sarkār'**.

5.4.5 Popular Perception of Institutional Credit: Repayment Unnecessary!

It has not been easy in Kinnaur to make it clear that loans have to be repaid and are not outright grants. Such a phalanx of subsidies and grants was available for S.Cs and S.Ts that people began to take it for granted that the 'sarkār' gave only grants. A historical overview[48] revealed that commercial banking was absent in Bushahr. The government had functioned as direct lender during the period of British-appointed managers in Bushahr State but only for larger traders carrying on trade with Tibet. People became used to grants from the government

[47] No bank manager in Kinnaur had a vehicle for touring the area at the beginning of 1986.

[48] Please see Chapter II - A of this work.

in the post-1948 phase when relief was distributed in times of distress caused by natural calamities. Bushahr had never developed an institutional credit network so that Kinnauras could get used to its ways and be aware that such loans had to be repaid just as promptly as the loans taken from moneylenders. The situation was further aggravated when Kinnaur was upgraded to a district. After the conflict of 1962 subsidies were pumped into the area indiscriminately.

In one specific case, typical of the early-1960s in Kinnaur, targets were set for giving housing loans. Since people were not keen to take these loans officials told reluctant borrowers that the loans were in fact grants which did not have to be repaid. This fact stood corroborated by the district office staff and by villagers. 31 cases received loans. They were told that the problem of repayment would not arise. Nothing happened till 1969-70 when notices were received by surprised borrowers asking them to repay their loan amounts. They replied that the money had been given as grants and not loans. They were informed that there was no question of grants and that penal interest was going to be levied @ 8% per annum. By 1978, accumulated interest payments had become seven to eight times the principal amounts in 27 out of 31 cases. Audit parties demanded recovery of these loans every year. The matter hung fire till 1980 when the D.C. recommended to the government that these loans should be written off since the villagers had been misled by the official machinery. The government, however, saw things otherwise and did not accept the D.C.'s recommendation. The matter still lay unresolved in 1985. Interest payments were accumulating and the borrowers were going to lose land and property for original loan amounts of Rs 500 to Rs 700 which they had never wanted in the first place.

Since government were treated as synonymous with subsidies, nationalization of banks made some Kinnauras feel that banks too had now become government departments and would hand out doles. In their anxiety to fulfil I.R.D.P. targets officials sometimes tended to underplay the recovery aspect of institutional credit. It was not adequately explained how the programme could not go on if recoveries got choked. As Dr Michael Lipton points out, the word ***"used for 'loan from the government' (tagai, taccavi) means 'assistance, grant', and the confusion of concepts corresponds to major and recurring defaults".***[49] In addition, popular perception has rightly observed that richer borrowers manage to evade repayment through political influence; personal relations with bankers/officials and collusion with lower staff. Contrary to the bankers' utterances in meetings, poor borrowers were not higher credit risks than richer borrowers. Being poor, they were easier to coerce; less likely to exert political pressure; more likely to be cowed into repaying loans and more liable to be made the first targets of special drives/campaigns to enforce recovery. In villages Chaura, Roghi, Pooh and Sangla field surveys carried out for the present research showed that out of 300 sample households, 94 had taken institutional loans. Of these 94, 57 were defaulters who had fallen behind on repayments. The most defaulters (33) did not belong to the poorest class, meaning the landless and those with land up to 2.5 bighās but to the category holding between 15 and 25 bighās of land. Only 14 defaulters belonged to the poorest groups while 10 belonged to the group owning more than 25 bighās of land. Of these 10, at least 7 admitted after much prodding that they did not much fear recovery proceedings because they could get these stalled in cahoots with lower officials. Here again, institutional finance was refinancing further lending operations in five cases by richer defaulters. The institutional credit network had been reduced to a refinancing institution. It has been pointed out that institutional loans become a *"random handout, not mainly to the poor, but to some of those strong enough to escape repayment...Where some default, moreover, others lose the incentive to repay..it is big farmers whose default/loan ratio is the highest. Subsidized institutional credit, overwhelmingly reaching big farmers of whom many default is extremely regressive".*[50] In

[49] Lipton, Michael, 1976, Part 4, p. 548.

[50] Ibid.

Kinnaur, it is not an integral part of popular perception even now that loans have to be repaid. The subsidy culture distorts proper perception of loans. This problem is compounded by political interference in bank loans.

5.4.6 Interference in Recovery of Bank Loans: Vote Catching!

Right from the level of the village political hack to the legislator from Kinnaur, interference in the form of pressure on banks to go slow on recoveries has become frequent. In some cases, this pressure at the higher levels is not exerted directly but indirectly through concerned government officials. The latter comply either to further their careerist aims by seeking to please politicians or to cool down public fears about repayments that make targeted beneficiaries unwilling to accept loans, thereby endangering official achievements. Pressure is also exerted on bank staff to give loans to ineligible borrowers who are conscious of their clout and ready to default. "Outsiders" may be willing to oblige politicians to get transferred out of Kinnaur while "insiders" may not be objective since they have a large number of local relatives and acquaintances. Finally, it all depends on the individuals concerned but pressure to slow down recovery has become more and more frequent. It hinders recovery and fosters default.

The problem is acute in the cooperative sector. Of the five non-official members of KINFED in 1981, three were defaulters of cooperative loans. A list of chronic defaulters prepared for the KINFED's Board of Directors at the D.C.'s insistence revealed 46 names. 19 of them were former/sitting members of boards/governing bodies of cooperative societies. Obviously, hardly any efforts had been made to recover loans from them. The hedge was eating the crop! Prominent defaulters were the rule rather than the exception in the cooperative sector in Kinnaur, setting a bad example for other borrowers. The result has been that crop loans were not being given any more in 1985.

The D.C. got criminal cases registered against three prominent defaulters who were panchāyat pradhāns in 1981. This created a political storm. Recoveries did, however, pick up as a consequence.[51] People found it hard to believe that cooperative loans could actually be made into something other than financial empires controlled by factions led by prominent persons, many of whom were themselves major moneylenders. They merrily used cooperative loans given to proxies as means of refinancing their moneylending or marketing operations. Rules were blatantly ignored. Defaulters were repeatedly given loans and false No-Dues Certificates by Secretaries of cooperatives under interference from influential persons, themselves defaulters and in control of the cooperative structure. This spilled over into the sector of commercial banks also, causing problems there as well.

5.4.7 Liaison between Banks and Cooperatives: Gaping Holes!

In a sparsely populated area like Kinnaur where commercial banks and cooperative societies were both concentrating on virtually the same target groups under government steered programmes, it was important to ensure good liaison between them so that chronic defaulters could not further choke up the institutional credit outlets by going from commercial banks to cooperatives or vice versa. Unfortunately, this practice has been all too frequent in reality. On paper, institutional lenders require No-Dues Certificates (henceforth referred to as N.D.Cs) from other institutional lenders before giving loans but sometimes under pressure from officials bent upon fulfilling their targets this was honoured more in the breach.

Asked to point out what safeguards were there to check if a loan applicant was already a defaulter or not, the manager of the PNB at Rekong Peo listed out the following steps:

[51] Personal experience.

(a) No-Dues Certificates from cooperative societies, banks;
(b) Local Enquiry.[52]

Personal experience and enquiries suggest that the only part of this package that worked in practice was that pertaining to N.D.Cs from other commercial banks. Bankers took care to warn their fellow bankers about chronic defaulters. Cooperatives had no such scruples. Even chronic defaulters were able to obtain N.D.Cs from cooperative societies. Their Secretaries bowed before pressure from the Chairman or other members of the governing body. 14 such cases were observed in village Sapni alone. Accustomed to getting away with defaults on cooperative loans, such chronic defaulter-borrowers carried their habit over to commercial banks as well. Local enquiries made by banks about financial bona fides of prospective borrowers were almost non-existent. Where such enquiry did take place, it was cursory and useless, with the Field Officer briefly visiting the village. The PNB, for example, had only one Field Officer, stationed at Rekong Peo, for the whole of Kinnaur, without a jeep or motor cycle. The UCO Bank had one Field Officer stationed at Sangla to look after Sangla, Aren Jhula, Spillo and Yangthang branches. It had a second Field Officer at Tāpri to look after its branches at Tāpri, Katgāon and Nāthpa Jhula.[53] These Field Officers were supposed to visit UCO Bank branches *"at least once in every month with a stay of one week in each branch, depending upon the quantum of work in the branch"*.[54] Needless to say, the Field Officers spent most of their time in their bank branches' locations and not in other villages making local enquiries. In villages Namgya, Sunnam, Gyabong, Moorang and Thangi, all very important villages, borrowers had never seen a Field Officer from any bank. All these villages could be reached with a jeep or motor cycle. Whatever contact the villagers had had with bank officials had been in bank branches and not in their own villages. Till stringent measures are taken to ensure that no false N.D.Cs are issued by Secretaries or Chairmen of cooperative societies, overdues will go on mounting. This problem is further aggravated by untimely release of loans.

5.4.8 Untimely Release of Loans: Ignorance is not Bliss!

It is not only important to know when to demand recovery but also when to release the loan so that the recipient can make optimum use of the benefit to be in a better position to repay. This implies at least a basic knowledge on the part of bankers of cropping patterns, agro-climatic conditions, marketing operations and general economic activities of Kinnaur. It was possible to find bank managers there who had no clear idea of even the difference between the Rabi and the Kharif crops.[55] They had no idea that in many areas of Kālpa and Pooh Sub-Divisions two crops were being obtained in a single cropping season (Kharif - May to November, mostly) by reaping the first crop around July/August followed by immediate sowing of the next crop, to be reaped in October. In such cases if loans were delayed it meant delayed sowing if seeds had to be purchased with such loans. Delayed sowing meant poor germination in the extremely short crop-maturity period. Poor germination meant low yield and consequently lower income meaning little or no repayment of loans and hence poor recovery!

[52] Personal Communication No. Nil dated Nil from Mr Negi, Manager, PNB, Rekong Peo, to the author. Handed over in person in Peo on December 15, 1985.

[53] Personal Communication from Mr S.C. Girotra dated May 13, 1985, op. cit.

[54] Ibid.

[55] Personal observation. Bank managers were not the only ones so ill-informed! Many government officers could not tell the difference either!

As a banker himself points out, bank branches in rural areas like Kinnaur have *"more or less untrained staff in rural development and agricultural finance. Urbanites appointed in rural branches find it difficult to cope up with the environment prevailing in the development work and are always looking for an opportunity to get themselves transferred to an urban area having better facilities".*[56] Little effort was made by bank staff of urban origin to familiarize itself with prevalent conditions so as to be acutely conscious of the need for quick loan sanctions and releases at the appropriate time. Cases were found in villages Hāngo and Chuling in which seven persons had applied for crop loans for potato production since potatoes grow well in both these villages. The nearest bank branch being then at Pooh (now there is one available at Yangthang which is about 20-25 kms away on foot), 18 kms away over the 12,000 feet high Hangrang Pass, the loanees had to keep shuttling back and forth over this hard track. By the time the bank's procedural formalities had been gone through, it was already October and the time for sowing of potato seeds was well past. However, the bank was anxious to claim credit for having financed cases in such remote villages and released the loans anyway. It was unrealistic to hope for proper recoveries in such cases because delay by bank officials in releasing loans had caused the borrowers' missing the proper sowing time for their principal cash crop. Similarly, loans were released in December in Nichār in a severe winter (1981) for purchasing jersey cows. Such cows were not available in Kinnaur for sale so the Purchase Committee proceeded to buy them from areas in Haryana as far away as Karnāl, areas much warmer than Kinnaur. Of the eleven cows that were brought to Kinnaur, four died within 45 days because they could not get used to such cold weather. The same transaction may have yielded better results had the loans been released in June, July or August. Fixation of repayment instalments was also a problem.

5.4.9 Fixation of Instalment Periods: Haste Makes Waste!

Having bogged poor borrowers down in procedural merry-go-rounds and delayed timely release of their loan amounts, bankers compounded the problem by exhibiting an unnecessary zeal in beginning repayment instalments as early as possible. This eagerness to obtain loan repayment as quickly as possible disregards whether income generation has meanwhile been sufficient to support such repayment. Loan instalments payable in durations shorter than recommended periods cause economic hardship to borrowers who default. If banks give a medium-term loan over three years, their staff should not manifest undue zeal by trying to enforce repayment in two years or even less time. In their hurry to recover loaned money by insisting on payment earlier than promised, bankers only contribute to a piling up of defaults. To this process is linked also the resistance of bankers to reschedule recovery instalments in times of natural calamities. Borrowers do not then have a disposable surplus and cannot repay their loans as per schedule. Haste in recovery only aggravates the problem. Where the first instalment of repayment fell due after about a month or so, or even a few days after when the benefit of the asset acquired through the loan had hardly begun accruing, it was unrealistic to expect prompt recovery.

A senior banker taking cognizance of this situation opines that it was desirable for bankers to be realistic while fixing instalment periods and not show too much eagerness to get their money back as quickly as possible.[57] *"Loan instalments payable in shorter duration than the recommended period put the borrower in hardship and thus he defaults. For instance, where a bank has fixed a repayment period of say, 9 years and the banker tries to recover in say, 5 years, this has led to difficulty in recovering the money. In case of natural calamities sometimes bankers do not rephase the loan or renurse the account resulting in hardships to the farmers who then avoid paying instalment due to non-surplus with them".*[58]

[56] Singh, Ajit, 1985, p. 370.

[57] Ibid, p. 374.

People in Kinnaur mostly generated such surplus as met their essential limited needs but was not ample, except for a few major traders. They had no experience of having contact with institutional lenders for loans but were dependent on village moneylenders, headed by the village deity. The latter fixed repayment periods well in advance, keeping in view local conditions. Instalments were always repaid on time as a consequence. The devta was flexible in time of natural calamities and did not attempt to recover his short-term loans before term. Banks can learn from the functioning of the devtas as moneylenders. This is discussed at length in Chapter VII.

Particularly in case of small and marginal farmers early fixation of repayment instalments causes acute financial hardship. In cases where the first instalment falls due after about a month or even after a few days after acquisition of the asset which has hardly had time to yield any returns, it is unrealistic to expect timely repayments. Bankers have the option in such cases of charging interest only for the gap period whereas the regular instalments could be deferred to the succeeding harvest when the repaying capacity of the borrower would be higher. It might in some cases be appropriate to defer the entire first instalment even to the next ensuing harvesting season by which time the acquired asset would have had time to yield at least some preliminary returns. It seems self-evident that in case of crop loans, instalments should be fixed only after the crop has been harvested. Such an obvious reality has not always been followed in practice by bankers in Kinnaur. Borrowers in villages like Roghi, Kangos, Meeru and Chagāoṅ showed repayment notices received 140 to 150 days before harvest. Instalment periods had been fixed for repayment in disregard of harvest times. No care had been taken to follow this elementary common sense principle. Apart from lack of local knowledge, such ignorance reflected a complete lack of research and analysis by banks to try and determine why recoveries were so slow.

5.4.10 Research and Analysis about Recovery: Remarkable Absence

While a lot of effort has gone into producing reams of reports and proceedings of meetings, no bank has made serious effort to establish a research wing to undertake comprehensive studies to find out exactly why recovery performance was not up to the mark in Kinnaur. Such an important aspect of the institutional credit infrastructure as recovery has not received its due share of research. This failure has meant that not enough literature was available for giving proper orientation courses/training to bankers being sent to Kinnaur. They could not be properly familiarized with detailed analyses about why recoveries lagged behind targets; what could be done to improve performance and how popular perceptions could be altered to ensure better receptivity to the importance of timely repayment. Without such a change in attitudes and voluntary involvement of borrowers in timely repayment, the entire recovery edifice would continue to be based on coercion by the Revenue Department as its backbone. Coercion or threat of coercion can never be good motivating agents fostering smoothly running recovery operations. Unless borrowers in Kinnaur can be made to see benefits for themselves in timely repayment, difficulties will continue.

This is not to suggest that firmness and coercion should not form part of recovery processes. Only, that coercion by itself cannot be as effective as when it is accompanied by a serious effort to comprehensively mould public attitudes in such a way as to reduce the necessity of using coercion. Laxity in applying coercive processes, especially against richer defaulters, creates a snowballing effect in defaults. For a healthy functioning of the institutional credit system, *"a tougher policy on defaults is a key...defaults must be collected using the full process of the law"*.[59] Since banks tend to prefer secured loans to unsecured ones, expansion of institutional credit into pre-specified channels has an effect on risk as a

[58] Ibid, p. 370.

[59] Lipton, Michael, 1976, p. 548.

determinant of interest rates in Kinnaur. Informal moneylenders cope with increased risk determinant by increasing interest rates, for a start. Banks are not allowed this leeway and seek to discourage high risk borrowers by increasing their transaction costs, as discussed.[60] Increased recovery thus becomes necessary to motivate institutional lenders away from resorting to such dilatory practices negating official goals.

5.5 SECURED LOANS: WIDELY PREFERRED

Normally, the premium for risk is inversely proportional to the adequacy of collateral on the loan. This premium is based on the estimated value of the collateral or security offered, relative to loan size. If institutional or other credit augments the borrowers' asset value relative to loan amount, it enables them to offer better security value. This motivates the lender to reduce his premium for risk progressively. His risk is reduced as the value of the security offered first approaches and then exceeds the value of the loan. Two major factors influence risk determination of secured loans:[61]

(a) Marketability of collateral; and
(b) Movements in the market value of the collateral

5.5.1 Marketability of Collateral: Quite Important

Collateral offered in Kinnaur on loan amounts generally consists of:

(a) Fixed assets such as land, capital equipment and gold or other ornaments; and
(b) Current assets such as crops under production or storage.

Prospective borrowers face difficulties regarding marketability of their fixed assets, as do institutional lenders. It is not always easy to establish title to land, particularly in the case of erstwhile forest lands belonging to the Rājā and his Jāgirdārs which were brought under the plough over the years. Land by itself thus may not be a foolproof security on loans. Even where titles could be clearly established there was no guarantee that somebody would bid for land offered for sale upon foreclosure. The devta might frown upon any potential buyer from thus harming his worshipper (the defaulter) in case the buyer belonged to a different village in Kinnaur or outside with its own deity. Non-tribals were in any case forbidden[62] to purchase land in Kinnaur. Only tribals could bid at such auctions. This absence of "*clearly defined set of legal rights to assets offered as collateral, and the existence of...social pressures raises the risk of lending against security*".[63]

5.5.2 Movements in the Market Value of Collateral

Kinnaura farmers under debt sometimes allow the value of collateral under their care to decline. This could happen where loans had been obtained against the security of crops in store. In village Ribba, of seven persons who had obtained loans for horticultural purposes, four had allowed collateral in the form of stored crop and fruit produce to deteriorate for want

[60] Please see Sections 4.10.1.1.3 and 4.11.1, Chapter IV of this work.

[61] Bottomley, Anthony: The Premium for Risk as a Determinant of Interest Rates in Underdeveloped Rural Areas, Part I, Pp 639-641, in: The Quarterly Journal of Economics, Vol. LXXVII, 1963, Pp 637-647.

[62] Under the provisions of the H.P. Transfer Of Land (Regulation) Act 1968.

[63] Bottomley, Anthony, op. cit., 1963, Part I: Secured Loans, p. 639.

of proper storage facilities. Metallic bins had not become very popular as items of storage even till 1985. Crop and fruit produce was found stored in wooden chambers. Its value could deteriorate by as much as 25% in some cases. Collateral of this kind was *"of steadily declining worth as a means of securing the lender against the possibility of failure to repay"*.[64] Defaults were perceptibly higher when the prices of produce fell. For example, in 1980 when neoza prices fell in the open market, defaults were higher, particularly in neoza producing villages like Roghi, Kothi, Brélingi and Telingi. "Not only will security in growing crops decline in value at such a time, but the desire and the ability of otherwise solvent farmers to bid for assets offered for sale on foreclosure will be much reduced. Furthermore, the sharpness of this tendency will always be correlative with what might be called the narrowness of the market. If the sale of crops or land faces the normally inelastic demand of a market which is narrowly limited in terms of area as well as purchasing power...then relatively small fluctuations in supply will drastically alter the value of either current or fixed asset collateral when it comes to sale".[65]

Mere coercion can thus not be totally effective. Clear determination of titles to land; modification of social attitudes; flexibility in laws pertaining to alienation of security; encouragement of farmers to preserve fixed assets and crops under production or storage, as well as broadening of markets for sale of produce should be integral parts of a wholistic package designed to reduce the premium for risk on loans against security. Well stored produce, accompanied by proper grading, can open access to a wider, presumably stabler national or regional market.

Efforts are underway in Kinnaur by the Agriculture, Horticulture and R.I.D. Departments to foster diversification of production. Production of saffron and cummin seed in Sangla area and Shong; of cauliflower seed in Kālpa; of peas in Bārang, Ribba, Sangla and Mébar; and of hops in Kālpa Sub-Division are all attempts at accelerating this trend. If diversification takes place, poor harvests or unfavourable market conditions would not afflict all crops in the same way at the same point of time. It is extremely unlikely that markets for potato, cummin seed, saffron, fruit and hops would crash at the same time. Such diversification, apart from other benefits such as a higher income, would serve as a stabilizing factor for farmers willing to risk moving into such new crops; thereby increasing their asset value and consequently their credit rating.

However, lest the diversification idea be treated as a major panacea ensuring improved credit ratings, it may be cautioned that *"innovation of any kind will normally involve an initial increase in the premium for risk, and this certainly applies to the cultivation of new crops. Until a new crop has proven its practicability the risk on its introduction, and consequently the interest on loans for its finance, will tend to be above average, and this situation constitutes a significant obstacle to growth. Perhaps, therefore, some convincing governmental demonstration of the efficacy of growing certain new crops might ultimately be effective in bringing down the rural interest rate"*.[66] Efforts in this direction are being made through the H.P. Agriculture University's demonstration-cum-research stations at Kālpa, Sangla, Shārbo, Gyabong and Leo. This aspect emphasizes the role of the government in almost all aspects of economic life in Kinnaur. This realization has been shimmering in the background during the discussion on commercial banks and cooperative credit in Kinnaur. We can now examine the role of the Government in the institutional credit set-up there.

[64] Ibid, (b) Movements in the market value of collateral, p. 640.

[65] Ibid.

[66] Ibid, p. 641.

CHAPTER VI

THE ROLE OF THE GOVERNMENT IN THE SANCTIONING OF CREDIT

The preceding discussion about cooperative credit, commercial bank credit and recovery of institutional credit has already hinted at the importance of the government in the entire framework of institutional credit. The 'sarkār' may not be directly involved in everyday loan transactions made by bank managers and cooperative societies but its long shadow falls all across the credit structure. It even extends its role into the informal sector through legislative action to regulate the functioning of moneylenders. Through its capacity to alter the very coordinates within which all the actors of the credit network have to operate, government have a unique position as arbiters of the institutional credit system. They operate through a web of incentives and dissuasive practices; subsidies and governing bodies/committees. Nothing seems to move in the sector of institutional finance without the government being somehow involved in it, directly or indirectly. If institutional credit flows more easily towards I.R.D. Programmes or towards certain specified social groups, it is only because government have laid down that these groups are to be given priority. If a bank manager refuses to sanction loans where government in the form of the D.C. and his subordinates are of a contrary opinion, the latter can bring almost unbearable pressure to **'persuade'** the manager to revise his decision. If people are not keen to take loans for adopting certain practices deemed desirable, like adoption of high yielding varieties of crops, modern cultivation practices and marketing through cooperative bodies, government can aid this process by liberal doses of subsidies as sweeteners. When banks did not conform to the guidelines laid down by the government in the period before 1969, the latter altered the rules of the entire ball game by nationalising 14 major banks at one stroke. It was a striking example of just how government can change the framework of operation of the credit structure.

This had not always been the case in Kinnaur, as already pointed out.[1] In the area of government intervention Bushahr had been remarkably laissez faire. Government over centuries had meant the person of the distant Rājā of Bushahr and his handful of visiting functionaries while Kinnauras had lived pretty much on their own. Captain C.P. Kennedy felt that they possessed "*a greater freedom than in any other district in these hills*".[2] Another attestation of the fact that government in Kinnaur were not very central to life there comes from Dr J.G. Gerard, brother of the famous Capt. Alexander Gerard. In his words, "*Koonawur, in spite of the defects of the Bussahir government and its remoteness from the capital, ranks above every other State in point of intelligence, active industry and good feeling*".[3] This was the state of affairs when an institutional credit infrastructure was totally absent. The creation and expansion of such a network since 1952 has been accompanied by an ever increasing dependence on the government for finding solutions to all problems, not just those of credit supply. Non-Kinnaura officials complain in private that Kinnauras lack enterprise and are not ready to strain themselves to make best use of funds that have liberally come their way since 1962, thanks to changed perceptions of their strategic geographical location. To a certain extent, this change from an enterprising lot to dependence on official doles has been nourished by the expanding network of subsidies doled out by the government. The situation had become such that non-official members of the Project Advisory Committee (henceforth

[1] Please see Chapter II of this work.

[2] Kennedy, Capt. C.P.: Report On The Protected Hill States, Para 43, p. 278, in: Chapter VIII: Reports on Lapsed and Reserved Territory in the Protected Sikh and Hill States and on the latter generally - 1824, in: Punjab Government Records, Vol. I: Delhi Residency and Agency 1807-1857, Lahore: Punjab Government Press, 1911, Pp 229-324.

[3] Report by Dr J.G. Gerard on Education In The Hills, Para 11, p. 315, Ibid.

referred to as the P.A.C.) repeatedly demanded that the rate of subsidy for government sponsored programmes in Kinnaur should be raised from the existing 50% to a whopping 75%.[4] Detailed personal discussions with them revealed that they did not find this demand unreasonable at all. Expansion of the institutional credit agencies and available direct government finance had accustomed them to the fact that government could always be relied upon to fork out more and more funds, a far cry indeed from the days of Bushahr State when it was only in the early 20th century under the prodding of British-appointed managers that government had begun thinking about providing institutional finance at all.

Government were, however, the first institutional lender in Kinnaur when traders were given the facility of direct loans from the Treasury towards the beginning of this century. To borrow a phrase from the planning process in India pertaining to the creation of a public sector, it can be said without exaggeration that government are in a position of **"commanding heights"** in the institutional credit network. The average Kinnaura borrower treats banks, cooperative societies and direct government loans as parts of one comprehensive **'sarkāri'** arrangement and not as different institutional channels of credit input. There exists no perception of the cooperatives' being autonomous institutions. In the public mind everything belongs to the government which alone counts. Defaulters do not sometimes go to bankers for discussing rescheduling of their loan repayment instalments but come direct to government offices for this purpose. It was quite common to hear Kinnauras pleading that bankers could not refuse a **'huqam'** (order) from the D.C. who should directly order the bankers to help the defaulters. Since government are quite an important actor in institutional finance, it is relevant to examine the schemes and laws through which their presence is felt in Kinnaur. Subsidies form a major prop of this presence.

6.1 SUBSIDIES: NOT JUST THE E.E.C., KINNAUR AS WELL!

The basic objective of allowing 50% subsidy to match loan amounts to poor borrowers in Kinnaur was not just to ensure an increase in their income but also to prevent a further erosion of their already meagre living standards. It was to prevent the so-called ***"Matthew Effect"*** as defined by Robert K. Merton,[5] *"For whoever hath, to him shall be given, and he shall have more abundance; but whosoever hath not, from him shall be taken away even that he hath (St. Matthew, 13:12)".*[6] Robert W. Jackman's application of this term to the widening gap between richer and poorer countries[7] can be extended to the widening gap between the rich and the poor within a developing country like India and even to a region like Kinnaur. Richer Kinnauras have achieved higher rates of economic growth than poorer Harijans. The **"Matthew Effect"** in the institutional credit network means that richer Kinnaura pradhāns and other persons of influence have developed large orchards, set up sawmills and constructed shops to rent out while the poor have sometimes lost what little they had in coercive proceedings to effect recovery. This disparity in development rate is a basic fact of life in Kinnaur. Just as Jackman calls the widening gap between the rich and the poor "commonly accepted",[8] inequality of social status and economic opportunity is a fact of life in Kinnaur

[4] Personal experience as Chairman of the Project Advisory Committee for three years between 1980 and 1983.

[5] Merton, Robert K.: The Matthew Effect In Science, in: Science, Vol. 59, January 1968, Pp 56-63.

[6] Ibid.

[7] Jackman, Robert W.: Dependence on Foreign Investment and Economic Growth in the Third World, in: World Politics, Vol. XXXIV, No. 2, Jan. 1982, Pp 175-196.

[8] Ibid, p. 175.

that has come to be accepted without too much agony. Religion, fatalism, belief in destiny and tradition contribute to such acceptance. Just as inequality between nations has been sought to be explained on the basis of a core (industrialized countries) and a periphery,[9] a core of richer families dominates a periphery of economically depressed families in Kinnaur.

In some writings, development has meant capitalist development. This form of development, in the periphery as well as the core, produces as it evolves, in a cyclical way, wealth and poverty, accumulation and shortage of capital, employment for some and unemployment for others. The notion of such development did not mean the achievement of a more egalitarian or just society. These were not consequences expected of capitalist development, especially in peripheral economies.[10] In Kinnaur, the notion of development in the mind of government planners was not in such ideological terms. They generally understood it to mean a more egalitarian distribution of wealth that would enable the poorest of the poor to improve their purchasing power to satisfy at least their basic needs. These basic needs stood pre-determined for them from outside, mainly under the I.R.D.P. While providing credit facilities, government planners did not worry about whether a capitalist development model was being introduced with its in-built inequalities, thereby perpetuating the underdevelopment of the "periphery" (mostly Harijans). Subsidies were built into the credit network to try and prevent the poor from being sidelined. Also, subsidies are a powerful tool of patronage by which government seek to keep their hands on the steering wheel of credit inputs. That subsidies can be misused has not changed the fact that they have become an integral part of the credit system in Kinnaur. They are handed out by different departments under different schemes.

Subsidies in Kinnaur can broadly be grouped under three categories:

(a) Departmental subsidies;
(b) Subsidized 'fair prices'; and
(c) Loans sponsored by the government at rates of interest below the 'market rate'.

While a per capita estimate can be attempted for (a) and (c), it is not possible to have such an estimate for (b) because funds under this category are released in a consolidated block by departmental heads in Simla for the entire State. It was not possible to get district-wise break-ups for making such calculation. For (c) also, such an estimate is quite approximate because rates of interest of the private sector are not very much higher than those of institutional loans, as will be discussed in Chapter VII, so that it is difficult to say that loans sponsored by the government are at rates of interest below the "market rate". Also, only nominal rates of interest are considered while talking of institutional loans and the costs of transaction are left out. If we include these costs, the real rates of interest for government loans may even work out to be sometimes higher than those for informal loans.[11] Considering that nominal rates of interest for loans under the D.R.I. scheme and the I.R.D.P. are @ 4% and 10% respectively, for estimating the per capita subsidy given in Kinnaur under head (c), we just take the amounts disbursed under these schemes (without bothering about transaction costs and real rates of interest) and divide them by the total population of Kinnaur according to the 1981 Census (= 59,547 persons) to get a rough per capita estimate. Data about these two schemes is sketchily available till 1985 when it began to be compiled in a systematized form. According to the quarterly banking statistics report for Kinnaur for 1983, Rs 3,003,000 had been advanced as I.R.D.P. loans and Rs 2,544,000 as D.R.I. loans in Kinnaur. The two figures were not mutually exclusive because many (if not most) of the I.R.D.P. beneficiaries

[9] Ibid.

[10] Ibid, p. 181.

[11] Please see Table 4.21, Chapter IV of this work.

were covered under the D.R.I. scheme. It is thus better to take the I.R.D.P. figure as more representative. With 59,547 as the population base, we get a per capita figure of **Rs 50.43** for I.R.D.P. concessional rate of interest loans. A similar figure for the D.R.I. scheme is Rs 42.72 only. For the period from January 1983 till September 1985, Rs 4,109,000 had been given as I.R.D.P. loans for 1,730 beneficiaries. This gives a per capita figure of Rs 2,375.15 per beneficiary and Rs 69 for the whole population for nearly three years. If we divide it by three we get a per capita per annum figure of Rs 23 for the entire populace and of Rs 791.72 for the beneficiaries. Considering only 1985, figures were available from January 1 to June 30 - Rs 1,344,000 for 803 accounts (beneficiaries) while funds advanced under D.R.I. scheme were Rs 3,647,000. Here we see that unlike the case for 1983, D.R.I. advances are higher than I.R.D.P. advances. Banks had given loans outside I.R.D.P. under the D.R.I. scheme. For 1985 we thus get per capita figures equalling Rs 61.25 D.R.I. advance for the total population and Rs 22.57 for all schemes. Per beneficiary figure comes out to Rs 1,673.72 for 803 account holders.

Coordination of the distribution of government subsidies is supposed to be done at joint decision-making forums like the D.R.D.A., the P.A.C.. and the D.C.C.C.[12] which decide about institutional loans. Since subsidies are generally matching amounts, these are considered automatically regulated once it has been decided how many beneficiaries are to be covered under each scheme. The problem is that in practice there is no close coordination of subsidies being disbursed. There is no single agency exclusively responsible for their distribution. Each department's district head and his/her staff disburse subsidies. They are supposed to keep the D.C. and the B.D.O. informed of the amounts distributed by them. Such information is delayed many times or is not accurate. Government departments do not by themselves make significant efforts to liaise with each other to ensure that applicants do not get subsidies from more than one source. They are generally anxious to fulfil targets and do not always insist on production of No Dues Certificates (N.D.Cs) from banks, cooperatives or other departments nor do they make enquiries to verify whether the applicant has already availed of subsidies from other departments. Intelligent people manage to get subsidies from more than one source by not divulging that they have already obtained subsidies. Bank ledgers are supposed to indicate whether an applicant has already received subsidy help or not but this can be avoided by sending another family member to get the new subsidy. The P.O., I.T.D.P., is supposed to keep track of money being spent under the tribal sub-plan but he functions purely as a compiler of information sent by departments. He has no authority over the departments and must always rely on the D.C. to pull his chestnuts out of the fire if some department either does not send information on time or sends wrong data. There are endless rounds of meetings but actual control of subsidies on the ground leaves much to be desired. Unscrupulous elements can and do profit from the diversity of the palette of subsidies being proffered by the government. Richer people manage to get subsidies through poor proxies beholden to them for favours. Enquiries by banks and cooperatives are still sketchy. The whole grid of subsidies leaks profusely.

6.1.1 I.R.D.P. Subsidies: A Whole Plethora

The I.R.D.P., being the main programme of development in Kinnaur, has to be considered first. Under different schemes of this programme,[13] matching subsidy to the tune of 50% was allowed, subject to a ceiling of Rs 5,000 total subsidy. The programme was first launched in 1978-79 in Nichār Block only.[14] It was extended to the remaining two Blocks of the District

[12] Please see Sections 6.3.1 to 6.3.3 of this Chapter.

[13] Please see Section 4.3.1, Chapter IV of this work.

[14] Demi-Official (D.O.) Letter No. M-11012/2/78-IRD dated October 7, 1978 from the Additional Secretary, Ministry of Agriculture and Irrigation, Department of Rural Development, Government of India, New Delhi. File No. IRDP - 1/78, Vol. I, D.C.'s Office, Kālpa, p. 2.

(Kālpa and Pooh) from October 2, 1980. All Scheduled Caste and Scheduled Tribe families with an income not exceeding Rs 3,500 per annum are eligible for benefits under the I.R.D.P. Benefits are to be provided according to choice in the primary sector (agriculture and allied activities), the secondary sector (industries and mining) and the tertiary sector (small vocations and mining). 600 poorest families were to be benefited every year in each Block, of which at least 200 families were to be given benefits in the secondary and tertiary sectors. Thus, at least 33.33% of the families were to be covered in the non-primary sectors.

Table 6.1 gives data about the Block-wise position in Kinnaur about families identified

Table 6.1: Coverage of Families under the I.R.D.P. in Kinnaur

sn	*Block*	*NFI*	*nfd*	*IRD*	*FB*	*BL*
01	Kālpa	1,682	009	1,673	1,975	000
02	Nichār	2,347	287	2,060	2,702	000
03	Pooh	1,830	018	1,812	1,445	367

Code: **Block = Development Block,**
NFI = number of families identified, nfd = number of families deleted by the Grām Sabha (Village Assembly), IRD = balance of families to be covered under the I.R.D. Programme, FB = families benefited up to 1985-86, BL = balance left to be given benefits.
(Source: Special Note entitled "Note on the Integrated Rural Development Programme in respect of Kinnaur District from the Date of Inception", Prepared for the author by Mr Lāl Singh Verma, I.R.D.P. Assistant, D.C.'s Office, Kālpa on December 7, 1985 from the files of the I.R.D. Branch)

and families provided benefits under the I.R.D.P. as on November 30, 1985. According to these official figures, all the families identified had been covered in Nichār and Kālpa Blocks. Only in Pooh Block were 367 families left still to be provided benefits under the programme. In official calculations a family was reckoned to have crossed the poverty line (defined at Rs 750 per capita per annum or Rs 3,500 per family per annum) once it had been provided a benefit under the I.R.D.P. By such ad hoc reckoning no identified families in Nichār and Kālpa Blocks remained below the poverty line, a most commendable result, if really true in the field!

Table 6.2 gives the yearwise break-up of families benefited under the programme and financial outlays involved. In all cases we see that loan amounts exceeded the subsidy amounts every year except for 1985-86 but only by very small amounts. The table shows that commercial banks did not give out much more extra credit over and above the amounts to match subsidies provided by the government. Borrowers stayed by and large within the standard pattern of 50% loan and 50% subsidy. More than Rs 10 million had been doled out as subsidies under the I.R.D.P. till November 30, 1985. Maximum achievement in terms of number of families covered was in 1982-83 while in terms of subsidy amounts released it was in 1983-84 respectively. Only in one year (1983-84) could the target of benefiting 600 families per Block be achieved. The remoter Pooh Block has lagged behind the other two Blocks in achieving I.R.D.P. targets. The I.R.D.P. was complemented by a youth training scheme.

6.1.1.1 Training of Rural Youth for Self-Employment (TRYSEM)

Under TRYSEM, eligible youth of target groups listed below are given training subsidies for being trained in a vocation of their own choice by a master craftsman for a period not exceeding one year. It is learning on the job and not theoretical knowledge. The trainees are to be chosen from among:

Table 6.2: Loan and Subsidy Amounts under the I.R.D.P. in Kinnaur

sn	*Year*	*FBB*			*Total*	*Subsidy*	*loan amount*
do	**-do-**	**Blocks**			**Fmls**	**Involved**	**released**
do	*-do-*	*N*	*K*	*P*	*Bnftd*	*(Rupees)*	*(Rupees)*
01	1980-81	268	000	000	268	283,525	285,600
02	1981-82	243	004	010	257	454,036	455,550
03	1982-83	710	607	500	1817	2950,537	2952,630
04	1983-84	600	609	601	1810	2979,444	2981,400
05	1984-85	610	536	146	1292	2340,000	2341,035
06	1985-86	271	209	188	668	1217,000	1217,000
07	Total	2702	1965	1445	6112	10224,542	10233,415

The figures for 1985-86 are till November 30, 1985 only.
Code: **FBB = families benefited Development Block-wise,**
Fmls = families, Bnftd = benefited, sn = serial number,
K = Kālpa, N = Nichār, P = Pooh.
(Source: As for Table 6.1)

(a) Small Farmers;
(b) Marginal Farmers;
(c) Agricultural Labourers;
(d) Rural Artisans; and
(e) Persons between 18 to 35 years of age in families below the poverty line.

Training subsidies were provided @ Rs 75 per month if training was imparted within the trainee's own village itself. For training outside home-village, the trainee received Rs 150 per month if accomodation was provided and Rs 200 per month if no accomodation was available. The programme was launched in Kinnaur in 1980-81. Local influential figures have quickly discovered therein a new source of patronage which they try and steer towards sons and daughters of their own supporters. TRYSEM is a preparatory programme after which the trainees are to be given loans and subsidies under the I.R.D.P. to establish them in vocations that they have chosen to be trained in. The amount of subsidies paid out under this programme is given in Table 6.3 . It can be seen that TRYSEM was used as a means of obtaining money from the government. The number of trainees settled after training crossed 50% of the number of those trained only once (in 1984-85). This percentage fell drastically in 1985-86 when only five trainees were settled out of 94 who had been trained. The amount of subsidy given out had accumulated in six years to just under half a million rupees. There was no regular pattern of increase or decrease in this subsidy. In addition to the I.R.D.P., other departments handed out subsidies as well.

6.1.2 Subsidies given by the Horticulture Department in Kinnaur

The Horticulture Department gives subsidies on horticultural inputs like fruit plants, pesticides, spraying of plants, pruning instruments, saws, irrigation pipe for watering orchards, irrigation tanks, wire for fencing, spray pumps, tarpaulins, orchard ladders or boundary walls. Approximately 2,000 orchardists were provided such subsidies in Kinnaur, according to the

Table 6.3: Financial Outlays under TRYSEM in Kinnaur

sn	*Year*	*Block In Which*			*Trns*	*Trgt*	*Subsidy*	*Total*
do	-do-	Trainees Trained			Stld	Fxd	Dstbtd	Trns
		N	*K*	*P*				
01	1980-81	000	004	011	003	120	37,540	015
02	1981-82	038	050	040	057	120	33,470	128
03	1982-83	045	005	009	027	120	124,545	059
04	1983-84	038	003	036	035	120	97,024	077
05	1984-85	000	028	056	052	120	126,000	084
06	1985-86	031	021	042	005	120	28,000	094
07	Total	152	111	194	179	720	456,579	457

The figures for 1985-86 are till November 30, 1985.
Code: **sn = serial no., Trns = trainees, Trgt = target,**
Stld = settled, Fxd = fixed, Dstbtd = distributed.
Subsidy distributed is in Rupees.
N = Nichār, K = Kālpa, P = Pooh Development Blocks.
(Source: As for Table 6.1)

District Horticulture Officer (henceforth referred to as the D.H.O.).[15] When Kinnaur became a district in 1960, only 290 hectares were under fruit plants, yielding around 300 metric tonnes of fruit. In 1984-85 i.e. in about a quarter of a century, corresponding figures were 3,677 hectares for the area and 8,821 metric tonnes for the produce.[16] ***The yield per hectare had more than doubled.*** It shows the subsidies handed out by the Horticulture Department in Kinnaur. As can be seen from Table 6.4, subsidies were given under special central assistance (S.C.A.) and centrally sponsored schemes (C.S.S.). The progression of subsidy amounts shows no consistent pattern, which is in line with most of the other results that have been observed till now.

6.1.3 Subsidies given by the Cooperative Department in Kinnaur

Cooperative societies in Kinnaur were assisted by the government by way of managerial subsidy; subsidy for the construction of godowns/sheds; subsidy for the purchase of machinery or implements and purchase of furniture/fixtures. The Cooperative Department was able to furnish subsidy data for only the year 1984-85, shown in Table 6.5 .

[15] Personal Communication entitled "Information regarding subsidy given to the orchardists of Kinnaur District", dated December 13, 1985 from the D.H.O., Kinnaur District at Rekong Peo to the author.

[16] Ibid.

Table 6.4: Subsidies given by the Horticulture Department

sn	*Year*	*S.C.A.*	*C.S.S.*	*Total*	*Pct*
01	1977-78	517,244	0,000	517,244	xxx%
02	1978-79	573,445	0,000	573,445	+11%
03	1979-80	486,551	29,942	516,493	-10%
04	1980-81	379,614	72,362	451,976	-12%
05	1981-82	625,036	23,500	648,536	+43%
06	1982-83	515,457	86,684	602,141	-07%
07	1983-84	472,956	311,792	784,743	+30%
08	1984-85	537,492	132,719	670,211	-14%

Code: sn = serial no.; S.C.A. = Special Central Assistance subsidies,
C.S.S. = under centrally sponsored schemes,
Pct = percentage change from preceding year,
xxx% = not applicable.
(Source: Personal Communication from the District Horticulture Officer, Kinnaur District, dated December 13, 1985)

Table 6.5: Subsidies given by the Cooperative Department in 1984-85

sn	*Society*	*S.S.*	*I.S.*	*M.S.*	*O.S.*	*Total*
01	KINFED	165,000	18,280	8,000	892,750	1084,030
02	Tahsil Union	0,000	0,000	20,000	343,579	363,579
03	Specialized Marketing	70,000	12,454	32,500	917,000	1031,954
04	A.M.P. and Service	0,000	0,000	84,000	239,000	323,000
05	Agricultural Non-Credit	0,000	0,000	,600	0,000	,600
06	Industrial	87,400	0,000	24,000	39,650	151,050
07	Consumer Stores	10,000	0,000	0,000	0,000	10,000

Code: A.M.P. = agricultural multipurpose, sn = serial number,
S.S. = share subsidy, I.S. = interest subsidy,
M.S. = managerial subsidy, O.S. = other subsidies,
All amounts are in Rupees.
(Source: Note prepared for the author by the District Cooperative and Supply Officer, Kinnaur District in December 1985.)

A total of Rs 2,964,213 or just under three million were doled out as subsidy to various cooperative societies in Kinnaur in 1984-85.

6.1.4 Subsidies given by the Food And Supplies Department

Kinnaur District was deficient in all the essential commodities of daily use and it has to depend on the adjoining states for the procurement of all essential commodities. Since the area faces a deficit in foodgrains, is tribal and inaccessible, the government give subsidies on the following commodities:

- ***(a) Wheat;***
- ***(b) Wheat flour;***
- ***(c) Sugar;***
- ***(d) Iodized salt;***
- ***(e) Palm oil and rapeseed oil.***

These commodities are being sold to consumers through fair price shops or depot holders under the Public Distribution System (henceforth referred to as the P.D.S.). Nobody seems to be aware of this aspect but the P.D.S. is clearly an attempt to reduce consumption credit needs for purchase of essential commodities by keeping their prices low through these subsidies. If essential needs could be met at controlled low prices, institutional credit inputs could then stand a better chance of being utilized for productive purposes rather than being diverted to purchase of essential items, so necessary in a chronically deficit area like Kinnaur. The P.D.S. is thus an adjunct of the institutional credit system even though it involves no direct loans. At the end of 1985, there were 44 fair price shops functioning in Kinnaur - 36 were being run by cooperative societies and 7 by individual depot holders, with one being run by the H.P. State Civil Supplies Corporation.[17]

Wheat was being issued according to a prescribed scale of 12 kg. per adult per month and 6 kg. per child per month at the end of 1985. The retail issue price was Rs 1.72 per kg. . Table 6.6 gives the amounts of subsidy released under this programme through the P.D.S. The subsidy attained an unprecedented high of more than a million rupees and a quarter in 1975-76, the heyday of the Emergency days.

During June 1981, the government decided to issue wheat flour at subsidized rates to consumers in Kinnaur in lieu of wheat with a view to restraining the rise in wheat flour prices in the open market. At the end of 1985, wheat flour was being sold @ Rs 2.20 per kilo at this controlled retail price. Table 6.7 shows the amounts of subsidy handed out under this scheme. For rice, levy sugar, rapeseed oil, exercise books, iodized salt, controlled cloth and levy cement, the D.F.S.C., Kinnaur was able to furnish no financial outlays in monetary terms. Subsidy amounts for these items had been released at the directorate-level in Simla for transportation from the point of supply to the distribution depot in Kinnaur. Subsidy amounts were higher than what are being shown here because of the difficulty of tracing such hidden amounts given out as consolidated blocks in Simla.

6.1.5 Subsidies given by the Animal Husbandry Department

The Animal Husbandry Department released subsidies under the Tribal Sub-Plan as well as under the Scheduled Caste Component Plan, both of which reserved specified percentages of budgetary allocations for Scheduled Tribes and Scheduled Castes respectively. Subsidies were provided to match loans for purchase of improved varieties of milch cattle, poultry units,

[17] Personal Communication entitled "Brief note on the working of the Food and Supplies Department in Kinnaur District", dated December 15, 1985 from Mr Sharab Gyachho Negi, District Food and Supplies Controller, Kinnaur District at Rekong Peo to the author, p. 2.

Table 6.6: Subsidy doled out for Supplying Wheat under P.D.S.

sn	*Year*	*subsidy amount*	*%change*
01	1975-76	1,374,222.43	xxx%
02	1976-77	205,094.80	-85%
03	1977-78	153,448.97	-25%
04	1978-79	194,454.09	+27%
05	1979-80	227,287.69	+17%
06	1980-81	366,450.30	+61%
07	1981-82	323,162.00	-12%
08	1982-83	414,462.48	+28%
09	1983-84	450,370.13	+09%
10	1984-85	441,402.15	-02%

Code: %change = percentage change from preceding year, sn = serial no.,
All amounts given are in Rupees, xxx% = not applicable.
(Source: Special note entitled "Brief Note on the Working of the Food and Supplies Department in Kinnaur District", prepared by Mr Sharab Gyachho Negi, District Food and Supplies Controller, Kinnaur District for the author in December 1985, Pp 4-5.)

Table 6.7: Subsidy on Retail Sale of Wheat Flour through the P.D.S.

sn	*Year*	*subsidy amount*
01	1982-83	66,131
02	1983-84	114,428
03	1984-85	72,784
04	Total	253,343

(Source: As for Table 6.6)

sheep units, ram breeding, donkey units, yak breeding and mules. Information about such subsidies is shown in Table 6.8 The average subsidy amount per beneficiary varied sharply from Rs 529 in 1982-83 to Rs 5,700 in 1983-84 to Rs 1,007 in 1984-85 respectively. It rose sharply and fell equally sharply.

6.1.6 Programmes of the Social Welfare Department in Kinnaur

Apart from programmes like the old-age pension scheme, widow pension scheme, disability pension scheme and special nutrition programmes for children and nursing mothers, the Welfare Department runs a Follow-Up Programme which "*aims at providing livelihood to local citizens or those who have undergone training in the R.I.T.Is or any other centres*

Table 6.8: Subsidies given by the Animal Husbandry Department

sn	*Year*	*SA*	*NB*	*ASBP*
01	1982-83	31,755	060	529.25
02	1983-84	969,050	170	5,700.35
03	1984-85	98,725	098	1,007.40

Code: SA = **subsidy amount, NB = number of beneficiaries,**
ASPB = average subsidy amount per beneficiary.
All amounts are in Rupees.
(Source: Detailed Chart entitled "Directory of Schemes Completed", prepared by the District Animal Husbandry Officer, Kinnaur District for the author in December 1985)

under various trades. In order to rehabilitate trainees coming out of the R.I.T.Is after getting training or otherwise conversant with any other trades, are supplied with equipment not exceeding Rs 300 each in case of sewing machines and Rs 200 each in case of other trades, so as to enable them to follow the respective trade and earn their livelihood. Artisans or newly trained persons whose annual income does not exceed Rs 6,000 are eligible to get benefit under this Scheme".[18] Table 6.9 gives the financial outlays doled out under this scheme. The average subsidy per beneficiary was around Rs 300, with two declines to around Rs 250. There was no consistence at all in the number of beneficiaries, which swung between a low of two and a high of 88. In ten years, just over Rs 100,000 had been distributed out as subsidy, giving an average per annum figure of Rs 10,000. The Welfare Department also gives housing subsidy. Financial outlays under this scheme are shown in Table 6.10 . The average subsidy handed out per beneficiary for Kinnaur District, Kālpa Sub-Division, Pooh Sub-Division and Nichār Sub-Division from 1978-79 to 1985-86 was Rs 1,578; Rs 1,497; Rs 1,821 and Rs 1,392 respectively. The figure for the Sub-Division with the maximum population (Nichār) was thus the least; that for the Sub-Division with the least population (Pooh) was the most, with Kālpa inbetween. The distribution of subsidy funds was most even between the three Sub-Divisions between 1980-81 and 1981-82. Otherwise the variations were greater. These subsidies were distributed by the District Welfare Committee, headed by the D.C. In general, non-official members of this committee sought to spread available housing subsidy allocation thinly by covering as many beneficiaries as possible, while officials sought to reduce the number of beneficiaries but increase the subsidy amount per beneficiary. Less than Rs 2,000 was too small an amount per beneficiary for constructing or repairing a house in Kinnaur. The subsidy was for poor, deserving S.Cs and S.Ts who had no house to live in or whose houses were in a dilapidated condition. Maximum subsidy limit for new construction was Rs 5,000 and for repair Rs 2,500 per beneficiary. S.Cs/S.Ts having an annual income from all sources of not more than Rs 6,000 are eligible for housing subsidy. A beneficiary had to contribute an amount equal to 25% of the grant from his/her side. The actual average amounts distributed were far below this maximum limit, insufficient for either construction or repair.

6.1.7 Subsidies given by the Soil Conservation Office

Soil conservation schemes were introduced in Kinnaur in August 1966. The District Agriculture Officer (D.A.O.) supervised the work of soil conservation in addition to his own work from 1974 till July 1979. Since August 1979 a Soil Conservation Wing has been headed by a regular Assistant Soil Conservation Officer (A.S.C.O.) at Peo. From January 1982 till

[18] Personal Communication dated December 6, 1985 from Mr P.N. Negi, District Welfare Officer, Kinnaur District at Rekong Peo to the author, Para entitled "Follow-Up-Programme".

Table 6.9: Follow-Up Programme Outlays in Kinnaur District

sn	*Year*	*PB*	*AD*	*%Change*	*AA*
01	1976-77	002	,600	xxx	300
02	1977-78	050	12,500	+1983%	300
03	1978-79	024	7,000	-44%	292
04	1979-80	042	12,600	+80%	300
05	1980-81	036	8,650	-31%	240
06	1981-82	015	4,500	-48%	300
07	1982-83	025	7,500	+67%	300
08	1983-84	025	7,500	+00%	300
09	1984-85	088	26,200	+249%	298
10	1985-86	051	15,200	-429%	298
11	Total	358	102,250	xxx	286

Code: **PB = number of persons benefited, AD = amount distributed in Rupees,**
%Change = percentage change from preceding year,
AA = average amount per beneficiary, xxx = not applicable.
(Source: Personal Communication dated December 6, 1985 from Mr Prem Nāth Negi, District Welfare Officer, Kinnaur District to the author.)

May 1983 this Division was under the newly created Soil Conservation Department formed by merging the soil conservation wings of the Forest and Agriculture Departments. The newly created department was abolished in May 1983 and status quo restored. In Kinnaur, soil conservation authorities provided incentives by providing 50% subsidy and 50% loan at the rate of Rs 5,000 to Rs 6,250 per hectare since 1974 irrespective of the land holding. From April 1984, this rate of assistance was raised by the government. Rs 7,500 per hectare became the upper limit for bench terracing and Rs 10,000 per hectare for irrigation, subject to a ceiling of Rs 6,000 per beneficiary. Soil conservation was and is of extreme importance in an erosion-prone area like Kinnaur where indiscriminate blasting for road construction and deforestation have aggravated the problem of soil erosion. Valuable farm land was rapidly being eroded in villages Akpa, Rispa, Mālling and Jāngi for example. This meant reduction of income particularly because culturable land was scarce in Kinnaur. Soil conservation measures, by trying to halt such declines in income, seek to improve the credit-worthiness of beneficiaries by improving their land, apart from raising income levels. The value of land with such works was higher and hence worth a greater credit rating, both in the institutional as well as the informal sectors. Table 6.11 shows the subsidies distributed by the Soil Conservation Division in Rekong Peo. Its overall financial achievements are shown in Table 6.12 . As usual, no consistent pattern of increase or decrease in the average amount per beneficiary or the total financial outlay could be discerned. It all depended on allocations made in Simla.

Table 6.10: Housing Subsidy Figures for Kinnaur District

sn	*Year*	*Sub-Division*						*Total*	*avgttl*
do	-do-	Kālpa		Pooh		Nichār		Amount	sbypbf
do	*-do-*	*NB*	*Amount*	*NB*	*Amount*	*NB*	*Amount*	*Rupees*	*rupees*
01	1978-79	021	42,000	043	129,000	030	60,000	231,000	2457
02	1979-80	016	35,400	032	79,000	017	34,300	148,700	2288
03	1980-81	021	23,200	021	25,800	034	27,000	76,000	1000
04	1981-82	021	25,000	017	24,500	017	24,000	73,500	1336
05	1982-83	011	15,500	021	40,500	013	19,000	75,000	1667
06	1983-84	059	71,000	057	68,000	068	74,000	213,000	1158
07	1984-85	051	70,300	046	65,500	048	63,700	199,500	1376
08	1985-86	015	39,500	029	52,000	027	51,500	143,000	2014
09	Total	215	321,900	266	484,300	254	353,500	11159,700	1578

Code: sn = **serial no., avgttl = average total subsidy per beneficiary,**
sbypbf = subsidy per beneficiary in Rupees,
NB = number of beneficiaries. Amounts are in Rupees.
(Source: As for Table 6.9.)

Table 6.11: Expenditure Incurred on Soil Conservation Works

sn	*Year*	*Block*									
do	-do-	Kālpa			Nichār			Pooh			Total
do	*-do-*	*NB*	*Loan*	*Subsidy*	*NB*	*Loan*	*Subsidy*	*NB*	*Loan*	*Subsidy*	*-do-*
01	1977-78	022	4,481	13,443	28	6,593	19,780	61	18,547	55,640	88,863
02	1978-79	038	16,554	49,661	41	11,594	34,781	119	25,345	76,036	160,478
03	1979-80	012	4,625	12,863	09	1,967	3,764	64	22,773	36,739	53,366
						CENTRAL ASSISTANCE					
01	1979-80	030	26,608	26,608	36	26,658	26,658	133	100,986	100986	154252
02	1980-81	023	15,894	20,817	73	53,381	92,615	77	46,420	67,025	180,457

Code: **NB = number of beneficiaries, sn = serial number,**
Loan and subsidy amounts are in Rupees.
(Source: Personal Communication dated October 29, 1981 from Mr Y.R. Thākur, Assistant Soil Conservation Officer, Kinnaur District to the author as D.C., Kinnaur at Kālpa.)

Table 6.12: Soil Conservation Outlays in Kinnaur District

sn	*Year*	*FA*	*NB*	*AOPB*
01	1974-75	56,787	038	1,494
02	1975-76	107,629	049	2,197
03	1976-77	115,830	148	,783
04	1977-78	145,167	203	,715
05	1978-79	213,969	165	1,297
06	1979-80	240,725	210	1,146
07	1980-81	296,160	063	4,701
08	1981-82	301,892	190	1,589
09	1982-83	164,660	080	2,058
10	1983-84	181,034	083	2,181
11	1984-85	303,838	116	2,619
12	1985-86	130,007	056	2,322

Code: FA = financial achievements, NB = number of beneficiaries,
AOPB = average outlay per beneficiary in Rupees.
(Source: Personal Communication dated December 8, 1985 from Er R.K. Singha, Assistant Soil Conservation Officer, Kinnaur District to the author.)

6.1.8 Subsidies given by the Agriculture Department in Kinnaur

The net cultivated area in Kinnaur was 7,962 hectares in 1985, with average size of holding = 1.76 hectares and with 60% of the cultivated area under irrigation.[19] Since agriculture was the basic way of life of most Kinnauras, the Agriculture Department offered a wide ranging package of subsidy schemes as follows:

6.1.8.1 Seed Distribution Programme

This scheme aimed at production of high yielding varieties of various kinds of seeds to meet local demand and demonstrate improved techniques for adoption in the area for increase in yields. Central and state governments supply agricultural inputs at 50% subsidized cost. The seed distribution scheme under the Tribal Sub-Plan involves distribution of seeds of high yielding varieties at 50% subsidy.

[19] Letter No. Agr-5-12/80-3919, dated Kālpa the 4th February, 1982 from the D.A.O., Kinnaur District at Kālpa to the author as D.C., Kinnaur, Enclosure entitled "A Brief Note Pertaining to Agricultural Activities in respect of Office of D.A.O., Kinnaur District", p. 1.

6.1.8.2 Fertilizer Distribution Programme

To encourage higher fertilizer consumption in Kinnaur, 50% subsidy was provided on the cost of fertilizers till the year 1984-85 when the rate of subsidy was lowered to 40%.

6.1.8.3 Plant Protection Scheme

Various kinds of insecticides and fungicides were distributed to farmers under this scheme. Material was supplied at 50% subsidy for pesticides and plant protection equipment.

6.1.8.4 Temperate Vegetable Seed Production Programme

Agro-climatic conditions in Kinnaur make it a suitable area for raising good quality temperate vegetable seeds. Seed production programme was begun in 1968-69 in collaboration with the National Seeds Corporation (N.S.C.). Sugarbeet, cabbage, turnip and chicory seed production is now being done on a large scale. Onion cultivation as off-season crop has been introduced under long-day conditions in Pooh Sub-Division. Lincoln variety of peas and September cabbage seed production programmes have been introduced. From 1983 to 1984, 255 kg. and from 1984 to 1985, 334 kg. of cabbage seed, valued at Rs 20,016, were produced in Kinnaur and supplied to the Government of Tamil Nadu. Seeds were distributed free at 100% subsidy under this scheme.

6.1.8.5 Improved Implements

To popularize agricultural implements for improving agricultural yields, the most suitable hand tools and ploughs were being distributed to farmers. The implements had been procured and stocked at district headquarters at subsidized cost for being given on 50% subsidy.

6.1.8.6 Development of Oil Seeds and Pulses

Under this scheme all kinds of oil seeds and pulses were being distributed to farmers on 50% subsidy, besides laying out of demonstration plots/trials to guide Kinnauras about the improved technology to be adopted for raising soyabeans, sunflower seeds and pulses.

6.1.8.7 Dry Land Farming

In order to demonstrate the latest dry land farming techniques to farmers in Kinnaur, demonstration trials were being conducted on their fields on 100% subsidy, for which agricultural inputs like seeds, fertilizers and plant protection materials were supplied. The amount of subsidies distributed under these schemes in Kinnaur is shown in Table 6.13 . There is no consistency in the pattern. Total amount of subsidy touched Rs 506,836 in 1978-79 and Rs 611,931 in 1983-84; falling to Rs 243,436 in 1979-80 inbetween. Subsidies have evolved into a mainstay of institutional finance.

6.1.9 Subsidies Provided by the Industries Department

Kinnaur has traditionally been witness to small-scale household industries like blanket weaving, carpet weaving and shawl making. From Gartok in Tibet to Rāmpur, 'gudmās', blankets and shawls made in Kinnaur were familiar articles of trade. Major industries could not be viable in Kinnaur because of its location. As the 7th Five Year Tribal Sub-Plan 1985-90 document puts it, the tribal areas are industrially severely handicapped because of *"remoteness, lack of adequate and all-weather communications and scattered and sparse population which makes the end-product uneconomic...It is therefore imperative that the development of industries in these areas is made to cater to the local needs of these areas, encourage such industries as are labour intensive and possess touch of the local handicrafts*

Table 6.13: Subsidies Distributed by the Agriculture Department

sn	*Year*	*SCS*	*SSS*	*TAS*
01	1976-77	85,137	51,998	137,135
02	1977-78	241,555	68,875	310,430
03	1978-79	368,134	138,702	506,836
04	1979-80	191,167	52,269	243,436
05	1980-81	232,629	74,212	306,841
06	1981-82	228,786	250,868	479,654
07	1982-83	259,624	133,184	392,808
08	1983-84	513,460	98,471	611,931
09	1984-85	370,323	46,160	416,483
10	1985-86	141,085	19,608	160,693

Code: SCS = **Subsidy in the Central Sector in Rupees,**
SSS = **Subsidy in the State Sector in Rupees,**
TAS = **Total amount of subsidy in Rupees.**
Figures for 1985-86 are only till November 30, 1985.
(Source: Personal Communication No. Agr 5-12/80-3919 dated February 4, 1986 from Mr Jagmegh Singh Chaudhary, District Agriculture Officer, Kinnaur District to the author.)

for which the consumer can pay reasonable amounts".[20] No large or medium industries were possible. "*The present policies aim at promoting rural-based industries to provide maximum employment to all people on decentralized basis and stop exodus of people to urban areas besides generating additional employment opportunities*".[21]

Subsidies have been made available in pursuit of these objectives of fostering rural cottage industries in Kinnaur to provide additional income. An industrial estate already exists at Rekong Peo. Behind this grand sounding name, only a H.P.M.C. canning unit was functioning there. Other plots had only signboards or derelict looking sheds at the end of 1985. However, under a scheme of incentives and subsidy, industrial units were to be aided in initial stages from 5 to 10 years to make them competitive after meeting extra overhead charges by giving a package of exemption from/reduction of various taxes, interest free loans on C.S.T. (Central Sales Tax) and interest subsidies. In order to furnish every type of assistance and facility to entrepreneurs under one roof, a District Industries Centre (D.I.C.) was established at Rekong Peo. It provided financial assistance in the shape of margin money, subsidy and technical know-how. Table 6.14 shows the amount of subsidies disbursed in Kinnaur by the D.I.C. The Tribal Sub-Plan document for 1985-90 shows an allocation of outlays as shown in Table 6.15. The actual amount disbursed as subsidy in 1983-84 and the

[20] Sātvin Panchavarshiyé Jan-Jātiyé Up-Yojanā, 1985-90 Aivam Vārshik Yojanā 1985-86 - Prārūp, Jan Jātiya Vikās Vibhāg, Himāchal Pradesh Sarkār, Simla 171002, November 1984, Chapter XII: Sectoral Programmes (State Plan), Item VI: Industry and Minerals, p. 33.

[21] Ibid.

Table 6.14: Subsidy Disbursed to Industrial Units in Kinnaur

sn	*Year*	*NB*	*SbDbd*
01	1979-80	02	9,000
02	1982-83	14	41,964
03	1983-84	12	48,130

Code: **NB = Number of units benefited, sn = Serial Number,**
SbDbd = Subsidy disbursed in Rupees.
(Source: Statistical Outline of Himāchal Pradesh 1983, Directorate of Economics and Statistics, Himāchal Pradesh, Simla, Part XVI-Industries, Pp 180-181 for 1979-80 figures; and Ibid 1985, p. 185 for figures for 1982-83 and 1983-84.)

Table 6.15: Tribal Sub-Plan Outlays for Industries in Kinnaur

sn	*Years*	*Expenditure Head*	*AO*
01	1985-90	Industrial Estate	500,000
02	1985-90	Incentives & Subsidy	800,000
03	1985-90	District Industries Centre	1800,000
04	1985-86	Industrial Estate	50,000
05	1985-86	Incentives & Subsidy	400,000
06	1985-86	District Industries Centre	275,000

Code: **sn = serial number, AO = allocated outlay in Rupees.**
(Source: Draft 7th 5-Year Tribal Sub-Plan 1985-90 and Annual Plan 1985-86, For office use only, Tribal Development Department, Government of H.P., Simla, November 1984, Statement GN-2(TSP)SP, Item VI: Industry and Minerals, Pp 66-67.)

projected outlay for 1985-86 reveal financial assistance of around Rs 40,000 to Rs 50,000 per annum, not a large amount but one that is explicable in view of the unfavourable geographic conditions. Aid was provided more effectively by the Handlooms and Handicrafts Corporation through provision of raw material at controlled rates and through purchase of finished products from artisans.

To render Kinnaura weavers credit-worthy, the preceding Corporation and the H.P. Khādi and Village Industries Board have been running a procurement scheme in Kinnaur; weaving production centres at Kālpa, Gyabong and Spillo; Kinnar Textiles at Nichār and a Sales Emporium at Kālpa. Statement GN-2A(TSP)(SCA) of the Draft Tribal Sub-Plan 1985-90 shows an allocation of Rs 3,000,000 to the H.P. Khādi and Village Industries Board and Rs 3,000,000 to the Handlooms and Handicrafts Corporation for the quinquennial plan period, with Rs 500,000 for each of them earmarked as grants-in-aid for the Annual Sub-Plan 1985-86.[22] These amounts were earmarked for all tribal areas in Himāchal and district-wise allocation was not given for these funds being provided as Special Central Assistance (S.C.A.)

[22] Ibid, Pp 82-83.

by the Union Government. The following purposes were meant to be achieved with these grants-in-aid:

(a) Construction of work sheds/community work sheds for carpet weavers;
(b) Discount on the sale of handloom products/handicrafts;
(c) Subsidy for the cost of tools and equipment;
(d) Establishment of raw material depots;
(e) Purchase of handloom products/handicrafts from artisans;
(f) Revival of extinct crafts;
(g) Market research;
(h) Procurement and supply of raw material to artisans; and
(i) Provision of sales outlets to artisans.

We can now try and estimate the volume of subsidy amount per person being doled out in Kinnaur.

6.1.10 Subsidies given Per Capita in Kinnaur: Cornucopia!

The estimate being attempted is only approximate and not exact because there are some hidden subsidies which have not been accounted for in financial terms. For example, fencing and barbed wire provided free of charge by the Forest Department for community forest lots. Free barbed wire provided by the Horticulture Department. Transportation subsidies provided by the Food and Civil Supplies Department under the P.D.S. and free insemination facilities provided at breeding centres of the Animal Husbandry Department, to name a few. The Health Department provides free medicines at its hospitals and dispensaries, if available (a really big **IF!**). Medical care is free to the extent of availability of hospital beds. All these are hidden subsidies which attempt to lower consumption expenditure of households. Health care costs, for example, could otherwise be much higher; not just because of medical fees but because of the transportation costs that would be involved in travelling to Simla or even to Rāmpur for buying the necessary medicines or for being examined by a qualified doctor. As it is, vacancies in hospitals and dispensaries remain unfilled for so long that such costs have to be borne anyway. The estimate made here is thus lower than the actual amount of average per capita subsidy in Kinnaur.

Table 6.16 shows the summation of subsidies listed till now from Tables 6.1 till 6.15 under departmental schemes. Only such years have been considered as had figures available for all departments. Table 6.16 shows that while percentage changes in the amount of subsidy released from one year to the next increased around 20% on the average, there was a sharp rise of +63% in 1982-83. We are now familiar enough with the working of political forces from Chapters III and IV to be able to predict that such a sharp rise could only have been caused by some important political event. There were elections in Himāchal in 1982 which were very closely contested and it was not known whether the ruling Congress party could eclipse the opposition Bharatiya Janata Party. Added to this political fact of funds being made liberally available in an election year was the fact that the D.C. had decided to launch a coordinated drive to give subsidy liberally in some selected areas like Sungra and Kangos to see whether concentration of institutional finance on selected target points would not yield better results than spreading it thinly all over Kinnaur. The drive was to see whether private moneylenders could be brought to lowering their rates of interest through selective but increased injection of institutional funds into Kinnaur. The fact that the rate of rise fell immediately to 19% in the succeeding year means that such a tempo could not be sustained as a matter of routine. The election had brought victory to the ruling party and things had taken on a less urgent aspect! This sudden increase in subsidies pumped into Kinnaur could not be maintained and even though subsidies increased in absolute terms they never managed to reach the same spectacular level of sharp rise in Kinnaur till 1986. The population figure used (59,547 persons) for calculating per capita subsidy figures is that taken from the 1981 Census, the latest available. For the years where Tables 6.2 to 6.14 had missing values for some

Table 6.16: Approximation of Total Subsidy Amounts given in Kinnaur

sn	*Year*	*AOS*	*SPC*	*%change*
01	1979-80	2315,242	039	xxx
02	1980-81	2822,142	047	+22%
03	1981-82	3340,750	056	+18%
04	1982-83	5433,503	091	+63%
05	1983-84	6456,654	108	+19%
06	1984-85	7704,356	129	+19%
07	Total	28072,647	471	xxx

Code: AOS = **amount of subsidy in Rupees,**
SPC = average per capita subsidy in Rupees,
%change = percentage change from preceding year, sn = serial number, xxx = not applicable.

departments like the Animal Husbandry, Cooperative and Industries Departments, estimated expenditure figures have been taken from the corresponding Tribal Sub-Plan figures for that year. However, total population used includes non-adults and small children as well. A more effective per capita estimate could be had by trying to leave out children. Since census figures did not give population figures by age-group, a rough approximation has been attempted by counting main and marginal workers and leaving out the non-workers, all of which are available in the census data. These categories included males and females even under 18 years of age since people assist in family labour from an early age onwards in Kinnaur, in some cases from 14/15 years itself, if not earlier. But very young children were not included. Also, very old people were excluded, being beyond working age. Definitions of main and marginal workers excluded age factors. Main worker for census purposes was a person *"who has primarily worked for a major period of the year...By major part of the year, it is intended to find out that the person has worked for 183 days or more or in other words worked for 6 months or more"*.[23] On the other hand, marginal worker was a person *"who has worked for less than six months or 183 days but worked at least a day during the year before enumeration"*.[24] Primary census abstracts of 1981 yield figures of 19,481 males; 13,071 females as main workers and 347 males, 1,198 females as marginal workers.[25] This gives a total figure of 34,097 workers on which we can base per capita subsidy calculation. Table 6.17 gives the results of such a calculation. Thus, by 1984-85, the government were pumping in about Rs 226 per (marginal + main) worker in Kinnaur, showing to what extent this **subsidy culture** had pervaded the entire spectrum of institutional finance there. Tables 6.16 and 6.17 show a continuous rise in subsidy figures, absolute as well as per capita. In no other table till now could such an unbroken rise be observed. Variations were always fluctuating, but here we see that subsidies consistently went up, regardless of non-quantifiable factors like political or administrative pressures. More than 28 million rupees had been given out in Kinnaur from 1979-80 to 1984-85, giving a mean figure of Rs 4,678,775 or around Rs 4.7 million per annum as subsidy for this sparsely populated area of around 60,000 people. No such calculation has been made

[23] District Census Handbook, Kinnaur District, 1981, p. 20.

[24] Ibid.

[25] Ibid, Pp 118-119.

Table 6.17: Per Capita Subsidy for Marginal/Main Worker Groups

sn	*Year*	*AOS*	*SPC*	*%change*
01	1979-80	2315,242	068	xxx
02	1980-81	2822,142	083	+22%
03	1981-82	3340,750	098	+18%
04	1982-83	5433,503	159	+62%
05	1983-84	6456,654	189	+19%
06	1984-85	7704,356	226	+20%

Code: AOS = **amount of subsidy in Rupees,**
SPC = average per capita subsidy In Rupees,
%change = percentage change from preceding year,
xxx = not applicable, sn = serial number.

for other tribal or non-tribal areas of Himāchal so that a comparison could be made. This gamut of subsidies was distributed under the overall framework of the Tribal Sub-Plan.

6.2 TRIBAL SUB-PLAN: 'ANNADĀTA' OF TRIBAL AREAS

The concept of a Tribal Sub-Plan is a *"plan within the plan, for accelerated socio-economic development of tribal majority areas"*.[26] This strategy was adopted only at the beginning of the V Five Year Plan in 1974-75 to try and give effect to the provisions of Article 46 of the Constitution of India, laying down special emphasis on the promotion of the educational and economic interests of the weaker sections, in particular of the Scheduled Castes and Scheduled Tribes[27] within the general cadre of planning outlined in Articles 38 and 39. Till the end of the IV Plan, development programmes for S.Ts *"tended to be formed in an ad hoc manner without any perspective and were in the nature of welfare schemes. Special programmes for these groups were conceived as a supplement to the total development effort under general sectors of development. In practice, these special programmes merely substituted the benfits available to the scheduled tribes under normal development schemes. This resulted in much lower investment for their development than envisaged. To obviate such a situation perpetrating further the strategy of tribal sub-plan was devised to ensure equitable share in plan investment to this backward tribal community"*.[28]

The primary responsibility for development of tribal areas devolved on the flow of state plan funds to such areas. This was augmented by the S.C.A. funds from the Central Pool at the disposal of the Union Ministry of Home Affairs (M.H.A.) for tribal development in states. The ambit of the Tribal Sub-Plan was widened in the VI Plan to include tribal pockets where in a population of 10,000 or more in contiguous areas the Scheduled Tribes constituted 50% or above of the total population. *"The planning strategy for tribal development during the VII*

[26] Draft Tribal Sub-Plan, 1985-90, op. cit., Chapter I, p. 1.

[27] Ibid.

[28] Ibid.

Plan will continue to be a mix of beneficiary-oriented and infrastructure and human resource development programmes".[29] Kinnaur, with its area of 6,401 km^2, constituted 27.06% of the total tribal area of 23,655 km^2 in Himāchal. While only 3.13% of total population was concentrated in tribal areas, flow of State Plan funds to these areas was targeted at 5.36% for the V Plan. The actual achievement during the V Plan period (1974-78) touched 5.75%. With this as backdrop, flow of State Plan funds was targeted at 8.48% of total funds for the VI Plan period (1980-85), while actual achievement reached 8.62%. Table 6.18 shows the increasing importance of the Tribal Sub-Plan concept, how beginning with 3.65% of State

Table 6.18: Tribal Sub-Plan Outlays for Tribal Areas of Himāchal

sn	*Year*	*TSPO*	*TTSPO*	*PCT*
01	1974-79	23,895.00	1,281.00	5.36 T
02	1974-75	3,066.00	111.81	3.65
03	1974-78	15,743.00	904.81	5.75
04	1974-79	23,043.00	1,491.05	6.47
05	1980-85	56,000.00	4,747.40	8.48 T
06	1980-85	62,833.56	5,415.31	8.62
07	1985-90	133,800.00	12,039.00	9.00 T
08	1985-86	20,000.00	1,806.65	9.03

Code: **sn = serial number, T = target figure,**
Amounts in lakhs, 1 lakh = 100,000.
TSPO = Total State Plan Outlay in lakhs of Rupees,
TTSPO = Total Tribal Sub-Plan Outlay (State Share) in lakhs of Rs,
PCT = Percentage of TTSPO to TSPO.
(Source: Draft Tribal Sub-Plan 1985-90 and Annual Plan 1985-86, For Office Use Only, Tribal Development Department, Government of H.P., Simla, November 1984, Chapter 1, p. 3)

Plan flow in 1974-75 it had risen to 9% by 1985-86. The percentage of total State Plan funds channelled into the Tribal Sub-Plan has been rising consistently. Achievements overshot targets for both the V as well as the VI Plan periods. An important innovation in the Tribal Sub-Plan process was the introduction of the Single Consolidated Demand (Demand No. 35) in 1981-82. This system of single demand ensured cent per cent expenditure because allocated funds could neither be diverted to other demand-heads nor allowed to lapse from then on. Departments could no longer divert these funds to schemes in other areas. Moreover, unlike for State Plan funds, the unspent balance of S.C.A. allocation was permitted to be carried over to the following year by the M.H.A. during the period of the VI Plan. Normally, unspent balances lapse at the end of the financial year. The institutional finance covered under the Tribal Sub-Plan was further regulated in three or four important committees.

[29] Ibid.

6.3 DISTRICT COMMITTEES: FORUMS FOR LETTING OFF STEAM!

Each district has a plethora of committees consisting of official and non-official members for overseeing expenditure of funds or their distribution. Some important committees are the 20 Point Programme Review Committee; District Welfare Committee; District Grievances Committee; District Food Advisory Committee and the Governing Body of the Desert Development Project. These committees are the battlegrounds where non-officials and officials or competing departments interact and try to steer programmes along their own lines. It would be simplistic to think that officials line up united on one side and non-officials on the other. There are internal differences of opinion in both these groups. Sometimes officials use non-officials as mouthpieces for expressing opinions which they want aired without identifying themselves as the source of such opinions. The web of relationships is quite intricate and a whole dissertation can be written on this aspect alone but every participant seeks to derive maximum advantage - career advancement for officials and political gain for non-officials. For the present study, only three committees need brief mention.

6.3.1 Project Advisory Committee: Verbal Storms and Meagre Results!

Kinnaur has been designated as an Integrated Tribal Development Project (I.T.D.P.), like the other four tribal areas of Himāchal (Lahaul, Spiti, Pāngi and Bharmaur). The I.T.D.P. is the operational unit towards which Tribal Sub-Plan funds are directed. To oversee both the implementation and formulation of the Sub-Plan, as well as dispensing nucleus budget funds, Project Advisory Committees (P.A.Cs) have been constituted for each of the five I.T.D.Ps. Members of Parliament from the area, Grām Panchāyat Pradhāns, local members of the Tribes Advisory Council, members of the Legislative Assembly, Chairman Zila Parishad, Chairmen Panchāyat Samitis all constitute the non-official section while district heads of offices constitute the official section of this committee. The P.A.C. is headed by the D.C. in Kinnaur, It had a ridiculously large membership of about 75 members to be of much practical use as a decision making forum. Its meetings generally lasted from 10.00 hours to well past 17.00 hours, exhausting everyone in the process. It resembles the General Assembly of the United Nations in that it generates a lot of speeches and verbal hot air but meagre practical results! Rather than confine itself to urgent tasks at hand, it becomes a forum for making sweeping demands for more buses, more roads, more subsidies. Minutes of its meetings show that officials get away with evasive replies and do not seem to be taking these meetings very seriously. Items drag on because officials do not send replies on time. The P.A.C. in Kinnaur has become a sort of debating society for up-and-coming panchāyat pradhāns.

6.3.2 District Consultative and Coordination Committee (D.C.C.C.)

This committee is the principal forum for reviewing progress made by banks and government agencies under the LBS and the D.C.P./A.A.Ps, as well as for sorting out coordination problems between bankers and government officials. It consists of representatives of the lead and other banks present in the district, representatives of financial institutions like the National Bank for Agriculture and Rural Development (NABARD) and concerned government officials like the S.D.Ms; B.D.Os; D.A.H.O.; D.A.O., D.H.O.; D.P.R.O.; D.C.S.O.; G.M., D.I.C.; P.O., I.T.D.P. . It is presided over by the D.C. or his nominee. This forum has smaller membership than the P.A.C. . Its relative compactness makes for increased efficiency. Its main functions can broadly be classified as follows:

(a) Ensure better coordination between various financial institutions to avoid overlapping of loans;
(b) Evolve better formulation of bankable schemes, especially for small and marginal farmers;
(c) Review actual performance of banks for framing better coordinated plans of action on time-bound basis;
(d) Allocate specific areas (Blocks or villages etc.) among different banks in the district;

(e) Recommend expansion of banking facilities through branch expansion programmes for chosen villages;
(f) Help the banks increase their liquidity through deposit mobilization;
(g) Thrash out any issue of mutual interest having a bearing on development of the area;
(h) Hold workshops and seminars for training government officials to better comprehend the functioning and problems of the banking system; and
(i) Suggest practical measures for reducing procedural red-tapism in sanctioning of bank loans, and for speeding up recoveries.

6.3.3 District Rural Development Agency (D.R.D.A.)

The D.R.D.A. is the governing body of the I.R.D.P. which forms the backbone of the institutional credit/subsidy inputs in Kinnaur. It is also a compact forum presided over by the D.C. and consists of members of Parliament/State Assembly from the area (one each for Kinnaur); Chairman, Zila Parishad; Chairmen of Ṗanchāyat Samitis (three for Kinnaur - Pooh, Kālpa and Nichār) as non-official members while the S.D.Ms; B.D.Os; G.M., D.I.C.; D.C.S.O.; D.A.H.O.; D.A.O.; D.H.O.; H.D.O. and the G.A. to the D.C. were official members. Managers of all bank branches in the district were also members. This forum was concerned with the I.R.D.P. but a lot of topics discussed were similar to those raised in the D.C.C.C. The presence of non-official members, all senior political figures, made the discussions more meaningful. Bank managers spoke up more freely here than in the D.C.C.C. in which their seniors (R.Ms/D.Ms) were present. Bankers or officials seem to succumb in the presence of their seniors to the habit of telling the latter what they want to hear rather than what they should hear! It is relevant to consider the role of the D.C. who presides over the meetings of most of these district committees. He is a key figure, perhaps the most important figure in the entire institutional credit set-up. A lot depends on how he functions.

6.4 ROLE OF THE D.C. AS AN 'ECONOMIC UMPIRE': A TRAPEZE!

The D.C. in Kinnaur is involved in making economic decisions which in a free economy would be determined by demand-supply relations or regulated at a higher centralized level in a socialist/communist planned economy. This aspect covers fixation of profit margins for all sorts of commodities ranging from fruit or vegetables to pressure cookers; fixation of freight/transportation charges; fixation of daily wages under the Minimum Wages Act and overall functioning as a sort of watchdog over the ebb and flow of economic life in the district. The regulatory aspect of the pre-1947 district set-up headed by the D.C. was primarily maintenance of law and order. Such maintenance may still have great importance in other areas but in a relatively crime-free area like Kinnaur has definitely taken a backseat to the development and economic roles. Law and order has never been a problem in Kinnaur. A British administrator had this to report about the area in 1824: ***"In no part of the protected dominion, and I may give a wider scope and say the world, is there less crime known"***.[30] While this ideal state of affairs is not true nowadays, Kinnaur continues to remain a low crime area. Tribal development and institutional finance are more important than maintenance of law and order for the D.C. there. The major law and order problem seems to be drunkenness!

The D.C. has evolved into a kind of ***"economic umpire"***[31] who holds the ring within which the infrastructure of institutional credit functions. He has the possibility of intervening decisively, should he so desire. He has enough legal powers, apart from the extra-legal power

[30] Kennedy, Capt. C.P., 1824, op. cit., Para 44, p. 279.

[31] Term so aptly coined by Prof. Dr D. Rothermund who has guided the present research. Amongst so many other debts of gratitude owed to him is this term.

of the mystique associated with his position because of the long legacy carried over from British times. An energetic D.C. can play an important role in price level fixation in his district and in the functioning of the institutional credit outlets. It is useful to examine the legal framework, procedure and actual functioning of the D.C. as an economic umpire.

6.4.1 Legal Framework: Laws, Ordinances and Rules

There are any number of ordinances and executive orders issued by the government which authorize the D.C. to act in the economic sphere. Only four or five important legal bases need to be reviewed here. A separate dissertation would need to be written if all statutory and administrative measures available to the D.C. were to be discussed.

6.4.1.1 The Essential Commodities Act: Shopkeepers' Bète Noire

This is an old piece of Union legislation which has been since its promulgation in 1955 amply supplemented by local and special laws passed by the H.P. Assembly. It still remains in force and is used by district authorities to act against hoarders and profiteers. A sustained campaign of raids and prosecutions under this Act can over the short-term marginally lower price levels by unearthing hoarded stocks of scarce commodities thereby increasing supply in the market. It would, however, be unrealistic to expect such raids to compensate for basic disequilibria of credit flow, demand and supply over a long-term. More practically, major bank loan defaulters, if they are also shopkeepers, can be nudged towards repayment of bank loans if the D.C. wants to help bankers. A series of raids and seizures, followed by indirect hints that the pressure could be eased provided bank defaults were liquidated can be a big help to the bankers.

6.4.1.2 the Excise and Taxation Act, 1961: Another 'Dandā'

This law has been supplemented in Himāchal by additional provisions. It provides powers of inspection, controls and imposition of penalties in case of shopkeepers/liquor vend owners not paying requisite excise duties and taxes. Excise duties/sales tax are periodically revised by the annual budget or through ordinances. The task of policing shopkeepers/liquor vend operators through this Act falls on the D.C. assisted by S.D.Ms and the hierarchy of the Excise and Taxation Department - the Excise and Taxation Officer (E.T.O.), the Assistant E.T.Os (A.E.T.Os) and Excise Inspectors. An extremely important excise item is liquor, an item of mass consumption (never mind the hoopla about prohibition and temperance!). Liquor vends are auctioned publicly every year by the D.C., aided by the E.T.O. and his staff. Retail price per bottle is fixed for each vend and cannot be exceeded under the law. Liquor contractors defaulting on bank loans can be subjected to sustained raids and even sealing off of their retail outlets till they decide to repay due instalments on their loans. There is hardly any liquor vend contractor not infringing excise laws in one way or the other.

6.4.1.3 The Agricultural Produce Marketing Act, 1972

This Act creates regulated markets for marketing of agricultural produce. A marketing committee is constituted at the district-level with the D.C. as its Chairman. This committee supervises the implementation of the Act's provisions. Functioning of commission agents (ārhtiyās) can be brought to heel to some extent by this Act, depending upon how active the D.C. is. The Market Committee fixes maximum commission charges (ārhat) that may be charged on agricultural produce being brought to the regulated market. It can levy penal interest and cancel 'ārhat' licences in case of violation of rules. Strict supervision and implementation of regulated market bye-laws affect price levels for agricultural produce. By curbing the proverbial rapacity of the ārhtiyās to the extent possible, corresponding benefits can be extended to sellers who are bank clients. Market committees earn income from ārhtiyās through imposition of market fees and spend this income providing facilities like irrigation schemes, rest houses, cemented auction platforms for crop produce, calibrated balances etc. to help agriculturists.

6.4.1.4 The H.P. Commodities Price Marking & Display Order, 1977

Just as the preceding Act of 1972 for commission agents, this Order and its accompanying Order became the bètes noires of the trading community. Heavy pressure was brought to bear on the government to withdraw these orders. Demonstrations and strikes were widespread but the Orders were not withdrawn though officers were asked to go easy on shopkeepers to diffuse this pressure. Under Section 2 (b), a dealer was defined as a person carrying on "*wholesale or retail business of selling or storing for the sale of any commodity whether or not such business is carried on in addition to any other business*".[32] Even handcart owners (réhriwālās) were covered by this definition. Section 3 (a) made it obligatory for every dealer to conspicuously display a list of prices and opening stocks in Hindi. The commodities in respect of which such display had to be made were specified in an attached Schedule and covered all foodstuffs, toiletry goods and almost all articles of general everyday use.

6.4.1.5 The H.P. Hoarding & Profiteering Prevention Order, 1977

This Order empowered the D.C., wearing his hat (or turban!) of District Magistrate (D.M.), to fix by notification in the official gazette the following in respect of any article:[33]

(a) The maximum quantity which may at any one time be possessed by a dealer or a producer;
(b) The maximum quantity which may at any one time be possessed by any consumer;
(c) The maximum quantity which may, in any one transaction, be sold to any person by a dealer or a producer; and
(d) The maximum margin of profit that may be charged by a dealer or a producer over his costs.

In addition, under Section 10(1), the Director of Civil Supplies, the District Magistrate or police officers of the rank of Sub-Inspector and above may:[34]

(A) Inspect or cause to be inspected any books or other documents belonging to or under the control of a producer or a dealer;
(B) Enter or search the premises of a producer, a dealer or a consumer;
(C) Seize any article in respect of which he has reason to believe that a contravention of this order or any notification issued thereunder has been, is being or is about to be committed.

An accompanying Schedule lists out a whole gamut of articles of everyday use to which this Order applies. Section 3(2) deals with fixation of profit margins. While fixing the margin of profit, the D.C. has to take into consideration "*the nature of the commodities and also all relevant local conditions and that such margin of profit shall in no case be less than 1.5% and more than 10%. But in the case of fresh vegetables the margin may extend up to 25%*".[35] Depending on the cost of transportation, prices could differ from trader to trader even for the same commodity. However, an upper ceiling is placed on the profit that a trader can extract from buyers. Each trader has thus to work out the retail prices for each consignment received. Price lists have to be changed each time if the trader claims that procurement or transportation costs have changed the retail price. The Order thus seeks to cap the price level. Free market forces are free to sway price levels but only within the profit margins specified. This measure and the power to raid and confiscate is a powerful weapon in the hands of the

[32] Notification No. FDS. A(3)-2/77, dated Simla-171002 the 5th. August, 1977, Govt. of Himāchal Pradesh, Food and Supplies Department, Section 2 (b).

[33] Notification Ibid, H.P. Hoarding and Profiteering Prevention Order, 1977, Sections 3 (1)(a) to 3 (1)(d).

[34] Ibid, Clauses 10(1)(a) till 10(1)(c).

[35] Ibid, Clause 3 (2).

economic umpire. Even the biggest shopkeepers fear this coercive potential, which has further been reinforced.

6.4.1.6 The Essential Services Maintenance Act, 1980 (E.S.M.A.)

This is a central act; a sort of post-1980 reincarnation of the notorious Maintenance of Internal Security Act (M.I.S.A.) of Emergency days. Specified categories of economic offenders, hoarders, smugglers, black marketeers can be put under preventive detention for up to one year, subject to approval by the E.S.M.A. Advisory Board constituted specially for such review. The D.C. can make it clear to traders that maintenance of the price line at a certain specified level should be considered as an essential service. Economic activities such as hoarding tended to create an artificial scarcity so as to push up prices and could be punished under this Act. The D.M. can pass detention orders. The Act is a severe measure but a very useful sword of Damocles to hang over the heads of traders.

In practice it can be observed that shopkeepers/traders do not mind paying fines as punishment because such amounts can always be recuperated in a couple of dubious transactions. What they really fear is extended detention which dislocates their trade activities and brings them into sharp public focus, harming their social clout. Most traders fear the E.S.M.A. strongly. In a regular trial the trader can easily furnish bail and carry on business activities while on bail. E.S.M.A. forecloses the bail option. The only remedy is the Advisory Board. But any D.M. using E.S.M.A. against traders must reckon with a storm of political pressure, manipulated protest and even transfer. Not many officers today are prepared to be so bold.

6.4.2 Procedure of the D.C.'s Economic Role

Apart from the statutory and administrative coercive powers at his disposal, the D.C. exercises his economic functions through meetings of numerous district-level committees. Besides formal meetings, most special interest groups like the Beopār Mandal, Truck Union, Zamindāra/Kisān Union, Arhtiyās' Union, Sawmillers' Association[36] or other bodies representing specific economic interests meet the D.C. frequently. Each such meeting is a protracted bargaining session in which the traders/growers/sawmillers highlight their difficulties and demand higher profit margins while the D.C. uses the carrot and stick approach to persuade them to hold the price line. The carrot lies in holding out hopes of an increase in the fixation of profit margins, holding steady or decreasing the costs of carriage and pressing bankers to make institutional credit more easily available. The stick lies in raids, prosecutions, arrests, choking off institutional credit lines and speeding up of recovery proceedings against defaulters.

These bargaining sessions involve trade-offs between different pressure groups. Traders want fixation of transportation/freight rates at low levels to reduce their own overhead costs. Truck Unions and cooperative depot holders press for higher carriage charges pleading that diesel rates have gone up, tyre/tube prices have increased or truck chassis have become more expensive. Fixation of rates for articles of general consumption is done by the D.C. after elaborate collective bargaining in the Food Advisory Committee. Prices of packing cases for apples, so important for Kinnaur, are fixed by the D.C. after meetings of the Apple Marketing Committee. Sawmillers seek higher prices for packing cases while apple growers seek lower prices. Some apple growers are also sawmill owners but they demand higher packing case prices because of the subsidies involved. The government pay a subsidy for keeping packing case prices low for growers. The retail price in Kinnaur for a 20 kg. wooden packing case had been fixed at Rs 5 per case, against an open market price of Rs 6.50 to Rs 7.00. The difference

[36] Beopār Mandal = Merchants' Association, Arhtiyās = Commission agents, Zamindāra/Kisān Union = Farmers' Association.

was subsidized by providing sawmillers cheap wood through allocation of trees in government forests at artificially low rates, lower than the market rates for these trees. The Forest Department has standardized tables specifying how many boxes can be made out of how many cubic metres of wood. It releases tree quotas on the basis of a demand recommended by the D.C. who can recommend less or more quota depending on his judgement of the needs of the sawmillers. In return for getting this subsidized wood, sawmillers are supposed to sell packing cases at rates fixed by the D.C. In this way felling of trees is subsidized in the name of horticultural development. Carriage charges for muleback and manback were fixed for Kinnaur taking into consideration local geographical conditions.[37] Upper limits were thus fixed for price levels of all essential commodities. Market forces could come into play within this ring held by the economic umpire.

6.4.3 Economic Umpire's Operation: Carrot and Stick!

The D.C. is not, however, an unfettered economic Czar. In reality prices are fixed on the basis of political and administrative realities and not purely on economic grounds. The Truck Union is usually a powerful lobby. A poor man, by definition, cannot be a truck owner! This Union groups together affluent, politically well-connected members who are also popular with bankers. Bankers are happy to give loans for purchase of trucks because a few such loans show up as large sums while giving bank loan figures; a small number of borrowers make follow-up for recovery much easier; hypothecation of the purchased truck is a good risk insurance because a truck, unlike land, can easily be sold or auctioned. Truck owners need repeated bank finance to renew or expand their fleets so that they cannot afford to default. They repay regularly to keep bank managers happy and institutional credit flowing. Truck owners are frequently called upon to perform a modern version of the traditional system of ***'bégār'***[38] in-as-much-as they are asked to transport people free of cost for political rallies or for visits by political bigwigs involving mass meetings; liberal "donations" to various district funds (Red Cross Fund, Flood Relief Fund etc.); transportation of household goods/building materials at very low rates or free of cost for politicians or officers and free use of trucks for non-official purposes. The D.C. cannot ignore this lobby.

Equally, he cannot ignore the Beopār Mandal which is made to 'donate' money for various funds; furnishes commodities free of cost or at artificially low cost during visits by V.I.Ps. It is the principal source of money for financial collections that the D.C. may be required to make. Meals for visiting V.I.Ps (politicians or officers) are generally lavish. Very few visitors bother to pay at all or to pay fully or question as to who pays for the food and drink given during their stay. Officially approved hospitality rates are ridiculously low and can be used only for persons formally declared as state guests. The D.C. has to squeeze truck owners and/or shopkeepers through his subordinates to meet these unofficial expenses. Obviously, he cannot be too harsh towards the hand that gives the "donations".

With increasing accent on provision of more and more consumer goods through the P.D.S. outlets, the D.C. is supposed to really function as a sort of merchant to revitalize fair price shops. Since cooperatives and individual depot holders were being told repeatedly to sell items of general consumption like lentils, soaps, exercise books, cloth fabrics etc. at fixed rates, incentives had to be provided in terms of higher carriage rates than the actual rates then prevailing in Kinnaur. If the actual cost of freight was, say, Rs 35 per quintal for some commodity in a remote area of the district, the rate would be fixed at Rs 40 per quintal, leaving a margin of Rs 5 or so per quintal, provided that additional consumer goods specified by the D.C. were stocked and sold. Depot holders were particularly prone to such persuasion. The consumer would pay a slightly higher price but would have essential items available in or

[37] Please see Section 1.2.4, Chapter I of this work.

[38] Please see Section 2.B.2, Chapter II - B of this work.

very near to his place of residence thereby reducing expenditure of time and money on having to travel far to fetch the same items. Items were supplied through the H.P. Civil Supplies Corporation and the KINFED, with carriage rates fixed for each retail P.D.S. outlet. It all demanded hard work, a study of prevailing procurement/carriage rates, knowledge of the desirability or otherwise of marketing certain commodities and a totally business-like approach. The D.C., enmeshed in so many other duties, may not always have the time for such an approach. Sometimes rates are taken from the preceding year and reissued as such or after a hike of 2%-2.5% in a new notification for the succeeding year. The focus in Kinnaur was more on providing commodities at specified rates through the P.D.S. outlets rather than rigid enforcement of price ceilings in the open market. By a sort of evolved consensus, a hike of more than 5% was not to be allowed in profit margins from one year to the next. Increases would by and large hover around 2.0 to 2.5% regardless of actual economic conditions. Or, the preceding year's notification may just be reissued as such for the succeeding year to save time and botheration and gain some popularity points.

The entire profit/price margin fixation mechanism is a weapon in the D.C.'s hands to put a brake on the trading community from pushing the price level above a politically unacceptable range. It is a good handle for whipping shopkeepers into line if they prove recalcitrant in coughing up favours when demanded. A non-cooperative trader may find his premises being raided frequently, his records seized and his shop even sealed. If nothing works there is always the menace of the E.S.M.A. which was, however, never used in Kinnaur.

Controls on prices of apple/fruit packing cases were lax. Sawmillers exploited the perishable nature of horticultural produce to charge higher rates. Growers could not afford to wait too long to obtain boxes at prescribed rates. They were willing to pay higher rates. Smaller orchardists could not afford to store their produce in distant cold storages in Parwānoo, Simla or Chandigarh and were forced to sell. Only bigger orchardists could use these remote cold storage facilities. They were in many cases themselves sawmill owners so that they could send their own produce in subsidized crates while making others pay inflated prices for packing cases, thereby pushing up their own competitive edge in fruit markets in Chandigarh and Delhi. Considering the political importance of large orchard owners in Himāchal, few campaigns of harassment have been launched against orchardists-cum-sawmillers. The D.C. has thus to function within a system buffeted by mutually conflicting pressure groups, each seeking to maximise its gain through official manipulation of market forces. Detailed knowledge of Marxian or Keynesian theories or monetarist precepts is not of much help in fixing the profit margins/prices of 'dāl roti' (staple food) for a small 'dhāba' (cheap eating place) in Kinnaur! In addition to all these functions, the D.C. directly controls some loans.

6.5 LOANS DIRECTLY CONTROLLED BY THE D.C.

Under British-appointed managers, Bushahr State had begun giving direct loans for trade.[39] This system of direct loans marked the first attempt by Bushahr to provide any sort of institutional finance. These loans were referred to in common parlance as taccāvi loans, even though this word denoted government assistance to agriculturists in times of flood, famine or similar emergencies. This system had been traditional in India and had been continued by the British who even passed a number of taccāvi acts.[40] An attempt was made to systematize loan operations subsequent to the proposals made by the Famine Commission of 1880 and the Agriculturists' Loans Act 1884, both of an enabling character. They conferred powers to frame

[39] Please see Section 1.2.4, Chapter I of this work.

[40] Act No. XIX of 1883, Act No. XII of 1884; also see: Rothermund, D., 1978, p. 85.

rules governing the sanctioning and disbursement of loans on provincial governments. By and large, financial assistance from the government was limited to the purposes specifically stipulated in the Acts. These purposes were as follows:[41]

(a) Construction of wells, tanks and other works for the storage, supply or distribution of water for the purpose of agriculture, or for the use of men and cattle employed in agriculture;
(b) Preparation of land for irrigation;
(c) Drainage, reclamation from rivers or other waters, or protection from floods or from erosion or other damage by water, of land used for agricultural purposes or waste land which is cultivable;
(d) Reclamation, clearance, enclosure or permanent improvement of land for agricultural purposes;
(e) Renewal or reconstruction of any of the foregoing works, or alterations therein or additions thereto;
(f) Such other work as government may, from time to time declare to be improvements for the purpose of the Act;
(g) Relief of distress;
(h) Purchase of seed or cattle; and
(i) Any other purpose not specified in the Land Improvement Loans Act but connected with agricultural objects.

The D.C., functioning as District Collector, was the competent authority for sanctioning loans, but for loans exceeding Rs 2,000 the previous sanction of the Divisional Commissioner was required and for those exceeding Rs 5,000 previous sanction of the government was necessary. Under the Agriculturists' Loans Act 1884, the S.D.O.(Civil) could sanction loans up to Rs 250, the Collector up to Rs 500 while loans exceeding Rs 500 required the prior sanction of the Commissioner and those exceeding Rs 3,000 required prior sanction of the government. For short-term loans, the average loan per head was not to exceed Rs 15 and the maximum was not to exceed Rs 25. But, as pointed out by Prof. D. Rothermund, *"Even the old institution of taccavi loans with which previous governments had helped the landholders so as to increase their revenue paying capacity had decayed under British rule, because the bureaucratic formalities which had to be observed in order to get such a loan proved to be almost prohibitive"*.[42] The object of the taccāvi system is, generally, to supply funds and not articles. Distribution in kind is only admissible where crop diseases decimate standing crops or a large-scale scarcity in fodder or grain is noticed, particularly for seed purposes. The taccāvi system applies mainly to advances under Act XII of 1884 but cases may occur where it may be used mainly for land improvement purposes. For example, when a special drive is being launched to encourage construction of masonary wells or lining of 'kutcha' (earthen) wells as a precautionary measure against famine. In cases under the Land Improvement Loans Act, if an agriculturist wants to improve his lands, taccāvi loans are available keeping in view the character of the improvement for which the loan is applied for. In considering loan applications the deciding authority has to first decide whether the need for taking a loan is established at all and whether the security available is adequate; how much loan is to be advanced; the instalments in which it is to be advanced and the period to be allowed before repayment commences. The sanctioning officer has to have regard for the circumstances of the borrower, as for instance in determining the advances under the Agriculturist Loans Act 1884, the area of the land cultivated by the applicant, the amount of the seed required by him and the price of the seed are all to be taken into account. Taccāvi loans are also available for the purchase of bullocks. The whole procedure here was ridden with safety catches and formalities. What were these formalities ?

[41] The All-India Rural Credit Survey: Report of the Committee of Direction, Volume I: Part 2 (Credit Agencies): The Survey Report, Bombay: Reserve Bank of India, 1957, Chapter 19: Sections 19.1.6 and 19.1.7, p. 62.

[42] Rothermund, D., 1978, p. 85.

6.5.1 Formalities involved in Sanction of Taccāvi Loans

Applications under the two Acts referred to in the preceding lines had to be on prescribed proformæ. If a loan appeared prima facie warranted, the Collector or S.D.O. would order an enquiry by an official not below the rank of Kānungo to ascertain area of land owned or occupied; status of the applicant; nature and value of immovable property offered as security; existing encumbrances on the property; names, status and means of sureties; suitable date for repayment of the first instalment with reference to the circumstances under which the loan was applied for; proposed instalments and period of repayment and the date on which the loan should be received by the applicant.

Objections were invited through a public notice to the grant of such loan. Having weighed the evidence produced by the objectors, an order would be made in writing accepting or rejecting the objections. The S.D.O. would then forward the loan case to the D.C. with a specific recommendation whether the loan should be sanctioned or not. The D.C. would have to determine whether enough security was on offer; what amount should be advanced; number of instalments to be specified for repayment and grace period allowed before repayment would begin. Anyone even vaguely familiar with the bureaucracy in India would know that this procedure would be extremely time consuming. To it were added conditions of security to be offered.

6.5.1.1 Types of Security Demanded on Government Loans

Under the Land Improvement Loans Act, 1883, security could be demanded in the following forms:

(a) If the amount of loan did not exceed 75% of the applicant's transferable interest in the land after the improvement to be effected, no collateral was required. In case this condition was not met, further security in the shape of transferable interests in other lands belonging to the applicant or to other persons willing to act as his sureties or of personal security, was demanded. Lands subject to the landlord's consent before transfer were ordinarily to be rejected as security. If this prior consent in writing of all the landlords in a specified way had earlier been obtained for the sale of this land in case of default such lands could be accepted as security;

(b) If five or more villagers jointly and severally bound themselves for repayment of the loan, their personal security would normally suffice provided the loan amount did not exceed five times the annual rental of the land held by members of the group, who had to agree to the following terms and conditions on a prescribed form:

(A) All and everyone of the applicants as well as their heirs and representatives were jointly and severally bound to the government for repayment of the entire loan amount due;

(B) In case of default in repayment of the loan in question or any part thereof, government had the authority and right to realize the entire and every part of the payment due from the person and movable or immovable property, whether mentioned in the bond or not, of all and every one of the applicants and of all and each of their heirs or representatives.

There were similar safeguards for loans given under the Agriculturist Loans Act, 1884 as follows:

(a) If an applicant possessed a transferable interest in immovable property of value sufficient to cover the entire loan amount such interest would normally be required to be mortgaged entirely or in sufficient portion to the government as security. In addition, the sanctioning authority could require or accept any other good security;

(b) *For applicants not in possession of transferable interests in immovable property sufficient to furnish security, loan could be given against guarantee of a third party possessing such transferable interest in immovable property of value sufficient to secure the whole amount;*
(c) *Lands not transferable without the consent of landlords were not ordinarily to be accepted as security. If such consent were given in writing on the prescribed proforma for sale of land in case of default, such lands could be accepted as security;*
(d) *Should the applicants be a body of five or more co-villagers who bind themselves jointly and severally to the government for loan repayment, their personal security could be accepted provided they agreed to terms and conditions as outlined for the Land Improvement Loans Act.*

6.5.1.2 Disbursement and Repayment: Red-Tape À La Carte!

After completion of formalities, loans up to Rs 500 could be disbursed in the village by the officer granting the loans, or by an officer not below the rank of Kānungo. In other cases payments were to be made before a gazetted officer at the district or sub-divisional treasury on presentation of the payment order by the applicant or his authorized agent. Unless specified otherwise by the D.C., loans were ordinarily to be released in three instalments; 40% before commencement of the work; 40% when the work was roughly half finished and 20% when the work was certified as fit after due completion.

Repayment would be in a number of instalments. The date of repayment of the last instalment of a loan was ordinarily to be not later than 20 years from the date of actual disbursement of the loan. If the loan had been disbursed in instalments, such date would be 20 years from the date of disbursement of the last instalment actually taken. This was subject to the overriding proviso that the entire amount of the loan due for recovery would in all cases have to be repaid before the expiry of the period for which the improvement was likely to be effective. Loans under the Agriculturists' Loans Act 1884 were ordinarily made repayable within one or two years, but a longer period could be given with the approval of the Divisional Commissioner. If the D.C. was convinced that whole or part of any loan had been misutilized for a purpose other than that for which it had been taken, he could proceed to order recovery of the entire loan amount with interest @ 12.5% per annum from the date on which the loan was made to the date of recovery. The D.C. would fix repayment dates with due regard to the dates of harvest of the principal crops. In single crop season areas, there would normally be only one repayment instalment per annum; in an area with two crop seasons there would be two instalments per year. In no case would the date of repayment of the first instalment be later than 2.5 years from the date of actual disbursement.

In Kinnaur such loans were being advanced till 1965-66 at rates of interest varying from 4% to 5% per annum. Recoveries were to be effected under easy instalments spread over a period ranging from one to 15 years depending on the type of loan. Loan amounts disbursed in Kinnaur are shown in Tables 6.19 and 6.20 respectively. These figures reveal straightaway how horticultural development has come to the fore in Kinnaur. Long-term loans given under the Act of 1883 have largely been supplanted by loans from the LDB and commercial banks. This falling off can be clearly seen in the figures compiled for land improvement loans under head '705-loans' given by the Revenue Department from 1975-76 till November 30, 1985, shown in Table 6.21 . From six and seven figure sums from 1960-61 to 1965-66, loans given by the Revenue Department under head 705 had fallen to a total of Rs 26,500 from 1975-76 till 1985-86. In fact, from 1976-77 to 1982-83 there was no loan disbursement at all under this head. Rates of interest had been raised by the government from the 4% to 5% earlier to 6.75% to 7.75% per annum as follows:

(a) *Improvement of land (other than horticulture) = 7.75%;*
(b) *Fire and flood sufferers = 7.75%;*
(c) *Agriculturists in distress = 7.75%;*
(d) *Purchase of seeds = 6.75%; and*

Table 6.19: Loans Advanced under the Land Improvement Loans Act, 1883, in Kinnaur District

sn	*Year*	*Loan Purpose*	
do	-do-	LIR	FFS
01	1960-61	350,000	100,000
01	1960-61	350,000	100,000
02	1961-62	400,000	,500
03	1962-63	350,000	0,000
04	1963-64	400,000	8,000
05	1964-65	100,000	0,000
06	1965-66	495,000	0,000

Code: **LIR = Land improvement loan amount in Rupees,**
FFS = loans for fire and flood sufferers in Rupees.
(Source: Gazetteer, 1971, Chapter IV, p. 155.)

Table 6.20: Loans Advanced under the Agriculturists' Loans Act 1884 in Kinnaur District

sn	*Year*	*LFHP*	*LEGC*
01	1960-61	3100,000	0,000
01	1960-61	3100,000	0,000
02	1961-62	4000,000	4000,000
03	1962-63	5375,000	3575,000
04	1963-64	5000,000	810,000
05	1964-65	3895,000	1883,000
06	1965-66	3321,000	969,400

Code: **LFHP = loan for horticultural purposes,**
LEGC = loan for establishment of garden colonies.
Loan amounts are in Rupees.
(Source: As for Table 6.19.)

(e) Soil conservation works = 7.75%.
(Source: File No. KNR-IV-5(DRA) of the D.R.A. Branch, D.C.'s Office at Kālpa).

Taccāvi loans in Himāchal are not based on multiples of land revenue paid as a measuring unit. The maximum amount under Act XIX of 1883 (Land Improvement Loan) is Rs 50,000; to be sanctioned by the Financial Commissioner in Simla; Rs 10,000 by the Divisional Commissioner; Rs 2,500 by the District Collector. Similarly, maximum loan amounts permissible under Act XII of 1884 (Agriculturist Loans Act) are Rs 10,000 by the F.C., Rs

Table 6.21: Loans under Head 705-Loans in Kinnaur

sn	*Year*	*Loan Amount Per Tahsil/Sub-Tahsil*							*BL*
do	-do-	H	P	M	K	S	N	T	do
01	1975-76	500	000	00	0,000	00	00	,500	00
02	1976-83	000	000	00	0,000	00	00	0,000	00
03	1983-84	000	2000	00	8,000	00	00	10,000	00
04	1984-85	000	000	00	7,000	00	00	7,000	00
05	1985-86	000	000	00	9,000	00	00	9,000	00

Code: **Loan amounts are in Rupees.**
sn = serial number, BL = balance left,
H = Hangrang, P = Pooh, M = Moorang, K = Kālpa, S = Sangla,
N = Nichār, T = total loan amount.
(Source: Information compiled by Mr Tegta, District Revenue Accountant, D.C.'s Office, Kinnaur District at Kālpa for the author in December 1985 from Register T-7 for each Tahsil.)

2,500 by the Divisional Commissioner and Rs 500 by the District Collector respectively. The admissibility of the taccāvi loan is to be calculated at half times the loan applied for. For example, if an agriculturist applies for a taccāvi loan of Rs 1,000, the cost of the land in which he has interest as a landowner should at least be Rs 1,500 worth. Multiples of land revenue are not considered. The following are the heads of account under which taccāvi loans are being disbursed:

(1) 704-Loans: land improvement loans; and
(2) 705-Loans: agriculturists' loans.

As already indicated in preceding lines the interest on such loans is charged at the rate fixed from time to time by the government. It used to be 6.25% per annum but the state government revised it upwards to 7% to 10% per annum.[43] The period of repayment should not in any case, except with prior sanction of the government, be longer than 20 years in the case of loans advanced for land improvement and not more than 10 years in case of agriculturists' loans. For fixation of instalments we can take an example. If a loanee chooses to repay a loan of Rs 100 in 10 annual instalments after two years, he will pay ten instalments of Rs 13.81 or Rs 138.12 in all. If he chooses to spread the repayment over 15 years and begins repayment after two years, he will pay 15 instalments of Rs 10.31 each or Rs 154.65 in all. If any instalment is not paid on a due date the whole of the loan with such interest as may be due thereon may, at the discretion of the Collector, be deemed to become at once due and be recovered in lumpsum. Normally in case of default penal interest is charged @ 12% per annum at the discretion of the Collector. There was no attraction left for borrowers for these loans at 7.75% rate of interest when they could get loans for the same purposes directly from banks or under the I.R.D.P. at annual rates of interest either 4% under the D.R.I. scheme or 10% under the I.R.D.P. . The loans under head-705 were direct from the Revenue Department under cast iron security in terms of transfer of titles to land. Tahsildārs were particular in recovering these loans on priority basis. They did not want their A.C.Rs spoilt. In cases of defaults on bank loans they could shift the blame onto bank authorities but here there was no such escape route. The D.C. would come down hard on any subordinates not recovering such

[43] Vide letter No. Fin-2-C(1)19/84-W & M, dated September 6, 1984 from the Finance Department in Simla.

loans. The borrowers also knew this quite well. Field surveys in villages Pooh, Sunnam, Kāmru, Roghi and Kothi made for this research showed that borrowers tended to use limited liquidity available to repay the Revenue Department's loans first; followed by repayment of loans from village moneylenders and finally, loans from banks, in that order.

The system of taccāvi loans designed by the British was not for replacing traditional moneylenders. As Prof. D. Rothermund so rightly points out, the concern of British rulers for the peasantry *"was only a rather narrowly conceived political one, and they were satisfied with the relief of debtors in general terms. When the immediate pressure subsided there was no further need for remedial legislation"*.[44] The accent on foolproof security meant that only more affluent landowners or tenants with clearly established occupancy titles to land would stand to benefit most. The really needy poor peasant could not furnish acceptable security in terms of unchallenged title to adequate land. *"The conservative law-and-order administrators were conscious about any responsibilities which may be thrust upon them, if they agreed to anything beyond remedial legislation which could then be enforced by the usual machinery of government. They did not want to bell the cat, i.e. control the individual moneylender, or take care of the kitten, i.e. build up rural credit institutions"*.[45] The British wanted to placate the larger tenants by giving the impression of being concerned about the economic distress of the peasantry. In reality the taccāvi loan system that they enacted involved heavy transaction costs for applicants who were required to fulfil a whole host of bureaucratic formalities which would push up the real rate of interest higher than the nominal rate of interest. Like the banks later, the system was sought to be loaded against credit risks (poor peasants) by pushing up transaction costs, all the while mouthing sympathy for the plight of the poor peasants!

6.5.2 Loans for Housing Schemes: 'Roti, Kapḍā aur Makān'?

Housing poses a problem for poor people who have to indebt themselves heavily to raise enough funds for repair or construction of some kind of shelter. Conscious of these problems, government gave loans for housing purposes under a variety of schemes for village housing.

6.5.2.1 Village Housing Projects Scheme (V.H.P.S.)

Loans under the V.H.P.S. Rules could be granted to the residents of villages selected for development under this scheme or to cooperatives of such persons for construction of new houses or for improvement of existing houses. The loan amounts could not exceed 80% of the estimated cost of construction or repair, subject to a maximum ceiling of Rs 3,000. Cost of land would be excluded from the estimates except in such flood affected villages where houses had to be rebuilt on new sites free from the danger of floods. No loans were to be granted to persons intending to build houses estimated to cost more than Rs 8,000. The loans were to be sanctioned by the D.C. or any other officer authorized by the government in this behalf. Applications were to be made to the D.C. through the B.D.O. No loans were to be granted without a local enquiry by the B.D.O. in regard to:

(a) *Title of the applicant to the property offered as security;*
(b) *Repaying capacity of the applicant with reference to his income over the preceding three years, his assets and liabilities. The applicants were to furnish such documents and evidence as might be demanded by the B.D.O.*

The D.C. or any other authorized officer would determine the amount of loan to be disbursed to each applicant, keeping in view the latter's repaying capacity and security offered. The applicant must own the house site and be willing and able to contribute at least 2% of the

[44] Rothermund, D., 1978, p. 85.

[45] Ibid.

cost of construction in cash or building materials or labour. House construction would have to begin within two months of the date of sanction and would have to be completed within a period of one year from such date. This period could be extended by the D.C. for a further period not exceeding six months in deserving cases. House improvements would have to be commenced within one month and completed within six months from the date of sanction. It could be extended up to a maximum of three months by the D.C. In case the work was not completed within the allowed period, the amount of loan was to be recovered summarily as A.L.Rs. The land and the house proposed to be constructed or repaired thereon would have to be mortgaged to the government as security for the loan and interest due thereon. Government would have first charge on the property during the pendency of the loan. In case of default in repayment of loan instalments including interest thereon, the government could order recovery of the amount due as A.L.Rs. Loan disbursement was to be in the following three stages:

(a) 30% only when a prescribed mortgage bond had been executed;
(b) 50% of the loan amount when construction reached plinth level stage; and
(c) Balance 20% when construction reached the roof level stage.

The loans were to be ordinarily recoverable in 20 equal annual instalments of principal and interest. The first instalment would fall due in 18 months in case of new construction and 12 months in case of improvement of existing houses. Loans had to be utilized for the purpose for which advanced and for no other purpose. No V.H.P.S. loan would be granted to an applicant who had already applied for or obtained a house building loan under the Low Income Group Housing Scheme (LIGHS) or any other government scheme. Table 6.22 shows

Table 6.22: Loans Advanced under the V.H.P.S. in Kinnaur District

sn	*Year*	*loan amt*
01	1960-61	0,000
02	1961-62	33,920
03	1962-63	8,480
04	1963-64	14,390
05	1964-65	9,750
06	1965-66	4,800

Code: Loan amount is in Rupees, amt = amount.
(Source: As for Table 6.19)

the magnitude of loans advanced under the V.H.P.S. in Kinnaur. The amounts were low, with no consistency in their variation. In Kinnaur where construction costs were high (estimated at around Rs 25,000 for one room by P.W.D. estimates for official buildings) such petty amounts had largely a symbolic value to show that the V.H.P.S. was being carried out. What the real state of affairs was shall be seen by considering the LIGHS.

6.5.2.2 Low Income Group Housing Scheme (LIGHS)

Loans were to be advanced under the LIGHS to applicants whose annual income did not exceed Rs 7,200 and who did not already own a house. A loan could be advanced to an eligible applicant already owning a house, provided the additional house was needed for his own bonafide residential purpose. Loans could be given to the extent of 80% of the actual expenditure on each house, including cost of land, subject to a maximum of Rs 14,500 per house. The remaining 20% of the cost would have to be borne by the applicant himself. Cost of land already in possession would be computed in this figure of 20%. Loans were to be advanced in three stages:

(a) 20% of the loan would be payable on execution of an agreement with the government on prescribed proforma;
(b) 50% on execution of a mortgage of the land and building to be constructed thereon in favour of the government and when construction reached the plinth level; and
(c) 30% to be paid only when construction reached the roof level stage.

The rate of interest in 1960-61 was 5% per annum, which had been raised to 7.5% per annum by 1985. Repayment of loan with interest was to be made in equal annual instalments not exceeding 30 years. Interest was to be levied from the date of disbursement. If no substantial progress was made within six months from the date of advance or if progress made had no relation to the amount of money advanced or if conditions governing the loan were not observed, the government could either withdraw or suitably curtail the loan. Except with previous sanction in writing of the government through the D.C., the applicant could not transfer by way of sale, gift or mortgage the land and the building erected on it or any right or title or interest therein till such time as the full amount of the loan and interest had been repaid to the government. Loan amounts actually given under LIGHS in Kinnaur are shown

Table 6.23: Loans Advanced under the LIGHS in Kinnaur District

sn	*Year*	*LIGHS*
01	1960-61	9,800
02	1961-62	68,000
03	1962-63	80,000
04	1963-64	74,670
05	1964-65	59,050
06	1965-66	49,000

Code: LIGHS = Low Income Group Housing Scheme loans in Rupees.
(Source: As for Table 6.19)

in Table 6.23 . The amounts were higher than those for the V.H.P.S. but not very much higher. Considering the bureaucratic formalities involved in securing these loans, it was no surprise that borrowers were not keen to offer cast iron securities. In fact, officials were having problems meeting loan disbursement targets under the V.H.P.S. and the LIGHS. In spite of repeated denials by officials, it was indicated by investigation in the field in several villages that the villagers had been told that they should not worry about accepting these loans as these were grants, not needing to be repaid. Kinnaur had then been newly created as a district and government were keen, particularly after the conflict with China in 1962, to see that targets were achieved for these loans. Officials in the field were under pressure to show results. Without thinking about long-term effects on recoveries or faith in the government as an institutional lender, field officials passed these loans off as subsidies. A case study of village Lippa reflects the consequences of this short-sighted quick-fix policy.

6.5.2.2.1 LIGHS Loan Cases in Village Lippa

A list of defaulters under the LIGHS loans for Kinnaur (as on March 31, 1985) was compiled from loan ledgers of the district office at Kālpa. Nine out of twelve defaulters belonged to village Lippa. The loans were all from March or August 1962. For Santan Sukh interest payments amounted to Rs 2,696.20 versus outstanding principal amount of Rs 2,833.22. In the case of Farboo Rām, interest due was Rs 1,096, more than double the outstanding principal of Rs 536.00. Accumulated interest exceeded pending principal amounts in the cases of Akal Jeet, Rām Kishan, Chhatandup, Karam Das, Wangail Chhering and Dharam Sukh; in all, for seven out of nine defaulters from village Lippa. Interest payments had accumulated to this extent because borrowers had been told that they did not need to repay since the loans would be written off by the government. They got a shock in 1980 when they were sent recovery notices asking them to repay else their property risked getting sequestered to ensure repayment. Convinced by the villagers' case that they had been misguided by officials, the D.C. took up their cause with the government and recommended writing off their loan amounts. There was prolonged correspondence in which the government demanded all sorts of details about the loan cases. After three years of such correspondence, the D.C.'s recommendation was rejected and recovery was ordered. The defaulters would have to pay interest even for these three years during which the matter remained under correspondence between the D.C. and the government. The former tried his best to help the villagers of Lippa but could achieve nothing concrete in the face of contrary orders from superior authorities.

The case of the villagers of Lippa became well known in Kinnaur. It was a setback to efforts to draw Kinnauras towards institutional credit by convincing them that doing so was in their own interest. In all the plans, projects and calculations, not much attention has been paid to the psychological aspect of making the Kinnauras feel involved in institutional credit programmes. It was taken for granted in official circles that Kinnauras should automatically see that official schemes were good for them. Officials were quite surprised that Kinnauras still seemed to be attached to their traditional practices and moneylenders rather than seeing how much the government were doing for them. In different discussions and workshops there were many suggestions about improving the functioning of the institutional credit network but attitudinal aspects were never discussed.

6.5.2.3 Attitudinal Aspect: Arrogant Officials and Bankers

There was a case in Nichār where the Reader to the S.D.M. and an office peon embezzled amounts repaid by villagers as instalments for V.H.P.S. and LIGHS loans taken by them. The Reader did not record the repayments in the ledger and was so brazen that he even issued receipts on white slips of paper. This defalcation of funds went on for three years after which villagers were sent notices for repayment. They came and produced the receipts which the Reader had been issuing to them. The concerned officials were both suspended from service and put on trial. They were convicted but the Reader was freed on probation. The then D.C. kept on dithering but his successor immediately dismissed both officials in 1980 since he felt that such persons had no right to be in government service. The Reader went in appeal against the D.C.'s order to the Divisional Commissioner who reinstated him in service on grounds of mercy on account of his young age. This concept of "mercy" seemed to always work in favour of employees, not in favour of debt-ridden peasants. In the case under discussion, 40 marginal farmers had systematically been swindled over three years; they had had to pay arrears with interest since their repayments had been embezzled. No mercy was shown to them by at least writing off the amounts repaid by them and embezzled by the Reader who in the name of mercy not only got his job back but also arrears of salary for the period for which he had not been paid. The poor villagers were handed notices threatening confiscation of their lands in case they did not repay their arrears.

It should not come as a surprise that borrowers subsequently lost confidence in government machinery's sense of justice and in its ability to help them. They turned to local moneylenders because they felt that official agencies would not understand their situation anyway. Very few government employees or bankers were imbued with a spirit of service or understanding which could help in weaning the Kinnaura peasantry away from village moneylenders. On the contrary, poorly paid employees indulged sometimes in bribe-taking and harassment of borrowers for obtaining pecuniary or other benefits, thereby nullifying in part the benefit of low rates of interest of institutional finance by pushing up transaction costs.

Procedures for obtaining loans from government agencies involved getting copies or attestations from a whole series of officials from the Patwāri and Grām Sėwak to the Naib Tahsildār/Tahsildār/B.D.O. on to the S.D.M. and the D.C. Each step may mean pecuniary losses plus several trips to concerned offices from remote villages. A high rate of absenteeism from duty of field officials aggravated this problem. For example, the Patwāri of Circle Chholtu was found missing from his place of duty for eight months. The Grām Sėwak of Circle Rupi went to his area of operation only once or twice a year, pleading ill health for his prolonged absences. Disciplinary action was sought to be taken against them but was stalled at higher levels because both officials had impeccable political connexions in Simla. In fact, the Patwāri boasted that he would get the D.C. transferred. When the latter transferred him to Circle Chāngo to at least distance him from his home district of Simla, the Patwāri (the juniormost revenue official) got cancellation orders sent from the-then Chief Minister's office. The D.C. stuck to his guns and the Patwāri had finally to proceed to Chāngo but the incident is typical of government functioning. A teacher in a single-teacher primary school in village Gharsu had not been on duty even for a single day but had sat at home in his native village in Kinnaur and continued to draw his salary. The Block Education Officer, Nichār had been showing him as present at his place of posting in inspection reports which had been written out at Nichār without ever having visited Gharsu. All these skeletons came out of the cupboard only because the D.C. personally visited Gharsu and prised information out of assembled villagers.

The functioning of institutional credit agencies cannot be delinked from the attitudes prevalent at various levels of government machinery towards prospective borrowers. Government may not now be the 'māi bāp sarkār' of British days for the average borrower but this changed perception has not fully seeped through as yet to all social layers in Kinnaur. Too many government functionaries still think that they have been sent to the area to lord it over the locals. Sending Kinnaura Patwāris and other officials does not always solve the problem. In fact, in some cases the problem got worsened. Some local field officials were close relatives of village moneylenders, coming from influential families being partly a reason for their having got into government service in the first place. Using political influence, such employees got posted close to their home villages in Kinnaur. Their caste background, their family network and their mental attitudes conditioned their attitudes which tended to be understanding towards village moneylenders who in many cases belonged to similar background or even to the same family or clan. They did not display motivation or zeal to loosen the clutches of village moneylenders. Apathy, indifference and collusion were unfortunately too frequent a constituent of the attitudinal makeup of field functionaries in Kinnaur.

In the absence of proper supervision and control, cooperative and government funds were embezzled by officials and non-officials in cahoots with each other. Such cases were discovered in Bari, Chhota Kamba, Rāmni, Jāni and Urni (to name a few!). Cooperative societies subsequently became defunct, leaving the field free for village moneylenders. The system as it exists today cannot function properly without due motivation and orientation of officials. No system of incentives or disincentives has been tried. An official who manages to turn a defunct cooperative society into a profitable undertaking could, for example, be allowed a fixed percentage of profits as bonus or an additional pay increment as an incentive. On the other hand officials who are negligent towards their duties should be penalized by reduction of benefits. Cooperative Department and other officials who allow embezzlement of public funds to go on unchecked should be prosecuted as co-accused before courts of law. Failure to curb embezzlement in spite of direct knowledge thereof is a crime. It has to be made more than clear that cooperative funds are not a pool of largesse.

Cooperative funds should be managed as carefully as personal funds and not as parts of a common till into which everyone can dip without fear of consequences. Police officials should be motivated to vigorously pursue cases of embezzlement of institutional funds by giving them a percentage of the amount they help to recover as bonus. At present, police officials are chary of pursuing such cases because documentary evidence is frequently destroyed or tempered with, reducing the chances of successful prosecution. Also, embezzlers are generally affluent and influential persons who furnish money and liquor. Steps have to be taken to make government employees more accountable for their actions. Donkeys, mules and horses tend to be treated alike in governmental work culture! It has to be made clear that acts of omission and commission would bring severe disciplinary action while a spirit of honest service would bring faster promotion and greater financial rewards. Government cannot just slumber on. Its róle as a direct credit giver was still quite important, as could be seen from a field survey done for the present research.

6.6 FIELD SURVEY DATA IN NICHĀR SUB-DIVISION

The field survey was carried out between December 1 and 15, 1985 with the help of the halqā (area) Patwāri and Grām Séwak in villages Bari, Paunda, and hamlets Kāshpo and Nigāni of village Nichār. According to the 1981 census, revenue estates Bari, Paunda and Nichār had 148, 41 and 476 households respectively.[46] Table 6.24 shows the number of households

Table 6.24: Field Survey Data for Nichār Sub-Division

sn	*VLG*	*nf*	*yf*	*npt*	*ypt*	*nc*	*yc*	*ncp*	*ycp*
01	Bari	18	15	54.50	45.50	18	33	54.50	100.00
02	Paunda	19	14	57.60	42.40	19	33	57.60	100.00
03	Kāshpo	21	13	61.80	38.20	21	34	61.80	100.00
04	Nigāni	08	20	28.60	71.40	08	28	28.60	100.00
05	Nagāni	02	04	33.30	66.70	02	06	33.30	100.00

Code: **sn = serial number, VLG = village,**
nf = frequency of households without official loans,
yf = frequency of households having taken institutional loans,
npt = percentage of households without institutional loans,
ypt = percentage of households having taken institutional loans,
nc = cumulative frequency of nf, yc = cumulative frequecny of yf,
ncp = cumulative percent of npt, ycp = cumulative percent of ypt.
(Source: own survey.)

covered in the survey. 33 households were sampled in villages Bari and Paunda each. 68 households were sampled in hamlets of Nichār, giving 134 sample households in all. 45.50% (15) of households surveyed in Bari, 42.40% in Paunda (14), 38.20% in Kāshpo, 71.40% (20) in Nigāni respectively had taken institutional loans. Households not having taken institutional

[46] District Census Handbook, Kinnaur District, 1981, p. 72, Pp 73-74.

loans had mostly taken loans from the informal sector for consumption purposes. Many of the households having taken institutional loans had in addition taken loans from village moneylenders.

From what has been discussed in Chapters III to VI, it would be expected that a large number of loans would be taken for an ostensible purpose where diversion to other purposes, including consumption purposes, would be the easiest. This is actually the case because most of the loans were for land development. Even if no land development works were observed on the ground, there was always the explanation that such work had in fact been done but that it had been obliterated by landslides or avalanches or other natural causes. It was just not possible to carry out a detailed enquiry in each case on the spot to find out the exact veracity of such assertions. Personal experience points to the fact that many, if not most, of the institutional loans taken for land development are diverted to other purposes. To fulfil targets, however, it is not possible to refuse loans under this head in spite of such knowledge.

It can also be predicted that government would be an important source of direct finance because till 1974 there were no commercial banks in Kinnaur at all and only one cooperative bank branch had been functioning since 1960. However, expansion of commercial bank network meant that the role of government as a direct source of institutional credit would not remain the most important source of institutional credit, yielding place to commercial banks. Borrowers were more willing to go to the banks than to the government because they could manage to delay repayment in case of banks but not in case of direct government loans where the Revenue Department did not permit such tardiness. Cooperative societies would be less important as sources of institutional finance because defaults and political manipulation had choked off their credit flow. The yearwise variation in the number of borrowers taking institutional loans, arranged according to the purpose for which loans had been taken, showed a preference for easily divertible loans cutting across source lines and was valid for each source.

6.6.1 Analysis of Field Survey Data

Table 6.25 shows the frequency distribution of the entire sample of 134 observations. It amply confirms that land development loans accounted for 34 cases out of 66 or more than half the total (51.50%). The next highest was animal husbandry with 10 cases (15.20%), a sizeable reduction. Horticultural loans had been taken in only one case. Deductions regarding the relative importance of the government as a source of direct finance were corroborated by bar charts.

6.6.1.1 Vertical Bar Charts

A histogram was plotted for the relative frequency distribution of purposes for which loans had been taken. Land development loans were by far the most preponderant, followed way behind by animal husbandry and sheep unit loans. In all these cases it was easy to offer explanations to mask actual utilization of loan amounts. The absence of milch animals or sheep could easily be explained away, as already mentioned earlier.[47] 51 loan cases out of 66 (77.30%) were for purposes where their diversion to so-called non-productive purposes could easily be explained away on the basis of extenuating circumstances.

[47] Please see Section 4.1.1, Chapter IV of this work.

Table 6.25: Frequency Distribution of Purpose of Loans taken in some Sample Villages of Kinnaur District

sn	*Type*	*n*	*%*	*cn*	*cp*
01	AH	68	0.00	00	0.00
02	AT	10	15.20	10	15.20
03	CL	04	6.10	14	21.20
04	HC	02	3.00	16	24.20
05	HL	01	1.50	22	33.30
06	LD	34	51.50	56	84.80
07	SH	07	10.60	63	95.50
08	SM	03	4.50	66	100.00

Code: sn = serial number, n = frequency, cn = cumulative frequency,
cp = cumulative percentage, % = percentage, Type = purpose of loan,
AH = animal husbandry, AT = artisanat tools, CL = combined loan,
HC = house construction, HL = horticultural loan,
Sh = sheep unit, LD = land development, and SM = sewing machine.

6.6.1.2 Vertical Bar Charts with Loan Source as Group Variable

The relative percentage bar chart grouping loan purpose according to the source of loans clearly showed that banks had replaced the government as the most important source of institutional finance. Government, however, continued to be a more important source of direct lending than cooperative societies. In all group variable values, land development loans were predominant. Sheep units were provided exclusively by banks and were more numerous than milch animal cases for banks but zero for other sources. House construction loans were as important as animal husbandry loans for loans directly granted by the government but much less important than animal husbandry loans for banks as loan source. A block diagram showed the same conclusions better visually.

6.6.1.3 Block Diagram with Source of Loans as Group Variable

A block diagram was plotted with source of loans as group variable and purpose of loans taken as block variable. Cooperative credit was visually seen to be less important than direct government loans which stood dwarfed by bank loans. After centuries of neglect, banking had found a foothold in Kinnaur! But as Table 6.25 shows, village moneylenders were far from being put in the shade by the development of the banking sector.

6.6.1.4 Village-wise Pie Charts

Land development loans accounted for 60% of the sample loans in Bari, 69.23% in Kāshpo, 25% in Nigani, 35% in Nagani and 57.14% in Paunda respectively. Nagani had only four loan cases so that its results are not really to be taken as representative. Otherwise, land development loans form by far the most important loan segment in all the villages surveyed. The possibility of easy diversion of land development loans cut across village boundaries. Government strategy of imposing a whole array of selection controls for channelizing institutional credit into pre-determined channels was leaking like a sieve and loans were being diverted to consumption purposes.

The number of households having taken institutional loans did not exceed 10.50% of total households in Bari, 34.20% in Paunda and 1% in case of Nichār respectively. These figures indicate that a majority of households were meeting their credit needs from a source of credit other than the institutional sector. Given that in an area like Kinnaur with a low degree of monetization of the economy, credit needs would be lower than those in areas like Punjab or Haryana but one can still not escape the obvious conclusion that the informal credit sector was playing an important role in meeting local credit needs in Kinnaur. To round off the credit infrastructure, we can now pass on to the informal sector as a finale.

CHAPTER VII

THE INFORMAL SECTOR: VILLAGE GODS AND MONEYLENDERS

Preceding chapters have made it amply clear that institutional credit agencies have met the credit needs of Kinnauras only in part and that, too, under well specified conditions designed to channelize such credit into so-called productive channels. It would be obvious to even the casual observer that credit for consumption purposes must be available from some sources even though institutional sources either do not allow it at all or do so in small driblets under stringent conditions.[1] It can be said at the outset itself that consumption credit needs of Kinnauras were being met and are being met almost entirely by the informal sector, meaning the non-institutional sector. Even with a primarily barter economy,[2] since Kinnaur was an area deficit in foodgrains the Kinnauras needed consumption credit in kind if not in cash. Need for credit in the form of foodgrains for seed and for consumption purposes was as true in the final two decades of the 19th century and the first decades of the 20th century as it had been over the preceding centuries.

First hand accounts from Moravian Missionaries in Kinnaur indicate this fact clearly. This aspect tends sometimes to be glossed over by authors idealizing the allegedly self-reliant and homespun Kinnaura economy and the frugal way of life of the Kinnauras.[3] The 12th Report of the Moravian Mission in the Western Himalaya refers to rampant poverty amongst the Christians of Pooh who belonged to the lowest caste.[4] This poverty and the need for consumption credit are a recurring theme in the papers sent by Moravian Missionaries from Kinnaur.

In his annual report for Chini for 1907, J. Bruske mentions that there was an acute scarcity of grain in the area. Merchants and grain dealers were not selling grain any more and were hoarding it.[5] In a personal letter dated June 28, 1906 to Bishop La Trobe in Herrnhut, Bruske talks of a lasting, widespread drought which had already raised the cost of living. Instead of wheat being sold @ 22 to 24 pounds per rupee, only 14 to 17 pounds were to be had per rupee. He even talks of the threat of starvation.[6] T. Schreve wrote from Pooh in 1901 that most of the poorer villagers stood indebted to the richer villagers and wanted the Moravian Missionaries to liquidate their debts as a kind of quid pro quo for converting to Christianity.[7] R. Schnabel reported from Pooh in 1903 that poor people were turning to the

[1] Please see Sections 3.3.3.5 (Chapter III), 4.3.2.1, 4.3.2.1.1 and 4.3.2.1.2 (Chapter IV) of this work.

[2] Please see Section 1.2.4, Chapter I, and Sections 2.B.4.1 to 2.B.4.5, Chapter II-B of this work.

[3] Please see:
(a) Negi, T.S., 1975, Pp 22-28; (b) Chopra, Pran, 1964, Pp 65-68.

[4] Twelfth Report of the Moravian Mission in the Western Himalayas, Simla: Cotton and Morris, 'Simla Courier Press, 1902, p. 3. The report is available in the archives of the Brüder-Unität at Herrnhut in the GDR under Rubric: N.B.VII.R 2.111(12), Report for 1892-1901.

[5] Jahresbericht der Station Chini - Jahr 1907, [Handwritten by J. Bruske in German], Unpublished. Available in the archives at Herrnhut under Rubric: Alte Sign. S.e.1.a, Prov. Missionsdirektion, Pert. West Himalaya.

[6] J. Bruske to Bishop La Trobe, Rubric: R.15.U.b.17: Briefwechsel mit Chini 1900-08, J.N. 248, FZ R 66, empf. 5/8/06, beant. 14/8/-, Unpublished. Available at Herrnhut.

[7] Jahresbericht der Station Poo, West Himalaya - 1901, Alt. Sign. S.e.5.a, Neu Sign. R.15.U.b.2.b: Berichte von Poo 1901-08, Prov. Missionsdirektion, Pert. West Himalaya, Unpublished, [Archives at Herrnhut].

J. N. 287
F. Z. ... 64
empf. 30/7/00.
beaut. 31/8/–

Chini, den 6. Juli, 1900.

Lieber Br. La Trobe!

Dein lieber Brief vom 27. März erreichte uns am 20. April in Pangi. Herzlichen Dank für die uns so wohl thuenden Worte freundlichen Zuspruches darin und für die gütige Bewilligung der Laterna magica und der homöopathischen Apotheke! Darf ich bitten, mir die von Dir bezeichnete, Leath & Ross Family Chest Nr. 12 complete zuschicken lassen zu wollen? Nach einer Nachricht von Warden & Co. ist Ofen und Lat. mag. in Bombay angekommen.

Dass wir am 7. April Chini erreichten, teilte ich bereits in einem Briefe desselben Datums mit, den Du wohl erhalten hast. Vom 9. bis 30. April bewohnten wir, da der Winter noch hier herrschte, das der Regierung gehörende Rest-house in Pangi. Am 1. Mai siedelten wir nach Chini über und leben seither im Zelt. Auch im Mai fiel noch verschiedene Male tüchtig Schnee, bis neulich kam fast täglich Regen, und es war bitter kalt. Dazu

(Specimen of the handwriting of the founder of the Moravian Mission at Chini, Rev. J. Bruske.)

priests for financial help in times of need. The rich seldom helped them. They exploited the latter as victims of their manipulation of credit. Wages were low. A landless labourer got 1.80 Marks per month apart from food. He had to manage clothing, shoes and wherewithal for winter. Daily wages consisted of food and two small measures of cereals, about three handfuls each. Women labourers were paid only one such measure instead of three. Indebtedness was rampant.[8] Schnabel further mentioned the scarcity of currency in circulation in 1905. The Mission, which had earlier paid its obligations in cash, resorted to the traditional local practice

[8] Jahresbericht der Station Poo, West Himalaya - 1902, Ibid.

of making payments partly in cash and partly in cereals, salt and wool.[9] It might appear retrograde on first appearance to adopt such a system, reported Schnabel, but it had positive effects. The labourers, mostly poor, were dependent on the rich villagers from whom cereals, salt and wool could be obtained. The rich would give only 12 or 14 measures of cereals, each about three handfuls, for one rupee instead of the usual 20 measures. The rich thus became richer and the poor poorer. Only the rich had disposable surpluses. Providing the poor only cash as wages was making them even more dependent on the rich who knew that the poor had cash disposable but no grains, with no possibility of converting their cash into goods and essential foodstuffs except to buy these from the rich. Accordingly, they reduced the amount given in cereals for one rupee. This artificial grafting of a money economy on a barter economy proved premature, as it had also at the time of the first Settlement Assessments in Bushahr.[10] Providing at least a part of the wages in kind made the poor that much less liable to exploitation by the rich who were out to garner their liquidity. Once the missionaries switched over to traditional forms of payment, the quantities of rarer cereals like buckwheat, millet and maize rose to 20 measures per rupee per day of physical labour, but for barley and wheat rose to only 16 measures per day. Schnabel, however, felt that even for better cereals the rich would sooner or later have to add in 4 measures more per day to match the 20 measures being paid out by the Mission.[11] H.B. Marx and his colleague H. Kunick reported from Pooh in 1910 that 14 feet of snow had fallen till April, leading to a bad cereal crop. The poor were forced to indebt themselves heavily.[12] Many years earlier, Edouard Pagell, the founder of the Moravian Mission in Kinnaur, had reported from Pooh in 1873 that he had had to assume repayment liability in respect of a loan of Rs 100 left unpaid by a Christian couple who had fled Pooh because of their inability to repay. They had fled to village Nésang.[13] Pagell indicated that the travails of Kinnauras were confined not only to a foodgrain deficit and hard nature but were complicated occasionally by an irregular taxation system as well. The Rājā of Bushahr's eldest daughter was betrothed to the Mahārāja of Benaras in the autumn of 1876. For Kinnauras, this otherwise happy event turned into a special **wall tax** *(besondere Mauersteuer)*. This meant a tax on walls or on all 'pucca' buildings. Since most houses, even of poorer classes, were built of stone and wood, the state could always consider the stones as constituting 'pucca' element liable to taxation. In addition to the annual specified tax amount of Rs 397, for Pooh, says Pagell, extra taxes of Rs 627, nearly two years' additional taxation, had to be paid without delay, causing extreme hardship to the poor people who had to sink further into debt to meet such periodic obligations.[14]

In a report from Pooh in 1887, Julius Weber explained that even though trade with Tibet had brought increased income to some families, he had not seen anyone really flourishing. Only four or six residents were in a position to carry on this trade with their own resources. All others were forced to obtain financing at 25% annual rate of interest.[15] Many

[9] Jahresbericht der Missionsstation Poo, West Himalaya für 1905, Ibid.

[10] Please see: Coldstream, W.: Fiscal History of Bashahr State, File No. 2, Pp 2-5, in: Report on the Settlement of Rāmpur Tahsil of the Bashahr State, in: Foreign Department, Native States, January 1894, Nos. 18-22.

[11] As in Footnote No. 9.

[12] Jahresbericht der Station Poo, West Himalaya für 1910-11.

[13] Jahresbeicht der Station Poo, West Himalaya - 1873, Alt. Sign. S.e.5.a, Neu Sign. R.15.U.b.2.a: Berichte von Poo 1865-1900, Prov. Missionsdirektion, Pert. West Himalaya. [Unpublished]

[14] Jahresbericht der Station Poo, West Himalaya - 1876, Ibid.

[15] Jahresbericht der Station Poo - 1887, Ibid. The original lines partly read: *"Durch solchen Handel ist bis jetzt noch niemand zu Vermögen gelangt, gar manche haben aber dabei ihr ganzes Besitztum eingebüßt, die*

lived constantly hand-to-mouth. The vast majority, however, lived off debts. They took cereals on loan during winter when they were unemployed. These loans would then be returned with an increment of 25% in summer through labour. A labourer receiveed one Rupee or two Marks as wages per month, apart from food. Pagell mentions extreme poverty in families with many children. This became really insupportable when somebody fell ill in the family. There was a custom in the area that a patient should eat as much meat as possible. The dāk (post) runner for Pooh had to indebt himself to the extent of more than 120 Marks in 1887 to procure sheep for slaughtering during the illness of his wife. Because of a high rate of interest, this sum was impossible to be repaid during the dāk runner's lifetime so that the burden of debt would be carried over as inheritance to his sons on his death.[16]

Julius Weber outlines another reason why many sank up to their ears into debt in the area. According to Buddhist tradition, wealth was distributed in charity if there was a death in the family, because such distribution would count as a factor of salvation for the departed soul in the Other World. It would be calculated in the deceased's favour to offset his/her sins.[17] Even though the dowry system was not widespread in Kinnaur (as in the plains), it did not mean that there were no social obligations creating a need for consumption credit. Sheep and goats had to be sacrificed to the village deities on festive occasions or when levied as 'dosh' (fine) by these divinities. Nobody dared defy the deity's wishes. Poverty could not be pleaded as an extenuating circumstance for escaping financial burdens imposed by obligations to the deity. Apart from offerings, at least one person per household had to accompany the deity's entourage on its tours. This could involve considerable time intervals. For example, Devta Badrināth of Kāmru went in procession to visit the guardian deity at Badrināth in U. P. once a year and then once in three years during the 1940s. The journey lasted weeks, involving a journey over the Dhaula Dhār range. For this duration persons accompanying the deity could not work and earn money. Richer Kinnauras could avoid such journeys by engaging poorer villagers to substitute for them or by paying fines in cash in lieu of absence. Poorer people could manage neither of these escape routes. They were obliged to forego their already meagre earning capcity. To this was added enforced absence due to bégār or corvée labour. Till reforms introduced under British prodding by which the period was reduced to one month, bégār had had to be performed for up to six months per year.[18] At least one fit adult per household was thus at the disposal of the Rājā and thus not in a position to contribute his earning capacity to his own household. While doing bégār for the Rājā, the labourer had to manage his food and board himself by draining his own household's resources. It is no wonder that bégār was highly unpopular. Possessing only meagre landholdings, poor Kinnauras were dependent on their physical labour for making ends meet. Deprived of even this facility for long periods by obligations to the Rājā and the devta, they were pushed towards indebtedness. Richer families could buy exemption from bégār by hiring substitutes or by making down payments as fines. An easy way of sending substitutes was by accepting repayment for loans in terms of physical labour from loanees. It suited both sides. The poorer borrower did not need to repay in cash which was scarce or in foodgrains, equally scarce. The rich needed such bégār substitution more than cash or foodgrains, both of which they had in adequate measure. Exploitation of physical labour in an area deficit in coinage and foodgrains

meisten aber fristen damit ihr dümmerliches Dasein. Nur 4 oder 6 Bürger betrieben diesen Handel mit eigenem Geld...Alle anderen aber müssen sich das Geld dazu gegen 25% Zinsen borgen". Free translation mine.

[16] Ibid.

[17] Ibid.

[18] Steedman, E.B.: Review of the Assessment Report of the Chini Tahsil, File No. 9, No. 6: Review of the Assessments of Tahsil Chini, Paras 12 and 26, Pages 3 and 6 respectively, in: Foreign Department, Native States, February 1897, Nos. 5-8.

was geared to actual realities of the system.

The need for consumption credit was widespread. Bushahr State never tried to provide an organized institutional credit network. Such a network, when it came after 1960, was geared only to pre-specified official programmes and took hardly any notice of this long tradition of widespread consumption credit need in Kinnaur. This need had been met over centuries by credit from the informal or non-institutional sector. This sector comprised principally village deities and village moneylenders. Having already seen how the devtas had evolved into the sine qua non of community life in Kinnaur, it is only to be expected that that they would have a major role to play as credit givers. They had been endowed by the Rājā and his Wazirs with the means of generating a surplus. They could then plough it back into moneylending. This set into motion a cycle of multiplication of their surplus by injecting it into the credit system. The devtas already had the necessary organizational wherewithal for efficient management of loans. Their lending operations are models of efficiency from which the cumbersome and creaking institutional credit agencies could learn a lesson. Village moneylenders were not so well organized as devtas but also ran their moneylending operations with exemplary efficiency. To get an idea of the extent of informal sector moneylending network in Kinnaur we consider the results of two field surveys.

7.1 INDEBTEDNESS SURVEY OF 1983: USEFUL BUT UNUTILIZED

This survey was carried out in July and August 1983. The idea was to estimate the extent of indebtedness, nature of debts, as well as sources and purposes of debts. The survey was carried out under the supervision of Mr B.C. Kāndpāl, D.S.O., Kinnaur by Mr M.C. Kochhar, Technical Assistant; Mr R.S. Negi, Investigator, and Mr S.R. Negi, Field Investigator Grade I; all from the Department of Economics and Statistics. The survey was carried out in ten villages. The period of reference related to transactions made from July 1, 1982 till July 30, 1983 for cash/commodity dues payable/receivable by sample households. Information collected about other items such as inherited loans, availability of financial institutions pertains to the date of survey. 100 households were surveyed in the sample. Villages with large population were divided into two or more compact area sub-divisions of nearly equal population content, called hamlet groups. The survey was conducted in one of the sub-divisions selected at random.

Official surveys generally tend to bring out conclusions favourable to government programmes, confirm what the bosses at headquarters want to hear. If even such a survey concedes that village moneylenders still exist and play an important role, we can safely presume that their actual role would be even more important than estimated. Legislative measures to restrict the operations of village moneylenders should not make much difference to the well established informal sector. The expansion of institutional credit outlets should by 1983 have made a dent, however, in credit markets in Kinnaur. The estimate of such influence would come out higher than its actual extent because 60 out of 100 households in the sample were owning land between 1.00 and 4.99 acres in the marginal and small farmer categories.

The I.R.D.P. and D.D.P. have focussed institutional credit onto these very categories so that impact tended to be magnified. Since the informal sector was almost the sole supplier of consumption credit in Kinnaur, most credit requirements would be short-term rather than long-term. Any reasonably accurate assessment of indebtedness patterns should highlight the significant role played by village deities as credit givers. The availability of institutional credit per se, even at lower rates of interest, nominal if not real, should not suffice to wean villagers totally away from the informal sector. The informal sector was very much more flexible than the rule- and procedure-ridden institutional sector. Loans taken from institutional agencies would ostensibly have been used for productive purposes because hardly any debtor would honestly declare that these loans had been diverted to non-specified purposes. No such restriction applied to loans from the informal sector which could honestly be declared to have been taken for consumption purposes. The average debt per family should not be very high as Kinnaur was traditionally not a money economy where large sums of money changed hands. Loans for productive purposes would predominate in the selected sample.

The percentage of loans in kind would not be high because with the extension of the P.D.S. and its subsidized commodities Kinnauras, unlike in preceding centuries and decades, can meet their essential needs without resorting to borrowing in kind. The money economy has got a foothold. In the past, apart from consumption, loans were also taken in kind for use as seed before sowing. After 1960, the Agriculture and Development Departments provide seeds on 50% or 100% subsidy through their extension outlets so that incidence of loans in kind would not be very high. To compete with a suddenly implanted and enlarged institutional credit infrastructure, the informal sector could not have extensively high rates of interest, even though transaction costs push up the real rates of interest of nominally low interest institutional loans above their nominal rates of interest.[19] They did not have a monopoly of the credit market any more. The rates of interest for loans from the informal sector would be competitive with the rates of the institutional sector. We can now examine whether the results of the survey bear these hypotheses out or not, at least in general trends. Before going on to tables showing data, it can be mentioned that the code for these tables is as follows:

(a) Occupation divisions (O.Ds) 0, 1 and 2 include professional, technical and related workers; administrative, executive and managerial workers;
(b) O.Ds 3, 4 and 5 include clerical and related workers, sales workers and service workers;
(c) O.Ds 7, 8 and 9 include production and related workers, transport workers, equipment operators and labourers;
(d) Occupation Group (O.G.) 61 includes all types of cultivators;
(e) O.G. 62 includes farmers other than cultivators such as planters, livestock farmers, dairy farmers, poultry farmers, insect rearers and orchard, vineyard and related workers;
(f) O.G. 63 includes all types of agricultural labourers;
(g) O.Gs 64 and 65 include plantation labourers, related workers and other farm workers like farm machine operators; animal, bird and insect rearing workers; gardeners and nursery workers; and
(h) All other groups (A.O.Gs) include other occupation classes not covered under any group or division mentioned earlier.

7.1.1 Data Tables of Survey Figures

The following Tables elucidate the information collected during the survey.

7.1.1.1 Distribution of Sample Households by Land Holding

Table 7.1 contains the distribution of sample households by land holding classes, meaning land owned and not land cultivated. Land cultivated could exceed land owned because a landowner could take land on lease or as a tenant. Table 7.2 contains data about the distribution of sample households by occupation. Tables 7.1 and 7.2 show that 69% of the sample households belonged mainly to the agriculturist class, of which about 53% owned land between 1.00 to 2.49 acres of land; 44% between 2.50 to 9.99 acres and only 3% possessed more than 10 acres of land. 16% had marginal holdings between 0.01 to 0.99 acres. This shows that a majority of landholders in Kinnaur owned land between 1.00 and 9.99 acres.

[19] Please see Section 4.10.1.1.3, Chapter IV of this work.

Table 7.1: Distribution of Sample Households by Land Holding

sn	*land owned*	*nhs*	*poh*
01	0.00-0.00	00	00.00
02	0.01-0.49	04	04.00
03	0.50-0.99	12	12.00
04	1.00-1.24	17	17.00
05	1.25-2.49	20	20.00
06	2.50-4.99	25	25.00
07	5.00-9.99	19	19.00
08	10.00-above	03	03.00

Code: sn = **serial no., Land owned is in acres and not hectares,**
nhs = **number of sample households,**
poh = **percentage of sample households.**
(Source: Field Survey of July and August 1983.)

Table 7.2: Distribution of Sample Households by Occupation

sn	*Occupation Class*	*nsh*	*poh*
01	O.Ds 0, 1 and 2	000	00.00
02	O.Ds 3, 4 and 5	001	01.00
03	O.Ds 7, 8 and 9	009	09.00
04	O.G. 61	069	69.00
05	O.G. 62	000	00.00
06	O.G. 63	008	08.00
07	O.Gs 64 and 65	000	00.00
08	A.O.Gs	013	13.00
09	Total of all	100	100.00

Code: sn = **serial number,** nsh = **number of sample households,**
poh = **percentage of sample households.**
(Source: As for Table 7.1.)

7.1.1.2 Outstanding Cash Loans on June 30, 1983

This information is contained in Table 7.3 which clearly shows that the sample households were under-reporting the extent of indebtedness. Only 27% of them reported loans totalling

Rs 2,369.90 or a mean figure of less than Rs 100 per indebted household. People are quite chary about giving exact information about their loan amounts and sources. They do not want to frighten their traditional creditors by sheltering behind government agencies. The informal

Table 7.3: Percentage of Households Reporting Outstanding Cash Loans on June 30, 1983 with Value of such Loans per Indebted Household by Occupation Class

sn	*Occupation Class*	*phr*	*vcl*
01	O.Ds 0, 1 and 2	000	00.00
02	O.Ds 3, 4 and 5	000	00.00
03	O.Ds 7, 8 and 9	003	389.33
04	O.G. 61	019	506.32
05	O.G. 62	000	00.00
06	O.G. 63	001	710.00
07	O.Gs 64 and 65	000	00.00
08	A.O.Gs	004	764.25
09	Total of all	027	2369.90

Code: sn = **serial number,**
phr = percentage of households reporting cash loans on June 30, 1983 in Rupees,
vcl = value of cash loans for indebted households on June 30, 1983 in Rupees.
(Source: As for Table 7.1)

sector operates in privacy! This was further supplemented by loans taken during the year preceding the survey. There was only one case reported in which loans had been taken in kind, whereas there were 27% of total sample households reporting loans in cash which worked out to Rs 2,370.00 in all. The percentage of households which borrowed loans in cash during the year 1982-83 was 31%. The amount of original loan borrowed per reporting household worked out to Rs 271.15. The value of cash loans outstanding on June 30, 1983 per household amounted to Rs 84.06 for all households.

7.1.1.3 Distribution of Cash Loans by Purpose and Loan Type

Broadly classified, a loan may be utilized for productive purposes or be exclusively used to meet immediate economic needs or to discharge religious as well as social obligations. Table 7.5 gives information about utilization of loans by purpose and type. 34 cash loans were reported, amounting to a total debt burden of Rs 58,459. This gives a mean figure of Rs 1,719.38 per household and an average of Rs 584.59 per sample household. The maximum number of loans i.e. 10 (or 29.41% of the total) were contracted for current expenditure in non-farm business. Household expenditure came next with 8 cases (23.53%), closely followed by current expendiuture in farm business with 7 loan cases (20.59%). However, in terms of money involved, the 7 loans of current expenditure in farm business involved Rs 17,700 whereas the 8 loans of household expenditure involved only Rs 7,734, giving an average loan size per loan of Rs 2,528.57 for the former category and Rs 966.75 for the latter. There were no short-term pledged loans. 32 out of 34 (94.12%) loan cases were short-term loans. Medium- and long-term loans accounted for only one case (02.94%). Table 7.6 gives the source-wise distribution of total loan amount. Table 7.7 gives the number of cash loans by

Table 7.4: Percentage of Households taking Cash Loans during 01-07-82 to 30-06-83 with Amount Originally Borrowed

sn	*Occupation Class*	*nbh*	*alt*
01	O.Ds 0, 1 and 2	000	00.00
02	O.Ds 3, 4 and 5	000	00.00
03	O.Ds 7, 8 and 9	004	1950.00
04	O.G. 61	021	1798.81
05	O.G. 62	000	00.00
06	O.G. 63	001	2600.00
07	O.Gs 64 and 65	000	00.00
08	A.O.Gs	005	2056.80
09	Total of all	031	8405.61

Code: sn = **serial number,**
nbh = number of borrowing households taking loans,
alt = amount of loan taken in Rupees.
(Source: As for Table 7.1)

credit-giving agency. Tables 7.6 and 7.7 together show that the most popular credit agencies were the government (23.53% of the loans) and the commercial banks (23.53% of the loans) with 8 cases each. Landlords were close on their heels as credit givers with 7 cases (20.59%). The complete absence of professional moneylenders confirms the absence of non-Kinnauras functioning as moneylenders in order to capture local property for reducing the locals to servitude. Local moneylenders were almost all landowners. Devtas accounted for 6 cases (17.65%). They, put together with the landowner-moneylenders, accounted for 14 loan cases (41.18%), almost as many as the loans given by the government and commercial banks put together (= 16, or 47.06%). Counting traders as well, the informal sector accounted for 15 loan cases out of 34 (44.12%) as compared to 19 cases of the institutional agencies. The informal sector accounted for nearly half the total number of loan cases. It was as important as the official agencies as a source of credit.

7.1.1.4 Distribution of Cash Loans by Credit Agency and Security

It is relevant to examine what kinds of security were demanded for loans in our sample. 16 loans (47.06%) were obtained on personal security; 9 (26.47%) on surety, security or guarantee by a third party; 7 (20.59%) on mortgage of immovable property and 2 (05.88%) were without security. The maximum amount (Rs 24,550 or 42% of the total amount) was loaned against guarantees by a third party; Rs 19,034 (32.56%) were given against personal security; Rs 13,875 (23.73%) on mortgages of immovable property and only Rs 1,000 (01.71%) without security, showing that credit givers were careful not to give uncovered loans. The devtas had demanded only personal security in all cases whereas the government had given no loans at all against personal security but had secured surety, security or guarantee on all loans given by it. The only uncovered loans given were those by landlords who would have enough influence and social coercive power to enforce repayment. Mortgages on immovable property, even though legally perhaps the most secure means of enforcing repayment, were resorted to only in 7 loan cases (20.59%). All these cases were commercial bank loans. No other credit giver had resorted to this security.

Table 7.5: Number of Cash Loans and Amount Originally Borrowed by Purpose and Loan Type

sn	*Purpose of Loans*	*STP*		*STNP*		*MT*		*LT*		*Total*	
do	-do-	no	amt	no	amount	no	amt	no	amt	no	amt
01	Capital Expenditure in Farm Business	0	0	2	2,500	0	000	0	000	2	2,500
02	Current Expenditure in Farm Business	0	0	6	14,200	0	000	1	3500	7	17,700
03	Capital Expenditure in Non-Farm Business	0	0	1	1,050	0	000	0	000	1	1,050
04	Current Expenditure in Non-Farm Business	0	0	10	24,175	0	000	0	000	10	24,175
05	Household Expenditure	0	0	7	3,734	1	4000	0	000	8	7,734
06	Litigation Expenditure	0	0	0	0,000	0	000	0	000	0	0,000
07	Debt Repayment Expenditure	0	0	0	0,000	0	000	0	000	0	0,000
08	Financial Investment Expenditure	0	0	0	0,000	0	000	0	000	0	0,000
09	Other Heads of Expenditure	0	0	6	5,300	0	000	0	000	6	5,300
10	Total Expenditure	0	0	32	50,959	1	4000	1	3500	34	58,459

Code: **sn = serial number, STP = short-term pledged, MT = medium-term,**
STNP = short-term non-pledged, LT = long-term,
amt = amount in Rupees, no = number.

7.1.1.5 Credit Agency-wise and Rate of Interest-wise Distribution of Loans

Table 7.9 shows the number of cash loans and amount originally borrowed by credit agency and rate of interest. There were no loans carrying interest higher than 18.75% per annum. The maximum amount of loans (Rs 29,425 or 50.33% of the total amount) were in the lowest interest rate range, followed by Rs 15,800 (27.03%) in the highest interest rate range. The devtas had given all their loans in the highest interest rate range while the government and commercial banks had given 14 of their 16 loans in the lowest interest rate range. These rates were nominal rates of interest, not including transaction costs which had not been calculated. Landowners had loaned their money in the two highest interest rate ranges. No loans were reported in which the rates of interest were only notional or designed not to be repaid and only to ensure a relationship of bonded servitude.

7.1.1.6 Other Survey Information

Three out of 34 (08.82%) indebted households reported inherited loans. The amount of inherited loans per reporting household was of the order of Rs 3,061 (Principal = Rs 2,850; Interest = Rs 211). The major sources of inherited loans were 66.67% from landlords and 33.33% from other sources, meaning devtas. All inherited loans were in case of agricultural households. The survey had to concede that moneylenders still existed despite legislative action to eliminate or regulate their activities. "*Their pivotal role is however on the decline as the institutional agencies now collectively account for a large share of the credit supplied to the farm sector*".[20] 94% of the families in the sample had taken short-term loans. "*The most striking*

[20] Indebtedness Survey among Tribal Population of Kinnaur, Issued by the District Statistical Office Kinnaur,

Table 7.6: Distribution of Cash Loans by Credit Agency and Purpose

sn	*Credit Agency*	*Purpose of Loan*						
do	-do-	cpex	crex	cpexn	crexn	hdexp	otexp	Total
01	Government	000	13,200	1050	5,300	000	000	19,550
02	Coop Society/Coop Bank	3000	3,000	000	0,000	000	000	6,000
03	Commercial Banks	000	0,000	000	18,875	000	000	18,875
04	Landlords	000	1,000	000	0,000	000	3700	4,700
05	Agricultural Moneylenders	000	0,000	000	0,000	4000	000	4,000
06	Professional Moneylenders	000	0,000	000	0,000	000	000	0,000
07	Traders	000	0,000	000	0,000	234	000	,234
08	Relatives & Friends	000	0,000	000	0,000	000	000	0,000
09	Others	000	0,000	000	0,000	5100	000	5,100
10	Total	3000	17,200	1050	24,175	9334	3700	58,459

Code: **cpex = capital expenditure in farm business,**
crex = current expenditure in farm business,
cpexn = capital expenditure in non-farm business,
crexn = current expenditure in non-farm business,
hdexp = household expenditure, otexp = other expenditure.
All expenditure figures are in Rupees.

feature of tribal indebtedness in Kinnaur is that on the average 20.6 per cent families had taken loans from landlords and moneylenders, as against 32.3 percent from government, cooperative banks and commercial banks. It is interesting to note that as much as 17.6 per cent families' loan needs in Kinnaur are met by the village deity".[21] According to the survey, on an average, 76% of the total credit requirements of all types were met by the government, cooperative institutions and commercial banks whereas landlords and moneylenders accounted for 14.9% of credit requirements, leaving 8.7% to the devta. When borrowers were asked why they were not meeting all their credit needs from institutional agencies which gave loans at nominally much lower rates of interest, a consensus of replies opined that there were principally two reasons for this:

(a) *Insistence of institutional agencies on securities and their consequent failure to completely meet people's demand for credit in time; and*

(b) *Procedural formalities which irk farmers who find it convenient to rely on village moneylenders.*

The rates of interest varied from one source to another, as well as from individual to individual. The usual rate of interest charged by cooperative societies lay between 6.25% to 9.36% per annum. The rate of interest charged by moneylenders, whose number per village came to a (sic) figure of 0.05, varied from 6.25% to 12.50%. These are average rates of

Rekong Peo, Unpublished, [Year not mentioned], Typewritten Document, p. 9.

[21] Ibid.

Table 7.7: Number of Cash Loans by Credit Agency

sn	*Credit Agency*	*Purpose of Loans*						
do	-do-	ce	cf	cn	crn	he	oe	Tl
01	Government	0	5	1	02	0	0	08
02	Cooperative Society/Coop Bank	2	1	0	00	0	0	03
03	Commercial Banks	0	0	0	08	0	0	08
04	Landlords	0	1	0	00	0	6	07
05	Agricultural Moneylenders	0	0	0	00	1	0	01
06	Professional Moneylenders	0	0	0	00	0	0	00
07	Traders	0	0	0	00	1	0	01
08	Relatives and Friends	0	0	0	00	0	0	00
09	Other Sources	0	0	0	00	6	0	06
10	Total	2	7	1	10	8	6	34

Code: **ce = capital expenditure in farm business,**
cf = current expenditure in farm business,
cn = capital expenditure in non-farm business,
crn = current expenditure in non-farm business,
he = household expenditure, oe = other expenditure, Tl = total.

interest, subject to minor local variations depending upon conditions prevailing in a particular area. The average rates of interest being charged by the informal sector were not much different from those being charged by institutional credit agencies in practice. The number of devtas advancing loans came to 0.60 per village and they charged interest rates varying between 4.50% and 12.50% per annum. Informal credit givers advanced loans but did not accept deposits like banks. Results of the survey showed that 70%, 60%, 100% and 50% of the sample villages had cooperative credit societies, commercial banks, post office savings bank and other institutional facilities available respectively. Nearly 50% of the sample villages had a cooperative credit society within one kilometre distance while about 50% had this facility within 5 kms distance or more. Nearly 30% of the villages had a commercial bank within a distance of 1 km while about 70% had this facility within a distance of 3 kms or more. Overall, the survey showed that 34% of sample households were under debt on the date of survey. Of these, 20.6% had obtained loans from village moneylenders at rates of interest varying from 9.37% to 18.74% per annum. They accounted for 14.9% of the total loan amount. As much as 77% of the total loan amount had been taken supposedly for productive purposes. Farm business accounted for 34% of these loans and non-farm business for 43%. The average debt burden per sample household came to Rs 584 and per indebted household to Rs 1,719 respectively. The survey found that of the 100 sample households, only two (one small farmer and one marginal farmer) had benefited under the H.P. Relief of Agricultural Indebtedness Act 1976.

The just mentioned Act of 1976 remains even today the major legislative endeavour in Himāchal to control the credit operations of the informal sector. It was a definitive recognition of the fact that significant expansion of official credit outlets had not succeeded in

Table 7.8: Cash Loans by Credit Agency and Type of Security

sn	*Credit Agency*	*Type of Security*										
do	-do-	prsnl scrty		ssogbtp		moip		no scty		Total		Pct
do	*-do-*	*no*	*amt*	*no*	*amt*	*no*	*amt*	*no*	*amt*	*no*	*amount*	-,,-
01	Government	00	0,000	8	19,550	0	0000	0	000	08	19,550	30
02	Cooperatives	03	6,000	0	0,000	0	0000	0	000	03	6,000	10
03	Commercial Banks	00	0,000	1	5,000	7	13875	0	000	08	18,875	30
04	Landlords	05	3,700	0	0,000	0	0000	2	1000	07	4,700	09
05	Agricultural Moneylenders	01	4,000	0	0,000	0	0000	0	000	01	4,000	08
06	Professional Moneylenders	00	0,000	0	0,000	0	0000	0	000	00	0,000	00
07	Traders	01	,234	0	0,000	0	0000	0	000	01	,234	--
08	Devtas	06	5,100	0	0,000	0	0000	0	000	06	5,150	09
09	Total	16	19,034	9	24,550	7	13875	2	1000	34	58,459	100

Code: **prsnl scrty = personal security, sn = serial number,**
ssogbtp = surety, security or guarantee by a third party,
moip = mortgage of immovable property, No scty = no security,

freeing debtors from the clutches of village moneylenders. Surveys were carried out to liberate debtors under the provisions of this Act (henceforth called the 1976 Act). They revealed that the informal sector was still a force to reckon with in the credit markets of Kinnaur. The state used its monopoly on power to alter the ground rules within which the informal sector credit markets had to function in favour of debtors and against village moneylenders. This legislation, however, failed to shake village moneylenders and touched only a fringe of private sector loans. It went the way of many government programmes, remaining marginal.

7.2 H.P. RELIEF OF AGRICULTURAL INDEBTEDNESS ACT 1976

This Act was passed during the Emergency and was meant to be part of a package of measures designed to alleviate the lot of rural poor. It was meant to be implemented in conjunction with land reform measures meant to give at least 5 acres of land to every farming household in H.P. To better understand the scope of this Act it is worthwhile to consider the legislative debate accompanying its passage. The debate shows that speeches made by some participating legislators were mostly rhetorical, without a careful analysis of its objectives or its implications. It was considered as a part of the 20 Point Programme which was (and is) sacred, beyond criticism. To just have a sample of the language used during the debate it suffices to consider portions of the speech made by Mr Dalip Singh, the first speaker on the bill.

Eulogizing the-then Prime Minister, Mr Dalip Singh said, "*...the rural population of India, particularly the landless labourers, agricultural labourers, downtrodden sections of society and marginal farmers and rural artisans will worship our honourable Prime Minister, our beloved*

Table 7.9: Credit Agencywise Rate of Interestwise Loan Distribution

sn	*Credit Agency*	*Rate of Interest in Percent*									
do	**-do-**	**3.13-6.24**		**6.25-9.36**		**9.37-12.49**		**12.50-18.74**		**Total**	
do	*-do-*	*no*	*Amount*	*no*	*amount*	*no*	*amount*	*no*	*amount*	*no*	*amount*
01	Government	07	15,550	0	000	0	000	1	4,000	08	19,550
02	Cooperatives	00	0,000	2	6,000	0	000	0	0,000	02	6,000
03	Commercial Banks	07	13,875	0	000	1	5,000	0	0,000	08	18,875
04	Landlords	00	0,000	0	000	2	2,000	4	2,700	06	4,700
05	Agricultural Moneylenders	00	0,000	0	000	0	000	1	4,000	01	4,000
06	Professional Moneylenders	00	0,000	0	000	0	000	0	0,000	00	0,000
07	Traders	00	0,000	0	000	1	234	0	0,000	01	234
08	Relatives & Friends	00	0,000	0	000	0	000	0	0,000	00	0,000
09	Others (devtas)	00	0,000	0	000	0	000	8	5,100	08	5,100
10	Total	14	29,425	2	6,000	4	7,234	14	15,800	34	58,459

Code: sn = serial number; no = number of loan cases.

Prime Minister for ever...Mr Deputy Speaker Sir, in India so many saints came, but they could not prove emancipators, they could not emancipate the rural poor from the clutches of slavery, social, political or economic. Hundreds of religious and thousands of sub-religious personalities in India could not emancipate the rural poor people from the clutches of slavery, economic, social or political. Similarly, so many thousands of our religious books, scripts including our Shastras could not provide emancipation to these rural poor people. It is only our beloved Prime Minister, who has done a lot of good to these rural poor people, who has proved that she is the real ***God*** *to these people. She has proved that she is the real* ***Masiha*** *of these people".*[22] The citation gives a flavour of the ambiance in which the bill was enacted into law and was to be implemented. A legislative pronouncement was meant to cut a swathe of emancipation amongst the rural poor; laying low the dragon of rural indebtedness! The debate proceedings show that only 45 minutes time had been allotted to the bill. How much analysis and scrutiny could be brought to the bill in this time can well be imagined!

Mr Dalip Singh did (naturally after his profuse eulogy of the Prime Minister!) find time to propose some amendments altering the definition of landless agricultural labourers and the income ceiling specified in the bill. Mr Kewal Rām Chauhān avoided high flown rhetoric and pointed out a practical difficulty that no alternative arrangements had been made for poor people dependent on the informal sector for loans. He suggested setting up of Grāmeen Banks (Rural Banks) or other banks, else the poor would be put to a lot of hardship and the whole

[22] The Himāchal Pradesh Relief of Agricultural Indebtedness Bill, 1976, p. 75, in: Himāchal Pradesh Vidhān Sabha Ki Kāryavāhi (Adhikrit Vivaran), Tratiya Vidhān Sabha, Khand 14, Ank 18, 26 February, 1976, Pp 74-87. Available in the H.P. Vidhān Sabha library at Simla with special prior permission only. It is not a public document.

objective of the bill would fail. "*The poor man would not have money for a coffin, would not have money for anything else, would not have money for needs of life, when he goes to borrow money the sāhukār says 'Go away, take from where it has been liquidated. Go to Dr Parmār, go to Des Rāj Mahājan, he will give money*".[23] Mr Chauhān felt that moneylenders charged exorbitant rates of interest but cautioned that they had practically given loans where loans had been needed. Potato growers had been taking loans from the informal sector in his constituency and had since been deprived of this facility because the moneylenders knew that a legislation was coming. Without private loans, potato growers had found it difficult to purchase seed. Without a rural bank being organized, they would face extreme difficulty. Mr Rangila Rām reiterated similar views. He wanted a bank branch opened in each Tahsil and rates of interest kept extremely low.

Mr J.B.L. Khāchi pointed out that operations of private moneylenders had flourished and been on the increase in spite of commercial banks simultaneously functioning as parallel credit institutions. "*All these institutions, in spite of the cooperative societies, in spite of the commercial banks going into the rural areas, the fact is that even in the past years the moneylenders who play a great role in the village's economy are of permanent importance, it was the biggest single factor responsible for rural credit. How are we going to replace this structure? Have we got a structure anywhere?* ***Sir, I am not interested whether the cat is black or white, all I am interested in is whether the cat can catch mice...*** *Small, marginal farmers will not easily be benefited by these banks. The Reserve Bank's restrictions and rural banks' restrictions are there...The moneylender of a village operates there as part of their family. He is one who has to provide money for the marriage of one's daughter, he is one who weeps with anyone when his son or any relation is dead...He has completely identified himself as rural creditor. Have we been able to create such like institutions in this country which have completely been identified like that?...What we really need, therefore, is to create a parallel welfare credit giving organization...The State of Orissa has introduced a Rural Indebtedness Bill where they have made a provision that all sāhukārs must be registered. There must be a code of conduct provided for them...It is immaterial to a person who is a loan-taker whether the money comes from Solan or somewhere else. It is immaterial to him whether it has come from the Reserve Bank of India or it comes from Lāla Nathu Rām. What is important is the repayment procedure, what is important is its interest that is charged, what is important is his capacity to get back that loan...Slogans cannot really help, slogans will destroy the concept of rural economy...Let us not consider something on a useless paper by making it really ridiculous, foolish and stupid. What is important, therefore, is that we must think about it before we remove this rural indebtedness...What is important is that the society, the government, the welfare state must provide parallel organizations which are rural based so that consumption credit is made available on easy terms to the debtors, and to the creditors in the villages*".[24]

Mr Hira Singh Pāl strongly criticised the functioning of institutional credit agencies. A certain Gopālu Rām, a marginal farmer of Shālāghāt, had had his loan case pending with a bank for 18 months. In spite of strenuous efforts by he himself (Mr Pāl), by the Project Officer, in spite of money having been sanctioned everywhere, the bank had not advanced the loan. The D.C.'s and the P.O.'s strenuous efforts did not push the bank to advance loans. "*The banks are beyond our circle. I would like to ask what is the cure for this. So long as some cure is not found for this, there will be a lot of difficulty*".[25]

[23] Ibid, p. 76.

[24] Ibid, Pp 79-81: Speech of Mr Jai Bihāri Lāl Khāchi.

[25] Ibid, p. 81: Speech of Mr Hira Singh Pāl in Hindi, Translation mine.

The debate was extremely cursory and propagandist. Opposition legislators did rightly point out that it was rash to talk about doing away with village moneylenders without providing institutional alternatives to replace their moneylending operations. One could not just wish away the pivotal role played by the informal sector in coming to the aid of rural borrowers needing credit. The government were very keen to sideline the informal credit structure by clamping down tight controls on how the village moneylenders could operate. It was felt that if rural moneylenders were deprived of repayment of their loans from marginal farmers and agricultural labourers, it would release these classes of debtors from their debt burdens. The Act made no provision for what should be done if the liberated debtors again sank into debt. Village moneylenders were considered as an unmitigated evil requiring to be eliminated, without considering how they were an integral part of village life which had evolved over centuries to cater to local credit needs. They were not necessarily the evil that they were made out to be. They understood local needs and conditions much better than institutional agencies. Their follow-up and supervision of loans was a model that could teach a lot to official agencies which proved weakest precisely in these spheres. Unable to emulate the performance of the informal sector, the government sought to cover up the deficiencies of the official credit agencies by imposing legislative hurdles on the operations of the informal sector.

7.2.1 Provisions of the Indebtedness Relief Act of 1976

The Act defined an agriculturist and a host of other terms[26] like rural artisan, marginal farmer and landless agricultural labourer but left traders who were in debt to moneylenders out of its scope. This meant practically in Kinnaur that erstwhile traders plying cross-border trade with Tibet who had piled up debts were not to be freed from their debt burdens. Labourers working on roads or on hydroelectric projects as casual labour were also not covered. In Sungra, where a large number of Kinnaura labourers working on the Sanjay Hydroelectric Project were indebted to shopkeeper-moneylenders this Act could not be used to liquidate their debts because they did not fall under the category of landless agricultural labourers. Nepali labourers working on timber extraction or on roads were held in bonded labour due to non-repayment of advances. They could not be helped. Only small sums of money were liquidated under this legislation which had limited impact in Kinnaur.

7.2.1.2 Liquidation of Debts: Modest even in Official Records

Under Section 3 of the Act every debt of the categories covered including the amount of interest was deemed to have been wholly discharged. All suits and proceedings for its recovery were barred. Creditors were to forthwith return every property/article pledged or mortgaged by debtors. Force could be used for this purpose by the Collector in case the moneylenders proved recalcitrant. Section 4 voided any agreement for labour in lieu of repayment of debt. It was good in intent but made illegal the sole means of repayment open to many poor debtor households - physical labour. Moneylenders would be chary of lending to debtors if the latter could not repay their debts through physical labour in case there were no other means of repayment available. Apart from bégār, there was a long tradition in Kinnaur of repaying debts of village moneylenders through physical labour. Retired Kānuṅgo Dharam Singh Negi mentioned a song from village Bārang which narrates the story of a boy who had to serve a lifetime of bonded servitude in lieu of repayment of a loan taken from a prominent family of the village, the Bārang Māthés family. The servant (named Rām Gopāl) supposedly complains in the song that thanks to his parents he has had to serve his entire lifetime in bonded labour.[27] Such bonded labour went on in some cases for generations till the entire

[26] Please see Sections 2(1)(a), 2(1)(g) and 2(1)(i), H.P. Relief of Agricultural Indebtedness Act 1976, Chapter I, in: H.P. Code, Volume V, p. 794.

[27] Personal interview with Negi Dharam Singh s/o late Mr Uma Saran r/o Chini, aged about 66 years (his own estimate), retired in 1978 after 26 years of government service, Interviewed on December 1, 1985 at 11.30

amount due had been repaid through labour in lieu of wages. Since wages were nominal and extremely low, repayment could be spread out over an extremely long time. Lāmā Shimed Chhéwang of Pooh was of the view that not only was bonded labour prevalent in the area as a means of repayment but people in many cases used to go and beg the sāhukār (moneylender) to employ them as labourers. The standard means of earning a livelihood were trade for the rich and physical labour for the poor. Labourers working for farmer-moneylenders received 6 ānnās daily wages. The Lāmā opined that this state of affairs continued till 1962 when new avenues of employment opened up for daily wage labour with the P.W.D. (Public Works Department) and the D.G.B.R. (Directorate General Border Roads).[28] Mr Khem Singh Negi, a serving B.D.O., mentioned that there was no system of regular bonded labour in the Sangla area. Debtors would put in three-four days' labour per month as repayment of loans but it was not done on a sustained basis.[29] This occasional labour stretched periods of repayment much longer. Negi Jeevan Lāl of Nugalsari and Negi Daulat Rām of Nichār corroborated the existence of bonded labour in the Nichār area.[30] All three sub-divisions of Kinnaur thus had had labour as a means of repaying loans.

7.2.1.3 Scaling Down of Debts of Small Farmers: Insignificant

Sections 16 and 17 put ceilings on the amount of debt that could be recovered from specified categories of borrowers. 20% of the estimated gross value of the agricultural produce in the preceding year and an annual rate of interest = 6% simple interest were specified as limits. This rate of 6% was lower than the 10% being charged by institutional lenders themselves on I.R.D.P. loans (other than D.R.I. loans). Bank loans carry higher rates of interest. Devtas and village moneylenders are all charging rates of interest higher than this limit. And all this in spite of the fact that stiff penalties (up to three years' imprisonment or a fine of up to Rs 2,000 or both) were provided for by Section 23 of the Act. No prosecutions were launched under this Section in Kinnaur. It is hard to understand the logic of using severe penalties to impose a maximum interest rate of 6% per annum on the informal sector when institutional lenders are charging double or even three times this value depending on the type of loan taken from them. Had such a step succeeded in practice, it would have driven more and more borrowers towards the informal sector rather than towards the official sector for loans. Low interest rates, combined with low transaction costs and absence of procedural formalities would have put the informal sector in an unassailable position which institutional lenders could not have matched.

7.2.2 Survey Data for Act of 1976: Lies, More Lies and Statistics!

The Act was implemented at full speed in Kinnaur. According to wireless message number KNR-III-41/74-43 dated March 14, 1980 from the D.C., Kinnaur to the Commissioner, Simla Division, 697 persons had benefited under the Act through delivery of possession of pledged property while wholly discharging them from their debts. Of these, 467 were S.Cs and 230 S.Ts. The amount written off for the S.Cs was Rs 64,019.80 and for S.Ts Rs 46,124.71 respectively. 203 bighās of land had been redeemed without payment of debt. These measures had been carried out in 1976 itself because the information from 1977 to 1980 was nil. These figures show that only the fringe of the indebtedness problem was being touched. The already

hours on the lawns of the D.C.'s residence at Kālpa.

[28] Personal interview with Lāmā Shimed Chhéwang alias Gautam Singh on December 10, 1985 at 19.45 hours in Suite No. 2 of the P.W.D. Rest House at Pooh.

[29] Personal interview with Mr Khem Singh Negi, then B.D.O., Paunta Development Block, District Sirmaur, in Suite No. 1 of the P.W.D. Rest House at Sangla on December 6, 1985 from 20.10 hours till 22.45 hours.

[30] Personal discussions after many district-level meetings in Rekong Peo between 1980 and 1982.

described tribal indebtedness survey[31] had shown more than one-third sample households in Kinnaur under debt. This figure itself was an underestimate. Field surveys made during the present research indicate that the percentage of indebted Kinnaura households is closer to one-half (50%) rather than one third.[32] Even if the figure of one-third given by the survey done by the Department of Economics and Statistics is accepted, it would mean around 4,100 indebted households in Kinnaur since there were 12,299 households in all as per the 1981 Census.[33] The 697 persons freed under the Act did not necessarily mean that 697 households had also been freed of their debt burden because many debtors were members of the same household. Looking at the data available in official files, it appears that around 400 households had been freed from debt, around 03.25% of the total number of households in Kinnaur in 1981. The Census of 1981 showed that 5.31% of the total population in Kinnaur were agricultural labourers and 61.97% were cultivators.[34] Even if we consider only 50% of the population as being small and marginal farmers, not unreasonable in an area with tiny land holdings because of extreme paucity of culturable land like Kinnaur, about 55% of the total number of households (around 6,764 households) would be eligible for relief under the Act of 1976. 400 households freed were peanuts, as the Americans might say!

The information conveyed in the wireless message dated March 14, 1980 was reiterated by the D.C., Kinnaur in his D.O. Letter No. KNR-II-41(Peshi)-7673 dated May 31, 1980, to the Financial Commissioner (Revenue) at Simla. This did not, however, mean that there was no confusion about data collected for indebtedness in the district. Letter No. KNR-III(PSH)-II-41/74-3711 dated March 31, 1981 from the D.C., Kinnaur to the S.D.O.(Civil), Kālpa directed the latter to issue directions to the Tahsildārs that they should not send their information always delayed and that it should not be wrong and fictitious 7B3). The S.D.O.(Civil) was directed to properly scrutinize information coming from the Tahsils and to forward it only after being fully satisfied about the veracity of its contents. The letter specifies that information received from the S.D.O.(C) vide his endorsement no. 911 dated March 17, 1981 did not tally with the information contained in his letter no. SDK-II-37(Reader)/74-693 dated March 16, 1979. It had not only been delayed but was also concocted and false. Tahsildārs kept changing the information being sent by them. Letter No. KNR-II-41(Peshi)/75-II- 11441 dated September 11, 1979 from the D.C., Kinnaur to the F.C. (Revenue) gave a different figure saying that 690 persons had benefited under the Act and not 697. As against the communicated figure of Rs 110,144.51 as the amount of debt written off, the figure mentioned here was Rs 87,725.74, with Rs 16,458 still under consideration, giving a total of Rs 104,183.74, about Rs 6,000 less than the other figure. A difference of Rs 6,000 on sums of the order of Rs 100,000 is not negligible. This confusion was partly the result of the tearing hurry in which the Revenue Department's field staff had had to collect data and implement the Act. Blitzschnell (very quick) remedies could not work against a centuries-old established credit network. Tahsildārs were also not always clear in their minds about how they were to proceed under the Act.

An illustrative example of such confusion was encountered in Kālpa Tahsil where the Executive Magistrate (Tahsildār) wanted to know how to proceed in a case in which the creditor denied having received any property from the debtor as security. The query by the E.M., Kālpa was sent vide letter no. T.K./Rdr/80-1093 dated November 13, 1980). The D.C. forwarded the query to the Divisional Commissioner Simla on November 20, 1980. The E.M.

[31] Indebtedness Survey, op. cit., Issued by the District Statistical Office Kinnaur.

[32] These surveys were carried out through the Halqa Patwāri or Grām Séwak in villages Nagāni, Chaura, Kangos and Sungra of Nichār Tahsil and villages Roghi, Yuwaringi, Khwāngi and Chini of Kālpa Tahsil.

[33] District Census Handbook, Kinnaur District, 1981, p. (x).

[34] Ibid.

had announced his decision in two cases under Section 3(e) of the Act of 1976 and sent these to the S.H.O. for execution. The latter sent the papers back with the observation that the creditor had denied having received security. Doubt arose over action to be taken. The Act allowed the use of force but was silent on what to do if the moneylender denied having received pledged security at all. The Commissioner's Office at Simla forwarded the matter to the government on July 13, 1982 nearly 20 months after the D.C.'s request for a clarification. The Under Secretary (Revenue I) to the government wanted to know from the D.C. whether the E.M., Kālpa had been authorized to act under Clause 3(e) or not before action could be taken in the matter. 3 years after his request, the only response that the D.C. had received was this question about a procedural transaction rather than a clarification. The latter confirmed in writing on January 2, 1984 what should have been obvious from the very beginning that the E.M. had indeed been duly empowered to act under Clause 3(e). He again requested a clarification. The long-awaited clarification was finally conveyed by the Secretary (Revenue)'s Office on July 19, 1984 It contained only a reiteration of Section 3(c) of the Act without a clarification. It had taken nearly four years and protracted correspondence to obtain a simple reiteration of a clause already known to the district authorities. We can see here how the buck gets passed. No wonder debtors prefer to go to the informal sector rather than wait for years for official clarifications to be received. The police had merely passed the buck back to the Tahsildār by just recording statements and sending the papers back. The Tahsildār, whether out of genuine confusion or a desire to postpone action, asked for a clarification. After four years came no clarification but a reiteration of what was already known. Efforts to find detailed survey data in district office files revealed only 283 cases and not 697 who had reportedly benefited under the Act.

7.2.2.1 Available Survey Data: Not Complete

283 cases were available in office files at Kālpa. Of them, 157 were S.Cs (referred to as Origin = C) and 126 S.Ts (Origin = T) spread over 30 villages. The villages were situated in all Tahsils of the district. The survey data was not complete because it cannot be presumed that rural indebtedness existed in only 30 out of 77 revenue estates of Kinnaur. Only 30 villages meant around 40% of this total of 77. Also, S.Cs accounted for 55.48% of this sample of 283 cases while S.Ts accounted for 44.52%. This shows that the S.Cs were more deprivileged. They constituted only 10.63% of Kinnaur's population in 1981 while S.Ts accounted for 74.87%.[35] This 10.63% of the population thus accounted for 55.48% of sample cases of rural indebtedness, giving a coefficient of 0.19 for S.Cs as percentage of population divided by their percentage of sample population. The same coefficient had a value of 1.68 for the S.Ts. Or conversely, the coefficient of indebted S.C. population divided by percentage of S.Cs in the total population was 5.26 whereas it was only 0.59 for the S.Ts. Roughly speaking, the chances of the S.Cs being indebted to village moneylenders were about nine times higher for S.Cs over those for S.Ts.

Survey data arranged village-wise shows after analysis with a computer that of the 283 sample cases, 156 had been freed of their debt burdens, making up 55.12% of the sample. Of these 156 cases, 54 (or 19.08% of the total in the sample) were S.Cs, while 102 (36.04%) were S.Ts. S.Cs were nine times as likely as S.Ts to be suffering debt burdens. Now we see that they were, however, only about half as likely as the S.Ts to be freed from this burden (going by these figures of 19.02% for S.Cs and 36.4% for S.Ts) for the debtors freed of their debt burdens. 127 cases were left unfreed (44.88%) of whom 103 (36.40%) were S.Cs and only 24 (8.48%) S.Ts. Thus a S.C. debtor was four times as likely as a S.T. debtor to be left unfreed from his/her debt burden. Regarding security found pledged, 146 cases (51.59%) were found where such security existed. Of these, 106 (37.46% of the total in the sample) were S.Cs and only 40 (14.13%) S.Ts. The percentage in parentheses refers to percentage with total sample number (283) as base. S.C. borrowers were thus nearly 2.5 times more likely than S.T.

[35] Ibid.

asked to furnish security in the form of a valuable article or ornament. 137 cases (48.41%) had obtained loans without security, of these 51 (18.02%) were S.Cs and 86 (30.39%) S.Ts. Clearly, a S.T. borrower was 1.5 times more likely to obtain a loan from village moneylenders without pledging security than a S.C. borrower. Not only were S.Cs less likely to reap the benefits of relief from indebtedness, they were more likely to be subjected to the necessity of having to furnish valuable security for securing loans.

7.2.2.2 Computer Anlaysis of Survey Data

The survey data was processed using the Statistical Analysis System (S.A.S.) programme. Till now this information had just lain in the files of the D.C.'s Office at Kālpa without any such analysis having been done on it or any conclusions having been drawn therefrom.

7.2.2.2.1 Descriptive Statistics for Loan Amounts

Maximum loan amount for the sample taken into consideration was Rs 9,900; with Rs 8,000 for S.Cs and 9,900 for S.Ts. Maximum interest amount was Rs 2,812.50; being Rs 1,476 for S.Cs and 2,812.50 for S.Ts. The mean figures show a mean loan size of Rs 473.90 (or less than Rs 475) for the entire sample, a rather low figure. Mean interest amount due was Rs 88.49 and family size 6.42 (around 6). Comparable figures for only S.Cs were Rs 412.21; Rs 68.86; 7.14 and for S.Ts Rs 550.29; Rs 112.79 and 5.52 respectively. Standard error value on sample mean was Rs 59.25 for loans and Rs 16.78 for interest due respectively. These figures show what we are already familiar with - the fact that S.T. borrowers found it easier to obtain credit than S.C. borrowers. Villagewise distribution of descriptive statistics shows significant differences in all variables under consideration. No correlation could be discerned for fluctuations. Even neighbouring villages had no similarity in their credit market patterns seen during the survey under discussion.

7.2.2.2.2 Correlation Coefficients

Since descriptive statistics showed no coherent correlation between indebtedness patterns of surveyed villages, any correlation test would show such dissonance. Interest amounts would obviously have a high correlation with loan amounts due. If loan amounts due piled up, interest due on them piled up as well. In an economy with low monetization like that in Kinnaur, borrowers would go to village moneylenders to fulfil basic consumption needs which depended not so much on family size as on capacity to repay. The surplus available to moneylenders for lending was not unlimited. Borrowers tended to demand moderate-sized loan sums linked to minimum needs which varied not very elastically with family size.

Analysis of loans showed an unsymmetrical distribution, needing a non-parametric correlation test. Hence Spearman's Correlation Coefficients had to be taken into consideration and not Pearson's Coefficients. The results confirmed the hypotheses outlined earlier. Loan and interest amounts showed a highly significant correlation with each other but no significant correlation with family size. We cannot, therefore, suppose that larger families necessarily borrowed more money from village moneylenders or that smaller families necessarily borrowed smaller loan amounts. The same correlations held good for S.C. borrowers but not for S.T. borrowers for whom even the correlation between loan and interest due amounts broke down. This showed that tribal borrowers received preferential treatment in the informal credit market. S.Ts' interest amounts due not being strongly correlated to interest amounts meant that these borrowers were less likely to be subjected to automatically increased interest payments if they delayed repayment than S.C. borrowers. The latter had no concessions and faced interest burdens proportionately correlated to loan amounts due.

7.2.2.2.3 G.L.M. and Regression Analysis of Survey Data

Having seen how weak the correlation between family size and loan amounts was, G.L.M. analysis was carried out with family size as the independent variable and loan amounts as the dependent variable. The R-Square value came to only 0.011 which means that there is only 1.1% reliability for the model being tested. The hypothesis that there exists some correlation between family size and loan amounts borrowed is thus conclusively rejected.

To see whether the results of the entire sample were equally valid for the S.Cs and S.Ts considered separately, regression analysis was carried out separately over these two categories. The R-Square value was 0.0039 for S.Cs and 0.474 for S.Ts respectively. The hypothesis that loan amounts are linked to and can be explained out of family size has thus to be rejected for each category as well, just as it had been for the whole. Loan amounts were independent of family size.

7.2.2.2.4 Vertical Bar Charts

Even though there were 157 S.C. debtors and 126 S.T. debtors, loan amounts and interest amounts would not be much higher for S.C. borrowers than for S.T. borrowers because the former were put under more unfavourable conditions for loans by the informal sector. They were allowed smaller loan amounts, being economically weaker than S.Ts. It should not be a surprise if 157 S.C. borrowers end up having smaller loan amount than 126 S.T. borrowers so that the sum of amounts due would be higher for fewer S.Ts than for more S.Cs. Vertical bar charts for these two groups corroborated exactly this presumption. 126 S.T. borrowers had a total outstanding debt burden of Rs 70,000 as against Rs 65,000 for 157 S.C. borrowers. Corresponding figures for interest burden were Rs 14,000 for S.Ts and Rs 10,500 for S.Cs respectively. We should not deduce from these figures that S.Ts had a greater debt and interest burden than S.Cs because of greater economic disability. It was because of the S.Cs' economic disability vis-a-vis the S.Ts and their consequent disadvantage in raising loans from the informal sector.

7.2.2.2.5 Block Diagram

To see family size-wise distribution of loan amounts, a block diagram was plotted with family size as the block variable and origin as the group variable with loan amounts summed up over family-size block. The maximum debt burdens existed in the three lowest blocks. For family size between 1 to 4 members debt amounts were Rs 23,332 for S.Ts and Rs 16,018 for S.Cs (Total = Rs 39,350); for family-size 5 to 8 members, debt amounts were Rs 20,577 for S.Ts and Rs 24,839 for S.Cs (Total = Rs 38,932) respectively. It gives totals of Rs 69,336 for S.Ts and Rs 66,394.50 for S.Cs over the whole sample. The S.Cs had more burden of debt than the S.Ts for family-size 5 to 8 members. In family-sizes beyond 13 to 15 members till 26-30 members, loan amounts fell sharply.

The block diagram shows an inverse relationship between rising family size and loan amounts due. Households with fewer members had higher debt burdens than those with more members. In Kinnaur, where households were many times polyandrous, this could partly be explained by assuming that larger households meant more working hands, more income and consequently lesser need for debt. It could also mean more hands to labour for moneylenders. Loans could be repaid faster. Debt burdens piled up more slowly than for smaller households whose lack of surplus working hands made it harder to repay loans through labour so that debt burdens piled up relatively faster. According to results of the sample, larger families seemed to be a boon rather than a curse in Kinnaur. The amounts involved show that the Act of 1976 touched only a fringe of the informal credit network and remained a cosmetic exercise. The total loan sum of Rs 135,730.50 in the sample was only a fraction of the total loan amounts transacted by private moneylenders in Kinnaur.

7.2.2.2.6 Selected Statistics: Act of 1976

To gauge how effective the Act of 1976 had been in freeing debtors from their debt burdens and in returning pledged securities to borrowers, we consider ten sample villages with the maximum number of debtors. These were villages Chāngo (17), Chini (22), Gyabong (13), Kilba (31), Lābrang (18), Leo (30), Mālling (17), Nāko (19), Shyalkhar (12) and Sunnam (33), a total of 212 out of 283 or 74.91% of the total sample cases. Figures in parentheses after the names of the villages represent the number of borrowers therein. Of these ten villages, five (Chāngo, Leo, Mālling, Nāko and Shyalkhar) were in Hangrang Sub-Tahsil, the most barren area of Kinnaur where the closure of trade with Tibet had hit the people really hard, there being little scope for profitable agriculture or horticulture in 1976. Since then horticulture has improved things but Hangrang still remains a hard area.

In village Chāngo all 17 loan cases were S.Ts. 14 of them had pledged securities for loans and 3 had obtained loans without security cover. All had been freed, giving an implementation rate of 100%. But we should not suppose that the problem of rural indebtedness was solved in Chāngo. It only means that there was substantial under-reporting and no accurate assessment of rural indebtedness. In the village with the district headquarters (Chini) all 22 detected loan cases were S.Cs and all had secured loans after pledging securities. Of these 22,15 (68.18%) had been freed and 7 (31.82%) still left in bondage. These 7 cases were shown as freed in the figures sent to the government in 1980, according to which all concerned debtors had been freed of their debt burdens. No reasons were found in survey files about why some loanees had been freed of their debt burdens but not others. In Gyabong village, all 13 debtors were S.Cs of whom 8 (61.54%) had secured loans without security and 5 (38.46%) with security. None had been freed. Of the 31 debtors in village Kilba, 19 were S.Cs and 12 S.Ts. 16 S.Cs (51.61%) and 11 S.Ts (35.48%) had been freed of their debt burdens. 17 S.Cs (54.84%) and 10 S.Ts (32.26%) had obtained loans with security while only 2 S.Cs and 2 S.Ts (each 6.45%) had obtained unsecured loans. In village Lābrang there were 18 debtors, all S.Cs, 6 of whom (33.33%) had pledged security and 12 (66.67%) had loans without security. All had been freed as per the survey report. Village Leo had 30 debtors of whom 23 were S.Ts (76.67%) and 7 were S.Cs (23.33%). 5 S.Cs (16.67%) and 19 S.Ts (63.33%) had obtained loans without having had to pledge security and only 2 S.Cs (6.67%) and 4 S.Ts (13.33%) had had to pledge security. 4 S.Cs (13.33%) and 12 S.Ts (40%) had been freed while 3 S.Cs (10%) and 11 S.Ts (36.67%) had been left unfreed. In village Mālling, of the 17 debtors detected, 5 were S.Cs and 12 S.Ts. All S.Cs and 11 S.Ts (64.71%) had obtained loans without pledged security while only one S.T. (5.88%) had had to give security for his loan. All the cases had been freed. Village Nāko had all 19 cases as S.Ts, 18 (94.74%) of whom had obtained loans without pledged collateral and only one (5.26%) with collateral. All had been freed. Similar was the case in village Shyalkhar where all 12 debtors were S.Ts of whom 11 (91.67%) had secured loans without collateral and all had been freed of their debt burdens. The largest number of cases had been detected in village Sunnam, the famous **Soongnum** of Alexander Gerard and others, where 28 of 33 cases were S.Cs and only 5 (15.15%) S.Ts of whom 16 (48.48%) comprising 12 S.Cs and 4 S.Ts (12.12%) had secured loans without security. 17 (51.52%) had loans with security, of whom 16 (48.48%) were S.Cs and one (3.03%) S.T. 6 debtors had been freed while 27 (81.82%), all S.Cs, remained unfreed.

These results indicate that S.C. borrowers were much more likely than S.Ts to be asked to deposit collateral for obtaining loans. Villages in Hangrang Sub-Tahsil had hardly any S.Cs and an overwhelming majority of S.Ts as detected borrowers. Most of those detected there, had had their debt burdens liquidated, at least on paper. The percentage of S.C. borrowers detected rises as we move southwards to other villages. Inevitably, the percentage of debtors not yet freed at the time of the survey also rose correspondingly. The informal sector was very much present and significant in Kinnaur. We can now evaluate how it functioned and what were its components.

7.3 ASSESSMENT OF THE INFORMAL SECTOR: GODLINGS AND MEDIUMS

How important the informal sector is can be seen from the frequency with which rural indebtedness crops up in official despatches and reports from British officers. In spite of repeatedly discussing the problem the British did not bring the Rājā of Bushahr to either establish an institutional credit network or enforce laws controlling village moneylenders. In his report on the assessment and revenue rate of Rāmpur Tahsil, the then Superintendent, Simla Hill States (W. Coldstream) mentions that the debts of agriculturists were posing a problem:[36] Still very old debts are realized, which is the source of their ruin. There is no period fixed for the payment of debts, nor is there any fixed rate of interest. The creditors strike out every year a balance of the amount due from debtors, and on account of the compound interest charged, their debt soon amounts to a large sum. This has made many leave their homes after making over their movable and immovable property to their creditors. The rate of interest amounts to at least Rs 2-8-0 per cent per month, which besides interest, includes many other items the agriculturists have to bear on account of their being in debt.

(a) When a cultivator goes to any moneylender to ask for a loan, he has to pay Rs 1 to the latter for loosening his purse, called ganthkhulai;
(b) For the purpose of realizing the debt each moneylender sends about eight men to each of his customers who may be indebted to him, who exact something from the indebted customers for themselves in addition to the actual debt with interest, which amounts to about four annas a month on each debtor. If the debt money is advanced for the payment of revenue then interest is charged for the whole year, although the money is kept by the cultivator for six months only'.

Debtors complained on some occasions against these exploitative practices but no action followed. However, G. Barnes issued an order on October 10, 1860 limiting the period of repayment of debt to 12 years.[37] In 1874, the agriculturists again petitioned the authorities about their debts, requesting that sāhukārs (moneylenders) should not send their men of their own accord for the collection of debts since this practice put them to great hardship, while it was no gain to the moneylenders. Indebtedness was rising so that they should be permitted to repay in instalments. The Rājā of Bushahr issued an order on December 2, 1874 directing the moneylenders not to send their men to their debtors in future and to allow repayment of their loans in instalments. W. Coldstream noted that except for Kinnaur this order remained a **"dead letter"**,[38] meaning that in Kinnaur repayments were allowed thenceforth in instalments and that moneylenders avoided sending their cohorts to extort repayments. The D.C., Simla reissued the same order on December 3, 1874.

Interestingly enough, the greater portion of the debts was due to the Wazirs and to other employees of the state. Therefore, this order for alleviation of the debt burden of cultivators was never properly carried out. *"On the contrary, they (Wazirs) are now realizing debts of past generations due to them"*.[39] According to Coldstream, the agriculturists were

[36] Foreign Department, Native States, January 1894, Nos. 18-22, (No. 21), Chapter III: Description of arrangements made in present Settlement, Para 49, Pp 30-31.

[37] Ibid.

[38] Footnote marked *, Ibid, p. 31.

[39] Ibid, Para 51, p. 31.

being ruined by such debts and there was no hope of improving the land revenue collection till they were protected from such improper demands because their debt burdens were on the increase and all their savings either from land or other sources were being mopped up by sāhukārs. Even at the time of reaping the harvest whatever they got went to the moneylenders, forcing them to incur fresh debts. Nevertheless, even many years later, taccāvi loans given by Bushahr State amounted to only Rs 10,178 in 1914-15, out of a total state expenditure of Rs 195,976.[40] This meant that only 5.19% of total state expenditure was given as taccāvi loans. This was for the entire Bushahr State, not just for Kinnaur which was only one of its three major territorial divisions. The Administrative Report of Bushahr for 1914-15 states that a sum of Rs 9,000 had been advanced by the state to traders, of which Rs 3,000 were distributed from Chini and Rs 6,000 from Rāmpur.[41] It is nowhere clarified in the Report whether these Rs 9,000 were in addition to the Rs 10,178 given as taccāvi loans or not. Since no such clarification was provided and only one head was given for taccāvi loans we can only deduce that this amount formed part of of the total taccāvi loan amount. Thus, of the 5.19% of the state budget earmarked towards taccāvi loans, Rs 9,000 (or 88.43%) were distributed for trade with Tibet and not to needy agriculturists requiring debt relief. The traders so favoured were mostly affluent Kinnauras with a proven capacity of repayment. The British were more concerned about optimizing collection of land revenue rather than about relief from rural indebtedness. In-so-far-as they provided debt relief it was only as a means to improving the surplus retention capacity of cultivators so that increased income could be tapped for increasing land revenue earnings. There was no idea at all of modern day concepts of social justice or elimination of poverty. No registration of moneylenders was required. Anybody could set himself up as an informal credit giver. No social opprobrium attached to being a sāhukār. If we consider that a major source of private sector credit was the village deity, it is clear that there was no question of opprobrium attaching to moneylending as an occupation. The devta was a prime actor on the informal credit scene. The informal credit market was shared mainly between village gods and resident moneylenders. The gods not only functioned as moneylenders but did so with amazing efficiency.

7.3.1 Village Gods as Moneylenders: Efficient Lending

We have seen how the devtas had served as agents of legitimation of authority for the Rājās of Bushahr.[42] This had not been a one-shot process in which, once established, the Rājā could ignore the devtas. It was a continuing process where the Rājā kept the devtas pleased through endowments of land and other gifts while the devtas served as reminders of the divine nature of the Rājā's authority. They themselves had a definite hierarchy.

At the apex was Goddess Bhimā Kāli of Sarāhan. She was followed by Devta Badrināth of Kāmru, the three Maheshras of Sungra, Bhāba and Chagāoṅ; and the Shuwang Chandika of Kothi. They were pargana-level deities. Kothi Devi had primacy in Pargana Shua from Ropa to Pāngi (Uparla Shua) and from Pāngi to Roghi (Nichla Shua).[43] Kāmru Badrināth used to tour Pargana Tukpa from Rispa to Chhitkul.[44] The Chagāoṅ Maheshras

[40] Mitchell, Alan, I.C.S.: Report on the Administration of the Bashahr State for the Year Sambat 1971, (March 13th 1914 - March 13th 1915), Simla: Liddell's Printing Works, 1915, Table D: Statement of Income and Expenditure, p. 15.

[41] Ibid, Appendix II: External Trade Report of the Simla District, 1914-15, p. 18.

[42] Please see Sections 2.4.4.3 to 2.4.4.5, Chapter II-A of this work.

[43] Personal interview with Negi Dharam Singh, 1985.

[44] Personal interview with Negi Uday Singh s/o Late Negi Bhoop Singh r/o Chini, aged about 69 years, Mohatmim of the Narénas Devta's Temple in Chini. Interviewed in the D.C.'s Office chamber at Kālpa on

had primacy from Meeroo to Wāngtu, Wāngtu to Rāmni, Jāni and Kilba. He had earlier also enjoyed predominance over Kanai, Baturi and Sapni villages which had subsequently passed under the sway of the Sapni Nāgés[45] as a result of disputes. Negi Uday Singh made it clear that the rise of the Sapni Nāgés from a purely village-level deity to a ghodi- or even a khund-level deity came about because of decisions by village chieftains. Powerful men made their village devta more powerful. The Bhāba Mahéshras held sway over Pargana Bhāba while the Sungra Mahéshras was predominant in areas southwards and westwards (downstream) from Wāngtu. The three Mahéshras are brothers who do not get along well with their sister Kothi Devi. Negi Uday Singh pointed out that Kothi Devi used to get along well with the Mahéshras of Bhāba till 1960-61 but that differences had cropped up since then *"because devi devtas develop differences when people of their corresponding areas develop differences"*.[46]

These major devtas used to tour their parganas on the Rājā's behalf, as props of and manifestations of royal authority. Since the rājās hardly ever visited remote areas of Kinnaur, the devi/devtas' frequent (once a year at least) tours were a sign of divine sanction for tax collection as well. A tax called pratishthā was imposed equally on all. In addition, 2 ānnās or 4 ānnās were recovered per person.[47] The founder of the Moravian Mission in Kinnaur, Br Edouard Pagell, gives an eyewitness account of such a visitation to Pooh village in October 1866. The Rājā sent his deities from Middle Kinnaur with an entourage of 130 persons. Local people had to bear all the costs of their stay. Such locals as could not pay cash, paid instead in wheat, barley, buckwheat and potatoes. The devtas moved in a chariot (rath).[48]

Representing the Rājā on one side, the devtas also represented, in a sense, the collective will of the populace against unchecked absolutism by the Rājā on the other side. Each deity had a managing committee composed of influential men of the village. These leading families had one leg in both camps. The Rājā's rule left their local hegemony intact so that it was in their own interest not to rock the boat by using the devta as an instrument of challenge to the Rājā's authority. On the other hand, should the Rājā's demands become insupportable, these local bigwigs could mask local resistance as the devta's will thereby avoiding direct danger to their own status that may have arisen had they been perceived as resisting royal authority. They could always pose as innocent subjects obeying the local divinity whose wrath could be implacable. Collective local will which may otherwise have seemed unacceptably rebellious appeared totally in another light when disguised as divine will of the devta. The Rājā of Bushahr himself had resorted to this device while annulling Lord William Hay's Assessment of 1856 on the outbreak of the mutiny of 1857.[49]

The Rājās of Bushahr did not establish any institutional credit infrastructure to act as an economic underpinning to their rule but provided the deities, consciously or otherwise, with the means of generating a surplus and functioning as moneylenders. Moneylending operations of the deities came to be so well organized in time that they came to constitute a kind of quasi-institutional credit network, lying somewhere between an official credit network and the network of village moneylenders. They functioned for some debtors as refinancing agencies for

December 3, 1985 at 16.45 hours.

[45] Interview with Negi Uday Singh, 1985.

[46] Interview with Negi Uday Singh, 1985.

[47] Interview with Negi Uday Singh, 1985.

[48] Pagell, Edouard: Jahresbericht der Station Poo, West Himalaya 1866, Entry for October 24, Alt. Sign. S.e.5.a, Neu Sign. R.15.U.b.2.a, Prov. Missionsdirektion, Pert. West Himalaya, [Unpublished].

[49] Please see Section 2.B.4.2, Chapter II-B of this work.

repaying loans from moneylenders. They gave (and give) loans regardless of purpose, unlik official agencies which give loans only for so-called productive purposes and almost refuse t admit the need of loans for consumption purposes. Since the devtas had sufficient propert endowed by the Rājā, they had no interest, unlike exploitative moneylenders, in using disbursement of consumption credit at exorbitant rates of interest as the thin end of a wedge to acquire tribal property, despoiling tribals and reducing them to servitude. They may well have helped in preventing ruthless exploitation of tribals by non-Kinnaura professional moneylenders. The devtas' interest lay not in reducing borrowers to landless servitude but in meeting their essential credit needs so that they would have enough surplus to repay the devta with interest, thereby increasing the latter's capacity for further lending. The devtas did not impose notional, insupportably high interest rates. The total absence of mārwāri seths from Kinnaur shows that the devtas have not done a bad job as moneylenders!

7.3.1.1 Sources of Surplus Generation: A Mix of Avenues

The Rājās of Bushahr had endowed many village deities with lands. Unlike other landowners, the devtas could use the major share of their income from land for credit giving. They had no families to support or daily consumption needs to meet. They had 'muāfis' (exemptions) of rent from the Rājā and were thus exempted from paying land revenue and other cesses as assignees. Taxation did not deplete their surplus for this reason. Information collected from the D.C.'s Office at Kālpa on muāfis shows that 23 village deities in Nichār Tahsil had been muāfidārs (assignees) to the tune of Rs 737.96. The three largest muāfidārs among them were the three Mahéshras of Sungra, Bhāba and Chagāoṅ with muāfis amounting to Rs 285, Rs 110 and Rs 194 respectively; accounting for Rs 589 or 79.82% of the total temple muāfis for the Tahsil. In the period since 1960, these muāfis have been resumed to the tune of Rs 641.15, leaving Rs 96.81 as muāfi amount. Sangla Tahsil had 13 muāfidār devtas with a total muāfi of Rs 357.75 of which Rs 257.20 now stand resumed. Devtas Bairing Nāgjee of Sangla, Badrināth of Kāmru and Nāgés of Sapni had muāfis of Rs 140, Rs 100 and Rs 70 respectively, accounting for Rs 310 or 86.65% of the total. Tahsil Kālpa had 11 muāfidār devtas with muāfi of Rs 130 of which Rs 100.91 now stands resumed. Kothi Devi alone had a muāfi of Rs 80 or 61.54% of Rs 130. Tahsil Moorang had 15 muāfidār deities with a total muāfi of Rs 121 (resumed amount = Rs 26.73) while Tahsil Pooh had 25 such deities with total muāfi of Rs 139.72 (all of which stands resumed). Hangrang Sub-Tahsil had 18 muāfidār deities with total muāfi of Rs 93.40 (resumed amount = Rs 91.28). Kinnaur District thus had 105 muāfidār deities with total muāfi of Rs 1,579.83.[50] Sometimes, though rarely, devotees also gifted landed property to deities as a sign of gratitude for some boon. Jawāhar Lāl Negi of village Chhota Kamba narrated how his Kuladevta (clan deity), Kota Nārāyan, had acquired 1.5 bighās of land in Chhota Kamba through a gift deed from a devotee.[51]

The devtas' lands were cultivated by tenants who paid in cash and/or kind for this privilege. This cash and/or kind went towards the devtas' income pool. The Wājib-ul-Arz (village administration paper) of Ghodi Kāmru prepared during the Revision Settlement of 1928 A.D. gives details of the conditions under which temple lands were cultivated by tenants. It lists out three kinds of payments:[52]

[50] List of Muāfidārs with details compiled for the author in Hindi by NaibSadar Kānuṅgo Jitendra Singh Negi of the Sadar Kānuṅgo Branch of the D.C.'s Office at Kālpa between December 1 and 10, 1985. The list was extracted from muāfi files for each individual muāfidār.

[51] Personal interview with Jawāhar Lāl Negi s/o Mr Gayajeet r/o Chhota Kamba, Peon in the D.C.'s Office at Kālpa. Interview held in the D.C.'s Chamber on December 3, 1985 at 15.45 hours at Kālpa.

[52] Wājib-ul-Arz Ghodi Kāmru, Pargana Tukpa, Tahsil Chini, Riyāsat Rāmpur Bushahr, Bābat Tarmim Bandobast Sambat 1984 Bikrami, Item 12: Zikar Muzāriyān, [In Urdu], Unpublished. Available in the District Record

(a) Tenants paying 50% of the produce in kind and rent/revenue in cash to the mandir/devta;
(b) Tenants paying only land revenue in cash but doing customary labour for the temple; and
(c) Tenants not paying any rent to the devta and cultivating the land as jāgir. They were tenants-at-will. Temple officials (kārdārs) and priests (pujāris) were recorded at some places as occupancy tenants. At some places the kārdārs were changed as tenants. Tenants-at-will called Béthus worked as cultivators on the devtas' self-cultivated land (khud kāsht). They were obliged to bring grass and fuelwood required in the devtas' temples. Sharecroppers giving 50% produce to the devta gave 50% of the produce without straw through the kārdārs into the deity's store (akhrājāt). Cash rent paying cultivators paid the fixed lease amount decided upon earlier. Some paid partly in cash and partly in kind.

The deities thus had income in cash as well as in kind from their lands.

Introduction of horticulture in a big way in Kinnaur turned many devtas into orchard owners. The Sungra Mahéshwar has one of the finest orchards in the district. This is auctioned publicly and the proceeds go to the devta's account. The orchard was earlier auctioned each year for one year but in 1984 it was auctioned off for three years @ Rs 20,000 per year, yielding Rs 60,000 in all.[53] Devta Mahéshwar had become a modern economist! Apple prices had been fluctuating in the 1980s and this auctioning off for three years at pre-specified sums was an attempt to dampen the effect of such open market fluctuations. The devta stood to lose if open market prices for apples rose so high that an annual auction could probably have fetched more than Rs 20,000 auction money. But he stood to gain if the open market price sank so low that the auction price would fall below Rs 20,000. Ukha Devi of Nichār owns about 30 bighās of orchard. This orchard is also auctioned openly. The fluctuation in market price can be seen from the fact that income from such auction varied a lot. The orchard is in two lots. In 1985 the two lots were auctioned off for Rs 700 and Rs 3,500 respectively because there was hardly any fruit on the trees. In 1984 they had fetched Rs 12,500 as auction money. In 1983 the auction had fetched Rs 4,500.[54] A strong attack of scab disease makes it doubtful that future auctions shall fetch substantial amounts. The importance of devtas as landowners in Kinnaur has already been seen from the fact that all five landholders affected under the Abolition of The Big Landed Estates and Land Reforms Act, 1953 were village deities.[55]

Another source of income for the deities were the offerings in cash and/or kind by devotees. Such amounts were, however, generally not very substantial in Kinnaur where people did not believe in conspicuous display of wealth. In any case, few people had such wealth in the first place. In Ukha Devi's temple at Nichār annual offerings from devotees are estimated to vary between Rs 2,500/3,000 minimum to Rs 5,000/6,000 maximum.[56] For the temple of Narénas Devta at Chini, annual offerings came to about Rs 8,000 to Rs 10,000.[57] Devotees sometimes gifted lands, cattle or other valuables to village deities. The annual

Room at Kālpa.

[53] Personal interview with Negi Daulat Rām, Chairman Zila Parishad Kinnaur, r/o Nichār on December 12, 1985 in the D.C.'s chamber at Kālpa at 13.00 hours.

[54] Information provided by Negi Daulat Rām; corroborated by other prominent figures of the Nichār area.

[55] Please see Section 2.B.5.1, Chapter II-B of this work.

[56] Source: Negi Daulat Rām, Mohatmim, Ukha Devi Temple.

[57] Source of information: Negi Uday Singh, Mohatmim Mandir.

income from offerings for the Sungra Mạhéshras varied from Rs 15,000 to Rs 25,000.[58] Nobody could point out a village deity richer than the Sungra Mahéshras in Kinnaur.

Interest from credit also accrued as income to the devtas' pool so that a kind of rotating fund came to be established. Each year credit was distributed and then collected back with interest the succeeding year. The divisible pool consisiting of cash and foodgrains kept on swelling from year to year unless natural calamities or bad climatic conditions reduced the surplus available. In villages like Pāngi, Chini, Kothi and Khwāngi it was a custom that even affluent residents took foodgrains on loan from the devta even if not necessary. They then returned the grains with interest. It was a system of voluntary taxation in which people paid the taxes to the devta in form of interest on loans. Being destined for a divinity, these taxes did not arouse the same indignation as direct taxes imposed by the state would have done. All these sources of income enabled the deities to have a surplus available for recycling into credit giving operations.

7.3.1.2 Management of the Devtas' Loans: A Model of Efficiency

Each temple had a temple committee to manage its affairs. There existed local variations in terms of composition of these committees in that the number of members, their terms of office or caste origins varied but the general features were similar. There existed no special committee for handling loans. Managing loaning operations was considered a normal part of its duties. The deity itself chooses committee members by making its choice known through its Grokch, also known as the Māli.[59] There is no democracy involved in this selection because the deity's word is final. Invariably, the deities' choice seems to fall on people from affluent and influential families of the village!

One-third to one-half of the committee membership gets changed every year by the deity. Hardly any one member lasts beyond a term of three years. And all this since generations, before modern Constitutions with such detailed provisions had even been heard of! This was an effective way of rotation by which all influential families were associated with the local power structure manifested through the local deity. Control of credit giving operations was an important aspect of this power structure.

The sole exception to this rule of rotation is the Mohatmim or manager. He is registered as such in the revenue record and continues in office till otherwise desired by the deity. For example, Negi Daulat Rām has been functioning as the Mohatmim of Ukha Devi's temple at Nichār since 11 years. Negi Uday Singh has similarly been Mohatmim of Narénas Devta's temple at Chini. The former is also Chairman, Zila Parishad; owner of sawmills and orchards; economically affluent and politically influential. The latter belongs to an affluent and politically influential family of famous erstwhile sāhukārs. These details are mentioned only to show the nexus between the devtas and influenṭial families as their agents. The Mohatmim acts as the chief overseer of the devta's lending operations, to which purpose he brings all his socio-economic predominance. Temple committeee officials are called kārdārs. They receive no salary. Working as the deity's agent had earlier been a social honour and a way of participating in the power structure. In the absence of institutional credit facilities, temple committees earlier controlled one of the two available sources of informal credit and could use it as a means of patronage for consolidating their own standing. Now such duties are more of a social obligation. People are also afraid of the deity's wrath in case of refusal to serve on the temple committee. Depending upon the annual income of the deity, however, special bonuses of the order of Rs 10 or 20 may be granted annually to the kārdārs by the deity as a mark of

[58] Information provided by an influential member of the temple committee, Sungra, on the condition that his name not be divulged. The promise is being kept.

[59] Please see Section 2.2.1, Chapter II-A of this work.

special favour. Only nominal sums are thus granted, more for honour than for financial gain.

7.3.1.3 Devtas' Distribution Procedure: Simple is Beautiful!

In contrast to the institutional credit sector's labyrynthine procedural formalities, the devtas' loaning procedures are a model of simplicity and efficiency. The temple committee announces a date for the distribution of loans. The Sungra Mahéshras's credit distribution takes place twice a year; once on 'Sāwan Sangrānd' and once in 'Poh', according to Negi Uday Singh.[60] Negi Bahādur Chand, Mohatmim of the Brahma Vishnu Temple in Chagāoṅ clarified that their loans were always distributed around Baisākhi (April 13).[61] Demands for loans are made orally to the kāyath (secretary) of the temple committee. He lists them out. Loan amounts to be given per demanding household are decided in an open meeting of villagers. Decisions of this assembly are put to the deity for approval through its Māthés (questioner). Nothing gets distributed without the deity's approval. After such approval, loans are distributed on the date announced earlier. In this way transaction costs are kept down to a minimum. Villagers do not have to go to distant places for credit. They do not have to waste time and money on repeated fruitless visits because dates for registration and distribution are announced well in advance. No complicated forms need to be filled in.

There is formally no ceiling on the amount of loan admissible but the system of distribution puts such a ceiling in practice depending on the surplus available for distribution. If the preceding year's income from lands, orchards or offerings had been good, loan amounts per household would be higher than if such income had not been adequate. The whole of the surplus available is not given out in general distribution. At least 10% to 20% is kept aside for meeting running expenditures and for giving loans in emergency cases. Anyone wanting loan amounts over and above the amount fixed for general credit disbursement has to make a separate request. Depending upon the availability of surplus kept aside after general distribution; the urgency of demand i.e. purpose for which funds are demanded, whether for a marriage in the family or some other social obligation; the decision of the temple committee and the final approval by the deity, additional loan amounts are released. Harijans are not discriminated against in loan distribution. The kārdārs carefully screen loan demands with respect to repaying capacity and past repayment record, filtering out past or suspected defaulters. Since they are all influential local men, they know the loan seekers personally in most cases. Unlike for banks, there are no problems of improper follow-up here. Temple committee members are themselves moneylenders in many case so that they not only have personal knowledge of the applicants' repaying capacity according to their net worth but also of their actual repayment behaviour on loans.

No security is demanded by the deity in form of jewellery or other valuables to be deposited as collateral for obtaining loans, unlike for many village moneylenders. Personal sureties had, however, to be furnished by bringing a guarantor. Members of the temple committee can also be guarantors but no guarantor can stand surety for more than one person at a time. Temple committee members can also obtain loans like other villagers but on exactly the same terms. No preferential treatment is meted out to them in the matter of obtaining loans by virtue of their having a particular status, that of temple committee members. The Sungra Mahéshras also gives loans on group guarantee basis to groups of 5 to 10 persons belonging to compact hamlets. The guarantors, who may be two or more in number, form a part of this group. These groups then decide between themselves how much loan amount goes to each member. This practice is not widespread though.

[60] Personal interview, 1985.

[61] Personal interview with Negi Bahādur Chand, Mohatmim, Brahma Vishnu Temple, Chagāoṅ on December 1, 1985 at 09.30 hours on the lawn of the D.C.'s Residence at Kālpa. Bahādur Chand had earlier been the author's official driver during his tenure as D.C. at Kālpa (1980-83).

Loan transactions are recorded in registers having mainly three columns viz applicant's name and address; surety's name and address; signature or thumb impression of the borrower and surety, with loan amount. No separate column exists for interest rate. Rate of interest is announced in a general assembly of villagers before loan distribution. They are decided by the temple committee and approved by the deity before being communicated publicly. No cash books are kept. The kāyath of the temple committee maintains a day-book in which he enters daily inflow and outflow of income in cash and/or kind. He has the temple registers in his custody but cannot take them home. They have to remain on the temple premises. They are not secret documents but are normally not shown to outsiders. The reason given is that the deity would get annoyed if these registers were shown to outsiders. The real reason seems to be apprehension that outsiders may be prying for the purpose of assessing and taxing the deity's income. The deity's permission is a pre-requisite for these registers to be shown to outsiders. Such permission is not easy to come by.

In case of excessive demand for loans, loan amounts distributed per household are reduced to conform to available supply of surplus rather than resorting to external refinancing to secure supplemental funds to conform to increased credit demand. No cases were reported in which a village deity used another deity or the Rājā of Bushahr as a refinancing agency for loaning operations. The Rājā did, however, use the deities as refinancing agencies for special occasions calling for heavy expenditure - like royal weddings, special yagnas and other religious ceremonies like the pranaut. Special demand lists (bāchh) used to be sent to each deity specifying the amount due from him/her. Deities were assignees of revenue at the Rājā's pleasure and these muāfis risked getting cancelled if the Rājā's demands were not met. Most loans given earlier by the deities were in kind. They all had storehouses (bhandārs) in which grains were stored before distribution. Loans in kind were mostly in wheat, barley and buckwheat. Nowadays most of their loaning is in cash because the P.D.S. caters to the demand for foodgrains for consumption while the Agriculture and Development Departments provide grain for seed purposes. Cash given by devtas is for consumption purposes. It is mostly taken for 'shādi, ghami' (marriage, sorrow) according to Kinnauras interviewed in the course of this research. That hardly any loaning in foodgrains takes place now could be discerned from the fact that during a field research visit to Kāmru fort in December 1985 three storerooms were found packed with cheena grains. The stores looked unused since long. Negi Ganga Lāl, the 68 year old kārdār accompanying the author, clarified that the kuthārs (stores) had remained full from before his times.

It may seem surprising that the Mohatmim is allowed to go on for an indefinite term while other kārdārs are changed regularly. But a closer examination of the actual working of the temple committee shows that the Mohatmim's longer term does not make him an unchallenged supremo. The system of rotation of committee membership ensures that participation in the power structure through association with the devta gets rotated amongst all dominant Khash clans and does not remain confined to a caucus which could use this monopoly to consolidate dominance over others. Rotation is a practical balance of power arrangement. There were generally between 15 and 25 families (depending on the size of the village) amongst whom committee membership rotates. It is not a device for democratic power-sharing. The Mohatmim belongs to one of these leading families. He is not in a position to function on his own in opposition to other members of the committee who are no lightweights in their own right. The Mohatmim can go on for a long time so long as he has the confidence of his colleagues. But he is not unchangeable. If he crosses swords with too many of his fellow-members on the temple committee, he can always be removed through the devta's express wish. The devta, divine that he is, knows when to dump him if he turns into a hindrance rather than an asset! Being in conflict with other influential families certainly does not further the devta's image and power.

Apart from the necessity of having the support of at least a majority of committee members the Mohatmim's authority depends on two other figures as well - the Grokch and the Māthés. The Grokch is the medium through whom the devta makes his wishes known, his 'voice' so to say. The Māthés is the person who puts questions to the devta who answers such questions through the Grokch. The latter is not just an oral source of history through his Chirāning[62] but an indispensable ally for the Mohatmim, as is the Māthés. Without these two personages on his side the Mohatmim can always be made the victim of a coup d'état in which the Māthés questions the devta whether a change were not desirable at the helm of the temple committee and the Grokch answers in the affirmative on behalf of the deity. The Māthés is generally from an affluent family. The Grokch's family may not be in the top bracket in terms of economic affluence but can not be ignored because of ritual status. Māthés and Grokch act as further brakes on the Mohatmim's ability to dominate the temple committee to the exclusion of other members with shorter terms. Like the Mohatmim, they, too, have indefinite terms and serve at the devta's pleasure. Both positions are hereditary and run within a closed group of families so that the Mohatmim cannot select a Māthés or a Grokch of his own volition. In any case he has usually a host of his own economic activities to supervise, leaving him not enough time to directly control the day-to-day functioning of the temple committee. He is a kind of influential umbrella over this committee which represents the balance of power between leading families of a village in Kinnaur. He is a sort of first amongst equals but in no way an overlord bossing over the others.

The day-to-day activities of the temple committee are supervised by its secretary called the kāyath. He is the custodian of its registers, records and documents. He is responsible for recording transactions, drawing up estimates of demand for credit and of the amount available for disbursement as loans. Even though the loan registers are not complicated and have only three or four columns for entries the kāyath needs to have a basic knowledge of book-keeping and accounting. It can be argued that it is a waste of talent to keep changing the kāyath every 2/3 years, once he becomes familiar with book-keeping. However, the kāyath could be tempted to misuse his position as custodian of loan registers and amounts if he had an unlimited tenure, the devta's wrath notwithstanding. Knowing that all accounts are going to be carefully scrutinized by incoming kāyaths, incumbents are careful about keeping their transactions generally above board. Incoming kāyaths are particularly careful in checking accounts because nobody wants to be tainted with the sin of having embezzled the devtas' funds. Apart from divine wrath it is also an invitation to social odium. There would certainly be problems if there were not existing in each village a group of persons with at least elementary knowledge of book-keeping enabling them to serve as kāyaths. The kāyath comes generally from an influential family. The circle of influential families among whom temple committee membership rotates are almost all (or have earlier been) moneylenders themselves and consequently possess the necessary experience in keeping accounts. This knowledge comes in handy in functioning as kāyaths/kārdārs. Moneylending as a profession having been widespread in Kinnaur, almost every village has a reserve pool of persons acquainted with accounts. This fact means that there is no disruption caused by rotation of kāyaths. It ensures a reasonably corruption-free system of management of the devtas' loans.

It has not been possible to achieve the same degree of absence of corruption in the institutional credit network in spite of a whole phalanx of deterrents like the Prevention of Corrūption Act, the Directorate of Vigilance, the Lok Ayukta (Ombudsman) and the like. Absence of corruption is not just a morally desirable phenomenon. It is also linked directly to borrowers' transaction costs and thence to real rates of interest on loans.[63] The higher the extent of bribes and corruption in the system, the higher the costs of transaction for borrowers and the higher the real rates of interest paid by them on their loans. The system of rotation of kāyaths and other members of the temple committee is a practical way of reducing the possibility of embezzlement of funds. It discourages kāyaths from raising the costs of transaction for borrowers in order to derive personal gratification. The devta forms the apex of

[62] Please see Section 2.2.1, Chapter II-A of this work.

[63] Please see Table 4.21, Chapter IV of this work.

this structure with his supernatural powers. His supremacy is practically manifested through the Mohatmim and his colleagues on the temple committee, alongwith the Grokch and the Māthés. Belonging to economically and socially important families these persons reinforce their hold on less affluent Kinnauras through their management of the devtas' loans.

Most loans from deities go to residents of the village in which the deity has its seat and influence. Pargana-level deities like the Sungra Mahéshras and Kāmru Badrināth do not refuse loans to villagers from villages within their parganas of influence. The instances of such cross-village lending are, however, rare. Unlike banks, devtas have not sought to defy geography by pitching their loaning operations too wide. Even though imbued with supernatural power in popular supposition, they have been sound bankers by confining their credit ranges to their immediate vicinity in which their influence and that of their committee members is optimal. In an area like Kinnaur, topography ensured that the range of socio-economic influence varied inversely as the square of the distance, an inverse square law. The law of diminishing returns set in early, as commercial banks discovered to their cost soon enough!

7.3.1.4 Rates of Interest Charged: Not Exorbitant

Contrary to the widely held belief in official circles that private moneylenders are an unmitigated evil because they seek to reduce borrowers to servitude through exorbitantly high rates of interest, the deities in Kinnaur always seem to have had well specified stable rates of interest which are even today not perceived as exorbitant by borrowers. Cash loans had to be repaid in cash and not in grain. Loans in grain could be repaid in terms of their cash equivalent or partly in cash and partly in kind. Prevalent folklore and memories of aged Kinnauras point to the fact that the traditional rate of interest was 25% per annum (Sawāi). Old account books (bahis) in possession of Negi Uday Singh speak of a rate of 'chawanni fi rupaiya' (25 paise per rupee) in Chini area. One bahi was from 1918. In Chhota Kamba, there was a measuring vessel called a kodu, measuring about 1 kg. of today. For every 4 kodus taken on credit, five had to be repaid into the devta's kuthār at the time of repayment after one year. If 8 kodus had been borrowed, 10 kodus-full had to be returned. For 16 kodus or 'bātis', 20 had to be returned. 16 pathé constituted a standard unit called one bār. 20 pathé (measuring vessels) constituted one khārin̊. 25 pathé constituted one nāṅko. Hence on one bār loan, one khārin had to be repaid. On one khārin loan, one nāṅko had to be repaid after one year. If there was default on repayment after one year, then on a loan of 4 kodus, for example, 6 kodus would have to be repaid after 2 years rather than 5 kodus after one year.[64]

In the Poāri area, the standard measuring unit was a pathā, equal to about a seer in weight. 20 pathās constituted one chharāri. The normal rate of interest on loans in kind was 5 pathās on one chharāri in this area. This information was given by Negi Amar Singh, scion of the Poāri Wazir family.[65] Negi Prabhu Sain of Moorang corroborated this fact by saying that in the Moorang area also, 5 pathās interest had had to be paid on a loan of 1 chharāri consisting of 20 pathās.[66] In the Pooh area, Seth Chhering Bhāg Sānā, Pradhān, Grām

[64] Source: Jawāhar Lāl Negi, personal interview, 1985.

[65] Personal interview with Negi Amar Singh Wazir, Pradhān, Gram Panchāyat Poāri on December 9, 1985 in his own house at Poāri village from 14.30 hours till 19.15 hours.

[66] Personal interview with Negi Prabhu Sain s/o Mr Chhering Dutt r/o Moorang, aged about 72 years, on December 11, 1985 in Moorang at 15.00 hours. The interview began just below the old 'Pandavas' Fort over the Satluj river and continued as we moved in the van of the procession of the two Ormik Devtas who had been brought out of their normal place of residence in the fort. This ceremony takes place once in every five years. The arrival of the author was a sheer coincidence. It was seen in detail how the devtas were dressed up and ceremonially decorated, what ceremonies took place and how the procession moved off, including the

Panchāyat Pooh, explained that the basic unit of measurement of foodgrains was one dheh. 20 dhehs constituted one hal. If one hal grain was taken as loan in kind from the devta, 5 dhehs had to be paid as interest so that 25 dhehs had to be returned after one year whereas 20 dhehs had been taken as loan. In case of default, either 10 dhehs would have to be repaid after 2 years or physical labour would have to be done in lieu of repayment. For such labour, wages would be calculated @ 2 dhehs per day for a male worker and @ 1 dheh per day for a female worker.[67] In the Nichār area, 5 pathās had to be paid as interest on a loan of 1 chharāri before 1945, according to Negi Daulat Rām.[68] Even though the names of measuring vessels were different and even if their quantities differed slightly, the rate of interest was fairly consistent at 25% per annum in all parts of Kinnaur till 1945 or so, even down till 1948.

Nobody could say when exactly a change took place but from about 1948 onwards, the rate of interest was cut from 25% per annum to 12.5% per annum. It became 2 ānnās per rupee per annum on loans in cash and 2.5 pathās per chharāri on loans in kind.[69] In 1980 the Sungra Mahéshra's reduced the rate of interest on his loans to 10% per annum.[70] Ukha Devi of Nichār followed suit in 1984 and cut the rate of interest down to 10% per annum as well.[71] The resemblence to a banking system here is striking. When a central bank or a major bank cuts its rate of interest, lesser banks follow suit in order not to be priced out of the credit market. The Sungra Mahéshras seems to be playing the role of a divine central bank for devi devtas in Kinnaur because more and more deities are now reducing their rates of interest on loans to 10% per annum, falling in line with the rate of interest floated by the Sungra Mahéshras.[72] The rates of interest charged by devtas are thus very much competitive in comparison to the rates being charged by the institutional sector. Coupled with minimal transaction costs, no procedural formalities and no restrictions on end-use of loans, it gives the deities an advantage over banks in the credit markets of Kinnaur.

7.3.1.5 Magnitude of Loan Transactions: In Thousands Not Lakhs

It remains extremely difficult to estimate the volume of loan transactions carried on by village deities because no kārdār seems willing to provide accurate information. Some are genuinely apprehensive of the deity's wrath should they divulge the scale of its lending operations. To cite just two examples of how difficult it can be to estimate the volume of such transactions, let us consider the cases of the Sungra Mahéshras and of Narénas Devta of Chini. Even responsible Kinnauras support the general popular view that the income of the former and his lending oprations are in lakhs. This is strongly contested by the temple committee of Sungra which quotes a much lower figure in thousands. Similarly, residents of the Chini area say that Narénas is a rich devta possessing a handsome income from his neoza trees. The devta's Mohatmim, however, refutes this belief. He maintains that earlier kārdārs had misused temple funds because of which he opposed giving of loans now. 8 or 10 earlier kārdārs had illegally usurped possession of about 60-70 bighās of chilgoza forest belonging to Narénas Devta, leaving the latter only about 25-30 bighās in balance. After Negi Uday Singh became the

author.

[67] Personally interviewed in Pooh with Lāmā Shimed Chhéwang, 1985.

[68] Personal interview, 1985.

[69] Negi Daulat Rām; corroborated by all others interviewed.

[70] Source: Negis Daulat Rām and Uday Singh, personal interviews, 1985.

[71] Source: Negi Daulat Rām, Mohatmim, Ukha Devi Temple, 1985.

[72] Source = Negi Daulat Rām, 1985; corroborated by personal observation.

Mohatmim, he got this usurpation vacated and restored the income from the chilgoza forest to the devta. Rs 25,000 to Rs 30,000 income now accrues to the devta per annum from this chilgoza jungle.[73] Personal contacts and observation have been used in making the following rough assessment of loan volume.

While the volume of loan transactions in cash seemed to be in the region of Rs 100,000 per annum for the Sungra Mahéshras, its value was almost certainly lower for other deities. In pre-independence days when loaning was mostly in kind, cash loans were in the region of Rs 5,000 for most deities. Nowadays, even with orchards, loaning in cash is still in thousands rather than in lakhs (hundreds of thousands), being around Rs 50,000 to Rs 60,000 per annum for the larger devtas. In the Nichār area, a ceiling of Rs 20 was put on the amount of cash each borrower could get from the deity before 1945. It was raised to Rs 100 in the 1950s and is now around Rs 1,000 for medium-level temples of deities like those of villages Nichār, Bari, Jāni and Rāmni.[74] In village Chagāoṅ the average loan amount per borrowing household was Rs 200 to Rs 250 for loans from the Brahma Vishnu Temple.[75] The Sungra Mahéshras gives cash loans of up to Rs 2,500 to Rs 5,000 per borrower, if necessary. Loan amounts in Kāmru were sometimes as low as Rs 10 or Rs 20 in cash.[76] On a very rough basis, since the list of muāfis revealed 105 deities in all, if we assume an annual lending figure of Rs 100,000 for the Sungra Mahéshras, of Rs 60,000 for five other major deities, of Rs 25,000 for about 20 smaller deities and of Rs 2,000 for the remaining 79 temples, we get an overall figure of Rs 1,223,000 per annum as loans from deities in Kinnaur. This means a per capita loan figure of Rs 20.54, taking 59,547 persons of the 1981 Census as the total population of Kinnaur. More

[73] Negi Uday Singh, personal interview, 1985.

[74] Negi Daulat Rām, personal interview, 1985.

[75] Negi Bahādur Chand, personal interview, 1985.

[76] Personal interview with Negi Ganga Lāl, then Up-Pradhān, Grām Panchāyat Kāmru and retired Forest Ranger, on December 6, 1985 at 12.30 hours in the old fort at Kāmru. He guided the author all over the fort to which entry is strictly restricted. This fort was the seat of the Thākurs of Kāmru who later on evolved into the Rājās of Bushahr. The author's turban was an advantage because according to tradition in Kāmru only persons wearing turbans, a traditional symbol of status, or specially designed round woollen caps could enter the fort after tying cummerbunds around their waists. The three companions of the author - Negis Khem Singh, Ganga Lāl and Sāgar Jeet (Grokch of Devta Badrināth) - put on these special caps to accompany him. All tied red woollen strings as symbolic 'Gāchhis' or cummerbunds. The author had to guarantee that he was not a Scheduled Caste. The question was put to him extremely indirectly and discreetly by Negi Ganga Lāl. Harijans are not allowed access into the fort. In 1982, Rājā Virbhadra Singh, present Chief Minister of H.P. and heir of the last ruling Rājā (Padam Singh) of Bushahr, came to Kāmru, his ancestral seat, to address a public meeting. The S.D.M., Kālpa, in whose jurisdiction Kāmru falls, accompanied him into the fort. The officer happened to be a Harijan. Ganga Lāl, Khem Singh and others who were present on this occasion told the author that they all knew the S.D.M.'s origins and tried to talk him out of going into the fort by saying that only the Rājā Sāhib should go in with his entourage. Nobody dared to forbid the S.D.M. directly. The officer, whether by accident or design, did accompany the Rājā into the fort, particularly since he was the officiating D.C. in the author's absence on leave. All the prominent persons of Kāmru and Sangla confirmed that after the departure of the party a special 'Shuddhi' (purification) ceremony was held since the fort had been considered defiled by the entry of a Harijan, be he the officiating D.C.! A lamb was sacrificed from the devta's treasury (Khazāna) as a part of this ritual. In earlier times the transgressor himself would have been required to offer such sacrifice to beg pardon. Since nobody dared to ask the officer to do so, the sacrifice was arranged out of the devta's khazāna. The author's companions were thoroughly relieved that he was not a Harijan. They told him that they could not have stopped him from having his way even if he had been a Harijan because they feared his official position but a similar purification ceremony would certainly have followed later. The author's not being a Harijan saved all this bother. That is why they are chary about letting officers visit the fort.

appropriately, this means Rs 99.45 loan per household as per the 1981 Census.

7.3.1.6 Recovery of Devtas' Loans: Needs Emulation!

Strikingly, while banks and cooperative credit societies are plagued by mounting overdues and defaults on loans, nobody in Kinnaur could recall even a single case of wilful default on loans taken from the devta. Penalties do, however, exist for possible default. In Chagāoṅ village, Rs 15 would be imposed as penalty per hundred rupees loan per day in case of default.[77] In Chini, it was a flat rate of Rs 5 penalty per day irrespective of loan size.[78] Defaulters risk getting cut off from further loans. Most important of all, they risk incurring the devta's 'dosh' (wrath) which could go on for two to three generations. If the defaulters later came to the deity for succour, the latter would impose 200% to 400% of the loan amount overdue as damages. It could also express a wish to camp in the defaulters' homes. For the duration of such visit the defaulters would have to bear the expenses of almost the entire village which would come visiting the deity. All amounts borrowed are returned on a specified day or days fixed for repayment well in advance and announced publicly. For smaller deities, only one day is fixed for repayment. For major deities, 2 or 3 days' time is announced for repayment. Once all the dues are in, fresh circulation of loans is done for the succeeding year after 5 or 6 days. Loans are returned mostly in October or November for most deities because that is when the harvest comes in. The loans of the Chagāoṅ Mahéshras had been recovered on November 19, 1985 for that year, while the author was on a field visit to Kinnaur.[79] Negi Bahādur Chand narrated how he personally had borrowed Rs 200 from the Chagāoṅ Mahéshras in 1982. He had provided a surety and signed on a revenue stamp on the loan register while taking the loan. At the end of the year he had returned Rs 225.[80] He, then himself the D.C.'s driver, had preferred to go to the deity rather than to a bank because banks had too many formalities to be gone through whereas the devta's procedure was simple. A most fitting commentary on the functioning of the institutional credit system that even the D.C.'s driver preferred the devta to the bank even though he knew fully well that a call from his boss could change the mind of even a recalcitrant bank manager! The devtas' loans are all short-term loans for one year. In the rarest of rare cases, the deity agrees to write off loans if borrowers are adjudged unfit to repay because of circumstances beyond their control. In rare cases, the borrower can request the devta for prolongation of the repayment period. If the devta consents to such prolongation then no penalty is imposed for the delay in repayment. Negi Balwant Singh, Chairman, Panchāyat Samiti Kālpa, pointed out that Kothi Devi had granted such extensions and exemptions in many cases. Ranséru, Mohatmim of the Devi, had got an exemption many times from repayment.[81] Even here, George Orwell's famous dictum seems to hold good. All Kinnauras are equal before village godlings but some Kinnauras seem to be more equal than others! The Mohatmim of Kothi Devi has been getting away with what would surely bring her wrath down on ordinary loan defaulters.

In any case, borrowers are by and large careful never to default on the deity's loans because they can get a fresh dose of loans 4 or 5 days after repaying the preceding year's dues. Even if they do not have the requisite amount available for repayment, they assemble it by borrowing from relatives, friends or other moneylenders. Once repaid, they get fresh loans from the devta and return this bridging loan obtained only to repay the devta on time. In case

[77] Negi Bahādur Chand, personal interview, 1985.

[78] Negi Uday Singh, personal interview, 1985.

[79] Negi Bahādur Chand, personal interview, 1985.

[80] Negi Bahādur Chand, personal interview, 1985.

[81] Negi Uday Singh, personal interview, 1985.

of unforeseen circumstances, the devtas can be approached for loans at times other than the pre-announced dates but such exceptions are kept rare. Under the umbrella of the devtas' divinity and supernatural attributes, recovery of loans functions smoothly and without hitches. It deserves emulation and due appreciation rather than being castigated as a primitive and unscientific practice. We can now examine how the other tier of the informal credit sector functions in Kinnaur - the much maligned moneylenders.

7.3.2 Village Moneylenders in Kinnaur: A Major Force

The informal credit sector was not entirely in divine hands! Even today, when banks have expanded into Kinnaur, moneylending or sāhukāri not only survives as a viable profession but carries no social stigma. This can chiefly be attributed to three factors:

(a) When the deities themselves indulge in sāhukāri, one could not attach social odium to such an occupation without automatically condemning the deities as well;

(b) Absence of an influx of non-tribal moneylenders into the area meant that moneylending remained associated with affluent local tribal families commanding positions of respect in Kinnaura society. They had a middling attitude towards poorer Kinnauras who did suffer exploitation at their hands but not to the extent suffered by tribals in other parts of India. Kinnaur did not possess culturable land in such quantities as would encourage usurious moneylenders to reduce people en masse to servitude for obtaining cheap labour to till their fields. Land holdings being small, there was hardly any tradition of absentee landlords getting their fields worked through penurious labour. The Rājā, the devtas, the Wazirs and others in positions of authority had unpaid labour through the system of bégār so there was no need for them to enlarge this pool of manual labour through high usury which generated much ill will; and

(c) Since a major part of the credit network relied on loans in kind before 1948, chronic foodgrain deficits in the area ensured that such loans in foodgrains served as succour of last resort in winter when available foodgrain stocks in poor families did not suffice for minimum nutritional needs. Poor people found it hard to brand as usurers and exploiters those who provided them foodgrains in times of dire need.

That village moneylenders were not the devils in Kinnaur that they are otherwise made out to be, can be gauged from the fact that even government publications, which normally pillory village moneylenders in severe terms, grudgingly admit that "*it was, however, noteworthy that the rate of interest charged by moneylenders in this area was much less and even today it is so as compared to the interest appropriated by moneylenders in other areas. This may be due to the fact that people here are simple and honest*".[82] This explanation is obviously too simplistic and ignores the fact that moneylenders in Kinnaur did exploit their debtors but that socio-economic conditions were such as to make overexploitation counterproductive. It was in their own interest to keep most debtors solvent so that their limited funds would not get choked up. Debtors' defaults en masse would have impaired income generation through this economic activity, one of the few gainful occupations available in that hard area. The state under the princely order did not have social justice, including a campaign against usurious moneylenders on its agenda and it is only in independent India that such efforts were concerted as part of state policy. Shorn of legal protection against moneylenders, borrowers had no institutional finance to turn to. Village moneylenders had pretty much a free run in the area till the 1960s. The word sāhukār is the same in Kinnauri as well! To get an idea of how village moneylenders function in Kinnaur we can consider a few sample cases.

[82] Gazetteer, 1971, p. 177.

7.3.2.1 Case Studies of Loans From Moneylenders

These case studies are persons who were interviewed personally. They had seen their families taking loans from moneylenders and how the latter functioned. The case studies reveal a flexible loaning structure with very low transaction costs.

7.3.2.1.1 Case Study from Village Chhota Kamba

Jawāhar Lāl Negi is a peon in the D.C.'s Office at Kālpa. He belongs to village Chhota Kamba of the former 15/20 Pargana. His family had taken cash loans of Rs. 100 and Rs 300 from Nargu Sain and Sunder Lāl of the same village in 1980. This was not an isolated transaction. Jawāhar mentioned that borrowing and repaying were a continuous process.[83] The loans were taken @ 12.5% rate of interest per annum. No 'likhat parhat' (documentation) was gone through for these loans because Sunder Lāl happened to be a relative, as was Nargu Sain. If the loan stood repaid in six months instead of in one year, only 6.25% would be charged as rate of interest instead of the annual 12.5%. Loans were needed to make bulk purchases in the Lavi Fair at Rāmpur. If the loan stood repaid in three months, then interest would be paid @ 3.125%. There was no fixed interval at which Jawāhar's family repaid loan amounts. Sometimes, they returned it much before one year and sometimes after two years when they had to pay 25% interest. In case of default, no penal interest was charged by the moneylenders. The already-agreed-upon rate of interest would be charged further for the period of extension. No security had been demanded from the family. Banks had not been approached for loans because they demanded lots of documents according to the family. This case study shows that moneylenders could be very flexible.

7.3.2.1.2 Case Study from Village Poāri

Wazir Amar Singh Negi mentioned that his family had been leading moneylenders in the area around their seat at Poāri. Their moneylending operations had continued till 1970 when a major fire reduced their ancestral house to ashes, including most bahi khātās of credit. In the absence of records, he could not recover loan amounts due to him and had stopped moneylending. Even after destruction of records, many honest debtors had come to him on their own and returned loan amounts with interest, in spite of the fact that no records existed to prove such transactions and that the Act of 1976 had liquidated many such debts. The Poāri Wazir family had charged 12.5% per annum as rate of interest and not 25% even in the lifetime of Amar Singh's father. The prevailing rate had then been 5 pathās on one chharāri but their family had demanded a rate of only 2.5 pathās on one chharāri and not 5 pathās. They did not require their debtors to bring sureties or guarantors. Being the leading Wazirs, they had already so much of social pre-eminence that such measures were unnecessary. Negi Amar Singh had employed two employees (Bhandāris) for carrying on loaning operations as his agents. No security was kept. He felt that Kinnauras were earlier very honest. Transactions had been recorded in the Tānkri script as reminders about credits given. There had been no sureties, no documents and no witnesses.[84] He did not remember defaults taking place on loans taken from him. People had always repaid their debts on time. His loans had mostly been in grain. On cash loans he had charged 2 ānnās per rupee (12.5%) as rate of interest per annum.

[83] Personal interview, 1985.

[84] Personal interview, 1985.

7.3.2.1.3 Case Study from Village Tāngling

Rām Singh of village Tāngling explained that his family had earlier taken loans from sāhukārs at rates of interest of 25% per annum. This rate had continued in practice till about 1965-66. His family had had to produce a guarantor as surety for getting loans. Since they were personally known to the moneylender, no advance deposit or mortgage had been demanded from them as security. Had they not been known to the moneylender, or if there had been doubts about their repaying capacity, valuables like ornaments or metal utensils would have had to be pledged as security. A 'tahrir' (agreement deed) was then drawn up by the moneylender. It always mentioned that in case of default on repayment, the pledged article would lapse in favour of the sāhukār. If even this step did not suffice to cover the default, the sāhukār used to begin a suit before an 'adālat' (court of law) for 'kurki' (confiscation). Loans were taken for purchase of consumer goods.[85]

7.3.2.1.4 Case Study from Village Chini

Duni Chand s/o Mr Kālu Rām r/o Chini, a Harijan aged about 42 years, stated that his grandfather, Mr Jiunar, had taken a loan in cash from Negi Bhoop Singh, father of Negi Uday Singh, of the Thurkyān family.[86] There was no record in writing to know what the amount of the loan had been. Jiunar had mortgaged land as security for this loan. He could not repay the loan. Bhoop Singh had then mortgaged this very land to the government and obtained money in lieu thereof. The khāta (land holding) was now in the name of 25 holders, Bhoop Singh's descendants. They paid land revenue to the government. Possession of the land was formally vested in the District Collector. As usual, this Harijan family seemed to have had to put up with more rigorous loan conditions than its tribal counterparts.[87]

7.3.2.1.5 Case Study from Village Pooh

Mr Médub Dandub s/o Mr Kunzang, aged 58 years, shopkeeper of Pooh talked about loans given by Kinnauras across the border in Tibet. He had been 22 times in Tibet, regularly till 1959, as a trader. He had followed the route Shipke, Kyuk, Tia, Māyāng, Rongtok, Domar Jot till the market of Gurché as final station. Each trader acted as moneylender to his Tibetan suppliers. The loan amount had to be a cash advance for the next year, equivalent to the value of all merchandise (chiefly wool, salt, sheep and goats) brought by the suppliers the preceding year. In return for this loan, the Tibetans undertook to supply their merchandise exclusively to the credit giving trader-moneylender. Médub Dandub estimated that in the area upstream of Rārang, roughly Rs 900,000 had been blocked in Tibet by the conflict of 1962. He himself had lost about Rs 17,000 as loaned out amount in Tibet. These loans in Tibet had been interest-free loans. Had some trader attempted to charge interest thereon, he would have received no supplies for the succeeding year. A trader from Pooh had been to Tibet in 1984. All his old debtors except for one were dead. Médub Dandub still had his old account books. He hoped that one day he and others like him would get repaid because Tibetan debtors did not let their loans lapse. Sons and grandsons repaid the debts incurred by their ancestors.

[85] Personal interview with Mr Rām Singh r/o Tāngling on December 9, 1985 at 19.30 hours. The author was returning in the D.C.'s vehicle from Poāri after interviewing Wazir Amar Singh and found Rām Singh walking by the side of the road. He was given a lift. The interview began in the vehicle itself and continued in his house in village Tāngling.

[86] Personal interview with Duni Chand on December 1, 1985 in the Tahsil Office at Chini.

[87] Idem; corroborated by the revenue record in the Tahsil Office at Chini.

Médub Dandub said that other traders and he used to obtain taccāvi loans from the Rājā of Bushahr @ 4 ānnās per rupee for 6 months. Loans used to be advanced in 'Jéth' (summer) when the traders used to go to Tibet and repaid in November/December after the Lavi Fair at Rāmpur. Only affluent traders used to be given such loans. "Am ādmi" (ordinary people) could not get such loans. The rate of interest in the area around Pooh used to be 2 ānnās per rupee (or 12.5%) per annum, as against 4 ānnās per rupee for 6 months, as was being charged by the Rājā on loans to traders from Kinnaur.[88]

7.3.2.1.6 Case Study from Village Sangla

Negi Khem Singh, B.D.O., explained how his family had borrowed money from one Rachhpāl of Sangla when he (Khem Singh) had been a child. They had borrowed Rs 200 at 12.5% rate of interest per annum. They had had to repay over many years and had repaid at least Rs 500. No security had been pledged, only a guarantor had given surety. A written deed (parnot) had been executed. Khem Singh's illiterate ancestors had signed the deed without seeing how much repayment had been written therein. The sāhukār had written more than double the amount which had to be repaid. His ancestors had not had to do bonded labour. Such labour had not been prevalent in the Sangla area. Debtors had sometimes done occasional labour for one or two days per month. Anyone could start sāhukāri and no licence was needed for it. There was no social resentment against moneylending as a profession which was considered as a normal activity. Since the devta could not meet the needs of the whole village, moneylenders filled in the gap. Since there had been no shops, purchases had had to be made at the Lavi Fair in bulk for the whole year. Credit used to be taken for these annual purchases. His own paternal grandmother (dādi) had given a loan of 20 silver rupees to a Harijan about 100 years before. The latter had pledged land as security for the loan, and this had been recorded in the revenue record. This land, measuring 2 bighās, was still in the possession of Khem Singh's family. No sāhukār used to borrow money for lending it further at higher rates of interest. Khem Singh mentioned that traders from the Pooh area used to lend cash to suppliers in Tibet. On closure of trade in 1962, Bābu Nihāl Chand of Spillo had lost lakhs of rupees blocked in Tibet. Pooh traders used to lend money to each other mutually. Students from that area studying with Khem Singh in school used to be better off than others because of extensive moneylending carried on by their trader-fathers.[89]

7.3.2.2 Deductions from Case Studies

These case studies show that terms of credit used to be flexible. Where debtors were well known to the creditors, no security had to be pledged. Surety used to suffice. In case of close relatives, even this requirement used to be waived. Harijans used to have severer conditions imposed on them in terms of requirement of security than others. Loans used to be taken chiefly for consumption purposes, for making purchases of essential commodities in bulk and for meeting social obligations. The Rājā himself functioned as a moneylender to a small number of affluent traders from the area around Pooh and charged high rates of interest (up to 50% per annum). Traders used to mutually give loans but at high rates of interest. Moneylenders used to be more likely than devtās to ask for collateral/security on loans. Shorn of the devtas' divine aura, moneylenders had to reckon with possible default on their loans to a greater extent. To cover this risk, they used to make debtors pledge articles as collateral, with value far in excess of the amounts being loaned out. The survey data of the Act of 1976 shows at least a hundred such cases out of 283 cases where the collateral pledged was

[88] Personal interview with Mr Médub Dandub on December 10, 1985 in Suite No.2 of the P.W.D. Rest House at Pooh at 20.45 hours. The interviews began with Lāmā Shimed Chhéwang and Chhering Bhāg Sānā. We were joined by Médub Dandub after an hour. After 21.30 hours, at least seven other villagers of Pooh joined the group. Discussions went on till well past midnight.

[89] Personal interview, 1985.

Table 7.10: Collateral Pledged against Loans in Kinnaur District

sn	*Name of Debtor*	*Name of Moneylender*	*Village*	*aol*	*Security Pledged*
1a	Inder Chhering(S.C)	Tulsi Rām(S.T)	Lābrang	38	26 T Silver Ornament
1b	Inder Chhering(S.C)	----do----	---do---	do	3 Brass Plates
1c	Inder Chhering(S.C)	Singha Jeet	Lābrang	140	1 Tola Gold Earrings
1d	Inder Chhering (S.C)	Kaldan Deva	Lābrang	80	1 Tola Gold
02	Krishan Das(S.C)	Kaldan Dewa(S.T)	Lābrang	120	40 T Silver Ornaments
03	Bhāg Sain (S.C)	Jeeta Mani (S.T)	Spillo	200	130 Tolās Silver
04	Rām Chand (S.C)	Bhagat Singh (S.T)	Kānam	10	1 Brass Vessel
05	Namgyal (S.C)	Amir Singh (S.T)	Kānam	100	1 Carpet
6a	Kunga (S.C)	Lobu Rām (S.T)	Sunnam	100	1 Wooden Box
6b	Kunga (S.C)	Lobu Rām (S.T)	Sunnam	100	1 Silver Chain
6c	Kunga (S.C)	Lobu Rām (S.T)	Sunnam	100	6 Tolās Silver
07	Panma (S.C)	Amir Singh (S.T)	Sunnam	25	2 Spades, 3 Hoes
08	Bhāgpur (S.C)	Guru Sain (S.T)	Chini	100	80 Tolās Silver
9a	Sunder Lal (S.C)	Yagtan (S.T)	Urni	150	41 Tolās Silver
9b	Sunder Lal (S.C)	Yagtan (S.T)	Urni	150	35 Tolās Garland
9c	Sunder Lal (S.C)	Yagtan (S.T)	Urni	150	10 Tolās Ornaments
9d	Sunder Lal (S.C)	Yagtan (S.T)	Urni	150	1 Pair Anklets
10	Budhya Pur (S.C)	Bharat (S.T)	Kothi	30	20 Tolās Silver

Code: **sn = serial number, aol = amount of loan in Rupees, T = Tolās.**

ridiculously out of proportion to loan amounts, as can be seen from Table 7.10 . It is a small sample of ten, all Harijans. Risk management by moneylenders in the form of high collateral demands is obvious from this sample. This reflects doubts about the repaying capacity of S.C. debtors.

7.3.2.2.1 Sources of Surplus Generation

Land holding was not a very remunerative occupation in Kinnaur because of geographical/climatic conditions. Only families like the Poāri Wazir family had large land holdings which yielded enough surplus for further moneylending. Orchards yielded some surplus but horticulture was not so remunerative in Kinnaur before 1960 as it is today. Besides agriculture and horticulture, other important sources of surplus generation, as pinpointed by T.S. Negi were:

(a) **Trade;**
(b) **Animal Husbandry; and**
(c) **Employment.**[90]

[90] Personal interview with Mr Thākur Sain Negi, former Speaker of the H.P. Legislative Assembly and retired

Enough has already been said on trade.[91] Government employment brought meagre salaries but government employees even at the lowest level belonged generally to influential families which were self-sufficient to a perceptible degree. The cash received as salary could be given out as loans, a process which then began a self-generating cycle because of interest. Goat and sheep breeders regularly went to the plains in winter. They sold some animals there for cash which they used as surplus for giving on credit back home in Kinnaur. Negi Goverdhan Singh's father Shri Hirpāl Negi built up his fortune from his sheep and goat flocks and through trade, for example. He became a major moneylender in the Sangla area, beginning a cycle which has kept his inheritors as one of the richest and most influential families in the area. The use of sheep and goats as pack animals gave flock owners an advantage as traders. Large flock owners came to be known as seths (moneylenders). Many important moneylending families in Kinnaur trace their moneylending operations to possession of sheep and goat flocks by their ancestors. A very large reserve of cash was in any case not required to begin moneylending operations in Kinnaur. The total monopoly of the informal sector on the local credit markets, coupled with a very low degree of monetization resulting in the need for loans more in kind than in cash meant that even a moderate cash surplus was sufficient to launch a moneylending career in Kinnaur.

7.3.2.2.2 Interest Rates Charged by Village Moneylenders

The picture was similar to that for loans given by devtas. Interest rates used to be 25% per annum till 1948. They fell to 12.5% p.a. around 1950. This was amply corroborated by entries in the bahi khātās of Sāhukār Bhoop Singh of Chini and of Dandub Rām of Pooh. Their bahis for the year 1950 show that the rate of interest charged per annum had been reduced to 2 ānnās per rupee as against 4 ānnās to the rupee in preceding years. Negi Goverdhan Singh showed some bahis from the time of his father around the turn of the century in which the annual rate of interest is mentioned as 4 ānnās per rupee or 25%. According to him, "*much later it was reduced to 2 ānnās per rupee*",[92] or 12.5% per annum. In the Nichār area, the rate of interest was 4 ānnās per rupee per year (25%) till about 1945 after which it fell to 2 ānnās per rupee or 12.5% per annum.[93] In the Pooh area, rate of interest had been 2 ānnās per rupee per half-year or 25% per annum.[94] Lambardār Keshwa Singh of Sangla pointed out that even some Harijans used to function as sāhukārs. They had charged the same rates of interest as those charged by other moneylenders. He specifically mentioned Dhansia of hamlet Thémgrang and Jiupur Halmandi of village Sangla as such Harijan moneylenders. They had charged their fraternity members the same 25% annual rate of interest as that charged by non-harijan moneylenders.[95] Wazir Amar Singh's family had reduced the rate of interest to 2

Chief Secretary to the H.P. Government, former Cabinet Minister in H.P., former President, Janata Party in H.P. He was formally interviewed on January 9, 1986 in the Adim Jāti Séwak Sangh complex at Salogra near Solan from 14.30 hours till 18.30 hours.

[91] Please see Section 1.2.4, Chapter I of this work.

[92] Personal interview with Negi Goverdhan Singh, retired Tahsildār and former Pradhān, Grām Panchāyat Sangla, in his house in Sangla on December 6, 1985 at 10.00 hours. At nearly 98 years of age, he is a treasure house of information about Kinnaur and Bushahr, a living participant in important events of Bushahr's history. He has a valuable collection of genealogical tables, bahi khātās, official letters and documents. He allowed the author access to his personal collection.

[93] Negi Daulat Rām, personal interview, 1985.

[94] Medub Dandub, personal interview, 1985.

[95] Personal interview with Lambardār Keshwa Singh of Sangla in his own house in Sangla on December 7, 1986 at 11.00 hours. He was 85 years old at that time and had been Lambardār for 46 years. He had a valuable

pathās per chharāri (10%) per annum instead of the generally prevalent 12.5%.[96]

7.3.2.2.3 Social Class of Moneylenders: Extremely Few Harijans

Village moneylenders had no supernatural attributes like devtas but belonged to leading and influential families in the village, often with members holding positions in the state hierarchy as employees. Parvenus could manage to break into this charmed circle since anyone could start moneylending operations. This happened frequently in the Pooh area where traders like Raghu Dās rose within one generation from socio-economic insignificance to a leading position in moneylending circles but the number of such cases making it to the big league remained small. Interviews with leading Kinnauras lead to a rough estimate that there were about 15 major moneylending families in Nichār division, about 20 such families in Kālpa division and about 50 such families in Pooh division. By major moneylenders is meant operations of Rs 5,000 per year or more given as loans. In addition, there was at least one medium-level sāhukār in each village, giving between Rs 500 and 5,000 as loans per annum. Moneylenders giving total credit of Rs 500 or less were too numerous to be counted.

Some renowned moneylenders of the Nichār area were Sita Rām Lambardār of Nichār; Lāla Bhagwān Dās Lambardār of Sungra; Shyāmā Nand Zaildār of Pānwi; Sukhnand of Pānwi and Jawāhar Singh of Rupi. A Lambardār used to be the head of a ghodi comprising a group of 8/10 or more villages. Zaildārs used to be heads of parganas, controlling 2 to 3 Lambardārs each. A large pargana could also have two Zaildārs or even more.[97] There were no professional moneylenders in the sense that they practised credit giving as their sole economic activity. Credit giving was generally a supplement to trade, animal husbandry, government service or agriculture. There was no mass alienation of land to non-tribals. In Chini, Bābu Narāyan Singh and Shyām Saran Negi, both large landholders, functioned as major moneylenders,[98] as did Wazir Amar Singh's family in Poāri. Leading moneylenders belonged to the Thurkyān, Machnaspāṅ, Boraspaṅg and Porpaṅg clans (who all claim to be Rājpūts) in the Chini area. Leading clans of the Nichār area were Nindan Māthés, Pailas, Kānsu and Somnya. According to Wazir Amar Singh, leading sāhukārs in Kinnaur were Opaṅg Negi of Kānam, Shāltu Khāndān of Lippa, Mazāraṅg Khāndān of Rispa, the family of Tāshi Sanam of Ribba, Gorinto Khāndān of Purbani, Bārang Māthés family of Bārang and Yamurth Sauraiya family of Kāmru.[99] The four leading clans of Kāmru were the Dudyāns, the Chaṅkum, the Bāgān and the Nyāmur. Leading moneylenders were the families of Sundar Lāl Mohatmim, Negi Harbans Singh and Badruwar.[100] The leading clans of Sangla were the Répalto, the Thongpon, the Nalgan, the Nālyān and the Chathāpaṅg; followed by the Lālipaṅg and other "chhotā motā" (unimportant) clans.[101] Since all these clans claimed to be Rājpūts, the only basis for differentiation was landed

collection of genealogical charts, bahi khātās and documents. He was much more hesitent than Negi Goverdhan Singh in allowing access to these documents. However, he translated many documents in Tānkri script for the author into Hindi and laboriously made copies of genealogical charts of the royal house of Bushahr in Tānkri.

[96] Negi Amar Singh, personal interview, 1985.

[97] Negi Daulat Rām, personal interview, 1985.

[98] Negi Dharam Singh, personal interview, 1985.

[99] Wazir Amar Singh, personal interview, 1985.

[100] Negi Ganga Lāl, personal interview, 1985.

[101] Negi Goverdhan Singh and Negi Khem Singh, personal interviews, 1985.

property and other assets. Leading clans of Pooh were the Chhau, the Linbo and the Lāmā.[102] Major moneylenders of the area were the Shyāso Bisht family, Bansi Lāl of Lippa and Jindub Rām of Kānam who is said to have put up a Lakhpati's flag in the early years of the 20th century when silver rupees were the legal tender[103] and not currency notes. Leading sāhukārs were called Chhokpu meaning Seth. Families of Raghu Dās, Chhering Bhāg, Lambardār Devā Rām and Lhondup Dandub were all Chhokpus.[104] All of these families could bring enormous pressure into play in case of recalcitrant debtors defaulting on repayment of loans.

7.3.2.2.4 Collateral Demanded on Loans by Village Moneylenders

Table 7.10 has already shown that poorer debtors, especially S.Cs, were perceived as credit risks and securities were demanded in the form of collateral to more than cover this risk. Of the 283 sample cases found under the Act of 1976, 146 had had to pledge collateral while 137 had obtained loans without collateral. Of these 146 loans with pledged collateral, 106 were S.Cs. This meant 37.46% of the total sample, 72.60% of 146 and 67.52% of the total number of S.Cs in the sample (= 157). For S.Ts, only 40 debtors (14.13% of 283) had had to pledge collateral. This was 27.40% of the total loans obtained with security (=146) and 31.75% of the total number of S.Ts in the sample (=126). The number of S.C. debtors having had to pledge collateral to obtain loans was thus more than twice the number of such S.T. debtors. The S.Cs constituted nearly three-fourths of the total number of loan cases with collateral. Village moneylenders were obviously demanding collateral not in all cases but only in 51.59% of sample cases, leaving 48.41% of loans without collateral. Since this sample was quite representative, we can deduce that about 50% of the loans from village moneylenders were released agiainst pledged collateral and about 50% were released without such collateral. This was much higher than the almost negligible percentage of loans from deities where valuables had had to be pledged as security.

50% loan cases without security did not mean no risk cover at all. Personal sureties had to be furnished in almost all cases. Tradition has it that most private loans used to be oral transactions (zabāni) without written documents. Field research done by the author unearthed account books from 1886 till down to 1976 where loan transactions had been recorded showing personal sureties or valuables pledged as security on loans being taken. The popular impression of moneylenders granting loans on purely oral transactions is not borne out by these documents. In many cases, though not too frequently, land had had to be formally mortgaged to the moneylender by getting the mortgage entered in the revenue record. Where jewellery or vessels or other valuables were pledged as security, a maximum time-limit of one year was specified, after which the article would lapse in favour of the moneylender. This was clearly spelt out in the bahi khātās. Negi Daulat Rām mentioned that ornaments would sometimes not be pledged as security at the start but would be handed over later in case of default.[105] Everybody seems to agree that in trustworthy cases (aitbār) no security used to be demanded except personal surety. This can be better understood if we see that defaults on loans were few and that most debtors repaid their loans, either in cash or in kind or through labour.

[102] Lāmā Shimed Chhéwang and Médub Dandub, personal interviews, 1985.

[103] Médub Dandub, personal interview, 1985.

[104] Lāmā Shimed Chhéwang, personal interview, 1985.

[105] Negi Daulat Rām, personal interview, 1985

7.3.2.2.5 Recovery of Loans by Village Moneylenders: Smooth

Unlike for the devtas, Kinnauras could recall defaults on loans from village moneylenders but these had remained few and far between, much lower than for banks. Moneylenders had such strong social, political and economic influence that it was not easy for debtors to default on repayment and get away with it. If the loans were not repaid in cash or kind, they had to be repaid through physical labour. Such conditions were usually written into loan agreements by moneylenders. Bonded labour in lieu of loan repayment existed only in the Hangrang area on a large scale. It was prevalent to a lesser extent in the area around Pooh and to a much lesser extent in Central and Southern Kinnaur. The bahi of Seth Dandub Rām of Pooh showed an interesting loan case illustrating repayment arrangements. One Fattu Kanait borrowed Rs 200 cash from Dandub Rām on 11 'Hād' sambat 2008 bikrami (1951 A.D.). The loan terms stated in writing on the bahi stipulate that the borrower would send his daughter Ghésar Māi to Sāhukār Dandub as servant for repayment. She would be paid @ Rs 35 per annum which would be offset against the loan and interest due thereon. Rs 35 per annum means a salary of less than Rs 3 per month, or virtually corvée labour. An interest of 2 ānnās per rupee per annum (12.5%) would also be levied on the loan amount, meaning practically that Ghésar Māi would probably be stuck as a bonded labourer for a good part of her life.[106]

Hangrang and Pooh areas were not favourable to agriculture. Trade brought prosperity to only a limited number of families. Shorn of much possibility of generating enough surplus to repay their loans poor debtors had to fall back upon servitude or corvée labour on a more regular basis than in areas of lower Kinnaur where nature was kinder and agricultural income was higher. Borrowers from the Hangrang area had to frequently pledge land as collateral. When they defaulted, this land was taken over by moneylenders, generally from Pooh. Bahi khātās found during field research in Pooh corroborate this fact. Forfeiture of land was rare in the Nichār area, not very widespread in the Chini area, more common in the Pooh area and on the largest scale in the Hangrang area, according to these bahi khātās. Lāmā Shimed Chhéwang of Pooh confirmed that poor debtors used to send their sons and/or daughters to sāhukārs as labourers in lieu of repayment of loans. The interest on loans used to keep on piling up and these labourers used to become quasi-bonded labour.[107] Chhering Bhāg Sānā, scion of one of the largest moneylending families of Pooh, corroborated this fact and said that similar cases had occurred in his father's time as well. The debt burden used to be passed on from one generation to the succeeding generation.[108]

The legal system of Bushahr State was on the side of the moneylenders when it came to enforcing recovery and not on the side of the debtors. Moneylenders were not required to register themselves with any government agency at all. Negi Goverdhan Singh explained that transactions above Rs 20 needed a revenue stamp as proof of transaction. The sale of such stamps for moneylending operations was a source of income for the Rājā.[109] The government were thus not interested in curbing moneylending operations of moneylenders thereby reducing its own income from sale of revenue stamps. Any effort to help the debtors with their repayment conditions was against the grain of Bushahr State's functioning. The State did not have many avenues of income generation and remained chronically short of funds. Captain C.P. Kennedy reported in 1824 that the total revenue of Bushahr at the time of the Gorkha

[106] Original bahi khāta (account book) given by Dandub Rām in Pooh. Now in possession of the author. The bahi has entries in Urdu, Tibetan and Tānkri scripts.

[107] Lāmā Shimed Chhéwang, personal interview, 1985

[108] Chhering Bhāg Sānā, personal interview, 1985

[109] Negi Goverdhan Singh, personal interview, 1985

invasion (1805) had been estimated by Captain Ross at Rs 67,000 per annum.[110] Even for carrying out settlement operations, Tikka Raghunāth Singh had had to ask for a loan from the British. W. Coldstream estimated the land revenue of Bushahr State in 1888 at below Rs 30,000 per annum, exclusive of jāgirs. He recommended giving the Tikka a loan of Rs 20,000, half of which was to be released forthwith and half after two years. Repayment was to be in instalments of Rs 2,000 each, commencing in 1893 A.D. and interest at 5% per annum was to be taken yearly on the unpaid balance. The amount of loan was to be given on the security of the revenue of the state.[111] A state that had to put its entire revenue on hock as security for such essential administrative operations as land settlement was obviously not going to further reduce its revenues by extending relief for rural indebtedness. Bahi khātās show that the use of Bushahr revenue stamps on loan transactions increased, albeit slowly, from 1935 onwards. Stamps were used when loan amounts were unusually large, around Rs 1,000 or more; the borrower was from another village or was considered as a risk. Most transactions did not have stamps affixed since the lender knew the borrowers fairly well. It also shows that recovery of loans was so high that moneylenders felt no necessity of putting revenue stamps as proof of transaction. This was useful only in litigation. Litigation would arise on default on repayment. Absence of widespread use of revenue stamps indicates that litigation was not being resorted to, which further points to the fact that the percentage of recovery of loans was quite high. Moneylenders did not need to resort to litigation.

Debtors had no locus standi to complain against moneylenders to Bushahr State officials who never audited or controlled the moneylenders' account books. In case of disputes over repayment, parties had to go to local Panchāyats, dominated by moneylenders, for redressal. After Tikka Raghunāth Singh abolished Panchāyats and established courts in the 1890s, sāhukārs could go to court for enforcement of their claims against debtors.[112] By showing the sāhukārs that the state would protect their rights, Bushahr authorities hoped that they would appreciate the use of revenue stamps as proofs of transaction. It was a quid pro quo of sorts. Shorn of any debt relief, debtors had to do corvée labour, in some cases over generations. And this, even though loan transactions were generally for small amounts, as shown by original bahi khātās.

7.3.2.2.6 Magnitude of Loan Transactions: Fairly Modest

To get an idea of the amounts involved in loan transactions, bahi khātās obtained during field research were used as sources. Since there were at least 2,000 loan transactions in the bahis, only two samples have been selected. Table 7.11 shows the magnitude distribution of loans recorded in a small bahi belonging to the Shong Māthés family of Negi Balwant Singh, Chairman Panchāyat Samiti, Kālpa in 1985. The loans date from 1937. The maximum concentration (59.46%) of loans (74) was in the range till Rs 25; followed by 16.22% in the range Rs 26-50. This means that 75.68% of loans were under Rs 50. This pattern conforms to the widespread assertion in Kinnaur that there existed a small money economy and a much larger barter economy. Money was needed only for those minimum basic needs for which exchange could not bring about the desired results - mainly to make purchases of essential commodities from shopkeepers in Rāmpur. Some loans (=7) were as low as Rs 5. The results of two bahis given by Dandub Rām of Pooh are summarized in Table 7.12. The loans were from 1950 A.D. till the beginning of 1954. Only 26 cases out of 247 were of loans in kind,

[110] Kennedy, Capt. C.P., 1824, Para 41, p. 278

[111] Letter No. 375 dated Simla, 19th December 1888 from W. Coldstream, Deputy Commissioner, Simla to Colonel L.J.H. Gray, Commissioner and Superintendent, Delhi Division, in: Foreign Department, Native States, February 1889, No. 1: Proposed Loan to the Tikka of Bashahr to enable him to complete the Resettlement of the State, Paras 7 and 8.

[112] Negi Goverdhan Singh, personal interview, 1985.

Table 7.11: Loan Statistics from Negi Balwant Singh's BahiKhātā

sn	*LARR*	*nb*	*PCT*
01	00-25	44	59.46
02	26-50	12	16.22
03	51-100	03	04.05
04	101-200	08	10.81
05	201-300	03	04.05
06	401-500	02	02.70
07	1001-2000	02	02.70

Code: **nb = number of borrowers in given range,**
LARR = loan amount range in Rupees,
PCT = percentage in terms of total number of borrowers.
(Source: Bahi Khāta (Account Book) of Shong Māthés Family)

showing that by the 1950s the money economy had begun to take hold in Kinnaur. 90% of the loan amounts had been taken in cash. Of the loans in kind, 17 out of 26 were in differing quantities of wool, 5 in grain and 4 in woven fabrics. This also shows that foodgrains had started being available in higher quantities than those described by J. Bruske towards the beginning of the present century.[113] It could also mean that the people were taking loans in foodgrains more from the devtas than from village moneylenders. Table 7.12 shows that 38.87% of the loans were up to Rs 100; 57.09% up to Rs 200; 67.21% up to Rs 300 and 76.12% up to Rs 400 respectively. Leaving aside the 10.53% loans in kind, it means that only 13.35% of total loans were between Rs 401 and Rs 2,000. There was no loan more than Rs 2,000. The loan distribution had moved into higher ranges on the average than the one in Table 7.11. Loans from the informal sector were becoming increasingly monetized. To round off the picture of the informal credit sector, we can consider a few case studies from the bahis of Sāhukār Dandub Rām.

7.3.2.3 Case Studies from Bahi Khātās found during Research

(a) Okal, caste Koli (S.C.) of village Jāngi, gave in writing on the bahi that he had taken fertilizer worth Rs 28 from Sāhukār Dandub Rām of Pooh on 12-08-samvat 2007 bikrami (1950 A.D.) which he would repay with interest @ 2 ānnās per rupee;
(b) Bhagwān Dās r/o Grosnam agreed on 20 bikrami 2007 that he had borrowed a goat worth Rs 30 which he would return in 'Jéth';
(c) Diwadar s/o Tandāman r/o Sumra borrowed currency notes worth Rs 150 on 1 Māgh samvat 2007 bikrami from Dandub Rām. He promised to repay Rs 100 with interest by Kātak 2008. He also agreed that if he failed to repay Rs 50, he would pay interest @ one ānnā per Rupee. "Mazqoora Tahrir Hosh Hawās Ké Sāth Likh Déta Hooṅ" (hereby write the above agreement document in full senses);
(d) Déwā s/o Tāndān r/o Sumra, caste Kanait (S.T.), took a loan of Rs 300 in currency notes from Dandub Rām on 3 samvat 2007. He committed himself to paying interest @ 2 'baranjās anāj' (measures of grain) for Rs 150 and interest @ 1 ānnā per rupee for the remaining Rs 150 which he promised to repay in full by the month of 'Jéth'.

[113] Jahresbericht der Station Chini - Jahr 1907, op. cit..

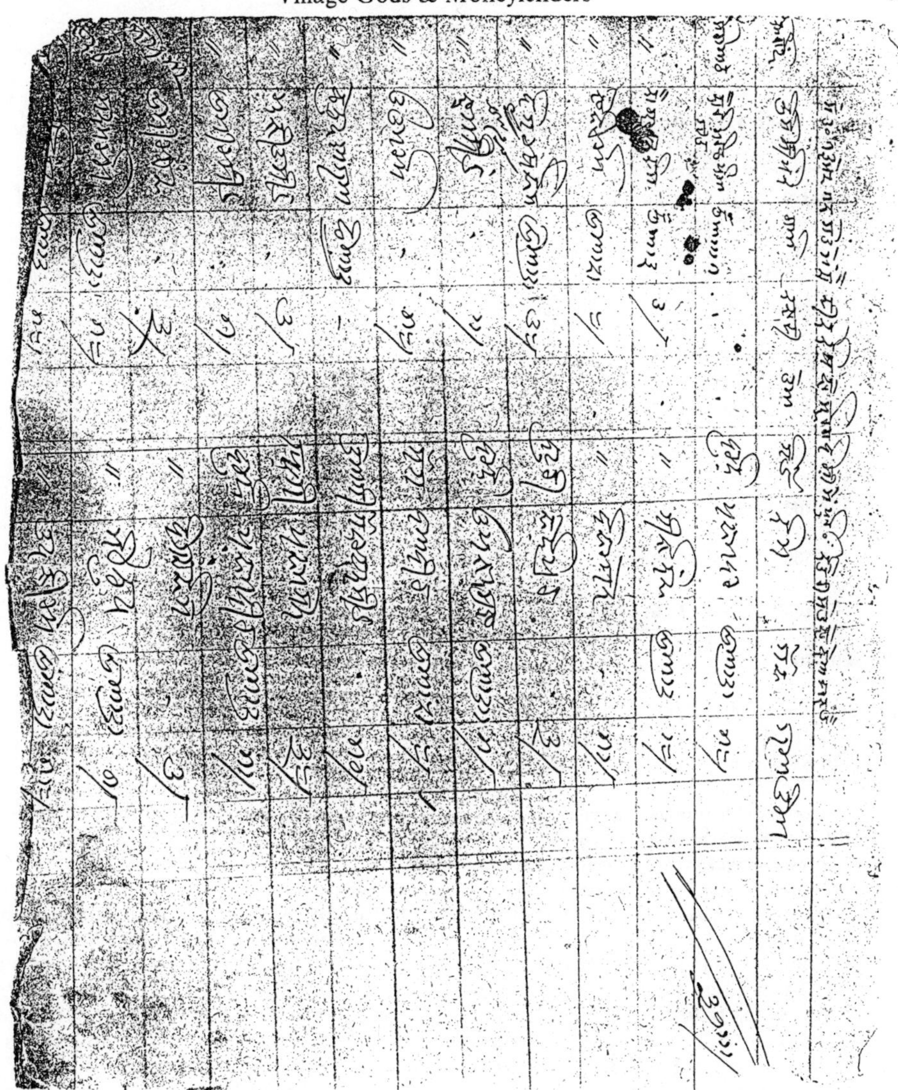

(Specimen of a page from the Bahi Khata of the Shong Mathes family.)

(e) Sanam Narboo s/o Sharab r/o Mālling, caste Rājpūt, borrowed Rs 400 in cash from Dandub Rām. He promised to pay interest @ 2 ānnās per rupee and to liquidate the debt in full at the time of the Lavi Fair at Rāmpur in one payment;

(f) Nandan, caste Kanait, r/o Nāko agreed that he had tallied up all his 'hisāb kitāb' (accounts) with Dandub Rām in Hād samvat 2008 bikrami (1951 A.D.) and agreed that Rs 400 had been found outstanding as debt against his name. He promised to repay the debt in full by the 11th of Kātak 2008 samvat bikrami. If he failed to repay on time, he gave the sāhukār full authority to recover the debt out of his property;

(g) Sharab Chhan; caste Kanait, r/o Moorang borrowed currency notes worth Rs 100 on 12 Hāḍ saṃvat 2008 bikrami from Dandub Rām. He promised to pay interest @ 2 ānnās

Table 7.12: Loan Data from the Bahis of Seth Dandub Rām of Pooh

sn	*LARR*	*nb*	*PCT*
01	00-25	21	08.50
02	26-50	26	10.53
03	51-100	49	19.84
04	101-200	45	18.22
05	201-300	25	10.12
06	301-400	22	08.91
07	401-500	16	06.48
08	501-1000	13	05.26
09	1001-2000	04	01.62
10	2001-Above	00	00.00
11	In-Kind	26	10.53

Code: **nb = number of borrowers in given range,**
LARR = loan amount range in Rupees,
PCT = percentage in terms of total number of borrowers.
(Source: Bahi Khāta (Account Book) of Dandub Rām Of Pooh)

per rupee (12.5%) and to repay the debt in full by Kātak. Nandan Sukh signed the transaction as guarantor-cum-witness. In a second transaction Sharab Chhan acknowledged that he accepted on his charge a 'bakra' (he-goat) of value Rs 45 total;

(h) A Rājpūt of Chini (name not legible) borrowed Rs 300 on 22 Hād 2009 samvat bikrami in currency notes from Dandub. He promised to repay the entire amount by Kātak samvat 2009 on time with interest @ 2 ānnās per rupee. If he did not repay in full as promised, the sāhukār would have the full right to recover the amount ot of his movable property;

(i) Neema Sain s/o Narjeet r/o Pooh, caste Rājpūt, borrowed 50 'batti' (measures) 'oon' (wool) assessed at a value of Rs 428 on 12 Hād samvat 2009 bikrami from Dandub. He promised to repay in full by Jéth 2010 samvat;

(j) Nandan Sukh, Rājpūt, r/o Nāko took a loan of Rs 1,000 in cash on 9 Hād 2010 bikrami from Dandub. He promised repayment by Kātak 2010 @ 2 ānnās per rupee interest. As security he pledged 3 plots of land, big and small, situated close to the irrigation channel in hock (bandhawi) to the sāhukār. In case of failure to repay on time, the borrower gave the lender full authority to appropriate this land through the medium of of a court of law. The borrower undertook not to raise objections to this. Signed on 22-06-1953 A.D.;

(k) Jugal Kishore s/o Lāla Tāra Chand r/o Rāmpur Bushahr took a loan in cash of Rs 1,000 from Dandub. He agreed to pay interest @ Rs 12 per 100 rupees per month, otherwise he would be liable to pay fine (nahiṅ to jurmānā kā zimmedār thaihrooṅgā). On 18.11-1953 A.D. came an entry for an additional loan amount of Rs 500 on the same terms and conditions as for the earlier amount;

(l) Gorkhu s/o Zālmu r/o Majoli, caste Koli, borrowed Rs 200 in cash for necessary consumption (barāéy kharch zaroori), pledging as security a plot of his land situated below the road with transfer of possession to the sāhukār. He promised to pay annual interest @ 3 maunds of grain (pukhta man anāj). In case of failure to repay the agreed-upon quantity of grains as interest, a further interest of 2 ānnās per rupee was to be imposed. The transaction was concluded with signatures of witnesses on 26 Kātak 2007 bikrami.

These sample loan transactions show how flexibly village moneylenders operated in Kinnaur. They were harder in imposing conditions on Harijan borrowers than on non-Harijan Kinnauras. There were also severe conditions on non-tribal outsiders like Jugal Kishore of Rāmpur. The circle of Dandub Rām's lending operations was widespread, extending from village Sumra, the last village of Kinnaur (opposite Hurling) on the Spiti river, through Chāngo, Mālling, Nāko to Pooh and on to Jāngi and Chini. This appears contrary to the normal traditional pattern of lending within a narrow circle of 5-10 kms radius.[114] Dandub belonged to a trading family which had wide contacts and could operate over an enlarged credit circle. The case studies speak for the ability of the informal sector to expand or contract its operations according to influence; to cover risk of default through innovative conditions of collateral and to function with a high degree of recovery at low transaction costs. It could teach a lot to the official agencies rather than being branded as unscientific and archaic. Having completed our survey of various credit giving agencies in Kinnaur it now remains only to suggest some changes and to draw some conclusions from what we have outlined till now.

[114] Please see Sections 1.2 and 1.2.1, Chapter I of this work.

CHAPTER VIII

CONCLUSIONS AND SUGGESTIONS

It remains now only to round off our review of the credit structure in Kinnaur by trying to concretize the deductions drawn during the present research. Even though nobody dare say it out publicly, it needs to be said that the present phalanx of subsidies in Kinnaur will some day have to be phased out because of overall financial constraints and for healthier overall development of the Kinnaura economy. Subsidies have distorted economic development in the area. The process of 'de-subsidifying', if one were to coin the term, Kinnaur's economic life will certainly need political courage of an order that does not exist at the present moment. Subsidized credit is refinancing private moneylenders in many cases.[1] A standard response to problems till now has been for government to extend its area of operation more and more into the sphere of credit through cooperatives, nationalized commercial banks and its own departments. Expansion of the role of the government into the economic sphere has been an all-India phenomenon and not one confined just to Kinnaur. This trend can be observed by

Table 8.1: Role of the Government in the Economic Sphere in India

sn		*1970-71*	*1976-77*	*1977-78*	*1978-79*	*1979-80*	*1980-81*	*81-82*	*1982-83*
01	GDP	36,736	71,464	80,466	87,046	94,978	113,584	131,747	145,148
02	Public	5,456	14,379	15,697	17,452	20,071	23,442	28,662	34,588
03	Private	31,280	57,085	64,969	69,594	74,907	90,142	103,085	110,560
04	Pct	014.90	020.10	019.50	020.00	021.10	020.60	021.80	023.80
05	Gdcf	07,344	17,669	18,548	22,933	26,228	31,443	36,680	40,435
06	Public	02,773	08,513	07,450	09,649	11,816	13,922	17,444	19,849
07	Private	04,571	09,156	11,098	13,284	14,412	17,521	19,236	20,586
08	Pct	037.20	048.20	040.20	042.10	045.10	044.30	047.60	049.10

Code: **GDP = Gross Domestic Product,**
Pct = share of public to total in per cent,
Gdcf = gross domestic capital formation,
All amounts are in crores of Rupees, 1 Crore = 10 million,
(Source: India 1984, A Reference Annual, New Delhi: Publications Division, March 1985, Basic Economic Data, Table 11.3, p. 193).

considering the statistical data given in Table 8.1 . The share of the government rose from 14.9% in 1970-71 to 23.8% in 1982-83 for the GDP and from 37.2% to 49.1% for gross domestic capital formation between the same years respectively. The government's share in gross domestic capital formation has risen without any substantial fall since 1977-78 and stands (at 49.1%) nearly equal to the contribution of the private sector (at 50.9%). Words cannot speak louder than these facts.

[1] Please see Section 4.11, Chapter IV of this work.

This extension of the role of the government involves increased borrower transaction costs, bureaucratization of the administration of loans and increasing defaults. Planning is needed from now itself for a future cut-back in the role of the government. Planners and policy framers must possess the "heroism of abandoning"[2] an ever increasing government role. This process has to be accompanied by recognition of the fact that private moneylenders are not necessarily an unmitigated evil but have their legitimate role to play in complementing the institutional credit network. Moneylending has not attracted social ostracism in Kinnaur, unlike for some mārwādi moneylenders in other tribal areas of India. The moneylending 'seth' was an honoured member of the aristocratic classes in some cases, e.g. the Wazir of Poāri. This was not something peculiar to Kinnaur. Members of the aristocracy functioned in many cases even in England as moneylenders. For example, Bess of Hardwick, wife of George Talbot, the Earl of Shrewsbury, was a *"builder, a buyer and seller of estates, a moneylender, a farmer and a merchant of lead and coals and timber"*.[3] The Wazirs of Poāri were moneylenders, farmers, traders, timber extractors and builders. The institutional credit network has to tailor its operations to offer competition to the informal sector so as to hold the latter to certain socially desirable guidelines rather than always seeking to run it out of business. The present research shows that the idea of driving village moneylenders into oblivion by trying to substitute them completely with institutional agencies remains a pipedream.[4]

It will take policymakers a good deal of time to accept the role of the informal sector. Tales about usurious moneylenders have been reinforced in their minds by *"endless repetition, numerous tales of horror, and religious teachings...It took Christian societies many centuries to view usury and lending with some logic other than passion"*.[5] Even where policymakers can view the role of the informal sector objectively, policy changes are not carried out to make its operation complementary to that of the institutional sector. This is due to the fact that the political system considers the current performance of rural financial markets as quite acceptable and even advantageous. Political forces in the country may be more than satisfied with the results of distortions caused by negative real rates of interest in rural financial markets because such rates lead to allocation of political patronage by means of implied income transfers to those influential people in the economy who ultimately garner most of the cheap credit. If the rates of interest were to be allowed to rise to equilibrium levels, politicians and their cohorts would have no cheap credit to grant to their favoured patrons and strong supporters who help in maintaining the status quo in place.

Subsidies have not proved a solution. Low interest rates strongly affect lender behaviour and administrative fiats and allocations are largely ineffective in reversing this behaviour. Low interest rates generate increased demand for cheap money. Institutional lenders seek to wriggle out of this situation by shifting a part of the loan transaction costs to the borrower; by preferring to lend to such persons as present the least risk of default; by insisting on substantial collateral, even in defiance of administrative guidelines; by attempting

[2] Aron, Raymond: Le spectateur engagé, Entretiens avec Jean-Louis Missika et Dominique Wolton, Paris: Julliard, 1981, p. 191. The phrase used in original is "l'héroisme de l'abandon".
Translation mine.
Aron was a leftist in his youth. He later on espoused opinions which were sometimes even considered as right-of-centre. This change was strongly criticised by Jean Paul Sartre. In reply, Aron uses the phrase cited when asked to explain his position by Missika and Wolton. He means that one should have the courage to change even long-standing opinions if objective facts point to the contrary. Recognizing that erstwhile opinions need change calls for courage of a high order.

[3] Fraser, Antonia: Mary Queen of Scots, St. Albans: Panther Books, Reprint, 1975, p. 486.

[4] Please see Section 7.1.1.6, Chapter VII of this work.

[5] Adams and Graham, 1981, p. 358.

to increase the average loan size and by discouraging new borrowers. Practically, such lender behaviour tends to channelize cheap credit towards the relatively affluent and experienced borrowers. Since the subsidies in Kinnaur are matching subsidies, i.e. are proportional to loan amounts, they follow the pattern of loans in gravitating towards affluent persons. The microeconomic interests of the lender swamp the policy directives from central authorities to ensure that loans and subsidies do not get focussed on wealthier borrowers. Policymakers are not in a position to ensure implementation of their fiats because of the large numbers of lenders and borrowers that are normally involved.

Four components can be identified in rural interest rates:

(a) The opportunity cost of the money involved;
(b) The premium for administering the loans;
(c) The premium for risk; and
(d) Monopoly profit.[6]

It is difficult to quantify what the opportunity cost of money will actually be. Nominal rates of interest cannot be manipulated in such a way as to ensure domination of free market interest charges by the opportunity cost. It can be the value to a rural saver of parting with his surplus or of foregoing the opportunity of investing in his own farming operations or of meeting social obligations like spending lavishly on religious ceremonies. Or it may be the nominal rate of interest plus the administration and risk costs which a bank levies on a wholesaler who relends with further increases in interest rates to village shopkeepers. If the retail trader fails to dovetail his loaning to farmers to his borrowing from a wholesaler through sale of goods, he will be compelled to charge a rate of interest that rises to compensate for the period during which the money lies inactive in rural shops.

Overheads are higher for banks than for informal lenders. Banking operations involve buildings conforming to strict specifications, paid staff, rigid rules and the like. This causes overheads to mount for bank loans, making the administration premium per unit loaned out higher in the institutional than in the informal sector. Administrative costs per unit loaned by banks can be reduced by lending to groups of borrowers who distribute the loan among themselves. Such groups can be cooperatives or groups of borrowers. Banks have not given such group loans too often in Kinnaur. Devta Mahéshras of Sungra has already been lending to groups of borrowers.[7]

The risk premium is not so simple that default is outright. Repayments can be delayed, partial payments may be received and renegotiation may be requested. The percentage charge on each unit loaned arises from, but should not be confused with being the same as, the percentage of default. Bottomley made a calculation for the risk factor as follows:

$$\rho = \delta (\pi + \lambda) / \beta$$

where ρ = Risk factor, π = Principal, λ = Lending costs and β = Principal actually repaid.[8]

Defaults on loans will rise with volume because, other things being equal, the larger the loan the higher the probability of default. Considered in isolation, the default rate is positively correlated to the volume of loan. This means that the risk of default is higher for larger borrowers who tend to be more affluent Kinnauras than for relatively poorer borrowers. Large

[6] Bottomley, Anthony: Interest Rate Determination in Underdeveloped Rural Areas, p. 279, in: American Journal of Agricultural Economics, Vol. 57, No. 3, August 1975, Pp 279-291.

[7] Please see Section 7.3.1.3, Chapter VII of this work.

[8] Bottomely, 1975, p. 282.

volume loans go only to borrowers possessing more assets to serve as collateral. This flies in the face of conventional banking wisdom in Kinnaur that poorer borrowers are credit risks while richer borrowers are desirable clients. Bottomley's general deduction for underdeveloped countries, that there *"appears to be a systematic tendency for larger farmers with greater asset values and higher incomes to borrow more than smaller poorer farmers throughout the third world"*,[9] has already been seen as valid for Kinnaur from field survey data.[10] If net incomes rise faster than the costs of borrowing, repayment performance tends to improve because ability to repay tends to rise correspondingly as well, as opposed to willingness to repay. There exists often a correlation between increases in the net income of borrowers and the extent of repayment of loans even though this correlation is not as significant as one might be led to expect.

The preceding discussion presumes that the borrower tends to repay loans. If he does not, which is often the case, the situation changes. Institutional loans become early casualties of recalcitrance on the part of borrowers to repay. The fact that official agencies are willing to tolerate even wilful negligence in repayment of institutional loans means that delinquency in repayment of loans will not remain confined to the poorer strata of society but affect the relatively affluent as well. In fact, the latter are prone to wield their political clout to persist with wilful default which the poor do not possess. The rich are better placed to avoid repayment. This is quite the case in Kinnaur. Coercive measures intended to cow down defaulters end up scaring poorer borrowers away from institutional agencies to the informal sector while the bigger defaulters, secure in their political and administrative connexions, manage to escape. It is clear that recovery campaigns have limited effect unless well-connected defaulters are subjected to coercive processes with the same severity as is used in the case of poorer defaulters. This is easier said than done. Given the prevailing political environment, few officials are willing to risk their careers by impartially applying coercive processes to enforce repayment. No standard formula can be laid down that so much severity should be used and no further. Each individual official finds his own equilibrium with his environment. Some individuals are more courageous and prone to take harsher measures, others less so. What the government can do is not to post such officials to Kinnaur as are known to be corrupt, incompetent or undesirable. Getting sent to Kinnaur as a punishment posting is no motivation to do good work. Without good officials the institutional credit system cannot function efficiently.

Institutional agencies as they are constituted now involve heavy administration costs and risk factors. It may seem unusual what is going to be suggested in the following paras but keeping in mind the findings of the present research about the functioning of the formal and informal sectors the whole picture falls into perspective. It is suggested that an effort be made to fuse together the official and the informal credit sectors in Kinnaur. The former has enough funds but high establishment and administration costs plus high rates of default on loans. The latter has a very low default rate and low costs of administering loans. We have seen from Table 4.21 that low nominal rates of interest do not draw borrowers away from the informal sector because borrowers' transaction costs push up real rates of interest on institutional loans to values comparable to or even higher than informal loans. Why should this reality not be faced squarely?

It emerges clearly from the present research that the devtas have been functioning in Kinnaur as efficiently managed, low-cost credit-cycling mechanisms. In earlier times, loans from them were taken more in kind and less in cash. The situation has reversed itself now. Only richer deities like the Mahéshras of Sungra have a cash surplus large enough to meet full credit needs of demanding borrowers in cash. Use can be made of the devtas' smoothly

[9] Ibid.

[10] Sections 3.5.1.2, 3.5.1.2.1, Chapter III of this work.

functioning credit operations by refinancing them from institutional agencies for short-term lending operations in Kinnaur. There is no need to go on opening more and more bank branches there. Better coverage can be ensured by utilizing the devtas as credit-input mechanisms for institutional funds. Temple committees exist in all villages and provide a low establishment-cost alternative to bank officials as managing agencies. Provided the concept is properly explained, it should not be too difficult to get temple committees and devtas to accept to borrow money from institutional agencies at, say, 8% to 10% p.a. rate of interest for loaning out further at 12.5% to 15%. Interest rates being charged by village deities are already in the range of 10% to 12.5% per annum in Kinnaur.[11] If they prove unwilling to avail of refinancing facilities at these suggested rates of interest, this rate can be cut down to 4% as is already the case for D.R.I. loans. Initially, even interest-free refinance facilities may need to be provided in order to get the devtas to accept this arrangement. Pecuniary incentives may have to be provided to temple committee members concerned with loan giving in order to get them to accept management of vastly increased amounts as cash loans. Fixed salaries generate laxity and inefficiency in loan management. Consequently, a fixed percentage of the amounts actually loaned out, say 1%, should be paid as incentive money into the devtas' account. The temple committee should be left free to spend this money for common local purposes as they and the devta deem fit to the extent of 25% of this bonus, while 75% would be used to supplement the devta's loaning operations. These amounts will be much lower than establishment and running costs of bank branches. The devtas' committees have all a finely balanced power-sharing arrangement between various village clans so as to check undue domination by any one person on loan giving operations.

The amounts given as refinance by the government to devtas should be subject to audit by audit parties from the Accountant-General's establishment, just as public moneys are. However, such audits should have no jurisdiction over the account books being kept separately for the devtas' own funds. Separate account books could be kept without too much difficulty by kāyaths but rules will have to be framed to exclude the devtas' officials from having to comply with bureaucratic ways of book-keeping demanded by audit parties - duplicate vouchers, special cash books and a whole set of antiquated and ridiculous financial rules based on the Britishers' inherent distrust of the Indians' honesty. The devtas' loan registers already contain essential items about loan transactions.[12] No attempt should be made to alter these traditional entries as a pre-condition for refinance. It should always be kept in mind that it is not the devtas who need institutional finance but institutional agencies who need the former for reducing rates of default, costs of transaction, and costs of administering loans. Devtas have functioned for centuries without the government and will not be amenable to attempts to bureaucratize their committees.

Recoveries will improve if institutional funds are channelled through devtas on a short-term basis for reasons already explained in the preceding chapter.[13] This means that short-term loan giving will not be stymied through blockage of limited funds available. Medium- and long-term loan facilities would in any case continue to be made available by the SCB, the LDB and by commercial banks as at present. These institutions will also keep their short-term facilities intact, leaving it to the borrower to decide whether a short-term loan is to be taken from an institutional agency or from the devta. It has to be recognized that fungibility of money makes it impractical to try and siphon off credit utilization towards so-called 'productive purposes' without close supervision of an order not to be found at present among the administrative apparatus in Kinnaur. As a consequence the borrower should be considered intelligent enough to know whether he needs a consumption loan or not.

[11] Please see Section 7.3.1.4, Chapter VII of this work.

[12] Please see Section 7.3.1.3, Chapter VII of this work.

[13] Please see Section 7.3.1.6, Chapter VII of this work.

Devtas have been giving consumption loans over centuries without this fact having led to defaults. Government can keep up present restrictions on supply of consumption credit through institutional channels, but should not try to impose similar limitations on devtas as a condition of proposed refinance. The idea is to benefit from the simplified, low-cost management of loans by devtas and not to turn such management into a distorted version of the high-cost, relatively inefficient loan management done by financial institutions operating in Kinnaur.

The proposal under discussion is certain to meet strong resistance in official and political circles. Officials tend to favour creation of more and more institutional establishments because this leads to new recruitment, more promotions and newer career advancement channels. Politicians will be loath to dilute their patronage over officially supplied cheap credit. It is easier for them to manipulate careerist employees who depend on them for advancement in service than centuries-old devtas who are in no way dependent on them. Secretariat officials will frown on this proposal because it necessarily means financial decentralization because each devta is an autonomous manager of loans, not involved in tangled bureaucratic hierarchies. The devta is a real grass-roots institution. Entrusting loan giving operations to the devta will foster a healthy practice of self-management of loans by Kinnauras. Such a system is well suited for an area like Kinnaur where topographical conditions make centralization an unworkable proposition. It will be a manifestation of reposing confidence in the ability of Kinnauras to manage their own loan transactions. It may mark a break with the present economically unhealthy trend of looking up to the 'sarkār' for any- and everything. Building up of such self-confidence is a pre-requisite to the gradual dismantling of subsidies in Kinnaur. How long can the area's economy be kept in a cocoon of subsidies to keep it from feeling the pinch of a market economy? It is a contradiction to encourage production of cash crops, fruit and handicrafts geared towards a free market money economy on the one hand and to attempt to perpetually insulate Kinnaur's economy from the effects of such a market money economy through newer and newer subsidy safeguards.

It may be argued by critics of the proposal under consideration that management of loans by temple committees out of funds provided by the government could lead to discrimination against Harijans and other poorer borrowers because temple committees are dominated by affluent non-Harijans. The surest rebuttal of this argument lies in observing the actual operation of loans by temple committees. There is much less discrimination to be seen against Harijans in loans granted by these committees than in institutional loans being distributed by banks and cooperatives. The latter may have given a sizeable portion of their loans to Harijans on paper. Reality shows that a significant percentage of such amounts are proxy loans for non-Harijan borrowers looking for low-interest 'sweet' loans. If official policymakers ignore this fact they are only deluding themselves. Harijans prefer to go to the devta in many cases because they can repay the latter through physical labour or customary services in case enough cash is not available. The temple committee should continue to have its present flexibility in deciding upon acceptable forms of repayment from borrowers. As incomes increase and the money economy extends its reach into Kinnaur, more and more borrowers will themselves prefer repayments in cash. If they preferred to repay in kind in the past it was because they did not have sufficient amounts in cash to meet the demands imposed on them and not because of any inherent love of doing physical labour! The government need not fear that its money would be in danger if devtas accept repayment from some debtors in the form of physical labour. This labour will in most cases be on the devtas' orchards or fields which generate surplus, part of which can be used to repay government funds taken for refinance. The exact percentages and modalities have to be left to temple committees for decision.

The problem of lagging recoveries on institutional loans has attained such proportions[14] as to call for drastic remedies, such as the one outlined in the preceding paragraphs. The institutional sector will term it as retrograde, unscientific and dangerous, chiefly to cover up the fact that any honest opinion suggesting a rolling back of institutional agencies' staff strengths or functions strikes at the very roots of vested interests of officialdom. Any idea of developing genuinely autonomous local institutions meets resistance. Cooperatives and Panchāyats are not in a position to fulfil the role suggested here for temple committees because of their too close connexions with government departments, because they are not autonomous enough and because they are ridden with time-consuming procedural norms carried over from government departments. These are not perceived by most Kinnauras as their own institutions but as extended arms of the 'sarkār'. They also lack the divine aura of the devtas' power, so essential to keep recoveries of loans flowing smoothly. Ever expanding bureaucratic fiefdoms are not the only icons that risk getting hit by the preceding proposal!

It brings into question the theory of integrated rural development which forms the foundation of institutional loan-giving in Kinnaur. Actual performance of integrated rural development programmes leaves room for doubt whether division of a given public rural outlay among specified components of an integrated package is really a better way of utilization of funds than concentrating them on removing major constraints on individual or group action. One of the most celebrated of integrated and cooperative schemes including rural credit, Comilla in Bangladesh, has been subjected to scathing criticism by its founder, Akhtar Hamid Khan, centering upon its replicability, cost and dependence on either charismatic leadership or mass commitment, neither sustainable for long in the absence of equity or shared goals. Progress in Comilla was, moreover, little better than in a neighbouring area little, if at all, affected by the scheme.[15]

In South Korea and Taiwan, where institutional credit programmes have proved successful, positive results followed radical equalization of rights in land through distributive reform. Without this assurance of being able to practically benefit from the produce of the land that they till through acquired rights, cultivators do not respond in a desired fashion to even an appropriate credit scheme. The mainstream institutional policies about rural credit have mostly achieved little at high cost. Political will to carry out such pre-requisite distributive land reform does not exist at the present moment in Kinnaur, Himāchal Pradesh or India for that matter. Even if it were to exist, topographical conditions limit the extent to which culturable land can be made available. The gradual eclipse of polyandry in Kinnaur means that already small land holdings risk becoming even smaller in time as polyandrous joint families yield place at an ever increasing rate to monogamous nuclear households.

Integrated development programmes cannot by themselves offer a panacea against underdevelopment and poverty. "*While the term underdevelopment implies occupation of a place on a continuum that is defined in terms of technological per capita capacity to produce, the term poor implies placement at the bottom of the scale of consumption, having less than others - less, usually, than most others*".[16] Development programmes have to be accompanied by distributive land reform measures, building up of genuinely autonomous local institutions to manage credit programmes, their refinancing through institutional funds to serve as outlets for short-term loans and other measures designed to enable the 'poorest of the poor' to join in the development process. The last has been tried through subsidies but only with very limited success in Kinnaur. Subsidies have, like cheap institutional loans, gravitated towards the more affluent. Other innovations are called for.

[14] Please see Sections 5.2.1, 5.2.1.1, 5.2.1.3, Chapter V of this work.

[15] Lipton, Michael, 1976, p. 550.

[16] Mead, Margaret: The Underdeveloped and the Overdeveloped, in: Foreign Affairs, Vol. 41, No. 1, October 1962, p. 80.

A major factor preventing productive utilization of institutional credit facilities by poor borrowers is the already existing debt burdens towards private moneylenders. Repayment to these credit givers diverts institutional funds away from the purposes for which credit has been given. Cheap loans and subsidies can be more effective if this starting hurdle were overcome. It is suggested that instead of pouring in ever increasing amounts of subsidies without first addressing the problem of indebtedness to the informal sector, government money should be used for paying off the devtas and village moneylenders on behalf of persons targeted as the poorest of the poor under official programmes. The Relief of Agricultural Indebtedness Act, 1976, attempted to tackle this problem by turning it on its head - by writing off loans from village moneylenders. The impact of this measure was quite limited in Kinnaur.[17] Many debtors were not willing to come forward to report their debts because they would thereby be shattering a decades- or generations-old credit relationship. Village moneylenders and their debtors are enmeshed in an intricate socio-economic matrix going beyond purely lender-borrower relationships. It would be better not to try and destroy such matrices through simplistic legislative measures without first being able to provide practical institutional alternatives. Since this is still not the case, relief should be tried another way, by paying off the moneylenders so as not to provoke them into choking off their supply of informal credit as an act of retaliation against persons benefitting under legislation.

Subsidy amounts ending up at present with moneylenders as low-interest refinance can be better utilized by being supplied in one initial dose as a welfare measure for liquidating the debts of poor Kinnauras. Income limits for persons falling within the category to be so helped can be fixed only in consultation with local representatives. These limits should be realistic, in the region of Rs 6,000 per annum, rather than ridiculously low like Rs 1,800 or 2,000 per annum as for the D.R.I. scheme at present. The government are already providing millions of rupees as subsidy,[18] they can afford to be generous in extensively liquidating rural indebtedness in Kinnaur by repaying the informal sector so that favourable circumstances are created for receptivity to official credit programmes. This process has to be accompanied by improvement in the quality of supervision. Without effective supervision, official credit programmes are bound to be either failures or only partial successes. Better supervision requires better recruitment, training and orientation, based more on ability plus aptitude and less on political interference and administrative nepotism. This is, indeed, a tall order.

Institutional credit could begin to function as an income transfer mechanism to remove inequities in income distribution in Kinnaur if the preceding suggestions were to be implemented. Using public credit institutions as part of a supervised credit package to induce traditional peasantry to adopt modern inputs helps if peasants are not obliged to obtain credit and sell their output through the same middlemen, being exploited in each transaction. The rural credit system in Kinnaur should ideally be judged by its contribution to achieving national development objectives. For this, coordination between development planning and development banking is called for. At the field, or the cutting-edge level, such precepts appear contradictory and confusing. The large numbers of persons to be covered by officially sponsored credit schemes, their diverse circumstances, the absence of yardsticks for measuring the effectiveness of official schemes and shoddy management have all contributed to the lack of a clear perspective at the field level. A pure credit mechanism has inherent limitations in achieving desired growth objectives. Unless economic programmes convey an overall coherent approach, credit in itself should not be treated as a kind of magic wand, waving which can produce miracles. Such a simplistic view may even be counterproductive. Integration of the credit system into the overall economic system faces numerous hurdles, often not fully appreciated. Rapid growth demands maximization of production from loans given for specific purposes for a specified period of time.

[17] Please see Sections 7.2.1.2, 7.2.2 and 7.2.2.1, Chapter VII, this work.

[18] Please see Section 6.1.10, Chapter VI of this work.

Integrated rural development, low nominal rates of interest on institutional loans and innumerable subsidies, both overt and covert, have become icons in the credit market in Kinnaur that nobody seems to question. It is ignored that hitherto discussed preliminary measures have not been implemented for creating the necessary pre-conditions for proper functioning of these shibboleths. Low interest rates have been accompanied by the fact that rates of interest on savings accounts have also been kept low, offering a maximum of 10% on long-term fixed deposits. Kinnauras have been traditionally a savings oriented people. This can be seen even now from the statistics for targets and achievements under the National Small

Table 8.2: Targets and Achievements under Small Savings in Kinnaur

sn	*Year*	*Target*	*Achieved*	*Pct*
01	1976-77	800,000	2016,124	252
02	1977-78	1000,000	1807,450	181
03	1978-79	800,000	2135,329	267
04	1979-80	840,000	2154,069	256
05	1980-81	840,000	2844,445	339
06	1981-82	924,000	2713,000	294
07	1982-83	2657,000	4092,000	154
08	1983-84	3000,000	3109,000	104
09	1984-85	3507,240	4560,000	130

Code: **sn = serial number, pct = Percentage of achievement to target**
All amounts are in Rupees.
(Source: Prepared by the Development Assistant, D.C.'s Office at Kālpa from relevant office files for the author in December 1985.)

Savings Programme for the district in Table 8.2 . Every year shows achievement exceeding target without exception. Kinnaur won several prizes for exceeding targets under the small savings mobilization programme. To further this trend, interest rate policies should be modified by raising interest rates on institutional loans[19] so as to offer higher rates of interest on savings in order to better mop up savings in Kinnaur. When Kinnauras begin to see that their savings bring them good returns and generate a reserve for recycling into loans in their area, they will feel more personally involved, will not mind paying higher rates of interest on institutional credit because institutional lenders will no longer be tempted to raise transaction costs for poorer borrowers in an effort to escape having to give them numerous loans at low unprofitable rates of interest.

There has to be recognition of the fact that unless the informal sector is roped into the effort to improve the quality of life of Kinnauras, official efforts will remain stymied. The informal credit sector has deep roots in Kinnaur and has not been too exploitative. Government officials have to change their perception of the credit structure in this area and not always think in terms of more official agencies and personnel as solutions. It is not being suggested that there should be a reduction in the number of already existing bank branches or

[19] Discussed in Section 4.11.1.1.3, Chapter IV of this work.

VARIATION OF TARGETS AND SAVINGS UNDER THE NATIONAL SMALL SAVINGS PROGRAMME IN KINNAUR DISTRICT

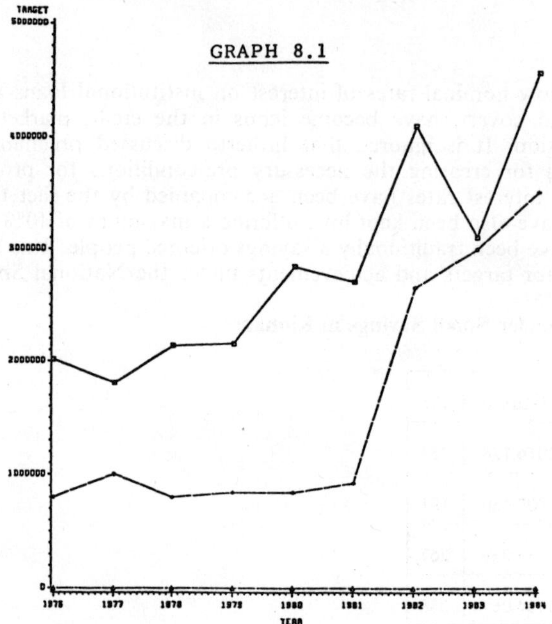

YEAR 1976 = 1976-77, 1977 = 1977-78.....1984 = 1984-85
UNBROKEN LINE JOINING SQUARES IS FOR ACHIEVEMENTS
BROKEN LINE JOINING STARS IS FOR TARGETS
BROKEN LINE JOINING TRIANGLES = PERCENTAGE OF ACHIEVEMENT TO TARGET FOR THE CORRESPONDING YEAR

VARIATION OF PERCENTAGE OF ACHIEVEMENTS TO TARGETS FOR THE NATIONAL SMALL SAVINGS PROGRAMME IN KINNAUR DISTRICT

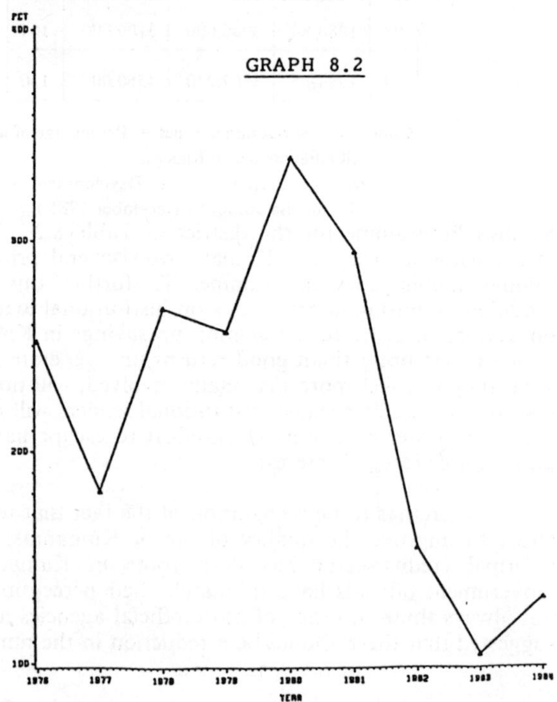

YEAR 1976 = 1976-77, 1977 = 1977-78.....1984 = 1984-85

credit schemes in Kinnaur. Expansion of official establishments is, however, not necessary provided the suggestions given in this work for utilizing local non-official institutions like devtas as partners in the credit-giving network could be implemented. Only time will tell whether Kinnaur goes the way of other districts in that it falls prey to excessive bureaucratization of its credit systems or manages to retrieve its centuries-old devtas as partners in the process of modern development aiming at the welfare of its masses.

ANNEXURES

BIBLIOGRAPHY

BIBLIOGRAPHY

I. ARCHIVAL MATERIAL: HERRNHUT

This refers to the material available in the archives of the Brüder-Unität (Moravian Mission) at Herrnhut in the German Democratic Republic. Some of the material used was in published form while most of it was unpublished.

I.A. Unpublished Documents

1. Rubric R.15.U.a.1: Aufrufe, Meldungen, Berufungen:

(a) Rubric R.15.U.a.1.10: Aufrufe, Meldungen, Berufungen Notizen über die Mongolen Mission 1851;

(b) Rubric R.15.U.a.1.14: Aufrufe, Meldungen, Berufungen Notizen über die Mongolen Mission 1853;

2. Rubric R.15.U.a.2 (Neu Sign.): Reise Berichte:

(a) Rubric R.15.U.a.2.4: Pagell nach Spitti und Kunawur, Bruchstück 1862;

(b) Rubric R.15.U.a.2.11: Heyde nach Ladak, Nubra, Spiti, Simla 1879;

(c) Rubric R.15.U.a.2.14: Weber, von Kleinwelka nach Poo 1883;

(d) Rubric R.15.U.a.2.16: Eine ärztliche Missionsreise 1890;

(e) Rubric R.15.U.a.2.17: Schnabel, Missionsreise 1900.

3. Rubric R.15.U.b.2.: Berichte Von Poo:

(a) Rubric R.15.U.b.2.a: Berichte Von Poo 1865-1900;

(b) Rubric R.15.U.b.2.b: Berichte Von Poo 1901-1908;

4. Rubric R.15.U.b.16: Briefwechsel mit Poo:

(a) Rubric R.15.U.b.16.a: Briefwechsel mit Poo 1875-1899;

(b) Rubric R.15.U.b.16.b: Briefwechsel mit Poo 1900-1908;

5. Rubric R.15.U.b.17: Briefwechsel mit Chini 1900-1908;

M.D. Register:

1. S.e. = Stationsberichte:

(a) S.e.1.a.3: Berichte von Chini 1900-07 (1905-06 fehlen);

(b) S.e.1.a.7: Protokolle der Konferenz in Poo 1899;

(c) S.e.1.a.12: Briefwechsel mit und über K. Marx 1883-1890;

(d) S.e.5.a: Stationsberichte von Poo 1899-1908;

(e) S.e.5.b: Stationsberichte von Poo 1909-1923;

2. S.f.: Statistiken 1901-1938:

3. S.h.: Stationsbriefwechsel:

(a) S.h.1.a: Briefwechsel mit Chini 1900-1908;

(b) S.h.5.a: Briefwechsel mit Poo 1899-1908;

(c) S.h.5.b: Briefwechsel mit Poo 1909-1923;

4. S.i.: Die Behörde in der Heimat:

(a) S.i.1: Memoranden u.A. der Missionsdirektion 1904, 1911, 1914;

(b) S.i.2: Visitationen der Missionsdirektion 1901;

5. S.k.: Verhandlungen mit Regierungsbehörden 1901-08:

(a) S.k.1.a: Verschiedenes, Briefwechsel mit Verschiedenem 1896-1905;

(b) S.k.1.b: Verschiedenes, Briefwechsel mit Verschiedenem 1906-1915;

(c) S.k.2: Verschiedene Akten (1896-1916);

I.B. Published Documents

1. Rubric R.15.U.a.3:

(a) Rubric R.15.U.a.3.1: Missions-Blatt, Mongolen-Mission, Nr. 10, 1850;

(b) Rubric R.15.U.a.3.2: Rechler: Die Mission in Tibet, Bericht, 1869;

(c) Rubric R.15.U.a.3.4: Englische Dokumente über die Mission, 1865;

2. Rubric N.B.VII.R 2.111:

(a) N.B.VII.R 2.111(1): Report of the Moravian Mission among the Buddhists in Lahoul and Kunawur, 1866, 14 pages;

(b) N.B.VII.R 2.111(2): Report of the Moravian Mission among the Buddhists in Lahoul and Kunawur, 1867-68, 15 Pages;

(c) N.B.VII.R 2.111(3): Report of the Moravian Mission among the Buddhists in Lahoul and Kunawur, 1869-70, 15 Pages;

(d) N.B.VII.R 2.111(4): Fourth Report of the Mission of the United Brethren (or Moravians) among the Buddhists in Lahoul and Kunawur in the North West Provinces of India, London: John Bithrey, 1873, 15 Pages;

(e) N.B.VII.R 2.111(5): Fifth Report of the Mission of the United Brethren (or Moravians) among the Buddhists in Lahoul and Kunawur in the North West Provinces of India, London: John Bithrey, 1875, 15 Pages;

(f) N.B.VII.R 2.111(6): Sixth Report of the Mission of the United Brethren (or Moravians) among the Buddhists in Lahoul and Kunawur in the North West Provinces of India, Nov. 1874-Dec. 1875, London: Norman and Son, 1876, 11 pages;

(g) N.B.VII.R 2.111(7): Seventh Report of the Mission of the United Brethren (or Moravians) among the Buddhists in Lahoul and Kunawur in the North West Provinces of India, Jan. 1876-Nov. 1877, London: Norman and Son, 1878, 10 pages

(h) N.B.VII.R 2.111(8): Eighth Report of the Mission of the United Brethren (or Moravians) among the Buddhists in Lahoul and Kunawur in the North West Provinces of India, Jan. 1878-Dec. 1879, London: Norman and Son, 1880, 10 pages

(i) N.B.VII.R 2.111(13): 13th. Report of the Mission of the United Brethren (or Moravians) among the Buddhists in Lahoul and Kunawur in the North West Provinces of India from 1901 to 1906, Rawalpindi: Egerton Press, 1907, 28 pages

(j) N.B.VII.R 2.112a 1941/564: A Brief Account of the Moravian Mission to Tibetan speaking Buddhists in the Himalayas;

(k) N.B.VII.R 2.116e FIV, B13b: The Journal of the Manchester Geographical Society: Western Tibet by F.B. Shawe, Pp 1-23.

II. ARCHIVAL MATERIAL: CHANDIGARH

The material cited here was found in the Punjab State Archives in Sector 35, Chandigarh, India. It had been shifted from Patiala and was in the process of being catalogued. It is, therefore, not possible to give the exact rubrics. The documents cited can be had with the help of Dr Harcharan Singh who works in this office.

Rubric: Foreign Department (Native States):

(a) February 1889, Nos. 1, 2, 27: Proposed loan to the Tika of Bashahr to enable him to complete the Resettlement of the State;

(b) January 1891, Nos. 3, 9, 10: Settlement Operations in Bashahr State;

(c) September 1893, Nos. 10-17: Boundary Dispute between the Pandrabis Kothi of Plach Tahsil and the Bashahr State, File no. 32;

(d) January 1894, Nos. 1-17: Boundary Dispute between the Pandrabis Kothi of Plach Tahsil and the Bashahr State, File no. 1;

(e) June 1894, Nos. 1-4: Boundary Dispute between the Pandrabis Kothi of Plach Tahsil and the Bashahr State, File no. 1;

(f) September 1894, Nos. 37-43: Boundary Dispute between the Pandrabis Kothi of Plach Tahsil and the Bashahr State, File no. 1;

(g) January 1894, Nos. 18-22: Report on the Settlement of the Rampur Tahsil of the Bashahr State, File no. 2;

(h) February 1897, Nos. 5-8: Review of the Assessment Report of Chini Tahsil, Bashahr State, File no. 9;

(i) April 1898, Nos. 48-52: Report on the disturbances in the Kowar Pargana of the Bashahr State, File no. 3 [confidential];

(j) June 1898, Nos. 39-47: Arrangements made for the carrying on of the Administration of the Bashahr State, File no. 3;

(k) July 1898, Nos. 17-23: State of Affairs in the Bashahr State and Appointment of Mangat Ram as Chief Wazir, File no. 3;

(l) September 1898, Nos. 44-46: Raja of Bashahr's personal allowances, File no. 3;

(m) September 1898, Nos. 58-59: Raja of Bashahr's personal allowances, File no.3;

(n) May 1899, Nos. 21-23: Report on the financial situation in the Bashahr State, Question of the Kaneti tribute, File no.4;

Rubric: Political Department (Native States):

(a) April 1905, Nos. 22-24: Proposed Allotment of a portion of the surplus income derived from the Bashahr forests to the clearance of the State debts, File no. 20;

(b) May 1905, Nos. 4-6: Proposed Allotment of a portion of the income derived from the lease of the Bashahr forests to repair the losses occasioned in Bashahr by the recent earthquakes, File no. 22;

Rubric: Political Department (General):

(a) December 1907, Nos. 11-22: Measures to prevent Europeans and others from crossing the frontiers of Bashahr, Spiti and Lahaul into Tibet, File no. 14;

(b) Report on the Administration of the Bashahr State for the Year Sambat 1971, (March 13th 1914-March 13th 1915), Simla: Liddell's Printing Works, 1915;

Unpublished Official Letters

(a) No. 419 dated Simla the 26th September 1919,
From: H.P. Tollington Esquire, C.I.E., I.C.S.,
Superintendent Hill States, Simla,
To: J.P. Thompson, C.S.I., I.C.S.,
Chief Secretary to Government Punjab, Simla E;

(b) No. 5370 dated Simla the 20th September 1922,
From: E.G.F. Abraham Esquire, C.B., I.C.S.,
Superintendent Hill States, Simla,
To: J.P. Thompson, C.S.I., I.C.S.,
Chief Secretary to Government Punjab, Simla;

(c) D.O. Letter No. 1291 I.C. dated Simla the 1st October 1917,
From: Signature illegible,
Superintendent Hill States, Simla,
To: J.P. Thompson,
Chief Secretary to Government Punjab, Simla;

(d) No. (illegible) dated Simla the 25th May 1917;
From: Lt. Col. P.S.M. Burlton,
Superintendent Hill States, Simla,
To: A.A.L. Roberts Esquire C.S.,
Under Secretary to Government Punjab, Simla;

(e) No. 163 dated Simla the 3rd July 1917,

From: Lt. Col. P.S.M. Burlton,
Superintendent Hill States, Simla,
To: The Hon'ble Mr J.P. Thompson C.S.,
Chief Secretary to Government Punjab, Simla;

(f) No. 242 dated Simla the 27th September 1917,
From: Lt. Col. P.S.M. Burlton,
Superintendent Hill States, Simla,
To: The Hon'ble Mr J.P. Thompson C.S.,
Chief Secretary to Government Punjab, Simla;

(g) Telegram dated 12 August 1914 from Prince Surendra Shah of Rampur Bishar, 17 Lyton Road, Dehra Dun to His Excellency the Viceroy, Simla;

(h) No. 2463 dated Simla the 7th July 1924,
From: Lt. Col. J.C. Coldstream, C.B.E., I.A.,
Superintendent Hill States, Simla,
To: The Chief Secretary to Government,
Punjab, Lahore;

(i) No. 4578 dated Simla the 17th September 1924,
From: Lt. Col. J.C. Coldstream, C.B.I., I.A.,
Superintendent Hill States, Simla,
To: The Chief Secretary to Government,
Punjab, Lahore;

(j) Letter No. 2819-S-(Pol) dated Simla the 26th of Sept. 1912;
From: C.A. Barron, C.I.E., I.C.S.,
Chief Secretary to Government Punjab;
To: The Superintendent,
Hill States, Simla,
sd. M.L. Darling, Under Secretary, for Chief Secretary,
[General Account of Mr Mackworth Young's Mission to Gartok];

(k) Letter No. 83 dated Simla the 9th of July 1912, [Note: "Kanawari Traders of Bashahr State" by G. Mackworth Young]

III. BANK DOCUMENTS

The items included here have been arranged alphabetically and within the same alphabetical groups chronologically.

All-India Rural Credit Survey, Report of the Committee of Direction, Vol. I: The Survey Report, Part 2: Credit Agencies, Bombay: Reserve Bank of India, 1957;

Annual Action Plan 1982
Kinnaur District (Himachal Pradesh), Cyclostyled Mimeograph, Simla: Punjab National Bank Regional Office, [Year of issue not mentioned];

Annual Action Plan 1984
Kinnaur District (Himachal Pradesh), Cyclostyled Mimeograph, Simla: PNB Regional Office, December 1983;

Annual Action Plan 1985

Kinnaur District (Himachal Pradesh), Cyclostyled Mimeograph, Simla: PNB Regional Office, [Year not mentioned];

Reserve Bank of India Annual Report 1984-85, Report of the Central Board of Directors on the working of the Reserve Bank of India for the year ended June 30, 1985 submitted to the Central Government in terms of Section 53(2) of the Reserve Bank of India Act, 1934, Bombay: Reserve Bank of India, 1985;

Annual Report, 1969 to 1980-81, Bombay: Reserve Bank of India;

Commercial Banks at District Kinnaur, [sic], Typewritten Manuscript, Simla: Prepared by the staff of the Divisional Manager, UCO Bank, Himachal Region for the author, January 1986;

Development of Cooperative Marketing, A Survey Report, Bombay: Reserve Bank of India; 1968;

District Credit Plan (1983-85) Kinnaur (H.P.), Cyclostyled Mimeograph, Simla: Punjab National Bank Regional Office, Himachal Region, [Year of issue not mentioned];

Gramin Rin ké kshétra mein Bhāratiya Reserve Bank ki bhumika, [Role of the Reserve Bank of India in the Rural Credit Sector], Bombay: Reserve Bank of India, October 1980, [in Hindi];

Guidelines for Advances to Priority Sector, Bombay: Reserve Bank of India, Rural Planning and Credit Department, June 1984;

New Light for Rural India
NABARD,
Articles brought out to mark the inauguration of the National Bank on 5 November 1982, Bombay: NABARD Publication, 1982, [NABARD = National Bank for Agriculture and Rural Development];

Report of the Agricultural Finance Sub-Committee, Bombay: Reserve Bank of India, 1945;

Report of the All-India Rural Credit Review Committee, I edn., Bombay: Reserve Bank of India, 1969;

Report on Trend and Progress of Banking in India, 1977-78 through 1980-81, Bombay: Reserve Bank of India, 1978 through 1981 respectively;

Report of the Study Group to frame Guidelines for Follow-up of Bank Credit, II Reprint/Bombay: Reserve Bank of India, 1981, [First published 1975];

Report of the Working Group on the Role of Banks in implementation of the New 20-Point Programme, Reference: RPCD No. PS.DC.21/C.682-83 dated February 7, 1983, Sent by the Reserve Bank of India's Rural Planning and Credit Department to all commercial banks, Bombay: R.B.I. Central Office, Cyclostyled Mimeograph, 1983, [R.B.I. = Reserve Bank of India];

Role of Commercial Banks in Kinnaur District, Typewritten Manuscript, Simla: Prepared by the staff of Mr Kapoor, Divisional Manager UCO Bank, Himachal Region, on the author's personal request, January 1986, [D.M. = Divisional Manager];

Role of Cooperative Banks in the Development of Agriculture, Typewritten Manuscript, Simla: Prepared by the staff of Mr Balbir S. Chauhan, H.A.S., Managing Director, H.P. State Cooperative Bank on the author's request to him, January 1986, [H.A.S. = Himachal Administrative Service];

Working of the H.P. State Cooperative Bank Ltd. in Kinnaur District with its Head Office at Shimla-171001, Typewritten Manuscript, Simla: M.D. of the SCB, January 1986,

IV. BOOKS, ARTICLES AND MONOGRAPHS

ABBI, B.L., and SABERWAL, Satish, (eds.)

Urgent Research in Social Anthropology,
Vol. 10, I edn., Simla: Indian Institute of Advanced Study, 1969;

ADAMS, Dale W., and GRAHAM, Douglas H.

A Critique of Traditional Agricultural Credit Projects and Policies,
in: *Journal of Development Economics,* Vol. 8, June 1981, Pp 347-366;

ADAMS, Dale W., and NEHMAN, G.I.

Borrowing Costs and the Demand for Rural Credit,
in: *Journal of Development Studies,* Vol. 15, January 1979, Pp 165-176;

AGRAWAL, Ramesh Chandra

An Analysis of the Contribution of Nationalised Banks in financing Indian Agriculture,
in: *Zeitschrift für ausländische Landwirtschaft,* Band 14, April/June 1975, Pp 144-158;

AHMAD, Zahiruddin

New Light on the Tibet-Ladakh-Mughal War of 1679-84,
in: *East and West,* New Series, Vol. 18, Nos. 3-4, September-December 1968, Pp 340-361;

ALLAMI, Abū'l Fazl

Ain-i-Akbari,
Translated into English by H. Blochmann, edited by S.L. Goomer, II edn., Delhi: Aadesh Book Depot, 1965, [I edn., 1871];

APPADORAI, A. and ARORA, V.K.

India in World Affairs 1957-58,
I edn., New Delhi: Sterling Publishers, 1975;

ARLÈS, J.P.

The Economic and Social Promotion of the Scheduled Castes and Tribes in India,
in: *International Labour Review,* Vol. 103, No. 1, January-June 1971, Pp 29-64;

ARON, Raymond

Le spectateur engagé,
Entretiens avec Jean-Louis Missika et Dominique Wolton, Paris: Julliard, 1981, [in French];

AZIZ, Sartaj

Rural Development-Some Essential Prerequisites,
in: *International Labour Review,* Vol. 123, No. 3, May-June 1984, Pp 277-285;

BAJPAI, S.C.

Kinnaur in the Himalayas
Mythology to Modernity,
I edn., New Delhi: Concept Publishing Co., 1981;

BAILEY, Rev. T. Grahame

A Brief Grammar of the Kanauri Language,
in: *Zeitschrift der Deutschen Morgenländischen Gesellschaft,* Dreiundsechzigster Band [Vol. 63], 1909, Pp 661-687;

BASU, A.R.

Tribal Development Programmes and Administration in India
With special reference to Himachal Pradesh,
I edn., New Delhi: National Book Organisation, 1985;

BECHLER, Th.

Kulturarbeit der Brüdergemeine im westlichen Himalaya,
in: *Beiblatt II zur Allgemeinen Missionszeitschrift,* Band 41 [Vol. 41], No. 2, März 1914, Pp 18-32, [in German];

BECK, Hartmut

Brüder in vielen Völkern
250 Jahre Mission der Brüdergemeine,
Erlangen: Verlag der Ev. Luth. Mission, 1981, [in German];

BERNARD, Jean-Alphonse

L'Inde
Le pouvoir et la puissance,
Sous l'égide de la fondation pour les études de défense nationale, Paris: Fayard, 1985, [in French];

BERNIER, Francois

Travels in the Mogul Empire,
Translated on the basis of Irving Brock's version and annotated by Archibald Constable (1891), II edn., Revised by Vincent A. Smith, London: Humphrey Milford Oxford University Press, 1916;

BERREMAN, Gerald D.

Hindus of the Himalaya
Ethnography and Change,
II edn. (Revised and enlarged), University of California Press, 1972;

BHATNAGAR, S.

Politics of Land Reforms in India: A Case Study of Land Legislation in Himachal Pradesh,
in: *Asian Survey,* Vol. XXI, No. 4, April 1981, Pp 454-468;

BINSWANGER, Hans P., and SILLERS, Donald A.

Risk Aversion and Credit Constraints in Farmers' Decision-Making: A Reinterpretation, in: *The Journal of Development Studies,* Vol. 20, No. 1, October 1983, Pp 5-21;

BOPEGAMAGE, A.

The Military as a Modernizing Agent in India, in: *Economic Development and Cultural Change,* Vol. 20, No. 1, October 1971, Pp 71-79;

BOTTOMLEY, Anthony

The Premium for Risk as a Determinant of Interest Rates in Underdeveloped Rural Areas, in: *Quarterly Journal of Economics,* Vol. LXXVII, 1963, Pp 637-647;

Interest Rate Determination in Underdeveloped Rural Areas, in: *American Journal of Agricultural Economics,* Vol. 57, No. 3, August 1975, Pp 279-291;

BUCHANAN, W.E.

In the Footsteps of the Gerards, in: *The Himalayan Journal,* Vol. II, April 1930, Pp 73-80;

CARNEIRO, Robert L.

A Theory of the Origin of the State, in: *Science,* Vol. 169, 1970, Pp 733-738;

CHAKRAVARTI, P.C.

India-China Relations, Calcutta: K.L. Mukhopadhyay, 1961;

CHANDRA, Ramesh

Ecology and Religion of the Kinner Mountain Dwellers of North Western Himalayas, in: Nature-Man-Spirit Complex in Tribal India, edited by R.S. Mann, Ranchi Anthropology Series-3, General Editor: L.P. Vidyarthi, New Delhi: Concept Publishing Company, 1981, Pp 269-293;

Types and Forms of Marriage in a Kinnaur Village, in: *Man In India,* Vol. 53, No. 2, April-June 1973, Pp 176-184;

CHIB, S.S.

Kanauras of the Trans-Himalaya, I edn., New Delhi: Ess Ess Publications, 1984;

CHOPRA, Pran

On An Indian Border, London: Asia Publishing House, 1964;

CLAESSEN, Henri J.M., and SKALNÍK, Peter (eds.)

The Early State,
The Hague: Mouton Publishers, 1978;

The Study of The State,
The Hague: Mouton Publishers, 1981;

COLEBROOKE, H.T.

On the Sources of the Ganges in the Himadri or Emodus,
in: *Asiatick Researches,* Vol. 11, 1812, Pp 429-481;

CUNNINGHAM, Alexander

Ladāk
Physical, Statistical and Historical,
Reprint/New Delhi: Sagar Publications, 1970, [First Published, London, 1854];

CUNNINGHAM, Joseph Davey [J.D. Cunningham]

Notes on Moorcroft's Travels in Ladakh, and on Gerard's Account of Kunawur, including a general description of the latter district,
in: *Journal of the Asiatic Society of Bengal,* Vol. 13, 1844, No. 147: Part I, Pp 172-222, No. 148: Part II, Pp 223-253;

DAS-GUPTA, Jyotirindra

Development and Poverty Reduction in South Asia - A Review Article,
in: *Journal of Asian Studies,* Vol. XLII, November 1982, Pp 105-117;

DATTA, C.L. [Chaman Lāl][1]

Significance of Shawl-Wool Trade in Western Himalayan Politics,
in: *Bengal: Past And Present,* Vol. XXXVIII, Part I, January-June 1969, Pp 16-28;

Zorawar Singh: Political Mission of J.D. Cunningham 1841-42,
in: *Bengal: Past And Present,* Vol. LXXXIX, Part I, January-June 1970, Pp 82-90;

Ladakh and Western Himalayan Politics 1819-1848
The Dogra Conquest of Ladakh, Baltistan and West Tibet
and Reactions by other Powers,
New Delhi: Munshiram Manoharlal, 1973;

DEUSTER, R.H.

Kanawar
Grundriß einer Volks- und Kulturkunde,
Studien zur Völkerkunde, Band 14, Leipzig: Druck und Verlag Jordan & Graimberg, 1939, [in German];

[1] The author was Dr C.L. Datta's student from 1973 to 1975 in Chandigarh. He had detailed discussions with Dr Datta about his research during his field visit to India in 1975-76 and is grateful to his former teacher for his help.

DUKA, Theodore

Life and Works of Alexander Csoma de Körös,
London: Trübner & Co., 1885;

ENGELS, Friedrich

Der Ursprung der Familie, des Privateigentums und des Staats,
Bücherei des Marxismus-Leninismus, Band 11, Berlin: Dietz, 1964, [in German];

The Origin of the Family, Private Property and the State,
(Edited with an introduction by Eleanor Burke Leacock), London: Lawrence and Wishart, 1972;

ÉTIENNE, Gilbert

L'agriculture indienne ou "l'art du possible",
I edn., Paris: Presses Universitaires de France, 1966, [in French];

Les chances de l'Inde
L'heure d'Indira Gandhi,
Paris: Éditions du Seuil, 1973, [in French];

Développement rural en Asie
Les hommes, le grain et l'outil,
Collection Tiers Monde, Paris: Éditions du Seuil, 1982, [in French];

FASBENDER, Karl

Strategy of Integrated Development-Some Remarks on the Development of Rural Areas in Developing Countries,
in: *Intereconomics,* Vol. 17, Nov./Dec. 1982, Pp 291-295;

FRANCKE, Rev. A.H. [August Hermann]

Die sprachlichen Verhältnissen der Himalaya-Mission der Brüdergemeine,
in: *Allgemeine Missions-Zeitschrift,* Band 25, 1898, Pp 439-447, [in German];

Die Jesuitenmission von Tsaparang im Lichte der tibetischen Urkunden,
in: *Zeitschrift für Missionswissenschaft,* Fünfzehnter Jahrgang [Vol. 15], 1925, Pp 269-278;

Antiquities of Indian Tibet,
Part I, Personal Narrative, Reprint/New Delhi: S. Chand & Co., 1972, [Archaeological Survey of India, New Imperial Series, Vol. XXXVIII, Calcutta, 1908];
Part II, Reprint/New Delhi: S. Chand & Co., 1972, [A.S.I., New Imperial Series, Vol. L, Calcutta, 1926];

A History of Ladakh,
With a critical introduction and annotations by S.S. Gergan and F.M. Hassanain, (Published originally as A History of Western Tibet), New Delhi: Sterling Publishers, 1977;

FRASER, Lady Antonia

Mary Queen of Scots,
Reprint/St. Albans: Panther Books, 1975, [I edn., 1970];

FRASER, James Baillie

Journal of a Tour through parts of the Snowy Range of the Himālā Mountains and to the Sources of the Rivers Jumna and Ganges,
London: Rodwell and Martin, 1820;

FRIED, Morton H.

The Evolution of Political Society,
New York: Random House, 1967;

GERARD, Alexander

Journal of an Excursion through the Himalayah Mountains, from Shipke to the Frontiers of Chinese Tartary,
in: *Edinburgh Journal of Science*, Vol. I, 1824, Pp 41-49 and 215-224;

Account of Koonawur in the Himalaya, Etc. Etc. Etc.
Edited by George Lloyd, London: James Madden & Co., MDCCCXLI;

Narrative of a Journey from Soobathoo to Shipke, in Chinese Tartary,
in: *Journal of the Royal Asiatic Society*, Vol. 11, Part I-New Series, 1842, Pp 361-391;

GERARD, J.G. [Brother of Alexander Gerard]

Observations on the Spiti Valley and circumjacent country within the Himālaya,
in: *Asiatick Researches*, Vol. XVIII, Part II, 1833, Pp 238-278;

GLOVER, H.M.

Round the Kanawar Kailas,
in: *The Himalayan Journal*, Vol. II, April 1930, Pp 81-86;

GODELIER, Maurice

La notion de "mode de production asiatique" et les schémas Marxistes d'évolution des sociétés,
in: Sur le "Mode de production asiatique", edited by Roger Garaudy, Paris: Éditions Sociales, 1969, Pp 47-100;

GORRIE, R. Maclagan

Two Easy Passes in Kanawar,
in: *The Himalayan Journal*, Vol. I, No. I, April 1929, Pp 75-77,

Through Kulu-Saraj,
in: *The Himalayan Journal*, Vol. V, 1933, Pp 85-89;

GOVINDA, Lama Anangarika (Anangavajra Khamsum Wangchuk)

The Way of the White Clouds
A Buddhist Pilgrim in Tibet,
Shambhala: Berkeley, III Printing, 1974, [I paperback edn., 1970];

GRIERSON, Sir G.A.

Linguistic Survey of India,
Vol. III: Tibeto-Burman Family, Part I: General Introduction: Specimens of the Tibetan Dialects, the Himalayan Dialects and the North Assam Group, Calcutta: Superintendent of Government Printing, 1909;
Vol. I, Part I: Introductory, Calcutta: Government of India (Central Publication Branch), 1927,

GRIFFIN, Sir Lepel H., and MASSY, Colonel Charles Francis

Chiefs and Families of Note in the Punjab,
A revised edition of "The Punjab Chiefs" by Sir Lepel H. Griffin and Col. Charles F. Massy, Vol. II, Lahore: Civil and Military Gazette Press, 1910;

HAMILTON, A.P.F.

Kulu,
in: *The Himalayan Journal,* Vol. V, 1933, Pp 75-84;

HEDIN, Sven

Trans-Himalaya
Discoveries and Adventures in Western Tibet,
Vol. III, London: Macmillan & Co., 1913;

HERBERT, Captain J.D.

An account of a tour made to lay down the Course and Levels of the River Setlej or Satūdrā, as far as traceable within the limits of the British authority, performed in 1819,
in: *Asiatick Researches,* Vol. XV, 1825, Pp 339-428;

HUNTER, W.W.

The Imperial Gazetteer of India,
Vol. V, London: Trübner & Co., 1881;

HUTCHISON, G. and VOGEL, J. Ph.

History of Punjab Hill States,
Vol. I and II, Lahore: Superintendent, Government Printing, Punjab, 1933;

HUTTON, Lieutenant Thomas

Journal of a trip through Kunawur, Hungrung, and Spiti, undertaken in the year 1838, under the patronage of the Asiatic Society of Bengal, for the purpose of determining the geological formation of those districts,
in: *Journal of the Asiatic Society of Bengal,* Vol. VIII, No. 7, November 1839, Part I: Pp 901-950; New Series, No. 101, Part II: Pp 489-513; Vol. IX, Part I, New Series, No. 102; 1840, Part III: Pp 555-581;

IQBAL, Farrukh

The Demands for funds by Agricultural Households: Evidence from Rural India,
in: *The Journal of Development Studies,* Vol. 20, No. 1, October 1983, Pp 68-86;

JACKMAN, Robert W.

Dependence on Foreign Investment and Economic Growth in the Third World,
in: *World Politics,* Vol. XXXIV, No. 2, January 1982, Pp 175-196;

JACQUEMONT, Victor

État politique et social de l'Inde du Nord en 1830,
Avec une introduction de M. Alfred Martineau, Paris: Librairie Ernest Leroux, 1933, [in French];

JOHNSON, Captain C.

Journey through the Himma-leh Mountains to the Sources of the River Jumna, and thence to the confines of Chinese Tartary: performed in April-October 1827,
in: *Journal of the Royal Geographical Society of London,* Vol. IV, 1834, Pp 41-71;

KENNEDY, Captain Charles Pratt [C.P.]

Report on the Protected Hill States,
in: Chapter VIII: Reports on Lapsed and Reserved Territory in the Protected Sikh and Hill States and on the latter generally- 1824, in: Punjab Government Records, Vol. I: Delhi Residency and Agency 1807-1857, Lahore: Punjab Government Press, 1911, Pp 255-299;

KIRSCH, Ottfried C., ARMBRUSTER, Paul G., KOCHENDÖRFER-LUCIUS Gudrun,

Self-Help Institutions in Developing Countries,
Studies in Applied Economics and Rural Institutions, Publications of the Research Centre for International Agrarian Development, No. 13, Saarbrücken: Verlag breitenbach Publishers, 1984;

KLEINERT, Christian

Siedlung und Umwelt in Zentralen Himalaya,
Geoecological Research, Editor: Ulrich Schweinfurth, Vol. 4, Wiesbaden: Franz Steiner Verlag, 1983, [in German];

KONOW, Sten

On some Facts connected with the Tibeto-Burman dialect spoken in Kanawar,
in: *Zeitschrift der Deutschen Morgenländischen Gesellschaft,* Neunundfünfzigster Band [Vol. 59], 1909, Pp 117-125;

KOSAMBI, D.D.

Ancient India
A History of its Culture and Civilization,
I American Edition, New York: Pantheon Books, 1965;

KOTOVSKY, Grigori G.

Certain Trends in India's Socio-Economic and Socio-Political Development,
in: *Asian Survey,* Vol. XXIV, No. 11, November 1984, Pp 1131-1141;

KULKE, Hermann

Kshatriyaization and Social Change
A Study in Orissa Setting,
in: Pillai, S. Devadas (ed.): Aspects of Changing India, Studies in honour of Professor G.S. Ghurye, Bombay: Popular Prakashan, 1976, Pp 398-409;

Legitimation and Town-Planning in the Feudatory States of Central Orissa,
in: Piper, Jan (ed.): Ritual Space in India, Studies in Architectural Anthropology, Special issue of Art and Archæological Research Papers (aarp), Vol. 17, [London], March 1980;

Tribal Deities at Princely Courts: The Feudatory Rājās of Central Orissa and their Tutelary Deities (Istadevatās),
in: Mahapatra, Sitakant (ed.): Folk Ways in Religion: Gods, Spirits and Men, Cuttack: Institute of Oriental and Orissan Studies, 1984, Pp 13-24;

Max Weber's Contribution to the Study of "Hinduization" in India and "Indianization" in Southeast Asia,
in: Kantowsky, Detlef (ed.): Recent Research on Max Weber's Studies of Hinduism, München & London: Weltforum Verlag, 1986, Pp 97-116;

KUMAR, Girja and ARORA, V.K. (eds.)

Documents on Indian Affairs 1960,
Issued under the auspices of the Indian Council of World Affairs, New Delhi, 1965;

KUTZNER, J.G.

Die Reise seiner königlichen Hoheit des Prinzen Waldemar von Preußen nach Indien in den Jahren 1844 bis 1846, Aus dem darüber erschienen Prachtwerke im Auszüge mitgetheilt,
Berlin: Verlag der königlichen Geheimen Ober-Hofbuchdruckerei, 1857, [in German];

KÖRÖS, Alexander Csoma de

Geographical Notice of Tibet,
in: *Journal of the Royal Asiatic Society,* Vol. I, No. 4, April 1832, Pp 121-127;

LAKHANPAL, B.R.

Assessment Report of the Second Regular Settlement of Nichar Tehsil of Kinnaur District of Himachal Pradesh (1977-81),
Unpublished Draft Manuscript, Under submission to the Government of Himachal Pradesh for approval, Simla: 1985;

LAMB, Alistair

Tibet in Anglo-Chinese Relations: 1767-1842,
in: *Journal of the Royal Asiatic Society of Great Britain and Ireland,* Part I: October 1957, Pp 161-176; Part II: April 1958, Pp 26-43;

LIPTON, Michael

Agricultural Finance and Rural Credit in Poor Countries,
in: *World Development,* Vol. 4, No. 7, 1976, Pp 543-553;

LLOYD, William, and GERARD, Alexander

Narrative of a Journey from Caunpoor to the Boorendo Pass in the Himalaya Mountains, via Gwalior, Agra, Delhi and Sirhind by Major Sir William Lloyd and Captain Alexander Gerard's Account of an attempt to penetrate by Bekhur to Garoo and the Lake Manasarowara, With a letter from the late J.G. Gerard Esq., detailing a visit to the Shatool and Boorendo Passes for the purpose of determining the line of perpetual snow on the southern face of the Himalaya,
Vol. I: Major Sir William Lloyd's Account, Vol. II: Captain Alexander Gerard's Narrative, alongwith a letter from the late Mr J.G. Gerard, edited by George Lloyd, London: James Madden & Co., 1840;

LONG, Millard F.

Why Peasant Farmers Borrow,
in: *American Journal of Agricultural Economics,* Vol. 50, No. 4, November 1968, Pp 991-1008;

LONGSTAFF, T.G.

Notes on a Journey through the Western Himalaya,
in: *The Geographical Journal,* Vol. XXIX, No. 1, January 1907, Pp 201-211;

MADDEN, Captain

Diary of an Excursion to the Shatool and Boorun Passes over the Himalaya, in September, 1845,
in: *Journal of the Asiatic Society of Bengal,* Vol. 15, No. 170 (New Series), 1846, Pp 79-135;

MAMGAIN, M.D.

Kinnaur,
Himachal Pradesh District Gazetteers, Ambala Cantt.: Quick Printers, 1971;

MASSIEU, Isabel

Népal et les pays himalayens,
Paris: Librairie Félix Alcan, 1914, [in French];

McMAHON, Colonel C.A.

Notes of a Tour through Hangrang and Spiti,
in: *Records of the Geological Survey of India,* Vol. XII, London: Trübner and Co., MDCCCLXXIX, Pp 57-69;

MEAD, Margaret

The Underdeveloped and the Overdeveloped,
in: *Foreign Affairs,* Vol. 41, No. 1, 40th Anniversary Issue, October 1962, Pp 78-89;

MERTON, Robert K.

The Matthew Effect in Science,
in: *Science,* Vol. 159, January 1968, Pp 58-63;

MISHRA, D.P.

Studies in the Proto-History of India,
I edn., New Delhi: Orient Longmans, 1971;

MISRA, S.D.

A Short Note on the Socio-Historical Geography of Himachal Pradesh,
in: *The National Geographical Journal of India,* Vol. VIII, Part 2, June 1962, Pp 164-171;

MOORCROFT, William

A Journey to Lake Manasarovara in U'n-d'es, a province of Little Tibet,
in: *Asiatick Researches,* Vol. 12, 1818, Pp 380-536;

MOORCROFT, William and TREBECK, George

Travels in the Himalayan Provinces of Hindustan and the Punjab, in Ladakh and Kashmir, in Peshawar, Kabul, Kunduz and Bokhara, from 1819 to 1825,
Prepared for the Press by Horace Hyman Wilson, Vol. I and II, Reprint/New Delhi: Sagar Publications, 1971, [Originally published from London in 1841];

MUKERJEE, Radhakamal

A History of Indian Civilization,
Vol. I: Ancient and Classical Traditions, II edn., Bombay: Hind Kitabs Publishers, 1958;

NEALE, Walter C.

Community Development in India,
in: *Asian Survey,* Vol. XXIII, No. 11, November 1983, Pp 1209-1219;

NEGI, Thākur Sain [T.S.]

Scheduled Tribes of Himachal Pradesh-A Profile,
Simla: Got published himself by the author, 1976;

NEWIGER, Nikolaus J.

Improving the operational efficiency of Agricultural Cooperatives providing credit,
in: *Zeitschrift für ausländische Landwirtschaft,* Jahrgang 12, 1973, Pp 298-304;

OPPENHEIMER, Franz

Der Staat,
Frankfurt-am-Main: Mohr Verlag, 1932, [in German];

OYA, Kenji

Environmental Dimensions of Regional Rural Development
A Report of a Study in three Asian Countries,
in: *Regional Development Dialogue,* Vol. 3, Spring 1982, Pp 72-116;

PADMANABHAN, K.P.

New Concepts for Rural Credit,
in: *Ceres,* Vol. 15, January/February 1982, Pp 21-25;

PALLIS, Marco

Gangotri and Leo Pargial 1933,
in: *The Himalayan Journal,* Vol. VI, 1934, Pp 106-126;

Peaks and Lamas,
II edn., London: Cassell & Co., 1948;

PAPIHA, S.S., CHAHAL, S.M.S., ROBERTS, D.F., and SINGH, I.P.

Genetic Studies among Kanet and Koli of Kinnar District in Himachal Pradesh, India,
in: *American Journal of Physical Anthropology,* Vol. 53, 1980, Pp 275-283;

PARMAR, Yashwant Singh [Y.S.][2]

Polyandry in the Himalayas,
Reprint/Delhi: Vikas Publishing House, February 1975, [I edn., January 1975];

PETECH, Luciano

The Tibetan-Ladakhi-Moghul War of 1681-83,
in: *The Indian Historical Quarterly,* Vol. XXIII, No. 3, September 1947, Pp 169-199;

The Kingdom of Ladakh
C. 950-1842 A.D.,
Istituto Italiano per il Medio ed Estremo Oriente, Serie Orientale Roma, LI, Rome, 1977;

Ya-ts'e, Gu-ge, Pu-raṅ: A New Study,
in: *Central Asiatic Journal,* Vol. XXIV, Nos. 1-2, 1980, Pp 85-111;

POTHEN, Paul

Fertilisers through Cooperatives,
in: *Agricultural Co-operative Bulletin,* Year XXII, No. 2/3, 1980, Pp 3-5;

PRAKASH, Buddha

Studies in Indian History and Civilization,
I edn., Agra: Shiv Lāl Agarwala & Co., 1962;

RAHUL, Rām, (ed.)

Social Work in the Himalaya,
Proceedings of the Seminar on Social Work in the Himalaya, Studies in Social Work, Publication No. 21, Delhi: Delhi School of Social Work of the University of Delhi, [Year not mentioned];

[2] Dr Parmār was the Chief Minister of Himāchal Pradesh and is respected as its founding father.

RAHUL, Rām

The Himalaya Borderland,
I edn., Delhi: Vikas Publishing House, 1970;

REEVES, H.C.

Notes on the Mountains of Bussahir and Spiti,
in: *Alpine Journal,* Vol. 27, 1913, Pp 332-334;

REICHELT, G. Th.

Die Himalaya-Mission der Brüdergemeine,
Gütersloh: Druck und Verlag von G. Bertelsmann, 1896, [in German];

ROSE, H.A.

A Glossary of the Tribes and Castes of the Punjab and North West Frontier Province,
Based on the Census Report for the Punjab, 1883 by the late Sir Denzil Ibbetson and the Census Report for the Punjab, 1892 by the Hon. Mr E.D. Maclagan and compiled by H.A. Rose, Reprint/Lahore: Aziz Publishers, [First edition published in Pakistan], 1978, [First Published, 1911];

Imperial Gazetteer of India
Provincial Series-Punjab,
Vol. II, Lahore: Aziz Publishers, 1979;

ROTH, Hans-Dieter

Institutioneller Agrarkredit und Traditionelle Schuldverhältnisse Distrikt Dhanbad/ Bihar (Indien),
Beiträge zur Südasien Forschung, Südasien Institut der Universität Heidelberg, Band 46, Wiesbaden: Franz Steiner Verlag, 1978, [in German];

Moneylenders' Management of Loan Agreements
Report on a Case Study in Dhanbad,
in: *The Economic and Political Weekly,* Vol. XIV, No. 27, July 7, 1979, Pp 1166-1170;

Indian Moneylenders at Work,
Case Studies of the traditional Rural Credit Market in Dhanbad District, Bihar, I edn., New Delhi: Manohar Publications, 1983;

ROTHERMUND, Dietmar

Government, Landlord and Tenant in India 1875-1900,
in: *The Indian Economic and Social History Review,* Vol. 6, No. 4, 1969;

The Record of Rights in British India,
in: *The Indian Economic and Social History Review,* Vol. VIII, No. 4, 1971, Pp 443-461;

Freedom of Contract and the Problem of Land Alienation in British India,
in: *South Asia,* Journal of South Asian Studies, [University of Western Australia Press], Vol. 3, 1973, Pp 57-78;

The Land Revenue Problem in British India,
in: *Bengal: Past and Present,* January-June 1976;

Government, Landlord and Peasant in India
Agrarian Relations Under British Rule
1865-1935,
Schriftenreihe des Südasien Instituts der Universität Heidelberg, Band 25, Wiesbaden: Franz Steiner Verlag, 1978;

ROTHERMUND, D., KROPP, Erhard, and DIENEMANN, Gunther (eds.)

Urban Growth and Rural Stagnation
Studies in the Economy of an Indian Coalfield and its Hinterland,
Dhanbad Research Project Report, General Editor: D. Rothermund, South Asian Studies No. IX (b), South Asia Interdisciplinary Regional Research Programme, New Delhi: Manohar Publications, 1980;

RUTTAN, Vernon W.

Integrated Rural Development Programmes: A Historical Perspective,
in: *World Development*, Vol. 12, No. 4, 1984, Pp 393-401;

RYDER, Major C.H.D.

Exploration and Survey with the Tibet Frontier Commission, and from Gyangtse to Simla via Gartok,
in: *The Geographical Journal*, Vol. XXVI, No. 4, October 1905, Pp 369-395;

SAHANI, Pandit Daya Ram, and FRANCKE, Rev. A.H.

References to the Bhottas in the Rajatarangini of Kashmir,
in: *The Indian Antiquary*, Vol. XXXVII, July 1908, Pp 181-192;

SAṄKRITYAYAN, Rāhul

Kinner Desh,
II edn., Allahabad: Kitāb Mahal, 1957, [in Hindi];

Méri Jeevan Yātra,
[The Story Of My Life], Part 4, I edn., Delhi: Rājkamal Prakāshan, April 1967, [in Hindi];

SCHLAGINTWEIT-SAKÜNLÜNSKI, Hermann von

Reisen in Indien und Hochasien,
Dritter Band [Vol. III]: Hochasien: II. Tibet, Jena: Hermann Gostenoble, 1872, [in German];

SCHNEIDER, H.

Ein Missionsbild aus dem westlichen Himalaya,
Gnadau: Verlag der Unitäts-Buchhandlung, 1880, [in German];

SCHULZE, Adolf

Abriß einer Geschichte der Brüdermission,
Herrnhut: Verlag der Missionsbuchhandlung der Missionsanstalt der Evangelischen Brüderunität, 1901, [in German];

200 Jahre Brüdermission-Das zweite Missionsjahrhundert,
Band II, Herrnhut: Verlag der Missionsbuchhandlung, 1932, [in German];

SCHUH, Dieter

Zu den Hintergründen der Parteinahme Ladakh's für Bhutan im Krieg gegen Lhasa, in: Kantowsky, Detlef and Sander, Reinhard (eds.): Recent Research on Ladakh: History, Culture, Sociology, Ecology, Proceedings of a Conference held at the Universität Konstanz, 23-26 November 1981, Schriftenreihe Internationales Asienforum, Band 1, Köln: Weltforum Verlag, 1983, Pp 37-50, [in German];

SENFT, E.A.

Les missions moraves
Actuellement existantes chez les peuples paiens,
Neuchâtel: Delachoux et Niestlé Éditeurs, 1890, [in French];

SERVICE, Elman R.

Origins of the State and Civilization,
New York: Norton Publishers, 1975;

SHERRING, Charles A.

Western Tibet and the Indian Borderland,
The Sacred Country of Hindus and Buddhists,
With an account of the Government, Religion and Customs of its Peoples, Reprint/ I Indian edn., Delhi: Cosmo Publications, 1974, [Originally published under the title 'Western Tibet and British Borderland', London, 1916];

SHEWEN, Major D.G.P.M.

The Way to the Baspa,
in: *The Himalayan Journal,* Vol. I, No. I, April 1929, Pp 67-74;

SINGH, Ajit

Rural Development and Banking in India
Theory and Practice,
New Delhi: Deep and Deep Publications, 1985;

SINGH, Hakim[3]

Application of the Technique of Farm Planning and Budgeting in the Punjab,
Thesis presented to the Faculty of the Graduate School of Cornell University, Ithaca (N.Y.), U.S.A., September 1961, Unpublished;

SINGH, Khushwant

A History of the Sikhs,
Vol. 1: 1469-1839, Third Impression, New Delhi: Oxford University Press, 1981, [First Indian edn.: 1977, First published by the Princeton University Press in 1963]; Vol. 2: 1839-1974, Second Impression, New Delhi: Oxford University Press, 1978, [First Published by the Princeton University Press in 1966, First Indian edn. : 1977];

[3] The author's late father, an agricultural economist and farm management expert, who worked for the F.A.O. and for the Government of Punjab.

SINGH, Miāṅ Durga

A Report on the Panjab Hill Tribes
From the Native Point of View,
(Communicated by H.A. Rose), in: *The Indian Antiquary,* Vol. XXXVI, 1907, September: Pp 264-284, October: Pp 289-315, December: Pp 370-375;

SINGH, Miāṅ Goverdhan[4]

Bushahr-Kinnaur Rājya,
Draft Manuscript in longhand, [With corrections in his own handwriting by Mr Thākur Sain Negi], Unpublished, [in Hindi. It is the draft of a history that Miān Goverdhan Singh plans to publish about Bushahr and Kinnaur with the collaboration of Mr T.S. Negi];

SINHA, Surajit

State Formation and Rajput Myth in Tribal Central India,
in: *Man In India,* Vol. 42, No. 1, March 1962, Pp 36-80;

SMITH, Clement M. [C.M.]

A Walking Tour through the Himalayas from Hindustan to Tibet,
in: *The Alpine Journal,* Vol. III, 1867, Pp 52-68;

SNELLGROVE, D.L.

Buddhist Himalaya
Travels and Studies in quest of the Origins and Nature of Tibetan Religion,
Oxford: Bruno Cassirer Publishers, 1957;

St.-MARTIN, Vivien de

Kounavar,
in: Nouveau dictionnaire de geographie universelle, Vol. 3, Paris: 1887, p. 203, [in French];

STEWARD, Julian H.

Theory of Culture Change,
Urbana: University of Illinois Press, 1955;

STOLICZKA, F.

Geological Sections across the Himalayan Mountains, from Wangtu Bridge on the River Sutlej to Sungdo on the Indus,
in: *Memoirs of the Geological Survey of India,* Vol. 5, 1866, Pp 1-154;

Das Setledsch-Thal im Himalaya,
in: Mitteilungen aus Justus Perthes' Geographischer Anstalt über wichtige neue Erforschungen auf dem Gesammtgebiete der Geographie von Dr A. Peterman, Band 16, Gotha: Justus Perthes, 1870, Pp 8-12, [in German];

[4] The librarian of the Secretariat Library in Simla and a well known author of books on Himachal Pradesh. The author is very grateful to him for his cooperation and help.

STRACHEY, Captain H.

Physical Geography of Western Tibet,
in: *Journal of the Royal Geographical Society of London,* Vol. XXIII, 1853, Pp 1-69;

STRIVASTAVA, Dru and SINGH, C.B.

Disparities in Cooperative Credit in India,
in: *Journal of Rural Cooperation,* Vol. III, No. 2, 1975, Pp 111-117;

SUKH CHAIN, Pandit, of Kumhārsain

Legends of the Godlings of the Simla Hills,
in: *The Indian Antiquary,* Vol. 54, 1925, June: Pp 101-113, July: Pp 129-140;

THEOBALD, W.

Notes of a Trip from Simla to the Spiti Valley and Chomoriri (Tshomoriri) Lake during the months of July, August and September 1861,
in: *Journal of the Asiatic Society of Bengal,* Vol. 31, No. V, 1862, Pp 480-527;

THOMAS, P.

Epics, Myths and Legends of India,
12th edn., Bombay: D.B. Taraporevala and Sons, 1961;

THOMSON, Thomas

Western Himalaya and Tibet
A Narrative of a Journey through the Mountains of Northern India during the Years 1847-48,
Reprint/Kathmandu: Ratna Pustak Bhandār, 1979, [Originally published in 1852 in London];

TÖKEI, Ferenc

Zur Frage der asiatischen Produktionsweise,
Berlin: Luchterhand, 1969, [in German];

TUCCI, Giuseppe

Indo-Tibetica
I. "Mc'od rten" e "Ts'a ts'a"
Nel Tibet Indiano ed Occidentale,
Roma: Reale Accademia d'Italia, 1932-XI, [in Italian];

Indo-Tibetica
III.
I Templi del Tibet Occidentale
E il loro Simbolismo Artistico
Parte I. Spiti e Kunavar,
Roma: Reale Accademia d'Italia, 1935-XIII, [in Italian];

Indo-Tibetica
III.
I Templi del Tibet Occidentale
E il lore Simbolismo Artistico
Parte II. Tsaparang,

Roma: Reale Accademia d'Italia, 1936-XV, [in Italian];

Santi e Briganti nel Tibet Ignoto,
(Diario della Spedizione nel Tibet Occidentale 1935), Milano: Editore Ulrico Hoepli, 1937-XV, [in Italian];

TUCCI, Giuseppe and GHERSI, Captain Emiliano

Secrets of Tibet,
Translated from the Italian Edition by Mary A. Johnstone, London and Glasgow: Blackie & Son, 1935;

UNBESCHEID, Günther

Göttliche Könige und Königliche Götter
Entwurf zur Organisation von Kulten in Gorkhā und Jumlā,
Typewritten Manuscript,[5] Heidelberg, Year not mentioned, [in German];

VOHRA, Rohit

Ethno-Historicity of the Dards in Ladakh
Observations and Analysis,
Paper delivered at the IV International Seminar on Tibetan Studies in München in July 1985, Unpublished, 1985;

WALDEMAR, Prince [of Prussia]

Zur Erinnerung an die Reise des Prinzen Waldemar von Preußen nach Indien 1844-1846, Band I und II, Berlin, 1853, [in German];

WALLERSTEIN, Immanuel

The Modern World-System I
Capitalist Agriculture and the Origins of the European World-Economy in the Sixteenth Century,
New York: Academic Press, 1974;

The Modern World-System II
Mercantilism and the Consolidation of the European World-Economy 1600-1750,
New York: Academic Press, 1980;

WARD, F. Kingdon

Tibet as a Grazing Land,
in: *The Geographical Journal,* Vol. CX, Nos. 1-3, July-September 1947, Pp 60-75;

WEBER, Max

The Religion of India
Sociology of Hinduism and Buddhism,
Translated by H. Gerth and Don Martindale, The Free Press, 1958;

[5] Kindly provided by Prof. Dr Günther Sontheimer of the Südasien Institut der Universität Heidelberg for which gratitude is expressed.

WESSELS, C.

Early Jesuit Travellers in Central Asia 1603-1721,
The Hague: Martinus Nijhoff, 1924;

WHISTLER, Hugh

In the High Himalayas
Sport and Travel in the Rhotang and Baralacha, with some notes on the natural history of that area,
London: H. F. and G. Wetherby, 1924;

WILSON, Andrew

The Abode of Snow
Observations on a Journey from Chinese Tibet to the Indian Caucasus, through the upper valleys of the Himālaya,
II edn., Edinburgh and London: William Blackwood and Sons, MDCCCLXXVI, [1876];

WILSON, H.H. [Horace Hyman]

Summary Review of the Travels of Hiouen T'sang,
From the translation of the Si-yu-ki by M. Julien, and the Mémoire Analytique of M. Vivien de St. Martin, in: *Journal of the Royal Asiatic Society of Great Britain and Ireland,* Vol. XVII, MDCCCLX, [1860], Pp 106-137;

WITTFOGEL, Karl A.

Oriental Despotism
A Comparative Study of Total Power,
New Haven: Yale University Press, 1957;

ZORZA, Victor

How the Poor were made to pay for Expert Help,
in: *The Times,* London: Monday March 24, 1986, p. 16.

V. GOVERNMENT DOCUMENTS

ACTS, STANDING ORDERS AND INSTRUCTIONS

The entries under this heading have been arranged chronologically and not alphabetically within each sub-group. The Standing Orders mentioned can be seen in File No. KNR-IV-(DRA), F.C.'s Standing Orders, of the District Revenue Accountant Branch of the D.C.'s Office at Kālpa in Kinnaur District.

Acts and Rules

The Himachal Pradesh Land Revenue Act 1954, Act No. 6 of 1954, With Rules, Edited by Ravinder Thākur (Advocate), Simla: Saraswati Publishing House, 1983;

The Himachal Pradesh Nautor Land Rules 1968, (As amended up-to-date), Simla: Saraswati Publishing House, 1983;

The Himachal Pradesh Transfer of Land (Regulation) Act 1968, Act No. 15 of 1969, in: File No. KNR-III-(PSH)-IX-4/74 [Previous File No. KNR-IX-4(PSH)/74], D.C.'s Office, Kālpa;

The Himachal Pradesh Holdings (Consolidation and Prevention of Fragmentation) Act 1971, Act No. 20 of 1971, As amended up-to-date, Simla: Saraswati Publishing House, 1985;

The Himachal Pradesh Agricultural Credit Operations and Miscellaneous Provisions (Banks) Act, 1972, Act No. 7 of 1973, [Cyclostyled mimeograph with author];

The Himachal Pradesh Agricultural Credit Operations and Miscellaneous Provisions (Banks) Rules, 1975, [Cyclostyled Mimeo provided by the D.M., UCO Bank, Simla];

The Himachal Pradesh Ceiling On Land Holdings Act 1972, Act No. 19 of 1973, H.P. Acts, Notifications and Rules: H.P. Code, Vol. II, Simla, Pp 451-466;

The Himachal Pradesh Ceiling On Land Holdings Rules 1973, H.P. Code, Vol. II, Pp 467-492;

The Himachal Pradesh Tenancy and Land Reforms Act 1972, Act No. 8 of 1974, As amended up-to-date, Simla: Saraswati Publishing House, 1985;

The Himachal Pradesh Tenancy and Land Reforms Rules 1975, Simla: Saraswati Publishing House, 1983;

The Himachal Pradesh Public Moneys (Recovery of Dues) Act, 1973, Act No. 22 of 1973, Simla: The Deputy Controller of Printing and Stationery Department;

The Himachal Pradesh Relief of Agricultural Indebtedness Ordinance 1975, File No. KNR-II-41(PESHI)/75-II, D.C.'s Office, Kālpa;

The Himachal Pradesh Relief of Agricultural Indebtedness Act 1976, Act No. 17 of 1976, H.P. Code, Vol. V, Pp 792-804;

The Himachal Pradesh Relief of Agricultural Indebtedness Rules 1978, File No. KNR-II-41(PESHI)/74, D.C's Office, Kālpa;

The Himachal Pradesh Commodities Price Marking and Display Order 1977, For official use only, Simla-3: Deputy Controller of Printing and Stationery of Himachal Pradesh, 1977, [Reference No. P & SHPS-1620-DCS/77-10-10-77-1,500], 1978,
File No. KNR-II-41(PESHI)/74, D.C's Office, Kālpa;

The Himachal Pradesh Hoarding and Profiteering Prevention Order 1977, For official use only, Simla-3: Deputy Controller of Printing and Stationery of Himachal Pradesh, 1977, [Reference No. P & SHPS-1620-DCS/77-10-10-77-1,500];

INSTRUCTIONS

Letter No. 1-13/72-Rev. I(II) dated Simla-171002, the 8th October 1976,
From: Shri U.N. Sharma,
Chief Secretary to Himachal Pradesh Government,
To: 1. All Administrative Secretaries to Himachal Pradesh Government,
2. All Heads of Departments in Himachal Pradesh,
3. All Deputy Commissioners in Himachal Pradesh,
Subject: Recovery of Government Dues-Instructions regarding;

Memorandum No. PCH-H-A(3)-2/76 dated Simla-2, the 18th of March 1977,
From: The Director of Panchayati Raj,
Himachal Pradesh, Simla-2,

To: All the Deputy Commissioners in Himachal Pradesh,
All the District Dev. and Panchayat Officers / District Panchayat Officers in Himachal Pradesh,
All the Block Development Officers in Himachal Pradesh,
Subject: H.P. Relief of Agricultural Indebtedness Act, 1976- Instructions Regarding,

File No. 2-A(3)-2/76 of the Revenue Department in the Secretariat at Simla;
Notification No. Rev-2-A(3)-2/76 dated Simla-2, 16 January 1978,

Government of Himachal Pradesh, Revenue Department, KNR-IX-4(PSH)/74, D.C.'s Office, Kālpa;

Demi Official Letter No. REV. 2.F.(2)-5/76-II, dated Simla 171002, the 28th of April 1980,
From: P.P. Srivastava, I.A.S.
Financial Commissioner,
To: Jogishwar Singh, I.A.S.
Deputy Commissioner,
Kinnaur District at Kālpa,
Regarding accuracy of the information to be sent to the Government under the Relief of Agricultural Indebtedness Act of 1976;

Letter No. 10-1/80-Commr, dated the 6th October 1980,
From: The Commissioner,
Simla Division, H.P.
To: All the Deputy Commissioners in Himachal Pradesh,
Subject: Purchase of land by non-agriculturists under Section 118 of the H.P. Tenancy and Land Reforms Act of 1972, File No. KNR-IX-4(PSH)/74, D.C.'s Office, Kālpa, p. 387;

Letter No. Rev. 2-F(2)5/76-II, dated Simla-2 the 1st August 1981,
From: Shri Anupam Dhar, I.A.S.
Financial Commissioner,
Himachal Pradesh
To: 1. The Divisional Commissioners, Simla and Kangra,
2. All the Deputy Commissioners in Himachal Pradesh,
Subject: Implementation of H.P. Relief of Agricultural Indebtedness Act 1976-Statistical Data regarding, File No. Rev. 2-F-(2)5/76-II, Revenue Department, The Secretariat, Simla;

Manual on Integrated Rural Development Programme, Government of India, New Delhi: Ministry of Rural Reconstruction, January 1980,
[Reference No. MGIPCBE-82-2MRR/ND/79-20.2.80];

Memorandum No. HPFC. 6338 dated Simla-171001, 9.9.1982,
From: Shri K.C. Pandeya, I.A.S.
Chief Secretary to Government of Himachal Pradesh and
Chairman, H.P. Financial Corporation,
To: i) The Financial Commissioner (Revenue), H.P.,
ii) The Divisional Commissioner Simla / Dharamsala,
iii) All the Deputy Commissioners in Himachal Pradesh,
Subject: Recovery of dues of the H.P. State Financial Corporation as arrears of Land Revenue under the H.P. Public Moneys (Recovery of Dues) Act, 1973, as amended by Himachal Pradesh Public Moneys (Recovery of Dues) (Amendment) Act, 1982;

STANDING ORDERS

Standing Order No. 5: Inspections, Gazette Extraordinary Himachal Pradesh, Simla, Saturday 28 July 1982, No. 1134-Rājpatra-28-7-82-1,572, Simla: Controller of Printing and Stationery;

Standing Order No. 29: Coercive Processes, III Reprint, Simla: Commercial Printing Works, 18th December 1951, [Original Issue = dated 28th July 1909];

Standing Order No. 55: Registers, II Reprint, Simla: Controller of Printing and Stationery Punjab, 13th September 1952, [Original Issue = 22nd July 1909];

Official Correspondence Other Than Instructions

Letter No. nil dated nil
From: Satish Mehra,
Manager, Punjab National Bank, Peo,
To: The Deputy Commissioner,
Kinnaur, Kālpa,
Subject: Rural Indebtedness: 20 Point Programme;

Letter No. 2656, dated Pooh the 6th of November 1976,
From: The Tahsildar Pooh,
District Kinnaur,
To: The Deputy Commissioner,
Kinnaur District, Kālpa,
Subject: Information regarding eradication of Rural Indebtedness under the Implementation of the H.P. Relief of Agricultural Indebtedness Act, 1976,
File No. KNR-IX-4(PSH)/74, D.C.'s Office, Kālpa;

Letter No. OK/76-3662 dated Nichar the 14th December, 1976,
From: The Tahsildar Nichar,
Kinnaur District, H.P.
To: The Deputy Commissioner,
Kinnaur District, Kālpa,
Subject: Survey of Persons benefited by the operation of the H.P. Relief of Agricultural Indebtedness Act, 1976,
File No. KNR-IX-4(PSH)/74, D.C.'s Office, Kālpa, p. 35;

Letter No. KNR-I-41(Peshi)/75-II dated Kālpa-172108 the 3rd of February, 1977,
From: The Deputy Commissioner,
Kinnaur District, Kālpa,
To: The Divisional Commissioner,
Himachal Pradesh, Simla-2,
Subject: Survey of Persons benefited by the operation of the H.P. Relief of Agricultural Indebtedness Act, 1976,
File No. KNR-I-41(PESHI)/75-Vol. II, D.C.'s Office, Kālpa;

Letter No. 18/KNR/SPK/82 dated 11th June 1982,
From: Mr P.C. Pande,
Private Secretary to the Speaker,
H.P. Vidhan Sabha,
To: The Deputy Commissioner,
District Kinnaur, Kālpa,
Subject: Contravention of the Himachal Pradesh Transfer of Land (Regulation) Act, 1968, [Letter marked 'URGENT'];

Letter No. KNR-IX-4(PSH)/74-8820 dated Kālpa-172108, the 20th September 1983,
From: The Deputy Commissioner,
Kinnaur District at Kālpa,
To: The Commissioner,
Shimla Division, Shimla-2,

Subject: Recommendations of the Commissioner for Scheduled Castes and Scheduled Tribes for the period 1979-81-Follow-Up Action;

Documents from the Directorate of Economics and Statistics, Government of Himachal Pradesh, Simla - 171001,

Review of Achievements, Kinnaur District, 1970-71;

Evaluation Study of Kinnaur District, 1971;

Statistical Abstract District Kinnaur 1974-75, Cyclostyled Mimeo;

Statistical Abstract District Kinnaur 1975-76, Cyclostyled Mimeo;

Statistical Abstract District Kinnaur 1976-77, Cyclostyled Mimeo;

Zila Sānkhyiki Sārāmsh Kinnaur 1978, [District Statistical Abstract Kinnaur. The title is in Hindi but the document is in English], Cyclostyled Mimeograph;

Zila Kinnaur Ek Drishti Méiṅ 1979, [Overview of District Kinnaur 1979], Cyclostyled Mimeograph in Hindi;

Zila Sānkhyike Sārāṃsh Kinnaur 1979, Cyclostyled Mimeograph;

Statistical Abstract of Kinnaur District 1981, Cyclostyled Mimeograph;

Brief Facts Himachal Pradesh 1983;

Statistical Outline of Himachal Pradesh 1983;

Statistical Outline of Himachal Pradesh 1985;

Development Profile of Himachal Pradesh 1985;

Economic Review of Himachal Pradesh 1985;

Documents from the Scheduled Castes Development Department, Government of Himachal Pradesh, Simla - 171002,

Special Component Plan for Scheduled Castes, Draft Annual Plan 1983-84, November 1982;

Special Component Plan for Scheduled Castes 1984-85, District-wise Outlays, May 1984;

Documents from the Tribal Development Department Government of Himachal Pradesh, Simla 171002,

Tribal Sub-Plan 1979-80, 1979;

Tribal Sub-Plan 1980-81, 1980;

Benchmark Survey of the Integrated Tribal Development Project Kinnaur, 1980;

Tribal Sub-Plan 1981-82, I.T.D.P.-wise Budgeted Outlays and List of Works, 1981;

Project Report of the Integrated Tribal Development Project Kinnaur 1980-85, October 1981,

Cyclostyled Document;[6]

Draft Tribal Sub-Plan 1982-83, November 1981;

Tribal Sub-Plan 1980-85 and 1981-82, For Official Use only, 1981;

Tribal Sub-Plan 1982-83, I.T.D.P.-wise Budgeted Outlays and List of Works, 1982;

Draft Tribal Sub-Plan 1983-84, November 1982;

Draft Tribal Sub-Plan 1984-85, For Official Use only, November 1983;

Sātviṅ Panchavarshiya Jan-Jātiya Up-Yojana 1985-90 aivam Vārshik Yojana 1985-86 Prārūp, November 1984, [Draft Seventh Five-Year Tribal Sub-Plan 1985-90 and Annual Plan 1985-86, Title in Hindi but document in English!];

Other Government Documents (Published)

Census of India 1961, Volume XX, Part VI, No. I: A Village Survey of Kothi (Kālpa Sub-Division, District Kinnaur), Simla: Government of India Press, 1963;

Census of India 1981, Series 7: Himachal Pradesh, District Census Handbook: Kinnaur District, Parts XIII-A & B: Village and Town Directory, Village and Townwise Primary Census Abstract;

Constitution of India, With short notes, Lucknow: Eastern Book Company, 1985;

Himachal Pradesh Vidhān Sabha ki Kāryavāhi (Adhikrat Vivaran), Tratiya Vidhān Sabha, The Himachal Pradesh Credit Operations and Miscellaneous Provisions (Banks) Bill 1972 par vichār aivam pāran, Khand 2, Ank 3, 7 Joon 1982, Pp 107-125, [Proceedings of the Himachal Pradesh Legislative Assembly (Authorized Version), Third Legislative Assembly, Vol. 2, No. 3, 7 June 1982, These proceedings are recorded in both Hindi and English depending upon the language used by the legislators. Not for general public];

Himachal Pradesh Vidhān Sabha ki Kāryavāhi (Adhikrat Vivaran), Tratiya Vidhān Sabha, Khand 14, Aṅk 18, 26 Farvari 1976, The Himachal Pradesh Relief of Agricultural Indebtedness Bill 1976, Pp 75-86, [Proceedings of the Himachal Pradesh Legislative Assembly (Authorized Version), Third Legislative Assembly, Vol. 14, No. 18, 26 February 1976.];

India 1984, A Reference Annual, Compiled and edited by the Research and Reference Division, Ministry of Information and Broadcasting, Government of India, New Delhi: Publications Division, March 1985;

Punjab States Gazetteer, Vol. VIII: Simla Hill States, Part 2 A: Bashahr State, Lahore, 1911;

Report of the Working Group on Development of Scheduled Tribes during the Seventh Five-Year Plan 1985-90, For official use only, Government of India, New Delhi: Ministry of Home Affairs, December 1984;

Survey Report on Handicrafts of Kinnaur District (Himachal Pradesh), Issued by the Director of Industries, Himachal Pradesh, Simla-4, August 15, 1965;

[6] Prepared under the direct supervision of the author in his capacity as Chairman of the I.T.D.P. Kinnaur.

Other Government Documents (Unpublished)

A Brief Note on Sixth Plan in Kinnaur [sic], Typewritten Manuscript, [Prepared by Mr B.C. Kāndpāl, D.S.O., Kinnaur];

An Economic Profile of Pooh Cold Desert Area, A bench mark survey, A study carried out for the Desert Development Agency, Pooh (Himachal Pradesh), Cyclostyled Mimeograph, [Year not mentioned];

Appeal under Section 14 of the H.P. Land Revenue Act against the Order dated 31-12-76 passed by the Assistant Collector I Grade Kālpa in Case No. 9/XIII/76
Case No. 2/77, Date of Institution: 28-4-1977, Date of Decision: 20-9-1977,
In the Court of Shri R.C. Sharma, Collector, Kinnaur District, Kālpa, Himachal Pradesh,
110 Villagers of village Chini through their Attorneys S/Shri Bhagwan Singh, Bhag Chand Dass, Maya Das, Keshav Ram, Charan Sukh and Sunder Dass
--- Appellants
Versus
Shri Daulat Singh etc. 40 persons of village Chini, Tahsil Kālpa through Shri Daulat Singh, Sukh Dev and Duni Chand, residents of village Chini
--- Respondents;

Desert Development Programme in Pooh Sub-Division of Kinnaur Distirct,[7] Cyclostyled Mimeograph, Rural Integrated Development Department, Government of Himachal Pradesh, Simla, [Year not mentioned];

Draft Pooh Desert Development Plan 1982-87, Cyclostyled Mimeo, R.I.D. Department, Government of H.P., Simla, [Year not mentioned];

In the matter of encroachment in Peo Township area by Sh. Samku Ram s/o Shri Kansho Dass r/o Village Kothi, Tahsil Kālpa, District Kinnaur,
Before Shri Jogishwar Singh, I.A.S., District Collector, Kinnaur District, Kālpa,
Case No. 11-XIII/80, Date of Institution: 27.6.1980, Date of Decision: 9-9-1980, Typewritten Order;

Indebtedness Survey among Tribal Population of Kinnaur, Issued by the District Statistical Office Kinnaur, Typewritten Manuscript, [Year not mentioned];

Letter No. 28(22)/62-H-II dated the 27th October, 1964 from the Government of India to the Secretary to the Government of Himachal, Subject: Implementation of the Middle Income Group Housing Scheme in H.P., Typewritten Copy, File No. KNR-III-3(Dev)/75, D.C.'s Office, Kālpa, p. 53;

Naqal Report Bandobast Tarmim, Tahsil Chini, San 1928, Naqal Kuninda: Bhagat Ram Kapret, [Copy of the Revision Settlement Report, Tahsil Chini, 1928 A.D., Copyist: Bhagat Ram Kapret], Handwritten Manuscript in Urdu;[8]

Notes recorded by Shri R.K. Rath, I.A.S., Joint Secretary, Ministry of Rural Reconstruction, Government of India, New Delhi after touring Himachal Pradesh between the 7th to the 13th May, 1981, Sent vide Memo no. 3(5)/2/80-DPAP dated the 20th May 1981, Cyclostyled

[7] Prepared by the author in his capacity as the founder-Chairman of the Desert Development Agency Pooh.

[8] This is the only copy existing of this document. It is in the custody of the Settlement Officer, Simla and Kinnaur Districts at Sanjauli near Simla. The S.O., Mr S.S. Negi, I.A.S., very kindly allowed the author to make a photocopy of this document in January 1986.

Document;

Office Order No. KNR-V-82(NB)/80-81 dated the 31st. March 1981 from Mr Jogishwar Singh, I.A.S., Deputy Commissioner, Kinnaur District at Kālpa, Addressed to all Heads of Department in Himachal Pradesh among others, File No. KNR-V-82(NB)/80-81, D.C.'s Office, Kālpa, [This order fixes the rates of carriage for man and beast in Kinnaur for the succeeding year];

Office Order No. KNR-V-82(NB)/83 dated 19 April 1983 from Idem to Idem, File No. KNR-V-82(NB)/80-81, D.C.'s Office, Kālpa;

Proposed Plan for Introduction of Desert Development Project in Pooh Sub-Division of Kinnaur District, Typewritten Draft Document,[9] File No. DDP-Pooh/80, Pp 100-130;

Rules for Grant of Loans for construction of houses under Village Housing Projects Scheme (as amended up to 31.8.61), Administration of Himachal Pradesh, Typewritten Document, File No. KNR-III-3(Dev)/75, p. 42 ff, D.C.'s Office, Kālpa;

Seventh Course on Development Perspectives on District Administration, December 2-12 1980, Course Material, For Restricted Circulation only, Cyclostyled Mimeo, Hyderabad: National Institute of Rural Development, 1980;

Wājib-ul-Arz [Village Administration Paper] Ghodi Kāmru, Pargana Tukpa, Tahsil Chini, Riyāsat Rāmpur Bashahr, Bābat Tarmim Bandobast Sambat 1984 Bikrami, Signed by Tanzin Darjé Patwāri and Shiv Lāl Naib Tahsildār, [in Urdu], [This document pertains to the Revised Settlement of 1928 A.D. and is available in the District Record Room at Kālpa];

Wājib-ul-Arz Ghodi Panchgāon, Pargana Dussow, Tahsil Rāmpur, Tarmim Bandobast, 1928 A.D., [in Urdu], [Available in the Record Room of the S.D.M. at Rāmpur, District Simla];

VI. PERSONAL COMMUNICATIONS TO THE AUTHOR

A brief note on the Cooperative Movement in Kinnaur District, Handwritten Note, Prepared by the District Inspector Cooperatives, Kinnaur District, Rekong Peo, December 1985;

Brief Note on the National Employment Programme, Typewritten Note, Prepared by Mr Lāl Singh Verma, I.R.D. Assistant, D.C.'s Office, Kālpa, December 1985;

Brief Note on Soil Conservation Activities in Kinnaur District of Himachal Pradesh, Typewritten Note, Prepared by Er R.K. Singha, A.S.C.O., Kinnaur District, Rekong Peo, December 1985;

Brief Note on the Working of the Food and Supplies Department in Kinnaur District, Handwritten Note, Prepared by Mr Sharab Gyachho Negi, D.F.S.C., Kinnaur District, Rekong Peo, December 1985;

Crime Statement, Handwritten Document, Got prepared by Mr Ajit Lāl, I.P.S., Superintendent of Police, Kinnaur District, Rekong Peo, [Sent to the author vide Memo No. 1809 dated Rekong Peo 11th February 1982], 1982;

[9] Prepared post-haste by the author as D.C., Kinnaur because he was told that the Government of India needed the document for sanctioning funds for the project.

Distribution of High Yielding Varieties under Agriculture Production Programmes since inception of the District of Kinnaur, Cyclostyled Mimeo, [Communicated by Mr B.C. Negi, D.A.O., Kinnaur District, Kālpa to the author vide letter no. Agr 5-12/80-3919 dated Kālpa the 4th of February 1982], 1982;

Economic Upliftment [sic], Typewritten Note, Prepared by Mr P.N. Negi, D.W.O., Kinnaur District, Rekong Peo, December 1985;

Letter dated November 5, 1982 from the Hon. Lady Betjeman [née Chetwode],[10] in Manāli to the author in Kālpa;

Letter dated January 9, 1983 from Idem in New Delhi to the author in Lausanne, Switzerland;

Letter dated February 10, 1983 from Idem in London, England to Idem in Cari, Switzerland;

Letter dated March 20, 1984 from Idem in Hay-on-Wye, England to Idem in Paris, France;

Letter dated 27.VII.85 from Idem in Hay-on-Wye, England to Idem in Heidelberg, West Germany;

Letter dated February 22, 1986 from Idem in Hay-on-Wye, England to Idem in Heidelberg, West Germany;[11]

Letter dated May 13, 1985 from Mr S.C. Girotra, Assistant General Manager, UCO Bank, Bombay to the author in Heidelberg, West Germany;

Letter dated July 13, 1985 from Idem in Bombay to Idem in Heidelberg, West Germany;

Letter No. 21 April 1986 from Dr N.J. Allen of the Institute of Social Anthropology, Oxford University, in Oxford to the author in Heidelberg, West Germany;

Note on the Integrated Rural Development Programme in respect of Kinnaur District (H.P.) from the Date of its Inception, Typewritten Note, Prepared by Mr Lāl Singh Verma, I.R.D. Assistant, D.C.'s Office, Kālpa, December 1985;

Socio-Economic Problems of Kinnaur, Typewritten Note, Prepared by Mr B.C. Kāndpāl, D.S.O., Kinnaur District, Rekong Peo, December 1985;

Submission of Statistical Data in respect of Education Department, Handwritten Statement, Prepared by Mr A.S. Kapoor, D.E.O., Kinnaur District, Rekong Peo, [Communicated to the author vide Letter no. EDN- KNR (Board Branch) 8A/ 81- (Meeting 20 + 5 Point) dated Rekong Peo the 11th February 1982], 1982;

Veterinary Institutions in Kinnaur District, Typewritten Note in Hindi, Prepared by Dr M.S. Chahal, D.A.H.O., Kinnaur District, Rekong Peo, [Communicated to the author vide letter no. AHY- KNR- (C) 9/80- 285 dated 23rd January, 1982], 1982;

[10] Wife of Sir John Betjeman, poet laureate of Great Britain. Daughter of Field Marshal the First Baron Chetwode, Commander-in-Chief of the British Indian Army. A well-known writer of travelogues, an intrepid guide to selected tourist groups and an expert on temple architecture in the hills.

[11] This was just a few days before Lady Betjeman left to conduct a guided tour in Himachal Pradesh. She died there in the Outer Saraj area of Kulu District in March 1986.

VII. PROCEEDINGS OF VARIOUS COMMITTEE MEETINGS

These proceedings are all cyclostyled mimeographs. They have been classified here according to Committee alphabetically and then for the same committee chronologically.

District Consultative and Coordination Committee, Meeting held on May 28, 1980 under the Chairmanship of Mr Kashmir Chand, G.A. to D.C., in the absence of Mr Jogishwar Singh, I.A.S., D.C., Kinnaur, [in English];

District Consultative and Coordination Committee, Meeting held on October 6, 1980 under the Chairmanship of Mr Jogishwar Singh, I.A.S., D.C., Kinnaur District at Kālpa, [in English];

District Consultative and Coordination Committee, Meeting held on January 16, 1981 under the Chairmanship of Mr Parthasarathi Mitra, I.A.S., Officiating D.C., Kinnaur District at Kālpa, [in English];

District Consultative and Coordination Committee, Meeting held on May 21, 1983 under the Chairmanship of Mr Vivek Srivastava, I.A.S., D.C., Kinnaur District at Kālpa, [in English];

District Consultative and Coordination Committee, Meeting held on June 24, 1985 under the Chairmanship of Mr Vivek Srivastava, I.A.S., D.C., Kinnaur District at Kālpa, [in English];

District Consultative and Coordination Committee, Meeting held on Sept. 30th, 1985 under the Chairmanship of Mr Vivek Srivastava, I.A.S., D.C., Kinnaur District at Kālpa, [in English];

District Consultative and Coordination Committee, Meeting held on Nov. 28th., 1985 under the Chairmanship of Mr Vivek Srivastava, I.A.S., D.C., Kinnaur District at Kālpa;

District Grievances-cum-Food Advisory Committee, Meeting held on June 19, 1981 under the Chairmanship of Mr Thākur Sain Negi, Speaker, H.P. Vidhan Sabha, [in Hindi];

District Welfare Committee, Meeting held on April 20, 1981 under the Chairmanship of Mr Thākur Sain Negi, Speaker, H.P. Legislative Assembly, Simla, Meeting held in Kālpa, [in Hindi];

District Welfare Committee, Meeting held on August 17, 1981 under the Chairmanship of Mr Jogishwar Singh, D.C., Kinnaur District at Kālpa, [in Hindi];

Governing Body of the Desert Development Project Pooh, Meeting held on September 20, 1982 under the Chairmanship of Mr Jogishwar Singh, I.A.S., D.C., Chairman, D.D.P. Agency, [in Hindi];

Governing Body of the Desert Development Project Pooh, Meeting held on October 7, 1982 under the Chairmanship of Mr G.P. Chawla, Deputy Secretary, Government of India, Ministry of Rural Reconstruction, New Delhi, [in Hindi];

Governing Body of the I.R.D. Agency Kinnaur, Meeting held on March 25, 1980 under the Chairmanship of Mr Jogishwar Singh, I.A.S., D.C., Kinnaur District at Kālpa, [in Hindi];

Governing Body of the I.R.D. Agency Kinnaur, Meeting held on June 27, 1980 under the Chairmanship of Mr Jogishwar Singh, I.A.S., D.C., Kinnaur District at Kālpa, [in Hindi];

Governing Body of the I.R.D. Agency Kinnaur, Meeting held on March 26, 1981 under the Chairmanship of Mr Jogishwar Singh, I.A.S., D.C., Kinnaur District at Kālpa, [in Hindi];

Governing Body of the I.R.D. Agency Kinnaur, Meeting held on August 19, 1982 under the Chairmanship of Mr Jogishwar Singh, I.A.S., D.C., Kinnaur District at Kālpa, [in Hindi];

New Twenty Point Programme Committee, Meeting held on August 5, 1983 under the Chairmanship of Mr Thākur Sain Negi, Speaker, H.P. Vidhān Sabha, [in Hindi];

Proceedings of the Meeting of Heads of Department concerned with the Desert Development of Pooh area, Held on 30th April 1981 at 3.00 P.M. in the Chamber of the Agricultural Production Commissioner, H.P., Simla under the Chairmanship of Mr B.C. Negi, I.A.S., A.P.C., Himachal Pradesh, [in English];

Project Advisory Committee, Meeting held on November 15, 1980 under the Chairmanship of Mr Jogishwar Singh, I.A.S., D.C., Chairman, P.A.C., [in Hindi];

Project Advisory Committee, Meeting held on February 2, 1981 under the Chairmanship of Mr Jogishwar Singh, I.A.S., D.C., Chairman, P.A.C., [in Hindi];

Twenty Point Economic Programme Committee, Meeting held on September 5, 1984 under the Chairmanship of Mr Vivek Srivastava, I.A.S., D.C., Kinnaur District at Kālpa, [in Hindi];

VIII. PRIVATELY OWNED UNPUBLISHED DOCUMENTS

Copy of a Sanad conferring the Poāri Jāgir on the Wazir of Poāri by Rāja Mahindar Singh of Bushahr, dated 4-8-1816, in possession of Wazir Amar Singh Negi of Poāri;

Copy of an Order dating from 1831 issued by Rāja Shamsher Singh specifying the arrangements to be made for Devta Badrināth of Kāmru and forbidding people from hunting in his jungles;[12]

Copy of an Order dating from 1930, issued by Rāja Padam Singh, forbidding people from dishonest behaviour in loan transactions;

Copy of an Order from Rāja Padam Singh directing Miāṅ Sundar Singh to accompany the Tikka to Simla;

Copy of an Order of Rāja Padam Singh from Chaitra 1979 Sambat laying down directions for the entourage supposed to accompany the Tikka Sahib to Simla;

Copy of a Court Judgement under Section 188 Indian Penal Code in the case of Devta Bairiṅg Nāg of Sangla versus Devta Badrināth of Kāmru, dated 13-12-1925;

Copy of a Court Order dated 6-1-1917 in the case of the Thākurdwāra, Ghodi Kāmru, Pargana Tukpa;

Copy of a Court Judgement on judicial stamp paper in a case under Section 500 Indian Penal Code without any date;

Draft of a letter from Rāja Padam Singh of Bushahr to Sir Edward Douglas Maclagan, K.C.S.I., K.C.I.E., I.C.S., Governor of the Punjab, about the former's political status, [in English, with corrections in the Rāja's own handwriting];

[12] Unless otherwise indicated, all the documents listed here are in the possession of Negi Goverdhan Singh of Sangla.

Draft of a Report from the Acting Dewān of Bushahr State to the Dewān of Bushahr State at Rāmpur giving details of the disturbances led by Master Anu Lāl in Gaura Village, Dated 9/1/2005, [1948 A.D.];

Genealogical Chart of the Royal House of Bushahr, [in Tānkri], [in possession of Lambardār Keshwa Singh of Sangla];

Genealogical Chart of the Royal House of Bushahr, [in Urdu];

Genealogical Chart of the Royal House of Bushahr, [in Tibetan];

Genealogical Chart in Persian showing the last 14 Rājās of Bushahr on one side and the last 14 Wazirs of Poāri on the other side with the name of each Wazir being shown parallel to that of the Rāja under whom he served as Wazir, [in possession of Wazir Amar Singh of Poāri];

Handwritten copy of the proceedings of a public assembly (Ijlās) in 1935 in Rāmpur under the chairmanship of the Rāja of Bushahr;

Letter dated 21/ K/ 2002 [1945 A.D.] from Rāja Padam Singh of Bushahr to Negi Goverdhan Singh in Sangla, [in Urdu, in the Rāja's own handwriting];

Memorandum No. C.2/7-(4)/47 dated Simla, the 9th August 1947 from J.E.A. Bazalgatte, Political Agent, Punjab Hill States, Simla to the President, Council of Administration, Bashahr State, Simla, ordering division of property of the deceased Rāja Sir Padam Singh of Bushahr, [in English. Negi Goverdhan Singh was to supervise this operation];

Memorandum dated 22nd December 1947 from Rāni Sāhiba Katochi of Rāmpur Bushahr to the President, Council of Administration, Rāmpur Bushahr; [in English. The Rāni's signatures are in broken Hindi];

Order [Copy] dated the 5th December 1898, passed by A. Meredith Esquire, Superintendent, Hill States, Simla, on the claim of Ran Bahādur Singh to proprietary and other rights in Dodra Kwar, [in English. Certified true copy.];

Order dated 31-05-04 [1947 A.D.] by the President, Council of Administration, Bushahr State, directing Negi Goverdhan Singh to draw up a list of the deceased Rāja's property and to supervise its division, [in Hindi];

IX. OTHER SOURCES

B.B.C. World Service Broadcast, Report from the B.B.C.'s Beijing correspondent Mark Brain reporting from Tibet about conditions there, Produced by Adam Raphael, July 24, 1985, 06.30 hours G.M.T., [Listened to at 08.30 hours at Heidelberg by the author]

INDEXES

INDEX I (GENERAL TERMS)

INDEX II (NAMES OF PERSONS)

INDEX III (NAMES OF PLACES)

INDEX IV (GEOGRAPHICAL TERMS)

APPENDIX

OTHER ACCOUNTS: UNWARRANTED CONCLUSIONS.

S.C. Bajpai suggests in his book on Kinnaur that the "earliest traditional organized political or social life in these hills was that of the janapada type, and the area being inaccessible to a greater extent the same type of organization continued up to a much recent period. Perhaps there is much truth in the claims of certain ruling families who trace their origin in a much remote past going back to Mahabharata times".[1] This is intelligent guesswork, not researched history. Bajpai goes on to suggest that Kinnaur must have formed a part of Ashok's, Kanishka's and Samudragupta's empires.[2] No convincing proof is cited as evidence for this assertion. It is mentioned only that these empires were extensive and included territories to the east and west of Kinnaur. Similar speculation is used by Bajpai to make Kinnaur a part of Yashodharman of Malwa's and of Harsha Vardhana's kingdoms.[3] The presence of an Ashokan rock edict at Kālsi in the Dehra Doon district, far from serving as a basis for inclusion of Kinnaur in the Ashokan empire, as has been argued by a scholar,[4] can serve exactly the opposite purpose. These rock edicts were generally set up near the boundaries of the empire. Kālsi is separated from Kinnaur by the Dhaula Dhār range, a high ridge. It is more logical to presume that the frontier remained near Kālsi, which was far more easily accessible from the plains than Kinnaur, and did not not extend over the intervening snow-bound high ranges to Kinnaur. Similarly, if Kinnaur were a part of the Kushana or Gupta empires, why do we not find any inscriptions, architectural remains or documents to establish this fact? Kushana inscriptions have been discovered in Ladakh, an area equally remote or even remoter than Kinnaur. One cannot argue that such evidence has not been found because of the hard climatic and geographic conditions in Kinnaur. In this case why is such evidence found in Ladakh? It seems more reasonable to deduce that Ladakh was a part of the Kushana empire and not Kinnaur, if discovery of inscriptions can be taken as an indicator to this effect.

Bajpai offers a novelty in that he questions the entire thesis of there having ever been some kind of Tibetan (Bhot) period in Kinnaur's history.[5] He maintains, "it appears that the Tibetan thrust was only northwards along the river Indus leading them to Sinkiang. They never crossed the Sutlej and hence there was no Tibetan rule in Kinnaur".[6] In his zeal to prove this hypothesis, Bajpai goes on to say, "Had they ever crossed Sutlej and proceeded to Kinnaur, what stopped them from reaching the fertile plains of Punjab, and why had they taken the trouble to proceed across the entire mountainous region of Ladakh and Sinkiang?...From cultural and religious points of view, even now we do not have the Bhot influence in the interior regions of Kinnaur. It is only on the borders of Tibet with Kinnaur that has the influence of Buddhism and Bhot culture...To me it appears the assertion of Rāhul Sānkrityāyan which had found place in the Gazetteer of Kinnaur regarding the Bhot rule's

[1] Bajpai, S.C., 1981, p. 49.

[2] Ibid, Pp 50-51.

[3] Ibid, Pp 51-52.

[4] Sānkrityāyan, Rāhul, 1957, Pages 2 and 295.

[5] Ibid, p. 54, p. 56, p. 137.

[6] Ibid, p. 56.

first phase is thoroughly...erroneous".[7] Regarding the second phase of Bhot rule, Bajpai is equally emphatic. He feels that the "activities of Ladakh rulers never came below Spiti. To trace any kind of Bhot rule in Kinnaur in the second phase also seems to be as much misleading as that in the first phase".[8]

Bajpai's reasoning appears simplistic. It reflects a world view[9] treating Punjab and the Northern Indian plains as the sole objective of foreign incursions into India. He seems to ignore the fact that the Tibetans, unlike invaders from the North West across the Khyber Pass, would simply not be interested in conquering or marching to Punjab. This would have meant going to a climatically insupportable area for them at low, hot altitudes. It would have also meant organization of an intolerably long supply line across mountainous terrain involving crossing several high ridges; encountering much stronger military opposition in the North Indian plains; and, perhaps most important of all, it was just not in the strategic religio-political designs of the Tibetan State. The Tibetans extended their empire westwards because their trade routes, ethnic and religious affinity and the climatic conditions dictated such expansion. Striking out on a hazardous detour towards Punjab would have made no sense for them. They did not have the ambition of ruling in Delhi.

As far as the religious and cultural influence of Bhot rule in Kinnaur is concerned, even a casual visitor to the area cannot fail to be struck by the strong influence of Buddhism of the Tibetan type on extended areas of Kinnaur. It is a fallacy to deny this and maintain that such influence exists only in border areas and not in the interior areas. In fact, such influence is quite perceptible precisely in the most interior areas like Asrang, Lippa, Hanǵrang valley, Pooh, Moorang, Kuno, Chārang and Nesang of the Pooh Sub-Division. It can also be seen in areas of Central Kinnaur like Kālpa, Poāri, Ribba, Rispa, Bārang, Purbani and Roghi, albeit to a smaller extent. This influence has been so pervasive that some writers have described Kinnaura religion as a hybrid or mixed blend of Buddhism and Hinduism.[10] A traveller in Kinnaur can notice Buddhist chhortens (m'cod-rten) as far south as Tranda and Chaura on the border with Simla District. Lāmas, food habits, housebuilding forms and language have all been strongly influenced by the Tibetans. This influence is weaker in the south towards Simla District but never absent. It gradually increases as we move northwards towards Pooh and reaches its peak in the Hangrang valley. Hindu and Buddhist temples sometimes share even the same courtyards, as at Sangla. The importance of Buddhist cultural influence can be gauged from the fact that a Buddhist temple was constructed under state patronage at Rāmpur. It flies in the face of reality to deny Buddhist cultural influence. What can be debated is the limit of its extent, not the fact of its existence.

[7] Ibid.

[8] Ibid, p. 57.

[9] The German word Weltanschauung is meant here.

[10] Please see the following:

(1) Massieu, Mme. Isabelle, 1914, p. 22. The original text reads: *"Le peuple Kanauri ne parait pas susceptible d'évangélisation. Sa religion tient à la fois du brahmanisme, du lamaisme et surtout du démonisme".*
Translation mine;

(2) Bruske, J.: Jahresbericht der Station Chini - Jahr 1900, Rubric S.e.1.a., M.D., J.N. 81, empf.10/3/01, [Herrnhut Archives];

(3) Deuster, R.H., 1939, p. 77;

(4) Cunningham, J.D., 1844, p. 195.

All these authors describe the religion of Kinnaur as an inseparable amalgam of Buddhism of the Tibetan variety and Hinduism of the hill variety.

S.S. Chib, who has published an account of Kinnaur in 1984,[11] does take a more balanced approach in making deductions out of the available plethora of myth and legend but even he cannot resist making some sweeping generalizations. For example, "The entire Kinner tract also came under the Gugé empire of Tibet. The Gugé rulers governed these people from Lhasa...The agents of the Gugé ruler, who lusted after women, power and money started facing defiance by the hitherto innocent and weak Kinnauras. The incidents of defiance and rebellion came as eye openers for the Lhasa emperor. He established his seat of rule near the border of Kinnaur and started redressing the grievances of the people".[12]

There is absolutely no historical evidence that the entire area of Kinnaur was under Gugé rule. It is a complete fallacy to claim that the Gugé rulers governed from Lhāsa. Their seat of government was at Tsaparang on the upper Satluj.[13] There is absolutely no evidence to show that the capital of Gugé was shifted near the Kinnaur border to enable the ruler to ensure speedier redressal of Kinnaura grievances. These are flights of imagination. From what little is known of the rulers of Gugé, some of them were priest kings. Kinnaur was never a very important constituent of the Kingdom of Gugé, else better supporting evidence would be available.[14]

Chib makes a manifestly apparent error when he says, "Rāja Kehri Singh died in 1811. He was succeeded by his minor son Mahinder Singh. The administration was, however, carried (sic) by the hereditary wazirs and Rāja Kehri Singh's widow...The Gurkhas...started raiding and plundering during the last days of Rāja Kehri Singh".[15] These repeated references show that no printer's devil is involved here. The author writes correctly in the preceding paragraph of his book that in the Tibet-Ladakh-Mughal War "Rāja Kehri Singh helped Tibet to emerge victorious".[16] This war is dated to the mid-17th. century by A.H. Francke and to 1681-83 A.D. by Luciano Petech.[17] This would make Rāja Kehri Singh between 145 to 185 years old

[11] Chib, S.S.,: Kanauras of the Trans-Himalaya, New Delhi, 1984.

[12] Chib, S.S., 1984, p. 9.

[13] For information about Gugé, please see:

(1) Wessels, C., 1924, Pp 63-64;

(2) Young, G. Mackworth: General Account of Mr Mackworth Young's Mission to Gartok, Report enclosed with letter No. 2819-S-(Pol.) dated Simla, the 25th of September 1912 from C.A. Barron, Chief Secretary to Government Punjab, to the Supdt., Hill States, Simla, Section III, p. 10;

(3) Fraser, J.B., 1820, p. 291.

All these documents mention that Tsaparang was the capital of Gugé and not Lhāsa, as maintained by S.S. Chib.

[14] For information about the rulers of Gugé, please see:

(1) Francke, A.H., 1926, [Vol. II], Pp 167-171;

(2) Govinda, Lāma Anangarika, 1970, Appendix 2, Pp 294-297;

(3) Petech, L., 1980, Pp 85-111;

(4) Tucci, Giuseppe, Indo-Tibetica III, 1936;

(5) Francke, A.H.: Die Jesuitenmission von Tsaparang im Lichte der tibetischen Urkunden, in: Zeitschrift für Missionswissenschaft, Fünfzehnter Jahrgang, 1925, Pp 269-278.

[15] Chib, S.S., 1984, p.13.

[16] Ibid.

[17] Petech, L., 1947, Pp 169-199.
However, the chronology of the war has been revised to 1679-1684 A.D. by Zahiruddin Ahmad on page 349 of his article. Please see: Ahmad, Zahiruddin: New Light On The Tibet-Ladakh-Mughal War Of 1679-84, in: East and West, New Series, Vol. 18, Nos. 3-4, Sept.-Dec. 1968, Pp 340-361.

at the time of his 'death' in 1811 A.D., presuming he was about 25 years old at the time of this war. Also, genealogies show well that Rāja Ugar Singh was the father of Rāja Mahinder Singh.[18] It is a clear mistake to try and fit Kehri Singh into the period of the Gorkha invasion of Bushahr. Such could have been the case only if the ruling chief had taken the same name, in this case Kehri Singh, as was the case with certain chiefs in the Dérājāt area of Punjab and Baluchistan.[19] This was not the case in Bushahr.

Works on Kinnaur have borrowed, with acknowledgement or otherwise, from Rāhul Sānkrityāyan's book 'Kinner Desh'. Rāhul toured the area at length and got excavations conducted at certain places. His analysis is original and informative but not always sound. He divides Kinnaura history into five periods:-

(A) Period of the Ancient Kinnaras and of the Pre-Khash (Copper Age).
(B) Pre-Bhot Period (till 7th Century A.D),
(C) Bhot Period (till the 13th Century A.D.),
(D) Thākurshahi Period (Till the end of the 15th Century A.D.),
(E) Period of the Kāmru (Rāmpur) Dynasty (Till February 1948 A.D.).[20]

On the basis of visual identification of some idols in Kothi village and the traditional renown of the wine made in Pargana Shua, Rāhul tries to establish that Kothi was the seat of a Gurjara-Pratihara prince from Kanauj.[21] His identification of the age of the idol in question is challengeable as it is in a dilapidated condition. Without scientific methods like carbon dating we cannot build up an entire sequence of events on such visible dating. While wine from Shua may well have been carried by Kinnaura shepherds to areas across the Dhaula Dhār range to Garhwal from where it may have found its way into the palaces of the rulers of Kanauj, as maintained by Rāhul, we cannot deduce therefrom that a prince from Kanauj fled to Kothi and established his rule there. It amounts to making a mountain out of a molehill. Rāhul himself cautions that a final decision can be made only after "discovery of some inscription, finding which is not impossible".[22] No such inscription has been found till today to support Rāhul's hypothesis.

These few examples show how we should not try to establish elaborate chronological sequences or explanations on insufficient evidence. We should base our findings on the sources available which, even if not copious, yield some cogent evidence. The problem appears to be that all the interpretations of Bushahr's history tend to see its evolution as the result of the decline of some earlier existing larger empire; be it the Maurya, the Kushana, the Gupta, the Gurjara-Pratihara or the Bhot. This predilection also stresses the role of conquest and of the ingress of foreign powers as the sole causal agents in the evolution of Bushahr. This is just not justifiable with the source material available.

[18] Please see:

(1) Petech, L., 1947, Footnote 8, Pp 175-176;
(2) A genealogical chart in Tānkri script in Lambardār Keshwa Singh's possession in Sangla village. This chart contains 96 names and is said to be a copy of the original in Tholing in Tibet;
(3) Genealogical chart in Urdu in possession of Negi Goverdhan Singh in Sangla village. It contains 121 names;
(4) Gazetteer, 1971, Appendix IV, Pp 366-368.

[19] Information given by Dr Inayatallah Baloch in Heidelberg. According to him, a certain chief in the Dérājāt always took the name Ismail Khan.

[20] Sānkrityāyan, Rāhul, 1957, p. 299.

[21] Ibid, Pp 302-303.

[22] Ibid, p. 212.

BEITRÄGE ZUR SÜDASIENFORSCHUNG

Stuttgart: Franz-Steiner-Verlag-Wiesbaden
ISSN 0170-3137

1 *Cultures of the Hindukush*: selected papers from the Hindu-Kush Cultural Conference held at Moesgård 1970 / ed.by Karl Jettmar. In collaboration with Lennart Edelberg. - 1974. XIV,146 p. ISBN 3-515-01217-6

2 Die Holztempel des oberen Kulutales: in ihren historischen, religiösen und kunstgeschichtlichen Zusammenhängen / von *Gabriele Jettmar*. - 1974. XI,133 S. ISBN 3-515-01849-2

3 Regionalism in Hindi novels / by *Indu Prakash Pandey*. - 1974. 179 p. ISBN 3-515-01954-5

4 *Community health and health motivation in South-East Asia*: proceedings of an international seminar organized by the German Foundation for International Development and the Institute of Tropical Hygiene and Public Health, South Asia Institute, University of Heidelberg, 22 October to 10 November 1973, Berlin / ed. by Hans Jochen Diesfeld and Erich Kröger. - 1974. VIII,199 p. ISBN 3-515-01990-1

5 Die britische Militärpolitik in Indien und ihre Auswirkungen auf den britisch-indischen Finanzhaushalt 1878-1910 / von *Werner Simon*. - 1974. VI,296 S. ISBN 3-515-01978-2

6 Die *wirtschaftliche Situation Pakistans nach der Sezession Bangladeshs* / von Winfried von Urff; Heinz Ahrens; Peter Lutz; Bernhard May; Wolfgang-Peter Zingel. - 1974. - XIX,453 S. ISBN 3-515-01979-0

7 Muslime und Christen in der Republik Indonesia / von *Wendelin Wawer*. - 1974. 326 S. ISBN 3-515-02042-X

8 The Muslim microcosm: Calcutta, 1918 to 1935 / by *Kenneth McPherson*. - 1974. VII,162 p. ISBN 3-515-01992-8

9 Adat und Gesellschaft: eine sozio-ethnologische Untersuchung zur Darstellung des Geistes- und Kulturlebens der Dajak in Kalimantan / von *Johannes Enos Garang*. - 1974. X,193 S. ISBN 3-515-02048-9

10 The Indo-English novel: the impact of the West on literature in a developing country / by *Klaus Steinvorth*. - 1975. III, 149 p. ISBN 3-515-02049-7

11 The position of Indian women in the light of legal reform: a socio-legal study of the legal position of Indian women as interpreted and enforced by the law courts compared and related to their position in the family and at work / by *Angeles J. Almenas-Lipowsky*. - 1975. IX,217 p. ISBN 3-515-02050-0

12 Zur Mobilisierung ländlicher Arbeitskräfte im anfänglichen Industrialisierungsprozess: ein Vergleich der Berufsstruktur in ausgewählten industrienahen und industriefernen Gemeinden Nordindiens / von *Erhard W. Kropp*. 2. unveränd. Aufl. - 1975. XVII, 231 S. ISBN 3-515-01976-6

13 Die Sozialisation tibetischer Kinder im soziokulturellen Wandel, dargestellt am Beispiel der Exiltibetersiedlung Dhor Patan (West Nepal) / von *Gudrun Ludwar*. - 1975. XI,209 S. ISBN 3-515-02063-2

14 Die Steuerung der Direktinvestitionen im Rahmen einer rationalen Entwicklungspolitik / von *Leo Rubinstein*. - 1975. XI,260 S. ISBN 3-515-02064-0

15 Ein erweitertes Harrod-Domar-Modell für die makroökonomische Programmierung in Entwicklungsländern: ein wachstumstheoretischer Beitrag zur Entwicklungsplanung / von *Axel W. Seiler*. - 1975. VII,230 S. ISBN 3-515-02092-6

16 *Islam in Southern Asia*: a survey of current research / ed. by Dietmar Rothermund. - 1975. VIII,126 p. ISBN 3-515-02095-0

17 *Aspekte sozialer Ungleichheit in Südasien* / hrsg. von Heinz Ahrens und Kerrin Gräfin Schwerin. - 1975. VII,215 S. ISBN 3-515-02096-6

18 Probleme interdisziplinärer Forschung: organisations- und forschungssoziologische Untersuchung der Erfahrungen mit interdisziplinärer Zusammenarbeit im SFB 16 unter besonderer Betonung des Dhanbad-Projektes / von *Dieter Blaschke*. Unter Mitarbeit von Ingrid Lukatis. - 1976. XI,201 S. ISBN 3-515-02131-0

19 Einflüss des Bergbaus auf die Beschäftigungsstruktur in ländlichen Gemeinden: gezeigt am Beispiel des Dhanbad-Distriktes, Bihar, Indien / von *Erhard W. Kropp*. - 1976. XII,184 S. ISBN 3-515-02132-9

20 Drei Jaina-Gedichte in Alt-Gujarāti: Edition, Übersetzung, Grammatik und Glossar / von *George Baumann*. - 1975.XVIII,176 S. ISBN 3-515-02177-9

21 Eigentumsbeschränkungen in Indien / von *Franz-Josef Vollmer*. - 1975. VIII,147 S. ISBN 3-515-02307-0

22 Nomaden von Gharjistān: Aspekte der wirtschaftlichen, sozialen und politischen Organisation nomadischer Durrani-Paschtunen in Nordwestafghanistan / von *Bernt Glatzer*. - 1977. XII, 234 S. ISBN 3-515-02137-X

23 Buddhistische Politik in Thailand: mit besonderer Berücksichtigung des heterodoxen Messianismus / von *Walter Skrobanek*. - 1976. VII,315 S. ISBN 3-515-02390-9

24 Lohnpolitik und wirtschaftliche Entwicklung: ein Beitrag zur Analyse der Verteilungsproblematik unter besonderer Berücksichtigung Indiens / von *Gunther Dienemann*. - 1977. VII,318 S. ISBN 3-515-02389-5

25 Der Gleichheitssatz in der Praxis des indischen Zivilverfahrens / von *Dierk Helmken*. - 1976. XII,286 S. ISBN 3-515-02134-5

26 Der Einfluss von Produktionstechniken auf die Produktion der Hauptfruchtarten im pakistanischen Punjab: methodische Probleme der Erfassung und Quantifizierung / von *Bernhard May*. - 1977. XVIII,403 S. ISBN 3-515-02580-4

27 Tai-Khamti phonology and vocabulary / by *Alfons Weidert*. - 1977. 92 p. ISBN 3-515-02582-0

28 Rudras Geburt: systematische Untersuchungen zum Inzest in der Mythologie der Brāhmaṇas / von *Joachim Deppert*. - 1977. LX, 396 S. ISBN 3-515-02583-9

29 Der Reisanbau im unteren Kirindi Oya-Becken: Analyse einer Reisbaulandschaft im Südosten der Insel Ceylon / von *Gisela Zaun-Axler*. - 1977. XIX, 286 S. ISBN 3-515-02584-7

30 *Faktoren des Gesundwerdens in Gruppen und Ethnien*: Verhandlungen des 2. Rundgesprächs 'Ethnomedizin' in Heidelberg vom 29. und 30. November 1974 unter Schirmherrschaft des Südasien-Instituts, Institut für Tropenhygiene und Öffentliches Gesundheitswesen und Seminar für Ethnologie / herausgegeben von Ekkehard Schröder. - 1977. XIII,125 S. ISBN 3-515-02585-5

31 Von Armut zu Elend: Kolonialherrschaft und Agrarverfassung in Chota Nagpur, 1858-1908 / von *Detlef Schwerin*. - 1977. XIX, 551 S. ISBN 3-515-02407-7

32 The Nilgiris: weather and climate of a mountain area in South India / by *Hans J. von Lengerke*. - 1977. XVIII,340 p. ISBN 3-515-02640-1

33 The social setting of Christian conversion in South India: the impact of the Wesleyan methodist missionaries on the Trichy-Tanjore diocese with special reference to the Harijan communities of the mass movement area 1820-1947 / by *Sundararaj Manickam*. - 1977. VIII,296 p. ISBN 3-515-02639-8

34 Religiöses Volksbrauchtum in Afghanistan: islamische Heiligenverehrung und Wallfahrtswesen im Raum Kabul / von *Harald Einzmann*. - 1977. IX,346 S. ISBN 3-515-02652-5

35 Untersuchungen des Königswahlmotivs in der indischen Märchenliteratur: Pañcadivyādhivāsa / von *Gabriella Steermann-Imre*. - 1977. XII,316 S. ISBN 3-515-02597-9

36 Schichtungsmodelle, Schichtungstheorien und die sozialstrukturelle Rolle von Erziehung: eine theoretische Diskussion und eine empirische Fallstudie aus Indien / von *John P. Neelsen*. - 1976. XII,240 S. ISBN 3-515-02638-X

37 Innovationsfaktoren in der Landwirtschaft Indiens: gezeigt am Beispiel ausgewählter Dörfer des Dhanbad Distrikts, Bihar, Indien / von *Harald Hänsch*. - 1977. XII, 277, 34, 4 S. ISBN 3-515-02704-1

38 Der indisch-pakistanische Konflikt und seine wirtschaftlichen und sozialen Kosten für Pakistan in den Jahren 1958-1968 / von *Hans Frey*. - 1978. XIX,234 S. ISBN 3-515-02716-5

39 Arleng Alam: die Sprache der Mikir; Grammatik und Texte / von *Karl-Heinz Grüssner*. - 1978. 222 S. ISBN 3-515-02717-3

40 Indian merchants and the decline of Surat, c. 1700-1750 / by *Ashin Das Gupta*. - 1978. X,305 p. ISBN 3-515-02718-1

41 Bangladesh: constitutional quest for autonomy, 1950-1971 / by *Moudud Ahmed*. - 1978. XVI,373 p. ISBN 3-515-02908-7

42 Bestimmungsgründe und Alternativen divergierender regionaler Wachstumsverläufe in Entwicklungsländern: eine theoretische und empirische Analyse unter besonderer Berücksichtigung der Regionalentwicklung in Ost- und Westpakistan 1947-1970 / von *Heinz-Dietmar Ahrens*. - 1978. XV,392 S. ISBN 3-515-02827-7

43 Das tibetische Handwerkertum vor 1959 / von *Veronika Ronge*. - 1978. VIII, 181 S. ISBN 3-515-02793-9

44 Hunza und China (1761-1891): 130 Jahre einer Beziehung und ihre Bedeutung für die wirtschaftliche und politische Entwicklung Hunzas im 18. und 19. Jahrhundert / von *Irmtraud Müller-Stellrecht*. - 1978. VII,139 S. ISBN 3-515-02799-8

45 Interdependenzen zwischen gesamtwirtschaftlichem Wachstum und regionaler Verteilung in Pakistan / von *Heinz Ahrens und Wolfgang-Peter Zingel*. - 1978. XXXVI,882 S. ISBN 3-515-02830-7

46 Institutioneller Agrarkredit und traditionelle Schuldverhältnisse: Distrikt Dhanbad, Bihar, Indien / von *Hans-Dieter Roth*. - 1978. XIX,364 S. ISBN 3-515-02795-5

47 Comparative evaluation of road construction techniques in Nepal / by *Hans C. Rieger and Binayak Bhadra*. - 1979. XIII,257 p. ISBN 3-515-03120-0

48 Labour utilization and farm income in rural Thailand: results of case studies in rural villages, 1969-70 / by *Friedrich W. Fuhs* in cooperation with Gregory Capellari and Fred V. Goericke. - 1979. XVI, 371 p. ISBN 3-515-03001-8

49 *Aruṇantis Śivajñānasiddhiyār*: die Erlangung des Wissens um Śiva oder um die Erlösung. Unter Beifügung einer Einleitung und Meykaṇṭadevas Śivajñānabodha aus dem Tamil übersetzt und kommentiert von Hilko Wiardo Schomerus. Hrsg. von Hermann Berger, Ayyadurai Dhamotharan und Dieter B. Kapp. 2 Bde. - 1981.XVI,745 S. ISBN 3-515-03874-4

50 Tamil dictionaries: a bibliography / by *Ayyadurai Dhamotharan*. - 1978. 185 p. ISBN 3-515-03005-0

51 Die Problematik regionaler Entwicklungsunterschiede in Entwicklungsländern: eine theoretische und empirische Analyse, dargestellt am Beispiel Pakistans unter Verwendung der Hauptkomponentenmethode / von *Wolfgang-Peter Zingel*. - 1979. XIV,554 S. ISBN 3-515-03002-6

52 Viêt-Nam: die nationalistische und marxistische Ideologie im Spätwerk von Phan-Bôi-Chau (1867-1940) / von *Jörgen Unselt*. - 1980. XIII,304 S. ISBN 3-515-03133-2

53 Auswirkungen der Nahrungsmittelhilfe unter P.L. 480 auf den Agrarsektor der Entwicklungsländer: dargestellt am Beispiel Indiens / von *Joachim von Plocki*. - 1979. 240 S. ISBN 3-515-03144-8

54 Paschtunwali: ein Ehrenkodex und seine rechtliche Relevanz / von *Willi Steul*. - 1981. XIV,313 S. ISBN 3-515-03167-7

55 The *Stūpa*: its religious, historical and architectural significance / ed. by Anna Libera Dallapiccola in collaboration with Stephanie Zingel-Avé Lallemant. - 1980. VII, 359, [103] p. ISBN 3-515-02979-6

56 Faktorproportionen, internationale Arbeitsteilung und Aussenhandelspolitik: eine theoretische und empirische Analyse unter besonderer Berücksichtigung von Singapur, Westmalaysia und Pakistan / von *Norbert Wagner*. - 1980. XV, 333 S. ISBN 3-515-03300-9

57 Jyotiṣa: das System der indischen Astrologie / von *Hans-Georg Türstig*. - 1980. XVIII,343 S. ISBN 3-515-03283-5

58 *Naṉṉūl mūlamum Kūḻaṅkaittampirāṉ uraiyum* / ed. by Ayyadurai Dhamotharan. - 1980. XXVIII,246 p. ISBN 3-515-03284-3

59 Britische Indien-Politik, 1926-1932: Motive, Methoden und Mißerfolg imperialer Politik am Vorabend der Dekolonisation / von *Horst-Joachim Leue*. - 1981. XI,259 S. ISBN 3-515-03395-5

60 *Städte in Südasien*: Geschichte, Gesellschaft, Gestalt / hrsg. von Hermann Kulke; Hans Christoph Rieger; Lothar Lutze. - 1982. XVIII,376,41 S. ISBN 3-515-03396-3

61 Die Erörterung der Wirksamkeit: Bhartṛharis Kriyāsamuddeśa und Helārājas Prakāśa zum ersten Male aus dem Sanskrit übersetzt, mit einer Einführung und einem Glossar versehen / von Giovanni Bandini. - 1980. 200 S. ISBN 3-515-03391-2

62 Die landwirtschaftliche Produktion in Indien: Ackerbau-Technologie und traditionale Agrargesellschaft dargestellt nach dem Arthaśāstra und Dharmaśāstra / von *Johannes Laping*. - 1982. X, 155 S. ISBN 3-515-03521-4

63 Kānphaṭā: Untersuchungen zu Kult, Mythologie und Geschichte śivaitischer Tantriker in Nepal / von *Günter Unbescheid*. - 1980. XXXIII,197,16 S. ISBN 3-515-03478-1

64 Die Kasten-Klassenproblematik im städtisch-industriellen Bereich: historisch-empirische Fallstudie über die Industriestadt Kanpur in Uttar Pradesh, Indien / von *Maren Bellwinkel*. - 1980. XII,284 S. ISBN 3-515-03499-4

65 Tamang ritual texts 1: preliminary studies in the folk-religion of an ethnic minority in Nepal / by *András Höfer*. - 1981. 184 p. ISBN 3-515-03585-0

66 Tamang ritual texts 2 / by *András Höfer*. - (forthcoming) ISBN 3-515-03852-3

67 Towards reducing the dependence on capital imports: a planning model for Pakistan's policy of self-reliance / by *Heinz Ahrens and Wolfgang-Peter Zingel*. With a contribution by Syed Nawab Haider Naqvi. - 1982. XVI,337 p. ISBN 3-515-03853-1

68 Aspekte der regionalen wirtschaftlichen Integration zwischen Entwicklungsländern: das Beispiel der ASEAN / von *Alfred Kraft*. - 1982. X,298 S. ISBN 3-515-03801-9

69 Indien, Nepal, Sri Lanka: Süd-Süd-Beziehungen zwischen Symmetrie und Dependenz / von *Citha Doris Maass*. - 1982. XXI, 380 S. ISBN 3-515-03802-7

70 *Grundbedürfnisse als Gegenstand der Entwicklungspolitik*: interdisziplinäre Aspekte der Grundbedarfsstrategie / Norbert Wagner und Hans Christoph Rieger (Hrsg.) - 1982. VIII,220 S. ISBN 3-515-03838-8

71 The vagrant peasant: agrarian distress and desertion in Bengal, 1770 to 1830 / by *Aditee Nag Chowdhury-Zilly*. - 1982. XV,196 p. ISBN 3-515-03855-8

72 Orissa: a comprehensive and classified bibliography / by *Hermann Kulke* in collaboration with Gaganendranath Dash and Manmath Nath Das, Karuna Sagar Behera. - 1982. XXIII,416 p. ISBN 3-515-03593-1

73 Adat, Macht und lokale Eliten: eine Studie zur Machtstruktur der Pfarrei Habi in Sikka, Flores, Indonesien anhand der Einführung der Institution Gabungan Kontas 1975/76; eine empirische Untersuchung / von *Paul Rudolf Nunheim*. - 1982. XVI,345 S. ISBN 3-515-03834-5

74 Tamil: Sprache als politisches Symbol; politische Literatur in der Tamilsprache in den Jahren 1945 bis 1967; mit besonderer Berücksichtigung der Schriften der Führer der dravidischen Bewegung: E. V. Rāmacāmi und C. N. Aṇṇāturai / von *Dagmar Hellmann-Rajanayagam*. - 1984. VII,249 S. ISBN 3-515-03894-9

75 Moderne Gesetzgebung in Indien und ihre Auswirkung auf die Landbevölkerung: eine Dorfstudie aus Uttar Pradesh / von *Eva Prochazka*. - 1982. XI,133 S. ISBN 3-515-03893-0

76 Status and affinity in middle India / by *Georg Pfeffer*. - 1982. VII,104 p. ISBN 3-515-03913-9

77 *Indology and law*: studies in honour of Professor J. Duncan M. Derrett / ed. by Günther-Dietz Sontheimer and Parameswara Kota Aithal. - 1982. XI, 463 p. ISBN 3-515-03748-9

78 Über Entstehungsprozesse in der Philosophie des Nyāya-Vaiśesika-Systems / von *Hans-Georg Türstig*. - 1982. XIX,101 S. ISBN 3-515-03951-1

79 Cheap lives and dear limbs: the British transformation of the Bengal criminal law 1769-1817 / by *Jörg Fisch*. - 1983. VII, 154 p. ISBN 3-515-04012-9

80 Brata und Alpanā in Bengalen / von *Eva Maria Gupta*. - 1983. X, 210 S. ISBN 3-515-04063-3

81 The *Modī documents from Tanjore in Danish collections* / edited, translated and analysed by Elisabeth Strandberg. - 1983. 386 p. ISBN 3-515-04080-3

82 Agrarverfassung und Agrarentwicklung in Thailand / von *Friedrich W. Fuhs*. - 1985. XVIII,311 S. ISBN 3-515-04553-8

83 Mokṣa in Jainism, according to Umāsvāti / by *Robert J.Zydenbos*. - 1983. IX, 81 p. ISBN 3-515-04053-6

84 Fischerei und Fischereiwirtschaft im nördlichen Ceylon: Standort und Lebensraum der Fischer im Norden der Tropeninsel / von *Thomas Gläser*. - 1983. XV,196 S. ISBN 3-515-04054-4

85 Thailands Lehrer zwischen 'Tradition' und 'Fortschritt': eine empirische Untersuchung politisch-sozialer und pädagogischer Einstellungen thailändischer Lehrerstudenten des Jahres 1974 / von *Ingrid Liebig-Hundius*. - 1984. XII, 342 S. ISBN 3-515-04121-4

86 *Ethnologie und Geschichte*: Festschrift für Karl Jettmar / hrsg. von Peter Snoy. - 1983. 654 S. ISBN 3-515-04104-4

87 Malediven und Lakkadiven: Materialien zur Bibliographie der Atolle im Indischen Ozean / von *Thomas Malten*. - 1983. 101 S. ISBN 3-515-04125-7

88 Astor: eine Ethnographie / von *Adam Nayyar*. - 1986. XIII, 120 S. ISBN 3-515-04344-6

89 Zwischen Reform und Rebellion: über die Entwicklung des Islams in Minangkabau (Westsumatra) zwischen den beiden Reformbewegungen der Padri (1837) und der Modernisten (1908); ein Beitrag zur Geschichte der Islamisierung Indonesiens / von *Werner Kraus*. - 1984. X,236 S. ISBN 3-515-04286-5

90 Energie und wirtschaftliche Entwicklung in Entwicklungsländern: das Beispiel Nepal / von *Jürgen Steiger*. - 1984. XX,329 S. ISBN 3-515-04345-4

91 Kampf um Malakka: eine wirtschaftsgeschichtliche Studie über den portugiesischen und niederländischen Kolonialismus in Südostasien / von *Malcolm Dunn*. - 1984. XV,275 S. ISBN 3-515-04123-0

92 Portraits in sechs Fürstenstaaten Rajasthans vom 17. bis zum 20. Jahrhundert: Voraussetzungen, Entwicklungen, Veränderungen; mit besonderer Berücksichtigung kulturhistorischer Faktoren / von *Juliane Anna Lia Molitor*. - 1985. 179 S. ISBN 3-515-04346-2

93 Bangladesh: era of Sheikh Mujibur Rahman / by *Moudud Ahmed*. - 1984. XI,282 p. ISBN 3-515-04266-0

94 Die politische Stellung der Sikhs innerhalb der indischen Nationalbewegung, 1935-1947 / von *Christine Effenberg*. - 1984. VI,232 S. ISBN 3-515-04284-9

95 'Hir': zur strukturellen Deutung des Panjabi-Epos von Waris Shah / von *Doris Buddenberg*. - 1985. VIII,156 p. ISBN 3-515-04347-0

96 Dialectics and dream: an evaluation of Bishnu Dey's poetry in the light of Neo-Marxian aesthetics / by *Subhoranjan Dasgupta*. - 1987. X, 273 p. ISBN 3-515-05134-1

97 Das Tor zur Unterwelt: Mythologie und Kult des Termitenhügels in der schriftlichen und mündlichen Tradition Indiens / von *Ditte König*. - 1984. XII, 389 S.
ISBN 3-515-04410-8

98 Religionspolitik in Britisch-Indien 1793-1813: christliches Sendungsbewußtsein und Achtung hinduistischer Tradition im Widerstreit / von *Cornelia Witz*. - 1985. VIII, 137 S. ISBN 3-515-04527-9

99 Landschenkungen und staatliche Entwicklung im frühmittelalterlichen Bengalen (5. bis 13. Jahrhundert n. Chr.) / von *Swapna Bhattacharya*. - 1985. XIV, 171 S.
ISBN 3-515-04534-1

100 *Vijayanagara - city and empire*: new currents of research / ed. by Anna Libera Dallapiccola in collaboration with Stephanie Zingel-Avé Lallemant. - 1985.
ISBN 3-515-04554-6
Vol.1. Texts. - XIII,439 p.
Vol.2. Reference and documentation. - X,221 p.

101 Zur Relevanz mikroökonomischer Theorie für die Analyse des ökonomischen Verhaltens der Wirtschaftssubjekte in Agrarsektoren von Entwicklungsländern / von *Rainer Marggraf*. - 1985. IX,295 S. ISBN 3-515-04513-9

102 Zur Methodik kosten-nutzen-analytischer Bewertung verteilungsorientierter Preispolitik: mit empirischen Untersuchungen zur Agrarpreispolitik Thailands und der Europäischen Gemeinschaft / von *Lothar Oberländer*. - 1985. XV, 320 S.
ISBN 3-515-04490-6

103 Zentrale Gewalt in Nagar (Karakorum): politische Organisationsformen, ideologische Begründungen des Königtums und Veränderungen in der Moderne / von *Jürgen Frembgen*. - 1985. XII,441 S. ISBN 3-515-04588-0

104 *Regionale Tradition in Südasien* / hrsg. von Hermann Kulke und Dietmar Rothermund. - 1985. XXIV,256 S. ISBN 3-515-04519-8

105 Law and society East and West: dharma, li and nomos, their contribution to thought and to life / by *Reinhard May*. - 1985. 251 S. ISBN 3-515-04537-6

106 Darul-Islam: Kartosuwirjos Kampf um einen islamischen Staat Indonesien / von *Holk H. Dengel*. - 1986. VIII, 255 S. ISBN 3-515-04784-0

107 Aṅkāḷaparamēcuvari: a goddess of Tamilnadu; her myths and cult / by *Eveline Meyer*. - 1986. XII,329 p. ISBN 3/515-04702-6

108 Die Vāḍabalija in Andhra Pradesh und in Orissa: Aspekte der wirtschaftlichen und sozialen Organisation einer maritimen Gesellschaft / von *Elisabeth Schömbucher*. - 1986. IX,253 S. ISBN 3-515-04835-9

109 Guru-Śisya-Sambandha: das Meister-Schüler-Verhältnis im traditionellen und modernen Hinduismus / *Ralph Mark Steinmann*. - 1986. XI,312 S.
ISBN 3-515-04851-0

110 Herrschaft und Verwaltung im östlichen Indien unter den späten Gangas, ca. 1038-1434 / von *Shishir Kumar Panda*. - 1986. III,184 S. ISBN 3-515-04861-8

111 Tension over the Farakka Barrage: a techno-political tangle in south Asia *Khurshida Begum*. - 1988. X, 279 S. 3-515-05064-7

112 *Developments in Asia*: economic, political and cultural aspects / ed. by Christine Effenberg. - 1987. 545 p. ISBN 3-515-05049-3

113 Annotated bibliography of new Indonesian literature on the history of Indonesia / by *Holk H. Dengel*. - 1987. 114 p. ISBN 3-515-04988-6

114 Die Stadt Badulla: Strukturentwicklung und Zentralität eines Ortes im östlichen zentralen Hochland der Insel Ceylon / von *Siegbert Dicke*. - 1987. XII,311 S. ISBN 3-515-04995-9

115 Social accounting matrix als praxisnahes Daten- und Modellsystem für Entwicklungsländer / von *Elmar Kleiner*. - 1987. X,210,[20],3 S. ISBN 3-515-04997-5

116 The problem of 'Greater Baluchistan': a study of Baluch nationalism / by *Inayatullah Baloch*. - 1987. VIII,299 p. ISBN 3-515-04999-1

117 *Portuguese Asia*: aspects in history and economic history; 16th and 17th centuries / ed. by Roderich Ptak. - 1987. VIII, 219 p. ISBN 3-515-05136-8

118 Rahmat Ali: a biography / by *Kursheed Kamal Aziz*. - 1987. XXXIII,576 p. ISBN 3-515-05051-5

119 Sozio-ökonomische Determinanten der Fertilität der Landbevölkerung im Nord-Punjab: Fallbeispiel Muradi Janjil, Pakistan / von *Eva-Maria Herms*. - 1987. XII,256 S. ISBN 3-515-05058-2

120 Ziarat und Pir-e-Muridi: Golra Sharif, Nurpur Shahan und Pir Baba; drei muslimische Wallfahrtstätten in Nordpakistan / von *Harald Einzmann*. - 1988. IX, 185 S. ISBN 3-515-04801-4

121 Yantracintāmaṇiḥ of *Dāmodara* / critically ed. by Hans-Georg Türstig. - 1988. 166, 5, 40 p. ISBN 3-515-05212-7

122 Die sowjetische Entwicklungspolitik gegenüber der Dritten Welt unter besonderer Berücksichtigung Indiens / von *Klaus-Dieter Müller*. - 1988. XIII, 433 S. ISBN 3-515-05284-4

123 Effektive Protektion von Rohstoffproduktion und -verarbeitung: mit empirischen Untersuchungen zur philippinischen Volkswirtschaft / von *Markus Kramer*. - 1988. ISBN 3-515-05348-4

124 Sozialstrukturen im Kumaon: Bergbauern des Himalaya / von *Monika Krengel*. - 1988. ISBN 3-515-05358-1

126 Burmese entrepreneurship: creative response in the colonial economy / by *Aung Tun Thet*. - 1989. XVI, 197 p.

127 Redupliziertc Verbstämme im Tamil / von *Thomas Malten*. - 1989. IX, 283 S.

128 Islamisierung in Pakistan, 1977 - 1984: Untersuchungen zur autochthoner Strukturen / von *S. Jamal Malik*. - 1989. XVII, 475 S.

129 Banks, gods and government: institutional and informal credit structure in a remote and tribal Indian district (Kinnaur, Himachal Pradesh); 1960 - 1985 / by *Jogishwar Singh*. - 1989. XXXVIII, 410 S. ISBN 3-515-05396-4

SOUTH ASIAN STUDIES

University of Heidelberg, South Asia Institute
New Delhi Branch

(from vol.8:) New Delhi: Manohar
Stuttgart: Franz-Steiner-Verlag-Wiesbaden [in comm.]

[1] Helmuth von Glasenapp: interpreter of Indian thought / *Wilfried Nelle*. With a preface by Zakir Husain. - 1964. 108 p.

2 *South Asian studies II* / ed. by Heimo Rau. - 1965. 111 p.

3 The dialect of Delhi / *Bahadur Singh*. - 1966. 68 p.

4 *Some problems of independent India* / ed. by Lothar Lutze. - 1968. 54 p.

5 A grammar of Tirukkural / *A. Dhamotharan*. - 1972. X,257 p.

6 Goethe and Tagore: a retrospect of East-West colloquy / *Alokeranjan Dasgupta*. - 1973. XI,127 p.

7 The joint Hindu family: its evolution as a legal institution / by *Günther-Dietz Sontheimer*. - 1977. XXI,250 p.

8 The *cult of Jagannath and the regional tradition of Orissa* / ed. by Anncharlott Eschmann; Hermann Kulke; Gaya Charan Tripathi. South Asia Interdisciplinary Regional Research Programme, Orissa Research Project. - 1978. XX,537 p.

9a *Zamindars, mines and peasants*: studies in the history of an Indian coalfield and its rural hinterland / ed. by Dietmar Rothermund; D. C. Wadhwa. - 1978. XXI,236 p. - (Dhanbad Research Project report / South Asia Interdisciplinary Regional Research Programme; a)

9b *Urban growth and rural stagnation*: studies in the economy of an Indian coalfield and its rural hinterland / ed. by Dietmar Rothermund; Erhard Kropp; Gunther Dienemann. - 1980. XXVI, 493 p. - (Dhanbad Research Project report / South Asia Interdisciplinary Regional Research Programme; b)

9c *Social inequality and political structures*: studies in class formation and interest articulation in an Indian coalfield and its rural hinterland / ed. by John P. Neelsen. - 1983. XIII, 285 p.

10 History of the Chaitanya faith in Orissa / *Prabhat Mukherjee*. - 1979. 126 p.

11 *Memorial stones*: a study of their origin, significance and variety / eds: S. Settar; Günther D. Sontheimer. - 1982. [85], 393 p. - (I.I.A.H. series / Institute of Indian Art History, Karnatak University; 2)

12 The religious system of the Mahānubhāva sect: the *Mahānubhāva Sūtrapāṭha* / ed. and transl. with an introduction by Anne Feldhaus. - 1983. VIII,285 p.

13 Oriya nationalism: the quest for a united Orissa 1866-1936 / *Nivedita Mohanty*. - 1982. XIX,201 p.

14 Indian moneylenders at work: case studies of the traditional rural credit market in Dhanbad District, Bihar / *Hans-Dieter Roth*. - 1983. XII,112 p.

15 *India and the West*: proceedings of a seminar dedicated to the memory of Hermann Goetz / ed. by Joachim Deppert. - 1983. 263 p.

16 Hindi writing in post-colonial India: a study in the aesthetics of literary production / *Lothar Lutze*. - 1985. XII,227 p.

17 Religion and pilgrim tax under the Company Raj / *Nancy Gardner Cassels*. - 1988. XII,184 p. ISBN 81-85054-32-0

18 Two medieval merchant guilds of South India / *Meera Abraham*. - 1988. XII, 273 p. ISBN 81-85054-48-7